24th EG-ICE International Workshop on Intelligent Computing in Engineering (EG-ICE 2017)

Nottingham, United Kingdom
10 – 12 July 2017

Editors:

Christian Koch
Walid Tizani
Jelena Ninic

ISBN: 978-1-5108-4345-5

Printed from e-media with permission by:

Curran Associates, Inc.
57 Morehouse Lane
Red Hook, NY 12571

Some format issues inherent in the e-media version may also appear in this print version.

Printed by Curran Associates, Inc. (2017)

For permission requests, please contact the European Group For Intelligent Computing in Engineering (eg-ice) at the address below.

European Group For Intelligent Computing in Engineering (eg-ice)
c/o Andre Borrmann
Arcisstrasee 21
80333 Munich
Germany

Phone: 498928-925117
Fax: 498928-948789

anything@eg-ice.org

Additional copies of this publication are available from:

Curran Associates, Inc.
57 Morehouse Lane
Red Hook, NY 12571 USA
Phone: 845-758-0400
Fax: 845-758-2634
Email: curran@proceedings.com
Web: www.proceedings.com

Digital Proceedings of the

24th EG-ICE International Workshop on Intelligent Computing in Engineering 2017

The University of Nottingham, United Kingdom

10-12 July 2017

Editors:

Christian Koch, Walid Tizani and Jelena Ninić

Preface

This volume contains the papers presented at eg-ice 2017, the 24th International Workshop on Intelligent Computing in Engineering held between 10-12 July at the University of Nottingham. This workshop is part of the series organised annually by the European Group for Intelligent Computing in Engineering (EG-ICE).

The workshop brings together international experts working on the applications of computing to engineering problems. It is intended to be a small-scale, but high-quality and single-track event focussing on the promotion, dissemination and exchange of knowledge and ideas through intensive discussions.

The European Group for Intelligent Computing in Engineering (EG-ICE) has been established to promote research and applications of advanced informatics to all aspects of engineering. The primary goals of the group are to promote advanced informatics research across Europe by encouraging and improving contacts between researchers, fostering research collaboration and enhancing awareness of the latest developments. The group maintains active contact with similar groups in countries outside Europe and encourages membership by non-Europeans. Moreover, the group has a further aim to increase the awareness of industry of advanced informatics.

First, we would like to thank the authors of all papers for their excellent work in sharing their research ideas and findings, thus making the workshop a very successful event. Second, we would like to thank all the members of the programme committee who assisted in the peer-reviewing process of the submitted papers. Finally, special thanks to Diane Karim, the local event coordinator at the University of Nottingham.

July 10-12, 2017
Nottingham

Christian Koch
Walid Tizani
Jelena Ninić

Table of Contents

Program Committee

Burcin Becerik-Gerber	University of Southern California
Jakob Beetz	Eindhoven University of Technology
André Borrmann	Technical University Munich
Pieter de Wilde	Plymouth University
Philipp Geyer	Katholieke Universiteit Leuven
Ewa Grabska	Jagiellonian University
Timo Hartmann	Technical University of Berlin
Wolfgang Huhnt	Technische Universität Berlin
Christian Koch	The University of Nottingham
Markus König	Ruhr-Universität Bochum
Haijiang Li	Cardiff University
Jelena Ninić	The University of Nottingham
Uwe Rüppel	Technische Universität Darmstadt
Alcinia Zita Sampaio	Technical University of Lisbon
Kay Smarsly	Bauhaus University Weimar
Ian Smith	École polytechnique fédérale de Lausanne
Georg Suter	Technische Universität Wien
Walid Tizani	The University of Nottingham
Jennifer Whyte	Imperial College London

A system for crowdsourcing on-demand quantitative design space exploration in 3dspace

David Birch[1], Alvise Simondetti[2]
[1]Data Science Institute, Imperial College London
[2]Foresight and Innovation, Arup
David.Birch@Imperial.ac.uk

Abstract. Crowdsourcing feedback on proposed designs is an effective means of gaining insight and acceptance of a proposed design. Recently web based 3d visualisation systems (Dobos 2012; Bugs et al 2010; Wu et al 2015) have enabled crowdsourcing of design feedback on a larger scale. However such systems rarely present more than one design alternative in a limited design space and seldom provide quantitative analysis on proposed design scenarios. This precludes a more participatory approach (Borning et al 2004) including a wider audience and their insight in the design process. We propose a system to assist the design team by augmenting a 3d visualisation crowdsourcing environment with quantitative on-demand assessment of design variants run in the cloud. This enables crowdsourced exploration of the design space. Automated participant tracking and submitted feedback on effective design options are collated to aid the design team in balancing the demands of urban master planning.

1. Introduction

Urban master planning is a balancing act between a number of inter-related design parameters that are explicit and quantitatively measurable, a number of other aspects that are implicit, not easily measurable, and are dynamically driven by human preference and market forces. Optimization alone won't help find the most appropriate solutions. Hence we propose crowdsourcing augmented with a quantified design analysis to explore these aspects and guide us to a set of the most synergetic solutions.

The design process involves experts from many disciplines making a plethora of decisions which will affect the urban environment and those who live and work within it. The design space has a very large scope including not only choice of architectural forms but also a huge number of design decisions which must be made to implement the vision of the development. These range from the number of parking spaces to the amount of green space included.

Aside from such design decisions the threat of climate change imputes a requirement to minimize the carbon emissions of a development by the adoption of mitigation strategies. Such strategies have impact across multiple disciplines and Key Performance Indicators (KPI's) and requires multidisciplinary collaborative exploration to enable their implementation. Such strategies are, of course, constrained by cost both capital and operating costs as well as impacts upon other resources such as water or energy consumption, creating a challenging optimization problem, particularly as many of the constraints are either undefined or cross traditional discipline boundaries. Such optimization of the design for an urban masterplan is rarely conducted within detailed quantified assessment nor is that assessment repeated more than a couple of design cycles (Flager and Heymaker 2007) nor does it often involve the key group of stakeholders – the people who will live and work in such an environment.

In this context crowdsourcing of design feedback enables wider participation in the design process. This is particularly effective if conducted early in the design process through participatory design. In recent years online web based tools (Dobos 2012; Salim 2015; Corney 2010) are enabling residents and members of the public to submit their feedback on design choices on a large scale, tagging insight geospatially (Dobos 2012; Brabham 2009) to highlight design issues.

However such systems are generally used to gather feedback on a single design variant or a small number of design options. This presents a clear and constrained choice to the participants and focuses input to decisions of interest to the design team. However the design space is dramatically larger and there are many more design variants and improvements which could be made if the crowd was given tools to explore the design space and assess the performance of design variants.

2. Approach

In the context of a multidisciplinary optimization problem, a large design space and the need to involve a range of stakeholders and the public in design decisions we propose to augment a 3d visualization environment with a quantitative design assessment by providing online assessment of design choices in the cloud. Crowdsourced feedback is then recorded and analyzed to provide a guide to the design team to improve decision making. Specifically we propose the following approach, summarized in Figure 1:

1) An interactive, web based, 3d environment for exploring proposed designs, annotated with design performance and enabling exploration of the design space for carbon mitigation strategies.
2) We couple this with a detailed analytical model (Ayaz and Levitas 2008) and a computational framework for design exploration (Birch 2013) providing real-time quantitative analysis of the masterplans performance across a range of KPIs.
3) This enables exploration of the design space by a large number of participants each able to explore the implications of adopting carbon mitigation strategies on the macro (masterplan) and micro (building) level across the development.
4) Such crowdsourcing of the design space is tracked providing a quantified insight into how the design space is explored and areas of interest or otherwise identified by the participants.

This system enables quantified participatory design by a wide range of stakeholders and the public. The automated tracking of stakeholders through their interaction with the design, their crowdsourced insight and voting together with quantitative assessment of designs as the design space is navigated by user demand and systematic insight is proposed to provide the design team with insight to develop their design. This system is fully implemented and this paper reports initial results from small scale testing.

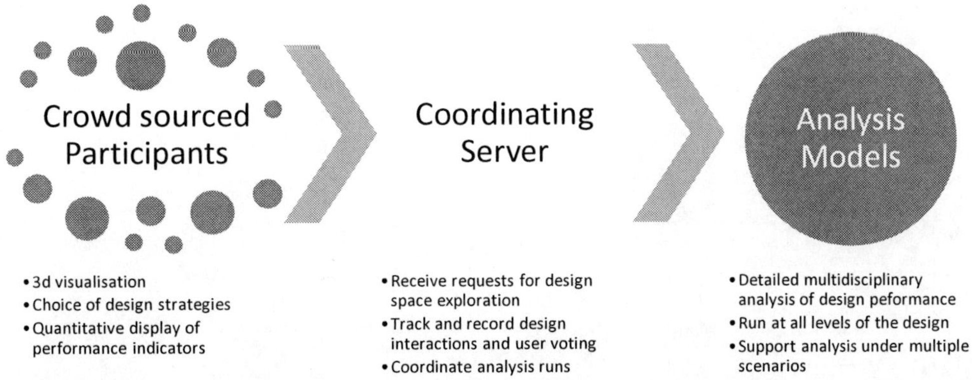

Figure 1: Our proposed methodology for enabling crowdsourced design space exploration backed by quantitative analysis of design variants

3. Architecture

To explore our proposed approach we have created a system which enables crowdsourcing of design input backed by the automatic analysis of design scenarios. The architecture of the system is shown in Figure 2 and builds upon the Hiersynth workflow system (Birch 2013) and is extended by the Concinnity analysis platform (Birch et al 2013).

The Concinnity analysis platform provides a workflow development environment for engineers and architects to configure and create analysis workflows interactively. The interface shown in Figure 3 provides infrastructure for configuring suites of analyses to the specific design site and scenario with a library of standard and partially configured analyses. The platform uses the Hiersynth engine (Birch 2013) to provide a multi-scale analysis capability, with the ability to run analyses at different scales of design. In this paper we consider a site wide analysis and a per-district analysis, this is enabled in Figure 3 by the use of design queries reading all districts in the design file.

Once the analysis workflow is created, a visualisation interface may be created interacting with the workflow system through a RESTful API server. We utilise the Unity3d game engine to create this interface due to its platform independence and ability to run within a website using WebGL. The visualisation environment enables participants to explore the design spatially and to comment upon it with geo-located comments. This aids exploring spatially analysis results, for example a lighting analysis or per district carbon emission analysis. Participants are provided with an easy to use interface to create design scenarios for analysis and view the results of such analyses at both an aggregate and per district level. Requests for analysis of design variants are submitted to the API server for analysis, this server is then polled for the results to be displayed. During this process tracking data of the user's movements in 3d, spatially located comments and voting on preferred KPI's are recorded in a database together with their design space exploration history.

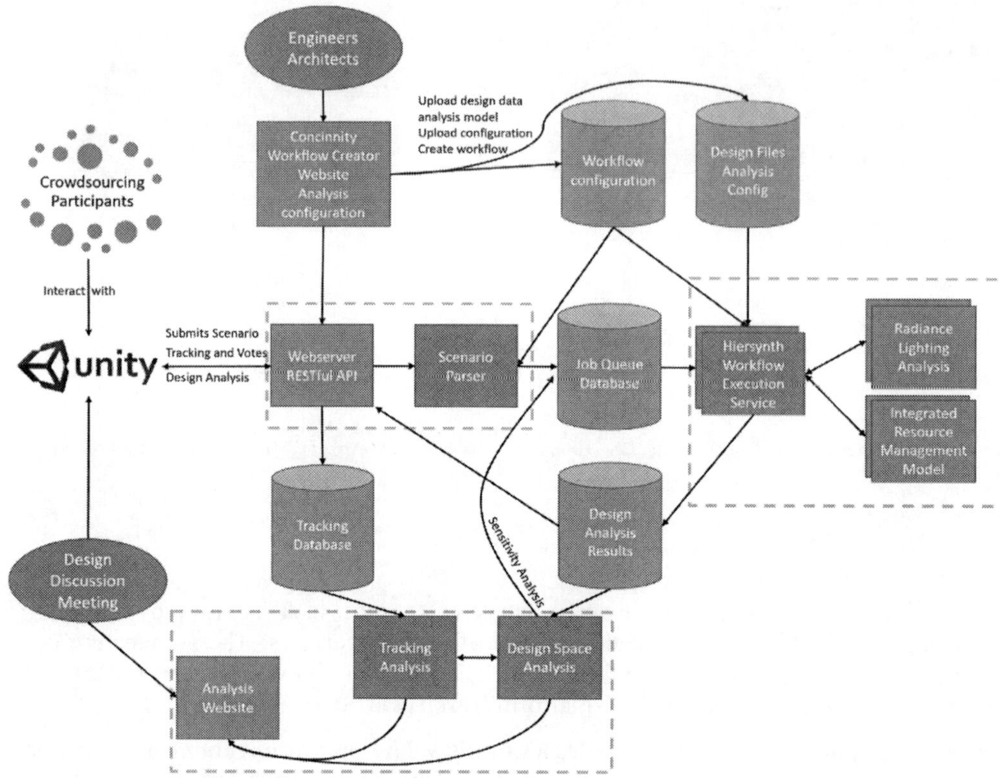

Figure 2: This architecture enables crowdsourcing of design insight with quantitative design analysis.

Once a request for analysis of a design scenario is submitted it is parsed and validated against the workflow and analysis configurations using the Hiersynth engine to ensure that all inputs are valid. Valid requests are logged in a database as jobs for worker nodes to analyse. This provides a scalability point by running many worker nodes to support crowdsourcing as while a webserver may scale easily, analysis of designs is compute intensive. We deploy our infrastructure to virtual machines on a private cloud using Openstack.

Once a job is received by a worker nodes, running an execution service, load and run the Hiersynth engine which manages the execution of a workflow, pulling all required analyses, design files and configurations from a MongoDB database onto the local computer. The engine then expands the structure of the workflow to reflect the design and scenario (e.g. one analysis per district) and concurrently runs the required analysis models with the design and scenario data. A local caching system of previous analysis results and queries provides a significant performance improvement. Once computed analysis results are post-processed, for example aggregating the performance of design elements and are stored in a database ready to be returned to participants through the RESTful API and to be used for subsequent design space analysis. We note that this system enables the security of analysis models and detailed design data to be protected and remain confidential as it is not included in the visualisation tool but resides solely upon the cloud system.

Finally throughout this process metrics on the participant's interaction with the design and requests for analysis of particular designs are stored for subsequent analysis. By enabling this crowdsourced data to include quantitative analysis of the design space we believe greater insight can be gained than by crowd exploration of a single or small set of proposed designs.

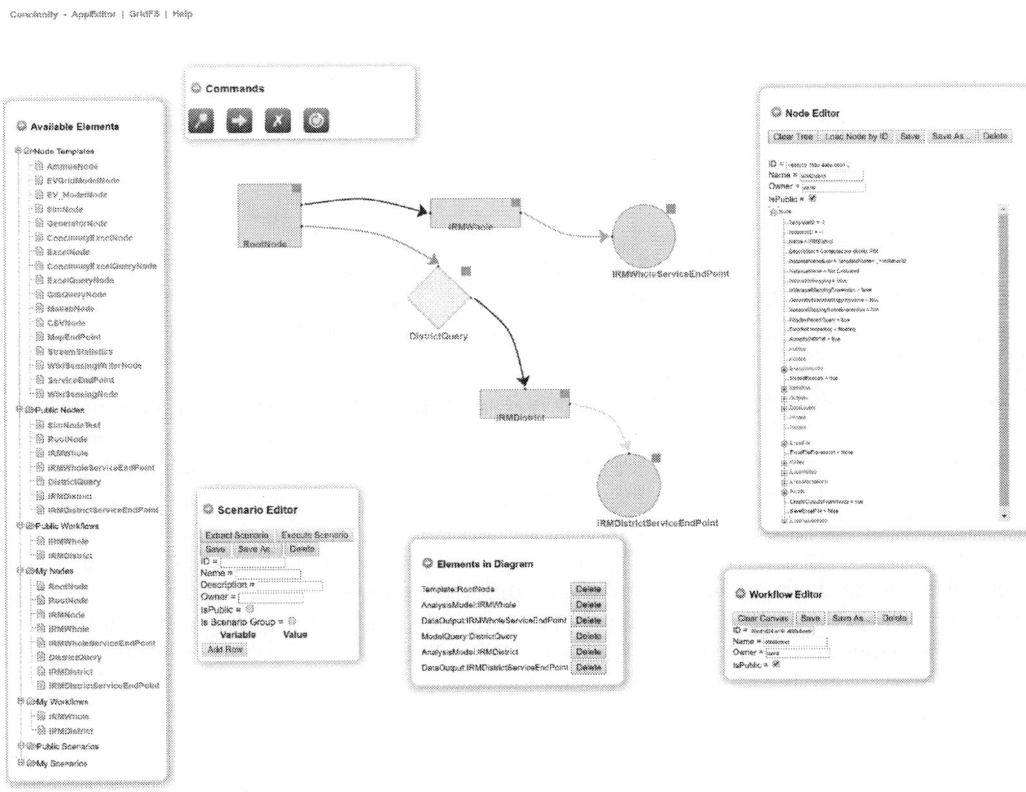

Figure 3: The Concinnity platform interface for creating analysis workflows to be used to analyse design scenarios created by crowdsourcing participants. Note the two analysis scales, whole site and per district analysis can be performed.

4. Case Study and Analysis models

To investigate what can be learned through our crowdsourcing approach we seek to apply our framework to an industrial case study. Partnering with Arup North America we apply our framework to a coastal development developing a new business district. The case study site comprises 29 districts over 39 hectares with a proposed total Gross Floor Area (GFA) of over 300,000 m^2. The key challenge we investigate in this development is how to achieve a more sustainable development. This presents a complex optimisation problem for which we require a number of analysis models to provide quantitative design insight.

The first of these models is an Integrated Resource Management (IRM) model (Ayaz and Levitas 2008). These models provide an integrated sustainability assessment of a masterplan design by coherently combining assessment models from several engineering disciplines. Discipline models contained within Arup's IRM model include Carbon Accounting, Energy consumption, Water, Waste, Transport, Materials and Economics. These models are tightly coupled with calculations and inputs in one model affecting calculations in the others. This allows the assessment of sustainability across a number of Key Performance Indicators (KPI's). Typical IRM models will contain several thousand design inputs and calculation assumptions, ranging from the site size to the carbon emissions for travelling 1km by bus. The models calculate several hundred KPI's which are summarised in 8 KPI's shown in Figure 4. These are the KPI's we provide to participants to enable quantitative assessment of the design.

Key Performance Indicator	Units
Total Primary Carbon	mton/yr
Energy Consumption	MWh/yr
Potable Water	ML/yr
Waste Water	ML/yr
Waste Landfilled	mton/yr
Transport Carbon	mtonCO2e/yr
Operational Expenditure	$/year
Capital Expenditure	$/year

Figure 4: The 8 primary KPIs calculated by Arup's Integrated Resource Management Model [todo cite] and used to provide quantitative assessment of designs during crowdsourcing.

The IRM model typically provides site-wide analysis. As described in (Birch 2013) the Hiersynth engine enables running of the IRM model at a per district level for a greater level of detail providing spatially decomposed results for analysis within a 3d environment. It should be noted that the IRM model does not assess geometric form other than assessing quantitative statistics about the development arising from its geometry, such as Gross Floor Area. To demonstrate the potential of our approach we include a geometric analysis model. We incorporate an analysis of the lighting conditions within the proposed masterplan's massing model by incorporating analysis using the open source ray-tracer Radiance (Ward 1994). Using this model we calculate an industry standard BRE209 (Littlefair 1991) daylight analysis, the results of such analysis can be seen in Figure 5.

Arup's IRM model also enables assessment of the impact of over 40 sustainability strategies. These strategies range from adopting "*low flush fixtures and fittings*" to "*water efficient landscaping*" and "*district energy supply*". The impact of these strategies is calculated across a number of the integrated resource models, for example a "*district energy supply*" may reduce energy and carbon consumption but may increase water consumption as heat is transferred between buildings as hot water. Capturing these interactions is the key strength of this modelling technique and supports exploration of this optimisation problem as a support to the design process. Design is primarily concerned with such trade-offs such as between increased build density which is good for lowering carbon emissions and increased green space which improves comfort and biodiversity.

These are the key optimisation problems and design challenges which we seek to gain crowdsourced insight upon within our 3d visualisation environment.

5. Crowdsourcing Environment

A 3d visualisation environment provides an intuitive environment for exploring a spatial design (Broll et al 2004; Dobos 2012). We provide a 3d web based and desktop visualisation environment through the Unity3d game engine. The environment is augmented with a heads-up display containing the performance of the whole masterplan design according to the 8 KPI's in Figure 4. When the participant clicks on any KPI the per-district performance is shown as a billboard above each district coloured on a red-green scale according to the relative performance amongst its peers in each scenario as shown in Figure 7. Participants are able interact with a list of sustainability scenarios which may be toggled on and off to propose a new design scenario, once complete this may be submitted for analysis which will take around 10-30 seconds depending on the level of detail requested. Results are then visualised and differential performance to the previous scenario in the 8 KPI's are displayed.

At any time participants may submit their comments in a number of ways as shown in Figure 6 including submitting a geolocated textual comment as in (Dobos 2012), voting for particular KPI's and for or against particular sustainability strategies. Participants are also invited to vote for a particular design scenario once they have had it analysed.

Figure 5: Our crowdsourcing environment developed in Unity3d showing a BRE209 daylight analysis calculated through Radiance. Participants are empowered to explore new design scenarios by choosing which sustainability strategies to adopt.

Specifically we ask participants to identify combinations of 49 sustainability strategies which should be applied to the masterplan to improve its sustainability, primarily through carbon emissions, while minimizing operational and capital expenditure to acceptable limits. This presents a design space of 2^{49} design options, which is infeasible for exhaustive exploration by human or machine methods. However we believe (Simondetti 2012) that the key finding from a crowdsourcing study is not an optimal design but rather feedback on directions and the most important strategies to be applied according to different stakeholders.

While techniques such as sensitivity analysis have (Birch 2013) been applied to this problem we believe that involving a wider range of participants within the design space exploration should lead to insight in the best synergies and approaches to improve the design.

Crowdsourced Data Source	Potential Insight
3d motion path at 1 second interval including look direction	Geospatial recording of areas of concern or interest. Key routes and paths through the development.
Submitted design scenario	Most applied sustainability strategies and their combinations.
Voting + and – for KPI's	Which KPIs matter most to different stakeholder groups.
Voting + and – for sustainability strategies	Which sustainability strategies are favoured by different groups
Votes for the current scenarios (set of strategies)	Preferred scenarios, optimised scenarios.
Username and type (Researcher, Resident, Architect…)	Stratification of results.
Textual comments located in 3d space	Design issue and performance issues located at particular buildings and views.
Which KPI's are viewed per building	Which KPI's matter for individual district performance.
Quantitative design performance	Design space exploration, impact of particular scenarios recorded per building.

Figure 6: Data recorded during crowdsourced quantitative exploration of the design space and its potential insight

Figure 7: Screenshot from our visualisation tool enabling crowdsourcing of quantitative design space exploration at all levels of an urban masterplan. Above each building a fine grained representation of primary carbon emissions per building is shown.

6. Preliminary Results

In conjunction with Arup we are in the process of applying this methodology and framework to an urban masterplanning project in North America. Here we present preliminary results from a small scale application of the crowdsourcing system. The goal of this pilot to demonstrate the potential of the insight which may be gained. Over 400 interaction events were collated.

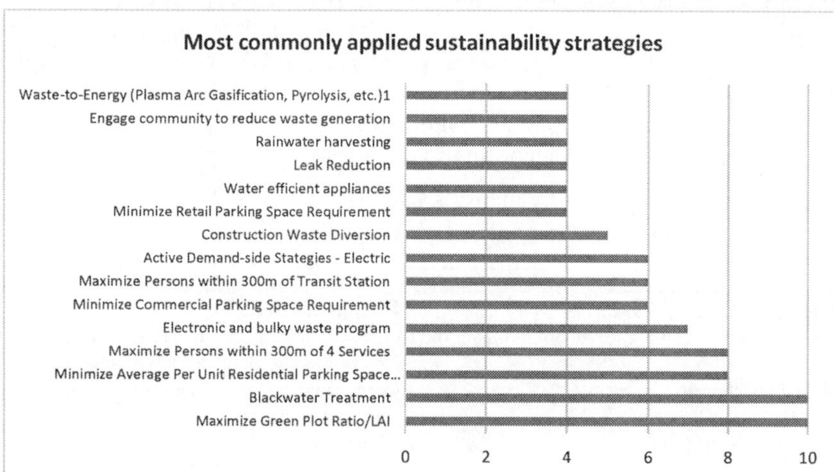

Figure 8: Crowdsourcing of the most commonly applied sustainability strategies

Figure 8 shows the most commonly applied sustainability strategies as submitted in design scenarios, on average 5 strategies were chosen per design variant. Notably most of the top strategies have spatial characteristics which, while modelled in the analysis model are not reflected in changes in geometry of the model, this is a key area of future work. Most of the applied strategies are straightforward to implement rather than requiring site wide design changes such as a district heating system which is more rarely applied but may have a larger impact upon the sustainability criteria. Such strategies may represent a common group to apply, with a larger crowdsourcing study we would expect to be able to identify common pairs or groups of applied strategies and identify the quantitative impact upon the design space.

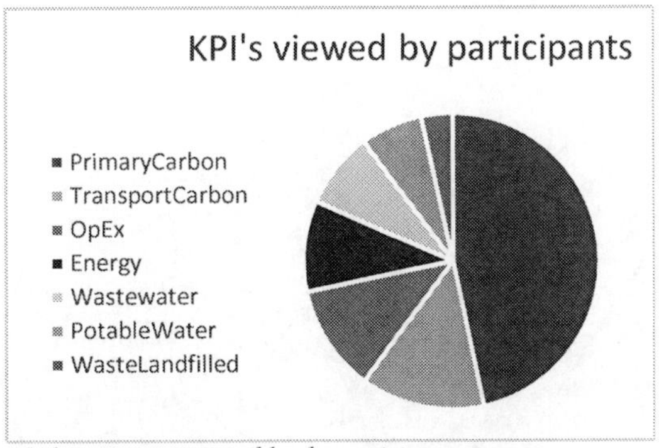

Figure 9: The Key Performance Indicators most viewed by the participants

Figure 9 shows the results of implicitly tracking which KPI's participants seek to view quantitative analysis results for on their design variants. It is striking that over 60% of requests are to view the carbon implications of design decisions. Next most popular is an interest in operational expenditure which varies dramatically depending on the implemented schemes. We would suggest this data could be used to create a weighting function for combining the KPIs into a single figure for subsequent optimization. Such functions could be created for different groups of participants – for example residents living within the development site compared to those adjoining.

Another data stream collected is motion tracking of users through the environment prior to the submission of new scenarios. From this we might infer whether participants were seeking to tackle a localized performance challenge or not, an example of this type of visualization can be seen in Figure 10.

Figure 10: Motion-tracking of participants prior to submission of a new scenario, potentially highlighting buildings of concern.

Figure 11 shows the results of 131 design analyses performed, per district, during our pilot study. Encouragingly these results show a wide potential to effect each of the KPI's considered. We note that groups of similar districts and wide differences between districts will account of the concentric rings in the radar plot. There is a clear trend within the design space to trade Capital Expenditure for reductions in resource consumption and carbon emissions, however this comes at the expense of Operation Expenditure (which is initially zero). The number of explorations that mitigate only a couple of KPIs might indicate that users are experimenting with the system and are adding one strategy at the time hence the large number of poor scores.

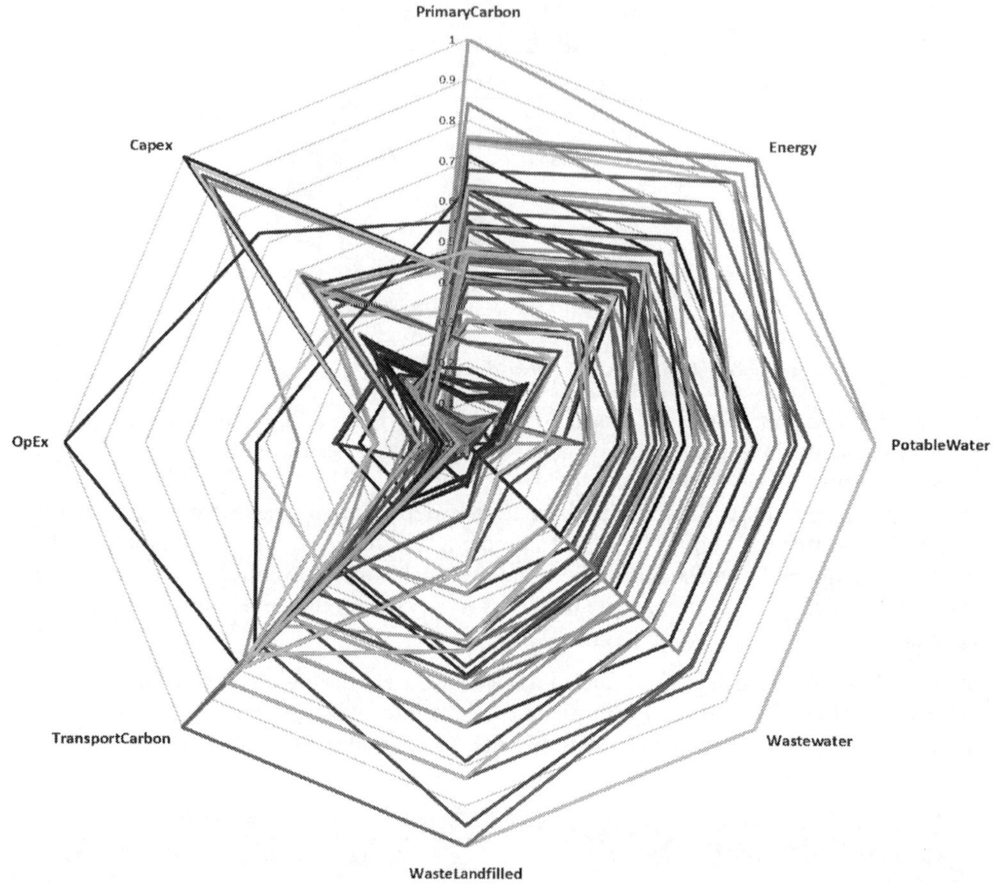

Figure 11: Radar plot of 131 analyses performed on demand during a crowdsourcing exercise.

Interactive segmentation of the analysis results according to specific groups of strategies involved would provide an interesting tool for designers to understand the implications of adopting that strategy and the design space including it. This would enable leveraging the wisdom of the crowd by asking how other participants designs performed when they followed similar steps to the design. For example if the strategy "Maximise Green Space" is enabled we could filter the analysis results to identify only scenarios where participants included this strategy and identify the best performing designs found within this reduced design space. By repeating this process with all of the most voted for analyses a "popular" and more constrained design space could be identified.

These preliminary results show the potential of the type of insight which may be gained from involving a wider audience with tools to quantitatively explore the design space, particularly with larger numbers of participants through an online system.

7. Conclusions

In this paper we have proposed a system for augmenting crowdsourcing with quantitative design analysis computed on demand in the cloud. We believe that this will enable inclusion of a wider range of participants in the design process and help them to explore the quantitative implications of design decisions. This is especially helpful as urban master planning is the process of balancing of design decisions and performance implications across many design disciplines. This system has the potential to provide an order of magnitude improvement in the number of design variants analysed in a typical project (Flager F 2007; Birch 2013).

Further we believe that tracking participants through their interaction with a design and the design space will lead to further insight for the design team. This can be done both explicitly through voting for design variants, particular elements and important KPI's or implicitly through tracking a 3d motion path through the 3d environment to highlight places of design interest. This compliments traditional crowdsourced geospatial commenting systems.

We believe that combining these two techniques can provide guidance to the design team of their stakeholders' views and quantitative advice on the performance of design variants in the design space. We believe this will enable more informed balancing of the competing decisions inherent within urban masterplanning. Such techniques should be applicable to wider design problems common in architecture and engineering practice.

8. Further Work

This paper presents a working crowdsourcing environment augmented with online computation of design analysis in the cloud. The key next step is to run a field trial of the system during the development of an urban masterplan. This would enable all architects, engineers and policymakers access to the system to explore the design space enabling quantified testing of hypotheses. We would further seek to open the platform to use by the general public in the area of the proposed masterplan to seek wider views. A large scale test would enable the implicit tracking of users to generate aggregate insight on the most interesting or contentious areas of the design and the most valued KPI's.

One limitation of the current system is that it does not allow variation of physical geometry, this could be amended by provision of design tools within the game engine environment. To compliment this further analyses which compute upon physical form – e.g. walking distances, these could easily be added to the Hiersynth engine. The potential of this can be seen in Figure 5 with the integrated Radiance lighting analysis. This would also enable moving beyond the massing model level of detail to provide greater geometric fidelity and design variance.

Finally we would seek to explore the possibility of adding an element of gamification to the crowdsourcing environment. This would enable participants to view each other's design scenarios and share designs which are local optima in the design space via a multi-parameter leader board system. This element of competition would gamify the experience and potentially induce the crowd to further explore the design space, identifying new improved design solutions which push the Pareto Front toward better optimality. We believe that the lessons learned through this system will be valuable for many engineering practitioners where similar multi-disciplinary optimization challenges are experienced.

References

Birch D, Kelly PHJ, Field AJ (2013) Computationally unifying urban masterplanning, Proceedings of the ACM International Conference on Computing Frontiers,

Simondetti A, Roberts S, Birch D, (2012), A Practical Perspective on Computer Tools for Sustainable Building Design, Proceedings of the 2012 International EG-ICE Workshop on Intelligent Computing, Herrsching, Germany

Ayaz E. and Levitas J. (2008) Spatially linked integrated resource management (IRM): A tool to inform eco-city planning. Proceedings of the 8th International Eco-city Conference 2008, 2008.

Flager F. and Haymaker J. (2007). A comparison of multidisciplinary design, analysis and optimization processes in the building construction and aerospace industries. 24th International Conference on Information Technology in Construction. I. Smith. Maribor, Slovenia, pages 625 – 630, 2007.

Daren C. Brabham (2009) Crowdsourcing the Public Participation Process for Planning Projects, Planning Theory, Vol 8, Issue 3, pp. 242 – 262

Geisa Bugs, Carlos Granell, Oscar Fonts, Joaquín Huerta, Marco Painho, (2010) An assessment of Public Participation GIS and Web 2.0 technologies in urban planning practice in Canela, Brazil, Cities, Volume 27, Issue 3, June 2010, Pages 172-181, ISSN 0264-2751,

Jozef Doboš, Alvise Simondetti (2012), and Anthony Steed. 2012. Visualizing 3D models in aid of public consultation. In SIGGRAPH Asia 2012 Symposium on Apps

Borning, Alan, Batya Friedman, and Peter H. Kahn Jr. (2004) "Designing for Human Values in a Urban Simulation System: Value Sensitive Design and Participatory design." PDC. 2004.

Birch, D., Tsinalis, O., Van Dam, K. H., Lee, C. H., Silva, D., Wu, C., & Guo, Y. Paper: Concinnity: A Digital City Exchange Platform. Digital Economy 2013 MediaCityUK, Salford

Gregory J. Ward (1994). The radiance lighting simulation and rendering system. Computer Graphics (Proceedings of '94 SIGGRAPH conference).

Littlefair P J. (1991) Site layout planning for daylight and sunlight: a guide to good practice. Building Research Establishment.

Flora Salim, Usman Haque 2015 Urban computing in the wild: A survey on large scale participation and citizen engagement with ubiquitous computing, cyber physical systems, and Internet of Things ☆ International Journal of Human-Computer Studies Volume 81, September 2015, Pages 31–48

Corney J.R., Torres-Sánchez C., Jagadeesan A.P., Yan X.T. , Regli W.C. , Medellin H., 2010 Putting the crowd to work in a knowledge-based factory Advanced Engineering Informatics Volume 24, Issue 3, August 2010, Pages 243–250

Hao Wu, Jonathan Corney, Michael Grant (2015) An evaluation methodology for crowdsourced design Advanced Engineering Informatics Volume 29, Issue 4, October 2015, Pages 775–786

Broll, W., Lindt, I., Ohlenburg, J., Wittkämper, M., Yuan, C., Novotny, T., Strothmann, A. (2004). ARTHUR: A Collaborative Augmented Environment for Architectural Design and Urban Planning. *Journal of Virtual Reality and Broadcasting*, *1*(1), 1–10.

A framework for ontology-based design assessment for human behaviour during fire evacuation

Calin Boje, Haijiang Li
Cardiff University, United Kingdom
BojeCP@cardiff.ac.uk

Abstract. The current procedures in assessing fire performance designs are costly and inefficient, as they require the preparation and analysis of several scenario models, which may change at every design iteration. To address this, this paper presents a way to leverage BIM model data using OWL ontology tools to integrate, automate and provide feedback to the design decision-making process. The paper introduces methodologies from research which are relevant to the presented concept, then expands on a problem identification section, arguing why crowd simulation analysis might also benefit the ontology-based approach. The core emphasis of the paper is the framework required to achieve the process where ontology rules, reasoning and inference are leveraged from existing IFC models, with minimal user input. The framework consists of several components which are described independently, based on a system currently under development. A use case presents the practical flow of the process and some of its requirements and limitations.

1. Introduction

With the gradual increase of interoperable tools and the proliferation of the IFC format, BIM centric design and management has led to the use of BIM and IFC as a means to assess code-compliance in performance-based design (Eastman et al. 2009). However, most of the tools and methods are less suitable in performance-based design situations, where the regulation process needs to include modelling assumptions such as data input and their sources, as well as the analysis results. Conventionally, these factors are usually at the discretion of the designer, based on personal and professional judgement and knowledge. In this sense, we aim to explore how more advanced information formats which support basic semantic reasoning can fill this gap, by adopting ontologies as tools to integrate information, automate the processes and provide adequate feedback. Several studies have already adopted similar methodologies when considering either rules checking or other building performance design criteria, which will be presented and discussed, along with the reasons we believe ontologies can leverage BIM information.

This paper aims to identify how semantic web applications can be used to integrate and automate the performance based design for safe fire evacuation. Based on this, the methodology we adopted looks to: a) identify the problem with fire escape design analysis and rules checking and b) propose a framework which describes the process of using semantic linked data and reasoning for performance based design of human behaviour analysis. A short use case example is presented at the end.

2. Related work

Pauwels et al. 2011 is one of the pilot studies investigating the capabilities of semantic web rule checking, applied to acoustic building design. They state that limitations in the IFC schema expressivity of concepts are overcome by an ontology approach. Another pilot study on using ontology tools is Scherer and Schapke 2011, which describes a framework for using ontologies as a means of integration on the project level, which can include multiple models and processes. Such approaches allow the rule checking process to go beyond the schema scope, thus allowing for more flexible model view definitions, which is crucial in including non-traditional design analysis under the BIM umbrella.

Venugopal et al. 2015 investigated the current state of exiting Model View Definitions (MVDs) and concluded that the processes behind them are inefficient and not future-proof as the industry expands its use of the IFC. The authors consider ontology representations of the IFC schema to allow for a flexible and more robust backbone for interoperability requirements. The computer-interpretable features of ontologies allow for validation methods and easier extensibility of other disciplines into the design process. Their ability to represent knowledge is better suited for the underlying BIM models, as is more robust than the IFC schema, while also being a good interoperability tool (Venugopal et al. 2015). There have been several applications of ontology data linking for specific applications in the AEC sector, mainly focused on energy, cost and risk analysis, but limited focus on human behaviour design analysis.

Buildings are designed to achieve minimum levels of safety regarding fire design. This usually comes down to prescribed regulations, which vary by region. However, prescriptive regulation design can restrict design in other fields, and thus simulation tools for human behaviour or fire fluid mechanics are used to assess building performance, where they are not met. Over the last decades, dozens of tools capable to simulate human behaviour in buildings have emerged, each with its own benefits and limitations, as reviewed more recently by Ronchi and Nilsson 2013.

Regarding fire design, there have been several attempts to explore integration of fire tools with BIM (Wang et al. 2015, Wang and Wainer 2015), with a small number aimed at regulation checking standardisation (Dimyadi et al. 2016), and even fewer aimed at performance design review. In most cases these attempts use IFC data in a static way, and mostly rely on the 3D information, making the process inefficient and lacking in interoperability. Wang and Wainer 2015 developed a system to provide crowd simulation as a service, integrated with BIM tools to some degree using IFC. This study however fails to address the complexities regarding information input specific to occupant data apart from geometric building data, or how simulation results can relate to existing BIM models and its object components.

Dimyadi et al. 2016 is one of the first comprehensive attempts to include fire rules in checking applications by importing IFC models. This is a more traditional approach in terms of rule-checking environments, expressing design rules in code format and using Regulatory Knowledge Models (RKMs). However, most of these implementations were initially intended for prescribed regulations checking, rather than for performance design. Dimyadi et al. 2015 explored the potential to link the above-mentioned RMKs to ontology concepts, for a more efficient compliance audit model, in order to give it more interoperability with other tools, while also being seen as more suitable for performance assessment, due to increased expressivity. However, there have been no actual implementations of such methodologies to the best of our knowledge, so far.

3. Problem identification

Building design is becoming increasingly complex in terms of process due to the need for optimised designs in multiple disciplines, project size or complex architecture. This puts a lot of pressure on designers to deliver safe, optimized and aesthetically pleasing buildings, in a limited amount of time. As the ability to improve or change a design diminishes over time during a project, design decision making must be precise and based on adequate scenario analysis in order to achieve the best results. Thus, building performance design audit domains need to be more efficient and collaborative across multiple disciplines, a gap which could solved automating several processes involved.

With design analysis tools and the proliferation of BIM technologies and processes, the potential to deliver better designs has improved. BIM not only improves the process, but it also offers new ways to manage and use data in a more integrated way. According to a recent study on industry and academic trends on BIM related subjects (Leite et al. 2016), some of the biggest challenges under consideration are the processes of simulating and predicting building behaviour and verification and validation of the simulation output. The authors also note that there are virtually no standard data sets or methods for predicting human behaviour in terms of energy usage or building usage in general. This increases the need to predict occupant behaviour, from the earliest design stages, across all fields.

Interoperability and integration of structured data sit at the core of BIM. The IFC format has been developed over the last 20 years in the hopes of solving this issue. While IFC has become a strong base for carrying out BIM level 2 projects, it cannot include every aspect of the building design across its lifecycle. Many studies in the area of costs or energy analysis try to work directly on the IFC schema and several IFC schema extensions have been proposed, including for fire safety models (Dimyadi et al. 2016), limited however to prescriptive design checking.

When considering the act of creating a specific scenario for analysis, there are several factors and input information channels which contribute to the final results, including: building layout and geometry data, predicted building occupant behaviour profiles, design guides and regulations, as well as user input preferences. There is a need to define in what manner these factors contribute to the process, and how they are interrelated within the scope of automation.

Out of some tools able to integrate with BIM models, like Wang et al. 2015 via different geometry imports, or Wang and Wainer 2015 through the use of IFC, information importing is restricted to the building geometry, whereas simulation scenario contextual information is usually not available and hard to express programmatically. This needs to be provided by specialists via manual input.

Crowd simulation analysis usually involves several iterations for two different reasons: the probabilistic nature of crowd simulation tools and the variety of scenarios to be assumed by designers, where different layouts or building capacities are evaluated. This can be a very time consuming process, and because of this, the lack of continued and thorough analysis might leave the building design underperforming. In addition to their intrinsic limitations at simulating realistic behaviours, simulation tools require a lot of assumptions which develop into very specific scenarios. In order to move the domain towards automation, representing such assumptions programmatically is required.

Ontology tools enable us to capture expert and regulations knowledge directly into our computational systems, allowing us to leverage information and cloud computing processing, where crowd simulation analysis can become an integrated service towards the BIM design and decision making processes.

Since ontologies are regarded as a good interoperability tool, we believe they have the potential to integrate the whole process and deliver faster scenario generation and improved analysis. Furthermore, from the perspective of the iBIM paradigm (or level 3 BIM), web semantic integration appears to be the next step. This suggests that ontologies are the means to achieve

BIM level 3, allowing data integration across several domains, along with the integration of Internet of Things (IoT), and other structured data formats available across the web.

In light of the above, we see ontologies as the only tool able to meet our needs in the way forward for integrated and automatic tools, for the time being.

4. Methodology and hypothesis of overall research

The hypothesis of our research is that current BIM technologies and processes can be leveraged to enable more automatic and integrated performance designs regarding human behaviour analysis in buildings, making the process more efficient and allowing knowledge feedback into the design stage for review and analysis. The methodology of the research involves several steps: integration of Crowd Simulation Models (CSM) with IFC models in OWL format, representation of simulation scenario from design rules, description of the framework for a fully functioning system, validation and testing.

This paper presents part of the overall research, the architecture of the system along with sample testing scenarios.

5. A framework for ontology-based fire escape analysis

The process of the proposed concept, described in Figure 1, showcases an automated process where crowd simulation scenarios are generated automatically, according to design input and ontology rules and reasoning. Feedback to designers is provided by ontology reasoning and interfaces, which considers input variables and simulation results. In order to achieve such a process, there are component requirements. The framework for such a system is best described by its components and their functionality in the entire process:

1) Input data models – provides all relevant input from building model information, user preferences and design constraints; any other additional data such as sensor data or design variable tables, depending on the context, can be included;
2) Ontology core – framework component which stores all the required information in RDF format, including representations of software components, model data, alignment models and reasoning rules;
3) Output models – refers to two types of output modes. The first is the generated analysis scenarios to be run and their respective additional generated data used for analysis. The second is the output provided by the ontology reasoning for design feedback;
4) Interfacing plug-ins - refers to the customised interfaces which are used for providing a user-friendly experience.

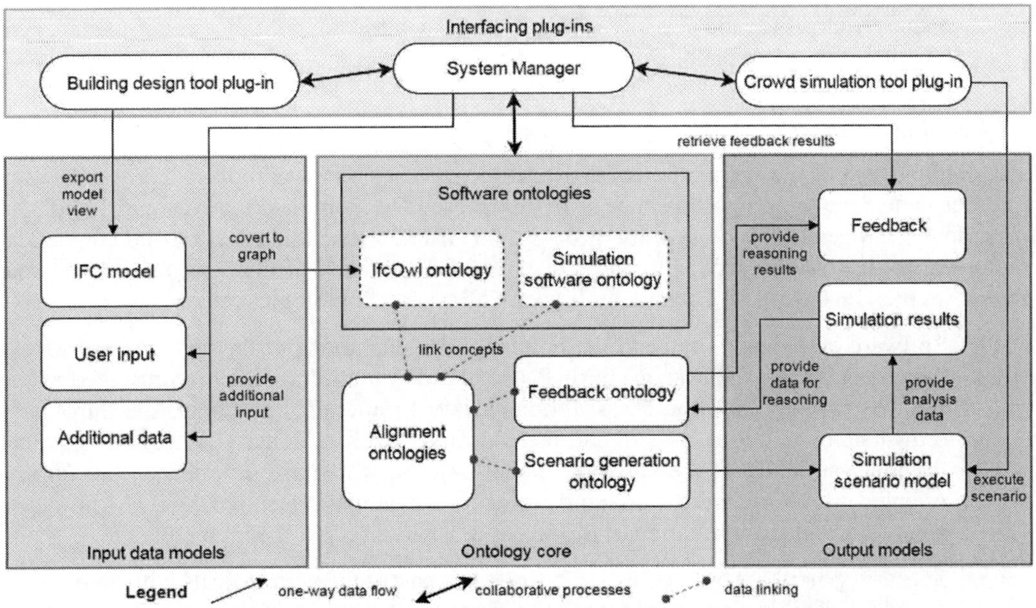

Figure 1: Framework components categories by their functionalities and their interaction

Each of the main framework components has specific roles to fulfil, depending on the stage of the process:

I. Scenario generation automation stage – all required inputs are aggregated into a valid crowd simulation scenario, which is then executed for analysis;

II. Scenario analysis and feedback stage – executed scenario data is queried, ontology reasoning is used to assess design rules or objectives, which provides feedback to users.

5.1 Input data models

The input models refer to several independent elements, which provide the required input for the entire process to work, as follows:

- IFC building model – a view of the IFC model as exported by a proprietary BIM platform. A full view is not required, but a specific MVD for crowd simulation analysis is not yet released, as such a normal coordination view is sufficient as it provides full geometry data as well as all other relevant annotation objects. The IFC model can store customised textual and numeric properties which could represent the design requirements, such as space occupancy numbers, densities or classification of spaces. This is probably the most efficient method to ensure a full model view for this purpose, as object data is easily mapped to each object instance through the IFC semantics, and thus requires less reasoning by the ontologies.
- User input – in addition to the specific data requirements present in the IFC model, user input needs to complement the data by adding specific contextual information, such as types of scenarios, objectives of the analysis process and including other sources of information if the IFC model only provides partial data (e.g. occupant densities)
- Additional information – this refers to any other contextual or data input channels, which vary based on the BIM lifecycle stage. For example, designers will use design

values from tables and classification systems (such as Uniclass), but building managers might prefer to use historical or sensor data.

5.2 Ontology core

The ontology core is the aggregation of the semantic representations of tools and processes used in order to achieve the proposed concept, by leveraging the input data via reasoning, and also providing interoperability to the entire process. To ensure a functional system and convenient maintenance, it is recommended to adopt a segregated approach of the core ontologies used, which are then linked via alignment ontologies. The types of ontologies required are:

- Software ontologies – refer to the ontology representations of the different BIM tools which are part of the system. In this case, the IFC building model, represented in the IfcOwl ontology, and the MassMotion (Oasys Limited 2017) model, the third-party crowd simulation tool chosen, and its respective ontology. These ontologies represent the inner structure of the software model objects, which are described in an object-oriented way. Since there is no standard for crowd simulation, unlike the IFC, this means an ontological representation of the software is necessary at the moment.
- Scenario generation ontologies– at its core, this part of the system deals with automation of model data. In the crowd simulation domain, it needs to define concepts such as: spaces and their types (inhabited, uninhabited, fire refuge, etc.), occupants and their behaviour, as well as other contextual knowledge like type of scenario (e.g. at full or partial building capacity). It consists of many rules able to reason according to input: what spaces are used and how, which parts of the building are populated by agents and their number, and where the input data is coming from. A scenario generation ontology needs to be precise and comprehensive in representing design knowledge and intent. It can become a mixture of best practices, in terms of knowledge representation, but it should also be able to encompass concepts related to user input preferences. For the approach adopted here, we have chosen to represent design knowledge from UK British Standards codes of practice, namely BSI PD 7974 2004, part-6, when using crowd simulation tools. While the codes can sometimes be vague or allow for designer lee way, it is necessary to represent the choices available to the users as well. This allows more variety of scenarios and brings more complexity and potentially more relevant information to the results feedback stage.
- Feedback ontologies – similar to the previous, the feedback ontologies represents design knowledge, but the evaluation and analysis perspective. They need to encapsulate various reasoning rules, which are in line with analysis objectives. These may relate to evacuation times, bottleneck points, agent behaviour, assemblies of objects which influence results. Like with the previous, to ensure relevant and precise knowledge feedback, input data, user preferences & objectives and software limitations should ideally be taken into consideration when representing this field.
- Alignment ontologies – this provides the interoperability of all the different knowledge and application domains involved, mapping data across the different ontologies mentioned above. The alignment ontology can also resemble the role of an MVD data transfer protocol. The main difference however, is that all the data in the other models can still be present, and with the correct mappings, accessible for future extensions.

The approach adopted in our research was to host a series of different ontologies on a commercial RDF server, namely Stardog (Stardog Union 2017), which enables easy access to the database via HTTP protocols using java APIs.

5.3 Output models

There are two types of output, corresponding to each process stage mentioned above:

- Simulation scenario model – represents the output of the automation process, consisting of a specific scenario, which is then executed to generate results;
- Simulation results – refers to the additional data provided by the crowd analysis software, after executing scenarios. The output data depends on the software tools used. In our developments, data is provided in SQL format. The alignment and feedback ontologies need to access only the required data, thus separate queries to the data were implemented to integrate the SQL.
- Feedback rules output – refers to the output provided by ontology rules execution and reasoning, as mentioned in 5.2. The reasoning is handled by the feedback ontology, but querying for the answers should be handled by the interfacing software.

5.4 Interfacing plug-ins

While the previous components collaborate in the background and manipulate data, the interface plug-ins have the role of managing the querying of the ontology embedded knowledge according to user preferences. The secondary role of the interfaces is to restrict the ontology reasoning scope and complement any limitations which ontology rules might not be able to perform, such as data format conversions, or the creation of new ontology individuals. The interface is vital to conducting a logical process of the underlying services, and act as connectors to the entire system.

5.5 Multi-layered architecture system

In order to achieve a federated modelling approach, we have adopted a multi-layer architecture for our developed system, as described in the figure below.

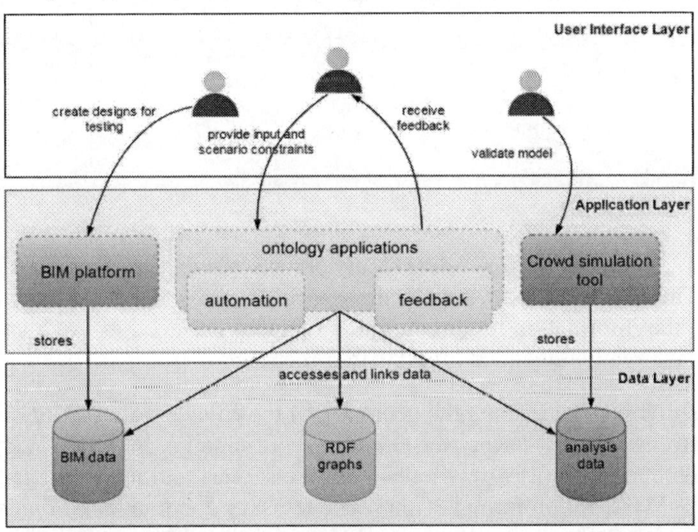

Figure 2: System architecture used in research, its layers and basic components

The main layers have the following functionalities:

1. Data Layer – stores all the data in different federated databases, including BIM models, RDF graphs which contain all the mentioned ontologies and SQL data from the analysis software.
2. Application Layer – while the different BIM applications and tools to not need to collaborate explicitly, collaboration is achieved via the ontology applications. They manage the performance review process, and have access to all the data in the lower layer. The BIM platform and crowd simulation tools are both provides or data in this case.
3. User Interface Layer – consists of all the separate interfacing plug-ins, which allow user input and feedback of the underlying layers.

6. Use case example

The current development of the system consists of a main Java application which interacts with the Stardog RDF servers. The IFC models are initially created in Autodesk Revit, and then converted to IfcOwl format. The ontologies and the rules were implemented using the Protégé software. Partial tests were carried out during the software implementation, and the ontologies were constantly checked using several reasoners.

When generating the scenarios, for automated crowd model generation, all the required data was provided in the IFC model, such as roles of space and their occupancies. Building components from the IFC model were directly mapped to the MassMotion ontology, thus any IFC model individual that has a MassMotion corresponding type, is also a MassMotion individual. As such, the *first step* involved selecting the required information from the IfcOwl model, as a reasoning query in SPARQL:

```
PREFIX mmOnto:  <http://icompe.engineering.cf.ac.uk/MassMotionOntology#>
PREFIX express: <http://purl.org/voc/express#>
PREFIX ifcowl:  <http://www.buildingsmart-tech.org/ifcOWL/IFC2X3_TC1#>
SELECT DISTINCT ?ifcId
WHERE {
  ?instance rdf:type ?class .
  ?instance ifcowl:globalId_IfcRoot ?guid express:hasString ?ifcId .
FILTER (?class = mmOnto:Actor) }
```

In the case above, "mmOnto:Actor" refers to any objects which have a geometric representation in MassMotion models, such as: floors, walls, spaces, stairs, etc. The query above is the first step in filtering the information required, which replaces the need to use a specific MVD for this purpose, as it already imbedded into the alignment ontology.

The *second step* involved generating the geometry of the objects from the IFC format (also now stored in the ontology model) to the MassMotion representation in XML. We have developed a software which queries the IfcOwl model from the servers and reconstructs the geometry of every object into MassMotion format. This was necessary due to a lack of an existing API for the crowd simulation software to date. Knowledge of the structure of the IFC schema and the crowd software geometry is required to perform this step. The IFC schema and its Owl representation are object-oriented, thus it usually generated lengthy queries to the IfcOwl model, to retrieve basic datatypes, such as strings and integer values. This can become very costly in terms of reasoning time, if the SPARQL query is long and if it contains vague triples, or multiple UNION operation of results. To optimise this, the geometry was queried without any reasoning flags, while storing in memory the global "IfcId" of the objects in question, which was used to identify individuals across multiple queries.

Unlike the geometry, contextual information present in the IFC (such as types of space, occupant number) varies with the situation. As such it was expressed in SWRL rules and reasoning was used to obtain it for scenario by scenario basis. For example, the SWRL rule below, seeks to identify which space is inhabited, based on its corresponding occupancy number:

```
Space(?space) ^ hasAgentNumber(?space, ?agentNumber) ^ hasInteger(?agentNumber,
?value) ^ swrlb:greaterThan(?value, 0) -> InhabitedSpace(?space)
```

These sort of rules can become very useful in finding inferences from data and semantics present in the IFC model. However, due to the expressivity of the SWRL syntax, it becomes quite challenging to express certain rules. For example, considering the rule above, if a "Space" type individual meets the requirements, it automatically becomes an "InhabitedSpace" type as a sub-class of "Space", but we cannot state in the same rule what happens if the result is false. As such, the contrary rule needs to be implemented to classify a space as "UninhabitedSpace" type:

```
Space(?space) ^ hasAgentNumber(?space, ?agentNumber) ^ hasInteger(?agentNumber,
?value) ^ swrlb:equal(?value, 0) -> UninhabitedSpace(?space)
```

It's important to distinguish between "inhabited" and "uninhabited" types of spaces correctly in order to make the correct scenario assumptions. For example, crowd simulations guidelines (PD 7974 2004) usually do not consider circulation spaces as inhabited, which is not possible to distinguish from the IFC model alone, without some ontology reasoning on top. We have implemented several rules in establishing this, according to specified occupant numbers, as expressed above, or according to Uniclass codes, where each space code corresponds to either of the two categories. Unfortunately, due to the Open-World Assumption (OWA) which OWL adheres to, there is no way to check if the space is inhabited or uninhabited if the required information to assess it is not present in the ontology. To overcome this, the ontology representation needs to be tested in multiple scenarios.

After the scenario automation stage, the *third step* involved running the MassMotion simulation model. The model contained all the geometry, as specified in the alignment process, as well as all the other contextual data provided by the data and ontology reasoning. These could be considered the initial parameters and assumptions of the simulation input. The simulation tool executed the scenario, providing a database in SQL of raw data.

For the *fourth step*, the data was queried according to the feedback ontology requirements. For example, a parameter of interest to designers considered was the total travel time of agents, which was looked up the SQL database and transformed as an ontology individual in the RDF graphs. A rule was then applied to check the results against user requirements:

```
TravelTime(?time) ^ InputTravelTime(?requiredTime) ^ swrlb:lessThan(?requiredTime,
?time) -> AcceptableTravelTime(?time)
```

The last step involved querying the RDF graphs for specific feedback, which is handled by the interface. As imbedded rules and inferences are present in the ontologies, data about specific individuals needs to be selected using specific SPAQRL queries and the results need to be presented in a user-friendly format. The last two steps of the development described are still a work in progress.

7. Summary

Current procedures for fire escape performance design are hard to assess and require significant input from designers, making the entire process costly and inefficient. In this paper we have presented a way to leverage BIM model data to provide integration of several tools, automation of data and ways to provide relevant feedback to designers. Based on a short literature review of similar concepts, the use of semantic linked data paradigm seems to show promise in complementing the IFC schema and integrating multiple design knowledge domains. A short problem identification raised the most important factors which might be beneficial for a performance based human behaviour analysis design case.

The framework for using crowd simulation analysis is dependent on a correct ontological representation of the tools, design regulations, user input and simulation results. Thus we have suggested a modular approach, where every component and its ontology representation are individually implemented, and all common concepts are mapped via an alignment ontology. The framework presented is based on our experience with implementing a similar system in practice, according to the described architecture.

The use case scenario provided shows a few simple examples of the ontology linking, reasoning and rules which are used as part of our overall research. The scenario showcases a few of the steps in the process of using ontology tools for integration, automation and feedback, along with some limitations of the ontology approach.

References

Dimyadi, J. et al. 2016. Computerizing Regulatory Knowledge for Building Engineering Design. *Journal of Computing in Civil Engineering* 30(5), p. C4016001.

Dimyadi, J. et al. 2015. Querying a Regulatory Model for Compliant Building Design Audit. *Proc. of the 32nd CIB W78 Conference 2015, 27th-29th October 2015, Eindhoven, The Netherlands*, pp. 139–148.

Eastman, C. et al. 2009. Automatic rule-based checking of building designs. *Automation in Construction* 18(8), pp. 1011–1033.

Leite, F. et al. 2016. Visualization, Information Modeling, and Simulation: Grand Challenges in the Construction Industry. *Journal of Computing in Civil Engineering*, p. 4016035.

Oasys Limited 2017. MassMotion [Online] Available at: http://www.oasys-software.com/products/engineering/massmotion.html.

Pauwels, P. et al. 2011. A semantic rule checking environment for building performance checking. *Automation in Construction* 20(5), pp. 506–518.

PD 7974 2004. *The application of fire safety engineering principles to fire safety design of buildings. Human factors. Life safety strategies. Occupant evacuation, behaviour and condition (Sub-system 6)*. British Standards Institution Group London UK.

Ronchi, E. and Nilsson, D. 2013. Fire evacuation in high-rise buildings: a review of human behaviour and modelling research. *Fire Science Reviews* 2(1), p. 7.

Scherer, R.J. and Schapke, S.E. 2011. A distributed multi-model-based Management Information System for simulation and decision-making on construction projects. *Advanced Engineering Informatics* 25(4), pp. 582–599.

Stardog Union 2017. Stardog [Online] Available at: http://stardog.com/.

Venugopal, M. et al. 2015. An ontology-based analysis of the industry foundation class schema for building information model exchanges. *Advanced Engineering Informatics* 29(4), pp. 940–957.

Wang, S.-H. et al. 2015. Applying building information modeling to support fire safety management. *Automation in Construction* 59, pp. 158–167.

Wang, S. and Wainer, G. 2015. A simulation as a service methodology with application for crowd modeling, simulation and visualization. *SIMULATION* 91(1), pp. 71–95.

Combined Super-Structured and Super-Structure Free Optimisation of Building Spatial Designs

Boonstra, S.[1*], Van der Blom, K.[2], Hofmeyer, H.[1], Emmerich, M.T.M.[2]
[1]Eindhoven University of Technology, The Netherlands
[2]Leiden Institute of Advanced Computer Science, Leiden University, The Netherlands
[*]s.boonstra@tue.nl

Abstract. This paper proposes a new method for multi-disciplinary optimisation of building spatial designs in the preliminary design stage. First it discusses two recently developed building spatial design optimisation methods, one using a super-structured approach and the other applying a super-structure free approach. Subsequently, a combination of the two methods into a new hybrid method is presented. A case study is demonstrated to compare the three methods based on their performance and the characteristics of their design evolution. First results show that the hybrid method could aid in the effective exploration of large design search spaces by selecting more confined design search spaces based on engineering knowledge.

1. Introduction

The process of building design optimisation is still strongly dependent on input from numerous engineers and designers, simply because the design search space is too large to be overseen by any single stakeholder. This limitation motivates computer scientists to constantly develop new techniques that try to find the global optimum by considering as many solutions as possible without bias. Taking into account every possible solution is, however, computationally infeasible. This paper proposes a new method that uses engineering knowledge to steer the process into interesting sub-domains of the design search space to increase the efficiency of and limit the strain on optimisation algorithms.

One domain in the research on optimisation focuses on multi-objective optimisation by use of evolutionary algorithms, which find a subset of designs to approximate the Pareto optimal front in a predefined search space. Here, a Pareto optimal front is a set of solutions that are characterized by being non-dominated, i.e. no other solutions are defined that perform better for any objective without there being a decrease of performance for any of the other objectives first. State-of-the-art optimisation algorithms such as NSGA-II (Deb *et al*, 2002) or SMS-EMOA (Beume *et al*, 2007) use random selection of solutions and random mutation or crossover on previously found solutions to find the Pareto front. The Hypervolume-based Subset Selection Problem (HSSP), as presented by Kuhn *et al* (2016) and Bringmann *et al* (2014) focuses on the selection of the solutions: If the found Pareto Front Approximation (PFA) contains more points than desired, a reduction should take place; if—on the other hand—fewer points than desired are found, all non-dominated and a diverse selection of dominated points can be selected to reach the desired number.

A drawback of evolutionary algorithms is that they are computationally costly when a rigorous search of large search spaces is attempted. So-called heuristic methods do not have this drawback, as they use a directed and thus fast way to obtain improved designs from the design search space. Heuristic methods are, however, prone to finish the search process when they find a local optimum, rather than the global optimum. An example of a heuristic method is the simulation of Co-evolutionary Design (CD) processes. This method tries to simulate evolutionary processes that are seen in nature where two species interact in a manner where they depend on each other in their evolution. Maher & Tang (2003) present a general method for co-evolutionary design optimisation. Hofmeyer and Davila Delgado (2015) use the principle of CD for building design. They base a simulation of a co-evolutionary design process on the interaction that building design engineers have during the design of buildings. A relatively new development concerns meta-heuristic algorithms, which improve the performance of evolutionary algorithms by adding heuristic methods to the search using hybridisation (Talbi, 2002). Hybridisation is defined here as a combination of two or more methods that share a common goal, such that the hybrid method inherits the positive features of each method.

As mentioned, evolutionary algorithms use a predefined search space, which is often referred to as a super-structure. Thus, a super-structured optimisation method operates on a predefined design search space, meaning that the set of solutions in this search space is limited to a finite number. On the other hand, for a super-structure free optimisation method no limit is placed on the design search space, and parts of a design can be freely modified, added, or removed. Most optimisation methods cannot handle super-structure free optimisation, since they assume a fixed number and type of parameters. Voll *et al* (2012) show that it can be beneficial to consider a super-structure free method to find new and possibly unexpected solutions that would otherwise not be found because they were not included in the super-structure. Kim and Kwak, (2002) automatically adapt a super-structure over time, such that the design space is either refined, extended or reduced, based on previous optimisation results.

The need for the reduction of building footprints, both environmentally as well as financially, has driven extensive research on the optimisation of building designs. Díaz *et al* (2017) review Multi-Disciplinary Optimisation (MDO) in the built environment and present practical problems to be solved in future research. Geyer (2009) presents work on the implementation of optimisation methods in Building Information Modelling (BIM) that also take user interaction into account. User interaction is considered by Steiner *et al* (2016) too, who present an algorithm that generates structural layouts based on spatial designs produced by architects. Many papers present an implementation of existing optimisation methods in Computer Aided Design (CAD) or BIM design frameworks. For example, Rahmani Asl *et al* (2015) and Welle *et al* (2011) both present building thermal design optimisation in a BIM-based design search space. Caldas (2008) show the capabilities of an optimisation oriented CAD environment in which user defined design variables may be optimised by an evolutionary algorithm. A limited amount of work also focuses on considerations for tuning and the development of building specific optimisation methods. For instance Mora *et al* (2011) propose a method to provide designers with feedback on the life-cycle costs during the design process. Gero *et al* (1983) demonstrate a model to represent and compare design alternatives in order to asses an objective in a context with other objectives. Hamdy *et al* (2016) present a comparison between several tuned optimisation methods to study the efficiency and the performance of different algorithms. Finally, Hopfe *et al* (2012) propose a method to predict the impact of design variables on the design's optimality.

As indicated above, for building design optimisation, the distinction between super-structured and super-structure free methods has not been taken into account explicitly so far. Also, an MDO method for preliminary building spatial designs does not exist. And finally, no hybridisation between knowledge-based building design optimisation and state-of-the-art evolutionary algorithms has been developed. For this reason, Boonstra *et al* (2016) defined the basis required for the cooperation between super-structured and super-structure free optimisation for building spatial design. Included were two design representations for building spatial design optimisation: First, a so-called supercube, which was suitable for mathematical programming methods because of its parametric design space. The second being a so-called movable sizable representation that is intuitive for engineers, and applicable for rule based super-structure free optimisation. As a next step, this paper proposes a method to combine the best characteristics of the above methods.

Section 2 elaborates on the two previously developed optimisation methods and their combination into a new hybrid method. An academic case study to compare and demonstrate the existing and new methods is presented in section 3. This is then followed by the conclusions and an outlook in section 4.

2. Optimisation Methods

This section presents the developed super-structured and super-structure free optimisation methods. For this the two design search space representations are briefly discussed (Boonstra *et al*, 2016): SuperCube (SC, figure 1a), and Movable Sizable (MS, figure 1b). The supercube has sizable divisions that divide it into cells that can each be activated for a space within the design. The movable sizable representation defines a design by given spaces that are each defined with a location and dimensions. The workings of the super-structured and super-structure free optimisation methods are presented first. This is followed by a description of the new combined method.

2.1 Super-Structured Optimisation

The SuperCube (SC) representation has first been applied in building spatial design optimisation by Van der Blom *et al* (2016a). In this paper a canonical evolution strategy was used for single objective optimisation. Moreover, penalty functions were used to navigate away from infeasible solutions. This was followed by Van der Blom *et al* (2016b), where two state-of-the-art evolutionary multi-objective optimisation algorithms have been used, namely the Non-dominated Sorting Genetic Algorithm (NSGA-II, Deb *et al* 2002) and the S-Metric Selection Evolutionary Multi-objective Optimisation Algorithm (SMS-EMOA, Beume *et al* 2007). Van der Blom *et al* (2016b) also tailored the SMS-EMOA algorithm—specifically for the building spatial design optimisation problem—by introducing smart mutation and smart initialisation operators. By taking into account constraints these operators avoid infeasible designs entirely. The design search space is defined by the input for this method: the supercube size, the number of spaces and the total building volume. A comparison between the three techniques has indicated that the tailored version of SMS-EMOA found the most accurate Pareto front approximation, measured by the so-called hypervolume indicator. More recently, Van der Blom *et al* (2017) propose improved initialisation and mutation operators to eliminate bias. Additionally, parameter tuning algorithms have been utilised to find an improved set of parameters for the tailored version of SMS-EMOA. This method has proven to be successful in the optimisation of building designs, but has not yet been tested on larger problem sizes (i.e. supercube size and number of spaces) that are needed for larger buildings.

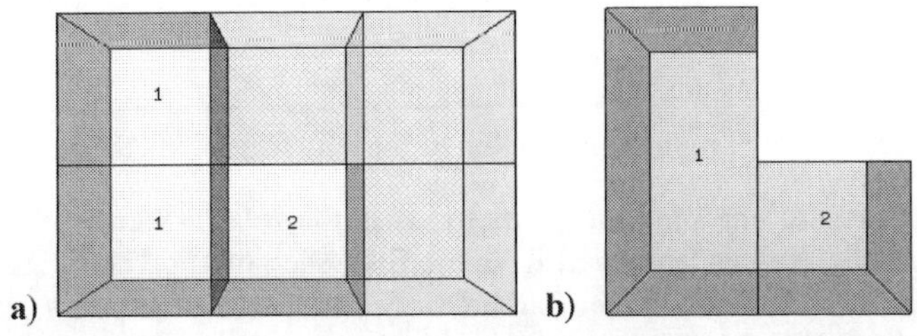

Figure 1: a) SC-representation, "active" cells (here yellow) describe a space within the supercube. b) MS-representation, each space is defined by its location and dimensions

2.2 Super-Structure Free Optimisation

Using the Movable Sizable (MS) representation, at Eindhoven University of Technology Hofmeyer & Davila Delgado (2015) performed simulations of Co-evolutionary Design (CD) as proposed by, among others, Maher & Tang (2003) to find structurally optimal building spatial designs. As part of these simulations, worst performing spaces were deleted from a given design, and some remaining spaces were split and the design was scaled to restore the number of spaces and volume of the initial design. Current research in Eindhoven focuses on finding a general approach of CD for multi-disciplinary optimisation of building spatial designs. This requires a technique to select a number of variables (which here are spaces) that should be removed or modified, for example by clustering the performance data of a design. Moreover, different modification techniques have to be developed that can modify designs to perform better for at least a single objective. Diversity in these modification techniques is desired as, firstly, it increases the chance that a solution can be steered towards Pareto optimality, and secondly it gives the possibility to consider more solutions in the design process. This method has proven to find better designs quickly, but it is sensitive to local optima.

2.3 Combination

A combination of the previously mentioned methods was proposed to employ the best of both without including their bad characteristics, i.e. employ speed and quality without computational costs. A combination does however also yield new parameters to consider. First of all is the scheme in which the different methods are executed. Useful suggestions for such schemes can be found in the research domain of hybrid metaheuristics, where local and global search methods are combined. Secondly, a selected scheme inevitably involves more new parameters, specific to the selected scheme and the used method. Finally, the information transfer between methods also involves parameters, e.g. which designs are selected for a computationally expensive local search? This subsection presents two (hybridisation) schemes from Talbi (2002) and relevant new parameters.

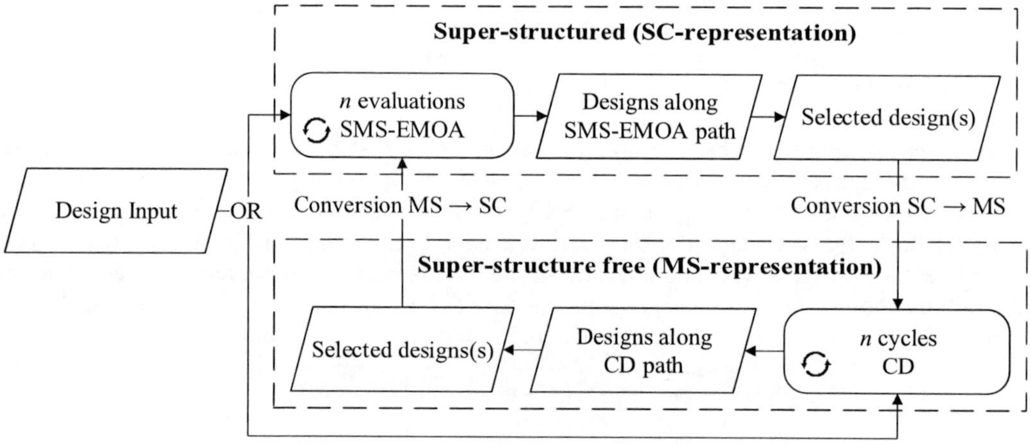

Figure 2: Relay combination of the optimisation methods

Relay. A straight forward combination of methods is the relay scheme as shown in figure 2. Methods are executed in relays, and apart from the first, each method is initiated with the results from the previous method. This scheme can be made more competitive by making the transfer to another method conditional: The next method is then conditionally called, depending on the performance of the previous. If the previous method performs satisfactory nothing changes, otherwise another method will be used.

Teamwork. The teamwork scheme as shown in figure 3 causes the combined methods to compete. Methods are run in parallel, where after selected solutions are used as starting points for a new parallel session of the methods.

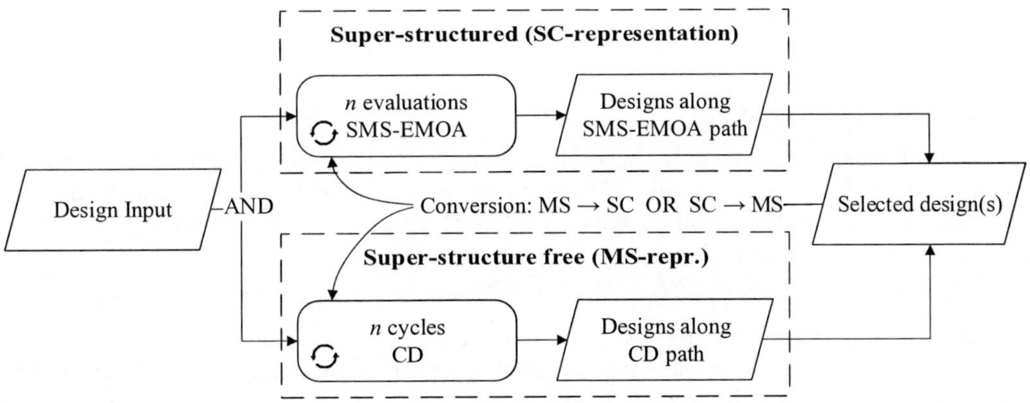

Figure 3: Teamwork combination of the optimisation methods

Parameters. A number of parameters has to be considered for the combination of the optimisation methods: with respect to the design selection; the initial method; the depth of search for each method; and the conversions between the representations.

Design Selection. For each iteration, a method generates a number of design solutions, of which one or multiple have to be selected for the next method. Pareto optimality could help in this selection; however, the number of designs that are contained in a Pareto Front Approximation (PFA) varies. Thus, selecting the entire PFA could lead to excessive computational costs, and in the case of SMS-EMOA it could result in an initial population larger than the chosen population size. Therefore, it could be considered to use the single so-called knee point, which is the point that lies closest to the minimum point. Hypervolume-based subset selection (Kuhn *et al*, 2016 and Bringmann *et al*, 2014) selects a representative subset (a specified number of points) from a PFA, and could be another approach to select the design to be continued.

Initial Method. The choice for the initial method determines the required design input. Namely the CD method needs an initial design consisting of spaces with their locations and dimensions, whereas SMS-EMOA requires the number of divisions in the supercube, the total building volume, and the number of spaces. Additionally, the choice for a sequence of methods will clearly affect the search path of the combined approach and thus will strongly influence the results.

Evaluation Budget. The evaluation budget, or the number of evaluations for each method, is of interest because a-priori it is not known how fast a method will find the optimum. If the budget is too low the method might find sub-optimal solutions, and if the budget is too large computation time is wasted. The optimal budget is problem and method specific and can only be found by tuning algorithms and by experience.

Conversion. A transfer between methods involves a conversion of the selected designs to another representation as described by Boonstra *et al* (2016). However, this is not straight-forward for a transfer from the CD method to SMS-EMOA because of the following: The input of SMS-EMOA is a supercube, thus a design is defined by a specific supercube plus a selection of activated cells. As such, either it has to be decided to regard the specific supercube as sufficiently describing the CD design, or to generate the initial individuals not only via the initialisation operators but also by activating cells such that the selected CD design(s) occurs.

Additionally, it should be noted that supercube sizes may differ when multiple designs are selected to initialise SMS-EMOA, which can only handle one supercube size. This can easily be solved by the addition of empty cells to each design's supercube, such that they can all be represented by the same supercube.

3. Academic Case Study

This section presents a case study concerning a building of eight spaces with a total volume of 300 m³. It serves as a demonstration and a first comparison of the developed methods. Settings are given for each optimisation method, as well as the results and a discussion.

3.1 Settings

Design Grammars. A building spatial design cannot be evaluated on discipline specific objectives without the corresponding discipline specific design properties. These design properties will be created by design grammars, which are sets of design rules that operate on the building spatial design. An alternative for grammars could be optimisation methods or computer learning techniques, but for demonstration purposes here grammars are used. Two design grammars are defined, one for structural and one for thermal building design.

Structural design. A grammar for structural design adds structural components like columns, beams, or slabs, and also structural loads and constraints to the building spatial design. For this case study, every surface in the building spatial design is structurally interpreted as a concrete slab of 150 mm thick with a Young's modulus E of $30000\ \mathrm{N/mm^2}$ and a Poisson's ratio ν of 0.3. Each slab is meshed into 100 flat-shell finite elements, i.e. with a division of 10 elements along each side. For the element formulation a combination of the formulations for in-plane-behaviour as presented by Cook (1974) and out-of-plane behaviour by Batoz & Tahar (1982) is used both with 2×2 numerical integration (Gaussian quadrature). All nodes in the model that have the global minimal z-coordinate are constrained for x- y- and z-displacements. A life load case in $-z$ direction with magnitude $5\ \mathrm{kN/m^2}$ is added to each horizontally oriented slab. Finally, four wind load cases are added to all exterior slabs, one in positive x, one in positive y, one in negative x and one in negative y direction. The magnitudes are determined with respect to the orientation of the slab and the direction of the load case: Three different magnitudes are defined: suction $0.8\ \mathrm{kN/m^2}$, shear $0.4\ \mathrm{kN/m^2}$ and pressure $1.0\ \mathrm{kN/m^2}$. Finite element equations are assembled into a system of equations, which is then solved using an LLT decomposition as found in the Eigen C++ library by Guennebaud & Jacob (2010).

Thermal Design. The thermal design consists out of walls, windows (not used here), and thermal loads. In this case study, the grammar will add to each surface of the building spatial design a concrete wall 150 mm thick, with a specific weight $\gamma = 2400\ \mathrm{kg/m^3}$, a specific heat capacity $C = 850\ \mathrm{J/(K \times kg)}$ and a thermal conduction coefficient $\lambda = 1{,}8\ \mathrm{W/(K \times m)}$. Furthermore, to each exterior surface an additional layer of 150 mm of insulation on the outside is added with $\gamma = 60\ \mathrm{kg/m^3}$, $C = 850\ \mathrm{J/(K \times kg)}$, and $\lambda = 0.04\ \mathrm{W/(K \times m)}$. Then a system of ordinary differential equations is developed by an RC-network of heat resistances and capacitances in which each wall and each space is represented by one temperature point—where that of a wall is located in its centre. The building is heated and cooled by means of an ideal power source of $100\ \mathrm{W/m^3}$ in each space, which is cooling when the temperature is higher than 25 °C and heating when it is lower than 20 °C. A ventilation rate of one air change per hour is defined per space. The outside temperature is imported from a real-world data set that is measured in De Bilt in The Netherlands by the Dutch Royal Meteorological Institute (KNMI, 2016) and a constant ground temperature of 10 °C is assumed. The building thermal behaviour is simulated over the period starting on 01/07/2014 01:00 until 31/07/2014 24:00. The simulator divides each hour into four time steps, which are eventually solved by a Runge-Kutta solver (Ahnert *et al,* 2011).

Objectives. For structural design (SD) the objective is defined as the sum of strain energy over all elements over all load cases. This is further referred to as structural compliance. The building physics (BP) or more specifically the thermal design objective is given by the sum of heating and cooling energy over the above-mentioned time period.

Constraints. The first and most natural constraint is no-overlap, which prevents building spaces to overlap. The next constraint is employed to guarantee correct conversion between the SC and MS representations by ensuring that for each design aspect the design solution conforms to the most demanding representation: This constraint enforces cuboid building spaces and consequentially also their ortho-convexity, which is necessary because the MS-representation can only represent cuboid (3D rectangular) spaces. To follow this constraint, in the supercube it is checked if the bounding box of a space can be formed by the corner supercube cells. If this is the case then it is checked if the space itself is ortho-convex, i.e. every supercube cell in between the corner cells is activated for that space. Finally, also an implementation specific constraint is defined, which prevents overhanging spaces. This constraint is introduced to make for a fast and efficient implementation of the cuboid and ortho-convexity constraints. Exact descriptions of the constraints and their mathematical notation are available in Boonstra *et al* (2016) and Van der Blom *et al* (2016a). Finally, dimensions of divisions in a supercube in SMS-EMOA are constrained to a minimum to prevent zero width divisions, but also to prevent unrealistic designs from being considered. The lower bounds are set to 500 mm for the width (x-direction) and depth (y-direction) dimensions and 3000 mm for the height (z-direction) dimensions in the supercube. The case study may seem simplistic in terms of the above constraints and problem size, however in (Van der Blom *et al*, 2016a) it is shown that these constraints are frequently violated and non-trivial.

The co-evolutionary approach automatically follows most constraints by using modification rules that are designed not to exceed them. However, this does not apply to the above constraints for minimal cell dimensions and no-overhang. For the CD approach, it is thus still required to check constraints and possibly exclude solutions before they would be used as starting point for the SMS-EMOA method, which has still been done manually for this study.

CD. A simple selection and modification rule set is used for this case study, thus only a single solution is generated after each co-evolutionary cycle. This selection and modification rule starts by evaluating the performance of each space in the design for each discipline. These performances are then normalised based on the minimum and maximum points. Here the minimum and maximum points are defined respectively as the points containing the lower and upper bound performance values of each discipline. Subsequently the space associated with the worst performance is removed, where the worst performance is measured by the shortest distance with respect to the maximum (anti ideal) point in the Pareto front for both disciplines. For finding the best performing space, a performance ranking is made in relation to the shortest distance to the minimum (ideal) point in the Pareto front. Finally, the best performing space is selected for splitting unless this splitting creates a space with a side smaller than twice the constraint on the supercube's minimal division width. In that case, the next best ranked space is considered for splitting, et cetera. This is carried out to prevent that too many constraint violating designs are generated by the CD method. A space is by default split in a vertical oriented plane (normal in (x, y)-direction) along a line parallel to the x-axis, or parallel to the y-axis when the space's side in x-direction is longer than its side in the y-direction. A space is never split in a horizontal plane (normal in z-direction). After splitting, the complete design is scaled up equally in the x- and y-directions to match the original design volume. Scaling of the design completes the selection and modification rule set. The case study is started with a design consisting of two spaces in x-, one space in y- and four spaces in z-direction, where each space measures 3500, 3570 and 3000 mm in x-, y- and z-directions respectively. The CD method will be run for 50 cycles in this case study.

SMS-EMOA. The tailored version of this method will be run using tuned parameters that were found in Van der Blom *et al* (2017). It should be noted that these tuned parameters were found for a design search space with five spaces and a different thermal performance objective, namely the minimal outside surface area rather than the minimal heating and cooling energy. The population size μ is set to 6 designs. Two types of mutation are used: binary, which mutates the cells that are assigned to a space; and polynomial, which mutates the continuous dimension variables. As a result of the tuning, the probability for the binary mutation operator is set to 0.4993 and the polynomial mutation operator is applied otherwise. The number of steps to be taken by the mutation operator is determined by a pooling technique, which chooses uniformly at random to do either a local move (one step) or an explorative move (three steps). A mutation probability of 0.4381 is set for each dimensioning variable in the case that polynomial mutation is selected. The volume constraint is maintained by an iterative repair function, in which the design is continuously scaled to the constrained volume and the dimensional values are continuously reset to their constrained values until the volume deviates at most one cubic millimetre. The remaining constraints are maintained by the smart initialisation and mutation operators, see Van der Blom *et al* (2017) for more details. The supercube for the case study is chosen to be three cells in x-direction two cells in y-direction and five cells in the z-direction, the volume constraint is set to 300 m^3. A budget of 5000 evaluations has been chosen for SMS-EMOA, for comparison reasons a Pareto front approximation will be made after 1000 evaluations and after 5000 evaluations.

Combined Method. Design selection is performed by selecting the knee point from the Pareto front of all found solutions. Selection based on HSSP (Kuhn *et al*, 2016) remains out of scope for simplicity and brevity. The CD method is selected as the initial method as it is believed that CD will suggest a better design search space before a computationally expensive run of SMS-EMOA is carried out. The combined method will iterate five times, with each iteration consisting of a CD run with 10 cycles and an SMS-EMOA run with a 1000 evaluations. The total evaluation budget of one run of the combined method is then 5050, thus creating the possibility to compare performances with the SMS-EMOA run after 5000 evaluations. During the conversion from MS to SC there will be an extra layer of cells added in the x-, y- and z-directions of the supercube, to prevent the supercube from being too restrictive for the SMS-EMOA design operators. SMS-EMOA will be initialised with an empty supercube, hence not with solutions containing a-priori activated cells, as it was found that such solutions are too dominant over randomly initialised designs. This dominance cannot easily be overcome by the current mutation operator in SMS-EMOA.

3.2 Results

Results contain outliers, causing graphs to only show a narrow bandwidth for most solutions. Graphs are therefore only visualised over the bandwidth of interest (i.e. the Pareto front approximation). Figure 4 shows the design path of the CD method, large jumps in performances show that the subtle selection and modification rule (i.e. the removal of only a single space) still has an aggressive impact in terms of performance. As a positive consequence, the CD method can rapidly move to other regions (but not necessarily better) in the design search space. For this case study CD can find a better solution after two cycles, but later iterations show worse performance and oscillation around solutions 7 to 10 after cycle 6.

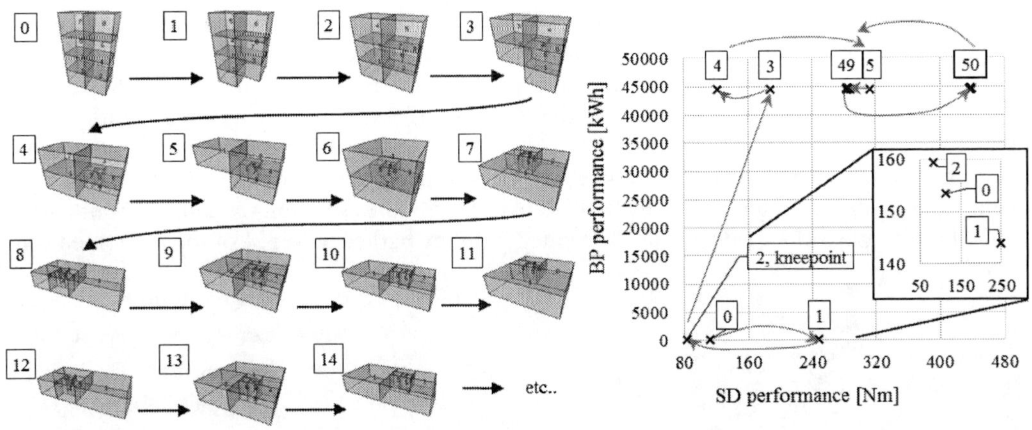

Figure 4: Designs along the design path of the CD only run, the knee point is found after the second iteration. The algorithm starts oscillating around solutions 7 to 10 after the sixth cycle. Note that each visualised design on the left of this figure is the final product of a single CD cycle.

Results for the SMS-EMOA run are shown in figure 5, two characteristic aspects can be noted. Firstly, at a 1000 evaluations the algorithm is not fully converged yet, as can be observed from the figure and from the irregular Pareto front. After 5000 evaluations, the Pareto front seems to have converged better, but it also shows that in a relatively late stage the algorithm found an improved solution space for the thermal design objective which has not fully been investigated yet. Secondly, the empty supercube cells at the top of the visualised designs indicate that better solutions could be obtained if more cells in the x- and y-directions were available, since this suggests that high buildings are non-optimal in this case study. On a general note, it should be mentioned that some tall slender spaces appear in the found design solutions. This is allowed for this case study but could be prevented by introducing constraints for either minimum floor surface or maximum aspect ratios of space dimensions.

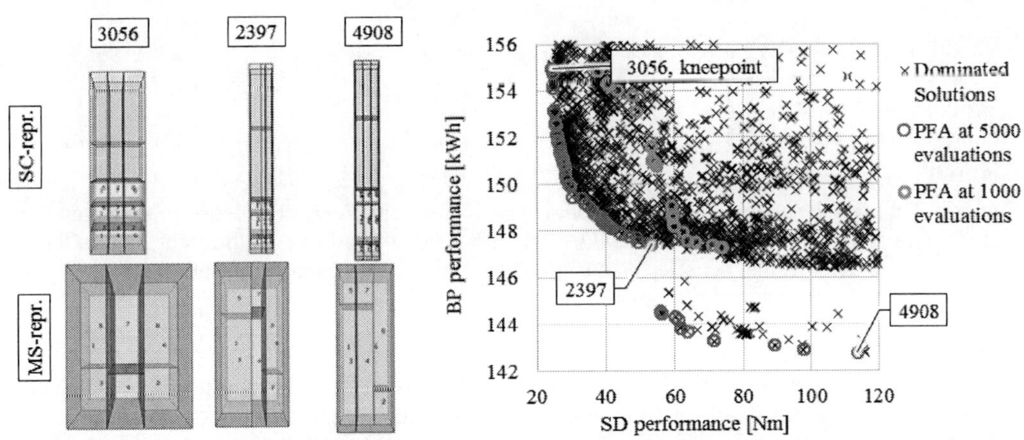

Figure 5: Results from the SMS-EMOA run. Some characteristic solutions are visualised on the left.

The combined method's results are presented in figure 6. The graph showing the Pareto fronts of the SMS-EMOA run in each iteration (figure 6, top) illustrates that only the first and fifth iteration of the combined method contribute to the eventual Pareto front approximation. This could be caused by the growing supercube size, since SMS-EMOA needs more evaluations to converge the PFA when a super-structure contains more solutions. The iterations with a larger supercube appear to be less converged judging by irregular Pareto fronts and the obviously non-optimal solutions. Moreover, it can be observed that the chosen design selection is sensitive to outliers in the results. Outliers in the BP performances of this case study are also considered in the computation of the knee points, therefore a preference for selection of SD optimal solutions (top left of PFA's) occurs. Additionally, the first run of SMS-EMOA has been continued an extra 4000 evaluations, this run shows that CD can find design search spaces that contain better solutions. Finally, comparing the total results of the run of the combined method with 5050 evaluations with the single run of SMS-EMOA after 5000 evaluations it can be seen that the PFA of the single SMS-EMOA run is extended with the part of the PFA of the combined run.

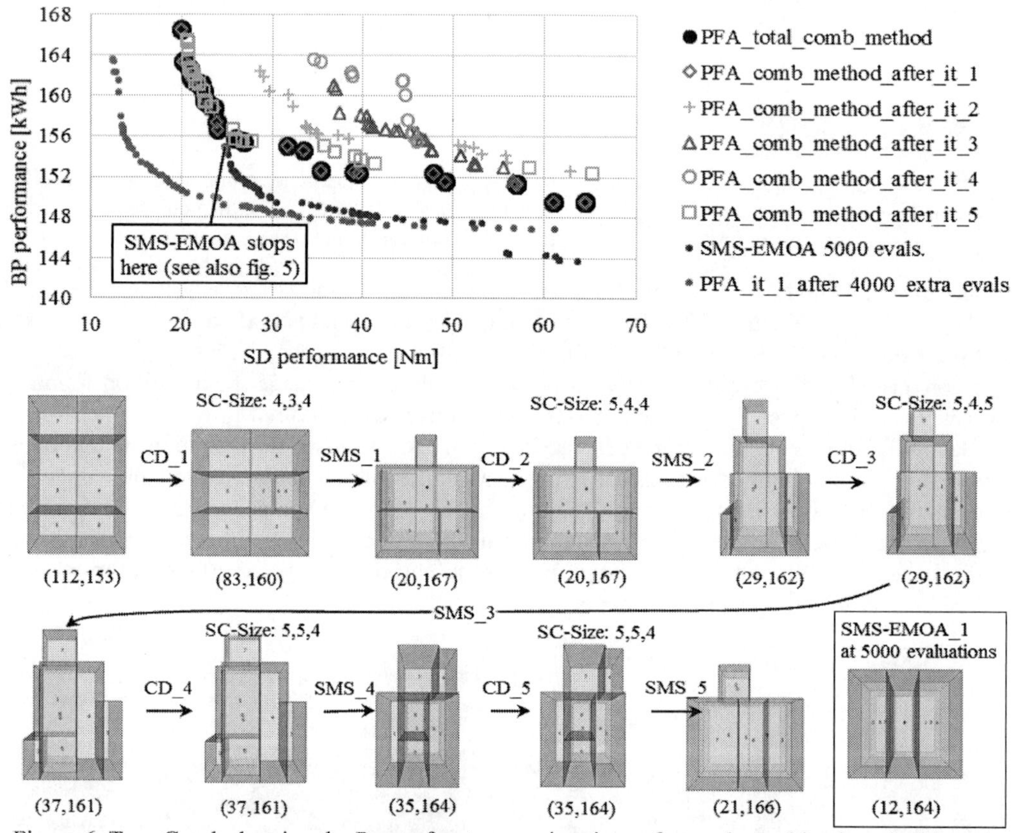

Figure 6: Top: Graph showing the Pareto front approximations after each combined method iteration and for comparison the single SMS-EMOA run with 5000 evaluations. Bottom: The path of the combined method, i.e. selected designs (knee points) after each optimisation run.

3.3 Discussion

The results show that the combination of methods proves to be able to suggest better design search spaces. It should however be noted that the presented results are a demonstration and somewhat arbitrary. For example, they are generated by a probabilistic algorithm and therefore new runs may not produce the same results. Additionally, SMS-EMOA has been tuned for different settings, namely for five spaces rather than eight and also for a different building thermal design objective. More tuning and experience should give more insight in the number of required evaluations for SMS-EMOA in the combined method. Moreover, the CD method has been presented using only one set of modification rules. Adding diversity to the rule set for modification will allow CD to explore multiple directions and steer towards Pareto optimality.

Comparing the results of the single SMS-EMOA run with the total results of the combined method it can be concluded that the combined method did not find improved solutions (with the exception of a slightly improved SD objective). Nevertheless, the 4000 extra evaluations of SMS-EMOA after the first iteration of the combined method prove that at least after the first CD run a better design search space has been found.

Currently no limitation on supercube size in the SMS-EMOA method is implemented, but it might be advantageous to constrain this size. The reason would be that larger problem sizes need more time to search for solutions and would thus have a slower convergence. Limiting the size leads to faster convergence, this will improve the performance of the combined method when the design selection and the CD methods are configured as such that they can select sub-design search spaces effectively.

4. Conclusion and Outlook

Three optimisation methods have been introduced: a super-structured; a super-structure free; and a hybrid method. The hybrid optimisation method has been explained, and its different schemes and new optimisation parameters were identified. A case study has been presented to demonstrate and compare the three optimisation methods. The co-evolutionary design method can quickly find better solutions, however, it is also prone to erratic behaviour. SMS-EMOA can find good Pareto front approximations within its design search space, but it cannot find better design search spaces. The combined method proves that the CD method can indeed shift the design search space of a super structured approach. It was shown that newly selected design search spaces can contain improved solutions, however this is dependent on the effectiveness of the used CD method(s).

The presented research is promising, and in the future, it may provide a method for designers that can quickly give insight in design problems. There is however still research to be carried out: A diversity in CD methods will be developed to offer the ability to steer solutions towards different parts of the Pareto front. An extensive investigation into parameter combinations with different case studies should provide more insight and experience with the hybrid method. Diversity maintenance in SMS-EMOA when initialised with a priori defined solutions will be investigated. Finally, hypervolume-based subset selection will be considered for design selection.

Acknowledgements
The authors gratefully acknowledge the financing of this project by the NWO-TTW (previously STW) Open Technology Program project number 13596.

References

Ahnert, K., Mulansky, M., Simos, T. E., Psihoyios, G., Tsitouras, C. and Anastassi, Z. (2011) 'Odeint – Solving Ordinary Differential Equations in C++', in AIP Conference Proceedings. Halkidiki, Greece, pp. 1586–1589. doi: 10.1063/1.3637934.

Batoz, J.-L. and Tahar, M. Ben (1982) 'Evaluation of a new quadrilateral thin plate bending element', International Journal for Numerical Methods in Engineering, 18(11), pp. 1655–1677. doi: 10.1002/nme.1620181106.

Beume, N., Naujoks, B. and Emmerich, M. (2007) 'SMS-EMOA: Multiobjective selection based on dominated hypervolume', European Journal of Operational Research, 181(3), pp. 1653–1669. doi: 10.1016/j.ejor.2006.08.008.

Van der Blom, K., Boonstra, S., Hofmeyer, H., Bäck, T. and Emmerich, M. T. M. (2017) 'Configuring Advanced Evolutionary Algorithms for Multicriteria Building Spatial Design Optimisation', in Proceedings IEEE Congress on Evolutionary Computation 2017. Jun 5-8, San-Sebastián, Spain.

Van der Blom, K., Boonstra, S., Hofmeyer, H. and Emmerich, M. T. M. (2016a) 'A super-structure based optimisation approach for building spatial designs', in Stefanou, G., Plevris, V., Papadrakakis, M., and Papadopoulos, V. (eds) Proceedings of the VII European Congress on Computational Methods in Applied Sciences and Engineering. Hersonissos, Greece: National Technical University of Athens: ECCOMAS, pp. 3409–3422.

Van der Blom, K., Boonstra, S., Hofmeyer, H. and Emmerich, M. T. M. (2016b) 'Multicriteria Building Spatial Design with Mixed Integer Evolutionary Algorithms', in Handl, J., Hart, E., Lewis, P. R., López-Ibáñez, M., Ochoa, G., and Paechter, B. (eds) Parallel Problem Solving from Nature – PPSN XIV. Edinburgh, Scotland: Springer International Publishing, pp. 453–462. doi: 10.1007/978-3-319-45823-6.

Boonstra, S., Van der Blom, K., Hofmeyer, H. and Emmerich, M. T. M. (2016) 'Super-Structure and Super-Structure Free Design Search Space Representations for a Building Spatial Design in Multi-Disciplinary Building Optimisation', in Electronic proceedings of the 23rd EG-ICE workshop. Krakow, Poland: Jagiellonian University ZPGK, pp. 1–10.

Bringmann, K., Friedrich, T. and Klitzke, P. (2014) 'Generic Postprocessing via Subset Selection for Hypervolume and Epsilon-Indicator', in Parallel Problem Solving from Nature - PPSN XIII, 13th International Conference. Ljubljana, Slovenia, pp. 518–527. doi: 10.1007/978-3-319-10762-2_51.

Caldas, L. (2008) 'Generation of energy-efficient architecture solutions applying GENE_ARCH: An evolution-based generative design system', Advanced Engineering Informatics, 22(1), pp. 59–70. doi: 10.1016/j.aei.2007.08.012.

Cook, R. D. (1974) Concepts and applications of finite element analysis: a treatment of the finite element method as used for the analysis of displacement, strain, and stress. John Wiley & Sons.

Deb, K., Pratap, A., Agarwal, S. and Meyarivan, T. (2002) 'A fast and elitist multiobjective genetic algorithm: NSGA-II', IEEE Transactions on Evolutionary Computation, 6(2), pp. 182–197. doi: 10.1109/4235.996017.

Díaz, H., Alarcón, L. F., Mourgues, C. and García, S. (2017) 'Multidisciplinary Design Optimization through process integration in the AEC industry: Strategies and challenges', Automation in Construction, 73, pp. 102–119. doi: 10.1016/j.autcon.2016.09.007.

Gero, J. S., D'Cruz, N. and Radford, A. D. (1983) 'Energy in context: A multicriteria model for building design', Building and Environment, 18(3), pp. 99–107. doi: 10.1016/0360-1323(83)90001-X.

Geyer, P. (2009) 'Component-oriented decomposition for multidisciplinary design optimization in building design', Advanced Engineering Informatics, 23(1), pp. 12–31. doi: 10.1016/j.aei.2008.06.008.

Guennebaud, G., Jacob, B. and others (2010) 'Eigen v3: a C++ linear algebra library'. Available at: http://eigen.tuxfamily.org.

Hamdy, M., Nguyen, A.-T. and Hensen, J. L. M. (2016) 'A performance comparison of multi-objective optimization algorithms for solving nearly-zero-energy-building design problems', Energy and Buildings, 121, pp. 57–71. doi: 10.1016/j.enbuild.2016.03.035.

Hofmeyer, H. and Davila Delgado, J. M. (2015) 'Coevolutionary and genetic algorithm based building spatial and structural design', Artificial Intelligence for Engineering Design, Analysis and Manufacturing, 29(4), pp. 351–370. doi: 10.1017/S0890060415000384.

Hopfe, C. J., Emmerich, M. T. M., Marijt, R. and Hensen, J. (2012) 'Robust multi-criteria design optimisation in building design', in Proceedings of Building Simulation and Optimization. Loughborough, United Kingdom, pp. 118–125.

Kim, I. Y. and Kwak, B. M. (2002) 'Design space optimization using a numerical design continuation method', International Journal for Numerical Methods in Engineering, 53(8), pp. 1979–2002. doi: 10.1002/nme.369.

KNMI Koninklijk Nederlands Metereologish Instituut (2016) 'Measured weather data in The Netherlands'. Available at: http://www.knmi.nl/nederland-nu/klimatologie/daggegevens.

Kuhn, T., Fonseca, C. M., Paquete, L., Ruzika, S., Duarte, M. M. and Figueira, J. R. (2016) 'Hypervolume Subset Selection in Two Dimensions: Formulations and Algorithms', Evolutionary Computation, 24(3), pp. 411–425. doi: 10.1162/EVCO_a_00157.

Maher, M. Lou and Tang, H.-H. (2003) 'Co-evolution as a computational and cognitive model of design', Research in Engineering Design, 14(2003), pp. 47–64. doi: 10.1007/s00163-002-0016-y.

Mora, R., Bitsuamlak, G. and Horvat, M. (2011) 'Integrated life-cycle design of building enclosures', Building and Environment, 46(7), pp. 1469–1479. doi: 10.1016/j.buildenv.2011.01.018.

Rahmani Asl, M., Zarrinmehr, S., Bergin, M. and Yan, W. (2015) 'BPOpt: A framework for BIM-based performance optimization', Energy and Buildings, 108, pp. 401–412. doi: 10.1016/j.enbuild.2015.09.011.

Steiner, B., Mousavian, E., Saradj, F. M., Wimmer, M. and Musialski, P. (2016) 'Integrated Structural-Architectural Design for Interactive Planning', Computer Graphics Forum, pp. 1–16. doi: 10.1111/cgf.12996.

Talbi, E.-G. (2002) 'A Taxonomy of Hybrid Metaheuristics', Journal of Heuristics, 8, pp. 541–564.

Voll, P., Lampe, M., Wrobel, G. and Bardow, A. (2012) 'Superstructure-free synthesis and optimization of distributed industrial energy supply systems', Energy, 45(1), pp. 424–435. doi: 10.1016/j.energy.2012.01.041.

Welle, B., Haymaker, J. and Rogers, Z. (2011) 'ThermalOpt: A methodology for automated BIM-based multidisciplinary thermal simulation for use in optimization environments', Building Simulation, 4(4), pp. 293–313. doi: 10.1007/s12273-011-0052-5.

Impact of zoning strategies for building performance simulation

Aurelien Bres[1], Florian Judex[1], Georg Suter[2], Pieter de Wilde[3]
[1]AIT Austrian Institute of Technology, Energy Department
[2]Design Computing Group, Center for Geometry and Computational Design, Vienna University of Technology
[3]School of Architecture, Design and Environment, University of Plymouth
aurelien.bres@ait.ac.at

Abstract. Building performance simulation (BPS) can provide detailed information on the thermal behaviour of buildings. Zoning is a key step in input data preparation for BPS. A simulation zone is typically composed of one or more rooms. Large spaces, such as open office spaces, may have multiple zones. Simulation zoning can be distinguished from HVAC zoning, which is a property of the HVAC system. An appropriate simulation zoning may depend on the simulation problem, and results from a trade-off between accuracy and simplicity. In current simulation practice, zoning is usually carried out based on the user's experience. This does not ensure consistency across modelled buildings and practitioners. This paper demonstrates how systematic bottom-up strategies can be applied to aggregate rooms into simulation zones. The impact of such strategies is investigated by applying them to several floors of residential buildings. Building performance simulation is carried out with either conceptual or detailed HVAC modeling. In the second case, variations in both simulation zoning and HVAC zoning are investigated. Simulation results are compared to those obtained with detailed one-zone-per-room models, to assess the deviations due to simulation zoning. A coarser simulation zoning is shown to cause significant deviations in certain cases. A fine simulation zoning may allow control inefficiencies due to coarse HVAC zoning to be quantified.

1. Introduction

Building performance simulation (BPS) can provide quantitative information on the processes that determine the energy consumption of buildings, notably in terms of heating, ventilation and air-conditioning (HVAC). The zone is a core concept in current BPS tools, and a central entity in their input models. Simulation zones determine the spatial discretization of the building model. Heat and mass balance is calculated for each zone. It is assumed that the air in a zone is perfectly mixed. As a consequence, heat transfer and storage surfaces, internal gains and air exchange rates are defined at the zone level (US DOE 2010). Outputs of simulated internal conditions also refer to zones. Geometrically, a zone is enclosed by a set of flat polygonal surfaces. One-dimensional heat conduction is calculated between the zone-facing side and the other side of these surfaces (Crawley et al. 2001). This other side may correspond to another zone, outdoor or ground conditions. Alternatively, it is sometimes assumed that there is no heat transfer across a boundary (adiabatic boundary), which allows the model to be simplified.

This papers deals with the impact of zoning strategies on BPS with either conceptual or detailed HVAC modeling. Zones, like rooms, are special cases of spaces. A space can be defined as a materially or theoretically bounded volume accommodating certain functions (Ekholm & Fridqvist, 2000). A room is a space which is typically enclosed by walls, floors, and ceilings. In the thermal domain, a zone is an aggregation of rooms related to a given purpose. We distinguish zones used in simulation from the zones defined in the context of HVAC systems. In the following, we refer to the former as simulation zones and to the latter as HVAC zones.

An HVAC zone, like a simulation zone, usually corresponds to a room or collection of rooms with common thermal characteristics, but it is defined in the context of HVAC design and operation, independently from simulation. ASHRAE (2013) defines an HVAC zone as a "space or group of spaces within a building with heating and cooling requirements that are sufficiently similar so that desired conditions (e.g., temperature) can be maintained throughout using a single sensor (e.g., thermostat)." Others tend to define HVAC zoning on the basis of the actuator. For air-based systems, Platt et al. (2010) define an HVAC zone as a group of adjacent spaces "serviced by a common air-handling unit (AHU) or air-terminal device". This definition leads to differences in meaning for various kinds of systems. Our distinction of HVAC zone and simulation zone broadly concurs with the ASHRAE (2013) distinction of HVAC zone and thermal block. The latter is "a collection of one or more HVAC zones grouped together for simulation purposes".

The modeling of HVAC systems in BPS may take place at different levels of abstraction, which can be summarized as conceptual modeling, system-based modeling, component-based modeling and equation-based modeling (Trčka and Hensen 2010). The increasing level of detail of these approaches makes greater accuracy possible, while complicating input data preparation. Within a component-based model, each component may be assigned to a simulation zone, and their thermal interaction simulated.

When determining simulation zones, one faces a trade-off between the accuracy of the model on the one hand, and its size on the other hand. The drawbacks of a high number of zones include greater computation intensiveness, as well as difficulties in creating, checking and modifying models, and interpreting simulation results. From a simulation accuracy perspective, two extreme approaches are, respectively, to consider each room (or even room sections) as separate zones, and to consider the whole building as a single zone. It may often be the case that neither is appropriate. While zoning is often left to the intuition and experience of simulation users, simulation zones could also be consistently derived from the grouping of spaces according to well-defined criteria. This paper aims at demonstrating this possibility, and determining which attributes and rules can yield effective simulation zonings. To this aim, a systematic study for multiple floor plans is proposed, including simulation experiments with known as well as unknown HVAC zoning.

2. Related work

The issue of building zoning for simulation has been addressed in various contexts, varying with the degree of definition of interior spaces. If interior spaces are not defined, as might be the case in conceptual building design, internal load properties cannot be considered. However, the building geometry may be discretized to account for differences in solar gains. ASHRAE (2013) recommends to divide floors into a core region and a perimeter region, and to subdivide the latter according to space orientation. Based on this recommendation, Dogan, Reinhart and Michalatos (2015) presented an algorithm to zone building massing models automatically.

If interior spaces are defined, a detailed building model can be created with one zone per room, and results of a simulation run with this model may allow zones to be grouped together based on their simulated behavior. Such an approach was followed by Georgescu, Eisenhower and Mezić (2012), as well as Giannakis (2015). With known interior spaces, thermal zones may also be determined without previous simulation run. In the context of a simulation project involving thousands of buildings, Ramirez et al. (2005) gave modelers the choice between three zoning schemes: one-zone-per-floor, perimeter/core and one-zone-per-activity-area. The last zoning was particularly recommended for restaurants, to account for differences between kitchen and dining areas. Looking at the influence of zoning on annual energy demand, Rivalin et al. (2014) concluded on the acceptability of large simplifications, including the grouping of rooms on different floors. For buildings with repeating floors, zone multipliers may also be used. Their use for the simulation of a high-rise building was shown to introduce very little error in annual cooling and heating energy (Ellis and Torcellini, 2005). The consideration of other performance indicators can lead to other conclusions. In a study of the performance of an office under climate change, De Wilde & Tian (2010) suggested that zonal resolution may significantly impact the predicted overheating risk, with coarser zoning likely to lead to an underestimation of this risk. Systematic studies investigating the influence of simulation zoning schemes in multiple buildings with defined interior spaces are not known to the authors.

3. Objectives and methodology

The objectives of the paper are to apply and extend an existing zoning method to simulation, and to evaluate this method in the context of automated BPS input preparation. This evaluation is to take place for two main cases, respectively with unknown and known HVAC zoning. In both cases, the deviations due to simulation zoning are evaluated, by comparing to results obtained with a detailed one-zone-per-room zoning.

In the first case, the zoning method is applied to a simulation of a building with unknown HVAC zoning. In this setting, simulation is carried out with an ideal HVAC system model, so that HVAC zoning is not taken into account, and no detailed HVAC model is used.

In the second case, the zoning method is applied to the simulation of a building with known HVAC zoning. In this case, we carry out detailed HVAC simulation with a component-based model, for the case of hydronic heating systems. This component-based model is derived from the zoned building model with the help of an automated method (Bres et al. 2017). While a simple decision in this case would be to use the HVAC zoning as simulation zoning, we investigate the impact of using a simulation zoning differing from the HVAC zoning.

4. Zoning method

Zones are generated based on a space aggregation operation that has been defined for a space modeling system (Suter 2013). A space model in this system consists of space layouts which model multiple views, such as architectural or pedestrian circulation views. Spatial relations between spaces and space elements (e.g. windows or walls) in a layout form a geometric network. In the space aggregation operation, spaces are merged based on their properties and connectivity (Suter et al. 2014). Space geometries are modeled as solids. Geometries of merged spaces are obtained by the solid union of original space geometries. Spatial inconsistencies due to operation processing are automatically detected and resolved. In case of space aggregation, doors and walls that separate merged spaces may not be included in the result layout.

The aggregation operation is used to define four simulation zone views that are derived from an architectural view (Table 1). All views are derived by merging spaces (rooms) in the architectural view based on the space adjacency relation. Different space properties are considered to group spaces in the architectural view. In the perimeter/core zone view, spaces are grouped if they are perimeter or core spaces (Suter 2015). External spaces are modeled explicitly in the space modeling system. A perimeter space is adjacent to at least one external space, whereas a core space is not. Core spaces are typically less exposed to solar radiation than perimeter spaces. In the functional zone view, spaces in the architectural view must be part of the same functional group (Suter 2015). Spaces belong to a functional group if they have the same primary space property, or if they share certain secondary space properties. For example, bathrooms and storage rooms belong to the group of service spaces. Similarly, there are groups for primary and secondary circulation spaces. Primary circulation spaces include publicly accessible stair cases and elevators. Secondary circulation spaces include hallways in spatial units with restricted access.

Table 1: Zoning schemes.

Scheme Id	Description
PZ	Perimeter/core
FZ	Functional zones
OZ	Orientation zones
OFZ	Orientation and functional zones

The orientation zone view is generated based on the orientation of internal spaces relative to external spaces. Space orientation is determined in three steps. First, a convex decomposition of external spaces in the architectural view is performed. This accounts for changes in building orientation, e.g. at corners where facades meet. Second, connectivity of internal spaces with external spaces through transparent openings (such as windows) is determined. Spaces that are related to the same external spaces have the same orientation. Core spaces are not oriented to any external space. Third, connected spaces with the same orientation are merged.

The functional and orientation zone view is a combination of functional and orientation zone views. Conceptually, connected spaces in the architectural view that belong to the same functional group and have the same orientation are merged.

5. Simulation experiments

5.1 Overview

The zoning method is applied to multiple building floors, chosen to represent a variety of floor plan types possible in apartment buildings and summarized in Table 2.

Table 2: Buildings floors for case study.

Id	D1989	M1951	K2010	J1972A2	J1972A5
Location	Amsterdam, Netherlands	Chicago, USA	Chicago, USA	Stuttgart, Germany	Stuttgart, Germany
Building year	1989	1951	2010	1972	1972
Architects	Duinker, van der Torre	Mies van der Rohe	Krueck and Sexton	Jäger, Müller, Wirth	Jäger, Müller, Wirth
Gross floor area (m^2)	321	649	650	340	398
Number of rooms	36	38	35	27	32

The corresponding apartment buildings were all built in heating-dominated climates. One representative floor per building is simulated, or two for the residential complex in Stuttgart. D1989 and M1951 represent the same building, before and after a renovation that changed the interior structure. Default constructions corresponding to the buildings' years of constructions are assumed. Weather data files for the respective locations are used. Internal loads and schedules follow the Swiss data sheet SIA Merkblatt 2024, which provides detailed schedules for bedrooms/living rooms, kitchens and bathrooms. This results in the creation of input building models for the BPS engines (Crawley et al. 2001) EnergyPlus and TRNSYS (Klein & Beckman 1976).

Table 3: Differentiation of internal loads and set points by space use.

Parameter	unit	Residential	Bathroom	Kitchen	Circulation	Duct
Heating set point	°C	21	24	20	18	-
Area per person	m^2/person	50	5	5	100	-
Heat gains from light and equipment	W/m^2	11	13	57	6	0

5.2 Experiments with unknown HVAC zoning

Simulation experiments are carried out to investigate the impact of the presented zoning strategies. Simulation models obtained from the application of the presented zoning strategies to the selected building floors are simulated with ideal HVAC system representation. Results are ideal loads, which represent the exact energy rate to be delivered in each zone by an HVAC system for set point conditions to be maintained.

We compare three different approaches to internal loads, summarized in Table 4. With interpolated internal loads, the sums of internal loads are preserved. The majority approach is simpler to implement, and probably more representative of actual practice.

Table 4: Internal load variations.

Id	Description
Uniform	Same internal loads in all zones.
Majority	Internal loads corresponding to space use with largest area in aggregated rooms.
Interpolated	Internal loads interpolated (area-weighted) from aggregated rooms.

5.3 Experiments with known HVAC zoning

With a more detailed HVAC model, it is attempted to question the relation between simulation zoning and HVAC zoning. This second group of simulation experiments is carried out only with interpolated internal loads. Variations of both HVAC zoning and simulation zoning are simulated, as illustrated in Table 6.

Table 6: Simulated variations in thermal zoning and HVAC zoning. Each cell represents a simulation case, and cell color describes the relation between simulation and HVAC zoning. Identical zoning in green cells. Simulation coarser than HVAC zoning in blue if allowed by ASHRAE, otherwise in orange. Simulation zoning finer than HVAC zoning in yellow.

Compare to evaluate simulation zoning error

HVAC zoning \ Simulation zoning	RZ	OFZ	FZ
RZ	RZ-RZ	RZ-OFZ	RZ-FZ
OFZ	OFZ-RZ	OFZ-OFZ	OFZ-FZ
FZ	FZ-RZ	FZ-OFZ	FZ-FZ

Compare to evaluate control inefficiencies

The described zoning method is used to generate HVAC and simulation zonings. In the three considered HVAC zonings, only rooms with the same function, and hence the same set point temperature, are grouped together. For a given HVAC zoning of the modeled system, the simulation zoning may be equal to the HVAC zoning (green cells in Table 6). According to ASHRAE (2013), a simulation zoning coarser than HVAC zoning would only be acceptable if aggregated "HVAC zones have the same space use and orientation" (blue cell). On the other hand, a simulation zoning finer than the HVAC zoning (yellow cells) can be assumed to give more accurate results. In particular, it may allow the control inefficiencies deriving from a coarse HVAC zoning, i.e. local overheating or underheating, to be quantified. This cannot be simulated in EnergyPlus, where the simulation of air temperature and heat demand takes place at the same zone level. Thus, we resort to co-simulation for the simulation experiments in this section, with HVAC system simulation in TRNSYS. Air temperatures for each simulation zone are passed from EnergyPlus to TRNSYS, and heat delivered by each component is passed from TRNSYS to EnergyPlus. In terms of simulation, HVAC zoning is reflected only in TRNSYS, by modifying the temperature sensors controlling heat delivery in the HVAC control model. Temperature sensors in simulation zones corresponding to the same HVAC zone are replaced by a single temperature sensor. We assume this temperature sensor to be placed in the largest simulation zone of the HVAC zone.

6. Results

The results of the presented zoning schemes are examined in terms of their static structure and of the corresponding simulation results. In order to quantify deviations resulting from space lumping, we use the mean bias error MBE and the coefficient of variation of the mean square error CV(RMSE) (Equation 1), frequently applied to BPS calibration (Coakley et al. 2014). In all cases, the reference value is that obtained with the architectural view, i.e. with one zone per room. No particularly large or high room in the considered floor plans makes it necessary to further refine this most detailed simulation zoning.

$$MBE(\%) = \frac{\sum_{i=1}^{n} x_i - x_{Ref,i}}{\sum_{i=1}^{n} x_{Ref,i}} \qquad CV(RMSE)(\%) = \frac{1}{\sum_{i=1}^{n} x_{Ref,i}} \sqrt{\frac{1}{n}\sum_{i=1}^{n}(x_i - x_{Ref,i})^2} \qquad (1)$$

6.1 Zone properties

We define the zoning factor as the number of rooms in the architectural view divided by the number of zones in the zoning view. The zoning factor indicates how many rooms in average a given zoning scheme aggregates into a single zone. As can be seen in Figure 2, the perimeter core zoning scheme tends to yield the highest zoning factors.

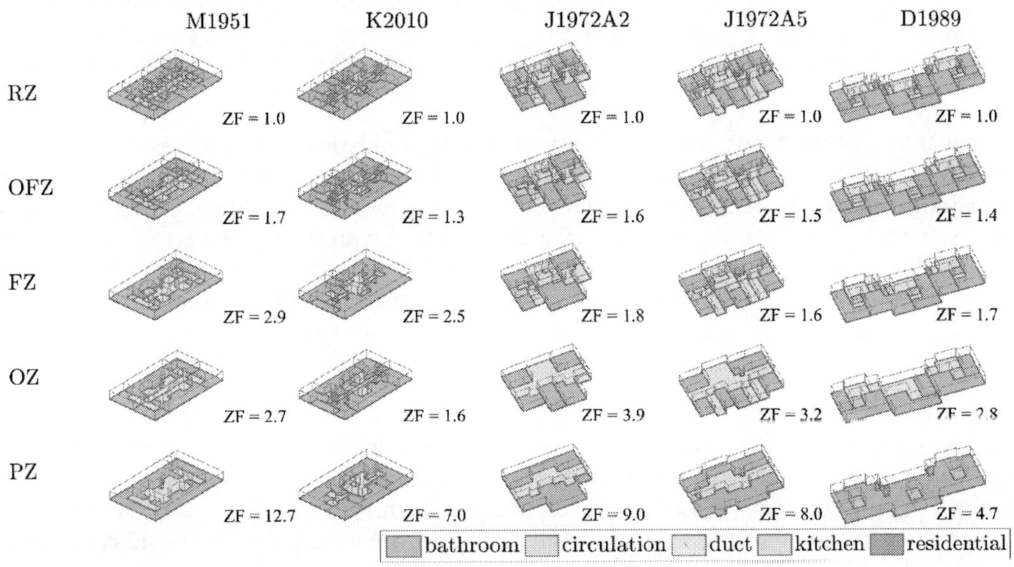

Figure 2: Resulting layouts for the selected floor models and zoning schemes, with the corresponding zoning factors (ZF).

6.2 Results with unknown HVAC zoning

Heating loads for a one-month simulation period in the peak heating month January are compared. As seen in Figure 3, the impact of the zoning schemes on heat load results can vary significantly for different floor plans. Only OFZ yields consistently lower deviations as the other zoning schemes. Also, results strongly depend on the way internal loads are treated. Uniform space uses result in the lowest zoning errors, especially for the orientation-conscious zoning. Indeed, zoning deviations with uniform internal loads are dominated by thermal interaction with the exterior. Also, uniform internal loads mostly lead to negative MBE values. These correspond to underestimating the heating load by having loads in spaces with different orientations compensate. On the contrary, with non-uniform internal loads, the bias can be positive as well as negative, as deviations due to internal loads are introduced.

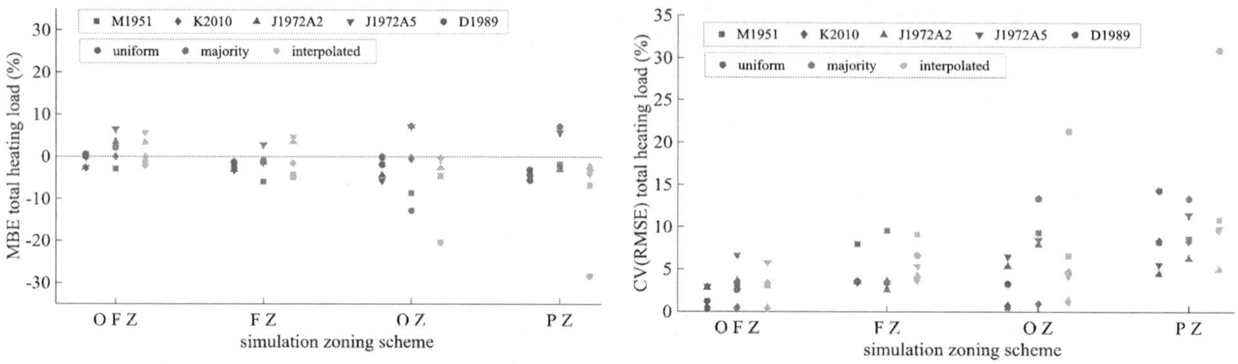

Figure 3: Error in total building heating load for buildings floors, zoning schemes and internal load variations relative to room-based zoning (RZ). Marker shapes represent building floors, and colors stand for internal load variations, as described in Table 4.

Interpolating internal loads from original rooms often yields lower errors than just deriving internal loads from the dominant space use. Sometimes it does not, as the deviations introduced by majority use internal loads may offset other deviations caused by lumping. This is especially the case with building D1989, which represents an outlier with the highest errors. Indeed, we can see that the majority approach for internal loads introduces a positive bias which compensates the exterior-dominated deviation assessed with uniform internal loads, whereas such compensation does not happen with the interpolated approach.

6.3 Results with known HVAC zoning

For the experiments with known HVAC zoning, heating control is not ideal, and temperatures can deviate from set point. The proportion of room temperatures below set point is shown in Figure 4. This indicator of underheating consistently increases with coarser HVAC zonings. The results with RZ simulation zoning, on the left third, are assumed to be the most accurate. Accordingly, the coarsest HVAC zoning, FZ, leads to unacceptably high proportions of underheating, particularly for the two Chicago floor plans. This can be detected with RZ or OFZ simulation zoning, but not when simulation zoning is as coarse as HVAC zoning.

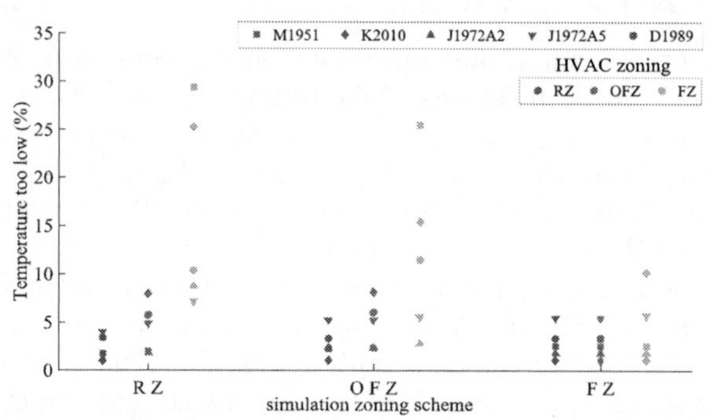

Figure 4: Proportion of time (during the simulation period January) and floor area in which simulated temperatures are lower than set point. Colors stand for HVAC zoning schemes.

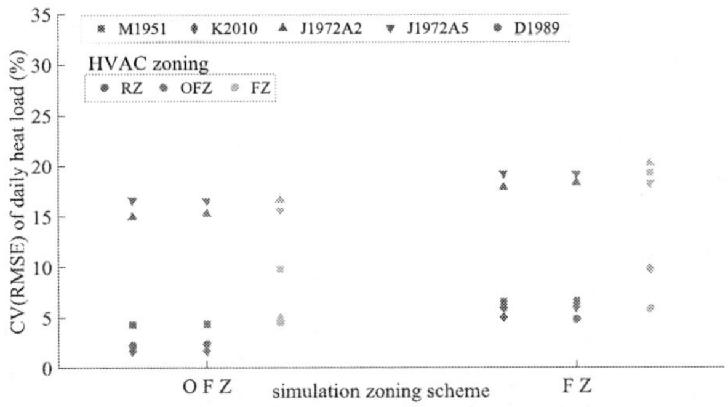

Figure 5: Errors in total heating load with several simulation zonings and HVAC zonings relative to room simulation zoning (RZ). Colors stand for HVAC zoning schemes.

Deviations in simulated heating load relative to room simulation zoning are illustrated in Figure 5. The more granular simulation zoning OFZ does result in lower errors than the FZ simulation zoning, but the difference are rather less marked than with ideal load simulation. This could be partially explained by interfering variations in achieved temperatures, as seen in the previous figure. Outliers with higher errors correspond to the two Stuttgart floor plans. It can also be seen that the errors due to simulation zoning rather tend to increase with coarser HVAC zoning. Like the temperature results, this contradicts the view that simulation zoning should correspond to HVAC zoning.

7. Discussion

Applying the presented method to selected floor plans and with several sets of parameters reveals that the effects of zoning schemes on simulation results may vary widely. Aggregating rooms with different uses into zones may lead to large errors, especially when grouping conditioned and non-conditioned (for instance circulation) rooms. The observation of outliers in the presented simulation experiments seem to indicate that building particulars play an important role.

A simulation zoning finer than the HVAC zoning may allow load differences due to coarse HVAC zoning to be evaluated. However, these differences can be expected to vary significantly with HVAC system, control scheme and sensor location. Also, at this level of detail, differences in thermal comfort should be taken into account. A coarse HVAC zoning should not lead modellers to choose an equally coarse simulation zoning, as this might result in significant errors in the evaluation of energy use and/or thermal comfort. Moreover, the amplitude of these errors is difficult to predict, as it was shown to vary strongly in the studied floor plans.

8. Conclusion

Systematic strategies for thermal zoning in the context of building performance simulation are presented and applied to multiple buildings. The method allows this aspect of model creation to be treated more consistently. Simulation experiments with multiple buildings show that the impact of zoning schemes on simulation results varies with individual buildings and parameters. Aggregating rooms with non-uniform internal loads can lead to significant errors. More experiments would be needed to investigate the trade-off between model accuracy and complexity on a more general basis. The presented method could also deal with cross-floor room aggregation. This has not been considered in the case study, which dealt only with floor plans. In the future, one could compare results obtained with floor-internal and cross-floor room aggregation, as well as with zone multipliers for zones on different floors. Zoning criteria have been built on parameters with discrete or nominal values. Zoning criteria based on quantitative and continuous values, such as window to wall ratio or shading ratio, could be introduced and used within a clustering approach.

References

ANSI/ASHRAE/IES Standard 90.1–2013. (2013). Energy Standard for Buildings except Low-Rise Residential Buildings, Appendix G. 2013. Atlanta, GA: The American Society of Heating, Refrigerating and Air-Conditioning Engineers.

Bres, A., Judex, F., Suter, G. & de Wilde, P. (2017). A Method for Automated Generation of HVAC Distribution Subsystems for Building Performance Simulation. *Submitted to Building Simulation 2017.*

Building Energy Codes Program (2017). "Glossary." Available from: https://www.energycodes.gov/resource-center/glossary/ [Accessed 1st March 2017].

Coakley, D., Raftery, P., & Keane, M. (2014). A review of methods to match building energy simulation models to measured data. *Renewable and sustainable energy reviews*, 37, 123-141.

Crawley, D. B., Lawrie, L. K., Winkelmann, F. C., Buhl, W. F., Huang, Y. J., Pedersen, C. O., ... & Glazer, J. (2001). EnergyPlus: creating a new-generation building energy simulation program. *Energy and buildings*, 33(4), 319-331.

Dogan, T., Reinhart, C. & Michalatos, P. (2015). Autozoner: an algorithm for automatic thermal zoning of buildings with unknown interior space definitions. *Journal of Building Performance Simulation*, 9(2), 176-189.

Ekholm, A., & Fridqvist, S. (2000). A concept of space for building classification, product modelling, and design. *Automation in Construction*, 9(3), 315-328.

Ellis, P. G., & Torcellini, P. A. (2005). Simulating tall buildings using EnergyPlus. *Proceedings of Building Simulation 2005,* 279-286.

Georgescu, Michael, Bryan Eisenhower, and Igor Mezic. (2012). Creating zoning approximations to building energy models using the Koopman operator. *Proceedings of IBPSA-USA's SimBuild 2012 conference*. Madison, Wisconsin.

Giannakis, G. (2015). *Development of Methodologies for Automatic Thermal Model Generation using Building Information Models*. PhD thesis. Technical University of Crete.

Klein, S. A. & Beckman, W. A. (1976). "TRNSYS – A transient system simulation program". *ASHRAE Transactions*, vol. 80.

Platt, G., Li, J., Li, R., Poulton, G., James, G., & Wall, J. (2010). Adaptive HVAC zone modeling for sustainable buildings. *Energy and Buildings*, 42(4), 412-421.

Ramirez, R., Sebold, F., Mayer, T., Ciminelli, M., & Abrishami, M. (2005). A building simulation palooza: the California CEUS project and DrCEUS. *Proceedings of Building Simulation 2005*, 1003-1010.

Suter, G. (2013). Structure and spatial consistency of network-based space layouts for building and product design. *Computer-Aided Design*, 45(8), 1108-1127.

Suter, G., Petrushevski, F., & Šipetić, M. (2014). Operations on network-based space layouts for modeling multiple space views of buildings. *Advanced Engineering Informatics*, 28(4), 395-411.

Towards Energy Efficient Operational Patterns in Air Handling Units in Highly Sensed Buildings

Gokmen Dedemen, Semiha Ergan
New York University Tandon School of Engineering, USA
gd1097@nyu.edu

Abstract. Building Energy Consumption accounts for more than 40 % of the total energy consumption in the U.S, and Heating Ventilating and Air Conditioning (HVAC) systems have a major share in the building energy consumption. Building Automation Systems (BAS) provide a valuable data source for energy savings in HVAC systems. However, there are a vast number of HVAC operational parameters stored in BAS, and not every operational parameter recorded in BAS is correlated with energy consumption. The facility management industry needs help to make sense of the captured BAS data and identify operational parameters relevant to the energy consumption. Data-driven approaches help facility managers monitor the patterns that occur between such parameters and energy consumption, and reveal energy efficient configurations of the parameters to prevent energy waste. This study provides a methodology that guides facility managers to define subset of operational parameters over a data captured and analyzed from a highly sensed building. Our results demonstrated that the number of AHU operational parameters dictate energy consumption can significantly be reduced to a subset by following the proposed approach. Case study analysis using the approach showed that pressure after cooling coil (PAC), supply air pressure (SAP), and fan speed (FSPD) were within the subset for the building analyzed.

1. Introduction

The energy consumption of residential and commercial buildings accounts for 41% of the total energy consumption in the U.S, and space heating and cooling has a share of 47% in this amount (DOE 2012). It is estimated that $20 billion per year can be saved by achieving energy efficiency in buildings (IPMVP 2001). Thus, energy savings in Heating Ventilating and Air Conditioning (HVAC) systems are a key in accomplishing energy efficient buildings and society. One way of achieving that is to examine how HVAC systems are running with respect to the energy use and identify configurations of HVAC system operational parameters that result in efficiency in the energy use. Although primary functions of Building Automation Systems (BASs) are monitoring and controlling the operation of HVAC systems, BASs are able to provide voluminous data on HVAC operational parameters over time. Utilization of this available data in BASs provides opportunities to gain insights on the efficient operation of HVAC systems and relate them to potential energy savings. However, BASs store the records of more than hundreds of HVAC operational parameters measured by sensors 24/7, some of which are irrelevant to energy consumption. For instance, humidity measurements of the conditioned air are expected to be more relevant to the indoor air quality rather than the energy consumption. In the current practice, the identification of operational parameters relevant to energy consumption is based on the domain knowledge of facility operators, although the vast amount of data stored in BAS is a valuable resource that can be utilized in the identification of these parameters. Therefore, an essential step to benefit from BAS data is to identify a subset of HVAC operational parameters that dictate the energy consumption of the system. Once such a subset is identified, patterns in the subset of HVAC operational parameters and in the energy consumption can be extracted to identify the energy efficient configurations of these parameters corresponding to lower energy consumption levels.

The vast amount of data stored in BAS enables utilization of data-driven approaches for knowledge discovery on building operations. Data-driven approaches focus on extracting knowledge from measured datasets (without detailed intervention from an expert) such as Support Vector Machine (SVM), clustering, Artificial Neural Networks (ANN), and feature selection algorithms (Miller, Nagy & Schlueter 2015). Feature selection algorithms aim for reducing the data dimensionality by eliminating irrelevant and redundant parameters from a data set (Sutha 2015). The objective of this study is to provide a way to identify a subset of HVAC operational parameters that contains only the parameters that dictate the energy consumption using data-driven approaches. Therefore, only feature selection algorithms has been used in this study. The authors proposed a feature selection approach to help facility operators identify relevant subset of operational patterns to configure systems that will result in lower energy consumption levels. The research method included categorization of feature selection algorithms, identification of feature selection algorithms that can be applied to this problem domain based on previous work and computational efficiency of the algorithms, and application and comparison of performance of the identified feature selection algorithms on a testbed building. The approach was tested using the data captured on one of the air handling units (AHU) of a case building. The building analyzed in this study is a highly sensed building, where AHU parameters have been collected for every minute and the energy consumption is segregated and measured at individual equipment level in the building.

2. Background

As the available data has become abundant, irrelevant and redundant variables as well as relevant ones to the target concept of interest are included in today's data sets (Piramuthu 2004). For instance, in the HVAC system monitoring and control domain, not only the energy consumption of the system, but also the indoor air quality, and thermal comfort are the target concepts of interests for facilities management. A variable that is relevant to thermal comfort might be irrelevant/redundant to other target concepts of interest. An irrelevant feature does not contribute to the predictive accuracy, and a redundant feature replicates the same information with the other features (Evangeline et al. 2013). It has been shown in numerous ways that data-driven approaches perform poorly in the presence of such irrelevant and redundant variables. In addition, feature selection increases the performance of data mining algorithms since they aim for eliminating irrelevant and redundant variables from the data set (e.g. Battiti 1994; Tsai 2009). Besides improving the prediction performance of the data mining algorithms, there are other advantages of utilizing the feature selection process, such as providing faster and more cost-effective models and gaining deeper insight into the underlying processes that generate the data (Saeys, Inza & Larranaga 2007).

Feature selection algorithms can be grouped into three categories as filter, wrapper, and embedded algorithms. The filter methods are usually known as correlation based feature selection algorithms. Given the problem at hand in this work, the correlation between selected AHU operational parameters and the energy consumption should be high, whereas the correlation among the selected parameters should be low for a sound selection performance. In other words, the selected subset of features should not be collinear, meaning that they do not replicate the same information (Hall 1999). Wrapper and embedded methods evaluate the goodness of different subset of features based on the predictive performance of an algorithm used. In these methods, prediction performance of the algorithms is compared for each and every possible subset of the features, and the features that give the best predictive accuracy are retained, while others are eliminated. In wrapper methods, since a predictor is trained for all possible subset of features evaluated, they are not computationally efficient. On the other hand, embedded methods are based on the selection of features in the training process, preventing recursive training of algorithms for each subset of the features. Therefore, they are computationally more efficient as compared to wrapper algorithms (Guyon & Elisseeff 2003). Therefore, wrappers are not considered in this study. In this study, collinearity in the data set is filtered by utilizing widely known Pearson correlation coefficient as a metric to identify correlations between different parameters. Pearson correlation coefficient shows the degree of linear relationship between two parameters, using a number between -1 and +1. A correlation coefficient of +1 indicates a perfectly positive linear relationship, whereas a correlation coefficient of -1 indicates perfectly negative linear relationship between two parameters. This coefficient is selected to be used in this study over the other correlation metrics available in the literature (such as Spearman correlation measure) since the parameters that have linear relationship with each other are desired to be captured. The Pearson correlation coefficient is known as a correlation metric to capture linear relationships between parameters, rather than monotonic relationships. Parameters with coefficient close to 1 replicate the same information with each other, and therefore they are collinear (Bolboaca & Jäntschi 2006). After detecting collinearity, most commonly used embedded algorithms in literature, namely boosting tree and random forest, were used to guide the selection of the least number of HVAC operational parameters relevant to the energy consumption (Tuv et al. 2009). Both algorithms aim to generate decision trees using a set of smaller trees. In the Boosting Tree algorithm, the boosting mechanism grows decision trees sequentially, using the already trained decision trees to build the next one (Hill & Lewicki 2006). In the Random Forest, however, data is resampled and every time a tree is trained independently from the rest of the samples (Liaw & Wiener 2002).

The advantage of using the feature selection process before the prediction of energy consumption has also been discussed in the HVAC domain. The Boosting Tree algorithm has been used in the feature selection process to build the prediction model with less amount of features for a better prediction performance. However, domain knowledge is also used in the feature selection process (Kusiak, Li & Tang 2010). The research presented in this paper is differentiated from the previous research efforts since the presented study envisions a completely data-driven process in the feature selection that is free of domain input, which could be subjective in nature and can bias the results. Moreover, the proposed methodology to guide FM operators rely on different feature selection algorithms to select the least number of AHU operational parameters most relevant to the energy consumption. In this way, operational configuration of these parameters that corresponds to lower energy consumption profiles can be identified for an energy efficient operation.

3. Research Method

A methodology is provided to guide facility operators in effective BAS data usage by analyzing the data-driven algorithms with respect to their fit in the problem domain and synthesizing the literature on data science field on efficiency and performance of these algorithms. The methodology is composed of the data pre-processing, filtering, and feature selection steps to deal with multivariate BAS dataset. Figure 1 shows the overview of the methodology. In order to select the operational parameters that are most relevant to energy consumption, first, the data for operational parameters for any equipment needs to be extracted from the BAS of a given building along with the corresponding energy consumption of that equipment. Next, a data pre-processing step is used to eliminate missing values and outliers in the data set, in addition to normalization of the data. Then, correlation coefficients between operational parameters are calculated in the filtering step to eliminate collinear features from the dataset. In the feature selection step, feature selection algorithms are applied on the filtered BAS data, and the importance factors of each operational parameter are given by the feature selection algorithms. Finally, the importance factors are interpreted to select the subset of operational parameters relevant to energy consumption. This methodology was implemented for an AHU of a case building as described next.

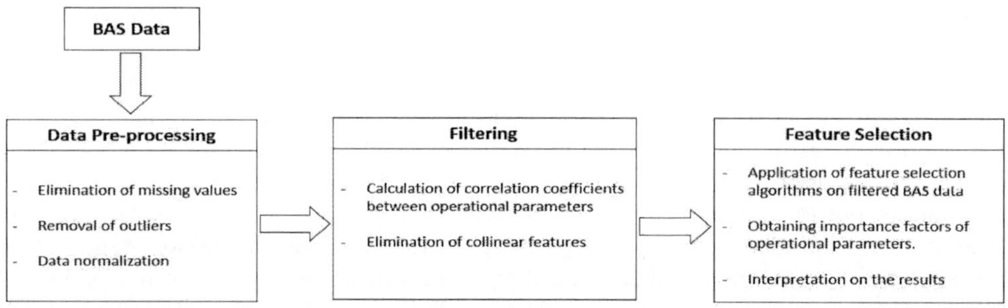

Figure 1: Overview of the Methodology

3.1 Overview of the Case Building

The case building analyzed is a three-story office building, which has 60,000 square feet of conditioned space. HVAC system of the building involves multiple air handling units (AHUs), each serving to different parts of the building. Only results of the analysis of one of the AHUs is reported in this paper. The methodology described above is implemented using summer and winter seasons of a year of continuous AHU performance data and electricity usage on that AHU. Available data set involves the measurements of 40 AHU operational parameters besides AHU energy consumption. The operational parameters include parameters such as temperature and pressure in different locations of AHU such as before or after cooling/heating coil, and status of sub-components (e.g., fan speed, damper position). The data collection frequency was one minute for every parameter. However, the data set is resampled to 15 minutes for a computationally more efficient analysis. Figure 2 illustrates the model of the AHU analyzed in the case building. The locations of filters, heating, and cooling coils, and fan are denoted in the figure as well.

The authors used the data of summer and winter seasons, separately, since the relevance of the AHU parameters to the energy consumption may change due to the effect of seasonality when the heating and cooling modes of the HVAC system is active for corresponding seasons. The summer and winter data sets used for the analysis involved 92 days from the summer season and 90 days from the winter season of a year analyzed (2015).

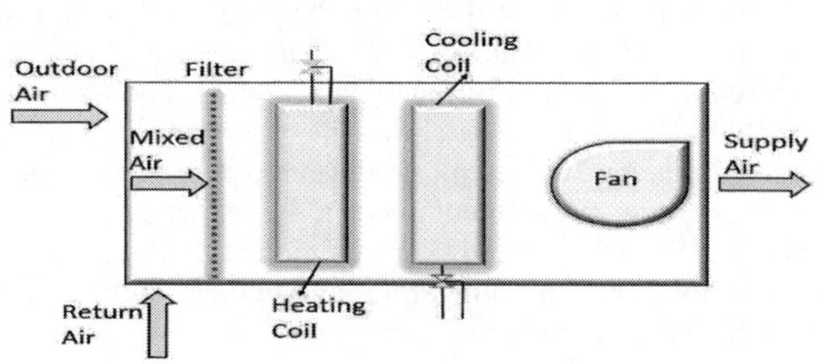

Figure 2: The Schematic Diagram of the Air Handling Unit Analyzed in the Case Study

3.2 Step 1: Data Pre-processing

Data pre-processing, which involves the elimination of missing values, removal of outliers, and normalization, is an essential step that should be applied before the application of feature selection algorithms on a given data set. The purpose of data pre-processing is to increase the quality of data. The performance of data-driven algorithms increases with increasing quality of data. However, the quality of BAS data is typically low due to intermittent missing values in the dataset, and outliers that makes the data set noisy. The reason of the existence of missing values in BAS data can be attributed to the sensor malfunctioning, while outliers exist mainly due to sensor misreading. In this study, if any of the operational parameters or AHU energy consumption data contained missing values at a timestamp, the entire data recorded across parameters at that time stamp was removed from the data set. An outlier has been defined as a value that falls outside the three standard deviations zone above and below the mean, which is a common way of labeling outliers (Miller, Nagy & Schlueter 2015). So, for a parameter, if a data point was outside the defined zone, it was labeled as an outlier and removed from the dataset. In addition, BAS data is a multivariate data set with different units and varying scales. For instance, the unit of the energy consumption data is kilowatt, whereas the units of temperature related parameters are Fahrenheit. Normalization is another step that must be implemented in the data pre-processing step to eliminate the effect of varying scales. Z normalization was used in this study so that each parameter had a mean of 0 and a standard deviation close to 1.

3.3 Step 2: Filtering

In this methodology, the Pearson correlation coefficient is used to calculate the correlation between different AHU operational parameters. In this methodology, the parameters that are highly correlated with each other (collinear features) are detected, and only one of them, having the highest correlation with energy consumption is selected, and the others are eliminated. Correlation coefficients of +0.9 and -0.9, which represent the two ends of high correlation expectations, were chosen to be the thresholds to label collinear features since they represent very high correlation between parameters (Batista et al. 2006). This methodology has been implemented in Python using SciPy module, which is widely used for implementing high-level scientific computing.

3.4 Step 3: Feature Selection

In the final step, Boosting Tree and Random Forest feature selection algorithms are applied on the filtered data set using Python scikit-learn module, which is used to implement machine learning algorithms. The reason to perform these algorithms on the filtered set of parameters is the wide use and high performance of these algorithms as discussed in the background section. These algorithms take the filtered data set composed of the AHU operational parameters and the AHU energy consumption as an input and calculate the importance factor for each parameter. The AHU operational parameters are ranked based on the importance factors obtained from the feature selection algorithms. The importance factors show the relevancy of AHU operational parameter with the AHU energy consumption. Higher importance factors illustrate that the parameter is more important/relevant to the energy consumption. Finally, the importance factors obtained from the algorithms are interpreted to finalize the feature selection process.

4. Analysis of Case Results and Discussions

Filtering process identified the collinear features in the data set. Figure 3 illustrates an example of bivariate relationship between three collinear features detected in the data set as a matrix. It is observed that these features (i.e., Pressure after filter, Pressure after heating coil, and Pressure after cooling coil) almost have linear relationships with each other. In other words, they replicate the same information and redundant. Instead of using all three, only the one having the highest correlation to energy consumption is kept for the following step of feature selection. Table 3(b) shows the correlation of these three AHU operational parameters with the AHU energy consumption. According to correlation values, the parameter PAC was kept in the data set, while the others were eliminated.

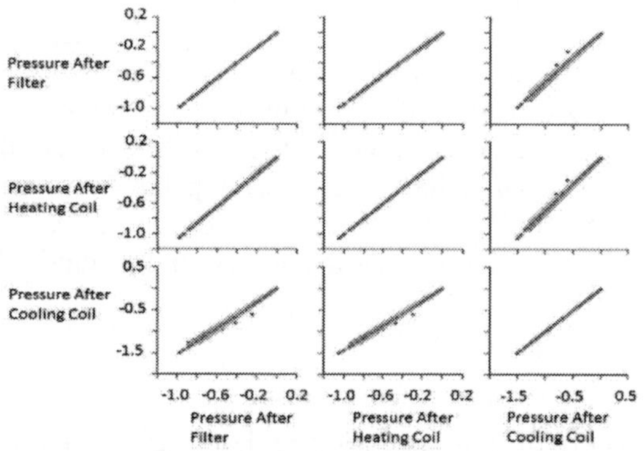

Parameter	Description	Correlation with Energy Consumption
PAF	Pressure After Filter	-0.73
PAHC	Pressure After Heating Coil	-0.74
PAC	Pressure After Cooling Coil	-0.79

Figure 3: Filtering example: Bivariate Relationships between Three Parameters (Left), (b) Corresponding Correlation Values (Right)

After the elimination of collinear features from the dataset using the filtering process, the number of AHU operational parameters in the filtered summer and winter data sets was reduced to 13 and 23, respectively. The remaining AHU operational parameters after the filtering process can be seen in Tables 1 and 2 for summer and winter seasons, respectively. Results of Boosting Tree and Random Forest algorithms are also provided in these tables. As shown in the tables, it was observed that Boosting Tree and Random Forest algorithm results were consistent with each other based on the rankings of the operational parameters. In addition, there was a sudden change in the importance factors of AHU operational parameters after fan speed (FSPD), especially for Random Forest results. Therefore, Pressure after cooling coil (PAC), supply air pressure (SAP), and fan speed (FSPD) were selected as the subset of AHU operational parameters that are most relevant to the AHU energy consumption. Monitoring the patterns that occur simultaneously in these three parameters with respect to AHU energy consumption may reveal operational configuration of these parameters corresponding to lower energy consumption profiles for an energy efficient operation. A facility operator may use the importance factor tables as a guideline to identify the AHU operational parameters that should be monitored for potential performance improvements. This process saves time in FM practice since the number of AHU operational parameters to be monitored is significantly reduced by using the proposed methodology.

Table 1: Feature Importance Factors for the Summer Season

Parameter	Description	Feature Importance (Boosting Tree)	Feature Importance (Random Forest)
PAC	Pressure After Cooling Coil	0.484	0.7144
SAP	Supply Air Pressure	0.226	0.1883
FSPD	Fan Speed	0.187	0.0810
HWTI	Hot Water Temperature, in	0.0308	0.0049
SAH	Supply Air Relative Humidity	0.0198	0.0030
RAT	Return Air Temperature	0.0166	0.0027
HVS	Heating Valve Status	0.0138	0.0020
AOAT	Average Outside Air Temperature	0.0092	0.0016
SAC	Supply Air CO_2 Concentration	0.0068	0.0007
RAH	Return Air Relative Humidity	0.0061	0.0004
DPRP	Damper Position	0.0002	0.0004
REF_P	Reference Pressure	0	0.0002
MAH	Mixed Air Relative Humidity	0	0.0002

As a final step, the goodness of the selected subset of the AHU operational parameters was evaluated by visualizing the correlation between the parameters. Figure 4 shows the bivariate relationships among the selected subset of AHU operational parameters. It was validated that the selected features were not collinear, and the same information is not replicated in the selected features.

Table 2: Feature Importance Factors for the Winter Season

Parameter	Description	Feature Importance (Boosting Tree)	Feature Importance (Random Forest)
PAC	Pressure After Cooling Coil	0.6310	0.9112
SAP	Supply Air Pressure	0.1572	0.0568
FSPD	Fan Speed	0.0550	0.0214
AFAV	Average Fresh Air Velocity	0.0326	0.0043
FAF	Fresh Air Flow	0.0324	0.0020
REF_P	Reference Pressure	0.0271	0.0007
RAT	Return Air Temperature	0.0156	0.0004
HWTI	Hot Water Temperature, in	0.0137	0.0004
HVS	Heating Valve Status	0.0088	0.0003
MAH	Mixed Air Relative Humidity	0.0072	0.0003
MAT	Mixed Air Temperature	0.0062	0.0003
HWTO	Hot Water Temperature, out	0.0051	0.0002
REF_T	Reference Temperature	0.0036	0.0002
DPRP	Damper Position	0.0033	0.0002
HWCF	Hot Water Coil Flow	0.0008	0.0002
HWH	Hot Water Heating	0.0001	0.0002
LSS	Liquid Solenoid Status	0.0000	0.0002
RAH	Return Air Relative Humidity	0.0000	0.0002
SAC	Supply Air CO_2 Concentration	0.0000	0.0002
AFAT	Average Fresh Air Temperature	0.0000	0.0001
SAT	Supply Air Temperature	0.0000	0.0001
ASAT	Average Supply Air Temperature	0.0000	0.0001
SAH	Supply Air Relative Humidity	0.0000	0.0000

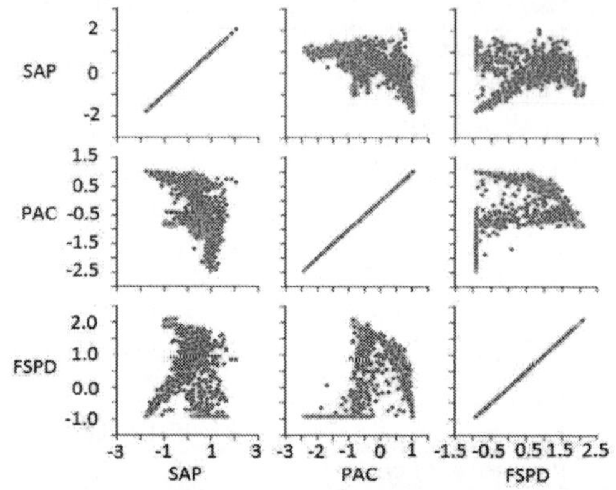

Figure 4: Bivariate Relationships between Selected Features

Since BAS data involves a great number of AHU operational parameters, it is challenging to identify the subset of the parameters relevant to energy consumption. The methodology can assist facility operators with the data-driven identification of the features that are most relevant to energy consumption. Although the feature selection process in this study is completely data driven, the methodology enables facility operators to check the importance factors obtained from the feature selection algorithms. The results can be interpreted by an experienced facility operator, and the subset of features that dictates the AHU energy consumption can be extended based on the domain knowledge of the facility operator. In addition, the selected AHU operational parameters can be used in the model formulation for the prediction of the energy consumption, since the feature selection algorithms improve the predictive accuracy of the algorithms.

5. Conclusion

In this paper, a methodology has been developed to identify the subset of AHU operational parameters relevant to energy consumption in buildings. The proposed methodology consists of a data pre-processing, filtering, and feature selection step. This methodology has been applied to a case study of one of the AHUs of a highly sensed building. Our results demonstrated that the number of AHU operational parameters can significantly be reduced by following the proposed approach. The subset of AHU operational parameters identified in the case study includes three out of 40 AHU operational parameters, namely, Pressure after cooling coil, fan speed, and supply air pressure. Future work includes analyzing the patterns in the identified subset of the AHU operational parameters, and AHU energy consumption to identify most energy efficient configuration of the operational parameters that corresponds to lower energy consumption levels.

References

Batista, L. H., Camargo, P. R., Aiello, G. V., Oishi, J., & Salvini, T. F. (2006). Knee joint range-of-motion evaluation: correlation between measurements achieved using a universal goniometer and an isokinetic dynamometer. Brazilian Journal of Physical Therapy, 10(2), pp. 193-198.

Battiti, R. (1994). Using mutual information for selecting features in supervised neural net learning. IEEE Transactions on neural networks, 5(4), pp. 537-550.

Bolboaca, S. D., & Jäntschi, L. (2006). Pearson versus Spearman, Kendall's tau correlation analysis on structure activity relationships of biologic active compounds. Leonardo Journal of Sciences, 5(9), pp. 179-200.

DoE, U.S. (2011). Buildings Energy Databook. Energy Efficiency & Renewable Energy Department.

Energy, D. (2001). International Performance Measurement & Verification Protocol. Handbook of financing energy projects, 249.

Evangeline, D.P., Sandhiya, C., Anandhakumar, P., Raj, G.D. and Rajendran, T., (2013). Feature subset selection for irrelevant data removal using Decision Tree Algorithm. In Advanced Computing (ICoAC), 2013 Fifth International Conference on Advanced Computing, Chennai, India, pp. 268-274.

Guyon, I. & Elisseeff, A., (2003). An Introduction to variable and feature selection. Journal of Machine Learning Research, 3, pp. 1157–1182.

Hall, M. (1999). Correlation-based feature selection for machine learning. The University of Waikato.

Hill, T., & Lewicki, P. (2006). Statistics: methods and applications: a comprehensive reference for science, industry, and data mining. StatSoft, Inc., Tulsa, OK

Kusiak, A., Li, M. & Tang, F., (2010). Modeling and optimization of HVAC energy consumption. Applied Energy, 87(10), pp. 3092–3102.

Liaw, A., & Wiener, M. (2002). Classification and regression by randomForest. R News, 2(3), pp. 18-22. Miller, C., Nagy, Z., & Schlueter, A. (2015). Automated daily pattern filtering of measured building performance data. Automation in Construction, 49(PA), pp. 1–17.

Piramuthu, S. (2004). Evaluating feature selection methods for learning in data mining applications. European Journal of Operational Research, 156(2), pp. 483-494.

Saeys, Y., Inza, I. & Larranaga, P., (2007). A review of feature selection techniques in bioinformatics. Bioinformatics, 23(19), pp. 1–10.

Sutha, K., (2015). A review of feature selection algorithms for data mining techniques. International Journal on Computer Science and Engineering, 7(6), pp. 63–67.

Tsai, C. F. (2009). Feature selection in bankruptcy prediction. Knowledge-Based Systems, 22(2), pp. 120-127.

Tuv, E., Borisov, A., Runger, G., & Torkkola, K. (2009). Feature selection with ensembles, artificial variables, and redundancy elimination. Journal of Machine Learning Research, 10(Jul), pp. 1341-1366.

An embedded algorithm for detecting and accommodating synchronization problems in wireless structural health monitoring systems

Kosmas Dragos, Kay Smarsly
Bauhaus University Weimar, Germany
kosmas.dragos@uni-weimar.de

Abstract. In wireless structural health monitoring systems, the inherent processing power of wireless sensor nodes enables the execution of structural health monitoring tasks in a decentralized manner. Decentralization may result in non-synchronized sets of structural response data, for example due to non-simultaneous triggering of the sensor nodes. Lack of synchronization is detrimental to the output of operational modal analysis (OMA), which is frequently applied in SHM, leading to erroneous structural mode shapes. From a computer science perspective, synchronization approaches in wireless SHM systems center around clock synchronization schemes. In this paper, an embedded algorithm is presented that enables wireless sensor nodes to detect and to accommodate synchronization problems. The proposed algorithm draws from the theory of OMA and the expected relationship between the phase angles of frequency components corresponding to mode shapes obtained from different sets of structural response data. The embedded algorithm is implemented into a wireless SHM system and validated through laboratory tests on a shear frame structure.

1. Introduction

Over the past decades, structural health monitoring (SHM) has been widely studied to assess the condition of large-scale engineering structures (Smarsly et al., 2012a,b). The advances in embedded processing technologies have enabled wireless sensor nodes to perform on-board computational tasks of increasing complexity. In wireless structural health monitoring, the enhanced computational capabilities of embedded microcontrollers take wireless sensor nodes one step further from serving merely as easy-to-install sensing devices that collect and communicate structural response data. Rather, in an attempt to address reliability issues associated with wireless communication, developing embedded algorithms to execute part of the monitoring process on board the sensor nodes has been the focus of extensive research (Dragos and Smarsly, 2015). Furthermore, it has been proven that on-board processing is less power-consuming than the wireless transmission of raw structural response data (Lei et al., 2010; Smarsly and Law, 2013).

Despite the merits of eradicating cables in SHM systems in terms of cost efficiency, the decentralized nature of wireless SHM systems may lead to synchronization discrepancies among different sets of structural response data. Specifically for system identification methods employed in SHM, which are typically based on the accumulation of different sets of structural response data, absolute synchronization is a prerequisite. For example, in operational modal analysis, which is applied in this paper, synchronization discrepancies may lead to erroneous mode shapes (García-Palacios et al., 2015).

In the field of computer science, research on synchronization in wireless SHM systems has been focusing on clock synchronization schemes. A comparison between various clock synchronization schemes along with discussion on clock synchronization problems, such as shifting and drifting, is given by Youn (2013). Moreover, a detailed survey on synchronization protocols can be found in Sundararaman et al. (2005). From an operational modal analysis (OMA) viewpoint, the characteristics of asynchronous structural response data, expressed through the respective power spectral density functions, has been investigated by Zhu and Au (2016). Maes et al. (2016) have presented a technique for the offline synchronization of data acquisition systems based on the mean phase difference of extracted mode shapes. Finally, Brincker and Brandt (2011) have proposed a synchronization method based on the cross correlation between different response data sets, assuming that a single mode is dominant in the structural response.

The aforementioned approaches aim at removing synchronization-induced errors in OMA, provided that the full sets of structural response data are available offline. This paper presents an embedded algorithm for wireless SHM systems attempting to detect and accommodate synchronization problems at an intermediate stage of the OMA, thus eliminating the need for transmitting raw structural response data. Drawing from the theory of structural dynamics and OMA, the sensor nodes estimate the time lags between the different sets of structural response data based on the differences among the phase angles of the frequency components corresponding to the fundamental (first) mode of vibration. The embedded algorithm is implemented into a wireless SHM system and validated through laboratory tests on a shear frame structure.

In the first section of the paper, the proposed algorithm is described. The second section covers the implementation of the algorithm into a wireless SHM system, while in the third section the validation tests are presented. The paper concludes with the summary and discussion as well as with an outlook on future research.

2. An embedded algorithm for accommodating synchronization problems in operational modal analysis

The proposed algorithm builds upon the fundamentals of structural dynamics and operational modal analysis. In this section, the mathematical background is briefly explained and the steps of the algorithm are presented.

2.1 Mathematical background

For detecting the time lag between two sets of structural response data, elements from the analysis of sinusoidal harmonic functions (signals) are adopted. Assuming the two non-synchronized sinusoidal signals $f(t)$ and $g(t)$ with the same frequency ω, amplitudes A_1 and A_2, and phase angles φ and θ, respectively, plotted in Figure 1, the time lag τ between the two signals is calculated in Eq. 1.

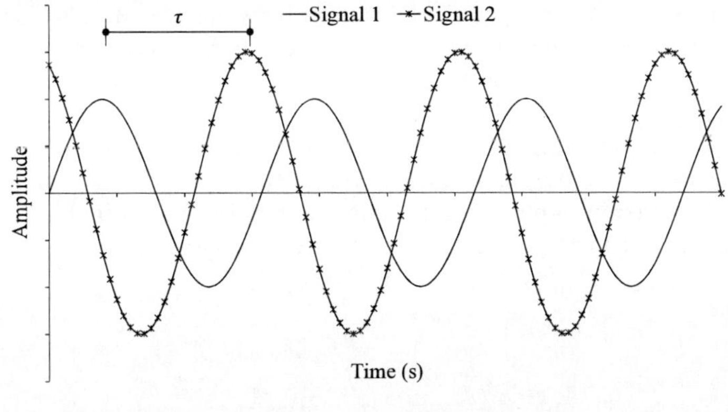

Figure 1: Sinusoidal signals with a time lag τ.

$$f(t) = A_1 \sin(\omega t + \varphi) \quad g(t+\tau) = A_2 \sin[\omega(t+\tau) + \varphi]$$
$$\Leftrightarrow g(t+\tau) = A_2 \sin(\omega t + \theta) \Leftrightarrow \tau = \frac{\theta - \varphi}{\omega} \tag{1}$$

According to the theory of structural dynamics, structural response can be represented by the superposition of "vibration modes", i.e. a sum of harmonic functions with different frequencies and oscillation amplitudes. Moreover, typically the response of a structure is dominated by one vibration mode, termed "fundamental mode", which is usually the vibration mode with the lowest frequency. In experimental structural dynamics, a common objective is to identify the frequencies of vibration modes using digital signal processing techniques, such as the fast Fourier transform (FFT) (Cooley and Tukey, 1965). The FFT transforms a time series, which in this case is a set of structural response data, from the time domain into the frequency domain, i.e. the FFT of a time series is a function of frequency ω, as shown in Eq. 2.

$$X_k(\omega) = \sum_{n=0}^{N-1} x_n \cdot e^{-2\pi i k \frac{n}{N}} \quad k \in [0, N) \quad N \in \mathbb{Z} \quad \omega = k \big/ (N \cdot \Delta t) \tag{2}$$

In Eq. 2, X is the kth element of the FFT transform of an N-point time series with elements x at frequency ω. The time step of the time series is denoted as Δt. From Eq. 2, it is evident that the FFT yields a complex-valued series, where each element represents a harmonic function. The modulus and the argument of each complex value correspond to the amplitude A and the phase angle δ of each harmonic function, as shown in Eq. 3.

$$A(\omega_k) = |X_k| = \sqrt{\text{Re}(X_k)^2 + \text{Im}(X_k)^2}$$
$$\delta(\omega_k) = \arg(X_k) = \arctan\left(\frac{\text{Im}(X_k)}{\text{Re}(X_k)}\right) \quad k = \omega_k \cdot \Delta t \cdot N \tag{3}$$

To estimate the time lag, for example, between two sets of structural response data, first the phase angles at the fundamental mode are retrieved. Since vibration modes describe physical oscillation, it follows that the harmonic functions of the fundamental mode from both sets of structural response data are either positively or negatively correlated. In terms of difference in phase angles, positive correlation is expressed as a difference between phase angles ("phase shift") equal to 0, while negative correlation is reflected on a phase shift equal to π. Assuming adequate knowledge on the correlation among the sets of structural response data at the fundamental mode, the time lags are estimated using Eq. 1 with phase angles computed from Eq. 3. Since the values of the phase angles computed from Eq. 3 are restricted within the interval $[0, 2\pi]$, the maximum phase shift cannot exceed 2π. Accordingly, the maximum time lag τ that can be estimated using the proposed algorithm is shown in Eq. 4.

$$\tau \leq \frac{2\pi}{\omega} = T \tag{4}$$

From Eq. 4, it is evident that the proposed algorithm can detect time lags that do not exceed the fundamental period T of the structure.

2.2 Description of the embedded algorithm steps

For applying the embedded algorithm proposed in this paper, prior knowledge or estimate of the fundamental mode ("fundamental mode shape information") of the structure is required. Specifically, the fundamental mode shape coordinates at the locations where structural response data is collected need to be estimated a priori. The sign difference among the mode shape coordinates indicates the correlation among the respective structural response data; coordinates of the same sign denote positive correlation, while coordinates of different sign express negative correlation. Accordingly, the expected phase shifts among the sets of structural response data at the fundamental mode are derived.

The embedded algorithm performs the following steps:

1. Collect structural response data (acceleration response data)
2. Transform collected acceleration response data into the frequency domain via FFT
3. Retrieve the phase angle at the fundamental mode of vibration
4. Exchange phase angles at the fundamental mode of vibration with the rest of the sensor nodes
5. Calculate the time lag with respect to a pre-defined reference sensor node
6. Shift the collected acceleration response data according to the calculated time lag
7. Send Fourier values at previously defined frequencies (corresponding to vibration modes) from the synchronized acceleration response data to a central server for modal identification

Finally, using the Fourier values of the synchronized sets of acceleration response data, the mode shapes are extracted by applying frequency domain decomposition (Brincker et al., 2000). In the following section, the implementation of the proposed algorithm into a wireless SHM system is described.

3. Implementation of the embedded algorithm into a prototype wireless SHM system

For implementing the embedded algorithm presented in this paper, a prototype wireless SHM system is devised. As shown in Figure 2, the SHM system is composed of wireless sensor nodes, a base station, and a centralized server. The tasks of detecting and accommodating time lags are entirely assigned to the sensor nodes, while the server is used for managing the SHM system, and the base station serves as a gateway between the sensor nodes and the server. The sensor nodes collect and transform acceleration response data, exchange the phase angles at the fundamental mode, calculate the time lags, synchronize their own collected acceleration response data, and transmit the Fourier values of the synchronized acceleration response data at frequencies corresponding to vibration modes to the server. The server initializes the SHM system, sends the fundamental mode shape information to the sensor nodes before applying the algorithm for the first time or when a change in structural state has been detected, and uses the Fourier values of the synchronized sets of acceleration response data to extract the mode shapes.

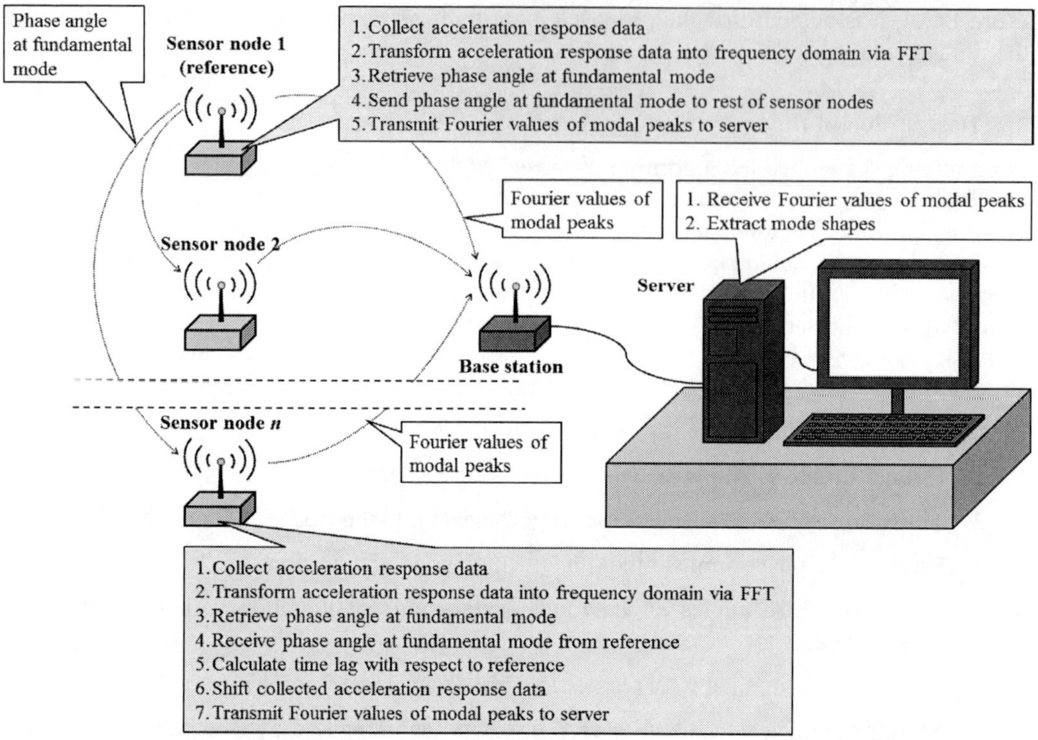

Figure 2: Architecture of the prototype wireless SHM and steps of the embedded algorithm.

The software for implementing the embedded algorithm, written in Java programming language, consists of two applications, one "host application" for the tasks of the server, and one "on-board application" for the tasks of the sensor nodes. The main class of the host application, named "`FDDonDesktop`", initializes the wireless communication links between the base station and the sensor nodes and sends the fundamental mode shape information to the sensor nodes. Upon receiving the Fourier values of the synchronized sets of acceleration response data, the mode shapes are extracted by calling the "`performFDD`" method, which uses the "`SingularValueDecomposition`" class of the JAMA library for matrix operations (JAMA, 2011). The on-board application comprises the "`FDDonNode`" main class, which, first, initializes the wireless communication links with the base station and the reference sensor node. Next, the `FDDonNode` class handles the collection of acceleration response data as well as the FFT transform via the class "`FrequencySpectrum`", which yields the Fourier series of amplitudes and phases, "`FFT`", yielding the complex-valued FFT series, and "`Complex`" to handle complex number operations. Then, class "`Synchronize`" is called to calculate the time lag and to synchronize the collected acceleration response data according to the phase angle at the fundamental mode of the reference sensor node, whose reception is managed by the `FDDonNode` class. Finally, the `FDDonNode` class sends the Fourier values of the synchronized acceleration response data at the previously defined frequencies corresponding to vibration modes to the server. The validation of the prototype wireless SHM system with the proposed embedded algorithm is presented in the next section.

4. Validation tests

To showcase the capability of the embedded algorithm of detecting and accommodating synchronization problems, laboratory tests on a shear frame structure are devised.

4.1 Experimental setup

The four-story shear frame structure employed for the validation tests consists of 15 mm thick, 300 mm × 200 mm (length × width) aluminum plates resting on four 20 mm × 2 mm (width × thickness) aluminum columns. The plate-to-column connections are fully fixed, while the four columns are clamped to a base plate, which is, in turn, fixed to a solid block, ensuring full fixity at the base of the structure. The story height is 300 mm. The aluminum alloy used for the shear frame structure has a density of ρ = 2700 kg/m^3 and a modulus of elasticity of E = 70 GPa.

The wireless sensor nodes employed for the validation tests are the Oracle SunSPOTs (Oracle, 2010). The sensor nodes feature a 400 MHz ARM microprocessor programmable in Java, 512 kB RAM, and 4 MB flash memory. The sensor nodes are equipped with IEEE 802.15.4 radio transceivers leveraging the ZigBee protocol. In terms of sensing, a 3D digital output accelerometer, a temperature sensor, and a light sensor are integrated in each sensor node. The accelerometer samples at 125 Hz, with selectable measurement ranges of ±2 g, ±6 g, or ±8 g at a resolution of 8 bit. The experimental setup is shown in Figure 3.

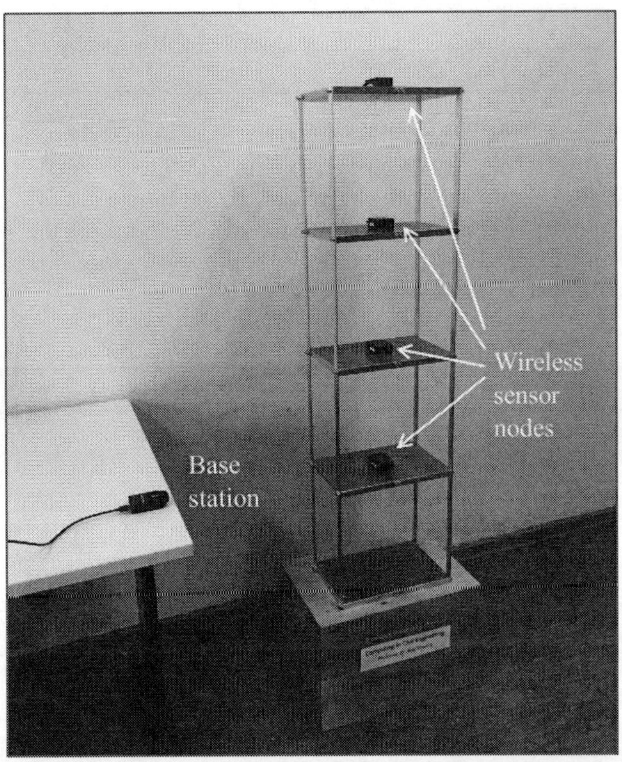

Figure 3: Experimental setup with the laboratory shear frame structure and the wireless sensor nodes.

4.2 Description of the validation tests

Prior to conducting the laboratory tests, the fundamental mode shape information is loaded to the wireless sensor nodes. Subsequently, the shear frame structure is excited by deflecting the top story. The sensor nodes are tasked to start collecting acceleration response data, once a predefined threshold of 0.1g, determined by engineering judgment, is exceeded. Due to the different input acceleration level introduced at each story by the excitation, the 0.1g threshold is not exceeded simultaneously at all stories, thus resulting in synchronization discrepancies.

The assessment of the algorithm is based on the comparison between the extracted mode shapes prior and after the synchronization. To provide a benchmark for this comparison, preliminary numerical analysis is performed on a numerical model of the laboratory test structure. The objective of the numerical analysis is to obtain estimates of the mode shapes. For the sake of simplicity, the analysis is restricted to the x-axis of the shear frame structure, which coincides with the length of the plates (300 mm). To verify the applicability of the algorithm, a total of two tests are performed. In both tests, the acceleration response data of the first story is taken as reference. The test results are summarized in Table 1.

Table 1: Time lags between the acceleration response data of the frame structure stories with respect to the first (reference) story.

Story	**Time lag (ms) – Test 1**	**Time lag (ms) – Test 2**
2	41	31
3	-10	48
4	-20	58

In the results of Table 1, negative values indicate that the respective set of acceleration response data needs to be delayed with respect to the reference set of acceleration response data. The extracted mode shapes from both tests, before and after the synchronization, are illustrated in Figures 4, 5, 6, and 7. The estimated mode shape from the numerical analysis is also plotted for comparison purposes.

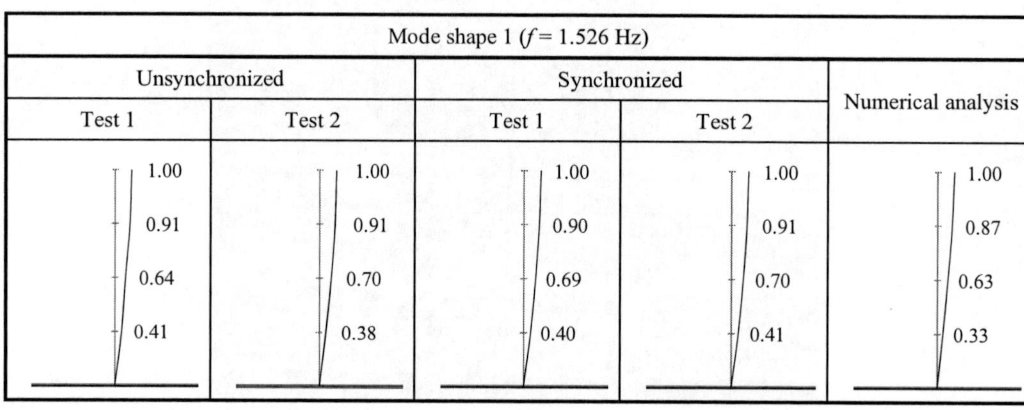

Figure 4: 1st extracted mode shape at f = 1.526 Hz.

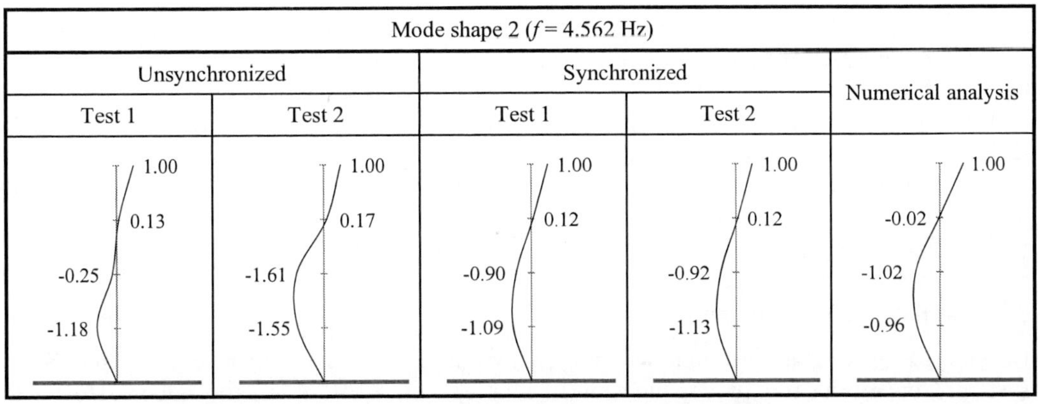

Figure 5: 2nd extracted mode shape at $f = 4.562$ Hz.

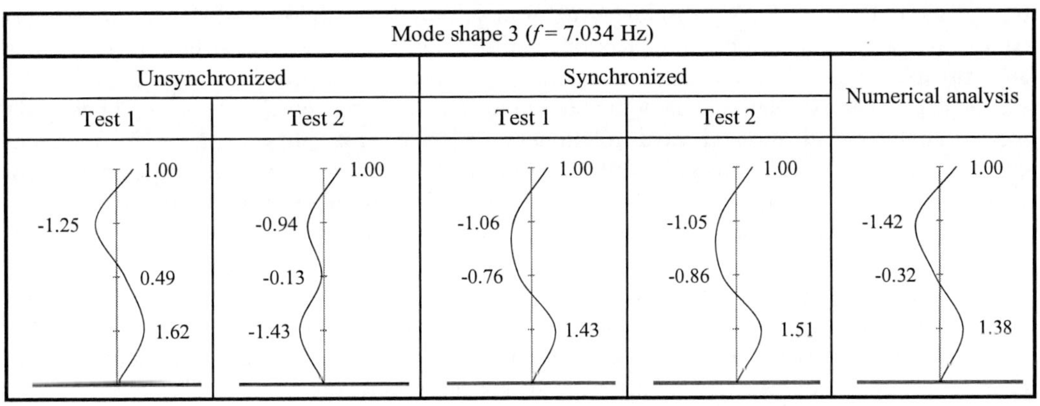

Figure 6: 3rd extracted mode shape at $f = 7.034$ Hz.

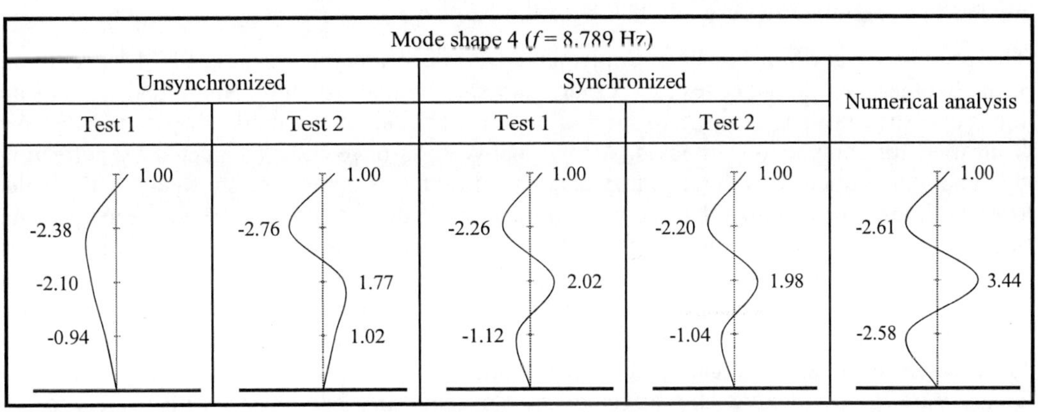

Figure 7: 4th extracted mode shape at $f = 8.789$ Hz.

From the results it is obvious that the synchronization performed by the embedded algorithms yields more realistic estimates of the mode shapes. As shown in Figure 4, the synchronization discrepancy effect is less obvious for the fundamental mode of the laboratory structure. This weak effect is attributed to the low frequency of the fundamental mode of vibration ($f = 1.526$ Hz) and, thus, to the long period of the respective frequency component

($T = 0.655$ s) with respect to the time lags; the respective phase shifts among the unsynchronized sets of acceleration response data are low. In Figures 5, 6, and 7, the effect of the synchronization discrepancies is visible, and the synchronized signals are in good agreement with the results of the numerical analysis. Deviations among the extracted mode shapes and the estimated mode shapes of the numerical analysis are expected, due to modeling uncertainties, to imperfect excitation of higher vibration modes, and to measuring inaccuracies.

5. Summary and discussion

Decentralizing structural health monitoring (SHM) tasks is common practice in wireless SHM systems, owing to the processing power inherent to wireless sensor nodes. However, decentralization may lead to synchronization discrepancies among the sets of structural response data collected by the sensor nodes. Moreover, in system identification methods, typically employed in SHM, absolute synchronization among the sets of structural response data is a prerequisite for obtaining accurate estimates of structural parameters. In this paper, an embedded algorithm for accommodating synchronization problems in wireless SHM systems has been presented. The embedded algorithm is based on the theory of operational modal analysis and the expected relationship between the phase angles of frequency components corresponding to modes of vibration. First, assuming adequate knowledge on the fundamental (first) mode of vibration, which typically dominates structural vibration, the expected differences among the phase angles of the fundamental mode (phase shifts) are derived. Next, the sensor nodes collect acceleration response data and transform the data into the frequency domain via the fast Fourier transform. Then, using the expected phase shifts, each wireless sensor node calculates the time lag between its own set of acceleration response data and the set of structural response data from a predefined reference sensor node, whose phase angle at the fundamental mode is wirelessly communicated to all sensor nodes. Finally, the sensor nodes synchronize their own sets of acceleration response data based on the time lags and send the Fourier values at previously selected frequencies, corresponding to vibration modes, to a centralized server.

The proposed algorithm has been implemented into a prototype wireless SHM system and validated through laboratory tests on a four-story shear frame structure. Numerical analysis on the frame structure has been performed to obtain estimates of the mode shapes, which have been used for comparison purposes. A total of two tests have been conducted by deflecting the laboratory structure at the top story and by letting the structure vibrate freely. The results from both tests have shown that the synchronization of the sets of acceleration response data according to the detected time lags yield mode accurate estimates of the mode shapes as compared with the numerical mode shapes. Moreover, the effect of synchronization problems has proven to be stronger in higher vibration modes, which are usually characterized by higher frequencies, and, thus, short periods with respect to the time lags. Future research will be directed towards investigating the performance of the embedded algorithm in cases of longer time lags. Moreover, the effect of the time lag on mode shapes with respect to the frequencies of the vibration modes can be quantified.

Acknowledgments

The authors gratefully acknowledge the support provided by the German Research Foundation (DFG) under grant SM 281/7-1. Also, the financial support through the DFG Research Training Group 1462 is gratefully acknowledged. Any opinions, findings, conclusions, or recommendations expressed in this paper are solely those of the authors and do not necessarily reflect the views of DFG or any other organizations and collaborators.

References

Brincker, R., Andersen, P. & Zhang, L. (2000). Modal identification from ambient responses using frequency domain decomposition. In: Proc. of the 18th International Modal Analysis Conference (IMAC), San Antonio, TX, USA, 07/02/2000.

Brincker R. & Brandt, A. (2011). Time synchronization by modal correlation. In: Proc. of the 4th International Operational Modal Analysis Conference, Istanbul, Turkey, 09/05/2011.

Cooley, J. W. & Tukey, J. W. (1965). An algorithm for the machine calculation of complex Fourier series. Mathematics of Computation, 19 (90), pp. 297–301.

Dragos, K. & Smarsly, K., (2015). A comparative review of wireless sensor nodes for structural health monitoring. In: Proc. of the 7th International Conference on Structural Health Monitoring of Intelligent Infrastructure, Turin, Italy, 01/07/2015.

García-Palacios, J., Tirando-Andrés, F., Soria, J. M., Díaz, I. M. & Araujo, Á. (2015). Effects of time synchronization on operational modal analysis. In: Proc. of the 6th International Operational Modal Analysis Conference, Gijón, Spain, 12/05/2015.

JAMA – A Java Matrix Package. Available at http://math.nist.gov/javanumerics/jama (Accessed: 29/03/2017).

Lei Y., Shen W. A., Song Y. & Wang Y. (2010). Intelligent wireless sensors with application to the identification of structural modal parameters and steel cable forces: from the lab to the field. Advances in Civil Engineering 2010, pp. 1-10.

Maes, K., Reynders, E., Rezayat, A., De Roeck, G. & Lombaert, G. (2016). Offline synchronization of data acquisition systems using system identification. Journal of Sound and Vibration, 381, pp. 264–272.

Oracle Corp. (2009). Sun SPOT Theory of Operation, 1.5.0. Santa Clara, CA, USA: Sun Labs.

Smarsly, K., Hartmann, D. & Law, K. H. (2012a). Structural Health Monitoring of Wind Turbines Observed by Autonomous Software Components – 2nd Level Monitoring. In: International Society for Computing in Civil and Building Engineering. In: Proc. of the 14th International Conference on Computing in Civil and Building Engineering, Moscow, Russia, 06/27/2012.

Smarsly, K. & Law, K. H. (2013). Advanced Structural Health Monitoring based on Multi-Agent Technology. In: Zander, J. & Mostermann, P. (eds.). Computation for Humanity: Information Technology to Advance Society. Pp. 95-126, Boca Raton, FL, USA: CRC Press – Taylor & Francis Group, LLC.

Smarsly, K., Law, K. H. & Hartmann, D. (2012b). Towards Life-Cycle Management of Wind Turbines based on Structural Health Monitoring. In: Proc. of the First International Conference on Performance-Based Life-Cycle Structural Engineering, Hong Kong, China, 12/05/2012.

Sundararaman, B., Buy, U. & Kshemkalyani, A. D. (2005). Clock synchronization for wireless sensor networks: a survey. Ad Hoc Networks, 3 (3), pp. 281–323.

Youn, S. (2013). A comparison of clock synchronization in wireless sensor networks. International Journal of Distributed Sensor Networks, 2013 Article ID: 532986, 10pp.

Zhu, Y.-C. & Au, S.-K. (2017). Spectral characteristics of asynchronous data in operational modal analysis. Structural Control Health Monitoring, 2017 Article ID: e1981, 15pp.

A computational paradigm for the optimisation of steel building structures based on cost and carbon indexes in early design stages

S. Eleftheriadis[a,c], C.F. Dunant[b], M.P. Drewniok[b], W. Rogers-Tizard[c]
[a]Department of Computer Science, University College London, UK
[b]Department of Engineering, University of Cambridge, UK
[c]Price & Myers LLP
stathiseleftheriadis@gmail.com

Abstract. The study explores a practical engineering paradigm that aims to augment the cost and carbon analysis of steel building structures. Cost and carbon functions were developed specifically for this purpose including raw material, fabrication, design, fire protection, and erection components. A customised computational model for the analysis of structural alternatives is investigated. The proposed model is tested in an actual building case where several benchmark designs are computed. The outputs from the model are compared with a small number of actual design alternatives which were developed by engineering practitioners. The proposed method can significantly increase the understanding of the design space's boundaries whilst the computed solutions have exhibited enhanced cost and carbon performance compared to actual designs.

1. Introduction

Although steel framed building structures are designed according to standards, which define minimum safety limits, their material efficiency is rarely being systematically addressed in practice. This inherently creates large inefficiencies in the way building structures are designed and constructed. Moynihan and Allwood investigated 79 steel-framed buildings, and concluded that unused mass of steel framed buildings could reach nearly 46% of the building's total mass due to over-specification of the steel sections (Moynihan & Allwood, 2014). Furthermore, Dunant et al. in their study confirmed that 35-45% of the steel by mass of the steel frame is not required in terms of structural efficiency (Dunant, et al., 2017).

Traditionally, the relationships between the cost of materials and the cost of fabrication in construction is considered to have a significant impact on the final design selection. In the literature, cost optimisation can be found in several instances: welded steel structures (Jarmai & Farkas, 1999), steel frames with semi-rigid connections (Hayalioglu & Degertekin, 2005), design, fabrication, and manufacturing (Sawada, et al., 2006; Heinisuo, et al., 2010; Haapio, 2012) and entire steel structures (BCSA & TATA, 2013). Cost as a single metric is easy to comprehend and quantify, however, its relationship with other environmental impact metrics is more complicated to determine. For example, even though material reductions are important in CO_2 optimisation this does not mean that material reduction will also yield cost optimum solutions.

Although optimisation methods are available to engineering practitioners for more than three decades, their implementation is limited by the different requirements addressed in every project (Prager, 1970). Even though mathematical techniques are well established in structural optimisation, which vary from construction scheduling (Zhou, et al., 2013), construction site layout (Zhou, et al., 2009), construction management (Suliman, et al., 2011), size, shape and topology optimisation (Frans & Arfiadi, 2014), and member optimisation in high rise buildings (Kingman, et al., 2015; Stromberg, et al., 2012; Stromberg, et al., 2012), more practical optimisation models are still needed. Despite the different optimisation studies of steel buildings found in the literature, the relationship between cost and carbon performance in early design stages has not been effectively addressed in the past. Understanding these relationships is a significant challenge and if appropriately addressed could offer structural engineers better ways to evaluate optimised design configurations. The study investigates a practical optimisation paradigm applied and validated in steel framed buildings developed to augment both cost and carbon performance of the structure during the early phases of the design development.

2. Research Approach

The objectives of the study are threefold: 1) To establish a cost and carbon model for the assessment of steel structures, 2) To develop the computational model for the analysis of structural alternatives, and 3) To verify the model in a real building case. In this study the results obtained from the computational model are evaluated against actual design solutions in a comparative study.

The study begins by defining the cost and carbon functions that are processed into a custom cost and carbon analysis model of steel structures. The cost and carbon functions use data factors from literature review and other empirical data sources. The analytical part of the study comprises of two components. In both components, the objectives are cost and embodied carbon minimisation of the steel structure. The functional unit of the study is defined as the floor system of the structure. In the first component of the study, engineering-based alternatives are developed using a manual trial-and-error design procedure. In this component, feasible designs are articulated by engineers and indicated as "actual" solutions. These designs depend on engineers' perception of optimality and due to time constraints only a small part of the solution space can be developed.

On the other hand, the second component includes theoretical design alternatives that are computed in the parametric structural model. In this component, designs are specified as "benchmark" solutions. Multiple configurations can be analysed rapidly and therefore the design space can be fully explored. At this phase of the study, the outputs from both components are used as inputs in the cost and carbon model in a separate process. However, an integrated cost and carbon model within the parametric structural model is currently under development. The cost and carbon model utilises the cost and carbon functions previously mentioned as well as material quantities, construction properties, etc. from the structural analysis models. The cost and carbon results for the actual and the benchmark solutions are evaluated and plotted in a 2D-graph that assess discrepancies between the two solution sets.

2.1 Cost and Carbon Functions

A database of embodied carbon and cost inventories is established and associated with the relevant material and structural type (beams, concrete, rebar). The review of the materials' type helps source the embodied carbon inventories: data input from Environmental Product Declarations (EPD) related data or other Life Cycle Inventories (LCI) are utilised. In addition, carbon data from GaBi and econinvent databases were utilised on several occasions. The cost assessment model has been developed based on a feature based cost methodology. Cost factors were used based on Spon's Architect's and Builder's Price Book 2017. In feature-based models, the manufacturing process of steel frames is divided into single processes. Each process is executed at separate cost centres. The comprehensive cost components include raw material, fabrication, design, fire protection, erection. The cost and carbon functions are developed using Microsoft Excel making allowances for manual data input for bill of materials from the structural analysis. The automatic query of cost and carbon functions is currently under development and it will be examined a later stage of the project. The cost functions are strongly related to the structural analysis as beam-level information is used to derive total lengths, total weights, number of elements and total surface area for painting and floor area. The function utilises cost factors for rolled steel sections, precast units, connections, fire protection, transportation, erection. The total cost of the structural system is adjusted in £/m^2. The embodied carbon component utilises concepts from the Life Cycle Assessment (LCA) theory and particularly on environmental standards developed under the CEN/TC350 framework. The scope of those standards follows a modular approach to buildings' life cycle impacts based on the corresponding life cycle stages starting from product and construction stages to use and end-of-use stages. The carbon functions use material quantities from the structural analysis to compute the embodied carbon of the structural steel, coating, precast concrete units, rebar and screed. The output from the carbon model is given in kgCO_2e/m^2.

2.2 Computational Model

To help guide early stage structural steel designs, the computational model explored in this study's principal role is to categorise technologies given the constraints which are often known. For example, for a given load and combination of spans, what type of flooring is preferable? If the ceiling height is restricted, is this different? In general, any number of restrictions in the possible spans, loads, etc. can be applicable. At the same time, the design space is very large: the number of commercially available options is considerable, and the grid, though it is frequently fixed, generally allows for some flexibility. The difficulty is thus to explore as completely as possible the complete solution space of possible floor solutions given a set of constraints.

An exhaustive search is not possible, therefore, the proposed computational model functions as a Monte-Carlo method, generating a large number of putative designs, rejecting those which do not match the constraints and selecting the best so that they can be used as hints for the design work of the structural engineers. The metric used to rank the solutions are predicted cost and carbon footprint, both calculated on the basis of a detailed bill of materials generated by the model. To generate putative designs, the model randomly generates bays from a user- provided length probability distribution which was built in a custom C++ algorithm. Each bay, composed of primary, secondary and tie beams is then calculated according to the prescribed loads. The load on each beam is computed according to the area of the bay, the average area of its neighbours, and its position as a corner, an edge or in the bulk of the floor. For each bay, all possible combinations of technologies are investigated.

The design process envisaged would be this: the engineer uses the model according to the specified spans and loads to choose the floor plate technology most appropriate for the project. In a second step, the engineer would create a preliminary design and evaluate it. The engineer would then use the design space described by the model to help them converge towards an optimal solution: knowing the design space boundary should help deciding whether cheaper or lighter designs are possible, particularly when the design of typical bays is suggested. The definition of the bays (Figure 1) can take three form:

1. Free: a statistical distribution of the possible spans is given. This is appropriate for general guidance where a general idea of the bay size is known, but is not fixed.
2. Semi-defined: the grid is defined in a single direction. This is typically the case for corridors which follow the main grid but which length can be variable.
3. Fixed: the dimension of the bay is fixed along both direction

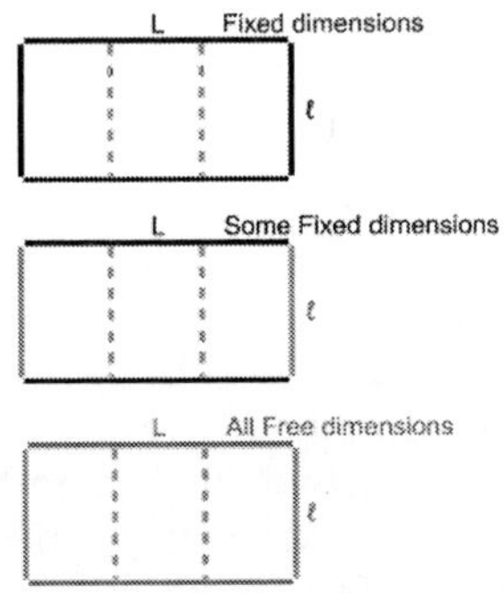

Figure 1: Bay type definition

The computational model (Figure 2) can compute both composite and precast floor designs. The study focuses on the analysis of precast systems only. A database of standard rolled sections has been built in the algorithm but fabricated sections can also be identified. For the purposes of this research the algorithm is searching for the optimum solution within the list of universal sections available on the list. The method for selecting the beams in the precast design is the following:

1. Universal sections are ranked according to their linear density
2. Each section, starting from the lightest is tested in turn for:
   2.1 Frequency
   2.2 Deflection
   2.3 Bending moment
   2.4 Shear strength
3. When a test is failed, the next section is tried
4. When no test fails, the section is selected.
5. Along the longest dimension of a bay, the opportunity to add secondary beams is tried
   5.1 The possible spans are selected
   5.2 The primary and secondary beams are selected as above, taking into account the additional stiffness.

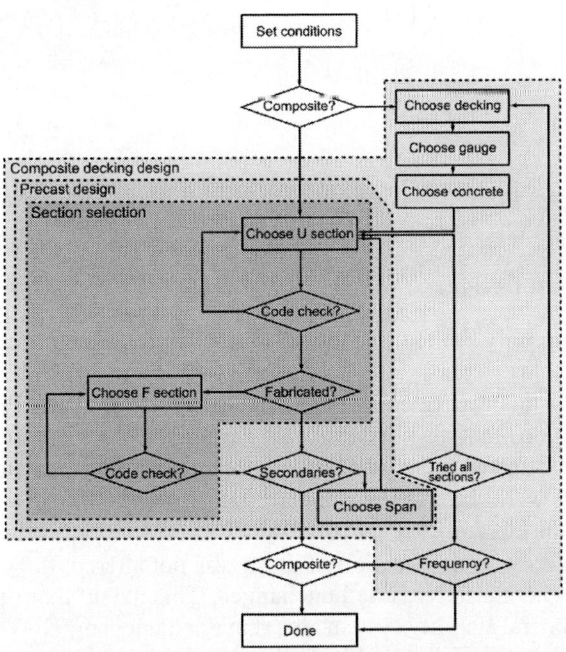

Figure 2: Representation of the computational model

3. Optimisation Scope

The optimisation options were separated into global and local levels. Components at global level refer to those elements that affect the project at high level, generally at the earlier stages of the design/concept, and were more heavily influenced by Architecture. Typically these factors could include: column grid, primary/secondary beam spacing, floor type depth, loadings, structural zone, and fire strategy. Local optimisation methods were those that could be decided upon at a later stage of design. These were factors that only really affected the beams independently, with little impact on the surrounding members, and were generally governed by the Engineer. Examples of these factors could be: member/section type, steel grade, connection type, cell/opening type, fire protection. The optimisation model in this study has focused on components from the global level analysis with aim to identify methods to augment early stage efficient design solutions.

4. Case Study

An in-depth investigation into the optimisation of a simplified steel frame was carried out. The frame selected was an actual design project. The building was part of a new 2 storey school block, with a single line of seven uniform classrooms with corridor down one side and circulation cores at either end (Figure 3).

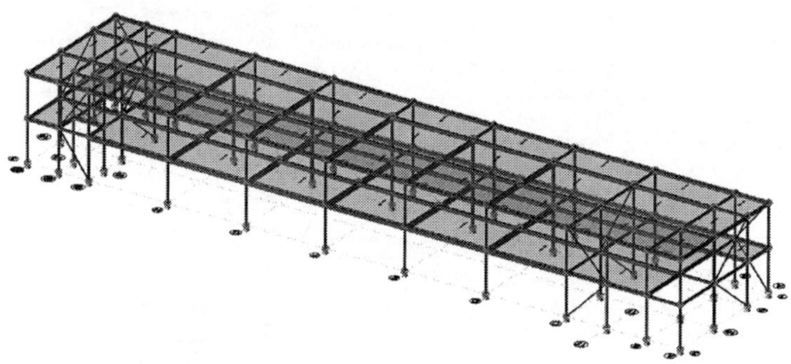

Figure 3: Typical layout of beams at first floor (the roof used an identical layout)

5. Engineering-Based Designs

Due to time constraints, only limited variations were looked at, with the other potential variables restricted. Fixed variables were:

- Column grid – this was fixed in this instance. Partly as it vastly reduced the potential number of options, but also because as a classroom block (room sizes fixed with non-negotiable clear spans) there was limited potential to alter this anyway.
- Imposed loads were fixed at the standard value for classrooms at 3.0 kPa + 1.0 kPa for partitions on the classroom level (first floor) and 0.75 kPa for the roof.
- Circulation cores – as the location of these was not altered, the general arrangement of beams within them also remained unchanged. This meant that the vertical bracing that provided the lateral stability system also remained unchanged. Wind loads were applied using a modeller tool built into the software, and this was also unchanged between each option.

- Cladding loads were ignored in all cases, as were the effect of any permanent partitions (e.g. around lift cores and stairwells).
- For all cases, the overall structural depth was left unrestricted. Whilst this may have provided some interesting results, it would have resulted in too many variables, and given that the primary load bearing members in all cases run along the perimeters of rooms it also was unlikely to be a restrictive issue in practice.

Table 1: The areas that were varied in the study were

Floor Type	Floor Depths	Floor Finishes	Beam Spacing
Precast planks	For precast this involved simply varying the depth of the planks in standard 50 mm increments (and allowing for secondary beams were necessary).	For the precast options, typically a 75 mm topping screed was added (as is usually necessary to provide an acceptable finish), however this was removed for comparison in two of the options.	Several variations of floor beam arrangement were considered, representing what were believed to be the various realistic patterns

5.1 Design Assumptions

Design was carried out on Tekla Structural Designer software in full accordance with Eurocode 3 (Steel). In each option, members were selected with the aim of achieving the section with the minimum possible weight to suit both ULS and SLS requirements – aiming for a utilisation ratio as close to 1.0 as possible. In principle, due to the relatively small variance between options only a small selection of member sizes were used across all options. Columns as well as beams were altered where necessary. Bracing was maintained as the same sections throughout.

5.2 Actual Solutions

In total, 11 precast options were identified. The layout and design options tested are shown in Figure 4. The material outputs were used to calculate the equivalent embodied CO_2 and cost for each option using the cost and carbon models previously described. This figure was then used for comparison between the options to determine which had the lowest value. Figure 5 shows the cost and carbon results for the entire structure of the 11 actual solutions analysed. Designs 1-4 were sized based on the optimum beam size, and plates were added to achieve the minimum 175 mm thickness needed for the bearing distance of 2 precast planks. Designs 4-8 were restricted, so that only beams with a minimum width of 175 mm were allowed, this meant that additional plates were not needed. All of designs 1-8 were designed assuming a propped construction. Designs 9-10 were designed as un-propped, and required torsion design for the temporary case where planks would be present on one side of the beam only. The final two cases are as per designs 1 and 2, but with no screed required. Designs 11 and 12 proved to be the most cost and carbon efficient solutions. The reduced screed lowered the volume of concrete and therefore the weight of the structure, subsequently reducing the steel weight. Designs 4 and 8 were both variations of beam layout 4, which required a larger number of steels with smaller spanning planks. This layout was not cost effective, and produced the largest cost and carbon solutions. There did seem to be a clear distinction between beams that had a limited minimum width of 175 mm, and in each case, the addition of flat plates to a smaller beam appeared to provide a most cost and carbon efficient solution. The results from Design 3 are interesting as it appears to have 5% less carbon and 5% more cost compared to Design 1. This can be attributed due to the larger number of total steel members used in Design 3 which increases erection, fabrication and fire protection costs. On the other hand, the total weight of steel is approximately the same with Design 1 but the use of 150 mm planks significantly reduces the carbon emissions in the floor construction. Design 9, which was equivalent to Design 1 with additional design contingency for torsion applied to the beam was more carbon intensive and costly than its counterpart (Design 1). However, this difference was smaller than many of the other factors. It should be noted that Design 10 encountered difficulties during the design stage and has been omitted from this results comparison.

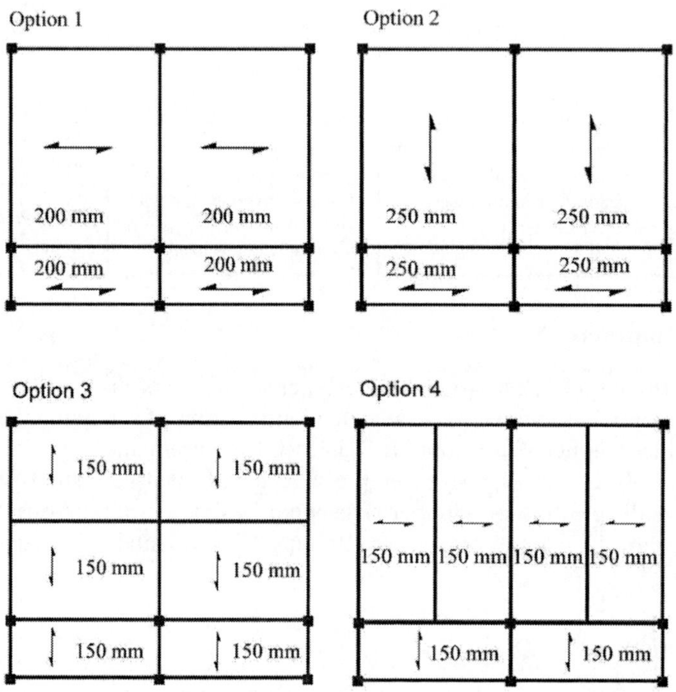

Type	Design No.	Beam Layout	Beam Restrain	Beam Type	Comments	Precast Type	Plank Depth (mm)	Screed Depth (mm)	Floor Areas (m^2)
Precast	1	Option 1	Pinned	Universal	N/A	Hollowcore	200	75	1259
Precast	2	Option 2	Pinned	Universal	N/A	Hollowcore	250	75	1259
Precast	3	Option 3	Pinned	Universal	N/A	Hollowcore	150	75	1259
Precast	4	Option 4	Pinned	Universal	N/A	Hollowcore	150	75	1259
Precast	5	Option 1	Pinned	Universal	No steel plate	Hollowcore	200	75	1259
Precast	6	Option 2	Pinned	Universal	No steel plate	Hollowcore	250	75	1259
Precast	7	Option 3	Pinned	Universal	No steel plate	Hollowcore	150	75	1259
Precast	8	Option 4	Pinned	Universal	No steel plate	Hollowcore	150	75	1259
Precast	9	Option 1	Pinned	Universal	Torsion	Hollowcore	200	75	1259
Precast	10	Option 4	Pinned	Universal	Torsion	Hollowcore	150	75	1259
Precast	11	Option 1	Pinned	Universal	No screed	Hollowcore	200	-	1259
Precast	12	Option 2	Pinned	Universal	No screed	Hollowcore	250	-	1259

Figure 4: Grid layout and design options for engineering-based designs

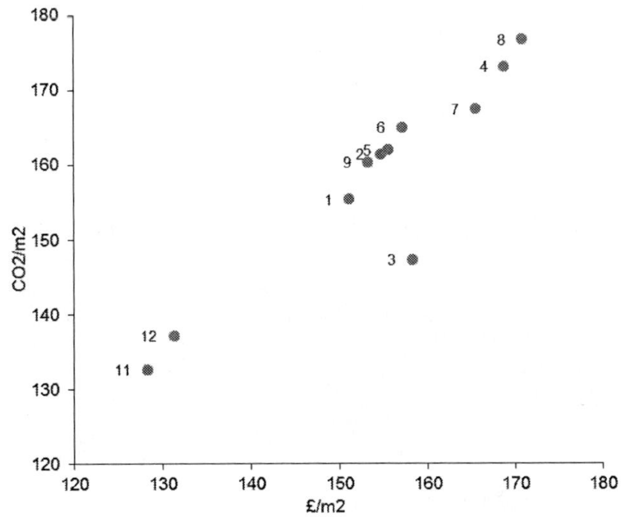

Figure 5: Results for Engineering-Based Designs for the whole structure

6. Computational-Based Designs

The design conditions and constraints used to populate the actual solutions were also implemented as input data in the computational-based designs. Based on the defined data input possible design configurations were computed to satisfy Eurocode 3 and the structural requirements set by the engineering practitioners. The resulting 20,000 designs were computed in less than 5 min. The material listings for these solutions were then compiled, using direct output from the structural analysis. In total the data collected included:

- Total steel weight by member type
- Total steel surface area – this is to calculate the area of paint needed.
- Total volume of precast planks
- Total volume of in-situ concrete. This included the infill concrete around and between planks for the precast options
- Total weight of reinforcing steel. For precast options it allowed a basic weight for the pre-stress tendons, as well as allowance for tying bars around the perimeter and between planks.
- Total weight of additional steel. This is to allow for plates and/or angles required where beams are selected that don't meet the required minimum bearing areas. No allowance has been made for connections for any of the options.

Figure 6 shows the representation of the design space as populated by the model for the steel beams of the structure. The swarm with the black nodes includes all the computational-based solutions and is combined with engineering-based designs which are represented by the red nodes. The comparative analysis with the actual designs only includes the first nine designs excluding the ones without screed (designs 11 and 12) in order to understand the impacts of the steel members on the cost and carbon results. It is evident that all the design solutions populated from the computational model are more economical than the cheapest actual solution by 12-18%. The carbon performance of the computational-based solutions lies on the lower boundary of the actual designs. Almost 50% of the swarm has similar carbon performance compared to the most carbon efficient actual solution. Furthermore, the design space showed that additional

6-8% carbon reductions could be achieved from the design of steel beams by optimising mainly the spans' distribution and the classification of more efficient beam sizes.

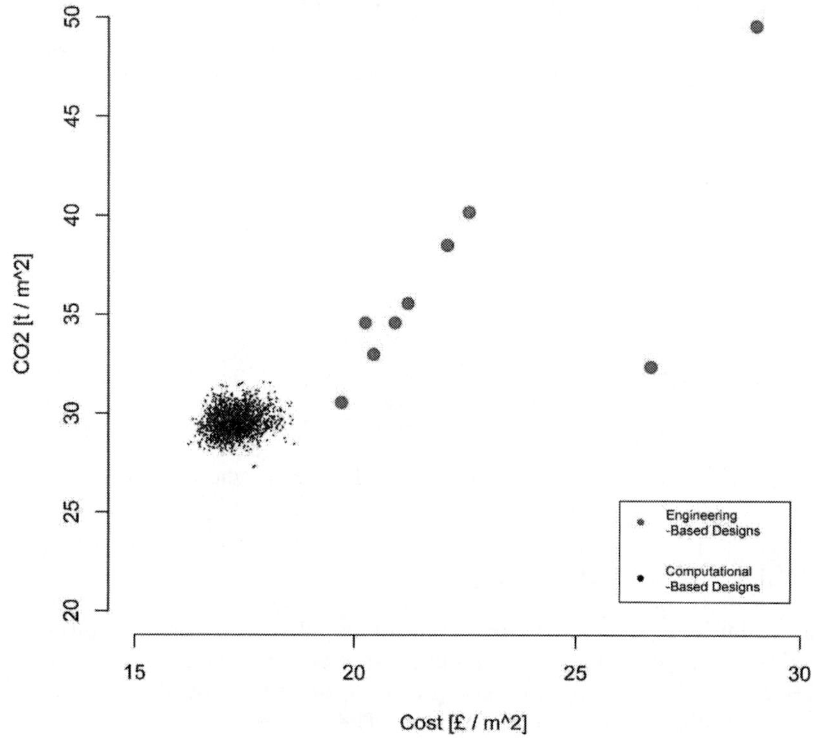

Figure 6: Design space and cost and carbon relationships

7. Conclusions

The study has focused on the development of a practical computational model for the optimisation of steel structures based on their cost and carbon performance. The research offers a new paradigm to structural engineers for the analysis of design alternatives during the early design stages where time restrictions often limit the exploration of the entire design space. The proposed computational model provides rapid analysis of the solution space which can increase the understanding of available designs and overall could enhance decision-making. Comprehensive cost and carbon functions were established using relevant material, manufacturing, fabrication, and construction factors which were then computed using the bill of materials generated by the computational model. An actual building was used to verify the proposed methodology. The engineering efficiency of the solutions was validated utilising an engineering-based approach. The results obtained from the completed computations on the tested building has showed that both cost and carbon performance could be enhanced when compared to the actual designs solutions by 12-18% and 6-8% respectively. The reasons for the enhanced efficiencies were mainly due to more appropriate use of spans and beam sections. This is part of a larger study and therefore additional investigations in multiple building scenarios are required in order to fully verify the efficiency of the computational model. Nevertheless, the initial findings are encouraging and could be used in the refinement of a new engineering paradigm for cost and carbon optimisation in steel building structures.

Acknowledgements

This work has been made possible through funding provided by Innovate UK, project 'Innovative engineering approach for material, carbon and cost efficiency of steel buildings' ref. 102477 and this is gratefully acknowledged here.

References

BCSA & TATA, S., 2013. Steel Construction – Cost. Technical report, s.l.: s.n.

Dunant, C. et al., 2017. Roles of regularity and optimisation practice in steel structural frames: A comparative study of real design cases. Construction & Building Material, p. Submitted.

Frans, R. & Arfiadi, Y., 2014. Sizing, Shape, and Topology Optimizations of Roof Trusses Using Hybrid Genetic Algorithms. Procedia Engineering, Volume 95, pp. 185-195.

Haapio, J., 2012. Feature-based costing method for skeletal steel structures based on the process approach, Tampere, Finland: Julkaisu-Tampere University of Technology.

Hayalioglu, M. & Degertekin, S., 2005. Minimum cost design of steel frames with semi-rigid connections and column bases via genetic optimization. Computers and Structures, 83(21), pp. 1849-1863.

Heinisuo, M., Laasonen, M. & Haapio, J., 2010. BIM based manufacturing cost estimation of building products. Cork, Ireland, ECPPM.

Jarmai, K. & Farkas, J., 1999. Cost calculation and optimisation of welded steel structures. Journal of Constructional Steel Research, 50(2), pp. 115-135.

Kingman, J., Tsavdaridis, K. & Toropov, V., 2015. Applications of topology optimization in structural engineering: High-rise buildings and steel components. Jordan Journal of Civil Engineering, 9(3), pp. 335 - 357.

Moynihan, M. & Allwood, J., 2014. Utilization of structural steel in buildings. Proc. R. Soc. A, Volume 470, p. 20140170.

Prager, W., 1970. Optimization of structural design. Journal of optimization theory and applications, 6(1), pp. 1-21.

Sawada, K. et al., 2006. A simple estimation of fabrication cost and minimum cost design for steel frames. s.l., Proceedings of the Fourth China-Japan-Korea Joint symposium on Optimization of Structural and Mechanical Systems.

Stromberg, L., Beghini, A., Baker, W. & Paulino, G., 2012. Design of structural braced frames using group optimization. Chicago, Illinois, United States, 20th Analysis and Computation Specialty Conference.

Stromberg, L., Beghini, A., Baker, W. & Paulino, G., 2012. Topology optimization for braced frames: combining continuum and beam/column elements. Engineering Structures, Volume 37, pp. 106-124.

Suliman, M. O., Kumar, V. S. & Abdulal, W., 2011. Optimisation of uncertain construction time-cost trade off problem using simulated annealing algorithm. Mumbai, India, Information and Communication Technologies (WICT), 2011 World Congress.

Zhou, F., AbouRizk, S. & Al-Battaineh, H., 2009. Optimisation of construction site layout using a hybrid simulation-based system. Simulation Modelling Practice and Theory, 17(2), pp. 348-363.

Zhou, J. et al., 2013. A review of methods and algorithms for optimizing construction scheduling. Journal of the Operational Research Society, 64(8), pp. 1091-1105.

BIM-Based Model for the Automatic Generation of Construction Sequences

Yasmeen A. S. Essawy[1], Khaled Nassar[2]
[1]PhD Candidate, Construction Engineering Department, School of Sciences and Engineering, The American University in Cairo (AUC), Cairo, Egypt; y_essawy@aucegypt.edu
[2]Associate Professor, Construction Engineering Department, School of Sciences and Engineering, The American University in Cairo (AUC), Cairo, Egypt

Abstract. With the rapid increase in complexity in the building industry, project managers are facing more and more complex decision environments and problems. Therefore, it would be beneficial to aid project managers in making sound decisions regarding the intelligent knowledgeable selection of the optimal construction methodology while making use of Building Information Modelling (BIM). BIM models' usage fused with modelling, and simulation tools allow efficiently prototyping a building and examining its construction activities before breaking the ground. For this purpose, an intelligent framework with advanced computational tools and algorithms is designed and created to achieve a higher degree of design-construction integration and spatial integration of individual building elements in order to achieve an optimized sequencing of building elements (in terms of time and cost).

This paper presents a model that extracts building elements, along with their topological relationships and geometrical properties, from an existing fully designed Building Information Model (BIM Model) to be mapped into a directed acyclic Elemental Graph Data Model (EGDM). Using graph search algorithms, Depth First Search (DFS) and topological sortings, possible construction sequences are generated. The model incorporates BIM-based search algorithms for automatic deduction of geometrical data and topological relationships for each building element type. It is implemented in a C# platform and verified with the aid of test cases.

Keywords: Building Information Modelling (BIM), Elemental Graph Data Model (EGDM), Geometric and topological data models, Graph theory, Depth-first Search, and Topological Sorting.

1. Introduction

Over the past 100 years, the building industry has changed dramatically. Buildings have become much more complex with many interconnected and integrated systems. Project managers are faced with complex decision environments and problems in the construction of the majority of the projects. For project managers to take sound decisions, they just rely on human value and judgment systems which contribute to the project problems as well. Accordingly, it is worthy to aid project managers to wisely select the optimal construction methodology. Consequently, professionals in the A/E/C industry began searching for better ways to model facilities/buildings and coordinate all this information together between all the involved parties throughout the project's life cycle (Krygiel, et al., 2008). These efforts were harmonized with research in the field of computer-supported building design, and, consequently, led to the continuous advancement in the development of building data models.

1.1 Building Data Model

Building data model describes the physical characteristics of building elements by means of their three-dimensional (3D) geometry and topology. Geometric data represents the building element's dimensions and location, whereas topological information represents spatial relationships among the building elements comprising connection, adjacency, containment, separation, and intersection (Nguyen, et al., 2005). Project participants/stakeholders consider topological information essential to perform various analyses during design and construction. For such complex tasks to be performed with the aid of building data models, advanced ways of extracting and presenting geometric and topological information should be adopted.

While geometric data of building elements can be manipulated and managed by a Computer-Aided Design (CAD) interface, their topological information are conventionally inserted into the model. However, the manual data representation is essentially a complex and challenging task as each constructed facility usually comprises of hundreds of elements with multiple types of topological and relationship information, such as connectivity, adjacency, containment, and intersection (Nguyen, et al., 2005). The lack of such building models that support geometric-topological analysis resulted in various research attempts in the field of computer-based representation of building elements over the last decade. These efforts have concentrated mainly on the development of a semantic object-oriented building model, also called Building Product Model or Building Information Model (BIM) (Borrmann & Rank, 2009).

1.2 Building Information Modelling (BIM)

BIM is a revolutionary technology which has transformed how buildings are designed, analysed, constructed and managed (Hardin, 2009). It was introduced to distinguish the information rich 3D modelling from the traditional 2D drawing, and is becoming a better known established collaboration process in the construction industry. General Services Administration (GSA) of the United States government defines BIM as: "Building Information Modelling is the development and use of a multi-faceted computer software data model not to only document a building design, but to simulate the construction and operation of a new capital facility or a recapitalized (modernized) facility. The resulting Building Information Model is a data-rich, object-based, intelligent and parametric digital representation of the facility, from which views appropriate to various users' needs can be extracted and analysed to generate feedback and improvement of the facility design" (The National 3D-4D-BIM Program, 2007).

The main benefits of BIM for construction professionals include, but not limited to: visualization, 3D coordination, construction planning and monitoring, and quantity take offs.

BIM opportunities that are currently being leveraged and explored by construction companies are staggered. As BIM becomes more widely adopted, information on buildings will increasingly be recorded in models, which can then be utilized for other purposes. (Langenhan, et al., 2013)

2. Current Practices/Problems in the Construction Industry

BIM not only helps in better visualization and documentation, but is also a catalyst for an enhanced and improved process in the design and construction industry. BIM models' usage fused with modelling, and simulation tools allow efficiently prototyping a building and examining its construction activities before breaking the ground. Such prototyping holds a lot of value, as it implores designers to avoid fudging practices, hence, improving quality and productivity while bringing out best practices (Montaser, 2015). To harvest BIM's true value, attempts to develop models that can support geometric-topological analysis of building elements are currently being explored.

3. Topological Data Models

Several contributions were performed to represent geometric data and topological relationships among building elements through topological primitives: (Wei, et al., 1998; Tse & Gold, 2003; Suter & Mahdavi, 2004; Paul & Borrmann, 2009; Grabska, et al., 2012; Plümer & Gröger, 1996; Lamarche & Donikian, 2004; Franz, et al., 2005; van Treeck & Rank, 2007; Borrmann & Rank, 2009), and (Lee & Kwan, 2005). Nevertheless, such models proved to be inefficient in handling various queries and complex network analysis, as they mostly store limited semantic information about rooms, openings and walls. Moreover, these models only deal with connectivity and adjacency neglecting any other type of topological relationship. However, BIM demands the availability of all the types of relationships (for example, connectivity, and containment) and their effective storage, in order to enhance the performance of spatial analysis such as construction sequencing, 5D simulation, energy simulation, emergency response and prefabrication optimization (Khalili, 2013).

4. Research Objective

Subsequently, BIM should be utilized to develop a reliable model to perform geometric-topological analysis of building elements that can support all types of spatial relationships. And, hence, aid professionals in the A/E/C industry to make sound decisions regarding the selection of the optimal construction methodology in order to obtain better cost and time trade-off. For this purpose, an intelligent framework with advanced computational tools and algorithms is designed to achieve a higher degree of design-construction integration and spatial integration of individual building elements in order to achieve an optimized coordinated construction plan. This could be accomplished by obtaining the optimal sequencing of building elements (in terms of time and cost), and, accordingly, recommending the Optimized Elemental Construction Method, Schedule & Resources, and, hence, generating 4D and 5D BIM models. The framework is, then, validated with the aid of a set of automatically generated test cases in order to assess the research findings.

Since graphs are highly versatile models for analysing a wide range of practical problems in which points and connections between them have some physical or conceptual interpretation, graph theory is used to represent the building elements and their relationships.

The framework is designed based on a three-level concept, namely:

1. Elemental Graph – In this level, all the BIM Model building elements are mapped into a set of vertices and their interrelationships are converted into a set of edges, thus, forming a directed acyclic Elemental Graph Data Model (EGDM), as shown in Figure 1.
2. Inter-Elemental – In this level, each element type can be built with a set of construction methods, as shown in Figure 2. By electing an appropriate construction method for each building element, the Elemental Construction Method Graph is formed.
3. Entra-Elemental – In this level, customized user-defined relationships are introduced to mimic any practical constraints, as shown in Figure 3.

This paper focuses on the first level of the framework, Level (1): Elemental Graph, and the generation of the subsequent construction sequence(s).

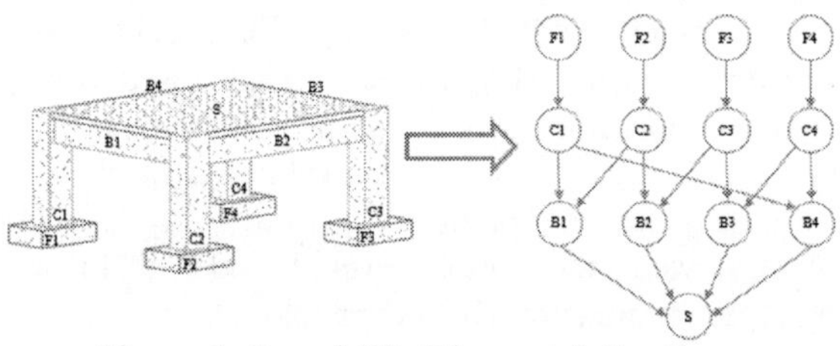

Figure 1: Level (1): Elemental Graph

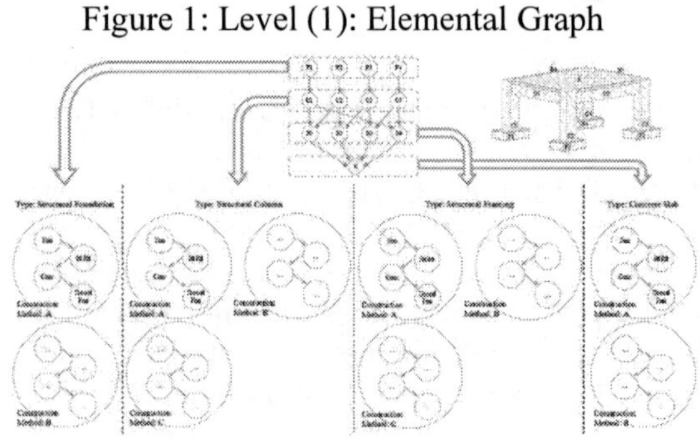

Figure 2: Level (2): Inter-Elemental

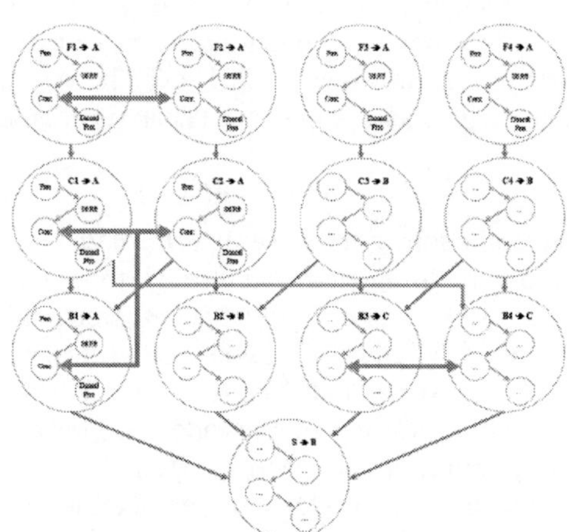

Figure 3: Level (3): Entra-Elemental

5. Proposed Model for Deriving the Elemental Construction Sequences

This section presents the proposed model for automatically extracting all building elements' topological relationships and geometrical properties from an existing fully designed BIM Model. The information is, then, presented in a directed acyclic Elemental Graph Data Model (EGDM). The EGDM, representing topological relationships and semantic information of building elements in micro-spatial environments, is utilized using graph search algorithms, Depth First Search (DFS) and topological sortings, to obtain possible construction sequences. The model is implemented in a C# platform.

5.1 Proposed Model Framework

Figure 4 shows the proposed architecture that derives the Elemental Graph Data Model (EGDM) with the aid of the building elements' topological/geometric representations, and, consequently, generates the Elemental Construction Sequences(s). The framework comprises three main modules, namely: Project Analysis, Elemental Graph Data Model Retrieval, and Elemental Construction Sequence(s) Retrieval.

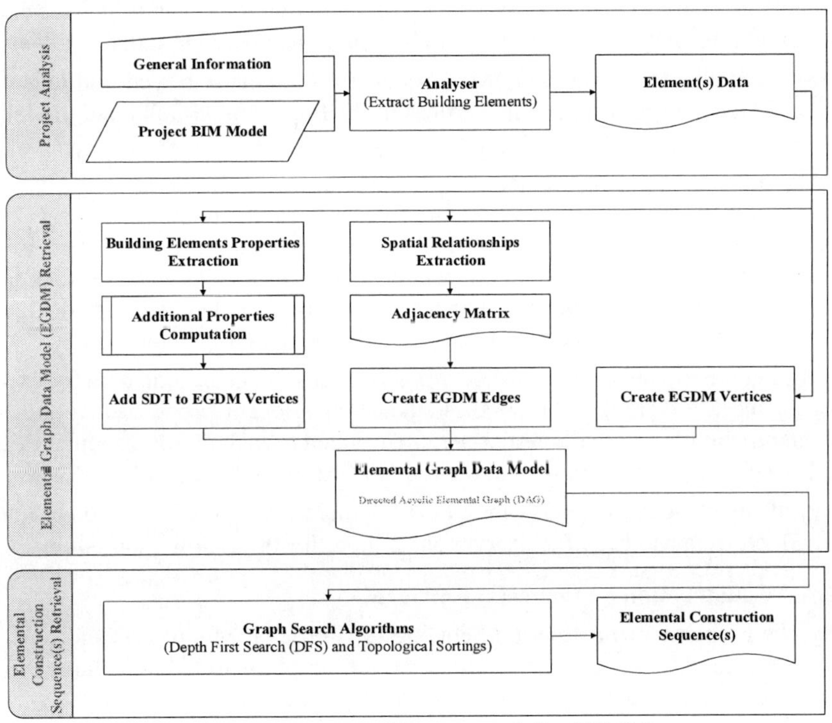

Figure 4: Proposed Framework for EGDM

1. Project Analysis Module

Essentially, the Project Analysis Module, as shown in Figure 4, is the first unit in the framework that, with the aid of the Analyser, parses the input data acquired from the Information Feeder (General Information and Project's BIM Model), and, then, builds an internal data structure to release Element(s) Data that would provide easy data access for its receptor, the Elemental Graph Data Model Retrieval Module.

The process starts with the Information Feeder in which the user feeds in General Information about the project along with the Project's fully designed BIM Model. Next, the Analyser imports building elements data, including topology/geometry properties, dimensions, materials, and functionality, from the BIM Model into the framework. It, then, builds an internal data structure to map the data obtained into the memory. The data structure is a linked list, comprising a list for each building element which gets linked together. Each building element's list carries the retrieved semantic data for that element and gets further extended in the following module to include additional imported and calculated data. This process finally categorizes and segregates all the building elements based on their element category to release the Element(s) Data that would serve as an input for the following module.

2. Elemental Graph Data Model (EGDM) Retrieval Module

The Elemental Graph Data Model Retrieval Module, as shown in Figure 4, is a functional unit in the framework that transposes the building elements, Element(s) Data, obtained from the Project Analysis Module to a graph model, Elemental Graph Data Model. This module, with the aid of the Spatial Relationships Extraction and Building Elements Properties Extraction, automatically deduces the geometric and topological information for all the building elements. Building elements along with their relationships and semantic data are mapped into a novel data representation model: directed acyclic Elemental Graph Data Model, in which vertices denote building elements; while edges represent the topological relations. The EGDM is enhanced by adding semantic information to the vertices to be able to handle wide ranges of queries.

The process starts with the Create EGDM Vertices in which the retrieved building elements in the Element(s) Data gets represented as vertices in the Elemental Graph Data Model.

The Spatial Relationships Extraction employs a "topology–driven" approach that further examines the project's building elements. It, firstly, checks for building elements' predefined relationships, and, thereafter, creates bounding boxes around building elements in order to automatically deduce the topological relationships among them, as described in following section. Hence, locating the building elements and their respective dependencies to form the Building Elements' Adjacency Matrix, which are, then, represented as directed edges with the aid of Create EGDM Edges in the directed acyclic Elemental Graph Data Model.

Next, the Building Elements Properties Extraction obtains the geometric data for each building element from the Element(s) Data, and, calculates its relevant properties by the Additional Properties Computation. These properties are, then, added to each building element's associated Semantic Data Table (SDT) with the aid of Add SDT to EGDM Vertices.

By the end of this process, the outcome is the Elemental Graph of the project under study, Elemental Graph Data Model, which serves as an input for the following module.

3. Elemental Construction Sequence(s) Retrieval

Ultimately, the Elemental Construction Sequence(s) Retrieval Module, as shown in Figure 4, is the last unit in the framework that, with the aid of Graph Search Algorithms, examines the Elemental Graph Data Model to generate possible construction sequence(s).

The Graph Search Algorithms employ Depth First Search algorithm, in its recursive form, to produce possible topological sortings. By the end of this process, the outcome is the Elemental Construction Sequence(s) of the project under study which could be used to form Elemental Construction Methods that can be evaluated against constructability rules to release the optimized/near-optimum elemental construction sequence and its associated schedule.

5.2 Proposed Model Elements

Performing geometric-topological analysis of building elements, that would aid professionals in the A/E/C industry in selecting the optimal construction methodology, is very difficult and in most cases impossible without the existence of a semantically rich representation of the building elements: a simple graph. Graphs are highly versatile models for analysing a wide range of practical problems in which points (nodes or vertices) and connections (links or edges) between them have some physical or conceptual interpretation. Depending on the complexity of the problem, the appropriate kind of graph is employed and advanced graph algorithms, such as spanning trees, shortest path, Hamiltonian paths, search algorithms and topological sortings, are utilized, resulting in a significant reduction in the computational time and storage as compared to dealing with the real-world application directly.

The proposed model abstracts and represents building elements and their relationships in a simple directed (all the edges are directed) acyclic (graph has no cycles or loops) graph, the EGDM, to generate Elemental Construction Sequence(s). The EGDM is composed of three main elements, namely: vertices, edges, and semantic data table (SDT). In the EGDM's graph structure, vertices represent building elements, and directed edges represent topological relations, whose direction identifies the interrelationships between the respective building elements and allow for assigning customized relationships that would mimic any practical constraints in a later stage: Level 3 of the Three-Level Concept. This simple directed acyclic graph is a logical network data model that can handle graph search algorithms, Depth-First Search (DFS) and topological sortings, to obtain possible elemental construction sequences. The building elements' semantic information required for such algorithms and a wide range of queries, are attached to their respective vertices by a data table, the SDT, which is the third element of the EGDM.

1. Graph Data Structure

The graph data structure is a definition for building elements from a specific group that are topologically related. In order to build the EGDM, a vertex is assigned for each building element, and paired vertices are joined with an edge on the condition that the corresponding building elements are interrelated. A beam and two columns, as shown in Figure 5, are mapped into vertices B1, C1, and C2 in the Elemental Graph Data Model. Since the beam B1 is supported on the two columns C1 and C2, two directed edges are mapped from the columns C1 & C2 (tails) to the beam B1 (head) respectively to denote the elemental dependencies between the elements.

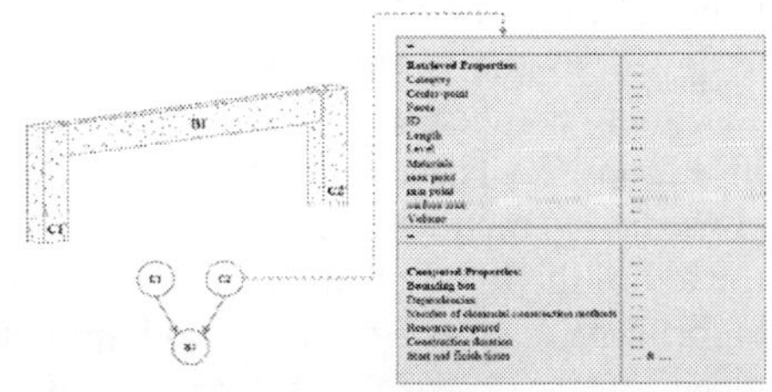

Figure 5: Mapping building elements to a directed acyclic EGDM

For an entire building, the EGDM defines the spatial relationships of its building elements. The types of topological relationships are represented through the direction of the edges, whereas the building elements' properties are included in the SDT, which are labels assigned to the associated vertices. Upon retrieval of all the building elements' properties, additional computed ones are added to the semantic data table (SDT) of each building element respectively, as shown in Figure 5.

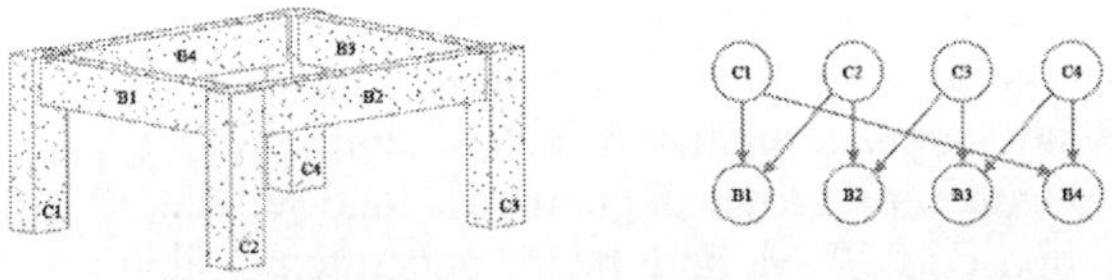

Figure 6: Example No. 1 and its Elemental Graph

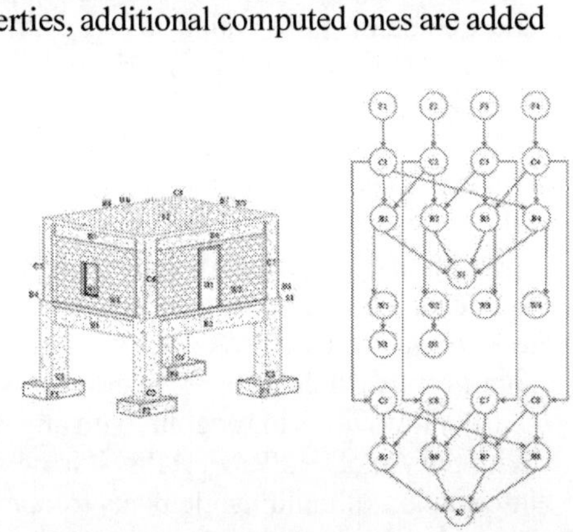

Figure 7: Example No. 2 and its Elemental Graph

A demonstration for the building-to-graph generation is shown in Figure 6 and Figure 7. Figure 6 shows an example of a simple concrete structure composed of 4 columns and 4 beams, which is represented as a DAG composed of 8 vertices and 8 edges. Figure 7 shows an example of a simple concrete structure composed of 4 foundations, 8 columns, 8 beams, 2 slabs, 4 walls, a door, and a window, which is represented as a directed acyclic graph DAG composed of 28 vertices and 38 edges.

The graph data structure in its presentation preserves the physical and topological characteristics of building elements, as well as the topological consistency through mapping all the building elements along with their topological relationships into a set of vertices and edges.

2. Graph Theory and Adjacency Matrix

Graph theory can be used to represent topological relationships in any graph G through the stipulation of sets of edges and vertices, namely E and V respectively. Since most of the building projects comprise of a relatively large number of vertices, the Elemental Graph can be stored in the form of a matrix to facilitate computational analysis and storage purposes. The matrix is often referred to as the Adjacency Matrix (Adj). For any structure composed of N building elements, the dimensions of its adjacency matrix is N x N, and Adj is represented in Equation 1, as shown:

$$Adj_{DAG}\,[v, v_h] = \begin{cases} 1 & if\ there\ is\ an\ edge\ from\ v\ and\ v_h \\ 0 & otherwise \end{cases} \quad \text{.......... Equation 1}$$

3. Semantic Data Table (SDT)

Upon the retrieval of the logical EGDM based on the spatial relationships among building elements of a facility, building elements' properties, such as: category, centre-point, faces, ID, length, level, materials, max point, min point, surface area, volume, etc…, are included in the SDT, which are assigned to the associated vertices. Upon retrieval of all the building elements' properties, additional computed ones are added to the SDT of each building element respectively, as shown in Figure 5. These properties include: bounding box, dependencies, number of elemental construction methods, resources required, construction duration, start and finish times, etc… With the aid of the building elements' SDT, the model can handle a wide variety of queries and search algorithms, such as BFS, DFS, and topological sortings, to obtain possible construction sequences.

5.3 Proposed Model Development

This sub-section discusses thoroughly how to develop the proposed framework.

5.3.1. Project Analysis

The BIM data structure is a semantically rich environment explicitly representing both topological and geometric information, along with non-geometric properties (e.g., material properties). To extract topological and geometric information, various research attempts in the field of Information Technology is and was undertaken to ensure a continuous flow of the required information from BIM Models. AutoDesk Revit, being a design and documentation platform that supports the design, drawings, and schedules required for Building Information Modelling (BIM) (Autodesk Revit, 2017), facilitated the smooth extraction and exchange of data between BIM Models and applications, hence, avoiding the time-consuming and error-prone process of obtaining and sharing such data. Data extraction is carried out using the AutoDesk Revit SDK and AutoDesk Revit APIs to communicate with AutoDesk Revit. AutoDesk Revit customization capabilities have been significantly extended over the past few years. AutoDesk Revit Application Programming Interface (API) allows users to program with any .NET compliant language such as VB .NET and C# .NET. With the AutoDesk Revit APIs, it is now possible to extract topological, geometric, and semantic information of building elements to complete the proposed EGDM, and, hence generate possible Elemental Construction Sequences(s).

5.3.1.1. Building Element Representation

Families are considered as the basic elements of Autodesk Revit platform where almost every object is based on a family definition. The family holds the geometric definition of the element and the parameters used by the element. Families, such as structural columns, structural framings, slabs, walls, windows, stairs, doors, etc…, are used to build the Building Information Model. Each family can have multiple types, such as different size, materials, parameter variables, etc… Any change to a type is updated in every instance throughout the project.

5.3.1.2. Building Element(s) Extraction

With the aid of AutoDesk Revit SDK and AutoDesk Revit API, building elements along with their data, including topology/geometry properties, dimensions, materials, and functionality, are retrieved, and mapped into an internal data structure. The data structure is a linked list, comprising a list for each building element which gets linked together. Each building element's list carries the retrieved semantic data for that element, which gets further extended and lengthened to include additional imported and calculated data. The extracted building elements are, finally, categorized and segregated based on their element category.

5.3.2. Elemental Graph Data Model (EGDM) Retrieval

AutoDesk Revit API is used to facilitate the implementation of the EGDM's topology-driven approach in deducing topological relationships by providing the required topological features, as well as predefined topological relationships in its hierarchical structure.

5.3.2.1. Topological/Geometric Representation of Building Elements

Each building element in the AutoDesk Revit BIM Model has a geometric/topologic representation. And each element category is modelled and represented in a distinct manner. For instance, structural columns, structural foundations, doors and windows are typically characterized by their "Location Point", while structural framing and walls are typically characterized by their "Location Curve". Figure 8 illustrates the structural column and structural framing representations along with the retrieved minimum and maximum points which will be utilized in the following section.

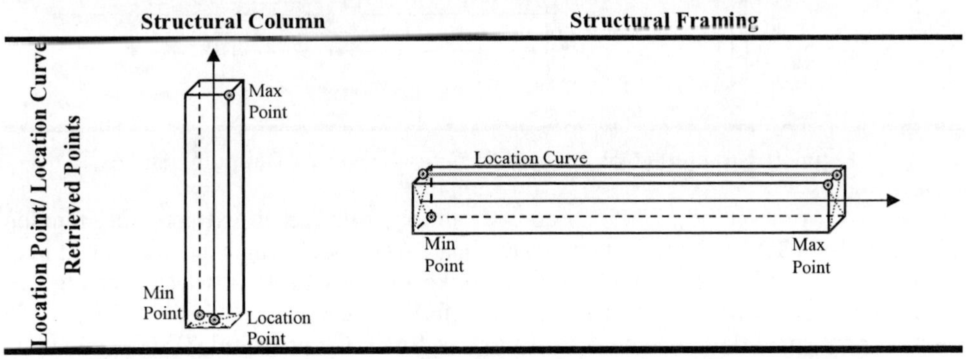

Figure 8: Structural Column and Structural Framing Representation

5.3.2.2. Obtaining Minimum and Maximum Points

To create the bounding box, in order to deduce the topological relationships among building elements, two (2) points (min & max points) should be identified with the aid of building element's geometry and the LocationPoint/LocationCurve. These two (2) points are simply computed and added to the building element's semantic data table (SDT) respectively.

In case of inclined building elements in 3D, minimum and maximum points can be computed in the element's local coordinates and transforming these coordinates to the Global Coordinates System through 3D Cartesian Coordinate Systems Transformation as indicated in Equation 2:

$$\begin{bmatrix} X \\ Y \\ Z \end{bmatrix} = \begin{bmatrix} X_{translation} \\ Y_{translation} \\ Z_{translation} \end{bmatrix} + \begin{bmatrix} 1 & 0 & 0 \\ 0 & \cos\alpha & -\sin\alpha \\ 0 & \sin\alpha & \cos\alpha \end{bmatrix} \begin{bmatrix} \cos\beta & 0 & \sin\beta \\ 0 & 1 & 0 \\ -\sin\beta & 0 & \cos\beta \end{bmatrix} \begin{bmatrix} \cos\gamma & -\sin\gamma & 0 \\ \sin\gamma & \cos\gamma & 0 \\ 0 & 0 & 1 \end{bmatrix} \begin{bmatrix} x_1 \\ y_1 \\ z_1 \end{bmatrix} \text{ .... Equation 2}$$

where the angle α resembles rotation about the x-axis, the angle β resembles rotation about the y-axis, and the angle γ resembles rotation about the z-axis

5.3.2.3. Predefined Topological Relations

Besides the topological/geometry representation of building elements, AutoDesk Revit BIM Model contains predefined relationships between certain types of elements. For instance, in the door and window type properties, the property: wall closure identifies the hosting element whether it is a wall or a skylight in a roof. Hence, the instance's properties define its hosting predecessor element (the element's topological relations).

5.3.2.4. Automatic Deduction of Topological Relationships

In order to automatically generate the EGDM, BIM-based algorithm is proposed to deduce the topological relationships among building elements by means of the creation of a bounding box (generated from element's retrieved min and max points) surrounding the elements, and, hence, deducing the predecessor/dependent elements, as demonstrated in Figure 9. The algorithm extracts the four major types of topological information: connectivity, containment, separation, and intersection as defined by (Nguyen, et al., 2005).

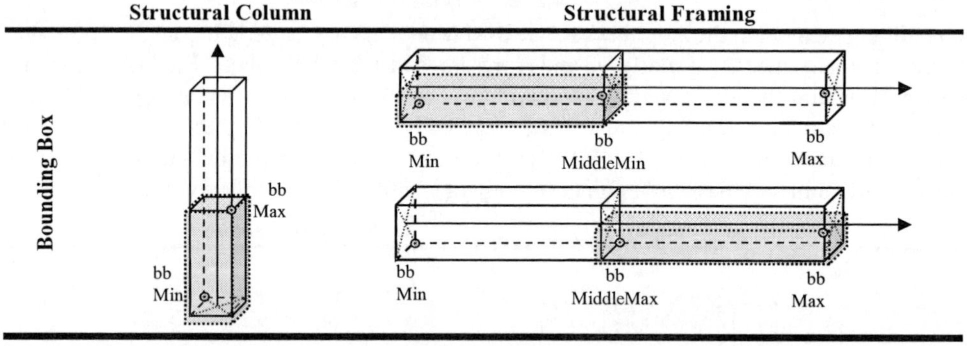

Figure 9: Structural Column and Structural Framing Bounding Boxes

Reference (Nguyen, et al., 2005) proposed an algorithm that extracts the topological relationships from 3D geometric data indicated in a CAD model, which is not efficient in terms of computation and data storage. Furthermore, unlike topology-driven models, geometry-driven models need geometric modifications for further analysis (Khalili, 2013). Using geometric/topological representations in AutoDesk Revit, the proposed BIM-based algorithm enhances deduction in three ways. First, AutoDesk Revit BIM Model may be used to directly extract the topological primitives and their geometric information instead of obtaining them from lines and points in a CAD environment. Second, the AutoDesk Revit BIM Model building elements representations cover a wider range of elements when compared to conventional CAD modelling. Third, AutoDesk Revit BIM Model comprises predefined relationships between certain types of elements, eliminating the need for deducing their relationships. Hence, reducing computation time and complexity.

Examples to demonstrate the deduction of the topological relationships are presented in Figure 10.

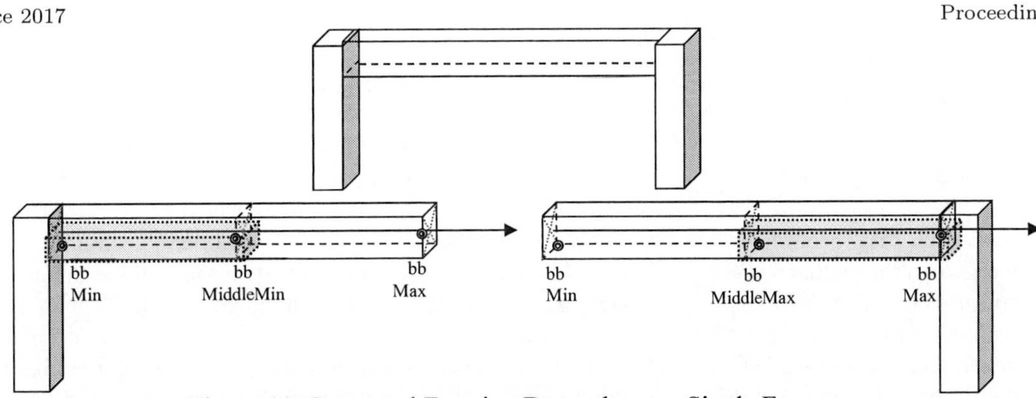

Figure 10: Structural Framing Dependency – Single Frame

5.3.3. Elemental Construction Sequence(s) Retrieval

Essentially, the model is designed to extract topological relationships and geometrical properties of building elements from the AutoDesk Revit BIM Model and map it to the proposed EGDM. Using graph search algorithms such as Depth First Search (DFS) and Topological Sorting, a set of possible elemental construction sequences are generated and compared against constructability rules.

5.3.3.1. Graph Search Algorithms

Depth-first search (DFS) is a tree-growing algorithm that is an integral part of numerous algorithms used in computer science, operations research, and other engineering disciplines.

The idea of the depth-first search is to select a frontier arc (A frontier arc for a given tree T in a DAG is an arc whose tail is in T and whose head is not in T, its non-tree endpoint) incident on the most recently discovered vertex of the tree grown so far. When that is not possible, the algorithm backtracks to the next most recently discovered vertex and ties again. Thus, the search moves deeper into the graph (hence, the name "depth-first"). (Gross & Yellen, 2006)

5.3.3.2. Topological Sorting by Depth-First Search (DFS)

A topological sort (or topological order) of an n vertex DAG (Directed Acyclic Graph) G is a bijection t_S from the set {1, 2, …, n} to the vertex-set V_G such that every arc e is directed from a smaller number to a larger one, i.e., $t_S(tail(e)) < t_S(head(e))$. The depth-first search is adapted to perform a topological sort on a directed acyclic graph. A source in a DAG is a vertex with in-degree 0, and a sink is a vertex with out-degree 0. Every DAG has at least one source and at least one sink.

DFS-Based Topological Sorting Algorithm:

Input: an n-vertex DAG G

Output: a topological sort tS of the vertices of G

Initialize graph H as graph G
Initialize k := n
Topo_Sort_DFS(v):
While VH ≠ Ø
Start at a source and grow a dfs-path until the first vertex t is finished
Set tS (t) = k
H := H – t
k := k – 1
Topo_Sort_DFS(k):
Return the function tS

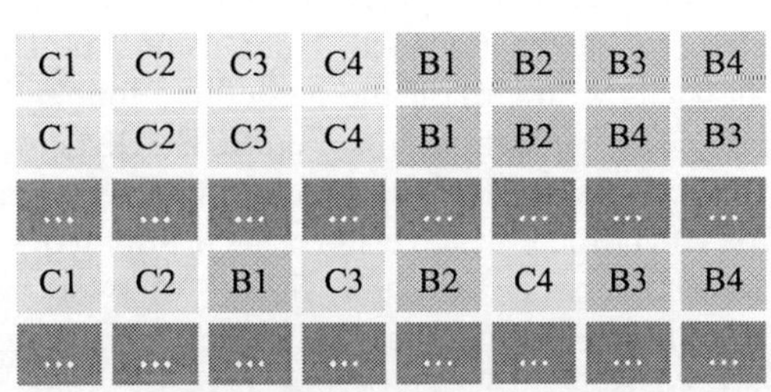

Figure 11: DNA Representation

For instance, the number of topological sortings for the example illustrated in Figure 6 is 1,088. That means that this structure can be built in 1,088 different elemental construction sequences. A sample DNA representation for selected elemental construction sequences is represented in Figure 11.

Accordingly, this model presents an algorithm that generates the possible elemental construction sequences for a given EGDM. This model can be further used to evaluate the elemental construction sequences, and recommend the optimal one while considering the user-defined constraints. It is worth mentioning that it is very difficult and in most cases impossible to determine all the elemental construction sequences (topological sortings) of a medium-sized buildings with more than 100 building elements, as this will take enormous computing time and memory. Hence, the model auto-generates a list of feasible elemental construction sequences and eliminates unnecessary ones based on user-defined constructability constraints. And evaluates these elemental construction sequences to recommend a near-optimum solution. This is done in Level 3 of the Three-Level Concept.

5.4 Computer Implementation

BIM is capable of recognizing building elements in its fixed asset hierarchy (Family-Type-Instance) while being user-friendly for visualizing the alternatives. AutoDesk Revit customization capabilities have been significantly extended over the past few years. AutoDesk Revit Application Programming Interface (API) allows users to program with any .NET compliant language such as VB.NET and C#.NET. The application main development language is C#, based on .Net framework 4.0 platform and has been written using Microsoft Visual Studio Integrated Development Environment (MS VS IDE). The application uses AutoDesk Revit SDK (programming package enabling programmers to develop applications) and AutoDesk Revit APIs to communicate with AutoDesk Revit Software.

6. Conclusions

This research established a new approach to achieve a higher degree of design-construction integration and spatial integration of individual building elements in order to achieve an optimized coordinated construction plan. Subsequently, an intelligent framework, with advanced computational tools and algorithms, was designed to generate possible construction sequences from a semantically enhanced, 3D topological data model, the Elemental Graph Data Model (EGDM). It exploits BIM capabilities for geometric/topological representation, thus simplifying the abstraction of the topological relationships among building elements using the vertex-edge structure of the graph, and employs graph search algorithms to obtain all possible elemental construction sequences.

Essentially, the EGDM presented in this paper contributes to the advancement of research in the area of 3D topological models for A/E/C applications and also overcomes several limitations of the existing models in the following ways: first, it explicitly represents the building elements (structural and non-structural) of buildings using a graph data structure; second, because the proposed model is not limited to any specific geometric representation of building elements, a wide range of building elements can be modelled. Third, using AutoDesk Revit APIs as a data-exchange platform enables the EGDM to exploit the predefined topological relationships in a BIM Model to significantly reduce the deduction time. Fourth, EGDM covers all four major spatial relationships for all A/E/C applications. Fifth, the proposed EGDM is enriched with the semantic information obtained from the BIM Model which enables the handling of complex semantic-based queries for different project stakeholders. Sixth, and finally, network-based analyses can be performed to maintain computational efficiency while avoiding storage of massive geometric data of complex buildings.

The EGDM forms the basis for obtaining possible elemental construction sequences using DFS-based topological sorting algorithm. The sequences can, then, be compared against construction rules to generate an optimized construction sequence and a better cost and time trade-off. And, finally, recommend the Optimized Elemental Construction Method, Schedule & Resources, and, hence, generate 4D and 5D BIM models.

The proposed model, serving as the first part of a research, has taken the first step towards implementing the concept of design-construction integration and spatial integration of individual building elements in order to achieve an optimized coordinated construction plan. The flexibility of the model facilitates applying more user-defined constraints in order to mimic any practical limitations.

References

Autodesk Revit, 2017. *Help - About Revit.* [Online] Available at: http://help.autodesk.com/view/RVT/2016/ENU/?guid=GUID-D8835F8E-1330-4DBC-8A55-AF5941056C58 [Accessed 25 02 2017]

Borrmann, A. & Rank, E., 2009. Topological analysis of 3D building models using a spatial query language. *Advanced Engineering Informatics,* pp. 370-385.

Franz, G., Mallot, H. A. & Wiener, J. M., 2005. Graph-based models of space in architecture and cognitive science - a comparative analysis. *Proceedings of INTERSYMP-2005, 17th International Conference on Systems Research, Informatics and Cybernetics (Architecture, Engineering and Construction (AEC) of Built Environments),* 1-7 August.

Grabska, E., Lachwa, A. & Slusarczyk, G., 2012. New visual languages supporting design of multi-storey buildings. *Advanced Engineering Informatics,* pp. 681-690.

Gross, J. L. & Yellen, J., 2006. *Graph Theory and its Applications.* Second ed. FL: Chapman & Hall/CRC.

Hardin, B., 2009. *BIM and Construction Management: Proven Tools, Methods, and Workflows.* s.l.:Sybex.

Khalili, A., 2013. *An IFC-based Framework for Optimizing Level of Prefabrication in Industrialized Building Systems (PhD Thesis).* s.l.:Department of Civil and Environmental Engineering, National University of Singapore.

Krygiel, E., Nie, N. & McDowell, S., 2008. *Green BIM: Successful Sustainable Design with Building Information Modeling.* s.l.:Wiley Publishing, Indianapolis, USA.

Lamarche, F. & Donikian, S., 2004. Crowd of Virtual Humans: a New Approach for Real Time Navigation in Complex and Structured Environments. *Eurographics,* 23(3), pp. 509-518.

Langenhan, C. et al., 2013. Graph-based retrieval of building information models for supporting the early design stages. *Advanced Engineering Informatics,* pp. 413-426.

Lee, J. & Kwan, M.-P., 2005. A combinatorial data model for representing topological relations among 3D geographical features in micro-spatial environments. *International Journal of Geographical Information Science*, pp. 1039 - 1056.

Montaser, A. M., 2015. *Value Engineering Using Building Information Modeling (M.Sc. Thesis).* s.l.:Faculty of Engineering, Ain Shams University, Cairo, Egypt.

Nguyen, T.-H., Oloufa, A. A. & Nassar, K., 2005. Algorithms for automated deduction of topological information. *Automation in Construction,* pp. 59-70.

Parvan, K., 2012. *Estimating the Impact of Building Information Modeling (BIM) Utilization on Building Project Performance (PhD Thesis).* s.l.:Graduate School, University of Maryland, USA.

Paul, N. & Borrmann, A., 2009. Geometrical and Topological Approaches in Building Information Modelling. *Journal of Information Technology in Construction (ITcon),* Volume 14, pp. 705-723.

Plümer, L. & Gröger, G., 1996. Nested Maps - A Formal, Provably Correct Object Model for Spatial Aggregates. *Proceedings of the 4th ACM International Workshop on Advanced Geographic Information Systems,* pp. 76-83.

Suter, G. & Mahdavi, A., 2004. Elements of a Representation Framework for Performance-Based Design. *Building and Environment (Elsevier),* Volume 39, pp. 969-988.

The National 3D-4D-BIM Program, U. G. S. A., 2007. *GSA Building Information Modeling Guide Series 01 – Overview (Version 0.6),* Washington, DC: U.S. General Services Administration.

Tse, R. O. & Gold, C., 2003. A Proposed Connectivity-Based Model for a 3-D Cadastre. *Computers, Environment and Urban Systems (Elsevier),* Volume 27, p. 427–445.

van Treeck, C. & Rank, E., 2007. Dimensional reduction of 3D building models using graph theory and its application in building energy simulation. *Engineering with,* Issue 23, pp. 109-122.

Wei, G., Ping, Z. & Jun, C., 1998. Topological Data Modelling for 3D GIS. *ISPRS Commission IV Symposium on GIS - Between Visions and Applications,* 32(4), pp. 657-661.

Constructability Assessment Model for Buildings Design

Abdelaziz Fadoul, Walid Tizani, Christian Koch
Centre for Structural Engineering and Informatics, University of Nottingham, UK
Abdelaziz.Fadoul@Nottingham.ac.uk

Abstract. Implementation of constructability principles in the construction industry has a potential return on investment concerning time and money. Prior research shows that reviewing the design constructability at the early design stages provides benefits to owners, contractors and designers. Considering the complexity of current building design process, there is a need to provide a decision support tool that can help designers in reviewing the design constructability based on embedded information within the design model. Such a tool would be most beneficial at the conceptual design stage so that constructability is factored into the design solution starting from its inception. Therefore, this research reviews how contemporary process- and object-oriented models can be used to assess the design constructability to inform the structural engineer's building design decisions at an early stage thus enabling design optimization.

1. Introduction

The Construction Industry Institute (CII) defines the term constructability as "The optimum use of construction knowledge and experience in planning, design, procurement, and field operations to achieve overall project objectives" (CII, 1986). Similarly, the Construction Industry Research and Information Association (CIRIA) defines term buildability as, "The extent to which the design of a building facilitates ease of construction, subject to overall requirements for the completed building" (Johnson and Jardine, 1995)

The design phase is a critical part of any project in the architectural, engineering, and construction (AEC) industry. Although the design process itself constitutes just 5% of the costs associated with a typical construction project, its success affects the build cost and the quality of the remaining 95% of the project (Egan and Williams, 1998, Latham, 1994). This includes the consideration of design constructability, which are often ignored by designers and building clients until the commencement of the construction phase, when they are confronted by the reality (CIRIA, 1983).

In recognition of the importance of designing for constructability, many studies were conducted to investigate the implementation of the concept. Various approaches were employed to benchmark the constructability of design solution and enable an objective evaluation of the abstract concept. One of the key approaches to improve and enhance constructability is through quantified assessment of designs (Wong et al., 2007).

This paper attempts to evaluate the practice in assessing the design constructability and associated challenges within such process, by reviewing current adopted approaches and methods to appraise the design constructability. The evaluation covers recent developed assessment tools that are presented to benchmark the design constructability, and hence designers could use obtained feedbacks to improve their designs solutions. It then identifies a set of requirements that should characterize any decision-support tool for assessing design constructability, given the advanced technologies available nowadays. It goes further to propose a model-based approach that can be utilized to employ current information technologies to assess design constructability. Such model can contribute significantly to address the identified gaps from the evaluation process. A proposed framework and its components will be described as well as the direction for future work.

2. Development of Constructability Concept

The separation of design and construction during the 1960s precipitated the emergence of the concept of constructability, but due to its inherently abstract nature it has been defined from different perspectives and approaches (Egan and Williams, 1998).

Previous studies came up with different perceptual attributes of constructability. Fig 1 below prototypes the commonalities amongst different interpretations of Constructability features, it categorizes them into 5 aspects, namely: Integration of construction knowledge and experience with design, application of constructability concept at various project stages, facilitation of ease of construction process, achievement of overall project objective/goals and optimisation of resource use to achieve results.

3. Benefits of Improved Constructability

Many studies explored the implementation of constructability assessments and recognized the potential benefits for owners, contractors and designers. Table 1 below shows some of these identified benefits.

Table 1: Benefits of improved constructability (Wong et al., 2007)

Domain	Impact	References
Cost	Saving 1-14% of capital cost	(Gray, 1983)
	Saving on total project cost	(Jergeas and Put, 2001, Elgohary et al., 2003, Trigunarsyah, 2004b)
	Lower cost of bidding	(Gibson Jr et al., 1996)
	Reduced site labour	(Lam, 2002)
	Increased cost effectiveness	(Pheng and Abeyegoonasekera, 2001)
	Better resources utilisation	(Eldin, 1999)
Time	Early competition	(GRIFFITH and SIDWELL, 1997, Eldin, 1999, Pheng and Abeyegoonasekera, 2001, Elgohary et al., 2003, Trigunarsyah, 2004b)
	Increased productivity	(Poh and Chen, 1998, Pheng and Abeyegoonasekera, 2001)
	Reduced outage duration	(Eldin, 1999)
Quality	Higher quality of built products	(Eldin, 1999, Pheng and Abeyegoonasekera, 2001, Pheng Low, 2001, Elgohary et al., 2003)
Safety	Safer environment on site	(Francis et al., 1999, Eldin, 1999, Trigunarsyah, 2004a)
Other	Reduction in unforeseen problems	(Francis et al., 1999, Pheng and Abeyegoonasekera, 2001)
	Improvements in industrial relations, teamwork, communication and client satisfaction	(Francis et al., 1999, Eldin, 1999, Geile, 1996)

However, benefits of constructability implementation may have further implications on the whole project and not only the construction process, this includes the improvements in the conceptual planning, conduct the procurement, construction methods and stakeholder involvement and satisfaction (GRIFFITH and SIDWELL, 1997).

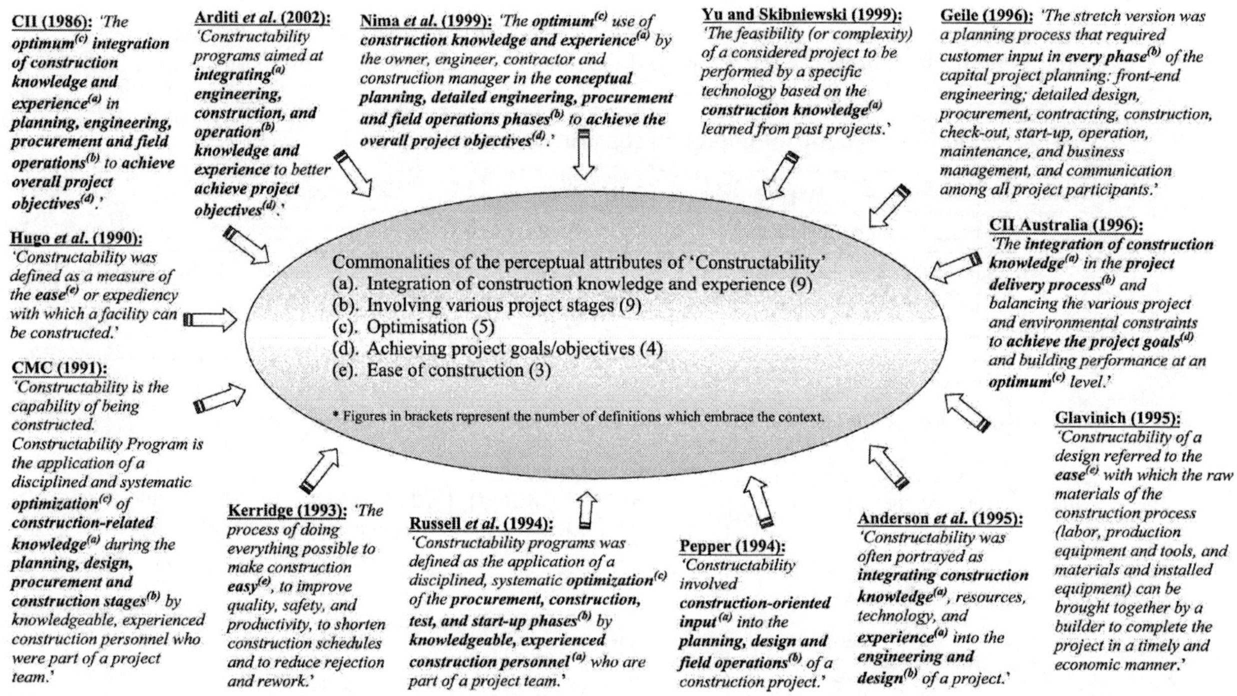

Figure 1: Commonalities amongst different interpretations of Constructability attributes (Wong, 2007)

4. Information Technology for Improving Design Constructability

BIM technologies can play a vital role in improving design constructability through the collaborative process with early construction input. It facilitates the integration between the design and construction processes that consequently leads to improved quality building with savings in project cost and time to construct (Eastman et al., 2008). Object-oriented models have a real potentiality in quantifying constructability application where designers can observe its factors using a fast, simple and a precise tool to assess their designs (Wissam Hijazi, 2009). In addition, BIM has the ability to electronically model and manage the vast amount of information encapsulated into the building design, from its conception to end-of-life, as can be seen in Fig 2. Such information can be employed to estimate, schedule, detail, advance bill production, automate shop drawing, and construction planning for all of the trades.

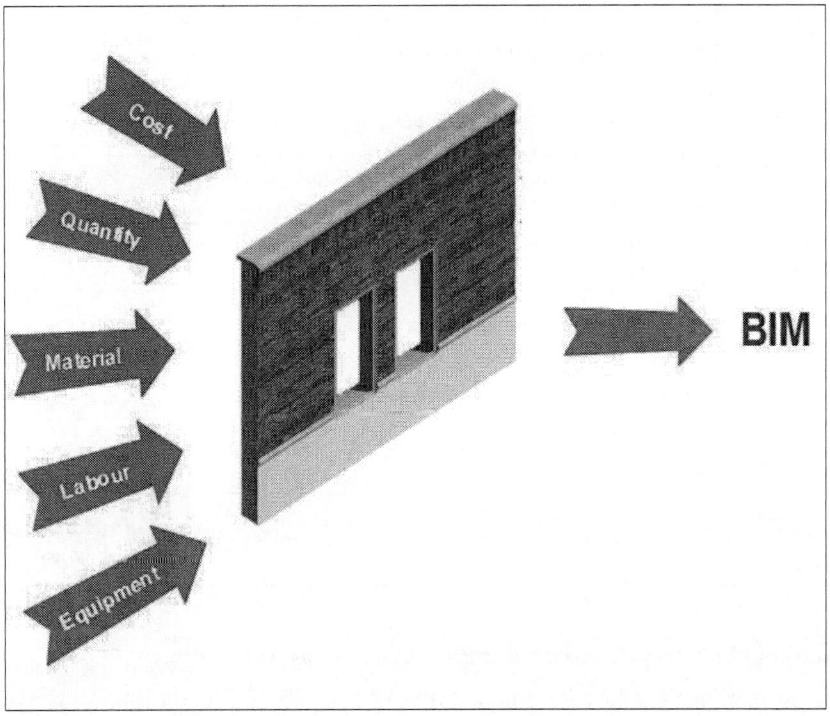

Figure 2: Building data model (Wissam Hijazi, 2009)

5. Adopted Approaches for Improving Constructability

As the importance of constructability concept is well recognized and its impacts on the total project performance, many studies investigated various approaches to enable an objective evaluation of the abstract concept. By reviewing different developed tools benchmarking the design constructability, it was found that most employed approaches for benchmarking design constructability are: quantitative assessment of constructability of design, constructability review and implementing constructability programs. Table 2 below shows previous studies that adopted each assessment method.

Table 2: Design constructability evaluation approaches and previous studies that adopted each approach (Hei, 2007)

Criteria	Previous Studies	References
Quantitative assessment of constructability of design	BDA in Singapore requires minimum score to be achieved	(Lam, 2002)
	Fuzzy Quality Function Deployment system	(Yang, et al., 2003)
	The knowledge models for automated assessment	(Ugwu, et al., 2004)
	The assessment framework of buildability in Malaysia	(Zin, et al., 2004)
Constructability Review	Using formalised buildability reviews at design & construction	(Ford, et al., 2004)
	Early implementation of design review in the conceptual stage	(Arditi, et al., 2002)
	Integration of buildability improvements into project development	(Anderson, 2000)
	Integration of analytical tools into the buildability review process	(Fisher et al., 2000)
	Implementation of buildability review at different design stages	((Young, 1998)
	In-house design-phase buildability review	(Glavinich, 1995)
	Carrying out buildability review by independent experienced team	(Pepper, 1994)
Implementing constructability programmes	Implementing buildability programmes at various project stages	Kog, et al., 1999, Jergeas, 2001)

6. Evaluation of Current Constructability Assessment Tools

Table 3 below summarizes the assessment of the 12 constructability tools employed (based on the quantification or knowledge-based approaches) in terms of their constructability evaluation. It can be clearly seen that the interview approach is the common way to acquire constructability knowledge from design and construction experts (Jiang, 2016).

By reviewing and evaluating those assessment tools, existing limitations can be identified as:

I. Their focus on single design elements, instead of considering a building design as a whole to make necessary trade-offs to optimize the overall constructability.
II. Their time of application indicates the assessment process lacks of inputs of construction knowledges at early design stages.
III. Nine out of 12 tools are separated systems from graphics design and lack the capability of visualization, which can cause communication issues and waste time during decision-making (Golparvar, 2006).

Table 3: Summary of current constructability tools (Jiang, 2016)

Constructability Tools		No.	Name	Constructability Knowledge Elicitation Methods	Level of Detail of Constructability Knowledge					Application Timing					References
					Building/ Site	System	Sub-System	Component	Elements	Conceptual Design	Schematic Design	Design Development	Construction Documents	Pre-Construction	
Knowledge-Based Systems (KBSs)	Non-Graphical-based	(1)	Structural frame selection system	N/A	X	X	X								Salazar & Brown (1988)
		(2)	Modular Construction decision support system	Interview	X	X									Murtaza et al. (1993)
		(3)	Automated constructability assessment system for structural steel design	Structured interview	X	X	X	X	X						Ugwu et al. (2004)
		(4)	Knowledge representation space for constructability analysis of concrete beam design	Machine learning		X	X	X	X						Skibniewski et al. (1997)
		(5)	Formwork selection system	Questionnaries, Unstructured & Structured interview	X	X	X	X							Hanna & Sanvido (1989)
	Graphical-based	(6)	Designer Fabricator Interpreter (DFI) system	Interaction with experts		X	X	X	X						Werkman et al. (1990)
		(7)	Automated rebar constructability diagnosis system	Interview		X	X	X	X						Navon et al. (2000)
		(8)	Fabrication issues checking system	N/A				X	X						Ernst & Roddis (1994)
		(9)	Construction Knowledge Expert System (COKE)	Literature review, Interview				X	X						Fischer (1993)
Qualitative Modeling Analysis		(10)	Buildable Design Appraisal System (BDAS)	Interaction with experts, Data collection		X	X	X							CIDB (1993), Pho & Chen (1996)
		(11)	Comparative analysis system of building upper structural systems	Questionnarie survey, Interview			X	X							Lam et al. (2007)
		(12)	Automated measurement of buildability factors affecting edge formwork labor productivity	Literature review, Data collection, Intermittent observation				X							Jarkas (2010)

7. Requirements for Modelling Constructability in Buildings

The comprehensive review of contemporary literature helps to identify the shortcomings of current assessment systems and what needs to be addressed in this area given the advanced technologies that are available nowadays. Hence, this research defined six requirements that need to be available in each appraisal system to facilitate the constructability assessment process and deliver it in an effective, faster and accurate way, as shown in Fig 3.

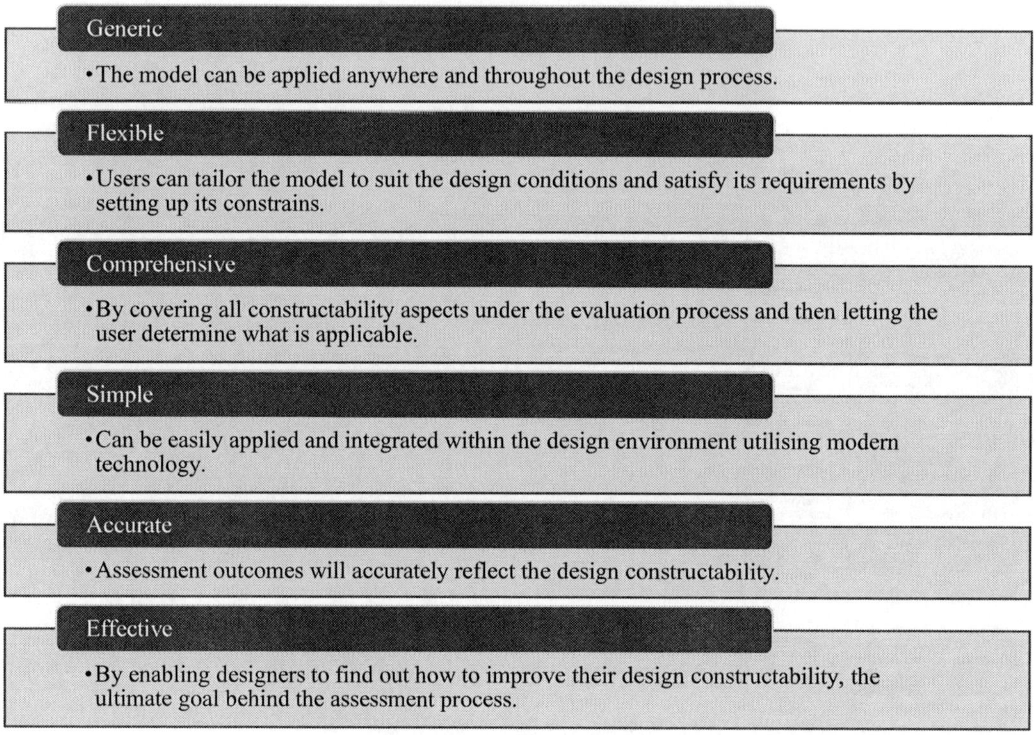

Figure 3: Requirements of constructability appraisal system

8. Current Limitations and Emerging Challenges

Despite the awareness of the potential benefits to facility design and construction from improving constructability, the application of a suitable method or constructability tools is still a significant challenge. The use of new technology-based tools to assess constructability of designs has not been fully realized. Now, the main challenge is how to use the potential capabilities that BIM provides to assess design constructability.

Therefore, a constructability decision-support tool is proposed as a solution to the identified problem, which is the subject of this study. It will provide a mechanism to assess the design constructability at an early design stage and deliver feedback that will enable designers to optimize their designs and make the necessary changes with minimum disruption and maximum efficiency (Lam et al., 2012).

9. A Proposed Framework for Constructability Assessment of Buildings Design

This section presents the constructability modelling framework and its implementation. It briefly discusses the components of the framework and how the various constituent objects relate in the operation of the model.

9.1 Modelling Framework

Fig 4 below illustrates the proposed methodology to assess design constructability using the embedded information within a BIM. The assessment process goes through four main stages, namely, development of the design model, development of constructability assessment model, the examination process and finally the decision making phase.

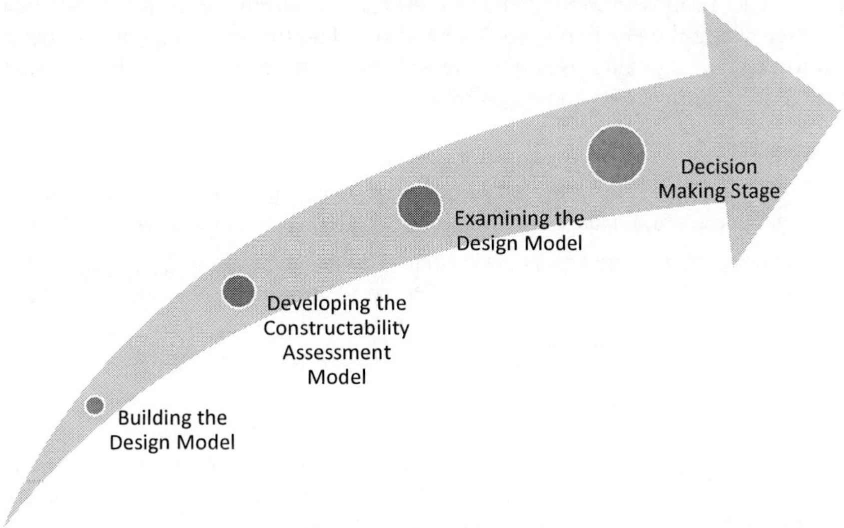

Figure 4: Constructability Assessment Methodology

The first stage is concerned with developing a design solution using a BIM software and providing the necessary information that the model should contain according to the agreed level of details (LoD). In the second stage, the constructability assessment model will be developed. This includes the identification of considered constructability factors and attributes, building the Construction Information Model (CIM) that extracts expertise knowledge and transfers it into design rules, and also assigning the design constrains for considered designs.

Once this is accomplished, then the developed design can be examined using the defined assessment model and deliver feedback to users for decision-making step. Based on the obtained feedback, designers will be able to decide whether to improve their developed design or to proceed to next project phase by achieving targeted constructability score goal.

9.2 Framework Implementation

The proposed framework will be implemented through a prototype using Application Programming Interface (API) as a BIM extension, which will allow constructability assessment to be embedded into the appraisal process of conceptual design options in BIM.

10. Summary

The current practice of designing for constructability fails to meet expectations and needs more improvement. The implementation of constructability concept is quite complicated and requires more serious efforts, resources and time than have hitherto been devoted to it, as evidenced by the studies discussed in this review.

This paper reviewed current conventional methods in assessing design constructability. It defines a set of modelling requirements that should characterize an ideal constructability tool. As a result, it proposed a model-based approach to quantify constructability of design. The potential of such model stems from its employment of the latest design techniques and contemporary information modelling technology, which means its integration with current design tools. The proposed model and its high-level components are described, and its implementation using the BIM concept is explained. The proposed system, if successful, is a major step towards design automation where a design can be automatically examined and the outcome be used to improve its constructability.

References

ANDERSON, S.D., FISHER, D.J. AND RAHMAN, S.P., 2000. Integrating constructability into project development: a process approach. Journal of Construction Engineering and Management, 126(2), pp.81-88.

ARDITI, D., ELHASSAN, A. AND TOKLU, Y.C., 2004. Closure to "Constructability Analysis in the Design Firm" by David Arditi, Ahmed Elhassan, and Y. Cengiz Toklu. Journal of construction engineering and management, 130(2), pp.302-304.

CII 1986. Constructability, a primer, publication 3-1. In: (CII), C. I. I. (ed.). Austin, TX. : University of Texas at Austin.

CIRIA 1983. Buildability: An Assessment. In: ASSOCIATION, C. I. R. A. I. (ed.). London.

EGAN, S. J. & WILLIAMS, D. [SUMMARY OF]"" RETHINKING CONSTRUCTION""-THE REPORT OF THE CONSTRUCTION TASK FORCE. ICE BRIEFING SHEET. Proceedings of the Institution of Civil Engineers-Municipal Engineer, 1998. Thomas Telford-ICE Virtual Library, 199-203.

ELDIN, N. N. 1999. Impact of employee, management, and process issues on constructability implementation. Construction Management & Economics, 17, 711-720.

ELGOHARY, M., FAIRCLOUGH, N. & RICCIUTI, R. 2003. Constructability--from Qinshan to the ACR. Nuclear Plant Journal, 21.

FRANCIS, V., CHEN, S., MEHRTENS, V., SIDWELL, A. & MCGEORGE, W. 1999. Constructability strategy for improved project performance. Architectural Science Review, 42, 133-138.

GEILE, R. J. 1996. Constructability," the stretch version". AACE International Transactions, VEC61.

GIBSON JR, G., MCGINNIS, C., FLANIGAN, W. & WOOD, J. 1996. Constructability in public sector. Journal of Construction Engineering and Management, 122, 274-280.

GRAY, C. 1983. Buildability: the construction contribution, Chartered Institute of Building Ascot, UK.

GRIFFITH, A. & SIDWELL, A. C. 1997. Development of constructability concepts, principles and practices. Engineering, Construction and Architectural Management, 4, 295-310.

GLAVINICH, T. E. 1995. Improving constructability during design phase. Journal of Architectural Engineering, 1, 73-76.

HEI, W. W. 2007. Developing and Implementing an Emprical System for Scoring Buildability of Designs in the Hong Kong Construction Industry. Doctor of Philosophy, the Hong Kong Polytechnic University.

HUGO, F., O'CONNOR, J. & WARD, W. 1990. 'Highway construct* ability guide. Investigation of highway project constructability improvement. Research Project No. 3-6-88, 1149.

JERGEAS, G. & PUT, J. V. D. 2001. Benefits of constructability on construction projects. Journal of Construction Engineering and Management, 127, 281-290.

JOHNSON, S. T. & JARDINE, F. M. 1995. Construction Industry Research and Information Association (CIRIA) Programme on Remedial Treatment of Contaminated Land: Phase 3—Case Study Demonstrations. Contaminated Soil'95. Springer.

KERRIDGE, A. 1993. Plan for constructability. II. Hydrocarbon processing, 72, 151-158.

LAM, P. 2002. Buildability assessment: the Singapore approach. Journal of Building and Construction Management.

LATHAM, S. M. 1994. Constructing the team, HM Stationery Office London.

NIMA, M. A., RAZALI ABDUL-KADIR, M. & SALEH JAAFAR, M. 1999. Evaluation of the engineer's personnel's role in enhancing the project constructability. Facilities, 17, 423-430.

PEPPER, H. 1994. The benefits of constructability reviews during the design of environmental capital projects. COST ENGINEERING-ANN ARBOR THEN MORGANTOWN-, 36, 19-19.

PHENG LOW, S. 2001. Quantifying the relationships between buildability, structural quality and productivity in construction. Structural Survey, 19, 106-112.

PHENG, L. S. & ABEYEGOONASEKERA, B. 2001. Integrating buildability in ISO 9000 quality management systems: case study of a condominium project. Building and Environment, 36, 299-312.

POH, P. S. & CHEN, J. 1998. The Singapore buildable design appraisal system: a preliminary review of the relationship between buildability, site productivity and cost. Construction Management & Economics, 16, 681-692.

RUSSELL, J. S., SWIGGUM, K. E., SHAPIRO, J. M. & ALAYDRUS, A. F. 1994. Constructability related to TQM, value engineering, and cost/benefits. Journal of performance of constructed facilities, 8, 31-45.

SKIBNIEWSKI, M. J. 1999. Quantitative constructability analysis with a neuro-fuzzy knowledge-based multi-criterion decision support system. Automation in Construction, 8, 553-565.

TRIGUNARSYAH, B. 2004a. Project owners' role in improving constructability of construction projects: an example analysis for Indonesia. Construction Management and Economics, 22, 861-876.

TRIGUNARSYAH, B. 2004b. A review of current practice in constructability improvement: case studies on construction projects in Indonesia. Construction Management and Economics, 22, 567-580.

UGWU, O.O., ANUMBA, C.J. AND THORPE, A., 2004. The development of cognitive models for constructability assessment in steel frame structures. Advances in Engineering Software, 35(3), pp.191-203.

WISSAM HIJAZI, D. S. A., P.ENG., AND DR. TAREK ZAYED 2009. Constructability Assessment Using BIM/4D CAD Simulation Model.

WONG, F. W., LAM, P. T., CHAN, E. H. & SHEN, L. 2007. A study of measures to improve constructability. International Journal of Quality & Reliability Management, 24, 586-601.

YANG, Y.Q., WANG, S.Q., DULAIMI, M. AND LOW, S.P., 2003. A fuzzy quality function deployment system for buildable design decision-makings. Automation in construction, 12(4), pp.381-393.

ZIN, R.M., NESAN, L.J. AND MOHAMMED, A.H., 2004. Constructability assessment framework. Journal of Building and Construction Management, 9(1), pp.44-58.

BIM for Asset Management: A taxonomy of non-geometric BIM data for asset management

KARIM FARGHALY, HENRY ABANDA, CHRISTOS VIDALAKIS & GRAHAM WOOD
School of the Built Environment, Oxford Brookes University, Oxford, OX3 0BP, UK
karim.ibrahim-2016@brookes.ac.uk

Abstract. Nowadays, the capabilities of collecting different sets of data from different sources (BIM, GIS, Sensors, Assets database) for asset management (AM) use have availed opportunitiess to provide benefits for project's owners and facility managers. Meanwhile, there has been a focus on asset management and the connection to effective documentation through BIM. However, this data integration came along with new issues and obstacles in terms of an effective process to extract, store, manage, integrate, and distribute this data to ensure interoperability. In addition to the foregoing, the issue is not only the interoperability, it is also about the decision regarding what data is relevant and what would provide value to asset owners. This paper explores the owners' needs from BIM in the operation and maintenance stage from an asset management perspective. A combination of methods consisting of literature review, face-to-face and focus group interviews was used in this study. This culminated in the development of a taxonomy that consists of 40 parameters. The developed taxonomy can help BIM professionals identify and recognise the required data to be submitted to facility managers which can be useful in AM practices.

1. Introduction

Asset Management (AM) is a sophisticated area of management with wide range of professional disciplines and activities (Spilling, 2016). Asset management is defined by ISO 55000 (2012) as "coordinated activity of an organization to realize value from assets". In other words, Asset Management is process in which a management system is bi-directionally linked to a record model to efficiently aid in the maintenance and operation of a facility and its assets. These assets, consisting of the physical building, systems, and equipment, must be maintained, upgraded, and operated efficiently to be of better value to the owner and the end users. Accordingly, asset management transforms business objectives into asset-related decisions and assists in financial decision-making, short-term and long-term planning, and generating scheduled work orders (Pocock et al, 2014). For the bi-directional link, these assets have to be available in electronic formats with proper classification and organization to simplify the access to the information. For that purpose, research efforts have been made to improve data interoperability between the different Facilities Management (FM) systems. However, the main challenge is creating and manually updating these assets data with the correct information linked to the relative documents in various databases and in various phases which is a timely process that leaves a lot of room to human errors. Building Information Modelling (BIM) model/database seems to be the ideal platform for collecting, capturing, visualizing data and information using different techniques such as standardized barcode and radio frequency identification (RFID) labels during different building phases such as planning, design, construction, and operation and maintenance phases. BIM for FM can be even described as "Better Information Management" (Thomas, 2017). BIM and Big Data technologies can achieve a good efficient database for asset management (Ibrahim et al, 2017). This good quality assets database can improve financial performance, improve asset investment decisions, manage risks and demonstrate compliance (Spilling, 2016).

Despite agreed benefits and exerted efforts, the implementation of BIM in FM generally and in AM particularly is rare and has been difficult (Eadie et al, 2015). Love (2014) argues that technology alone cannot deliver business outcomes and that the process of its implementation should be proactively managed to ensure that the organization obtains the results it expects. Researchers (Love et al, 2014; Mayo & Issa, 2015) identified that the slow implementation of BIM by owners and facility managers has been to an extent due to the complex nature of the assets information. Data Management was the main concern pertaining to the use and the adoption of BIM in FM in workshop titled "FM and BIM" (Ashworth et al, 2016). A case study at an educational institution (Thabet et al, 2016) has illustrated that the usual obstacles are that asset data is scattered and not structured and the data of components are not integrated or even referenced with other related data/information. Meanwhile, several publications (Ashworth et al, 2016; Becerik-Gerber et al, 2012; Carbonari et al, 2015) have criticized the lack of the connection between BIM deliverables and the owners'/facility managers' goals and ultimate use needs especially for assets management. This contrasts sharply to one of the key objectives of the UK Construction Strategy (2011) promoting an alignment of interest between those who design/construct a building and those who subsequently occupy and operate it. Mayo and Essa (2015) specified that the implementation of BIM in FM requires the owners to provide more details of the specific required information deliverables. Ibrahim et al. (2016) added that this required data has to be correctly added in the BIM models in early stages to build on even foundations.

Based on the discussion above and to improve the current practice of BIM implementation in asset management, a new framework is proposed (Figure 1). The proposed framework is particularly developed for assets that consume energy. The knowledge assets information facilities management (KAIFM) framework consists of four main aspects namely, 1) New classification of assets that consume energy based on the discipline of energy consumption, 2) Taxonomy for the required data for each asset, 3) Model of extracting the required data with appropriate classification for the assets consume energy, 4) A database for storing and integrating BIM data with assets consume energy databases.

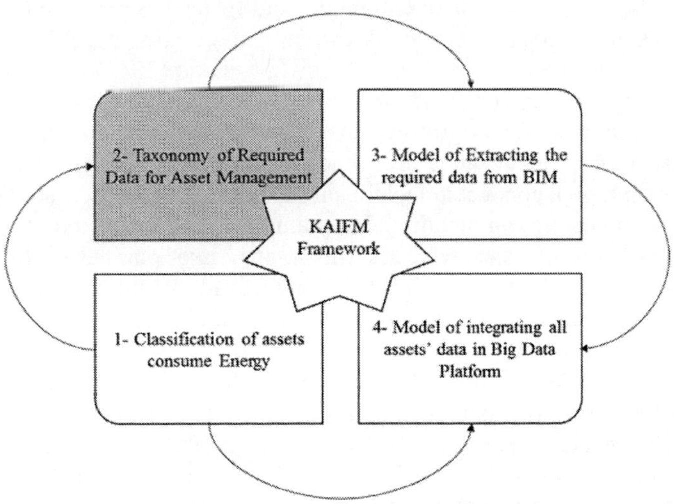

Figure 1: KAIFM Framework and the aspect covered in this paper is highlighted

It is clear from the above that there is a wide range of aspects related to integrating Building Information Modelling (BIM) and asset management (AM) data to be considered and they cannot all be addressed in this paper. This paper focus on the one of the KAIFM aspects, the development of a taxonomy for the non-geometric data required for assets that consume energy.

2. Methods

The main purpose of this research is to identify the non-geometric assets consume energy data required to support successful implementation of BIM in asset management practice. For this purpose, different research methods were utilized and interconnected such as peer literature review, semi-structured interviews and focus groups. Firstly, a literature review, including academic papers, project documents, case studies, international reports and practice guidelines and standards, has been carried out focusing on the recommended/proposed non-geometric assets data extracted from BIM models for asset management. Subsequently, semi structured interviews were conducted with facility manager and information manager involved in the decision making to adopt BIM in their companies. The interviewees were guided by the main questions; however they were free to elaborate on asset management challenges as experienced in their projects. The interviews were aimed at confirming and clarifying the required assets data from BIM found in the literature. Based on findings from literature and semi structured interviews, an analysis was carried out to develop the taxonomy of BIM parameters required. A focus group with eight BIM experts was conducted to evaluate and validate the developed taxonomy, and relate them to Revit - Most popular BIM platform - taxonomies/structures.

3. Literature Review

Most discussions and researches of BIM implementation in FM have been focusing on the geometric data requirements, while there is a serious need to concentrate on identifying the non-geometric ones to support successful implementation (Becerik-Gerber et al, 2012). In literature, some researches were conducted to identify the non-geometric required data, however, still more work has to be carried out. Becerik-Gerber et al. (2012) identified the data required in a pyramidal classification from the basic identification which can be captured in the early stages own to the operation and maintenance data which can be captured during building usage. Wang, Wang et al. (2013) proposed a structure of BIM database for FM in the early engagement of FM in the design stage. The database of equipment and systems is classified into two categories namely, attributes and data (vendor, location, etc.), and portfolios and documents (specifications, manuals, certificates, etc.). Meanwhile, Hunt (2011) proposed an hierarchical classification in the closeout and handover stage with two main levels namely description system level (location, manufacture information, vendor, ID name and number) and technical content level (warranties, maintenance instructions, etc.). Mayo and Issa (2015) further refined these taxonomies through a conducted Delphi survey with 21 FM expertise. They classified the required data based on the FM application. For example, they proposed four main data required for building asset management namely, asset locations, asset purchase information, bar code information and asset identifier. Also Construction Operation Building Information Exchange can be considered as a taxonomy of the required information for asset management. COBie - subset of IFC- is a data standard that was developed by the US Corps of Engineering to manage the non-graphical data received from BIM models into the client organization, particularly for the handover of Operation & Maintenance manual information (East, 2013; Spilling, 2016). COBie classified the data into ten main categories: facility (Project, Site and Building/Structure information), floor (the mandatory spatial structure), space (the spatial locations where inspection, maintenance and operation Jobs occur), zone (additional functional groupings of locations), type (mandatory grouping of Components as types or products, used to organize maintenance tasks), component (the physical assets), system (additional functional groupings of components), spare (the physical objects), job (the processes and tasks used to maintain and operate the assets) and resources (support the processes and the tasks). COBie UK 2012 extended with two more categories: cost and carbon (Spilling, 2016).

At the same time in the practice, several projects and guidelines recommended different required data. Sydney Opera House (SOH) is one of the first projects where BIM has been implemented for FM. Due to the long design life of SOH and its complexity and importance, the engagement of BIM was mandatory to provide open interoperability and a data management pool (Schevers et al, 2007). In SOH Model Management Plan (MMP) document, thirty-six parameters were identified as the required data from BIM models for asset management. The identified required data are classified into six main categories namely, BIM4FM, element details, element specification, warranty, certifications and asset control. Based on the building information manager of SOH, the MMP is a live document and consequently will be revised and updated from time to time to achieve successful asset management. Manchester City Hall (MCH) is another project where BIM has been implemented for asset management. Before BIM implementation, the asset information in Computer-aided facility management (CAFM) systems were inadequate and inaccurate and thus were inefficient in terms of creating an onward maintenance plan. Therefore, BIM was implemented to create an asset information model and new rules of measurements (NRM3) was selected as the guidance for the assets taxonomy (Oluteye & Marjanovic-Halburd, 2015). NRM3 is an asset classification standard for structuring the cost data of assets relevant to the operation and maintenance phase of built assets (Green, 2014). NRM3 information requirements for order of cost estimates and the purpose of BIM implementation influenced and formatted the collected/required assets data. The collected assets data included data related to assets location, assets maintenance history, assets operation history and assets costs. Generally in the current on-going BIM projects, the required information is identified based on plain language questions (PLQs) and/or educated experience, sometimes assumptions, of the data that might be needed for better asset management (Tune, 2017).

On the other hand, in the last couple years, three leading construction bodies in UK - Building Engineering Services Association (BESA), the Construction Products Association (CPA), and the Chartered Institution of Building Services Engineers (CIBSE) - have been working on and are still developing in standardized product information for successful implementation of BIM in all the phases of Architecture, Engineering and Construction (AEC) and Operation and Maintenance (O&M) (Caplehorn, 2017). CIBSE developed a working group and engaged industry experts to make standardized Product Data Templates (PDTs) under a project called BIMHawk (Caplehorn, 2017). The PDT is meant to be a standardized way through which manufacturers' product attributes/parameters can be made available in machine-readable format during all the phases of the building. CIBSE's PDT is an excel sheet of five columns. The first column defines the information category which is divided to three sub-categories namely, specification, suitability and asset management. Column two, three and four represent the parameter to be defined, the value of the parameter, and the value unit respectively. Finally column five is for guide notes. Only value column (column three) needs to be completed, all other are fixed for each asset. Once data of column three is added the PDT becomes product data sheet (PDS). The total number of fields - parameters - varies from PDT to PDT depending on the asset functions and its manufacturer (Thompson, 2016). Meanwhile, CPA with cooperation with the BIM Task Group and UK BIM Alliance are leading the development and implementation of LEXiCON, the plain language approach to product data definition and exchange in the UK (Caplehorn, 2017). As part of this development, the key source of product information requirements comes from the Harmonized European Standards (hENs), standards requirements, industry recognized requirements, and client requirements (Thompson, 2016). The concept of LEXiCON is to create so-called Product DNA – information that stays with a product and is added to through a product's lifecycle (Thompson, 2016). LEXiCON provides the governance to ensure the properties defined are the correct ones, and these will then be aligned with the buildingSMART Data Dictionary (Caplehorn, 2017). In other words,

LEXiCON will guarantee that the AEC and OM industries have one common fixed PDT for each product type including agreed parameters and their standardized naming convention, and managed by the CPA and relevant trade associations (Small, 2017). BESA, CIBSE, and CPA have agreed on the respective roles of the 'LEXiCON' and 'BIMHawk' to avoid any confusion or even competition (Caplehorn, 2017). Meanwhile, other parallel efforts have been exerted by National Building Specification (NBS) and Norway coBuilder. NBS produced its own PDTs as part of its BIM toolkit and it is completely different than the CIBSE's PDT. On the other hand, Norway coBuilder developed more than 700 PDTs based on IFC, the parameters included in the PDTs are aligned with the Construction Product Regulations (CPR) (Tune, 2017). To ensure the rewards form all these efforts, Small (2017) critiqued that all different industry stakeholders (manufacturers, architects and contractors) should lead and participate in working groups and associations involved in the development of tools for guidance and support when considering their PDTs to attain the most exhaustive results. The work of the preceding authors can summarize the academic research and some of the practice works contributing in identifying the required data for successful implementation of BIM in asset management.

4. Taxonomy Development

During the literature review stage, it was found that different classifications and long lists of diverse parameters have been produced. On the basis of the review, a preliminary taxonomy was developed to collate and consolidate results of these previous studies, and to work as a ground base for conducting the semi-structured interviews. After the interviews, the preliminary taxonomy has been modified and updated. Figure 2 is a diagrammatic presentation for the proposed taxonomy of the required data for successful implementation of BIM in asset management practice. The taxonomy adopts a hierarchical structure with two levels. The top level is classified into five main categories namely, space/location, BIM capex, specifications, warranty, and asset's capex and opex. While at the second level, forty parameters are presenting the required BIM data/parameters for asset management during handover stage. This data can be collected in different stages which include planning and design, construction, handover and closeout, and finally operation and maintenance. The five top categories are disused below together with their required parameters.

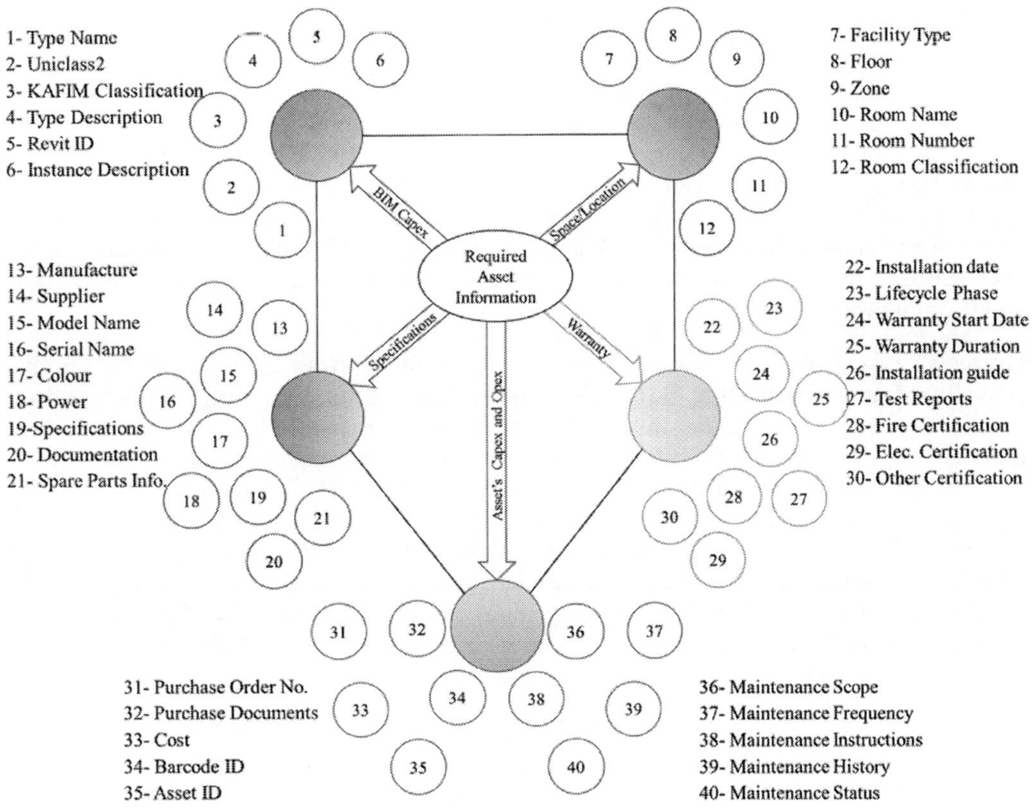

Figure 2 : Development taxonomy for required parameters for asset management

BIM capex category includes the following parameters: type name, Uniclass2, discipline, type description, Revit ID, and instance description. All of these parameters can also be collected during the design stage. Some of these parameters and parameters in the other categories (such as Uniclass2, specifications, maintenance duration …) have to be added to the Revit model as a shared parameter as it is not available by default in the Revit platform. Uniclass2 is the new UK implementation of the international framework for construction information. Uniclass2 classification is not identified in the Revit Database, however, it can be easily implemented. Classification parameter will be developed based on the proposed classification of the assets consume energy (Aspect 1 - KAIFM framework). Revit ID is a unique identification generated by Revit, while instance and type description are two blank parameter to be filled for comments related to the asset during the handover stage. Revit ID and Instance description parameters are instance parameters while the others are type parameters.

Space/Location category includes six parameters: facility type, floor, zone, room name, room number, and room classification. All of these parameters are related to the spatial location of the asset, and they can be identified and captured form the architecture models during the design stage. All of the space/location parameters are instance parameter which differs for the same type of assets depending on the location.

Specification category includes nine parameters namely, manufacture, supplier, model name, serial name, colour, power, specification, documentation and spare parts. These parameters are related to the specifications of the assets and all are type parameters except the serial name one.

These data can be collected during the construction and handover stage. Manufacture parameter includes the email address or the name for the organisation responsible for manufacturing the asset, while supplier parameter identifies the organisation responsible for supplying the asset. Model name is label of the asset assigned by the manufacture (most of the times, this parameter value equals to the type name parameter value), while the serial name is the product, item or unit number assigned by the manufacturer of the asset. Colour is the characteristic or primary colour of product/asset and the power parameter states the energy consumption rate for the asset. Specification, documentation and spare parts are URL value parameters for the documents stating the specification of the asset, any relative documents and the spare parts specifications respectively.

Warranty category includes nine parameters namely, installation date, lifecycle phase, warranty start date, warranty duration, installation guide, test reports, fire certification, electrical certification, other certification. Installation data is the date that the manufactured item was installed and this parameter is an instance parameter. Lifecycle phase states the duration of expected life of an asset (typical value in 'years'). Warranty start date is the date the warranty commences for an asset (mostly it has the same value as the installation date), while warranty duration is duration of warranties (typical value is 'years'). Some assets includes different parts with different warranty duration, in that case a new parameter is added which includes the URL for the document of the different warranty durations for the parts. Installation guide, test reports, fire certification, electrical certification, other certification are URL value parameters for the documents related to installation and certifications.

Asset's capex and opex category includes purchase order No., purchase documents, cost, bar code ID, asset ID, maintenance scope, maintenance frequency, maintenance duration, maintenance history, and maintenance status. Purchase order number and purchase documents are the two parameters related the procurement of assets. Purchase order number is a unique number for each purchase for easier classification and purchase documents parameter is a URL path for the document. Cost parameter indicates the cost of the purchase of an asset or even its replacement. The bar code ID parameter identifies the bar code (or RFID) given to an occurrence of the product (per instance), while the asset ID is the identification assigned to an asset that enables its differentiation from other assets. The remaining parameters of asset's capex and opex category are mainly related to the maintenance jobs.

Table 1 illustrates and summarises the forty parameters, their category, their unit and type or instance and the phase where the data can be collected.

Table 1: Forty required parameters for asset management.

No.	Category	Parameter	Unit	Type /Instance	Source Phase
1	BIM Capex	Type Name	Alphanumeric	Type	Phase 1
2	BIM Capex	Uniclass2015	Alphanumeric	Type	Phase 1
3	BIM Capex	Classification	Alphanumeric	Type	Phase 1
4	BIM Capex	Type Description	Alphanumeric	Type	Phase 1
5	BIM Capex	Revit ID	Numeric	Instance	Phase 1
6	BIM Capex	Revit Classification	Alphanumeric	Instance	Phase 1
7	Space	Facility Type	Alphanumeric	Instance	Phase 1
8	Space	Floor	Alphanumeric	Instance	Phase 1

Table 1 Cont.: Forty required parameters for asset management.

No.	Category	Parameter	Unit	Type /Instance	Source Phase
9	Space	Zone	Alphanumeric	Instance	Phase 1
10	Space	Room Name	Alphanumeric	Instance	Phase 1
11	Space	Room Number	Alphanumeric	Instance	Phase 1
12	Space	Room Classification	Alphanumeric	Instance	Phase 1
13	Specification	Manufacture	Alphanumeric	Type	Phase 2
14	Specification	Supplier	Alphanumeric	Type	Phase 2
15	Specification	Model Name	Alphanumeric	Type	Phase 2
16	Specification	Serial Name	Alphanumeric	Type	Phase 2
17	Specification	Colour	Alphanumeric	Type	Phase 2
18	Specification	Power	Decimal	Type	Phase 2
19	Specification	Specification	URL	Type	Phase 2
20	Specification	Documentation	URL	Type	Phase 2
21	Specification	Spare Parts	URL	Type	Phase 2
22	Warranty	Installation Date	Numeric	Instance	Phase 2
23	Warranty	Lifecycle Phase	Numeric	Instance	Phase 2
24	Warranty	Warranty Start Date	Numeric	Instance	Phase 2
25	Warranty	Warranty Duration	Numeric	Type	Phase 2
26	Warranty	Installation Guide	URL	Instance	Phase 2
27	Warranty	Test Reports	URL	Instance	Phase 2
28	Warranty	Fire Certification	URL	Instance	Phase 2
29	Warranty	Electrical Certification	URL	Instance	Phase 2
30	Warranty	Other Certification	URL	Instance	Phase 2
31	Assets' Capex & Opex	Purchase Order No.	Alphanumeric	Instance	Phase 2 or 3
32	Assets' Capex & Opex	Purchase Documents	URL	Instance	Phase 2 or 3
33	Assets' Capex & Opex	Cost	Decimal	Instance	Phase 2 or 3
34	Assets' Capex & Opex	Bar Code ID	Alphanumeric	Instance	Phase 3
35	Assets' Capex & Opex	Asset ID	Alphanumeric	Instance	Phase 3
36	Assets' Capex & Opex	Maintenance Scope	Alphanumeric	Instance	Phase 3
37	Assets' Capex & Opex	Maintenance Frequency	Alphanumeric	Instance	Phase 3
38	Assets' Capex & Opex	Maintenance Duration	Numeric	Instance	Phase 3
39	Assets' Capex & Opex	Maintenance History	Alphanumeric	Instance	Phase 3
40	Assets' Capex & Opex	Maintenance Status	Alphanumeric	Instance	Phase 3

5. Conclusion and Further Works

Required asset data is essential for the delivery, maintenance and operation of any built asset. Academic and practice efforts are conducted to identify the required data during BIM implementation in asset management. In UK, two main ongoing projects are working in developing standardised product data parameters and structures, and ensuring the properties defined are the correct ones. In an attempt to fill the gap, a taxonomy for the required data for successful implementation of BIM in asset management is developed in this paper based on peer literature review, semi-structured interviews and focus groups. The developed taxonomy consists of forty parameters classified into five categories including Space/Location, BIM Capex, Specifications, Warranty and asset's capex and opex. Each category contains related parameters which can be instance parameter or type parameter. All classification/taxonomy systems have inconsistencies or inaccuracies. The present effort is no exception. Nevertheless, the developed taxonomy represents the required data for effective implementation of BIM in asset management practice and it is created based on consensus of an international group of experts and it is hoped that the taxonomy will be useful to the academic research and contributes to the on-going related works by the construction, and operation and maintenance industry. Further work including pilot projects and case studies will be conducted for reliability and validity for the developed taxonomy.

Acknowledgement

The authors would like to thank Mr. Chris Linning - BIM Implementation Manager at Sydney Opera House - and Mr. Mahmoud Abdelmoneam - BIM Implementation and Development Manager at Virtual Projects - for their inputs and help. Also the authors would like to thank Virtual Project company employees for their participation in conducting the BIM-AM focus group.

References

Ashworth, S., Tucker, M. & Druhmann, C. (2016) The Role of FM in Preparing a BIM Strategy and Employer's Information Requirements (EIR) to Align with Client Asset Management Strategy, EuroFM's 15th research symposium at EFMC2016. Milan, Italy, 218.

Becerik-Gerber, B., Jazizadeh, F., Li, N. & Calis, G. (2012) Application areas and data requirements for BIM-enabled facilities management. Journal of construction engineering and management, 138(3), 431-442.

Caplehorn, P. (2017) Industry bodies agree single process for BIM product data

Carbonari, G., Ashworth, S. & Stravoravdis, S. (2015) How Facility Management can use Building Information Modelling (BIM) to improve the decision making process. Journal of Facility Management, 10(2015).

Eadie, R., Browne, M., Odeyinka, H., McKeown, C. & McNiff, S. (2015) A survey of current status of and perceived changes required for BIM adoption in the UK. Built Environment Project and Asset Management, 5(1), 4-21.

East, B. (2013) Using COBie. BIM for Facility Managers, 1st Edition, New Jersey: John Wiley & Sons, 107-143.

Green, A. (2014) 2014: New Rules of Measurement-NRM 3: Order of cost estimating and cost planning for building maintenance works. London: Royal Institution of Chattered Surveyors (RICS).

Hunt, G. (2011) Comprehensive facility operation & maintenance manual, 2011. Available online: https://www.wbdg.org/facilities-operations-maintenance/comprehensive-facility-operation-maintenance-manual [Accessed.

Ibrahim, K., Abanda, H., Vidalakis, C. & Wood, G. (2017) BIM Big Data system architecture for Asset Management: a conceptual framework, Proc. Lean & Computing in Construction Congress (LC 3). Heraklion, Greece: CIB W78.

Ibrahim, K. F., Abanda, F. H., Vidalakis, C. & Woods, G. (2016) BIM for FM: Input versus Output data, Proc. of the 33rd CIB W78 Conference 2016. Brisbane, Australia.

ISO-55000 (2012) 2012: Asset management-Overview, principles and terminology.

Love, P. E., Matthews, J., Simpson, I., Hill, A. & Olatunji, O. A. (2014) A benefits realization management building information modeling framework for asset owners. Automation in construction, 37, 1-10.

Mayo, G. & Issa, R. R. (2015) Nongeometric Building Information Needs Assessment for Facilities Management. Journal of Management in Engineering, 32(3), 04015054.

Oluteye, D. & Marjanovic-Halburd, L. (2015) The Application of NRM3 In Asset Data Classification in BIM: A Case Study Report. Chartered Institution of Building Services Engineers (CIBSE).

Pocock, D., Shetty, N., Hayes, A. & Watts, J. (2014) Leveraging the relationship between BIM and asset management. Infrastructure Asset Management, 1(1), 5-7.

Schevers, H., Mitchell, J., Akhurst, P., Marchant, D., Bull, S., McDonald, K., Drogemuller, R. & Linning, C. (2007) Towards digital facility modelling for Sydney opera house using IFC and semantic web technology. Journal of Information Technology in Construction (ITcon), 12(24), 347-362.

Small, A. (2017) A Standardised Future: LEXiCON and Product Data Templates. bim4manufacturers. BIM for Manufactures and Manufacturing (BIM4M2).

Spilling, M. (2016) Asset Management Surveying Practice. The British Institute of Facilities Management (BIFM).

Thabet, W., Lucas, J. & Johnston, S. (2016) A Case Study for Improving BIM-FM Handover for a Large Educational Institution, Construction Research Congress 2016.

Thomas, P. (2017) The role of FM in BIM projects. The British Institute of Facilities Management (BIFM).

Thompson, S. (2016) Product Data Definition. A technical specification for defining and sharing structured digital construction product information.

Tune, N. (2017) Manufacturers: BIM Objects don't make you BIM Ready, Bimplus.co.ukAvailable online: http://www.bimplus.co.uk/people/manufactu6rers-bim-objects-dont-ma5ke-bi4m-ready/ [Accessed.

Wang, Y., Wang, X., Wang, J., Yung, P. & Jun, G. (2013) Engagement of facilities management in design stage through BIM: framework and a case study. Advances in Civil Engineering, 2013.

Investigating solar envelope by making use of point clouds data

Miktha Farid Alkadri, Michela Turrin, Sevil Sariyildiz
TU Delft, Netherlands
M.F.Alkadri@tudelft.nl

Abstract. Dealing with solar envelope analysis in architectural design becomes crucial feature because it gives an impact to the building performance analysis in the real environment. Various simulation tools were used by architects play a significant role in determining the design process. However, these tools were not yet confirming the expected performance of the future building design. Manual modeling platform and actual information processing are delivering the main issue on the design operation. This analysis leads to the potential application of point cloud as design medium in architectural domain. This paper furthermore investigates a comparative analysis between point cloud data model-based and the conventional modeling. Some challenging tasks are discussed in related with the point cloud processing in the design framework. The main contribution of this paper is to propose a novel design method for exploring the solar envelope simulation as a part of conceptual design analysis.

1. Introduction

The rapid development of 3D laser technology inevitably has pushed the boundaries of design and engineering world. To date, however, practical implementation in the architectural area is predominantly remaining on heritage (DRAP et.al 2003; WHITE 2013) and landscape domain (LIN et.al 2016). Investigating point cloud as metadata processing in surveying data and digital reconstruction were assigned as the major subjects in these areas. Nevertheless, the provision and utilization of such information data have yet to be effective in most instances, and disconnections between point cloud processing and architectural design practice within design and analysis stage are obvious. However, the fundamental parts of enrichment of point clouds usability are as much as the hidden potential to the practical design implementations. Thus, by considering prospective applications in geosciences, computer graphics or photogrammetry are expected to wider architectural spectrum in data scan processing. As a data visualization, for instance, point cloud has been used in automation process for the planar 3D building interior modeling (SANCHEZ and ZAKHOR 2012), the automatic extraction of spatial arrangement (TAMKE et.al 2014) and visibility analysis techniques in the close range photogrammetry (ALSADIK et.al 2014). Regarding reverse engineering, it was found useful for surface road data management in the maintenance construction (FUJITA et.al 2014) and verification of as-built construction progress through photogrammetry techniques (SHIH and WU 2005). These existing literatures provide us the profound insight to step further into architectural design analysis. The utilization of point cloud as design medium particularly for solar analysis has offered a great potential to the exploration of solar envelope simulation.

Recently, the concept of solar envelope was firstly introduced by Knowles considering the amount of desirable sun access to the surrounding site based on a predefined time (Knowles 1974). This idea was then further elaborated by Capeluto & Shaviv (1997) using "solar rights envelope" and "solar collection envelope" to generate a final envelope that so-called "solar volume." Furthermore, Ratti & Morello (2005) have investigated the concept of "iso-solar surface" through image processing method, DEMs (Digital Elevation Models) which corresponds to the number of solar energy in the urban area. These approaches, however, were not sufficient to represent the solar envelope simulation when it comes to the real environment as a fundamental context. Dissemination impact of solar radiation value and sunlight hours analysis will result differently for both the existing building and the generated envelope.

The utilization of 3D laser data scanning is not only introducing the real atmosphere of built environment but also covering the existing complex geometry such as building blocks, vegetation or other site properties. The simulation outcome is also simultaneously responded to the number of deviation result from the current solar analysis approaches. This paper mainly aims to investigate the potential of using point clouds data in generating solar envelope. In a broad spectrum, it is intended to improve design support means in architectural design analysis that corresponds to the passive design strategies for sustainable building design.

2. Design Procedure

This paper discusses the following procedures:

1. Selecting a geographical context in parallel with identifying the relevant attributes information from the point cloud data. This pre-processing step is included in the selection of solar envelope generation variables.
2. Developing a design framework through solar envelope generation technique by selecting the attribute information of point cloud data.
3. Demonstrating the generated design framework by considering several indicators to make a comparative analysis with conventional modeling platform. The conventional modeling means that we use the same context but manually generated in the computer program, usually called CAD-based drawing, by constituting the plain surface model. There are three design values which have been measured in the simulation result: the geometric envelope, total radiation value, and sunlight hour analysis.

3. Data Collection

The selected site is located in Kruisplein area, Rotterdam-Netherlands, nearby the Rotterdam central station. This area represents city center of Rotterdam which shows the dynamic urban forms such as high rise building, wide span building, large open space, and vegetation in between of the buildings (see Fig.1). We cover these urban properties through the point cloud data collection as a part of the relevant site elements. On top of that, this data collecting method illustrates the ability of point cloud data to capture complex information in the real environment.

Figure 1: Selected site

The 3D point cloud data is obtained from the Digital Elevation Map (DEM) of Netherlands based on laser altimetry measurement (AHN Netherlands 2017), which is open source media and accessible for architects. Our primary concern is to extract this potential open information from the point cloud data to be used in architectural design analysis. It, however, still opens the possibility to obtain point cloud data in an accurate way by using such the Terrestrial Laser Scanning (TLS) device like Faro, Leica, Riegl and others.

Furthermore, we employed Cloud Compare (CC) for data preparation to be legible in Rhino and Grasshopper (GH) as parametric modeling platform. As a part of preliminary step of data processing, we converted the .laz format (original data format from DEM) to the .e57 file (designated format) and removed the outliers of point cloud in the selected site boundary. Then, we transformed the attribute information of point cloud data through the scalar field value. We used the height ramp feature in CC to obtain data colorization according the vertical unit. The scalar field value plays an important part in the development of design framework because it determines the type of variable input of point cloud data. For instance, by selecting the green (G) value for the color attributes, the point cloud data will show green color as the highest point geographically in the chosen area. We could also, by using CC, produce and calculate multiple values of scalar field for point cloud data such as R-G-B color, intensity, curvature, composite and so forth. However, calculation of this scalar field value depends on the type of extracted data which we selected from DEM, AHN. Each data format may correspond to the different scalar field value. The data preparation steps in CC enable us to identify and to extract such geometrical shape according to a certain level in the parametric modeling stage.

In the development of solar envelope design framework, we operated Ladybug component in Grasshopper (GH) and Volvox (Zwierzycki et.al 2016) for point cloud data processing. We also constructed the additional GH components to formulate a further analysis of point cloud data. Table 1 illustrates the workflow of data processing from the 3D raw point clouds data into the parametric modeling space.

Table 1: Workflow of 3D raw point cloud data processing

Step 1	**Step 2**	**Step 3**
	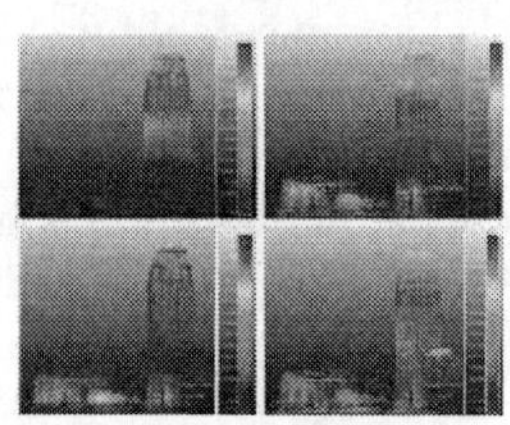	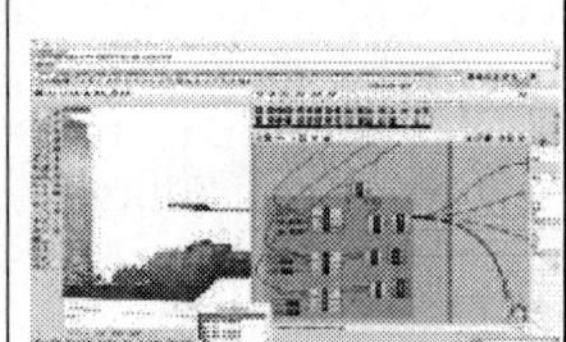
DEM, AHN	**Cloud Compare (CC)**	**Rhino+Grasshopper**
Site selection: - set type of data. - specify density of points. - import the selected data. - the data format is .laz	Data conversion: - trim the boundary of site - filter the outlier of points - convert to scalar field value - the data format is .e57	Development of design framework: - import .e57 file - make a classification of objects included ground level and relevant facades - generate reference plan for each surrounding building

		- run the meshing process - set the solar envelope simulation based on selected objects and variables.

4. Application of Case Studies

This paper constructs the solar envelope generation technique by making use of extension concepts from Capeluto & Shaviv (1997) considering two design principles "solar right envelope" and "solar collection envelope." The needs of obtaining sun access in our building (the proposed envelope) would be adjusted by following the floor level of surrounding buildings that we have set. This floor level will determine the maximum height of generated envelope in the design framework during a predefined period. It also simultaneously assigns the obtained envelope does not violate sun access for the neighboring buildings or the so-called "solar right envelope." As a result, the surrounding area where is located below the established floor level will get a shadow.

To some extent, the surrounding border can also be used to govern the lowest possible surface of our building (the proposed envelope) that could have sun access without being obstructed by the adjacent buildings. Afterwards, the defined surface could be used to determine position of the window and potential solar collector in our design or the so-called "solar collection envelope." However, the area located below the generated envelope surface will not get the sun access. As an architect, we should be able to explore and to maximize design possibilities of our designated envelope by constructing mutual dependency with the surrounding environment.

According to above-mentioned of the basic principle of solar envelope, we selected several parameters that could be relevant to our case study in this paper. Three considered parameters including in the design framework are climate, urban rules or zoning regulation, and surrounding environment (see Fig.2)

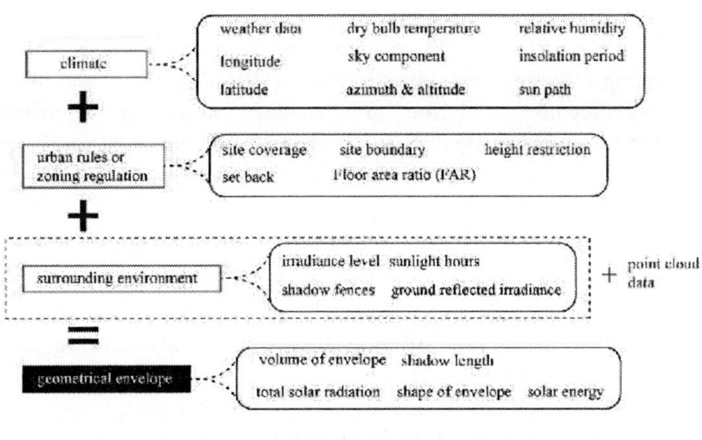

Figure 2: Parameters of Solar Envelope

In respect to these parameters, this paper extracted the climate data by using default formulation from Netherlands climate dataset. The selected site is 16,5 m x 42 m, which is located between the wide-span and high-rise building. The design simulation then sets the cut-off times during the period from June 1st to December 31st between 9 am and 10 pm. All connected variables in the design framework (see Fig.3) parametrically generate the solar envelope surface both solar rights and solar collection. According to this design framework, we enable to explore certain scenarios of design possibilities by making use of point cloud data.

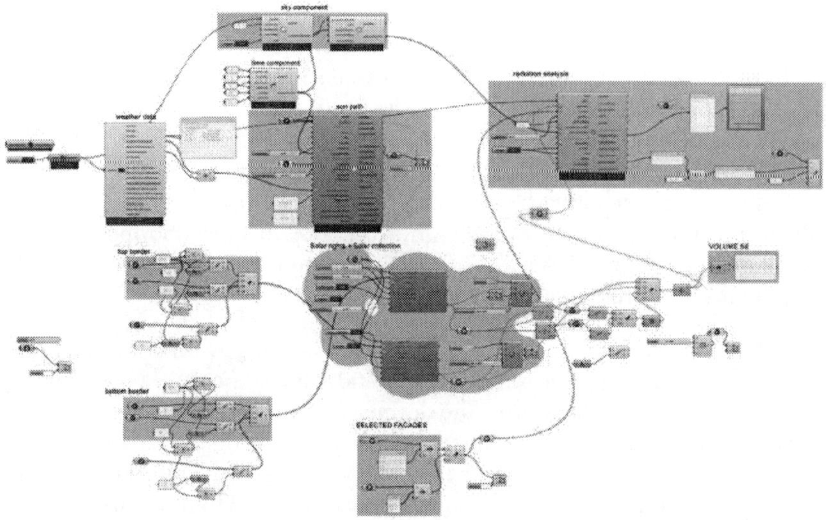

Figure 3: Design framework

As a set of data structure, point clouds is assigned as the detached of three-dimensional location (XYZ coordinates) that can have auxiliary metadata (WHITE 2013). Typically, it represents each record of point data such as color information, intensity, and position information. In this case, the 3D point cloud contributes to enhance the value of surrounding environment parameters by giving several impacts to the geometric envelope as follows:

- Consideration of vegetation as part of surrounding site variables is able to affect the shape and volume of the designated envelope. Plants could also be counted into the protected variable to have sun rights access (DEKAY 1997) like a solar community garden. The relevant vegetation in this case study has contributed to slightly increasing the volume and the radiation value of the generated solar envelope.

- Calculation of the total solar radiation value to the generated envelope produced a different result when considering only surrounding building facades which are facing to the site rather than measuring the whole surrounding building surface.

- Utilization of sunlight hour analysis on the surrounding building facade is useful to detect the most accessible area of solar access radiation. It further helps us to extract the possibility of locating solar collector and placing windows in the building façade. Moreover, we could discover disparity of generated total radiation value between point cloud surface-based and plain modeling surface by looking at the reflected radiation vector to those surfaces. The sunlight hour analysis is also potential to define the boundary of sun access area on the ground level of the site.

- The point cloud data opens further possibilities to figure out the complex building geometry of surrounding environment such as the roof shape, ground properties, building facades and so forth. Capturing the existing building blocks through the conventional way may end with the difficulty of geometric identification because building shape could overlap each other on a particular perspective. Thus, implementation of point cloud data offers more extensive analysis platform concerning the deeply understanding of relationship between our site and the surrounding environment in the real context.

The exported point clouds from CC consists the colored scalar field based on height ramp indicator. It however still represents the unclassified cloud of points. For example, the ground level, building shape, and vegetation remained in the same entity of points. Thus, we need to make a selection and classification for the object variables. The ground points are selected first based on the vertical unit to illustrate a different geographical level. This selection will help us to classify other objects above the ground level such as trees and buildings. Once classification is completed, we employed the extracted outline from the building's boundary as a threshold to set up the maximum height of the designated solar envelope. The threshold line acts as a floor limit representing both the bottom and top border of surrounding buildings. The aims of this threshold line are to manage the area that receives shading from the surrounding buildings and to control the maximum height of the generated solar envelope.

5. Result and Discussion

According to the simulation process, we compared two modeling platform approaches between point cloud and plain modeling. Three assigned indicators are used as a benchmark to investigate the simulation result as follows: the geometrical envelope that consists of volume and shape of the envelope, the produced total radiation value by the generated solar envelope, and the calculation of sunlight hours on the surrounding building facades.

Table 2: Comparison of total sunlight hours and radiation value between two model approaches

Plain model-based	**Total sunlight hours (n hours)**	**Deviation area* (m^2)**	**Total radiation (kWh)**
Building facade A (wide span)	27.476,68	161,888	248.328
Building facade B (high rise)	129.187,77	12,627	207.756
Selected site (ground level)	29.324,46	5,879	72.274,11
Point cloud-based	**Total sunlight hours (n hours)**	**Deviation area* (m^2)**	**Total radiation (kWh)**
Building facade A (wide span)	18.236,16	0,00785	51.822,194
Building facade B (high rise)	47.040,23	4,45021	114.613,314
Selected site (ground level)	17.387,45	0,9853	45.552,12

*deviation area represents the total area that receives sunlight hours and then divided by the calculated area that collects sun access smaller than 8.5 hours (desirable hours).

The simulation result in the Table 2 demonstrates significant disparities of radiation value between two different modeling platforms. There are two aspects taken into account in the existing area: the building facades and the selected site at the ground level. The plain modeling illustrates that the total sunlight hours and the received total radiation are inclined to produce the excessive value compared to the point cloud modeling-based. This is because the point vectors reflect in a perpendicular direction to the designated surface. Thus, the plain surface could collect a large number of total solar reflections which may affect the further design analysis.

On the other hand, the generated triangular irregular networks (TIN) surface from point clouds data illustrates the uneven surface morphology. The TIN surface basically constructs topographic depth referring to dissemination and the density of original point data. As such, the point vectors spread in a random direction by following the surface morphology. The projection of this mechanism navigates to more accountable results in terms of radiation analysis. The result in particular deals with the surface modeling platform that becomes crucial variable in the envelope generation process.

This paper moreover examines comparative analysis between the plain modeling and the point cloud data-based. We measured two simulation indicators: the total volume of generated envelope and the total radiation value. Each modeling platform is assigned by three scenarios based on the different level of threshold. These thresholds basically correspond to up and bottom level of the selected surrounding objects. The up level indicates the solar collection boundary and the bottom level refers to the solar rights boundary. In this case, the thresholds of the plain modeling are set only to account the surrounding building forms that include wide span and high rise building. By exploiting the point cloud data however we could set vegetation in the site as additional border variable. This means that we consider sun access to our building (the proposed envelope) without being blocked from the selected vegetation.

Table 3: Comparison of envelope's volume and total radiation value between two model approaches based on three different scenarios

Plain model-based	**Scenario A (m)** **Up : 50/20** **Bottom : 3/2**	**Scenario B (m)** **Up : 60/15** **Bottom : 7/5**	**Scenario C (m)** **Up: 80/10** **Bottom : 1/1**
Envelope's volume (m^3)	7.598,45	1.728,35	1.718,25
Radiation Value (kwh)	71.773,52	40.659,40	42.867,55
Simulation			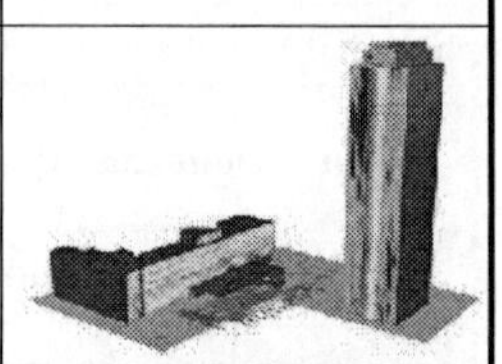
Geometrical envelope			
*up = highrise building / widespan building (meter)			

down = highrise building / widespan building (meter)

Point cloud model-based	Scenario A (m) Up : 50/20/14 Bottom : 3/2	Scenario B (m) Up : 60/15/14 Bottom : 7/5	Scenario C (m) Up: 80/10/14 Bottom : 1/1
Envelope's volume (m³)	7.658,44	1.858,60	1.779,23
Radiation Value (kWh)	94.124,96	59.469,86	49.202,94
Simulation			
Geometrical envelope			

*up = highrise building / widespan building / vegetation (meter)
down = highrise building / widespan building (meter)

According to the simulation result in Table 3, both models are nearly demonstrated the same envelope shape for the all scenarios. The largest envelope volume is illustrated by the scenario A, whereas the least dimension is obtained by the scenario C. The differentiation of these scenarios validates that the closest distance between up and bottom border will generate the greater volume. As a result, the plain modeling gains the smaller envelope volume compared to the point cloud-based. Another remarkable result is that vegetation which is considered as the up border confirms the volume alteration of the solar envelope.

Furthermore, the simulation measures radiation value for both model platforms. In this context, we account the relevant surrounding building facades in the site to obtain the more accurate result. The radiation value of point cloud model-based shows the significant upgrading. This means that the TIN surface from point cloud data has succeeded to enhance the radiation value of the generated envelope thoroughly. The result of this radiation value furthermore could encourage architects to explore more the potential information of surrounding context. In addition, architects can map the solar potential surface on the generated envelope to position the window and the interior building layout based on desirable sun access. Lastly, the simulation result is also useful to figure out the pre-determined material properties in the building surface in the conceptual design stage.

6. Conclusion

This paper generally proposes the idea of using point cloud as a context data in generating and analyzing solar envelope. The utilization of point cloud data has offered the architectural possibilities to step further into the design analysis. The important role for architects is the ability to manage the relevant site information properly in the real environment which simultaneously could enhance the accuracy of modeling simulation analysis in the conceptual design stage. Therefore, the point cloud data through color information and position information enables architect to select a certain area precisely among many objects. By using parametric design space, we could control the point cloud data more flexible that correspond to the geometrical shape of the developed design framework.

Furthermore, point cloud data has confirmed the positive contribution to the solar envelope analysis through three selected indicators: the enhancement of solar envelope volume, the total radiation value for generated envelope, and the sunlight hour analysis for the surrounding building facades. The TIN surface of point cloud data represents the extraction of surface morphology from the real building context which is assigned by the irregular surface pattern and the scattered point vectors. As a result, the total radiation and the sunlight hour value from the point cloud data shows a decreasing number compared to the plain modeling.

During the design simulation process, some acknowledged limitations of this study are addressed. For instance, the material properties from the point cloud data could not be displayed through meshing process because of extraction of the original data from DEM, AHN. Thus, design investigation of the point cloud data focuses on the utilization of point attributes such as color information and position information. Another considerable factor is the density of point that corresponds to the geometrical aspect, the accuracy of the TIN surface, and the robust information that could we extract from the data. However, the execution of the high resolution point cloud data still consumes expensive time due to a great number of hardware computer memories.

The potential fruitful areas for further research from this study are the possibilities in constructing solar energy distribution by adding multiple performance indicators such as shadow analysis, material properties, daylight factor, and other microclimate variables. This design method is expected to open a novel design framework for the future building performance analysis in the conceptual design phase. As it also responds the concept of "metabolism" Knowles by having a broad impact quality on the built environment.

Acknowledgment

This paper is part of the on-going research funded by the Indonesian Endowment Fund for Education (LPDP). We would also like to thank Ervine Lin for providing the point cloud data supporting tools in GH.

References

Drap, P., Sgrenzaroli, M., Canciani, M., Cannata, G., Seinturier, J. (2003). Laser Scanning and close range photogrammetry: Towards a single measuring tool dedicated to architecture and archaeology. In: CIPA XIXth INTERNATIONAL SYMPOSIUM, 2003, Turkey.

White, D.A. (2013). LIDAR, Point clouds, and their archaeological applications. In: Corner,D.C.,Harrower,M.J.(Eds.). Mapping Archaeological Landscapes from Space, New York: Springer Science+Business Media, pp.175-186

Dekay, M. (1997). The implications of community gardening for land use and density. In: Journal of Architectural and Planning Research. [Online] **14**(2).pp.126-149. [Accessed 27 October 2017]. Available from: https://www.jstor.org/stable/43029255

Lin, E., Shaad, K., Girot, C. (2016). Developing river rehabilitation scenarios by integrating landscape and hydrodynamic modeling for the Ciliwung River in Jakarta, Indonesia. In: Haghighat,F.(Eds.). Sustainable cities and society. [Online]. **20**.pp.180-198. [Accessed 17 October 2010]. Available from: http://www.sciencedirect.com/science/article/pii/S2210670715300378

Sanchez, V., Zakhor, A. (2012). Planar 3d modelling of building interiors from point cloud data. In: 19th IEEE International Conference on Image Processing, 2012, USA

Tamke, M., Blümel, I., Ochmann, S., Vock, R., Wessel, R. (2014). From point clouds to definitions of architectural space. In: Thompson,E.M.(Eds.). Fusion - Proceedings of the 32nd eCAADe Conference - Volume 2, Newcastle Upon Tyne:eCAADe, pp.557-566

Alsadik, B., Gerke, M., Vosselman, G. (2014). Visibility analysis of point cloud in close range photogrammetry. In: ISPRS Annals of the Photogrammetry, Remote Sensing and Spatial Information Sciences, 2014, Italy

Fujita, Y., Kobayashi, I., Chanseawrassamee, W., Hoshino, Y. (2014). Application of attributed road surface point cloud data in road maintenance. In: Journal of Japan Society of Civil Engineers, Ser. F3 (Civil Engineering Informatics).[Online].**70**(2).pp.I_185-I_192. [Accessed 24 October 2016]. Available from: https://www.jstage.jst.go.jp/article/jscejcei/70/2/70_I_185/_article

Shih, NJ., Wu, MJ. (2005). A 3D point-cloud-based verification of as-built construction progress. In: the CAAD futures 2005 conference, 2005, Vienna

Knowles, RL. (1974). Energy and form: an ecological approach to urban growth. Cambridge: MIT Press

Capeluto, I.G., Shaviv, E. (1997). Modeling the design of urban fabric with Solar rights considerations. In: Solar World Congress, ISES International Energy Society, Korea.

Ratti, C., Morello, E. (2005). SunScapes: extending the 'solar envelopes' concept through 'iso-solar surfaces'. In: PLEA2005 - The 22nd Conference on Passive and Low Energy Architecture. 2005, Lebanon

AHN Netherlands 2017, accessed 26 March 2017, <http://www.ahn.nl/>

Zwierzycki, M., Evers, H.L., Tamke, M., (2016) Parametric Architectural Design with Point-clouds – Volvox. In Herneoja, Aulikki; Toni Österlund and Piia Markkanen (eds.), Complexity & Simplicity - Proceedings of the 34th eCAADe Conference - Volume 2, University of Oulu, Oulu, Finland, 22-26 August 2016, pp. 673-682

Collaborative BIM Reconstruction on Mobile Consumer Devices

Steffen Franz, Robert Irmler, Uwe Rüppel
Technische Universität Darmstadt, Germany
franz@iib.tu-darmstadt.de

Abstract. This paper presents an approach for real-time web-based collaborative generation and visualization of 'as-built' BIM content based on Google Tango enabled devices. A client-server system was developed that allows for the collection and distribution of multi-sensor based indoor scan data. The server application assembles and aggregates scan data of multiple Tango devices and applies the data stream to a post-processing pipeline to detect rooms, walls and openings. The processed data is then distributed to all clients. On the client side, the aggregated scan data is merged into an envelope model of the investigated building and visualized in real-time. The system allows for a self-sufficient reconstruction of multi-room indoor scenes and enables on-site collaboration in real-time. These features make the system especially useful in situations that are time-critical and require concurrent collection and processing of data. Our targeted use cases include search and rescue scenarios, on-site construction progress tracking and crime scene documentation.

1. Introduction

The comprehensive digital representation of a building provides a great source for computational analysis, optimization and building operation. In recent years, the concepts and technologies of Building Information Modelling (BIM) have been adopted by a great share of the Architecture, Engineering and Construction (AEC) industry worldwide. Although Building Information Models are mostly created during the planning and design phase of construction projects, there is an increasing demand for 'as-built' building model reconstructions. The 3D reconstruction of semantically rich building models opens up a wide range of application possibilities ranging from the preservation of architectural knowledge (Beetz et al., 2016) to the forensic documentation of crime scenes (Franz et al., 2015). Buck et al. (2013) and Komar et al. (2012) for example, utilize a 3D crime scene reconstruction for documentation purposes and emphasis the resulting benefits for presentations and reenactments in court, testing theories or examining witness statements.

In this work, we focus on exploiting the advantages of next-generation mobile devices for the reconstruction of 'as-built' building models. Next-generation mobile phones and tablets combine multi-modal sensor technologies with significant computing power (Google Tango III, 2017). This provides the opportunity to develop self-sufficient indoor reconstruction systems that are capable of acquiring, processing and sharing scan data in real-time. Based on the Google Tango Technology we present an approach for real-time web-based collaborative generation and visualization of 'as-built' BIM content. A client-server system was developed that allows for the collection and distribution of multi-sensor based indoor scan data. The server application assembles and aggregates scan data of multiple Tango enabled devices and applies the data stream to a post-processing pipeline to detect rooms, walls and openings. The processed data is then distributed to all clients. On the client side, the aggregated scan data is merged into an envelope model of the investigated building and visualized in real-time. The system allows for a self-sufficient reconstruction of multi-room indoor scenes and enables on-site collaboration in real-time. These features make the framework especially useful in situations that are time-critical and require concurrent collection and processing of data. Our targeted use cases include search and rescue (SAR) scenarios, on-site construction progress tracking and crime scene documentation.

This paper consists of five sections including the introduction. Section 2 presents a brief review of methods targeting the reconstruction of 'as-built' building models. Section 3 provides an overview of the client-server architecture and elaborates on the collaborative workflow. In Section 4 we present our approach on adding semantic depth to the model by detecting rooms, walls and openings within the scan data. Finally, Section 5 summarizes conclusions and discusses topics for further research.

2. Related Work

The necessity for the digital reconstruction of cities and buildings arises from various application areas e.g., urban planning, pollution forecasting or disaster management. Over the past two decades the technologies for the digital reconstruction of our environment advanced rapidly.

Spatial data at city scale is usually collected via airborne LiDAR systems (Wu et al., 2017; Sohn et al., 2008). To improve data quality, the fusion of different data sources like images and GIS data has also been considered (Suveg et al. 2003). For the outdoor reconstruction of single buildings, stationary laser scanners (Previtali et al., 2014) and image-based techniques (Koch et al., 2016, Strecha et al., 2014, Schindler K., 2003) have been proven to be suitable. While the reconstruction of outdoor settings and exterior building geometries has already been well-researched and published, the robust reconstruction of complete indoor scenes remains a particularly challenging problem. Indoor environments often exhibit high levels of clutter and occlusion which can lead to noise, artifacts and missing data. Reliable indoor reconstruction methods therefore have to be particularly tolerant to missing data, occlusion and highly reflecting surfaces like windows. Prior work on this subject shows a great variety of different approaches each of which displays strengths and weaknesses. Many indoor reconstruction systems require substantial hardware setups (Ochmann et al., 2015; Turner et al., 2015; Corso et al., 2013), rely on user interaction (Du et al., 2011) or only generate meshed geometries, i.e. do not identify individual building elements, and therefore lack semantic depth (Yue H., 2014; Henry et al., 2012). Many of these techniques have been based on laser scanning and image processing methods (Ochmann et al., 2015; Okorn et al., 2010, Cabral et al., 2014; Furukawa B., 2009). In recent years, with the availability of consumer depth sensor devices, an additional research and application field emerged. Consumer depth cameras like the Microsoft Kinect or the Google Tango provide a cost-effective way to gather 3D measurements of the environment (Franz et al., 2015; Zhou et al., 2014; Newcombe et al., 2011). However, such devices do not themselves solve the underlying problems to extract higher-level models from the acquired raw point cloud data. The depth-camera-based collection of indoor point cloud data requires the camera to globally register a series of views along a complex trajectory and at the same time manage odometry drifts. Prior work on scene reconstruction with consumer depth cameras focused mainly on reconstructing a detailed mesh of the scanned environment (Yue H., 2014; Henry et al., 2012), rather than generating a semantically enriched building model composed of detected building elements (e.g. rooms, walls, openings).

Most of the current work in the field of indoor reconstruction focuses on achieving a high accuracy of scans and reconstructed geometry. Time aspects, hardware costs or computation resources are often of subordinate importance. Furthermore, the acquisition and the processing of the scan data is usually done on separate devices. This is a technology break which further limits the applicability of these approaches and excludes certain use cases where an immediate utilization of scan data is required. Applications that are time-critical and require the concurrent collection and processing of data can therefore hardly profit from these developments. Only little research has been conducted regarding the on-site semantically rich reconstruction of indoor environments. The same applies to research regarding the speed-up of the scanning and reconstruction process by using a collaborative approach. We therefore propose a method for an on-site real-time collaborative reconstruction of multi-room indoor scenes at low costs and with sufficient accuracy for the stated use cases.

3. A Framework for Collaborative BIM Reconstruction

Next-generation mobile devices like the Google Yellowstone tablet or the Lenovo Phab2 Pro provide the opportunity to collect and process scan data on a single mobile device. The combination of multi-modal data acquisition capabilities and mobile computing power makes these devices particularly suitable for tasks where mobile on-site processing of scan data is required. By connecting these devices to the web, it is further possible to share and combine information in real-time.

An example for a use case that could profit from such a system is the documentation of fire investigation sites (Franz et al., 2015). The immediate preservation of all available information at the scene is critical to the following investigation. This is especially true if the site is exposed to external influences, i.e. the weather. Today, stationary or mobile laser scanners are often used to produce a 3D model of the scene that can provide further evaluation possibilities. However, to make use of the 3D scan data, it has to be transferred to a computing device and processed by specialized software. Meanwhile, evidence is mainly collected in form of pictures, videos, sketches, notes and voice-recordings. Traditionally these distributed pieces of information have to be connected manually. Using a mobile device that provides a live reconstruction of its environment would allow for a direct annotation and localization of evidence within the scene. By instantly sharing this information over a network it would further be possible to have external experts participating 'live' in the documentation process. This approach is of course not limited to the documentation of fire investigation sites. For example, other targeted use cases include search and rescue (SAR) scenarios, on-site construction progress tracking and crime scene documentation.

3.1 Software Architecture

Our framework for collaborative BIM reconstruction is based on a client-server architecture that consists of four major components. The component model is shown in Figure 1.

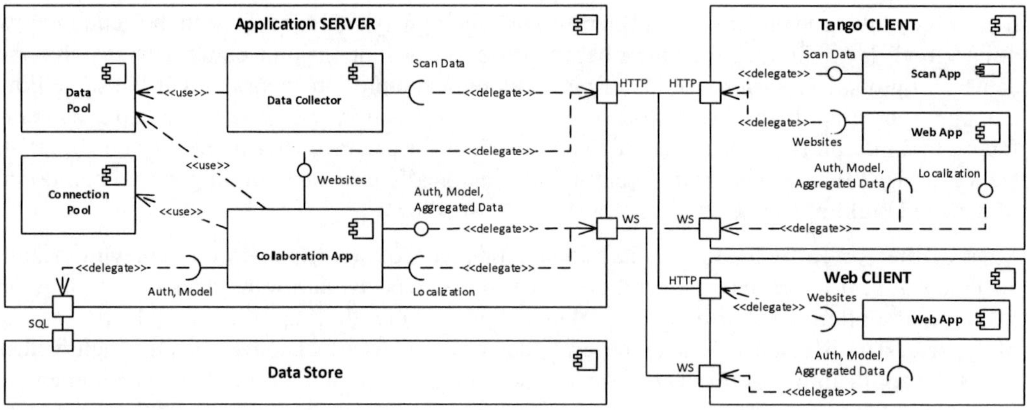

Figure 1: Component Model of the Collaboration Framework

Application Server. The central component is a simple Node.js server. The server provides static content (web sites), manages all client connections (Collaboration App) and acts as the central data receiver (Data Collector). Data received from Tango clients is processed and stored in a data pool. The Collaboration App distributes the data to all requesting clients.

Data Store. Session data and geospatial building models (CityGML) are stored in a central data base. The CityGML models provide the envelope geometry of a building which is later merged with the reconstructed indoor geometry.

Tango Client. A Tango client is a Tango device equipped with a specially developed android application. The application consists of two components, the Scan App and the Web App. The Scan App handles the scanning process through the Tango API and continuously posts collected data to the server. The Web App is a JavaScript application that includes a WebGL viewer. We are currently using the free Autodesk Forge Viewer as it provides convenient rendering capabilities and a comprehensive API. The Web App is used to initially localize the Tango device within the building envelope of the investigated site. It further receives the aggregated and processed scan data and visualizes it in real-time. For a better understanding of the recorded scene, we merge the reconstructed floor plan data with a CityGML (LoD2) model of the investigated building. The user interface of a Tango client is shown in Figure 3.

Web Client. The web client can be seen as a standalone version of the Web App. It only requires a web browser that supports WebGL. On the initial web site a user can pick a CityGML building by clicking on a map location. This opens the WebGL viewer which then displays the building envelope geometry and integrates all available scan data for this building in real-time.

3.2 Collaborative BIM Reconstruction

Figure 2 describes the basic communication sequence to realize a collaborative reconstruction of an indoor scene.

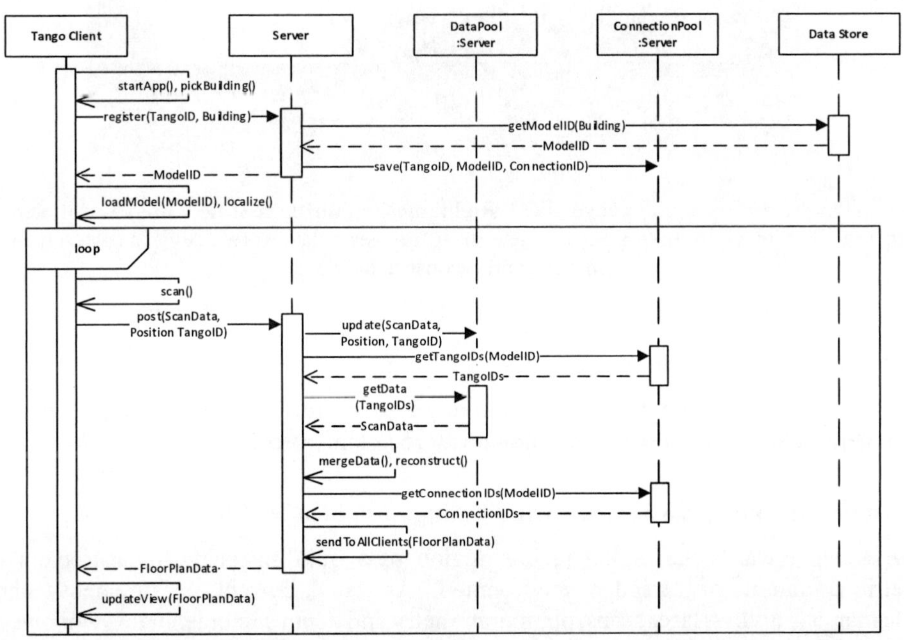

Figure 2: Sequence Diagram of the Client-Server Communication (Tango Client)

The process starts with the user picking the building where the scan should take place. Even though our current implementation assumes that a CityGML model of the investigated building is available, this is not a mandatory requirement. The client then registers with the server which saves the connection details and returns the model ID for the picked building. After loading the envelope model of the building into the viewer the user is required to pick the start location of the scan. This allows for the correct alignment of envelope and indoor geometry later in the process. After the scan has been started the application continuously posts the current scan data, which is provided by the Tango API, to the server. The server stores the scan data in the data pool and links it to the device ID ('Tango ID'). To enable collaboration, the server application then searches the connection pool for all connections that refer to clients which registered for viewing or scanning the same building, i.e. requested the same model ID. All available scan data for the particular model ID is merged and applied to the post processing pipeline to acquire a reconstructed floor plan. Afterwards, the reconstructed geometry data is send to all related clients via web socket connections. Back on the client-side the web application listens for incoming data and continuously updates the model view. This process enables the collaborative scanning of an indoor scene and provides instant feedback and availability of reconstructed geometry information. Figure 3 shows the user interface of the developed Tango application.

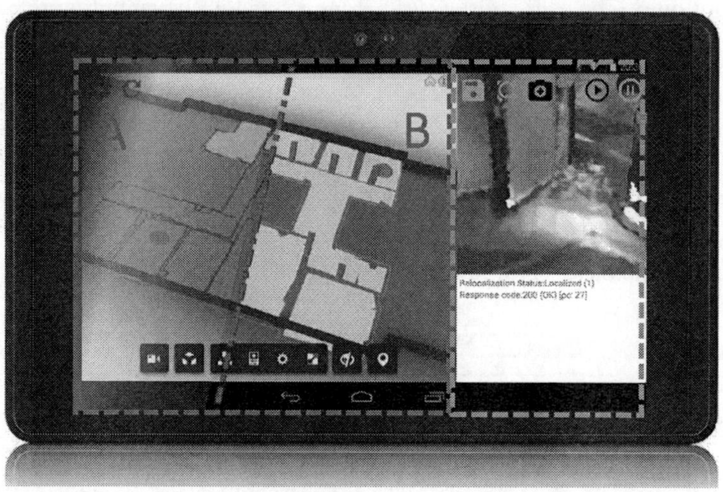

Figure 3: User Interface of the Tango client; Right: mesh of the current field of view, UI elements; Left: WebGL viewer (Autodesk Forge Viewer), A: raw scan data of two devices (blue/green), B: merged and reconstructed data

4. Reconstruction of Building Elements

This section describes the hardware setup used to perform scans of multi-room indoor environments and discusses the succeeding post processing steps.

4.1 Scanning Indoor Environments with a Tango Enabled Mobile Device

The first step towards the digital reconstruction of a building is the measurement of the geometric conditions of the indoor environment. As stated, current measurement techniques include manual surveys, laser scans, photogrammetry and depth cameras. In this work we utilize the Google Tango technology. Tango enabled devices are composed of dedicated hard- and software modules that allow for a cost effective scanning of indoor environments. In this work we used the Google 'Yellowstone' Development Kit (Android 4.4.2, Tango SDK 1.53) and the Lenovo Phab2 Pro (Android 6.0.1, Tango SDK 1.53) which is the first – and currently only – Tango enabled consumer device.

When scanning the environment, a Tango device is able to navigate fully autonomous via visual odometry and is therefore completely independent of any indoor navigation infrastructure like Bluetooth beacons, Wi-Fi or ultra-wideband. The lack of an external reference however makes the device prone to drift errors which might even increase over time. To compensate this effect a Tango device is capable of self-adjusting its position and orientation every time a loop closure is detected. Furthermore, the device can store a description of the scanned area, a so-called Area Description File (ADF). This enables the user to re-localize within a previously learned area. This procedure can be used to extend a previous scan or to share localization information between multiple users to collaboratively work on one site. The 3D image sensor of the Tango is based on Infineon's IRS1645C chip and uses a Time-of-Flight (ToF) measuring principle to create a 3D image with a resolution of 224 x 172 pixels. The sensor chip has a range of up to 4 meters (13 feet) and a measuring accuracy of 1 percent of the distance (Google Tango II, 2017). The Tango SDK delivers a support library to reconstruct meshes from the recorded pose and point cloud data. Aside from reconstructing a geometry mesh the software further provides methods to generate an approximate floor plan of the scene (Keralia et al., 2014; Google Tango I, 2017). The reconstructed floor plan data consist of two-dimensional polygons, each of which represents the coarse perimeter of a space.

When scanning walls and floors, the quality of detected indoor perimeters is often heavily affected by occlusion and clutter. To compensate this effect and to improve scan results Previtali et al. (2014) suggested the utilization of ceiling scan data because these building parts are usually less affected by occlusion. Nevertheless, the detection of building elements like rooms, walls and openings still requires a dedicated post processing of the scan data.

4.2 Post Processing and Reconstruction

Because this work targets the real-time processing of indoor scan data, the developed post processing pipeline only consists of simple geometric operations in 2-dimensional space to reduce computation time. Figure 4 shows the different steps of the pipeline.

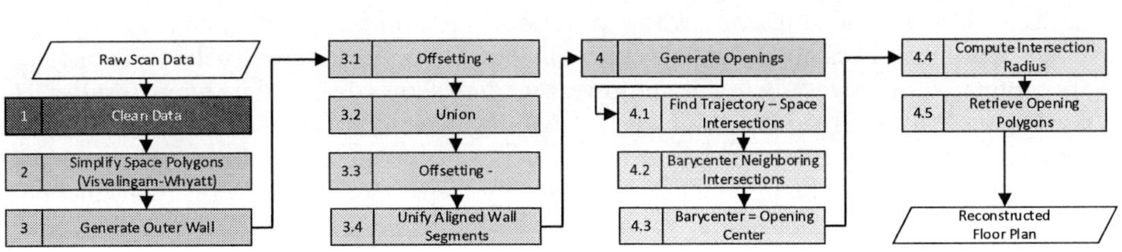

Figure 4: Flow-Chart of Post Processing Pipeline

Step 1: Clean Data. Scan data usually consist of the desired information and undesired artifacts. Artifacts originate for example from measurement errors. The Tango devices use a 3D ToF camera which is vulnerable to reflecting surfaces like windows, picture frames or mirrors. Falsely detected spaces are usually small and can be eliminated by a threshold for a minimum size of a space.

Step 2: Simplify Space Polygons. Scan data often shows low precession in occluded or not fully coverable areas and approximated space boundaries appear blurry and uneven. Before such data can be further processed it needs to be smoothed. Therefore, we apply the

Visvalingam-Whyatt algorithm (Visvalingam & Whyatt, 1993) on each polygon to achieve more regular space boundaries.

Step 3: Generate Outer Wall. By applying offsets and Boolean operations on the simplified space polygons, we approximate the outer contour of the limiting walls of the scene. This process breaks down to four steps. First, a positive convex offset is applied to all polygons. The offset amount is chosen reasonably high, so that it can be ensured that buffers of neighboring polylines overlap and artifacts are avoided. The buffered polygons are then unified which results in a rough contour of the scanned scene. Afterwards, another, this time negative, offset is applied to achieve a reasonable wall thickness. Lastly, all wall segments whose alignments do not differ more than a certain threshold from each other are being unified to achieve a more consistent description of the scene.

Step 4: Generate Openings. The trajectory of the scanning process is used to determine candidates for openings. Intersections between the trajectory and space boundaries are considered locations where openings have to be placed. We assume a standard opening width and place them evenly between neighboring points of intersection.

4.3 Test Results and Discussion

To validate our approach we chose three sites that are typical for the targeted application areas. The first site is an apartment of a late 19th century townhouse ('Apartment 1'), the second one is a flat in a 1990s residential building ('Apartment 2') and the third test environment is a floor in an office building that was built in the 1960s ('Office'). All three test sites offer a variety of common challenges for indoor reconstruction, like occluded areas, reflecting surfaces and walls that do not comply with the Manhattan Assumption.

Figures 5 to 7 show the different post processing steps for our test cases and should be understood as follows: a) Raw space polygons from Tango reconstruction procedure; b) Cleaned space polygons; c) Simplified space polygons; d) Offsetting; e) Reconstructed outer wall contour; f) Opening reconstruction; g) Reconstructed floor plan consisting of rooms, walls and openings; h) CAD plan based on manual surveying.

We can see that the post processing pipeline is able to reliably detect rooms, walls and openings. The quality of the reconstructed geometry is thereby strongly influenced by the quality of the scan data. It is noticeable that the whole process is very time-efficient. The scanning of an average apartment takes about half an hour. The smoothing and reconstruction of space and wall contours still leaves room for improvement but shows reasonably good results. The Visvalingam-Whyatt algorithm achieves a satisfying generalization of the geometry while keeping the typology and main features of the raw space polygons intact. However, the parameters that control the different post processing steps, like the generalization tolerance, buffers and intersection radiuses, are currently based on experience and can therefore not be expected to be always robust.

We further validated our scan and reconstruction results against manually conducted measurements. Some statistics and evaluations are given in Table 1. Area deviations between reconstructed and manually measured space geometries vary between 4 and 14 percent. The minimum deviation of - 3.76 % occurred for test site 'Office' and a maximum deviation of - 13.70 % occurred for the test site 'Apartment 1'. In most cases the reconstructed geometry shows smaller area values. It seems likely that such deviations are caused by occlusions and noise created by windows and big furniture objects like wall units and curtains.

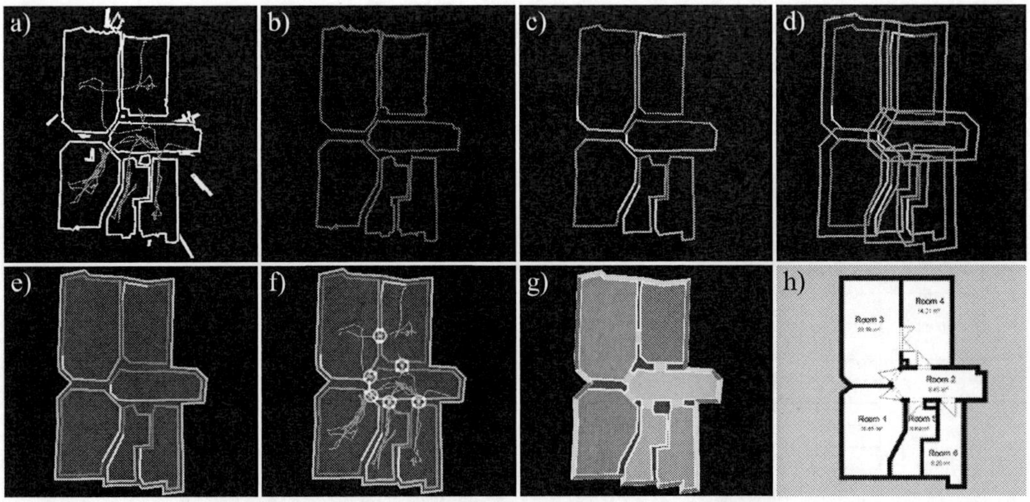

Figure 1: Post processing steps of the test site 'Apartment 1'

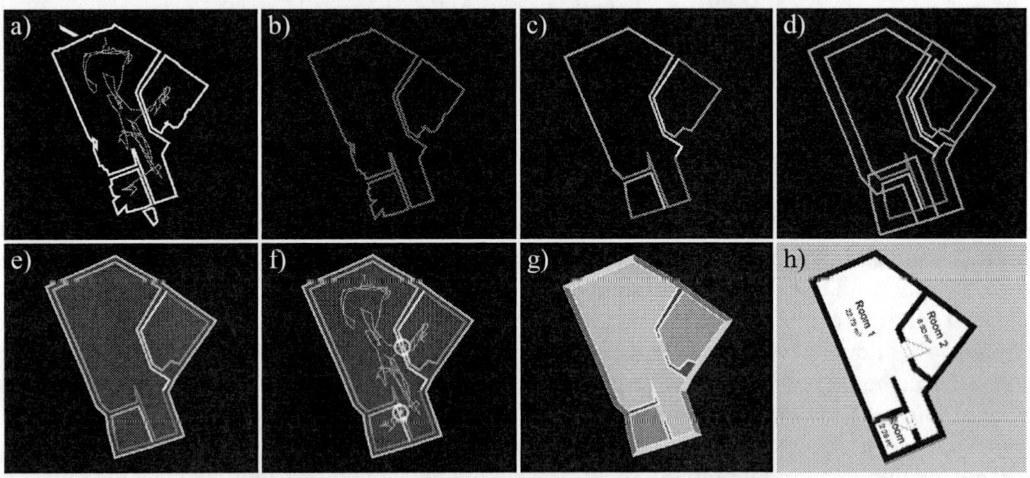

Figure 2: Post processing steps of the test site 'Apartment 2'

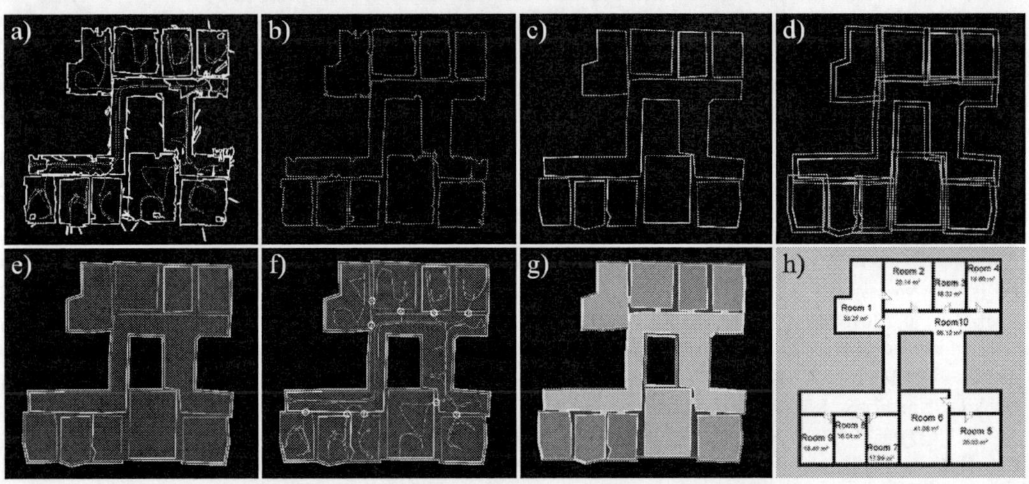

Figure 3: Post processing steps of the test site 'Office'

Table 1: Statistics and Validation for Test Sites

Site	Room No.	Raw Scan		Reconstructed		Manual Surveying		Deviation	
		Area [m²]	Σ	Area [m²]	Σ	Area [m²]	Σ	Raw Scan to Manual Surveying	Reconstructed to Manual Surveying
Apartment 1	1	14.07	64.41	14.03	64.11	16.55	74.29	-13.30%	-13.70%
	2	7.80		7.90		8.45			
	3	17.79		17.60		20.19			
	4	11.10		11.17		14.21			
	5	5.93		5.68		6.69			
	6	7.72		7.73		8.20			
Apartment 2	1	23.71	32.76	23.95	32.95	22.07	31.28	+ 4.73%	+ 5.34%
	2	6.45		6.41		6.30			
	3	2.60		2.59		2.28			
Office	1	30.02	305.75	30.51	306.10	33.27	318.05	-3.87%	-3.76%
	2	24.83		24.26		28.14			
	3	17.82		16.40		18.32			
	4	17.88		17.86		18.80			
	5	25.85		24.69		28.83			
	6	40.19		39.93		41.08			
	7	17.03		16.53		17.99			
	8	17.87		17.45		18.04			
	9	17.75		18.45		18.46			
	10	96.51		100.02		95.12			

5. Conclusion and Outlook

In this paper we presented an approach for real-time web-based collaborative generation and visualization of 'as-built' BIM content based on Google Tango enabled devices. A client-server system was developed that allows for the collection and distribution of multi-sensor based indoor scan data. A post-processing pipeline was developed that is capable of reliably detecting rooms, walls and openings. The system was tested on three test sites and proved to be robust against common challenges regarding the reconstruction of indoor environments. The presented framework allows for a self-sufficient reconstruction of multi-room indoor scenes and enables on-site collaboration in real-time. These features make the system especially useful in situations that are time-critical and require concurrent collection and processing of data. To the best of our knowledge, this work is the first attempt to enable real-time collaboration based on a live reconstruction of an indoor environment. We acknowledge that our approach is still subject to some limitations. In particular, the parameters that control the post-processing pipeline are based on experience and might not always be reliable. There are also still open questions regarding the geometric alignment of reconstructed data and pre-existing envelope models (e.g. CityGML). At this point the user has to manually pick the initial start position of the scan within the building footprint. This is not a very precise solution and should be improved in the future. Therefore, we see the current implementation as a first step towards a collaborative platform that goes beyond simple geometric reconstructions. Future work will include the implementation of a learning algorithm for parameter estimation and the detection of other scene objects.

References

Beetz J. et al. (2016) Enrichment and Preservation of Architectural Knowledge. In: Münster S., Pfarr-Harfst M., Kuroczyński P., Ioannides M. (eds) 3D Research Challenges in Cultural Heritage II. Lecture Notes in Computer Science, vol 10025. Springer, Cham.

Buck U., Naether S., Räss B., Jackowski C., and Thali M. J. (2013) Accident or Homicide – Virtual Crime Scene Reconstruction Using 3D Methods. Forensic Science International 225, no. 1–3.

Cabral R. and Furukawa Y. (2014) Piecewise planar and compact floorplan reconstruction from images. In CVPR.

Corso N. and Zakhor A. (2013) Indoor localization algorithms for an ambulatory human operated 3D mobile mapping system. Remote Sensing, 5(12).

Du H.,Henry P., Ren X., Cheng M., Goldman D. B., Seitz S. M., and Fox D. (2011) Interactive 3D modeling of indoor environments with a consumer depth camera. In UbiComp.

Franz S. & Rüppel U. (2015) Supporting forensic fire cause analysis with next generation mobile devices by assembling a BIM based on multiple integrated sensor data. In: Proceedings of the 22nd EG-ICE International Workshop, 13.-15. July 2015, Eindhoven, Netherland.

Furukawa Y., Curless B., Seitz S. M., and Szeliski R. (2009) Reconstructing building interiors from images. In ICCV.

Google Tango I (2017) https://developers.google.com/tango/ Accessed: 2017-04-20.

Google Tango II (2015) http://www.infineon.com/cms/en/about-infineon/press/market-news/2015/INFATV 201512-017.html Accessed: 2017-04-20.

Google Tango III (2017) https://get.google.com/tango/ Accessed: 2017-04-20.

Yue H., Chen W., Wu X. and Liu J. (2014) Fast 3D modeling in complex environments using a single Kinect sensor, Optics and Lasers in Engineering, Volume 53, Pages 104–111.

Henry P., Krainin M., Herbst E., Ren X., and Fox D. (2012) RGB-D Mapping: Using Kinect-Style Depth Cameras for Dense 3D Modeling of Indoor Environments. The International Journal of Robotics Research 31, no. 5, 647–663.

Keralia D, Khyati K.Vyas and Deulkar K. (2014) Google Project Tango – A Convenient 3D Modeling Device. In: International Journal of Current Engineering and Technology, Vol.4, No.5 (Oct 2014)

Koch, Tobias, Körner, Marco and Fraundorfer, Friedrich (2016) Automatic Alignment of Indoor and Outdoor Building Models using 3D Line Segments. In: Proceedings of Computer Vision and Pattern Recognition 2016, Seiten 10-18. IEEE Xplore. Conference on Computer Vision and Pattern Recognition, 27-30 June 2016, Las Vegas, USA.

Komar D. A., Davy-Jow S., and Decker S. J. (2012) The Use of a 3-D Laser Scanner to Document Ephemeral Evidence at Crime Scenes and Postmortem Examinations. Journal of Forensic Sciences 57, no. 1.

Newcombe R. A., Izadi S., Hilliges O., Molyneaux D., Kim D., Davison A. J., Kohli P., Shotton J., Hodges S., and Fitzgibbon A.. (2011) KinectFusion: Real-time dense surface mapping and tracking. In ISMAR.

Ochmann S., Vock R., Wessel R. and Klein R. (2015) Automatic reconstruction of parametric building models from indoor point clouds. In: Computers & Graphics, Volume 54, February 2016, Pages 94–103.

Okorn B., Xiong X., Akinci B. and Huber D. (2010) Toward Automated Modeling of Floor Plans.

Previtali M., Scaioni M., Barazzetti L. and Brumana R. (2014) A flexible methodology for outdoor/indoor building reconstruction from occluded point clouds, ISPRS Ann. Photogramm. Remote Sens. Spatial Inf. Sci., II-3, 119-126, doi:10.5194/isprsannals-II-3-119-2014.

Previtali M., Barazzetti L., Brumana and R. Scaioni M. (2014) Towards automatic indoor reconstruction of cluttered building rooms from point clouds. In: ISPRS Annals of the Photogrammetry, Remote Sensing and Spatial Information Sciences, Volume II-5.

Schindler K. (2003) A Model-Based Method For Building Reconstruction. In Proc. of the International Conference on Computer Vision workshop on Higher-Level Knowledge in 3D Modeling and Motion (HLK'03).

Sohn G.; Huang X., Tao V. (2008) Using a binary space partitioning tree for reconstructing polyhedral building models from airborne lidar data. Photogramm. Eng. Remote Sens. 74, 1425–1438.

Strecha C., Krull M. and Betschart S. (2014) The Chillon Project: Aerial/Terrestrial and Indoor Integration. https://support.pix4d.com/hc/en-us/articles/202557199-Scientific-White-Paper-The-Chillon-Project-Aerial-Terrestrialand-Indoor-Integration. Accessed: 2017-04-20.

Suveg I. &Vosselman G. (2003) Reconstruction of 3D building models from aerial images and maps. In: ISPRS Journal of Photogrammetry and Remote Sensing, Volume 58, Issues 3–4, January 2004, Pages 202–224

Turner E., Cheng P., and Zakhor, A. (2015) Fast, automated, scalable generation of textured 3D models of indoor environments. IEEE Journal of Selected Topics in Signal Processing, 9(3).

Visvalingam, M. & Whyatt, J.D. (1993) Line generalization by repeated elimination of points. Cartogr. J. 30, 46–51.

Wu B., Yu B., Wu Q., Yao S., Zhao F., Mao W., Wu J. (2017) A Graph-Based Approach for 3D Building Model Reconstruction from Airborne LiDAR Point Clouds. Remote Sens. 9, 92.

Zhou Q.-Y. and Koltun V. (2014) Color map optimization for 3D reconstruction with consumer depth cameras. ACM Transactions on Graphics, 33(4).

Construction Health and Safety Management – a Methodological Review Towards a Smart and Holistic Approach

Shang Gao, Haijiang LI
Cardiff University, United Kingdom
lih@cardiff.ac.uk

Abstract. Despite the significant efforts working on the improvement of safety performance on construction site, the statistics of injury, illness and fatality occurred still indicate that Health and Safety (H&S) issue remains a serious problem worldwide. Current H&S management approaches are often based on inaccurate and incomplete data, leading to information silos and single objective decision making. Therefore, devising new preventive strategies to manage H&S in an effective and holistic manner is indispensable for construction H&S management. The emerging Building Information Modelling (BIM) promotes life cycle accurate and comprehensive data and information reuse through life cycle standardization across domains. The recent development in knowledge engineering, e.g. ontology modeling, can provide a new way to extract domain knowledge and link different domains together to form up a smart decision making engine. Ontology has been widely used in health care, smart energy, but not yet fully investigated by construction H&S sector. This paper therefore reviews the abovementioned topics with an aim to provide an overall understanding for smart and holistic construction H&S management, hence to propose a roadmap for the future development.

1. Introduction

During the last few decades, construction industry has witnessed a rapid growth all around the world, especially in developing countries (Bryde, Broquetas et al. 2013). Because of the complexity and uncertainties inherent in the nature of the construction site (Malekitabar, Ardeshir et al. 2016), construction industry always has the bad reputation of accidents with high frequency and diverse hazard sources (Zhou, Goh et al. 2015). Therefore, devising new preventive strategies to manage H&S in an effective and holistic manner is indispensable for construction safety management (Koehn and Datta 2003).

However, current construction H&S management are often based on inaccurate and incomplete data, leading to an error-prone process. Experts identify possible risks based on their individual expertise along with design information that is normally provided in 2D construction drawings and schedules. Additionally, H&S is normally managed separately from the construction management (Hare, Cameron et al. 2006).
In summary, current construction H&S management are lack of (1) comprehensive and accurate data sets, information and knowledge that can be dynamically updated throughout life cycle; (2) smart ways to make a holistic decision by leveraging the inter-connected relevant sectors.

The emerging Building Information Modelling (BIM) promotes life cycle accurate and comprehensive data and information reuse through life cycle standardization across domains. Examples have been demonstrated on using BIM to improve the information environment for supporting a more effective and proactive H&S management (Ku and Mills 2010). The recent development in knowledge engineering, e.g. ontology modeling, can provide a new way to extract domain knowledge and link different domains together to form up a smart and holistic decision making engine. Ontology is defined as the formal conceptualization of knowledge in a certain domain (Zhang and El-Diraby 2011) and it has been used to structure the knowledge base for H&S management. Ontology reasoning based holistic decision supported by comprehensive and accurate data sets provided by BIM could offer a new clue to achieve a new way of H&S management, which is proactive, automatic, holistic and whole life cycle oriented. But there are no comprehensive reviews yet in these areas to investigate what is currently available and what the future might hold.

This paper therefore reviews the above-mentioned topics with an aim to provide an overall understanding for smart and holistic construction H&S management, hence to propose a roadmap for the future development. The structure of this paper is showed below. review of the current construction H&S practices (section 2) is explained first and methods used to improve the construction H&S management. With identified problems, BIM and its relevant applications for construction H&S management are reviewed thoroughly to provide the understanding for BIM to provide life cycle data and information reuse (section 3). Section 4 goes further to investigate the means to provide smart and holistic decision making with a focus on ontology. Section 5 discusses the findings, identified research gaps, and proposes a roadmap of leveraging both BIM, providing accurate and comprehensive data / information, and ontology, providing the capability to reasoning across inter-linked domain knowledge, towards a smart and holistic approach for construction H&S management. It is believed that this review could support in-depth investigation and motivate further studies on construction H&S management. It could offer potential chances for researchers and stakeholders with a new thought of innovation to the H&S problem in construction industry.

2. Current Practice of Construction H&S management

The construction sector has a long history, with some evidence of building structure dating back to the Palaeolithic (Koshevoy, 1995) and some evidence of building regulations dating back to 2200 B.C. (Clarke,1999). However, the number and frequency of accidents, injuries and fatalities occurring in this industry still remain the top of the list as one of the most dangerous industries in the world.

Construction H&S management is defined as "organized efforts and procedures for identifying workplace hazards and reducing accidents and exposure to harmful situations and substances which also include training of personnel in accident prevention, accident response, emergency preparedness, and use of protective clothing and equipment." (Business Dictionary Website). Construction H&S management can be divided into three stages including: (1) safety planning stage when designers' H&S considerations upstream in the creation of the artefacts and its associated hazards and risk consequences; (2) pre-construction stage when safety managers develop an H&S plan according to construction activities and schedule, and (3) construction stage that all H&S risks during construction for site personnel should be managed. Overall speaking, the current H&S management practice is regarded as insufficient as there are still some problems in each stage:

H&S Planning/Design Stage: Missing safety factors.
Pre-Construction stage: Incomplete H&S planning.
Onsite Monitoring stage: Insufficient site monitoring.

3. BIM supporting construction H&S data and information management

3.1 Related BIM overview

BIM is defined as "a digital representation of the physical and functional characteristics of a facility. A BIM is a shared knowledge resource for information about a facility forming a reliable basis for decisions during its life-cycle; defined as existing from earliest conception to demolition (National BIM Standard, 2013)". It could be employed in a virtual space to achieve high-quality and efficient construction and management throughout the life cycle of a facility. BIM can be leveraged as a tool in providing the whole building life-cycle data information. Taking Safety Analysis of Building in Construction (SABIC) proposed by Hu et al. (Hu, Zhang et al. 2008) as an example, this system can convert a BIM-based architectural model into a BIM-based safety analysis model with extra information of construction process, therefore static building model can be rebuilt according to safety analysis carried out at several time points.

General speaking, gaining economic profits is the main purpose of a construction project, many efforts have been directed to look at speeding up the progress and saving costs, which makes manage time and cost be the priority of a construction project. However, H&S management gains much attention recently as "people-first value" is gaining publicity with economic and cultural progress (Ding, Zhou et al. 2014).

3.2 BIM applications for H&S management

The main keywords "BIM", "Building Information Modelling", "Risk", "Health and Safety Management" were used in web searches from online academic publication resources including "Web of Science", "Scopus" and "Science Direct" Although the total number of the first round search was large, only 23 were kept for further analysis after closely inspection as most of them do not focus on BIM supported construction H&S management.

Figure. 2 presents the number of selected papers against their publication year. The earliest paper selected which is highly related to BIM for construction safety management was from 2008. It concentrated on the issue of supporting rescuers in finding the shortest way within a public building and providing them with important information in their particular spatial context (Rueppel and Stuebbe 2008). This requires to display the section where the user is located and to calculate routes to guide the user. The information needed here should be in a format as it would be used for data analysis and route calculation. BIM not only can provide all information needed but also with standardized international data formats.

The increasing pattern reflects the interest of the research community in the BIM for construction H&S management field. Figure 1 also indicates the benefits of BIM applications in other aspects of construction have been recognized and H&S concept is taken more seriously by industry. It is also noted that the amount of published articles steadily increases from 2012 to 2015; between 2015, there are 9 papers published related to BIM for construction H&S management.

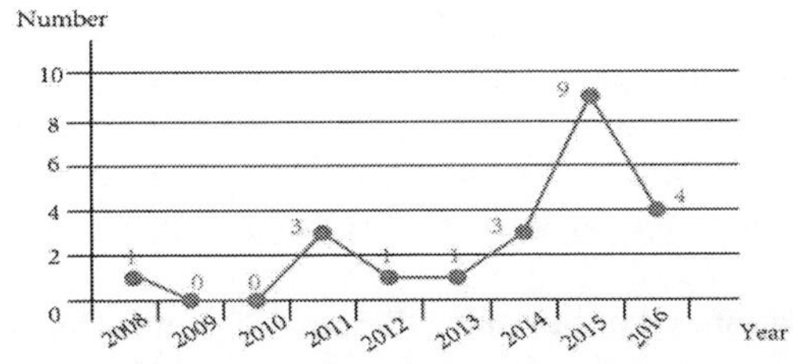

Fig. 1. Publications of BIM for Construction H&S Management

Based on the literature review, it is found that the current BIM for construction H&S management research still focuses on design stage as design review takes the highest number of published research articles.

There are a few publications for pre-construction and construction stages (5 and 4 papers respectively) A BIM-based approach for automate tower crane layout planning could be a typical example for pre-construction safety management (Wang, Zhang et al. 2015). This paper combines BIM and Firefly Algorithm (FA) to automatically generate an optimal tower crane layout plan and BIM is utilized as shared knowledge resource for information here to provide inputs such as site boundary, time-based materials consuming, size and number of material laydown yards, etc. for the mathematical model.

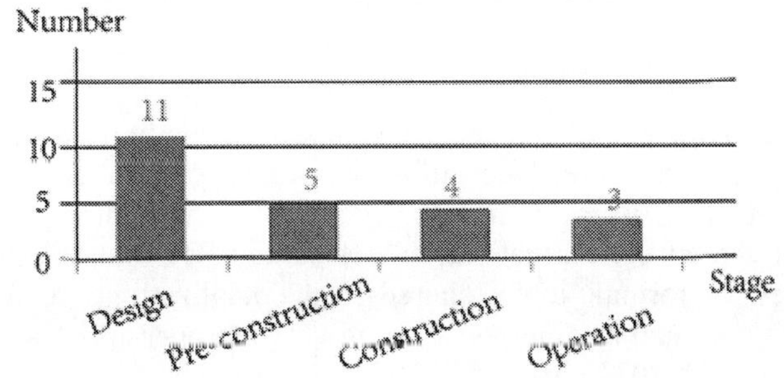

Fig. 2. (a) Publications of BIM for Construction H&S Management for different stages

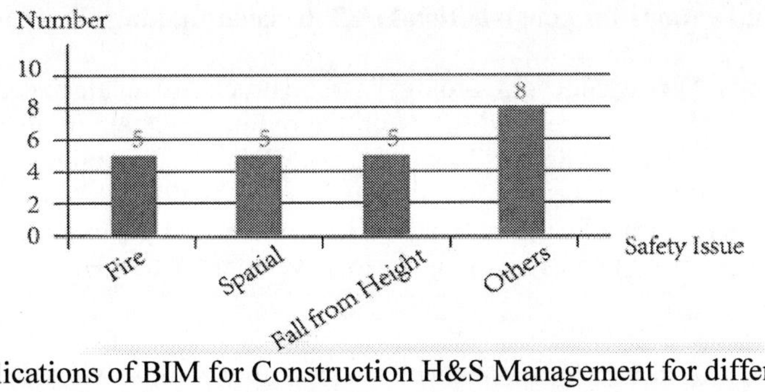

Fig. 2. (b) Publications of BIM for Construction H&S Management for different H&S issues

Considering different H&S risk types, Figure 2(b) indicates that researchers focus more on fall from height, fire evacuation and spatial clashes, which aligns with the fact that falling from height remains a major safety risk at construction sites. It takes up 33% of all injuries according to the report from HSE (2016). Fire evacuation problems and spatial clashes are also the highly risky safety issues as well. Zhang et al. investigate a BIM-based fall from height detection and prevention prototype system. A building model is not only well constructed here to include the required objects, attributes and relations used to carry out the rule checking, but also the schedule information is leveraged since fall prevention equipment is closely related to the status of the construction work (Zhang, Sulankivi et al. 2015).

In summary, the aforementioned studies have illustrated that BIM is capable of improving construction H&S management by providing the whole building life-cycle data sets/information. However, the relation between end user and information system is limited, as BIM typically could not be a repository storing all different parties involved during the building life cycle. Within the wider construction H&S management context, BIM models are single silos of information, with the contained information that is usually not being customised to the needs and requirements of the end user (Pauwels 2014). In this context, a knowledge gap exists between experts and the construction project team, a tool which could represent the H&S knowledge and share it with the project team is essential to narrow this knowledge gap and to achieve a holistic H&S decision-making system across different sectors. Therefore, ontology for construction H&S management is reviewed in the next section as a knowledge management tool.

4. Ontology supporting smart H&S decision making

4.1 Ontology overview

Using ontology to share domain knowledge is necessary. "An explicit specification of a conceptualization" is the most widespread definition of ontology (Gruber 1995) and was complemented by Studer et al. (Studer, Benjamins et al. 1998) as "ontology is a formal, explicit specification of a shared conceptualization". It contains formal vocabularies of a specific domain; it gives a formal logic shared conceptualization; it makes better communication between human and computers; it improves interoperability among diverse software (Valaski, Malucelli et al. 2012).

4.2 Ontology applications for construction H&S decision making

The main keywords "Knowledge", "Ontology", "Construction Health and Safety", "Risk", "Decision Making", "System" are used to search the online academic publication data-bases including "Web of Science", "Scopus" and "Science Direct" for collecting academic and applied publications related to the topic "ontology for construction H&S management". After the selection, the relevant publications was just 10. As the first paper started from the year 2009, it could be concluded that using ontology to solve construction H&S issues is still in its early stage.

The ontological approach for H&S management concentrates on solving the entire building life cycle H&S issues rather than working only for a specific period of construction process. Among those selected 10 papers, 4 papers emphasize in solving safety issues throughout the whole building life cycle. There is only one paper applying ontology-based decision-making for design stage. In addition, ontology-based H&S decision-making system tends to take all safety-related issues into account. There are 8 papers concentrating on eliminating H&S-related hazards while only 2 papers looking at collapse issue particularly.

As mentioned in the current H&S management practice section, JHA is highly complex and time-consuming. While some researchers have applied ontology as knowledge base to support smarter decision making for JHA. Wang et al. (Wang and Boukamp 2011) proposed a framework that uses ontologies for structuring knowledge about activities, job steps and hazards.

Other researchers use ontology as H&S knowledge base for safety checking. For example, Lu et al. developed a meta model named Construction Safety Checking Ontology (CSCOntology) for construction safety checking system. Therefore, this ontology-based safety checking system could realize a better health and safety decision-making.

5. Discussion

5.1 BIM applications in construction H&S management

BIM technologies and applications have the potential to support better information collection, storage, analysis, visualization and response. It does not only have the ability to store and update the whole building lifecycle information, but also can facilitate the conversion of specific requirements of building codes to machine readable rules to be checked automatically in BIM models (Eastman, Lee et al. 2009). As concluded in Table 1, BIM could represent the complex and dynamic construction information by providing fundamental standardization, dynamic information and structured information. However, there are some problems / gaps identified for using BIM for construction H&S management according the literature review on section 4. The full potential of BIM has not been achieved:

- As BIM could store the whole building life cycle information, it could be utilized to enhance construction H&S management throughout planning/design stage, pre-construction stage, construction stage and operation/maintenance stage. However, until now, researches only emphasize on one specific stage rather than developing a system that could benefit construction H&S management during the whole life cycle.
- Operation / maintenance stage has been largely overlooked. Building repair and maintenance work reviewed for six out of ten (66.7%) fatal cases in the construction industry of Hong Kong in 2010. H&S management during this stage indeed deserves more attention.
- With the assistance of BIM, different hazards could be studied and controlled. While most of the current researches (among 22 selected papers) only take one type of construction risks into account; and there are only 2 papers try to solve related hazards throughout the whole project process.

What's more, as current BIM practices mainly focus on the standardization for life cycle data and information processing, it could not be fully leveraged by existing decision making engine to achieve a holistic approach for construction H&S management. Ontology, in this context, is proposed to connect with BIM for construction H&S management due to its ability of representing domain knowledge and relationship between classes semantically. Integrating BIM and ontology-based knowledge system has already existed in other domains, but not yet in H&S management realm, e.g. Fruchter et al. (Fruchter, Schrotenboer et al. 2009) attempted to transform the BIM into the building knowledge model by linking the knowledge tool with BIM.

5.2 Research Trends

Knowledge base includes basic H&S information such as construction activities, hazards, As illustrated above, the combination of BIM and ontology could lead to a proactive and holistic approach to better manage construction H&S issues. Several recommendations are listed below:

1. Comprehensive knowledge base. As mentioned in the paper, there are gaps existed between H&S experts and construction project team. A comprehensive knowledge base will be invaluable for practitioners. The solutions and safety risk factors, which can be used for comparing different H&S methods. With the visualization capability of BIM, the result could be reviewed intuitively in BIM models. External risk factors such as surrounding environment, weather condition and so on can also be considered.

2. Ontology standardization. For researchers who develop their own ontology knowledge base, they use their own definition of class, hierarchy, semantic relationship between classes, which means these different ontology knowledge bases cannot be connected to each other easily or the process is time-consuming. If standardization could be achieved for ontology, different ontology knowledge bases could be connected to assist in a better decision-making process. For example, using IFC as a central exchanging format to map with construction H&S ontology and construction cost ontology respectively, so when H&S managers make decisions, they could do the cost estimation at the same time and are able to choose the cost-effective method for H&S management.

3. Holistic risk consideration. The existing researches normally only look at how to solve individual risk. There might be knock on impacts between risks, for example, if safety manager change project schedule in order to eliminate the hazard "fall from height", it may increase the risk for the hazard "electric shock". In addition, the external risk of weather or other delays, like congestion at certain times on the road, may also influence the overall decision making. Based on the comprehensive review and analysis, a BIM based ontological approach supporting holistic decision-making framework for construction H&S management is proposed as shown in Figure 3.

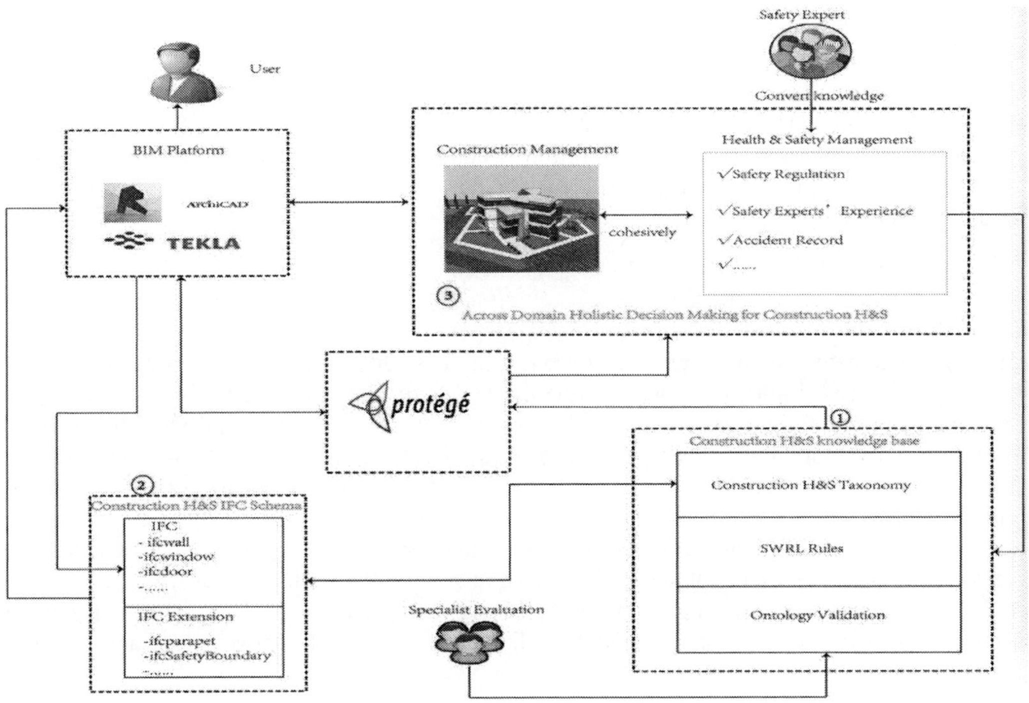

Fig.3. Ontological BIM-based Holistic Decision Making System for Construction H&S

Following the recommendations mentioned above, there are three key aspects in the proposed decision-making framework:

1. Knowledge base development. This is the fundamental step for the proposed decisionmaking system as the knowledge base will contain all related H&S information and semantic relationship to help the whole system to make a proper decision to avoid risks. This knowledge base consists two parts: internal elements and external elements. To be more specific, internal elements conclude location, the height of the building, task information, project schedule, the education level of workers etc. while external elements concludes weather information, traffic information and sustainability information etc. With the help of H&S experts, technical staff could convert all related H&S knowledge including safety regulations and standards, accident records and best practices into construction H&S classes and SWRL rules.
2. Construction H&S IFC schema development. Without BIM model providing the whole life cycle information of the real project, H&S knowledge base could not be fully exploited. BIM platform will also work as user interface for construction H&S management as well. The proper connection between H&S knowledge base and BIM model is the essential step to complete the decision-making system. Construction H&S IFC schema could be developed as the bridge to link the H&S knowledge base and BIM model. As many H&S related concepts do not exist in existing IFC, for example, safety boundary and parapet wall, a complete construction H&S ifc schema should be established with the extension of existing IFC. By mapping ontology classes and ifc schema, BIM model could be linked with H&S ontology knowledge base.
3. Holistic decision-making engine development. After linking ontology knowledge base with BIM model, Designers and H&S managers will need an engine to conduct decision

making for H&S management. The decision-making engine will provide a query interface & automatic warning system. Automatic warning system could remind the designers during the design stage, for example, different materials of external wall decorative surface would make the level of difficulty different during exterior wall construction processes, automatic warning system will give designers a warning when they choose a material which most likely trigger the hazard "fall from height'' during the construction task "exterior wall construction and decoration".

6. Conclusion

H&S management are still facing major issues across global construction industries due to the fatalities and injuries reported every year. With the recent sustainable and social development, gaining economic profits is no longer the major goal of project management, therefore much more attentions have been paid to H&S issues, which could also be illustrated by the growing research in this area worldwide. Through the review of current practice of H&S management, the result reveals that it is still mostly management-driven, and lacks of a smart and holistic approach considering the whole project life cycle and across different sectors for project team to make a better H&S decision making. More specifically, the current H&S management approaches are lack of (1) comprehensive data sets that can be dynamically updated and reused throughout life cycle; (2) intelligent way to make a holistic decision that crosses different sectors.

Therefore this paper methodologically reviews the potential positive outcomes of integrating innovation technologies with management practices. In respond to the identified gaps, two new recent technology advances, BIM and ontology are closely investigated. Through the review of current research about BIM-based H&S management, it shows that BIM has the capacity to provide life cycle comprehensive data set. The review goes further to identify the missing link between knowledge management and BIM based data and information processing in order to achieve a smart and holistic H&S decision making. Based on the requirement of knowledge management in construction H&S domain, ontology related literatures are reviewed, with a main focus on its advantages compared to ES, uncertain reasoning, semantic networks and so on. The different ontology applications in different domains supporting smart decision-making and construction H&S management are also reviewed.

Finally, the review suggests that it is necessary to leverage both BIM, for its comprehensive and standardized data presentation and information integration; and ontology, for its semantic richness representing domain knowledge, to create a new approach, that can take full use of life cycle design, construction and maintenance data and H&S knowledge to achieve truly holistic decision making to support construction H&S management. Furthermore, recommendations were concluded and corresponding proposal was developed in the discussion section, to demonstrate the key components to develop such novel approach, which aligns will with those identified further research directions.

Reference

Bryde, D., et al. (2013). "The project benefits of Building Information Modelling (BIM)." International Journal of Project Management 31(7): 971-980.

Ding, L., et al. (2014). "Building Information Modeling (BIM) application framework: The process of expanding from 3D to computable nD." Automation in Construction 46: 82-93.

Eastman, C., et al. (2009). "Automatic rule-based checking of building designs." Automation in Construction 18(8): 1011-1033.

El-Diraby, T. and J. Zhang (2006). "A semantic framework to support corporate memory management in building construction." Automation in Construction 15(4): 504-521.

Fruchter, R., et al. (2009). From building information model to building knowledge model. Computing in Civil Engineering (2009): 380-389.

Gruber, T. R. (1995). "Toward principles for the design of ontologies used for knowledge sharing?" International journal of human-computer studies 43(5-6): 907-928.

Hare, B., et al. (2006). "Exploring the integration of health and safety with pre-construction planning." Engineering, Construction and Architectural Management 13(5): 438-450.

Lee, S.-K., et al. (2014). "BIM and ontology-based approach for building cost estimation." Automation in Construction 41: 96-105.

Pauwels, P. (2014). "Supporting Decision-Making in the Building Life-Cycle Using Linked Building Data." Buildings 4(3): 549.

Rezgui, Y. (2006). "Ontology-centered knowledge management using information retrieval techniques." Journal of Computing in Civil Engineering 20(4): 261-270.

Rueppel, U. and K. M. Stuebbe (2008). "BIM-based indoor-emergency-navigation-system for complex buildings." Tsinghua Science & Technology 13: 362-367.

Studer, R., et al. (1998). "Knowledge engineering: Principles and methods." Data & Knowledge Engineering 25(1–2): 161-197.

Sulankivi, K., et al. (2010). 4D BIM for construction safety planning. Proceedings of W099-Special Track 18th CIB World Building Congress.

Valaski, J., et al. (2012). "Ontologies application in organizational learning: A literature review." Expert Systems with Applications 39(8): 7555-7561.

Wang, H. H. and F. Boukamp (2011). "Ontology-based representation and reasoning framework for supporting job hazard analysis." Journal of Computing in Civil Engineering 25(6). 442-456.

Zhang, J. and T. El-Diraby (2011). "Social semantic approach to support communication in AEC." Journal of Computing in Civil Engineering 26(1): 90-104.

Zhang, J. P. and Z. Z. Hu (2011). "BIM- and 4D-based integrated solution of analysis and management for conflicts and structural safety problems during construction: 1. Principles and methodologies." Automation in Construction 20(2): 155-166.

Rules Complexity Classification for Automated Compliance Checking

Seyedamir Hakim, Fulvio Re Cecconi, Mario Claudio Dejaco, Sebastiano Maltese
Politecnico di Milano, Italy
seyedamir.hakim@polimi.it

Abstract. Buildings are growing in complexity and so laws and standards; traditional code checking, as well as laws creation, are no more sustainable, especially in terms of information management (storage, elaboration, update, etc.). This research is focused on the creation of a new automated compliance checking process, looking not only at how rules are checked, but also at how rules are created; this involves the classification of rules in different categories and their elaboration, to translate them from plain language (although it usually is a "complex language") to computer-readable language, associated to attributes implemented in the Asset Information Model by the various stakeholders during building life (since early design to operation). This paper presents a preliminary classification of rules usually found in building codes, standards and laws. Some examples are shown to demonstrate the robustness of the classification provided.

1. Introduction

Automated compliance checking (ACC) is expected to reduce time, cost, and errors of compliance checking (Salama and El-Gohary, 2013; Hjelseth, 2012). Many efforts have thus attempted to automate the compliance-checking process, including: (1) SMARTcodes project by the International Code Council (ICC); (2) construction and real estate network (CORENET) project led by the Singapore Ministry of National Development; (3) REScheck and COMcheck software by the U.S. Department of Energy; and (4) the Solibri Model Checker (Eastman et al., 2009). However, despite their importance, these efforts are still limited in their automation and reasoning capabilities; the state of the art in ACC still uses ad hoc reasoning schema/methods, with lack of support for complete automation.

A common to automated code checking is systematic comparison, i.e. comparing each object or system in a building model representation with the constraints in a standard. The output is usually a non-conformant objects list (Dimyadi and Amor, 2013).

Rule checking on a building model is a complex problem. Much research work has been done in this area for the past 50 years, but with limited success. The complexity covers: (a) building data; (b) how the information is presented and how easy it is to access it; (c) rule specifications and requirements that present entirely different complexities with their construct and their limitless variations and various semantic meanings that often are domain dependent (Solihin and Eastman, 2015). Most of the efforts in rule checking often resulted in a very limited capability to solve building rules. Some solutions are too complex that the cost of implementation becomes prohibitively high, or too rigid that they are unable to adapt to even minor rules changes or variations.

This research is focused on the creation of a new ACC process, looking not only at how rules are checked, but also at how rules are created; this involves the classification of rules in different categories and their elaboration, to translate them from plain language (although it usually is a "complex language") to computer-readable language, associated to attributes implemented in the Asset Information Model (AIM) by the various stakeholders during building life (since early design to operation).

The aim of this paper is to provide an initial guide for creating a framework for rules classification that expresses both the process challenges and the technology needs to address rule automation. A preliminary classification is provided for the rules usually found in building codes, standards and laws. Some examples are shown to demonstrate the robustness of the classification provided.

2. State of the Art

This chapter contains a brief state of the art about the main topics held in the research, aiming at providing a context for the work developed. Here some of the most relevant works on building information complexity, interoperability and level of detail/information are presented.

2.1 Semantic Knowledge Representation of Building Rules

In recent years, several approaches have been proposed to capture building related rules into certain forms of knowledge representations. For example, El-Gohary et al proposed the use of Natural Language Processing (NLP) to "interpret" building codes (Salama and El-Gohary, 2013; Zhang and El-Gohary, 2013). Hjelseth and Beach used a methodology called RASE (Requirement, Applicability, Selection, Exception) to tag the building codes into four categories of ideas to drive the computer implementation of automated rule checking (Hjelseth, 2012; Beach, 2013). Both approaches focus on the structure of the rules and have not sufficiently addressed the semantic-interpretation issue of the rules and whether the building representation is sufficient to support the richness of language expression written in the rules. In this research, the rules are viewed as knowledge assets completed with their association with the building representation that they mean to check. As previously mentioned, in this research, only the widely used open standard IFC (Industry Foundation Classes) by BuildingSMART is used. IFC is now described in the ISO 16739:2013 and is supported by all major BIM authoring tools.

The first task needed is to choose a suitable representation to capture semantic knowledge of the rules. The most suitable method appears to be from the field of Knowledge Base (KB) that is a branch of Artificial Intelligence (AI). But even within KB, there are many different approaches including First Order Logic (FOL), Description 60 Logic (DL), and Conceptual Graph (CG). CG was originally proposed by Sowa in 1976 and further developed in 1984. The Conceptual Graph (CG) offers intuitive, easy to read and suitable to capture semantic knowledge representation of the rules (Chein, 2008). CG has its semantic foundation in FOL and the basic form of CG can be mapped 1-to-1 directly to FOL. Thus the goals in using the CG are:

- as an expressive tool to capture knowledge of rules in terms of their requirements for automation that are easily understood by the rule experts, who are typically not familiar with computer programming;
- ability to capture data requirements of the building objects and their relationships or interactions with other building objects, including constraints;
- direct mapping of the CG concepts into IFC entities, derived entities and extension functions. The mapping is important for both defining MVDs and for software development efforts;
- ability to breakdown complex rules into their atomic rules in a systematic and standardized way.

2.2 Interoperability

Interoperability is one of the most relevant issues about BIM (Grilo and Jardim-Goncalves, 2010), especially now that the level 2 (The National Building Specification, 2014) is under development and collaboration is an essential factor. Interoperability enables the exchange of data among different software and professionals, easing the collaboration and increasing the overall quality of a project, also by avoiding information repetition. A (perfect) interoperable world is characterised by: interoperable software (3D CAD Object-Oriented), database for life cycle data shared among operators, no need of specific software, costs reduction, less errors and an overall quality improvement. Of course the reality is characterised by a mixture of software and procedures more or less interoperable, as a result of different operators' background, organisation, ability and topic (traditionally the service sector is more advanced than the fabric one). Interoperability is not just a design issue, as the data gathered during the design stages affect all the other (longer) phases, like operation, maintenance and refurbishment; so organising the data in a proper way is extremely important to avoid losses in the future: converting the data from one format to another could be really expensive, as instance the International Facility Management Association (IFMA) Maintenance Survey in 2009, which states that the loss of information generates an added costs of 12.4% of total annual mean O&M costs.

The main exchange protocol is the Industry Foundation Classes (IFC) (BuildingSMART, 2015), currently at the IFC2x4 version, even if the most used is currently the IFC2x3. IFC is a standard to classify and describe electronically, in a software-readable format, objects that can be used in a construction product (from bricks to the entire building); it has been developed by BuildingSMART (formerly IAI – International Alliance for Interoperability) from ISO-STEP 10303, nowadays ISO 16739:2013 and it is available for all the BuildingSMART members, which can develop third party applications based on this standard.

2.3 Level of Detail and Information

It is important to highlight that BIM does not mean to provide the whole set of information at the same time: Level of Development and Level of Detail clarify how many data are required and when. The Level of Development is the degree to which the element geometry and attached information has been thought – the degree to which project team members may rely on the information when using the model. Level of Detail (LOD) is essentially how much detail is included in the model element (The Building National Specification, 2015). Level of Information (LOI) measures the amount of information (qualitative, quantitative, and alphanumeric) associated to a specific object.

In this research LOD and LOI are fundamental for the classification of the rules and for gathering input from objects; so rules can be categorised according to when they can be asked, which is directly connected to the moment in which the data are implemented (defined in LOD and LOI).

3. Research Methodology

This research aims to classify the complexity of the building rules into broad categories that require different approaches (e.g. qualitative, quantitative, production of certifications, etc.). Some relevant examples are discussed to highlight the complexity involved and the factors required to solve the problems are identified.

A literature review of main researches and projects related to ACC is undergoing, so to create a robust basis for this research. An analysis of the current efforts is applied for the purpose of identifying the real needs for rule checking. With this, the systematic and holistic approach to the problem in rule checking is described, with the identification of potential and criticalities related to the ACC approach. After this first phase, a preliminary classification of the rules has been drafted, aiming at testing it with some rules types commonly used in codes and standards. The third step, not included in this paper, is to translate current rules into computer-readable rules, as well as creating (or selecting from IFC, if natively existing) BIM objects attributes for storing input and output.

4. Rule Classification

A crucial foundation for rule checking are the semantics introduced on the schema level: in order to prevent false positives and negatives, elements and rules need to be classified correctly. Currently there are no or very limited provisions in the IFC schema that actually guarantee this formally. As a consequence, elements are misclassified, or classified in overly broad or meaningless categories, such as *IfcBuildingElementProxy* (Krijnen and Van Berlo, 2016). Elements that are misclassified result either in false negatives, as certain relevant checks are not performed, or in false positives, because irrelevant checks are performed.

In the following paragraphs the preliminary classification of rules, consisting in three main categories (each one divided in two sub-classes) is presented, together with some examples (Figure 1).

Complexity ↓			Totally IFC compliant
Class 1	require a single or small number of explicit data	Sub-class.1	✓
		Sub-class.2	✗
Class 2	require simple derived attribute values	Sub-class.1	✓
		Sub-class.2	✗
Class 3	require extended data structure and simulation	Sub-class.1	✓
		Sub-class.2	✗

Figure 1: Rules Classification Schema

The main goal of defining these subclasses is to take into account not only logic complexity of rules but also interoperability of checking parameters simultaneously. BIM dataset (IFC for instance) extensibility studies are highly demanded in order to build a robust basis for the future BIM-based fully automated compliance checking.

4.1 Class 1 – Rules that require a single or small number of explicit data:

Typical uses of this class of rules are:

1. The required attribute settings of entities for correctness checking.
2. Some simple building code checking.
3. Some model view business rules in MVDs restricting options allowed, for example Name and LongName attributes, which are optional in the IFC schema for *IfcBuilding*, are mandatory in the Basic FM Handover MVD.
4. Attributes and attribute values that are essential for consistent derived values required in other classes of rules. For example, to be able to derive a concept of an apartment

unit, all spaces within the unit must be members of an *IfcZone* and the *IfcZone* must be named and classified according to the standardized naming convention or classification.

Sub-Class 1.1. This class of rules checks explicit attributes and entity references that exist inside the BIM dataset (IFC). At this level, information is explicitly available from the model either directly from the entities or its associated properties with other entities using the explicit relationship entities. One example on how this type of rule can be processed:

"C.7.3 Double WC-flushes must be used."(CESBA- Public Buildings Refurbishment 1.1, 2013)

To process this rule, the model is queried for well-defined entities (Cistern unit and its components) and their relationship. The Single Flush property to be checked is obtained using explicit relationships from each of the entities being processed (Figure 2). All entities and relationships are usually explicit in the model and the rule is able to follow the links in a straightforward manner.

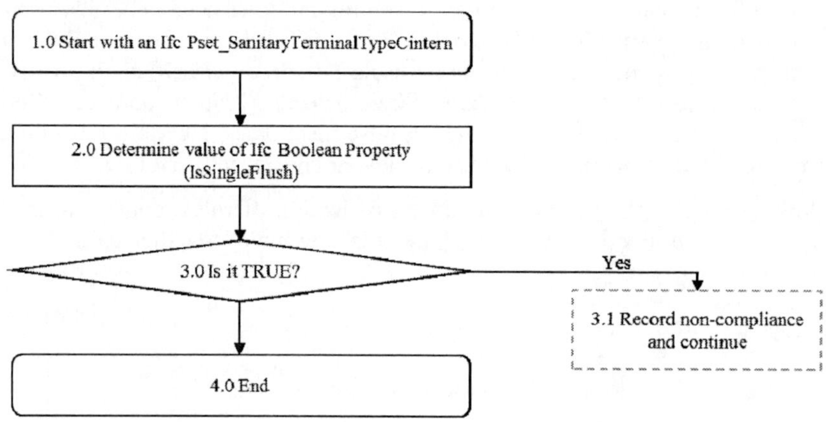

Figure 2: Checking Process of CESBA- Public Buildings Refurbishment C.7.3

Sub-Class 1.2. This class checks explicit attributes and entities that some of them are not existing inside the BIM dataset (IFC). At this level, some information should be added to custom dataset which is decided to work parallel to your IFC data. One example of this class of rules is:

"C.7.2 Contact free faucets must be used for sinks."(CESBA- Public Buildings Refurbishment 1.1, 2013)

For processing this rule, a custom-defined model is required for entities (Faucet unit and its components) and their relationship. The Sensor Using property to be checked is obtained using added custom valve property set to Faucet Operation Value (**Error! Reference source not found.**).

4.2 Class 2 – Rules that require simple derived Attribute Values:

This class of rule checks derive attributes or values but does not generate new data structures. This class of rule involves a trade-off between requiring the user to derive the data vs. rule checking-derived data. The rule checking-derived data has a clear benefit to the industry, which needs the work done once across all applications instead of including similar data derivations in each platform.

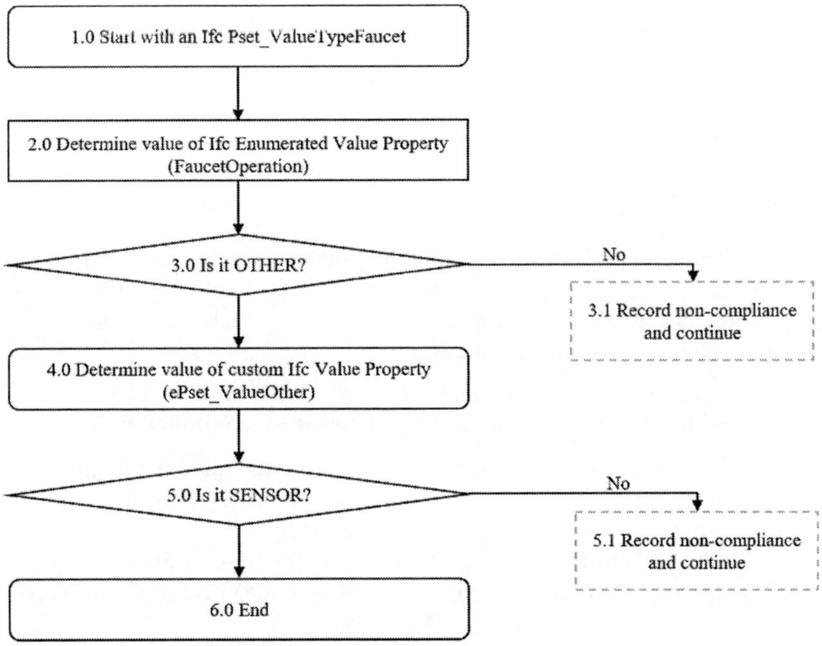

Figure 3: Checking Process of CESBA- Public Buildings Refurbishment C.7.2

Sub-Class 2.1. At this level, implicit relationships are often required to fulfil the checking requirements. BIM models do not usually capture this explicitly and the program needs to derive the value from the basic BIM model data and relationship. Here is an example to illustrate the process to check this type of rule:

"3.2.2 The discharge pipe shall not be located in places where it can cause health and safety hazards such as locating the discharge pipe above any potable water storage tank and electrical transformer/ switchgear. " (Design Criteria, Singapore, 2013)

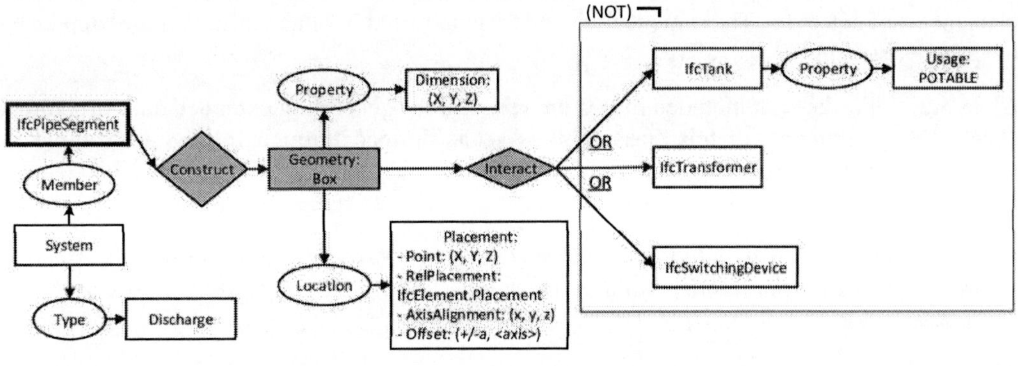

Figure 4: Conceptual Graph of Design Criteria, Singapore, 2013-3.2.2

This expression requires an extension function to construct a transient Box geometry based on a specified location and dimension (Figure 4). This Box is used to evaluate the existence of any type of object within the Box that is a type of a potable water tank, a transformer, or a switching device. Their existence within the Box is not allowed.

Sub-Class 2.2. This set faces some non-IFC data that are needed for checking the requirements based on derived values. One example for describing this set:

"10.0.Wst 02 Where the total amount of recycled or secondary aggregate specified is greater than 50% (by weight or volume) of the total high grade aggregate specified for the project. The contributing recycled or secondary aggregate must not be transported more than 30km by road transport."(BREEM, 2016)

This rule checks the amount of recycled aggregates and also the distance of transportation. The transportation distance requires an extension function based on the geometric location and dimensions. Aggregate properties of concrete are entities which are missing inside IFC and should be added during a customizing process.

4.3 Class 3 - Rules that require extended data structure and simulation:

This class of rule requires an extension to the data structure that encapsulates higher level semantic conditions of building data. The main idea is to be able to "compute once, use many" since such information typically requires extensive computation often involving geometry operations. Multiple data structure construction strategies may apply. We offer one of the possibilities. Typical use of this class of rules is building code checking that involves complex requirements.

Class 3.1: This sub-class is identified by extended data structure fully based on IFC entities, relationships and properties. One example on how this type of rule can be processed:

"Smoke alarm are ceiling mounted and at least 300 mm from walls and light fittings. Units designed for wall mounting may also be used provided that the units are above the levels of doorways opening into the space and they are fixed in accordance with manufacturer's instructions." (Fire Safety Clause 1.15.b)

This rule requires a sophisticated geometry engine to create a coverage map using distance triangulation between detectors (Fortune 1992). This allows identification of the nearest neighbour detectors and hence the distance between the detectors can be checked (**Error! Reference source not found.**). This example shows the need to "compute once use many" for generating the triangulated network, in that it can be re-used in many other rules related to the placements of detectors. The same technique is also required in other similar clauses applicable to sprinkler systems.

Class 3.2. Some data not included in IFC are required for generating extended data structure to check the requirements of this class. This is set is defined through following example for reduction of night time light pollution:

"13.0.Pol 02:

1. *Where external obtrusive lighting has been eliminated through effective design that removes the need for external lighting without adversely affecting the safety and security of the site and its users.*

OR alternatively, where the building does have external lighting:

2. *All external lighting (except for safety and security lighting) can be automatically switched off between 23:00 and 07:00.*
3. *Illuminated advertisements, where specified comply with:*
   - *3.1. The maximum luminance (CD/m²) outlined in Table 1*
   - *3.2. In Zone E1 (see Table 1) the maximum luminance value shall be zero post-curfew.*

4. *If safety or security lighting is provided and will be used between 23:00 and 07:00:*
   4.1. *Safety and security lighting complies with the lower levels of lighting recommended during these hours in accordance with CIE150-2003 and CIE126-1997, for example by using an automatic switch to reduce the lighting levels at 23:00 or earlier."*(BREEAM, 2016)

Table 1: Recommendations for maximum luminance (CD/m²)

Illuminated Area (m²)	**Zone E1**	**Zone E2**	**Zone E3**	**Zone E4**
< 10.00	100	600	800	1000
≥ 10.00	N/A	300	600	600

In this example you can see there are some entities and properties which are not inside the BIM dataset (IFC) such as advertisements and effective design description. Also as the sematic point of view, checking this rule needs an extended data structure due to its complexity and hierarchy.

Due to the generally complex form of rules, especially building codes, it is generally a good idea to try to separate one large rule into independent sub-rules. It will make the rule more discernible and hence easier to maintain. This is beneficial even if there are small redundancies between sub-rules due to some minor variations in the sub-rule (Solihin and Eastman, 2016).

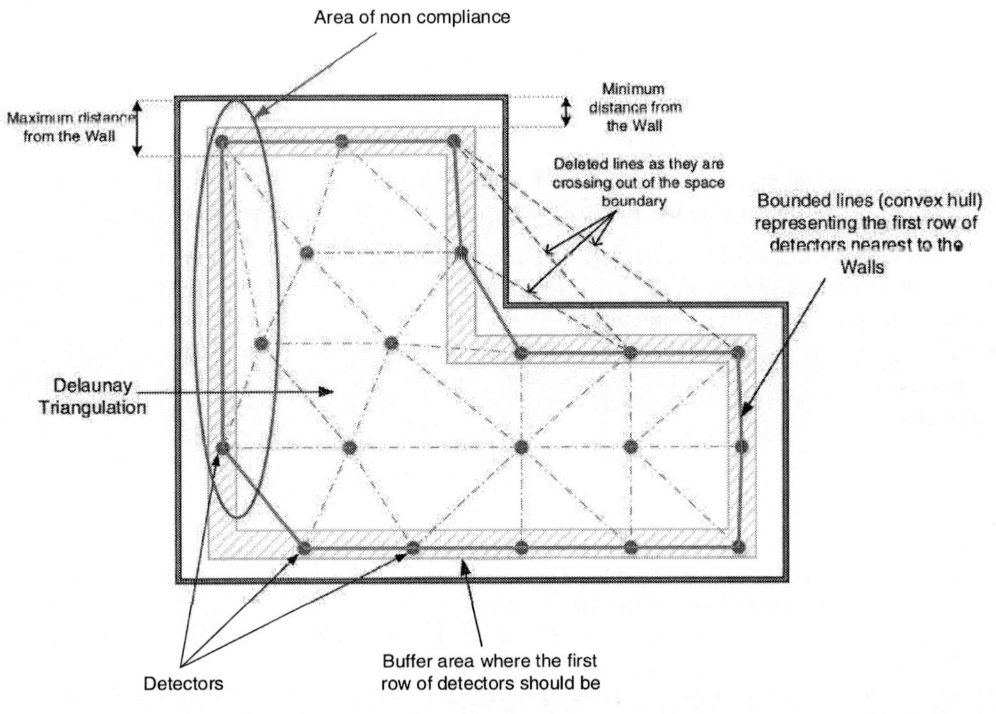

Figure 5: Coverage map of detectors for detection of distances and identifying the first row

5. Conclusion

This paper highlights the necessity of having a reliable classification of rules as the starting point of the creation of a robust ACC procedure. The six examples presented show that there is an increasing complexity of rules: from simple check of present/absence of a parameter to the creation of a "model" useful for data elaboration (e.g. **Error! Reference source not found.**). The second issue highlighted by this research is that not all input and output are natively included inside IFC, so probably some additional custom property sets will be necessary to fulfil all requirements (in terms of both input and output).

This paper presents the preliminary results of this research, which can be summarised in a rule classification made of six sub-classes:

- Class 1, rules that require a single or small number of explicit data:
  - Sub-Class 1.1, this set checks explicit attributes and entity references that exist inside the BIM dataset (IFC);
  - Sub-Class 1.2, set simple checks explicit attributes and entities that some of them are not existing inside the BIM dataset (IFC).
- Class 2, Rules that require simple derived Attribute Values:
  - Sub-Class 2.1, at this level, implicit relationships are often required to fulfil the checking requirements included inside IFC;
  - Sub-Class 2.2, this set faces some non-IFC data that are needed for checking the requirements based on derived values.
- Class 3, rules that require extended data structure and simulation:
  - Sub-Class 3.1, this sub-class is identified by extended data structure fully based on IFC entities, relationships and properties;
  - Sub-Class 3.2, some data not included in IFC are required for generating extended data structure to check the requirements of this class.

Future developments of this work include the classification of major rules (e.g. related to structures, energy, hygiene, safety, etc.), the definition of attributes (input and output) to fulfil the rules and procedures to manage them.

References

Beach, T. H., Kasim, T., Li, H., Nisbet, N., and Rezgui, Y. (2013). Towards automated compliance checking in the construction industry. In International Conference on Database and Expert Systems Applications (pp. 366-380). Springer Berlin Heidelberg.

BREEAM, (2016). New Construction Technical Manual. Version:SD233 – Issue:1.0.

Chein, M., Mugnier, M. L. (2008). Graph-based knowledge representation: computational foundations of conceptual graphs. Springer Science and Business Media.

Common European Sustainable Building Assessment (CESBA), (2013). Indicator Catalogue for Public Buildings Refurbishment 1.1.

Dimyadi, J., Amor, R. (2013). Automated Building Code Compliance Checking–Where is it at. Proceedings of CIB WBC, 172-185.

Eastman, C., Lee, J. M., Jeong, Y. S., and Lee, J. K. (2009). Automatic rule-based checking of building designs. Automation in construction, 18(8), 1011-1033.

Fortune, S. (1992). Voronoi diagrams and Delaunay triangulations. Computing in Euclidean geometry, 1(193-233), 2.

Grilo, A., Jardim-Goncalves, R. (2010). Value proposition on interoperability of BIM and collaborative working environments. Automation in Construction, 19(5), 522-530.

Hjelseth, E. (2012). Converting performance based regulations into computable rules in BIM based model checking software. eWork and eBusiness in Architecture, Engineering and Construction: ECPPM, 461-469.

HM Government, Building Regulations (2006): Approved Document B (Fire Safety) — Volume 1: Dwellinghouses, NBS, London, 2013.

Krijnen, T., van Berlo, L. A. H. M. (2016). Methodologies for requirement checking on building models.

ISO, T. (2013). 184/SC4, Industry Foundation Classes (IFC) for data sharing in the construction and facility management industries. International Organization for Standardization (ISO).

Salama, D. A., El-Gohary, N. M. (2013). Automated compliance checking of construction operation plans using a deontology for the construction domain. Journal of Computing in Civil Engineering, 27(6), 681-698.

Salama, D. M., El-Gohary, N. M. (2013). Semantic text classification for supporting automated compliance checking in construction. Journal of Computing in Civil Engineering, 30(1), 04014106.

Singapore (2013) Singapore building codes, http://www.corenet.gov.sg/einfo/Index.aspx.

Solihin, W., Eastman, C. (2015). Classification of rules for automated BIM rule checking development. Automation in construction, 53, 69-82.

Solihin, W., Eastman, C. (2016). A knowledge representation approach in BIM rule requirement analysis using the conceptual graph. Journal of Information Technology in Construction (ITcon), 21(24), 370-401.

Sowa, J. F. (1976). Conceptual graphs for a data base interface. IBM Journal of Research and Development, 20(4), 336-357.

Sowa, J. F. (1983). Conceptual structures: information processing in mind and machine.

The National Building Specifications – The NBS (2014), BIM levels explained. [ONLINE] Available at: http://www.thenbs.com/topics/bim/articles/bim-levels-explained.asp. [Accessed 7 September 2015].

The National Building Specifications (2015), NBS National BIM Report 2015.

Zhang, J., El-Gohary, N. (2012). Extraction of construction regulatory requirements from textual documents using natural language processing techniques. In Computing in Civil Engineering (2012) (pp. 453-460).

Zhang, J., El-Gohary, N. (2016). Semantic-Based Logic Representation and Reasoning for Automated Regulatory Compliance Checking. Journal of Computing in Civil Engineering, 31(1), 04016037

Application of graph databases and graph theory concepts for advanced analysing of BIM models based on IFC standard

Ali Ismail, Ahmed Nahar, Raimar Scherer
TU Dresden, Germany
ali.ismail@tu-dresden.de

Abstract. In this paper we present a workflow for automatic transformation of IFC schema and IFC models into an IFC Meta and object graph databases. The aim of this research is to study and demonstrate the potential of using graph theory concepts and graph databases in order to manage, visualize and analyse the huge information and complex relationships of BIM models based on IFC standard. For the validation a set data retrieval queries and advanced model analysis for model topology analysis and comparison of different IFC models are carried out in order to demonstrate the flexibility and advantages of the suggested approach.

1. Introduction

The very fast development in the sector of information technology has been successfully exploited in construction and engineering field to adopt new digital methods such as Building Information Modelling (BIM) for construction project managing. However, BIM models may contain a huge amount on information with complex relationships between the model entities. This information could remain inaccessible in several cases due to the use of closed property formats or the absent of suitable data management tools in case of using open standard formats like Industry Foundation Classes (IFC).

A lot of data retrieval queries are hard to be accomplished using currently available software's and most of them operate on single IFC models. The rigid and complex hierarchical structure of the IFC schema prevents simple manual extraction of building information and requires deep understanding of the IFC object model itself. The BIM query languages introduced so far have certain limitations, particularly with respect to the high level of knowledge about the IFC object model and about data mapping mechanisms required by the user (Tauscher, Bargstädt, & Smarsly, 2016).

Evidently, graphs have shown great capabilities in understanding and accessing complex and rich datasets in many different domains. Graph models are extremely useful for representation and description of the complex relationships among building elements and data within BIMs (Isaac, Sadeghpour, & Navon, 2013), hence converting of BIM models based on the IFC standard into an effective information retrievable model based on graph databases could significantly facilitate the efforts of exploring and analysing BIM highly connected data.

A graph-based schema, termed the graph data model (GDM) was presented by (Khalili & Chua, 2015). This schema can be used to employ semantic information, to extract, analyse, and present the topological relationships among 3D objects in 3D space, and to perform topological queries faster. Another generic approach towards information retrieval using the IFC object model based on graph theory was presented recently by (Tauscher, Bargstädt, & Smarsly, 2016). In this approach a directed graph was generated that serve as semantic data pools facilitating generic queries. This approach is limited to apply queries on single IFC models.

This paper presents a workflow for complete and automatic transformation of IFC models into a labelled property graph-based model using the world leading graph database Neo4J [1] as a graph database framework.

The proposed approach targets two kinds of graph models:

- IFC Meta Graph (IMG) based on the IFC EXPRESS schema
- IFC Objects Graph (IOG) based on STEP Physical File (SPF) format.

Beside the automatic conversation of IFC models into graph database this paper aims to demonstrate the potential of using graph databases and concepts of graph theory in order to (1) explore, check and analyse the complex relationships inside one or multiple BIM models, (2) run complex queries for information retrieval and (3) carry out advanced analysis of the building topology like escape route analysis and comparing of different IFC models.

2. IFC data model

IFC is a data model developed by buildingSMART International to support the exchange of building information in Architecture, Engineering and Construction (AEC) industry to improve collaboration, scheduling, cost and delivery time activities throughout the whole life cycle of the building project. It provides an object-oriented and semantic data model for storing and exchanging building information. This enables actors from different disciplines to effectively use BIM data and to fully exchange information in construction or facility management projects. IFC schema is described using EXPRESS specification language that defined by ISO 10303-11, as conceptual information modelling language. The specification specified also a graphical representation known as EXPRESS-G to provide graphical subset. The IFC data schema can be saved as Extensible Markup Language (XML) file structure per ISO10303-21 or STEP Physical file (SPF) document structure following ISO10303-28.

Each IFC model is composed of IFC entities built up in a hierarchical order, where each IFC entity includes a fixed number of IFC attributes, plus any number of additional IFC properties. The IFC attributes are the main identifiers of the entities, while the names of these attributes are fixed, having been defined by buildingSMART (buildingSMART) as part of the IFC standard code. The IFC data schema has three fundamental entity types as shown in Figure 1. These entity types are the first level structure of the IfcRoot entities hierarchical.

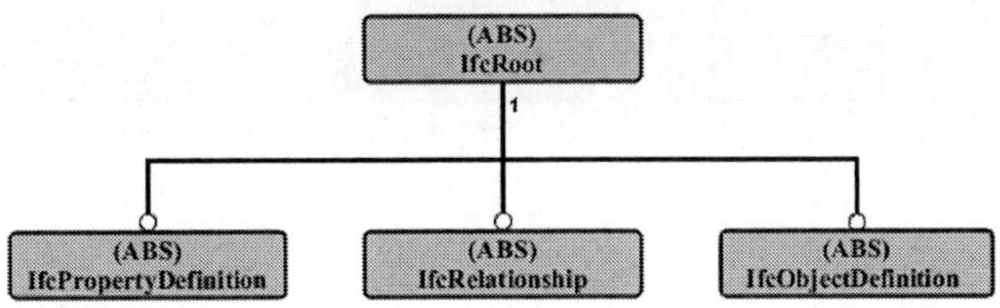

Figure 1: Fundamental entity types derived from IfcRoot class

- IfcPropertyDefinition describes all characteristics that may attach to objects. Thus, valuable information can be shared among multiple object instances. However, it may express the occurrence information of the actual object in the project context, in case that it is attached to a single object instance.

[1] www.neo4j.com

- IfcObjectDefinition stands for all handled objects or process. Where, all physical items and products such as roofs, windows, and slabs that can be touched and seen are classified as IfcObjectDefinition.
- IfcRelationship summarizes all the relationships among objects. This can enable users saving relationship specific properties directly at the relationship object and avoid duplication of relationship semantics from the object attributes. The abstract objectified relationship IfcRelationship and its subtype relationships are responsible for connectivity among objects, in which several properties can be attached to each relationship.

Figure 2 demonstrates the different types of objectified relationship within the IFC (Version 2x3) and their abstract super type IfcRelationship.

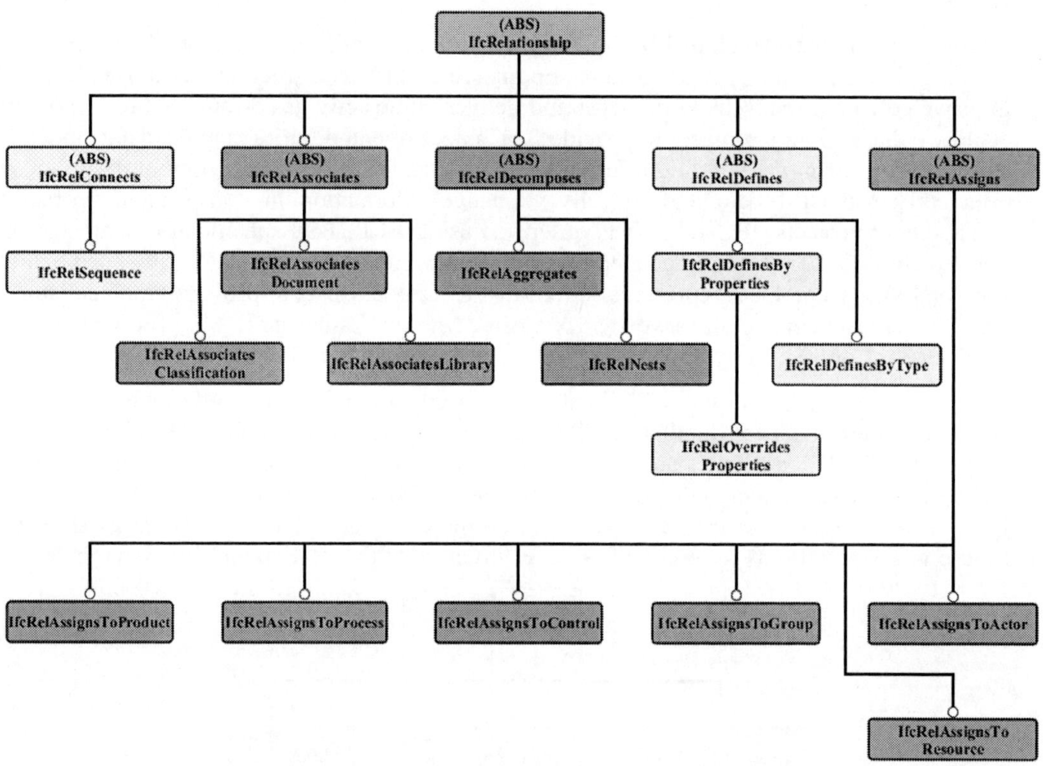

Figure 2: IFC abstract objectified relationship

IFC classes have direct attributes attached to them which could indicate a relationship to another object or they could just be attached as simple data type attribute, e.g. integer, string, logical, or Boolean. Therefore, IFC models distinguish between the attributes that are directly attached to object as entity attributes, and attributes that assigned to indicate a relationship to other objects. The second of two attributes are the most adopted approach to extend viable properties. However, as it is depicted Figure 3, each IFC class could have simple data attributes with referenced object attributes as in the case of the *IfcRoot*, or referenced object with relationship attributes as in the case of IfcProduct, or entity attributes and relationship attributes together as in the case of IfcObject.

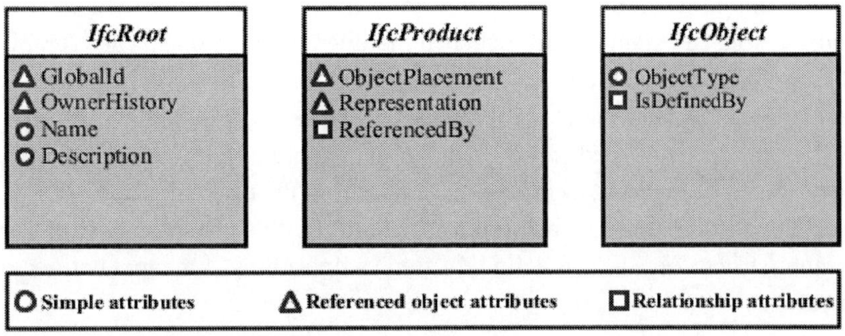

Figure 3 IFC Entity attributes and relationship attributes

In addition to the direct attached attributes, the objects can inherit attributes from their supertype classes, where, property pair can be assigned to almost any type of objects and thus to support enlarging their attributes base.

3. Graph data management

Graph theory is the branch of mathematics that dealing with the study of graphs (Hughes, 2016). While the concept of graphs itself is defined by graph theory as a diagrammatic representation of real-world scenarios in a form of points and lines (Wilson, 1996). The points are called vertices or nodes, while the lines that connect them are so-called edges, arcs or relationships. Each vertex in the graph is represented by drawing a dot or a circle, while the relationship between each pair of vertices is indicated by drawing an arc or line if they are connected by an edge.

The application of graphs has become an important technique to describe several scenarios in the real-world. One of the applications of graphs is to provide a simplified description of scenarios datasets in a way that produce a useful understanding of a complicated data. This has led to the birth of a special form of graph model, the so-called labelled property graph (Robinson, Webber , & Eifrem, 2015 "Second Edition"). Labelled property graphs are similar to simple graphs; consist of nodes and relationships which are often expressed as vertices and edges. However, labeled property graphs provide additional characteristics to facilitate graph understanding, where, nodes could have a single or multiple labels; in addition, they could have properties (key-value pairs). Relationships can also be named and contain properties while connecting each two nodes as start and end node.

Several graph processing systems have been developed in the last decade to meet the modern graph modelling and analysis tasks. Doekemeijer (Doekemeijer & Varbanescu, 2014- PDS-2014-003) has declared that more than 80 systems have been introduced in the period from 2004 to 2014, by academia and industry sectors together. However, the currently available systems can be divided into two main kinds, graph databases, and graph processing. In this section and for the objectives of the present study, we will express the concepts of graph database systems in general, with a focus on Neo4j graph database system particularly in some cases. However, all these efforts in the field of graph modelling express the importance of graphs for real-world scenarios. Angles (Angles & Gutierrez, February 2008) summarized the advantages of using graphs as modelling mechanism for data management as following:

1. Graphs enable users to model data exactly as they are represented in the real-world scenario, this can significantly enhance the operations on data. Thus, graphs can keep all the information about an object in a single node and display the related information by relationships connected to it.
2. Queries can be developed based on the graph structure. For instance, the finding of the shortest path can be considered as sub graph from the original graph.
3. Operationally, graphs can be stored efficiently within databases using special graph storage structures, and functional graph algorithms for application of specific operations.

4. Methodology and Transformation Workflow

The proposed methodology introduces a workflow to develop and build IFC-based graph models using IFC EXPRESS schema and IFC models in STEP physical file format. In this workflow the whole transformation is automated and done through connected web services (dynamic EXPRESS parser, IFC web data server and web-based graph database import interface) without the need for any local tools. The transformation supports any valid IFC schema.

In our approach a single graph database is used to storage various IFC models at the same time, where each node (object) will has a special attribute to identify the belonged model. In this way queries and advanced analysis are not limited to one IFC model. This feature allows to do merging queries on different disciplines BIM models (architecture, structural design, MEP) of the same project, or to compare different versions of the same model over time.

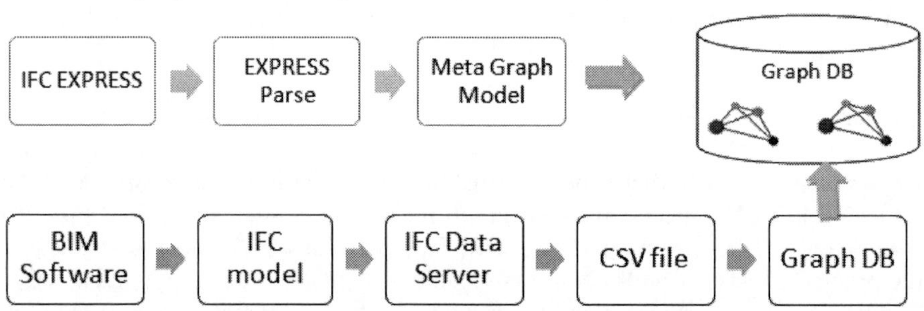

Figure 4: IFC to graph database conversation workflow

4.1 IFC Meta Graph Model

The workflow starts with analysing the IFC EXPRESS schema and developing a generic approach to generate an IFC Meta Graph Model (IMG), which represents all IFC classes, their attributes and the relationships between them (Figure 5).

IMG model will be used later in order to generate and check the relationships between IFC instance entities and validate IFC models. It can be also used to investigate changes between different IFC versions (e.g. IFC2X3 vs IFC4) or to run filters and information retrieval queries for a better understanding of IFC schema and analyzing its complex data connectivity.

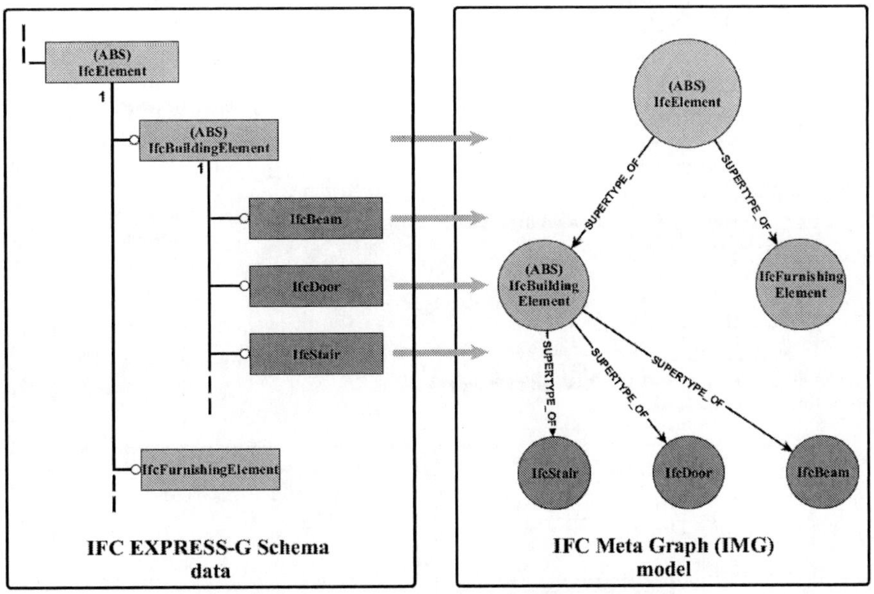

Figure 5 Mapping IFC EXPRESS into a Meta Graph Model

The mapping of IFC EXPRESS model into IMG is carried out through writing a special server script (in Ruby language) and run it on IFCWebServer.org (Ismail, 2011) which provides a dynamic EXPRESS parser and web script console. This script generates a set of Cyber commands, which create the Meta graph inside Neo4j database, where Cypher is a declarative, SQL-inspired language for describing patterns in graphs visually using an ascii-art syntax.

Figure 6 shows the scope of mapping for IFC classes, their attributes, data types and the relationships between classes. Both of IFC classes and the attributes are mapped into nodes and they are connected through various relationships like "has_property" to connect a class node with its direct attributes or "subtype_of" to connect a class with its sub-classes.

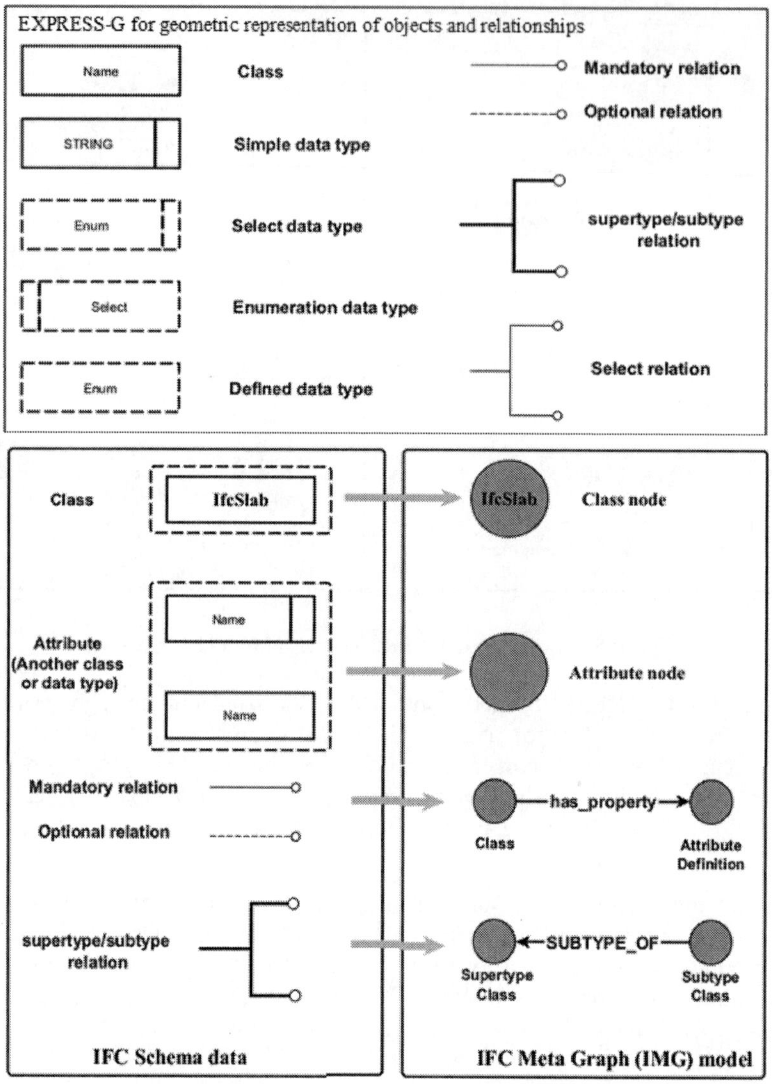

Figure 6 Mapping of classes, data types and relationships within IMG model

4.2 IFC Object Graph model

The next step in the workflow is to convert IFC models into IFC Object Graph (IOG). In this graph each IFC entity expect the relationships will be represented as a node and will hold information about the class of the entity and its basic attributes and will be connected to other entities through named relationships.

A special server script based on IFCWebServer.org has been developed in order to automate the process of extracting IFC data (objects, relationships) and creating all necessary Cypher commands for the data import and also relationship generation. The script include some options to exclude certain IFC classes, for example all low level geometry classes.

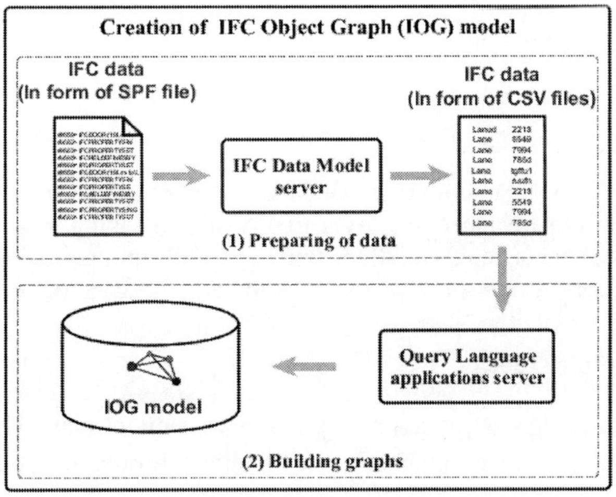

Figure 7 Creation of IFC Object Graph

IFC data are extracted and saved at first in CSV format then imported into Neo4j to create the graph-based models (Figure 7).

The Cypher snippet bellow shows the import command for IfcBuilding.

```
Load csv with headers from 'http://www.ifcwebserver.org/
/ahmednahar/Muster003.ifc/IfcBuilding.csv' as line FIELDTERMINATOR '	'
Create (u: IfcBuilding {Model: line.Model, label: line.label, IFCID: line.IFCID,
globalId: line.globalId, ownerHistory: line.ownerHistory, name: line.name,
description: line.description, objectType: line.objectType, objectPlacement:
line.objectPlacement, representation: line.representation, longName:
line.longName, compositionType: line.compositionType, elevationOfRefHeight:
line.elevationOfRefHeight, elevationOfTerrain: line.elevationOfTerrain,
buildingAddress: line.buildingAddress });
```

After importing the IFC data and with help of the Meta graph model the relationships for referenced, inversed and derived attributes will be created automatically. The scope of relationships transformation includes all IFC relationships, for example: (1) aggregation, (2) spatial and element composition, (3) spatial and element decomposition, (4) zone and group assignment, (5) building system assignment, (6) spatial structure, (7) element and path connectivity and (8) element filling.

The next step creates direct relationships between graph nodes and their connected information and deletes all redundant relationship. For example the building element nodes will be connected directly with their corresponding properties through a "isDefinedByProperties" relationships and all IfcRelDefinesByProperties and IfcRelDefinesByType can be deleted. As a result, the graph queries can be simplified by normalizing the property sets and non-direct attributes of building elements to be assigned as direct node attributes.

A further step will be assigning each node in the graph with a set of labels of all its parent classes and running a set of pre-defined queries for further classification and normalization of the building elements attributes according to their classes and property sets. For example all walls which have the property "Load bearing" set to true will be linked into a node "Load bearing walls" through a relationship "is-load-bearing".

5. Validation and Case Studies

After converting IFC models into a graph database it can be used as an IFC data server to run data retrieval queries and advanced analysis of BIM models taking in account the advantages of applying graph theory concepts and algorithms like path finding and shortest path method. In the following sections we present some simple and advanced examples.

5.1 Examples of Simple Queries

- **Retrieve the assigned property sets of a certain object:** This query returns all propery sets which are assigned to a ceartin object through its globalId value.

```
MATCH
(wall:IfcWallStandardCase{Model:'M.ifc',GUID:'3wP5TgnCHEPwsgi3SxIcXs'})-
[rel]-(property:IfcPropertySet)
RETURN DISTINCT wall,rel,property
```

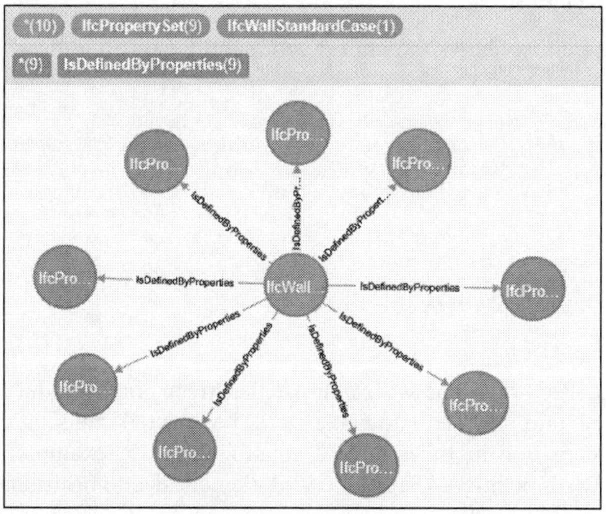

Figure 8 getting the assigned PropertySets for a certain object

- **Filter objects based on material:** This query returns a list of all doors and their material names. The connection between doors and material nodes is done automatically by the graph database engine (through IfcDoor–[*1..5]-IfcMaterial relation command) without the need to know how both IfcDoor and IfcMaterial are related to each other in the IFC schema.

```
MATCH (door:IfcDoor{Model:'Muster003.ifc'})-[*1..5]-
(material:IfcMaterial)
RETURN DISTINCT (material.IFCID)AS IFCID,(material.name)AS Material_name
```

- **Create new relationships to assign objects to layers:** This query creats the relationship "assignedItem" between defined layers in the model and their coresponding elements.

```
MATCH (n:IfcPresentationLayerAssignment{Model: "Office_A.ifc"})
UNWIND split(replace(replace(n.assignedItems,"(",""),")",""),",") as o
MERGE (assignedItems {Model: "Office_A.ifc",IFCID: replace(o,"#","")})
MERGE (n)-[:assignedItems]->(assignedItems);
```

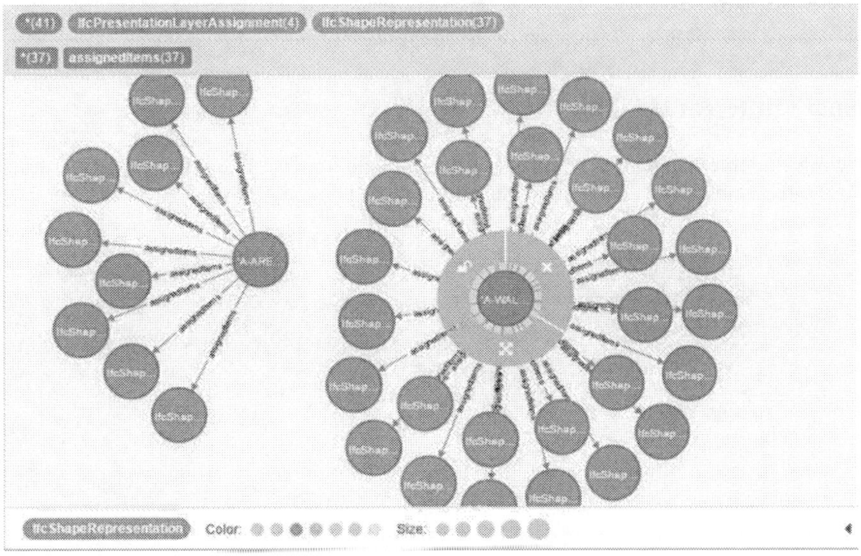

Figure 9 Assign objects to layers

5.2 Analysis of BIMs for Emergency Routes

In this example we used the graph database to do a simplified topology analysis of BIM models in order to analyse and generate emergency routes. The construction of possible escape paths is done in 2 steps:

(1) Through the relationship "BoundedBy" between IfcSpace and IfcDoor entities

(2) Through the relationship "RelatingSpace" between 2 IfcSpace neighbour objects.

```
MATCH p=(d:IfcDoor{IFCID:'9824',Model:'Muster003.ifc'})-[r:BoundedBy]-
>(s:IfcSpace)
RETURN p
UNION
MATCH p=(s1:IfcSpace{Model:'Muster003.ifc'})-
[r1:BoundedBy]-(d1:IfcDoor)-[r2:BoundedBy]-(s2:IfcSpace)
WHERE s1.IFCID > s2.IFCID
RETURN p
UNION
MATCH p=(s1:IfcSpace {Model:'Muster003.ifc'}) <-[r1:RelatingSpace]-
(r:IfcRelSpaceBoundary)-[r2:RelatingSpace]->(s2:IfcSpace)
```

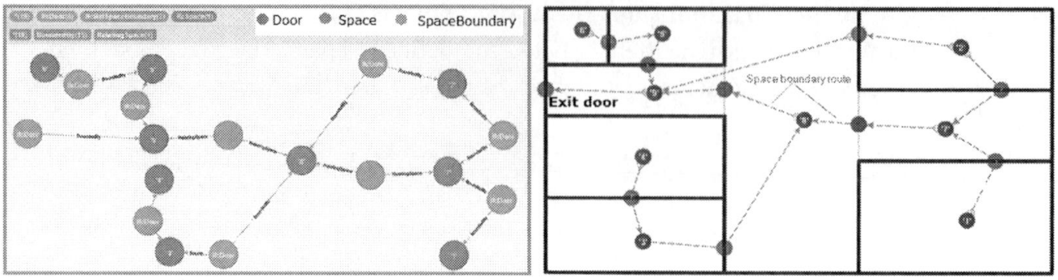

Figure 10 Creation of escape routes through graph query

5.3 Compare Different IFC Models

The following example compares 2 versions of IFC models for the same building and returns a list of all windows which have been added in the second model.

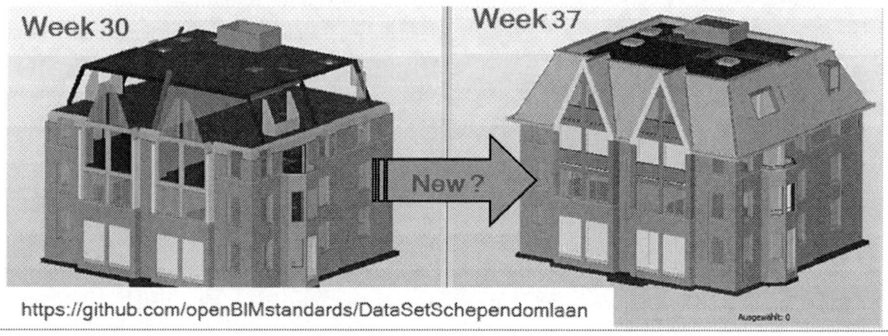


```
MATCH (W30 { Model: 'Week30.ifc' }),(W37 { Model: 'Week37.ifc' })
WHERE W30.tag = W37.tag
WITH collect(distinct W30.tag) as tags
MATCH (new) WHERE new.tag <> "" AND NOT new.tag  IN tags
AND new.label = "IfcWindow"
RETURN distinct new.label as Class, new.globalId, new.IFCID as
STEPID,new.name, new.tag ORDER BY new.tag
```

$ MATCH (w30 { Model: 'Week30.ifc' }),(w37 { Model: 'Week37.ifc' }) where w30.tag = w37.tag WITH collect(distinct w30.tag) as tags M

Class	GUID	STEPID	Name	Tag
IfcWindow	'2KsoxVt15Es8dH3L6KMVj0'	#108847	'dakkoepel 1000x_(769613)'	'281480A1-040A-48D1-A601-A1D6110BB331'
IfcWindow	'1aiPGZMJTBuOCj8nflqbyU'	#70771	'velux K08_(944800)'	'3461CF7D-134D-4C49-8212-00B3CB2FAA89'
IfcWindow	'0fexbeEOj7GxM6YwAainL9'	#293103	'dakkoepel 1000x_(1010566)'	'3EA47F39-44A3-44C7-A8F2-48A6D7B6F079'
IfcWindow	'2ZTlq5qx98Gg00NEGgsCu7'	#94339	'velux K08_(967504)'	'416FC727-C9B1-48B9-9170-B149BE80A18F'
IfcWindow	'0FbXSSF5b7$Or4awT$abIF'	#47203	'velux K08_(926256)'	'45C00328-2D0A-4E32-8D62-D9E365398AA8'
IfcWindow	'0y5r$haCX78Pq2BDkdcGl6'	#302403	'dakkoepel 1000x_(1018927)'	'481DE70F-AC2D-4599-864B-80BCD74EA453'
IfcWindow	'3OsF8vqm52GRculCVSAR6F'	#290003	'dakkoepel 1000x_(1019167)'	'727B48D4-9217-4F38-984E-DDD4AFF7252C'
IfcWindow	'2PhZ0Ahyn399ojlU1JuiEf'	#23635	'velux K08_(948940)'	'E0CC4923-AC54-46D1-96DF-3F7628C03F8A'
IfcWindow	'1uSpy8O7X6qvqZOAWOaRLe'	#296203	'dakkoepel 1000x_(1019087)'	'EEB2ECF2-163A-4985-A831-5E9F2FFE50EB'
IfcWindow	'1TLojM7ir6OReaPEG9rR1A'	#299303	'dakkoepel 1000x_(1019007)'	'FAB3F4BB-3B1F-4E1D-98BE-3FDFD0EA66A1'

Started streaming 10 records after 205 ms and completed after 206 ms.

Figure 11 Compare IFC models using graph query

6. Conclusions and Future Work

This paper presented a workflow for automatic transformation of IFC schema and models into a property graph database. The suggested approach have been applied on many IFC schema/models in order to explore the capabilities of the IFC-based graph models for data query and advanced analysis of the BIM models.

The current scope of transformation and queries doesn't take in account the geometry information or the process of creating geometry objects based on parameters or Boolean operations. A future research is needed in order to include the geometry information to be a part of the pre-defined queries by developing an interface between the graph database and an IFC geometry engine.

Future research could involve developing a user friendly web application for editing the information of graph database and developing an IFC export interface for sub-models or merging models. The future work will include also developing special stored procedures which allow accessing the Java API of Neo4j directly and running the import and data retrieval queries much faster compared with solely using of Cypher commands and followed with a benchmark to compare the performance with other existing query approaches.

Graph models can be considered a satisfactory tool to manage building information. However, writing user-defined queries for users without IFC and graph skills still quite challenging where advanced queries should be written by IFC and graph DB experts. This research can be considered as an initial step in the direction of IFC-based graph models formation management.

References

Angles, R., & Gutierrez, C. (2008). Survey of Graph Database Models. ACM Computing Surveys, 40(1).

Doekemeijer, N., & Varbanescu, A. (2014). A Survey of Parallel Graph Processing Frameworks. Delft: Parallel and Distributed Systems Group- Delft University of Technology.

Hughes, J. (2016). ECE 3020 Mathematical Foundations of Computer Engineering. Atlanta: Lecture notes from Georgia Institute of Technology.

Isaac, S., Sadeghpour, F., & Navon, R. (2013). Analyzing Building Information using Graph Theory. International Association for Automation and Robotics in Construction (IAARC)- 30th ISARC, (S. 1013-1020). Montreal.

Ismail, A. (2011). *IFCWebServer*. IFC Data model server and online viewer: http://ifcwebserver.org

Khalili, A., & Chua, D. (2015). IFC-Based Graph Data Model for Topological Queries on Building Elements . American Society of Civil Engineers, Vol.29 Issue3.

Robinson, I., Webber , J., & Eifrem, E. (2015). Graph Databases. Sebastopol: O'Reilly Media.

Tauscher, E., Bargstädt, H.-J., & Smarsly, K. (2016). Generic BIM queries based on the IFC object model using graph theory. The 16th International Conference on Computing in Civil and Building Engineering. Osaka,Japan.

Wilson, R. (1996). Introduction to Graph Theory (Fourth edition Ausg.). Harlow- England: Longman Group Ltd.

Using a Knowledge Based System for Automatic Site Equipment Planning

Katrin Jahr and André Borrmann
Technische Universität München, Germany
katrin.jahr@tum.de

Abstract. The site equipment (SE) planning is a fundamental part of the construction preparation. A suitable site equipment supports the timely, cost-efficient and qualitative execution of the construction progress. The use of scientifically based planning tools can both speed up the process of construction site planning and lead to better results. This paper proposes a rule-based knowledge inference system to support SE planners in a semi- or fully automated manner using input data from building information models and working schedules. The knowledge based system is built using the ASL 2 licensed business rule management system *Drools*. Exemplary rules for four types of site equipment have been developed and implemented. Using sample projects, the feasibility of the proposed approach has been proven by showing that site equipment can be generated instantly.

1. Introduction

A reasonable and appropriate site equipment planning supports the timely, cost-effective and high-quality implementation of a construction project. The purpose of the site equipment (SE) is to ensure an orderly, productive and safe execution of all tasks necessary during the construction, reconstruction or demolition of a building or construction. Poorly designed or inappropriately executed site layouts can slow down the construction process, generate unnecessary costs and even constitute actual safety risks, making the process of the construction site layout planning (CSLP) an indispensable step of the execution planning. The first step to create reasonable site layout plans is to identify all needed SE, and to determine the necessary dimensions of each element of the SE. To generate a site layout plan, the SE has to be placed on the available areas.

The necessary site equipment varies widely depending on the conditions of the specific construction project. Due to the large deviations of the circumstances and specific requirements in different construction projects, the site equipment has to be planned individually for each project. However, despite the large impact of the SE on the on-site overheads and productivity of the construction, the site planning process has been formalized very little. Usually, planners conduct the CSLP manually, without technological support. The dimensioning of the individual elements of the SE is mostly realized based on experience of the planners and rules of thumb, without qualitative or quantitative reviews. The results of the manual CSLP planning thus depend solely on the expert knowledge and practical experience of the executing planner.

A large set of information, which is traditionally acquired in very late planning stages, has to be considered during the CSLP process, and changes in the construction design and construction methods usually require the adjustment or re-planning of the SE. To reduce the planning efforts and prevent from repetitive re-planning phases, the CSLP is usually conducted only after decisions on the design and construction are final, depriving the possibility to include information about the necessary SE in the process. In this way, potentially expensive and inconvenient solutions might be condoned because the SE was not taken into account during the construction planning.

To be able to include aspects of the site layout in the planning considerations, a fast and easy way support planners in their decisions by partly or even completely automating the planning of the construction site. To support the planners during the generation of individual site facilities, knowledge based systems (KBS) form a very suitable basis. These systems are computer programs that formalize human knowledge in a strict logical and computable manner, allowing them to infer conclusions from given facts. They are used to assist humans in solving complex problems and tasks.

This paper presents an adaptable approach to efficiently automate the generation of construction site facilities, concentrating on the identification and dimensioning of individual site equipment. In the first part of the paper, an overview of the state of the art in construction site planning is given. In the second part of the paper, different types of knowledge based systems are presented. Furthermore, a rule-based KIS is defined as most applicable for the use case presented here. In the third part of the paper, an implementation of a rule-based KIS for automated construction site facility generation is introduced.

2. State of the Art

Up to now, the construction site equipment is generally planned by hand. However, there has been effort by several research groups to automate the planning process. In the next sections, a short overview over the traditionally site equipment planning and the state of the art in digitally aided site equipment planning is given.

2.1 Fundamentals of Site Equipment Planning

The site equipment on construction sites is used to prepare and conduct all individual construction processes in the best possible way in order to enable a fluent and continuous construction progress. The construction site equipment includes all producing and non-producing facilities required on site for the construction or renovation of a structure (Meyran, 1973). Depending on the state in which a construction project is to be carried out, different laws and regulations have to be applied. This work is primarily concerned with legislation in Germany. Construction-related regulations can be found, for example, in the workplace ordinance (BAuA, 2016) and various DIN standards. The site equipment can be classified in seven basic groups (see Schach and Otto (2011) and Albert and Schneider (2016)):

- Construction machinery (e.g. hoists and concrete pumps)
- Social and office facilities (e.g. office and sanitary containers)
- Storage areas (e.g. tool sheds, outside and inside storage)
- Traffic areas and transport routes (construction roads, entrances and exits)
- Media supply and disposal (e.g. power and water supply and waste disposal)
- Site security (e.g. fences, illumination, scaffolding)
- Excavation support

With ongoing progress, the requirements and conditions on the construction site change. The construction process is typically divided into several construction stages, where some facilities may not be required in each construction stage. Therefore, a dynamic construction site plan is required. At the beginning of each construction stage, items which are no longer needed are disassembled and replaced by other facilities (Kumar and Cheng, 2015).

During the planning process, all needed site equipment is identified, dimensioned, and finally placed on the construction site. In this paper, we concentrate on the identification and dimensioning of SE. Dimensioning—the determination of necessary and economic dimensions according to the specific conditions and requirements of a construction project—is especially crucial for producing, transporting and storing facilities. Under dimensioned elements can lead to a delay in the construction progress (e.g. non-sufficient storage areas). Individual work steps could become impractical (for example if a crane's reach is too small). Over dimensioned elements increase the costs (for example if the crane is higher than needed) and the travel times (if storage areas are too large and need to be crossed frequently).

2.2 Related Work

While digital assistance is widely available in other construction phases, the CSLP is supported little. Especially the automatic generation and dimensioning of site facilities are widely neglected. While various research groups have dealt with the optimization of construction site facility planning during the last decades, they generally use predefined site equipment and consider solely the positioning on site. Up to now, there is no comprehensive implementation of the construction site setup problem, requiring extensive manual inputs for all approaches.

First approaches on using knowledge based systems for construction related tasks have been published by Hendrickson et al. (1987) and Moselhi and Nicholas (1990). Both groups are using expert systems to create working schedules. Hamiani (1987) presented CONSITE, a knowledge-based expert system framework to solve the construction site layout problem. Tommelein et al. (1992) used an expert system to designing construction site layout. In both approaches, construction site equipment objects are represented by rectangular surfaces and arranged on a 2D building site. Limits of the program lie in the need of high amounts of manual inputs, as well as the lack of transparency and the possibility to influence the generation.

Newer approaches use the advantages of using information obtained from Building Information Models, but again, are neglecting the automated generation of the site equipment. Researchers concentrate on heuristic optimization of the site layout. Huang and Wong (2015) use a binary-mixed-integer-linear algorithm to optimize the site layout towards reduced travel times as well as little set-up costs. Shawki et al. (2010), Elgendi et al. (2014), and Kumar and Cheng (2015) propose the use of genetic algorithms to create construction site plans. The algorithms begin with random layouts, which are varied by crossing and mutation. The research also includes the use of meta-heuristic algorithms, such as swarm intelligence: Yahya and Saka (2014) use an algorithm based on the behavior within a beekeeper (artificial bee colony algorithm), Ning et al. (2010) use an ant-algorithm (max-min ant system). Wang et al. (2015) plan optimal crane positions on large-scale sites using firearm algorithm. Schwabe et al. (2016) use interactive rule checking to evaluate site layouts during the manual generation. An extensive literature review on prior approaches to optimize site layouts is also provided by Huang and Wong (2015).

3. Knowledge Based Systems

Knowledge based systems are computer programs using methods from the field of artificial intelligence. They are used to assist humans in solving complex problems and tasks, that are usually conducted by specialized decision makers. To that end, the algorithms mirror human thought processes and attempt to draw intelligent conclusions and action recommendations from given information (Lunze, 2016).

3.1 Characteristics and Architecture of Knowledge Based Systems

Knowledge based systems are characterized by the strict separation of knowledge (stored in a knowledge base) and techniques to retrieve information from that knowledge (called inference engine). Further components are needed to fill the knowledge base (expert interface and knowledge acquisition component) as well as to retrieve solutions for a specific problem (user interface, working memory and explanation facility) (Beierle and Kern-Isberner, 2008). The typical structure of a KBS is shown in Figure 1.

The core functionality of a knowledge based systems lies in the knowledge base and the inference engine. The *knowledge base* contains the permanent knowledge, which can be structured in rules and facts. While the knowledge usually consists of factual and certain knowledge,

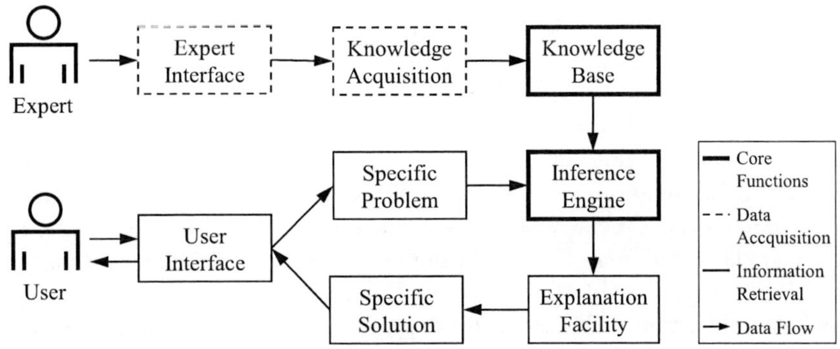

Fig. 1: Components and data flow of a knowledge based system

heuristic knowledge can be added. However, heuristic knowledge is less rigorous and may lead to unexpected results, and is therefore rarely used (Shen et al., 2010). The *inference engine* is the knowledge processing and reasoning component of the KBS. In analogy to the functionality of the human brain, it is able to generate answers, predictions or suggestions for a specific problem by the use of artificial intelligence. There are two types of inference that can be implemented in inference engines: forward chaining and backward chaining (Lunze, 2016). Forward chaining is the classical data-driven approach: the input data is known and a previously unknown solution is searched. Backward chaining is used, when the input data is not known, i.e. it generates possible input data to obtain a desired solution.

For the creation and expansion of the knowledge base with expert knowledge, a knowledge acquisition component and an expert interface are needed. The *expert interface* operates as input device for entering knowledge about the specific field of the KBS. The *knowledge acquisition component* inserts the data into the knowledge base. Knowledge can be entered and altered by human experts as well as by the KBS itself (Raza, 2009).

To generate and retrieve solutions for specific problems, a user interface, and an explanation facility are used. The *user interface* provides the communication between the user and the KBS. It may contain a graphical interface and different amenities to facilitate the interaction. The specific problems have to be converted to facts that can be processed by the inference engine. Temporary, case-specific data is stored in the working memory. This data includes both data inserted into the user interface as well as the determined solutions for this data. The *explanation facility* is used to control the generated solutions. An explanation of how the inference is drawn is substantial to better understand how the system generates a certain solution, and to supervise the results in case of unexpected outcomes (Beierle and Kern-Isberner, 2008).

3.2 Types of Knowledge Inference Systems

During the last decades, several different methods of setting up knowledge inference systems have been developed. In the following, a selection of these methods are briefly described. Finally, a well-suited method for the application in automated construction site layout planning is identified.

Logic Based Systems (LBS): In logic based systems, the knowledge is formulated as assertions in logic. They are well suited for problem domains that can be divided in small, logically solvable entities. LBS are usually represented using logic-based languages, such as Prolog. A disadvantage of using hard-coded LBS lies in the low flexibility and in the need to recalculate the whole program for each fact (Lunze, 2016).

Rule Based Systems (RBS): Rule based knowledge systems are related to logic based system. They are well suited for problem domains that can be represented in modular rules. Rules are used to precisely describe elementary circumstances. They are typically in the general form of *WHEN* <situation or condition> *THEN* <action> (Kostem, 1986), contrast to the first predicate logic of other logic based systems. More complex systems can be reduced to a set of elementary entities, with each entity being represented by one rule. To process the set of rules through inference, it is insufficient to merely execute one rule after the other. Several rules may refer to the same fact, which might lead to a loop – one rule changing the fact, and the other rule changing it back. This is why a rule engine is used. Rule engines are able to execute a set of rules in an intelligent manner by using algorithms such as Rete (Forgy, 1982). They are able to support additional features, such as priorities, preconditions, or mutual exclusion. Therefore, even complex, cross-linked sets of rules can be evaluated efficiently. An advantage of RBS is the human readable and comprehensible formulation of the rules, allowing for easy inspection and rule acquisition. However, more complex relations between pieces of knowledge may be impossible to represent accurately. Also, reasoning under uncertainty is a challenge to be considered.

Case Based Reasoning (CBR): In case based reasoning, the knowledge base is structured as a set of cases, where previously encountered experiences are stored. New problems are solved by adapting the solution of the most relevant known case. Subsequently, the problem and adapted solution are saved, gradually increasing the knowledge base ("learning by doing"). Case based reasoning is therefore not logic based, but rather a memory based process. CBR are well suited for problems with complex cases, that means large scale patterns that cannot be divided into smaller, logically solvable entities. Difficulties in CBR lie in the knowledge acquisition and in the adaptation of known solutions to new cases. Decisions based on imitation may lead to devastating consequences through incorrect adaption.

Network Based Reasoning: In network based reasoning, the knowledge is organized in decision trees or networks, where several attributes are used to describe one object. The knowledge trees or networks can be generated from known cases through machine learning techniques. However, for each case, the values of each attribute should be known. Each attribute is assigned to one node of the tree, whereby each node represents the query for the value of the attribute. The edges originating from a node represent the possible values of the attribute. Each end node (leaf node) is assigned a truth value or class representing the outcome of the decision tree for this end node. Network based systems are well suited and primarily used for classification problems (Beierle and Kern-Isberner, 2008).

Regulations and instructions concerning site equipment are usually formulated in clear and precise rules that can be broken down to elementary entities. Usually, the correlations between requirements and solutions are concise and definite (e.g. the number of washing facilities per worker or minimal required crane capacities). Therefore, a rule based knowledge system is a good choice for this application. The human-readability and comprehensibility of the rules helps to lower the acceptance threshold of engineers. Additionally, it facilitates the knowledge acquisition and control of results. In the past, rule based systems faced difficulties in user-friendliness and applicability. Limited resources in hard disk space and system memory restricted the scope and inference speed, impeding the broad implementation of rule based knowledge systems. With modern hardware and improved inference algorithms, new opportunities arise for user-friendly and comprehensive applications.

3.3 Rule Based Knowledge Inference Systems in Drools

For this work, the ASL 2 licensed business rule management system *Drools* is used. It contains an inference engine used to process data on specific projects (facts) depending on the knowledge base (rules). As most rule based systems, Drools uses an advanced version of the Rete algorithm (Forgy, 1982), which is able to scale to a large number of rules and facts by increasing the efficiency of the rule processing. The Rete algorithm generates a discrimination network using all conditions given in the different rules. The network contains different types of nodes: root, object, 1-input, 2-input and terminal. All objects enter through the root node. Each condition is represented by a 1-input node. If a rule contains more than one condition, a 2-input node is used to combine each two conditions in one 1-input node. The output of the last input node is used as input for a terminal node. The terminal node represents the action of a condition. During the first propagation of the fact, all conditions are checked and actions are performed when needed. The output of each node is stored. From the second propagation onward, the stored outputs are reused when the facts remain the same. Only conditions for altered facts must be checked, reducing the calculation effort significantly. However, as the interim results have to be stored, the memory usage can increase drastically (Forgy, 1982).

To better represent object oriented data and to reduce the calculation effort further, the Rete algorithm was adapted. Adding further node types, the developers of Drools implemented the ReteOO (Rete-Object-Oriented) algorithm (Sottara et al., 2010). The new node types are entry point nodes, object type nodes, alpha nodes, join nodes, and left input adapter nodes. Entry point nodes are located behind the root node. If several entry point nodes exist, the network can be split into several networks. For each object type used in the rules, an object type node is created. Object type nodes act as barrier—they only propagate facts that apply to the following nodes. This way, facts are only checked against rules whose conditions demand the same object type. Alpha nodes expand the function of 1-input nodes to evaluate literal conditions. Left input adapter nodes are used to convert objects to tuples for following joins. Join nodes, or beta nodes, expand the function of 2-input nodes to find matches for rules with several conditions. Additionally, ReteOO adds enhancements such as node-sharing, where nodes can be shared when rules follow similar patterns.

After further development, the PHREAK algorithm was introduced (JBoss Community, 2016). PHREAK is characterized as lazy and goal oriented, whereas Rete is characterized to be eager and data oriented. Instead of instantly firing all rules, rules with all inputs satisfied are queued. Rules are then fired depending on their salience. According to JBoss Community (2016), the PHREAK algorithm is additionally enhanced by adding three layers of contextual memory, stack based evaluations, isolated rule evaluation as well as rule, segment and node base linking.

4. Proof of Concept

To demonstrate and test the proposed approach, a prototype has been implemented using JavaFX. The prototype provides different features to support engineers during the planning of the construction process: generation of work schedules, generation of site equipment and generation of site layout plans.

4.1 Developement of the knowledge base

The knowledge base consists of a set of rules defining the required specifications of the site equipment. In the business rule management system Drools, rules can be formulated using both the MVFLEX Expression Language, which allows simplified syntax, as well as in plain Java when additional commands are needed. The rules follow the typical form of *WHEN...THEN...*. In this implementation, Java statements have been used in the *THEN* statements.

During knowledge acquisition, rules have to be identified and transformed in the rule format. Rules on how to create site equipment are available in technical documents such as standards, guidelines and drawings. Required dimensions and performance of the site equipment can often be derived from the demands of the construction and logistical considerations. Additionally, there are non-written rules and engineering knowledge arising from experience of the planners. Up to now, rules have been implemented for four main types of site equipment: tower cranes, concrete pumps, storage areas and social facilities. For better maintainability, an individual rule file has been created for each type of equipment. The characteristics implemented per site equipment type are depicted in Table 1. Several rules need to be implemented per characteristic, as they can be influenced by several conditions. To form the knowledge base, the rules have been formulated using a development environment. The knowledge base can easily be expanded with further information on the existing site equipment or with rules for the planning of further site equipment types.

Table 1: Characteristics of site equipments been implemented as rules

Site equipment type	Characteristics
Tower crane	hight, jib length, capacity
Concrete pump	capacity, reach
Storage spaces	minimum width, minimum length or minimum area
Sanitary and office facilities	number of offices, break rooms, first aid rooms, restrooms

An example rule for creating the needed size of a storage space is depicted in Figure 2. In a first step, a storage space is created for each material. It can be read as: when material of type rebar is needed, and a storage space of type rebar is planned, then calculate the minimum side lengths. For rebar, the minimum storage side length can be assumed as the length of the longest bar. The minimum side width can be depicted by the number of bundles, where a bundle is assumed to have the width of one meter. To get the required width in meter, the number of bars is divided by the number of bars per bundle. The number of bars per bundle is requested as user input and stored in the HashMap map.

```
rule "Storage size rebar"
    when
        $s : StorageSpace(type == "Rebar")
        $m : Material(type == $s.type)

    then
        double number = $m.getQuantity();
        double minWidth = number / (double)map.get("amountInBundle");
        double minLength = (double)$m.properties.get("Length");

        modify($s){setMinWidth(minWidth), setMinLength(minLength)}

    end
```

Fig. 2: Rule for rebar storage size calculation

4.2 Prototype Implementation

A process scheme for the proposed concept is depicted in Figure 3. As input for the site equipment generation, information from the BIM model and the working schedule is used (see Table 2). The working schedule provides additional information on the operation sequences of the individual construction processes. If certain site equipment elements are required only for a short time, the demolition and reconstruction of the site equipment may be considered. Additionally, the knowledge of the time operation is necessary for the determination of reserve quantities and the reasonable design of storage areas. For the generation of working schedules, the tool "ultimatum" has been integrated (Abdelaleim et al., 2014). Each construction component from the BIM-model is linked with a process pattern to retrieve all processes necessary to conduct the construction (cf. Marx and König (2011)). The processes are then sorted by an optimization algorithm to form a working schedule. Additionally, each process has a list of needed ressources, such as tower cranes, workers or concrete pumps. The working schedule, the correlating building components and the needed equipment (according to the pocesses) are stored in an SQLite database for data exchange. Using this input, the site equipment is generated using the knowledge based system presented in this paper. Additional information needed for the generation can be entered in an input prompt, for example if the workers are accommodated on site. The generation of site layout plans by placing the site equipment on the construction field is currently conducted by the user via keyboard input or drag and drop. An optimization algorithm to automate the positioning of site equipment is currently under development. After finishing the site layout planning, the generated site equipment is stored in a database (type, characteristics and location of each equipment) and used to simulate the construction again, this time considering the site equipment. For example, process times could speed up when two tower cranes are placed instead of one. If the working schedule has to be updated, the site equipment might change as well. If no changes are necessary, the process is terminated. In a next step, the generated site equipment could be integrated and visualized together with the BIM model using a VR system (Ebner et al., 2012). In this system, a 3D representation can be created for each site element using the generated dimensions.

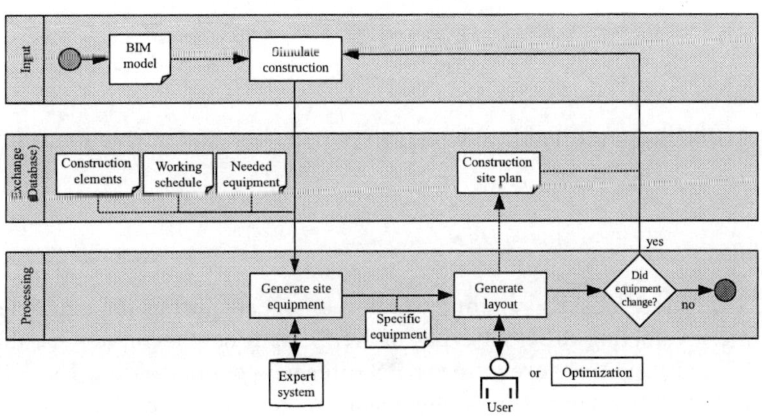

Fig. 3: Process scheme for a semi-automated site equipment planning system

Table 2: Information to be extracted from the BIM model

Category	Used Information
Conditions on site	property lines, approach and exit roads
Planned construction	floor area, coordinates of the highest point, building components
Material for prefabricated construction elements	number, weight and format of the parts
Material for in-situ concrete constructions	number and format of formwork, rebar, concrete volumes

The site layout planning is conducted in 2D using a graphical user interface (Figure 4). The main steps scheduling, dimensioning and positioning (yet to be implemented) can be accessed the buttons on the upper right corner. On the right hand site, a 2D representation of the construction field (light gray) with the planned construction (gray) is depicted. The site equipment is represented by their footprint. For a better overview, the positions of the elements can be shown as text. For construction machinery (tower cranes and concrete pumps), the reach is depicted, additionally. On the left hand site, all generated site elements are listed. If one element is selected in the list or on the 2D map, further information is depicted in the lower left corner. All site equipment can be altered towards special user requirements, and additional equipment can be easily generated by hand by using the buttons on the lower left corner.

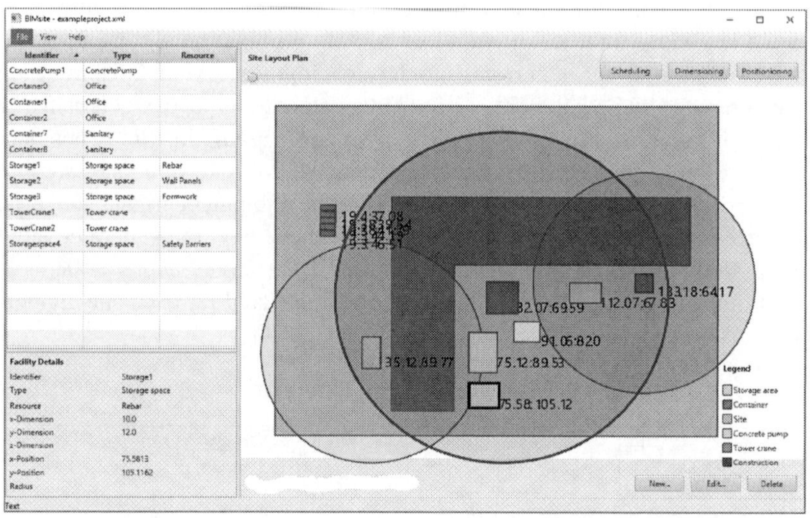

Fig. 4: Graphical user interface with plan presentation and interaction features

5. Conclusions

In this paper, a knowledge based system to support engineers during site equipment planning is presented after evaluating different types of KBS. With new technologies, that allow for larger databases and faster rule execution, KBS offer new opportunities. The KBS has been implemented in Java, using the business rule management system Drools. Dimensioning rules have been implemented for several site equipment types, allowing the automatic generation of site equipment for given working schedules and BIM models. However, the prototype is still open for extensions: further types of site equipment, such as supply facilities or traffic areas, can be added. Up to now, only rectangular storage areas are generated. If fuzzy input and uncertainty should be considered, another system might be necessary. However, Drools already announced to implement functionalities on fuzzy reasoning in further versions, so an upgrade could be sufficient (JBoss Community, 2016). Another idea currently investigated is the addition of a machine learning component, that is able to draw conclusion from a large amount of existing construction projects and site plans. This way, the generation is not reduced to rules, but also relies on experience. If needed, the site could be visualized in 3D using an external program. Additionally, the prototype is to be expanded by a site facility placing algorithm. The prototype will be tested and validated on several real-world pilot projects in the future.

Bibliography

Abdelaleim, O., Lin, Q., and Merkl, C. (2014). ultimaTUM - Intelligent Scheduling System. Technical report, Technische Universität München, Munich, Germany.

Albert, A. and Schneider, K.-J. (2016). *Schneider - Bautabellen für Ingenieure: mit Berechnungshinweisen und Beispielen*. Bundesanzeiger, Köln, 22 edition.

BAuA (2016). Arbeitsstätten. Arbeitsstättenverordnung, Technische Regeln für Arbeitsstätten. Verordnung, Bundesanstalt für Arbeitsschutz und Arbeitsmedizin (Hrsg.), Dortmund, Deutschland.

Beierle, C. and Kern-Isberner, G. (2008). *Methoden wissensbasierter Systeme: Grundlagen, Algorithmen, Anwendungen (German Edition)*. Vieweg+Teubner Verlag, Wiesbaden, Germany, 4. edition.

Ebner, A., Kammergruber, F., Horenburg, T., and Günthner, W. (2012). Logistics and layout planning of construction equipment on a vr-multi-touch-tablet. In *12th International Conference on Construction Application of Virtual Reality*.

Elgendi, E. M. O., Ahmed, V., Aziz, Z. U. H., and Shawki, K. (2014). A dynamic automated system for site layout planning in Egypt. In *14th International Conference on Construction Applications of Virtual Reality*, pages 52–58. University of Sharjah.

Forgy, C. L. (1982). Rete: A fast algorithm for the many pattern/many object pattern match problem. *Artificial intelligence*, 19(1):17–37.

Hamiani, A. (1987). *CONSITE: a knowledge-based expert system framework for construction site layout*. PhD thesis, Univ. of Texas,Austin, TX.

Hendrickson, C., Zozaya-Gorostiza, C., Rehak, D., Baracco-Miller, E., and Lim, P. (1987). Expert system for construction planning. *Journal of Computing in Civil Engineering*, 1(4):253–269.

Huang, C. and Wong, C. K. (2015). Optimisation of site layout planning for multiple construction stages with safety considerations and requirements. *Automation in Construction*, 53:58–68.

JBoss Community (2016). Drools Expert User Guide. `https://docs.jboss.org/drools/release/latestFinal/drools-docs/html/ch05.html#d0e4333`. Last checked on 2017/07/04.

Kostem, C. N. (1986). *Expert Systems in Civil Engineering: Technology and Application*. Amer Society of Civil Engineers.

Kumar, S. S. and Cheng, J. C. P. (2015). A BIM-based automated site layout planning framework for congested construction sites. *Automation in Construction*, 59:24–37.

Lunze, J. (2016). *Künstliche Intelligenz für Ingenieure: Methoden zur Lösung ingenieurtechnischer Probleme mit Hilfe von Regeln, logischen Formeln und Bayesnetzen (De Gruyter Studium) (German Edition)*. De Gruyter Oldenbourg, 3. edition.

Marx, A. and König, M. (2011). Preparation of constraints for construction simulation. In *Computing in Civil Engineering (2011)*, pages 462–439.

Meyran, G. (1973). *Optimierungsfragen der Baustelleneinrichtung*. PhD thesis, Technische Universität München.

Moselhi, O. and Nicholas, M. J. (1990). Hybrid expert system for construction planning and scheduling. *Journal of Construction Engineering and Management*, 116(2):221–238.

Ning, X., Lam, K.-C. K., and Lam, M. M. C.-K. (2010). Dynamic construction site layout planning using max-min ant system. *Automation in Construction*, 19(1):55–65.

Raza, F. N. (2009). Artificial intelligence techniques in software engineering (aitse). In *International MultiConference of Engineers and Computer Scientists (IMECS 2009)*, volume 1.

Schach, R. and Otto, J. (2011). *Baustelleneinrichtung: Grundlagen - Planung - Praxishinweise - Vorschriften und Regeln*. Leitfaden des Baubetriebs und der Bauwirtschaft. Vieweg+Teubner Verlag / Springer Fachmedien Wiesbaden GmbH Wiesbaden, Wiesbaden, 2. edition.

Schwabe, K., König, M., and Teizer, J. (2016). BIM Applications of Rule-based Checking in Construction Site Layout Planning Tasks. In *ISARC. Proceedings of the International Symposium on Automation and Robotics in Construction*, volume 33, page 1, Auburn, USA.

Shawki, K. M., El-Razek, M. E. A., and Maqboly, S. A. (2010). Optimal Arrangement of temporary Facilities in Construction Sites. *Journal of Engineering Sciences*, 38(4):949–960.

Shen, W., Hao, Q., Mak, H., Neelamkavil, J., Xie, H., Dickinson, J., Thomas, R., Pardasani, A., and Xue, H. (2010). Systems integration and collaboration in architecture, engineering, construction, and facilities management: A review. *Advanced Engineering Informatics*, 24(2):196–207.

Sottara, D., Mello, P., and Proctor, M. (2010). A configurable rete-oo engine for reasoning with different types of imperfect information. *IEEE Transactions on Knowledge and Data Engineering*, 22(11):1535–1548.

Tommelein, I. D., Levitt, R. E., and Hayes-Roth, B. (1992). SightPlan Model for Site Layout. *Journal of Construction Engineering and Management*, 118(4):749–766.

Wang, J., Zhang, X., Shou, W., Wang, X., Xu, B., Kim, M. J., and Wu, P. (2015). A BIM-based approach for automated tower crane layout planning. *Automation in Construction*, 59(AUGUST):168–178.

Yahya, M. and Saka, M. (2014). Construction site layout planning using multi-objective artificial bee colony algorithm with Levy flights. *Automation in Construction*, 38:14–29.

Deformation Monitoring of a Steel Structure Using 3D Terrestrial Laser Scanner (TLS)

Jatmiko[1], Panos Psimoulis[2]
[1] Ministry of Agrarian Affairs and Spatial Planning, Republic of Indonesia
[2]Nottingham Geospatial Institute, The University of Nottingham, United Kingdom
jatmiko@bpn.go.id, panagiotis.psimoulis@nottingham.ac.uk

Abstract. Terrestrial Laser Scanner (TLS) offers a new approach of deformation analysis. Different from conventional equipment such as Global Navigation Satellite System (GNSS) and Total Station (TS), the entire surface of observed structure can be analysed by contactless measurement. However, until recently the application of laser-scanner is still limited to long-term deformation monitoring. Using TLS to monitor dynamic response faces some challenges, such as scan time delay and its data characteristic. This project proposed a new approach by applying the function of helical mode of a TLS in order to solve these issues. The proposed method was tested on a high-rise artwork deformation monitoring case, the Aspire Sculpture in Nottingham. The result showed that scan time delay can be solved. Then TLS can be used to observe the sculpture dynamic deformation. New approach of point cloud processing was introduced in order to extract the deformation, leading to promising results that prove that there is potential of TLS to be used for monitoring the dynamic response of a civil engineering structure.

1. Introduction

Terrestrial Laser Scanner (TLS) has been introduced in deformation monitoring the last 15 years. Lichti et al. (2002) did the earliest attempt using TLS for structure deformation monitoring. They used TLS to monitor bridge deformation on loading test and compare the result with the result achieved using photogrammetry technique. Schneider (2006) used TLS to determine bending line of television tower and to observe the deformation of dam water. For long-term deformation monitoring, laser scanner has been proven to be a reliable technique. On the other hand, monitoring dynamic motion, such as structural response, is still a very challenging task. Even though, there are TLS with the capacity to scan in high sampling-rate (>1Hz), there are restrictions in the function of the TLS, which limit their application for monitoring of dynamic motion. Such a difficulty is the scan time delay between the successive scans, causing complication in the time-stamping of the scans and generally in monitoring moving or oscillating object.

2. Literature Review

In deformation monitoring applications, there are two main steps that are followed; the field measurements followed by the data processing and data analysis to extract the information expressing the deformation of the object, which was monitored. Furthermore, the estimation of the deformation is based on the comparison of each measurement/sample with a reference initial sample. Until recently, the main geodetic monitoring applications were based on GPS and conventional surveying techniques (levelling, total station), leading to monitor specific number of points, restricting the estimation of the deformation of the object only to the specific points. The latter may lead to limited information of the deformation, which could result to misinterpreting the response and the health condition status of the structure. On the other hand, the deformation monitoring using TLS allows getting massive points as point clouds, as it can be considered as remote sensing technigue. However, the main challenge with TLS deformation monitoring is the data process, as it may be difficult to assess some fix benchmarks on the surface of the deforming area (Tsakiri et al., 2006).

The TLS deformation monitoring aims in comparing same surface at different epochs. The accuracy of surface reconstruction based on point cloud data determines deformation-monitoring accuracy. Furthermore, sometimes the surface should be reconstructed from some scenes. One of the familiar methods of surface reconstruction from various scenes in deformation monitoring is Iterative Closet Point (ICP). A brief explanation of ICP approach in deformation monitoring can be found in Teza et al. (2007), they used ICP algorithm to do automatic calculation of landslide displacement field. This approach was also followed in monitoring applications of structures (Schneider, 2006; Sarti et al. 2009) and archaeological monuments (Pesci et al. 2011; Pesci et al. 2012; Teza and Pesci, 2013).

Deformation extraction can be achieved using different approach. In Monserrat and Crosetto (2007), the authors identified some methods commonly used to extract deformation from point cloud data. The deformation values can be obtained by directly comparing Digital Elevation Model (DEM) at different epoch measurements. In Schafer et al. (2004), the authors used Delaunay-Triangulation to create regular surface from point cloud data of a platform of hydropower station at different epoch measurements to achieve its deformation. In Teza et al. (2007), the authors proposed a procedure to calculate landslide displacements called the Piecewise Alignment Method (PAM). Base on this procedure, the first data of the point clouds processed become a first complete landslide model. Polynomial modelling was used as an approach to transform point cloud to surface model. This complete landslide model will be used as reference to calculate the deformation. Other deformation extraction that used Digital Terrain Model (DTM) approach can also be found in Wilkinson et al. (2012).

The approach that is commonly used in deformation monitoring extraction takes advantage of the shape of the observed object. Regular objects, such as circle, ellipse and cylinder have mathematical models, which are used to reconstruct the model of the object from point clouds. Then, the deformation is extracted by comparing the different models. In terms of achieving good quality of deformation result, choosing the right mathematical model is fundamental. In several studies, simple models, such as circular-shaped (Schneider 2006; Teza and Pesci 2013) or elliptical-shaped (Wei et al., 2014) models were used to model the monitored structure and estimate the deformation, while more complicate models, such as cylindrical-shaped model for modelling pillars of gas pipelines (Vezočnik et al., 2009) and parabolic-shaped model for modelling dam (Sarti et al., 2009), were used for structural deformation monitoring. Finally, there are applications, where even more complicated models have to be adopted, for instance in monitoring railway track (Liu et al., 2014).

However, most of the abovementioned approaches are for long-term deformation monitoring. There has been made though recent attempts in order to use TLS for dynamic deformation monitoring. For instance, Hong and Laefer (2014) used TLS to capture the dynamic displacement of a structure, where they tried to limit the problem of the time stamping by restricting the monitored area, which reduced the time delays of the successive scans but not solved the problem, as there were time delays and gaps on the captured data of. In the current study, we used a 3D TLS functioning in helical mode and modified version of the TLS interface, allowing for automatic time-stamping of the scans, to monitor the dynamic response of a steel structure. A methodology was developed in order to filter the TLS data and model the structural response, which allowed to estimate the dynamic characteristics of the structural response.

3. Methodology - Measurements

3.1 Faro Laser Scanner Focus^{3D} 120

In this study, the FARO Focus^{3D} laser scanner was used, which has helical mode function, where the laser scanner is forced to rotate only vertically and scan the profile of the object. Thanks to the open interface of the laser scanner, we developed an option to extract the time-stamping with 1μs resolution and the coordinates of each scanned point in a local coordinate system, where the TLS is the origin. Figure 1 are presented the Faro Focus^{3D} attached to Helical Adapter and Faro open interface application. The application was be used to export helical mode data into positions and their time-stamping in an ASCII file.

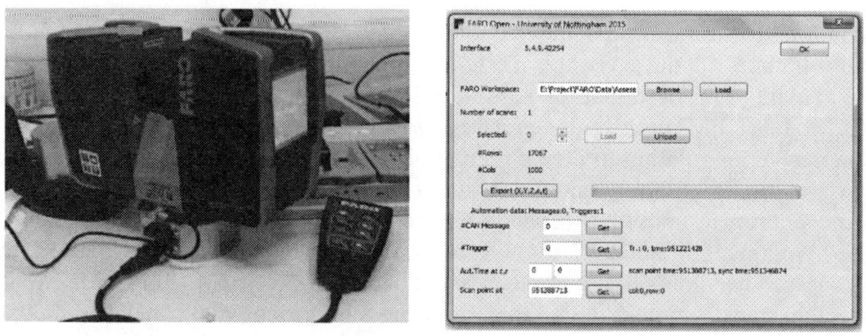

Figure 1: (left) Faro Focus^{3D} and (right) Faro open interface application

3.2 Preliminary experiments - Monitoring a stable wall

Figure 2: (left) The wall of Nottingham Geospatial Institute (NGI) and (right) the Aspire Sculpture

For the assessment of the performance of the developed method, a series of experiments were conducted, where the external 11m-tall wall of Nottingham Geospatial Institute (NGI) was scanned from different distances (Figure 2), ranging from 6 to 60m. Based on the scans, the accuracy of the scans of the helical modes was correlated with the distance from the observed object (the vertical wall) and with the vertical angle of the captured points, which affects the accuracy of the measurements. Apart from the assessment of the impact of the distance and the vertical angle on the measurement accuracy, the outcome of these measurements was used also to develop the methodology to extract the displacement from helical data for dynamic deformation monitoring purposes.

Due to the rigidity of the wall, it could be assumed that it remained stable during the experimental measurements and thus the measurements express the noise of the TLS scans. The wall was scanned several times from five different distances: ~3m, 7.5m, ~23m, 49m and 60m. From the several scans of each distance, the standard deviations of points, corresponding at specific levels of the wall, were calculated. In Figure 3 are presented the standard deviations, which corresponds at the 5m level of the wall, from where it is evident that the distance affects significantly the accuracy in the logntudinal direction (x-axis), as the standard deviation varies between 0.1 and 8.6mm. On the other hand, the lateral (y-axis) and vertical (z-axis) are not significantly affected by the distance, as the corresponding standard deviations vary between 0.1 to 0.8mm. This variation of standard deviation was due to error and noise of the TLS scans, which are affected by the distance and the vertical angle, which clearly shows that the longitudinal is mainly affected. Thus, for deformation monitoring applications with the current TLS, where accuracy of approximately 2mm is required, the distance between station and scanned object being observed should be approximately 25m. In range of 60m, the expected displacement should be more than 10mm.

3.3 Measurements and Deformation Extraction

The Aspire Sculpture (Fig. 2) is a steel structure in Jubilee Campus in the University of Nottingham and it is 60m high, consists of 8m of concrete cylindrical base and 52m steel structure, which has conical-shape, with the circular cross-section increasing with height. Aspire Sculpture is a flexible structure, affected by wind load, temperature variation and solar radiation. The structure was scanned, under no wind condition, in order to model the conical-shape of the profile, by determining the linear-shape of the profile and the circular cross-sections at different level, based on the approach of Schneider (2006). The model was extracted by developing a code on Python, where an algorithm was applied to fit a circular geometry at different heights, using x,y coordinates and least square method.

In Figure 4 is presented the deployment of the TLS for monitoring a structure in helical mode, and the characteristics which are recorded. More specifically, the TLS scans in a Cartesian coordinate system, where the TLS is the origin (0,0,0), *hi* is the height of the TLS, *hs*, *d* are the height and the distance of the structure/observed point from the TLS and *Z* is the height of the structure/observed point from the TLS level. The TLS records three values corresponding

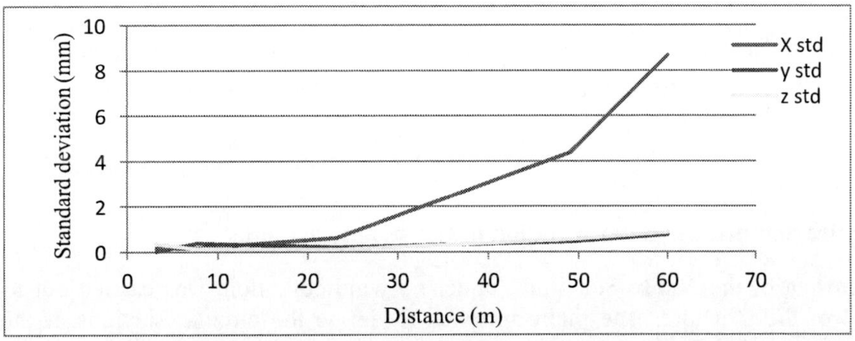

Figure 3: Estimate standard deviation and distance

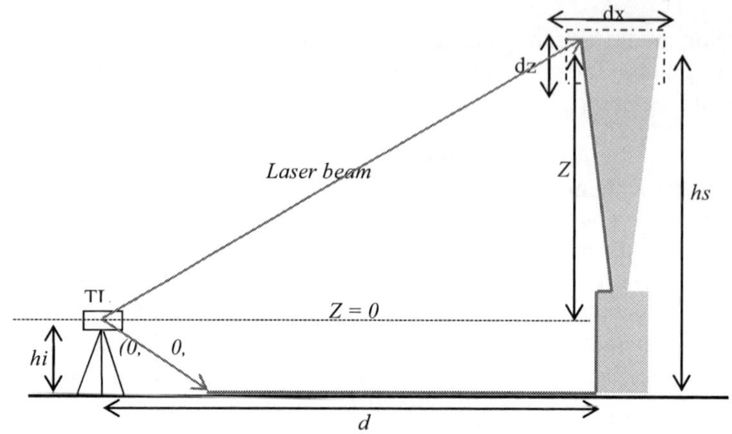

Figure 4: Sketch presenting the laser-scanning of the profile of the Aspire Sculpture

to x,y,z coordinates of each point. In helical mode, y coordinate expresses noise, while x- and z-coordinate express the longitudinal and vertical coordinates, relatively to TLS. Since TLS scans much more points than those corresponding to the structure, the required data are those which correspond to a range of *dx* and *dz* in the longitudinal (x-axis) and vertical (z-axis) for the monitoring of the structure. Thus, filtering of the TLS scan data is required to exclude all the points which are not relevant to the structure. This filtering can be made in two steps. Firstly, the first-twenty profile scans are removed to ensure that there are no noisy profiles, since FARO Focus^{3D} laser scanner data include noise in the first-twenty vertical rotations, due to calibration. The second step is to remove half of total profile, which in the helical mode, corresponds to objects which are on the backside of the TLS and not in the front side, where the monitored structure is. After the filtering, the displacement at specific levels of the structure was calculated by using several points that where in a range of ~0.2m around these levels. This approach gives better precision than using single point of helical mode data, as the noise of the individual points is reduced by using the average of the point cloud. Thus, the average of the points at specific levels of the structure was calculated for each profile and the displacements at each level was calculated, using the first reference as the reference. Each profile should have same number of points. However, in some cases there were profiles with less number of points, which could be due to the fact that the structure is not solid, but consists of several linear steel elements, which for large vertical angle may not be captured consistently. Furthermore, in case that the percentage of reflection of laser beam is small, the laser scanner ignores this point. For the shake of consistency, the average of each level was calculated when more than specific number of points for each scan was available. Profiles with number of points different from the majority of the profiles was removed. A filtering based on *mode* statistic data was applied in the Python program to filter these unwanted profiles. Finally, it was estimated the displacement of at 12 levels/points for each scan.

4. Results and Discussion

4.1 Aspire Sculpture – Determination of the structure model

The monitoring of the Aspire Sculpture, under no wind condition, was carried out to define the model of the structure. The main aim was to define the circular sections at the levels which were then used for the estimation of the dynamic motion. In Table 1 are presented the centre and radius of each circular cross-section and the standard deviation of the points which were used for each level. The top of sculpture could not be modelled duc to the non-circular shape. For the concrete basc, the standard deviation was 1 mm, while for part of the sculpture made of steel, it was between 15 to 32mm. The main reason for that difference, is that the concrete part is solid, with mode dense point cloud, while the steel part is formed by steel elements, forming a non-solid structure. Furthermore, there is observed difference in the estimation of the centres and radii of the circular cross-sections, small for the concrete part, while they increase in the steel part. Again, the concrete part due to its solid structure is more well-defined, with the differences of up to 5-6mm characterising the accuracy of the estimation of the centre and the radius. On the steel part the centre generally ranges in an area of 15mm x 10mm, apart from the the top two levels (50m and 53m) of the structure, where the potentially the corresponding points are more noisy due to the relatively large the vertical angle increases, leading to less accurate estimation of the cross-section centre. Likewise, the standard deviation ranges between 25mm and 30mm, while for the two top levels is much smaller, possibly due to the limited number of points. However, the deviation between the centre of the base of the structure (concrete) and the level of 53m of the steel structure, which corresponded to deviation of 0.14° from the verticality, could be attributed also to potential semi-static deformation of the structure caused by the temperature and the solar radiation.

Table 1: Determination of the circular cross-sections at different levels of the Aspire Sculpture

Cut of point cloud into thin layers/circles at different heights	Height of points (m)	Centre of circle X_m (m)	Centre of circle Y_m (m)	Radian (m)	Standard deviation (mm)	Material
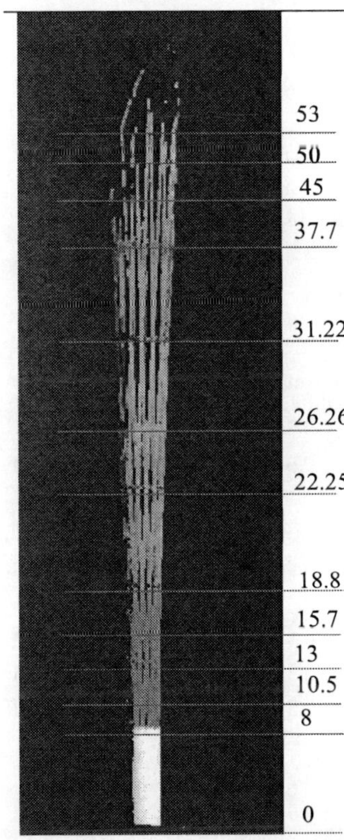	53	11.761	11.055	2.414	16	Steel
	50	11.710	11.054	2.246	15	Steel
	45	11.693	11.083	1.997	32	Steel
	37.7	11.681	11.121	1.726	26	Steel
	31.22	11.699	11.144	1.495	30	Steel
	26.26	11.702	11.154	1.342	30	Steel
	22.25	11.698	11.148	1.223	28	Steel
	18.8	11.692	11.149	1.141	30	Steel
	15.7	11.687	11.141	1.079	25	Steel
	13	11.687	11.145	1.041	28	Steel
	10.5	11.681	11.140	1.013	24	Steel
	8	11.717	11.187	1.098	1	Concrete
	0	11.719	11.193	1.102	1	Concrete

4.2 Aspire Sculpture Dynamic Motion

Several attempts of helical mode measurement were made, as there were many difficulties due to the sculpture structure and the limited capabilities of the TLS. First attempt was made by setting the TLS in distance of 40m from the sculpture, on 22nd June 2015. Local weather forecast showed wind speed was 19 km/h. The configuration setting of the TLS was ¼ and 3x of resolution and quality respectively, providing with 24 profiles per second (i.e. 24Hz). Not all part of structure from the bottom to the top could be scanned. Another successful attempt was on 24th June 2015, while the wind speed was only 14 km/h, in a distance of approximately 18m. The measurements used resolution and quality setting of ½ and 3x respectively, resulting to sampling-rate of 12Hz. Thus, the second laser scanner had better resolution than the first, resulting to larger number of scanned points. Figure 5 shows raw data plot in 3D and its xz-projection of second attempt.

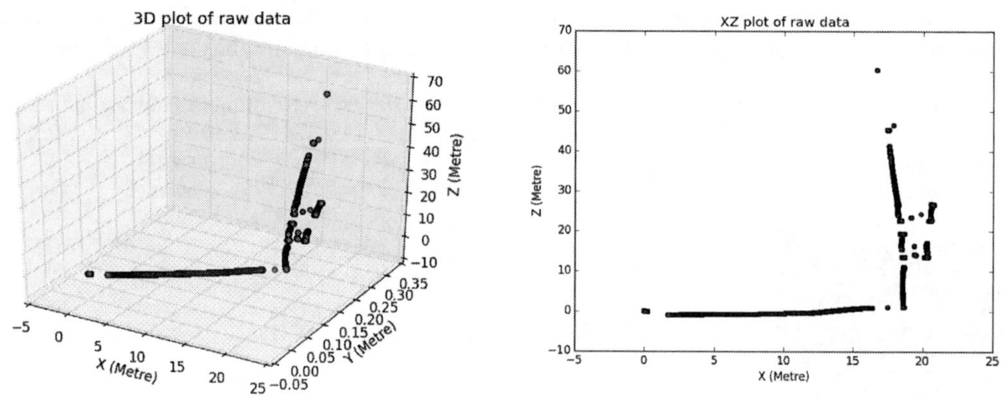

Figure 5: A typical data-set of the point-cloud of the its profile scanned with FARO Focus3D laser scanner (second attempt)

Table 2: Second attempt result (24th June 2015)

Height (m)	Recorded profile	Profile used	Profile unused	Total points	Estimate standard deviation			Decision
					σ_X (mm)	σ_y (mm)	σ_Z (mm)	
5*	100%	58.06%	41.94%	33	0.5	0.3	0.1	No
10	100%	39.27%	60.73%	20	0.7	0.3	0.4	Oscillated
15	-	-	-	-	-	-	-	-
20	-	-	-	-	-	-	-	-
25	100%	79.19%	20.81%	12	1.5	0.3	1.9	Oscillated
30	99.83%	48.79%	51.04%	10	1.8	0.3	2.9	Oscillated
35	89.19%	19.76%	69.43%	8	2.2	0.3	4.4	Oscillated
40	58.27%	19.76%	38.51%	6	2.6	0.3	5.8	Oscillated
45**	97.90%	41.53%	56.38%	7	1.3	0.3	3.3	Oscillated
50	-	-	-	-	-	-	-	-
55	-	-	-	-	-	-	-	-
60***	17.06	6.25%	10.81%	2	14.3	0.3	10.4	Oscillated

**concrete part **ring of sculpture ***top part of sculpture*

Table 2 summarises the displacement of sculpture for every 5m level. The percentage in recorded profile, profile used and profile unused columns were calculated from the total data of structure recorded from the measurement (the number of line inputted to the laser scanner setting), while the total points column data was used for calculating the average point. In general, the displacement magnitude increased as level increased, apart from height of 45m, where there was a circular ring increasing the rigidity at this level of the vertical steel linear elements. Also, the number of profiles which could be processed, decreased due to sculpture shape characteristic and laser scanner ranging limitation. In order to decide whether the trend in time-series was systematic error or the structure displacement, an assessment was made, where the standard deviation of the points of the structure was compared with the standard deviation of the points for the case of the vertical wall. More specifically, for distance of 18m the noise level based on the standard deviation of the vertical wall would be ~1mm (i.e. 95% confidence level 2x0.5mm). However, for the vertical component (z-axis), where is introduced also the error of the vertical angle, for large vertical angle (i.e. high points), the error could be larger by a factor of 2. The grey-highlighted standard deviations of Table 2 indicate the structure at these levels was oscillating.

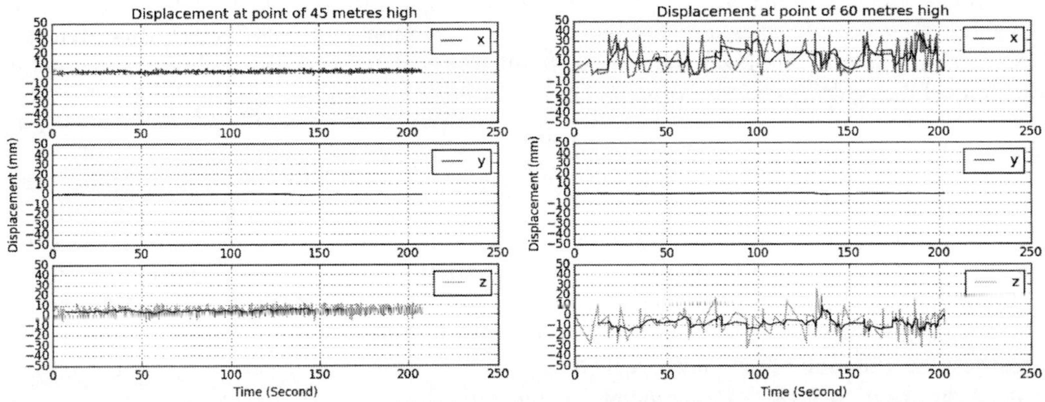

Figure 6: Time-series of displacements (coloured lines) and its moving average (black line) of second attempt (45 and 60m level)

Figure 6 shows time-series of displacements at 45 and 60m level and their 20-window moving average. At 60m level, the time-series has many gaps, due to the linear steel elements, which are not as dense as at lower levels. At higher levels of the structure, the displacement was observed to be larger than that of lower levels. However, for the level at 45m the displacement was lower, possibly due to the additional rigidity which is added by the circular ring at that level. height showed the opposite. From the time-series, amplitude in vertical axis (z-axis) was observed to be larger than that of the longitudinal axis (x-axis), even though the displacement on the longitudinal axis is expected to be larger. This can be attributed to the error which is introduced by the vertical angle, which for the higher points is large. The largest displacement of the sculpture was at the top part (60m). In x-direction, the amplitude of the displacement was approximately 40mm. Semi-static was detected clearly at approximately 140 seconds until the end of time-series.

Using time-series of displacement the frequencies of dynamic deformation could be drived, based on spectral analysis (Psimoulis and Stiros, 2008). The Discrete Fourier transform (DFT) was used for the analysis of the data corresponding to the second attempt. The later was chosen since it has most complete data from botom to the top of structure. The spectral analysis was only focused on displacement in x- and z-directions as the dynamic movement of

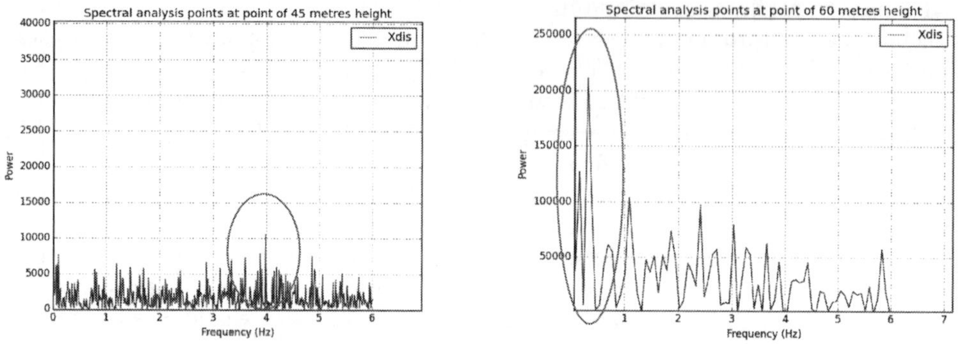

Figure 7: Spectral analysis of point 45 and 60m level

structure in y-direction was not recorded by helical mode. The second attempt was using resolution and quality setting of ½ and 3x. It gave 12Hz of sampling rate data. Therefore, the maximum frequency that can be detected by this spectral analysis is 6Hz. The spectral analysis focused on highest peak in the spectrum corresponding with the structure dynamic motion. At point of 45m level, the peak of frequency detected was 4Hz. While at the point of 60m level the peak was 0.25Hz (Figure 7).

In general, frequency approximately of 0.25 Hz was detected at points 25, 40 and 60m level, while the frequency of 1.7 Hz and 4 Hz were detected at point of 30 and 45m level. The larger frequencies at levels of 30 and 45m was due to the additional circular which added rigidity to the sculpture at those levels. However, most levels detected a frequency of 0.3Hz. For the point of 45m level, the frequency, which was detected, was the largest, probably due to the circular ring; possibly the laser scanner observed the ring instead of the columns, resulting to very rigid response. Hence, it seems that the ring of the circular cross-section at 45m height, restricts the vibration of the linear steel elements. This is the main reason, why the response at higher or lower position, is larger than of that height.

5. Conclusion

In the current study, it was examined the potential use of TLS in monitoring dynamic response of civil engineering structure. This application is made possible thanks the helical mode function of FARO Focus^{3D}, which was used in the current study. More specifically, the developed methodology solved the scan time delay problem turning off the horizontal rotation and also the access to the open source interface gave the opportunity to extract all the important information. Helical mode accuracy had been tested using simple procedure. In short-range measurements with distance less than 25m, it can achieve up to millimetres precision. The developed methodology was applied on the monitoring of the Aspire sculpture, a steel structure which is in Nottingham, UK. Firstly, the developed method was applied in a stable structure, assessing the accuracy and its dependency on the distance and vertical angle. Then, the method was applied on the structure to create the model of the structure, based on fitting circular cross-section along the height of the structure, identifying potential inconsistencies due to laser-scanning. Finally, the developed method was applied in order to model the dynamic motion of the structure for specific levels of the structure. The dynamic displacement was estimated approximately 40mm at the top of structure during measurement when wind blew with speed of approximately 14 km/h, with the frequency at the more stiff section being of 4Hz.

Thus, in the current study, there was developed a methodology, using the FARO Focus^{3D}, the helical mode function and the developed modifications on FARO Open source software, which proved that there is potential of TLS for monitoring the dynamic response of civil engineering structures. Further investigation is required to enhance the developed method and make it more reliable, accurate and robust. Finally, this method can supplement other techniques (e.g. RTS), which can monitoring limited number of points.

References

Hong, L, T, & Laefer, D, F 2014,'Using terrestrial laser scanning for dynamic bridge deflection measurement', *Istanbul Bridge Conference,* Istanbul, 2014, viewed 21 July 2015, http://istanbulbridgeconference.org/2014/ISBN978-605-64131-6-2/papers/060.pdf

Lichti, D, D, Gordon, S, J, Stewart, M, P, Franke, J & Tsakiri, M (2002), 'Comparasion of digital photogrammetry and laser scanning', Viewed 7 November 2014, http://www.researchgate.net/publication/245716767_Comparison_of_Digital_Photogrammetry_and_Laser_Scanning?enrichId=rgreq-b68fd2ba-1d6d-4f0f-b05f-bf9166f11a01&enrichSource=Y292ZXJQYWdlOzI0NTcxNjc2NztBUzoxNDI5NjQyMTQ5OTY5OTNAMTQxMTA5NjczMzc4Nw%3D%3D&el=1_x_2

Liu, C, Li, N, Wu, H, & Meng, X 2014, 'Detection of high-speed railway subsidence and geometry irregularity using terrestrial laser scanning, *American Society of Civil Engineers.*

Monserrat, O, & Crosetto, M 2007, 'Deformation measurement using terrestrial laser scanning data and least squares 3D surface matching', *ISPRS Journal of Photogrammetry & Remote Sensing*, pp. 142–154.

Pesci, A, Bonali, E, Galli, C & Boschi, E 2012, 'Laser scanning and digital imaging for the investigation of an ancient building: Palazzo d'Accursio study case (Bologna, Italy)', *Journal of Cultural Heritage*, pp. 215–22.

Pesci, A, Casula, G & Boschi, E 2011, 'Laser scanning the Garisenda and Asinelli towers in Bologna (Italy): detailed deformation patterns of two ancient leaning buildings' *Journal of Cultural Heritage*, pp. 117–127.

Psimoulis, P, A, & Stiros, S, C 2008, 'Experimental assessment of the accuracy of GPS and RTS for the determination of the parameters of oscillation of major structures." *Computer-Aided Civil and Infrastructure Engineering*, pp. 389–403.

Sarti, P, Vittuari, L & Abbondanza, C 2009, 'Laser scanner and terrestrial surveying applied to gravitational deformation monitoring of large VLBI telescopes primary reflector', *Journal Of Surveying Engineering*, pp. 136-148.

Schafer, T, Weber, T, Kyrinovič, P, & Zámečniková, M 2004, 'Deformation measurement using terrestrial laser scanning at the hydropower station of gabčíkovo', *FIG Regional Central and Eastern European Conference on Engineering Surveying.* Bratislava, 2004.

Schneider, D 2006, 'Terrestrial laser scanning for area based deformation analysis of towers and water damns'',*12th FIG Symposium.* Baden, 2006, viewd 8 November 2014, https://www.fig.net/resources/proceedings/2006/baden_2006_comm6/PDF/LS2/Schneider.pdf

Teza, G., Galgaro, A, Zaltron, N & Genevois, R 2007, 'Terrestrial laser scanner to detect landslide displacement fields: a new approach', *International Journal of Remote Sensing*, pp. 3425–3446.

Teza, G, & Pesci, A 2013, 'Geometric characterization of a cylinder-shaped structure from laser scannerdata: Development of an analysis tool and its use on a leaning bell tower', *Journal of Cultural Heritage*, pp. 411–423.

Tsakiri, M, Lichti, D & Pfeifer, N 2006, 'Terrestrial laser scanning for deformation monitoring', *12th FIG Symposium.* Baden, 2006, viewd 13 November 2014, https://www.fig.net/resources/proceedings/2006/baden_2006_comm6/PDF/LS2/Tsakiri.pdf

Vezočnik, R, Ambrožič, T, Sterle, O, Bilban, G, Pfeifer, N, & Stopar, B 2009, 'Use of terrestrial laser scanning technology for long term high precision deformation monitoring', *Sensors*, pp. 9873-9895.

Wei, Z, Huadong, G, Qi, L & Tianhua, H 2014, 'Fine deformation monitoring of ancient building based on terrestrial laser scanning technologies', *International Symposium on Remote Sensing of Environmen,* 2014, viewed 26 November 2014, http://iopscience.iop.org/article/10.1088/1755-1315/17/1/012166/pdf

Wilkinson, M.W, McCaffrey, K.J.W, Roberts, G.P., Cowie, P.A., Phillips, R.J., Degasperi, M, Vittori, A, M, & Michetti, A, M 2012, 'Distribution and magnitude of post-seismic deformation of the 2009 L'Aquila earthquake (M6.3) surface rupture measured using repeat terrestrial laser scanning', *Geophysical Journal International*, pp. 911–922.

Towards Precedent Based Design Foundations for Parametric Design Systems

Vasiliki Kondyli[1], Mehul Bhatt[1], and Timo Hartmann[2]

[1]Human-Centred Cognitive Assistance (HCC Lab), and
The DesignSpace Group. University of Bremen, Germany
[2]Department of Civil Systems Engineering, Civil Engineering Institute, TU Berlin, Germany
vasiliki@design-space.org

Parametric design systems serve as powerful assistive technologies in the design process by aiding the generation of a vast number of design alternatives. However, with their focus on low-level engineering and structural form, parametric systems do not automatically fulfil cognitively founded people-centred behavioural design criteria. We propose a precedent-based design approach for parametric systems that introduces people-centred criteria according to empirical behavioural evidence. As an example, we identify people-centred precedents for navigation design in large-scale buildings, and verify a number of them through perceptual data analysis based on cognitive vision theory and high-level semantic analysis of multimodal data as part of an empirical study conducted in two health-care environments. As running examples, we present design constraints about visibility and the morphology of decision points in navigation routes, and an example of integrating precedents into parametric modelling.

1 A People-Centred Parametric Approach to Design

Parametric design is a well-established method in several engineering and manufacturing design domains such as architecture, product design, construction [Gun et al., 2010]. Decoupling *form* from physical *structure*, parametric and generative approaches offer the ability to rigorously explore many design alternatives and reveal new solutions during design problem-solving process [Rybczynski, 2013, Boucherie et al., 2012]. They are used to replace traditional shapes with eccentric morphologies and provide adaptability and flexibility in the design procedure [Boucherie et al., 2012]. The Trade Fair ceiling project (Fig. 1(a)) and the Walt Disney Concert Hall (Fig. 1(b)), are some examples of optimisation of the construction, while the Al Bahr Towers project, incorporates environmental variables dynamically into design process (Fig. 1(c)).

Whereas parametric design leads itself well to the manipulation of numerical, geometric features and relationships between object parameters (e.g. width, height, positions), it currently fails to integrate the dimension of human behaviour as a variable of morphological formulation. For instance, the geometric form of the London Aquatics Centre failed to take into consideration the dynamic performance of users and predict specifically a perception-related problem concerning visibility. According to reports, the curve of the roof obscure the view for a vast number of the audience (Fig. 1(d)). This experience,

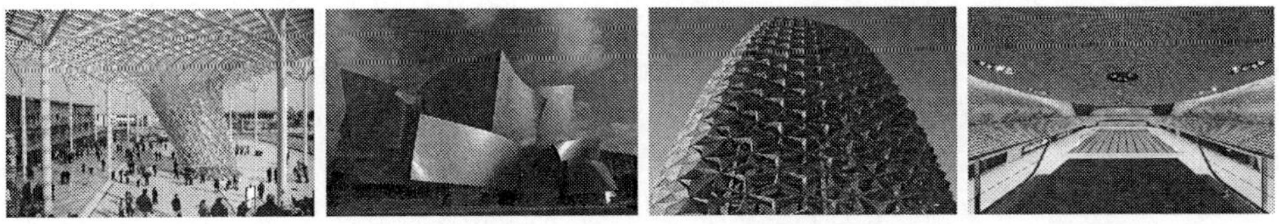

(a) (b) (c) (d)

Figure 1: (a)New Trade Fair of Milan (Fuksas Studio), (b) Walt Disney Concert Hall (Frank Gehry), (c) Al Bahr Towers (Aedas Architects), (d) London Aquatics Centre (Zaha Hadid Architects)

earned in practice, is a valuable precedent for large-scale buildings design in the future. To incorporate people-centred precedents into parametric design synthesis, we need to specify the properties of the elements present in the encountered topology [Norton, 2003]. Our approach to provide a primary role to the user during the design procedure, requires a wide range of behavioural evidence, obtained by previous behavioural studies as well as by additional focused behavioural experiments for the particular functional building case [Bhatt et al., 2016a]. Towards this direction, a better understanding of people-environment interaction, spatial perception and spatial cognition about user's spatio-temporal experience is required.

2 Visuo-locomotive Experience Driven Parametric Design.

People interact daily with their surrounding environment so that they formulate their visuo-locomotive experience. Users of built up spaces depend mostly on external information of the environment during this process. Designing for facilitating and best formulating people's daily experience is overtaken during the design process, or it is considered at a late stage of design. In our approach, we seek to influence efficiently designer's work, by formulating a well-defined method to bridge the gap between user's spatial behaviour analysis and contemporary design tools, such as parametric design tools. This method includes the following parts:

Identify People-Centred Precedents. In architecture practice, precedents are widely used; they are established by long practice or they serve as examples or rules to authorise and justify a subsequent design decision. To identify precedents from a people-centred perspective, we focus on the state of the art and the empirical studies in the interdisciplinary field of Evidence-Based Design, Environmental Psychology, and Spatial Cognition. In this context, a range of factors that contribute to people's experience in space emerges. These factors are categorised into:

- **environmental characteristics** of the built-up space (e.g. geometry, layout, colour, manifest cues, architectural differentiation, light conditions),
- **individual differences** among the users (e.g. spatial knowledge acquisition, spatial memory, gender, age),
- **building type** (e.g. airport, museum, clinic, train station, care centre), and
- **locomotive task** (e.g. navigation, wayfinding, exploration, emergency exit).

For instance, healthcare design, needs an *inclusive* guided design perspective, that gives priority to precedents related to functionality and circulation of different user-groups (e.g. patients, families, physicians, and nurses). In this framework, evidence-based design platform collects knowledge by post-occupancy evaluations or behavioural studies. To make use of this data in design, Ulrich et al. [2010] for instance, structure this knowledge and demonstrate nine design categories to represent the built environment: audio environment, visual environment, safety enhancement, wayfinding system, sustainability, patient room, family support spaces, staff support spaces, and physician support spaces. Each category indicates different precedents, that can be used as design rules.

Analyse Embodied Visuo-locomotive Experience. To establish valuable precedents we investigate the cognitive aspects of visuo-locomotive experience in space. In practice to approach the interaction of people with space, we employ a range of sensors for measuring the embodied visuo-locomotive experience of building users: eye-tracking, egocentric gaze analysis (from video), external camera-based visual analysis to interpret fine-grained behaviour (e.g., stopping, looking around, interacting with other people), and also manual observations made by human experimenters [Bhatt et al., 2016a]. New cognitive-assistive technologies aim at generating narratives of visuo-locomotive user experience from digital computer-aided architecture design (CAAD) based on this collected behavioural knowledge. The combination of multi-modal behavioural data analysis with morphological analysis of space and computational geometric structure analysis; helps us to study systematically the built-up space and the relations developing between variant structural characteristics, as well as to draw conclusions about the parts of the built environment that provoke problematic behaviour [Bhatt et al., 2016b].

Define Parametric Design Constraints. Our approach to establish behavioural based qualitative constraints aims at integrating cognitive thinking into architectural and engineering design processes. These constraints, defined as design rules, are correlated with environmental features that contribute to user's experience, e.g., geometry, layout [Kondyli et al., 2017a]. Thereafter, the resulting design rules are systematically formulated and embedded into parametric design systems. In this paper, our core focus is on positioning the process of bridging the dynamic spatial experience of users directly within parametric systems following the method in Kondyli et al. [2017b], Schultz et al. [2017].[1] We present examples of implementations with Grasshopper in Rhino. The key crux of the presented examples is to demonstrate the manipulation of geometrical features based on people-centred design constraints.

3 Precedent-Based Design for Navigation

An example about our people-centred precedent-based design approach is examined in the context of the navigation experience in large-scale built environments, with the contribution of our behavioural data analysis from a case study, conducted in the old and the new Parkland Hospital in Dallas (Texas)[2]. We combine state of the art knowledge about

[1]For the implementation of indicative design rules, we extend industry-standard parametric systems to support a range of qualitative and visuo-locomotive spatial constraints: incidence (points interior or exterior to regions), mereotopology (disconnected, inside, touching), size (smaller, larger), visibility and movement. The technical details of the implementation within parametric systems is beyond the scope of this paper; however, complete implementation details and several examples based on evidence-based rules realised within FreeCAD system are available in [Kondyli et al., 2017b].

[2]As part of the collaboration between the DesignSpace Group and the Corgan Associates (Dallas)

design precedents related to navigation performance, with the outcome of our multi-modal behavioural analysis, as well as the insights of human spatial cognition (sections 3.1 - 3.3). We demonstrate an overview of the empirically confirmed precedents about navigation (sections 3.4), and we focus on the two most significant ones (involved in our case study): the geometry of the decision points in a building layout and the rate of visibility or the available visual range along the navigation path.

3.1 Embodied Navigation Experience

People's navigation in unfamiliar large-scale buildings is a common problem in everyday life. Human's experience in space is based on interactions between individuals and the environment [Weiss, 1999]. It is an embodied experience constantly intangible and bodily related with other cues in space [Csordas, 2008]. These interactions between architectural space and human, occur at discernible levels: that of the space of the body, that of the space in reach or in sight of the body, that of the space of navigation (too large to be apprehended at once), that of the space of external representations, or graphics (constructed to augment human cognition) [Tversky, 2005]. This is also depicted on users' movement patterns. Navigation according to this classification includes two components, locomotion, and wayfinding [Montello, 2005]. Locomotion is associated with human perception; and wayfinding are related to human spatial cognition [Kaplan and Kaplan, 1982, Carpman and Grant, 2002]. Indicatively, the human-environment relationship, on a perceptual level, is interpreted through the notion of affordances (environmental cues that provide behavioural options for immediate action without reasoning) [Gibson, 1979] and in a spatial cognition level through image schemata (cognitive concepts which structure a meaning of our perception and action).

3.2 Cognitive Aspects of Design Composition

Design for navigation, as a cognitive task, and for different user groups is a challenging process. For instance, complex building facilities such as hospitals usually present wayfinding problems of users, as a result of complicated layouts that lead to stress [Arthur and Passini, 1992]. Numerous studies have demonstrated that many navigation problems are caused by the problematic arrangement of complex decision points, their linking paths, the vertical incongruence of floors [Weisman, 1981, Arthur and Passini, 1992] or other environmental aspects as location, size, distance, direction, separation and connection, shape, pattern, and form [O'Neill, 1991]. To summarise, navigation performance for various user-groups is correlated with affordances [plan configuration, geometry of the environment, geometry of the scenes (formulated during user's locomotion), available visual range, architectural differentiation] and manifest cues [signage, landmarks] [Devlin, 2014, Evans, 1980]. Among the environmental factors that influence navigation, we investigate the ones strongly related to the architectural composition such as the morphological characteristics of decision points along a navigation route, and the dynamic change of the available visual range along the navigation route.

Morphological Features of Decision Points. Decision points in navigation have a crucial role to play concerning decision making and orientation; as well as an major impact on user's spatial experience and navigation performance (delays, confusion, fluctuation of the stress rate). Previous studies indicate that the boundaries of the environment are crucial for determining the place cell representation of the location, which is weakly affected by the global geometry of the environment [Hartley et al., 2004]. Gallistel [1990] notices that disoriented people reorient themselves by matching geometric properties of the perceived and the recalled environment. Concerning the locomotive performance, the geometry of the scene has a great behavioural impact while at the same time is easily manipulated my the designer. Moreover, the eligibility of the layout - depended on the arrangement of settings and a reasonable amount of geometrical complexity [Baskaya et al., 2004, Tversky, 2005] - is a significant variable for an effective navigation task. For instance, symmetrical settings make people feel lost [Baskaya et al., 2004], too simple floor plans are also insufficient for navigation in unfamiliar environments [Weisman, 1981].

Visual Range. The perceived visual space has dimensions very different from the geographic or measured space, and as a consequence also different affordances that influence the way spatial information is encoded and maintained in working memory. This is a result of humans' binocular field of vision (120 degrees forward-facing horizontal) [Snowden et al., 2006] and that is why spatial experience is highly depended on the eye, head, and body movement. The available visual field, as an important environmental factor, influences navigation and locomotion particularly in the level of interaction with the reachable or visible space around the body [Weisman, 1981, Arthur and Passini, 1992]. For example, empirical studies provide evidence about people moving towards the direction of the pictured area with the longest line of sight [Wiener et al., 2012]; about visual access towards the external environment that enhances the legibility of interiors [Gärling et al., 1986]; or about inter-visibility among various parts of the building that make people to rely on information directly available in their field of vision [Gibson, 1979].

3.3 Behavioural evidence from empirical case study

The behavioural analysis reveals that users get confused in particular decision points during the route. Together with the morphological analysis, we observe that this behavioural outcome is related to the spatial configuration, the environmental features and the position of the manifest cues (Fig. 2). Combining the computational eye-tracking data analysis of participants, with external camera data analysis and computer vision techniques, we are able to justify some key parts of the detected problematic navigation performance [Kondyli et al., 2017b,a]. For instance, user's visual patterns in decision points, which are correlated to decision making, confirm previous behavioural evidence about the tendency of people to move towards the direction with the longer line of sight [Wiener et al., 2012]. Moreover, based on visual attention heatmaps, scan maps, and fixations on annotated objects in egocentric scenes (obstacles, other people, distraction element, functional features, edges, surfaces etc.) [Bhatt et al., 2016b], we confirm existing design precedents such as: narrow spaces are not preferable for decision points as they tend to accumulate people, block the view towards manifest cues (landmarks and signage), enforce various visual distractions (by obstacles, by other people, by functional features of the scene) and consequently have a major impact on user's navigation performance.

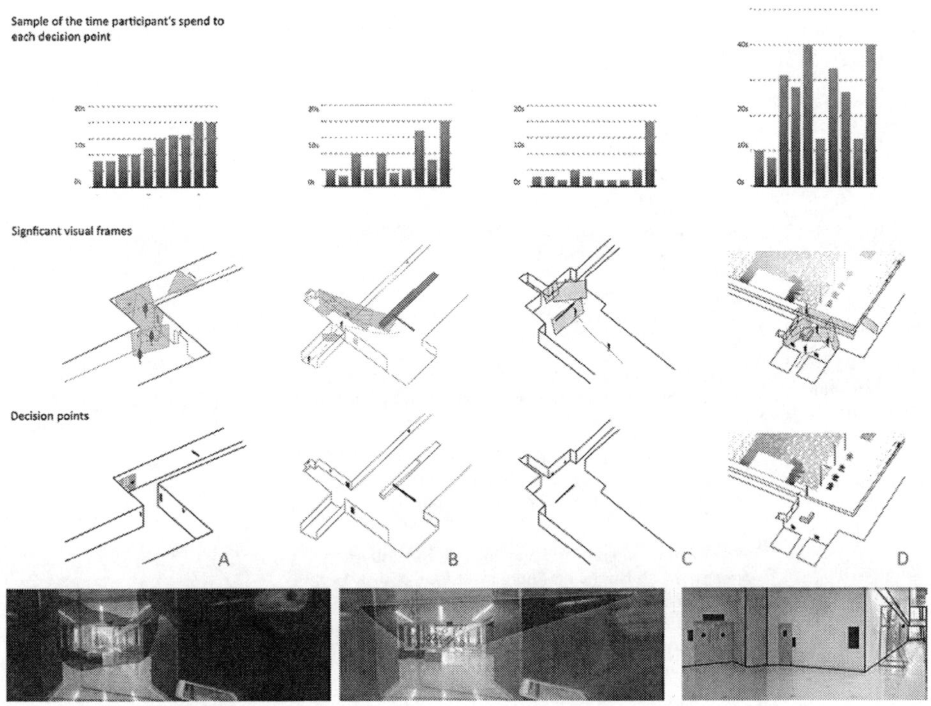

Figure 2: The comparison of users' multi-modal behavioural analysis between four decision points during a navigation route at new Parkland hospital, shows the correlation between the spatial geometry, the average visual perception patterns, and the navigation performance. Major delays are observed in the first decision point (A) as a result of the narrow corridor that obscure visibility; and the last decision point (D) where the average user's behaviour is characterised by a misleading visual attention patterns provoked by the spatial geometry (atrium is more visually attractive that the navigation route).

3.4 Indicators for Design Precedents

The outcome of the case study confirm a number of well-known precedents about the effect of the available visual range and the spatial geometry on navigation performance, as for example the role of the atrium, the distance between the detection point of a landmark and the decision point, or the spatial configuration of a decision point. Furthermore, we observe that the visual perception is formulated, to an extent, by the designed geometry and the affordances. Combining the state of the art about behavioural and cognitive studies in navigation, together with our observations from the empirical studies, we demonstrate a list of precedents that can be implemented as parametric design constraints (Fig. 3). The precedents included in the table are selected according to the main environmental features as they revealed from the case study.

4 Shape the Empty Space of Navigation

People-centred design approach consider user's visuo-locomotive experience, as the primary element of design. Under this principle, the architect organizes the empty space

Environmental Characteristics	Indicators for Design Precedent	State of the art	Our Behavioural Observations
Decision point_ Geometry	people follow the path with the longer line of sight	✓	✓
Path_ Geometry	non-orthogonal/curved paths can be more attractive than linear paths during decision making but they could also provoke confusion		✓
Path_ Visibility	visual connection between different parts of the route help navigation performance	✓	✓
Landmark_ Visibility	visual connection with a landmark in different parts of the route helps orientation and navigation performance	✓	✓
Decision point_ Geometry	a decision point positioned in a narrow space are more likely to provoke confusion to the user than a decision point in wide space	✓	✓
Manifest cues_ Visibility	manifest cues are better detected when they are positioned in accordance with the fixation zones, which depend on spatial geometry and the geometry of the dynamic egocentric scene of the user during locomotion		✓
Perforation_ Visibility	transparent materials and openings extend visual connectivity with landmarks (indoor/outdoor) and promote navigation performanc	✓	✓
Layout_ Geometry	symmetry of the layout is helpful for navigation as soon as important parts remain discrete	✓	✓

Figure 3: Indicators for design precedents according to the state of the art and the outcome of our empirical navigation case study.

by building up structures and artifacts of the everyday life. Designing the space is about defining and organizing functional space, operational space, empty space, spatial structures etc. [Bhatt et al., 2012], or as Ching categorize them: the notions of structure, function, and purpose [Ching, 2012]. Positioning the user in the middle of the design procedure means that the designer considers the visuo-locomotive experience of the user in several stages of design, from the morphological composition until the structural details of the construction. Through this process, a people-centred parametric design system should reassure that important design principles (such as visibility connection between defined positions, or layout legibility of functional places) are satisfied while other variables can be manipulated (functional routes, emergency routes, position of objects, position of signage, position of decision points), and consequently a range of morphologies can be generated.

Decision points. Based on the indicators presented on the table (Fig. 3e), we implement an example related to the *decision point - geometry*. We use the precedent as a design precondition, where the decision points of the main route should be formulated in a wide empty space (wider in relation to the geometry of the route). We introduce an open space (referring to the first stages of a design composition) (Fig. 4a) and we draw curves as potential routes inside the built environment. The intersections of the routes-curves indicate decision points (Fig. 4b). Based on the *decision point - geometry* precedent, we formulate a wide empty functional place in these particular points marked (Fig. 4c). The designer can choose which line is considered the main route. Consequently, the boundaries of the main route (Fig. 4d) and the decision points are combined to a new morphology (Fig. 4e). The outcome constitutes a primary morphology of the empty

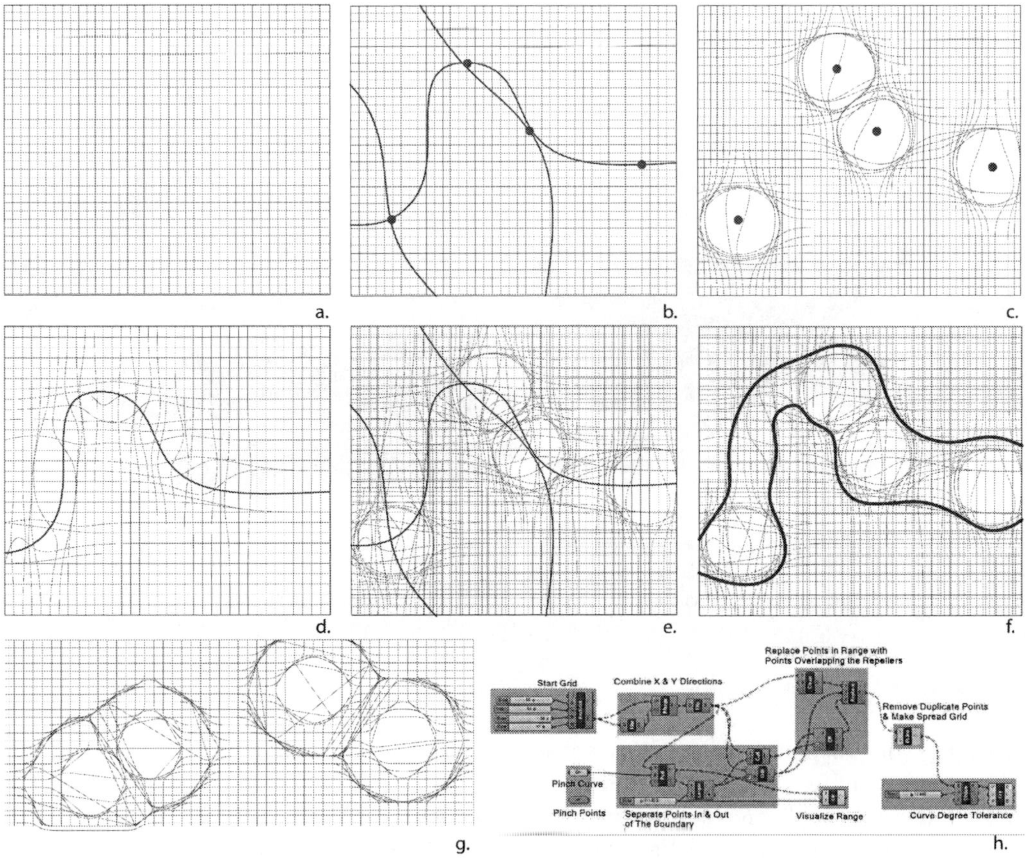

Figure 4: Step by step the implementation of the morphological structure as it is modified by the variables of the minimum functional space around each decision point and along the main navigation path. The points and the lines should be provided as input by the designer.

space with respect to the *decision point - geometry* precedent. The suggested morphology can be modified further, as new boundaries or levels of functional space can be depicted in the drawing (Fig. 4g), and further extensions of the main point attractor code in Rhino-Grasshopper can be added (Fig. 4h).

Visibility connection. In this example we use the precedent from the table 3 about *perforation - geometry*. We hypotheses that the morphological structure around a navigation route should reassure visual connectivity between the user and an outdoor landmark, for a number of times during the navigation process and especially on chosen the decision points. We provide user's line of route as an input together with a landmark position. A connective line between the point on the route (that indicates user's position) and the stable position of the landmark, represents the visibility connection. When an obstacle intersects with the visibility line - that can represents surfaces or volumes (walls, roofs, etc.) - then the designer is able to manipulate the openings dynamically in the parametric model according to the position of the user (Fig. 5).

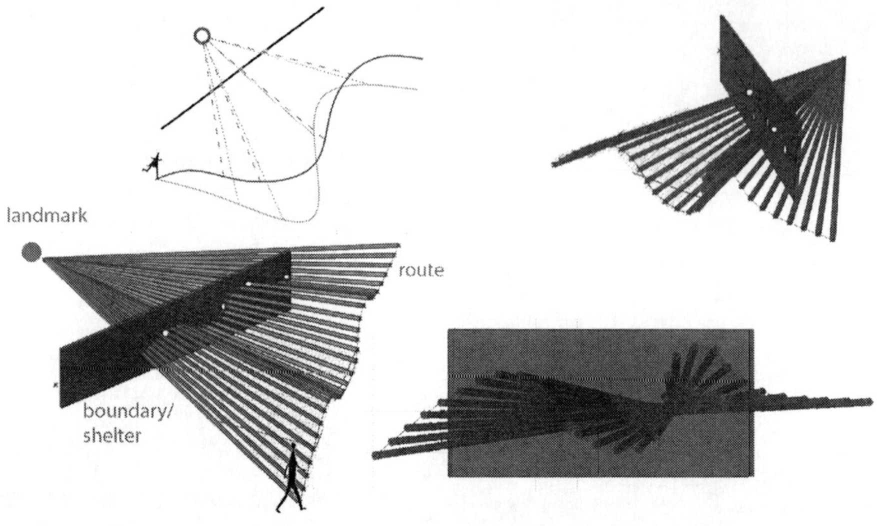

Figure 5: Indication of openings position that keep visibility connection between the landmark and the dynamic position of the user during a navigation route.

5 Outlook and Discussion

Tracking and analysing people's behaviour in large-scale buildings provides evidence about users' embodied visuo-locomotive experience and leads to confirmation of known precedents or establishment of new ones, useful for design decision making. Focusing on visibility and geometrical features of the layout, we explore how cognitive-assistive technologies contribute to precedent's evaluation and how they validate them for further integration into parametric modeling. The indicative implemented examples of this paper, suggest how simple parametric design, acquires a people-centred value under an established behavioural precedent. A number of further implementations in parametric design tools, for a range of design precedents related to cognitive aspects of design, will be needed to demonstrate the design improvement that they can provide into parametric design thinking. Further experimentation aspires to promote people-centred evaluation tools for the numerous morphological outcomes of the contemporary parametric systems.

References

P. Arthur and R. Passini. *Wayfinding: people, signs, and architecture.* McGraw-Hill Book Co., 1992.

A. Baskaya, C. Wilson, and Y. Z. Özcan. Wayfinding in an unfamiliar environment. different spatial settings of two polyclinics. *Environment and Behavior*, 36, 2004.

M. Bhatt, C. Schultz, and M. Huang. The shape of empty space: Human-centred cognitive foundations in computing for spatial design. In *IEEE Symposium on Visual Languages and Human-Centric Computing, VL/HCC 2012, Austria*, pages 33–40, 2012.

M. Bhatt, J. Suchan, V. Kondyli, and C. Schultz. Embodied visuo-locomotive experience analysis: Immersive reality based summarisation of experiments in environment-behaviour studies. In *Proceedings of ACM SIGGRAPH Symposium on Applied Perception (SAP 2016)*, Anaheim, USA., 2016a.

M. Bhatt, J. Suchan, C. Schultz, V. Kondyli, and S. Goyal. Artificial intelligence for predictive and evidence based architecture design: Integrating spatial reasoning, cognitive vision, and eye-tracking for the analysis of embodied visuo-locomotive experience in the built environment. In *Proceedings of the 30th AAAI Conference on Artificial Intelligence (AAAI 2016)*. AAAI Press, 2016b.

R. J. Boucherie, W. H. Erwin, and T. Hartmann. Health care logistics and space: accounting for the physical build environment. In *Winter Simulation Conference*, 2012.

J. R. Carpman and M. Grant. *Handbook of Environmental Psychology*, chapter Wayfinding: a broad view, pages 427–442. Wiley, New York, 2002.

F. Ching. *Architecture: Form, Space, and Order*. Wiley, 2012.

T. J. Csordas. Intersubjectivity and intercorporeality. *Subjectivity*, 22(1):110–121, 2008.

A. S. Devlin. Wayfinding in healthcare facilities: Contributions from environmental psychology. *behavioral Sciences*, 4:423–436, 2014.

G. W. Evans. Environmental cognition. *Psychonomic bulletin*, 88:259–287, 1980.

C. R. Gallistel. *The organization of learning*. Learning, development, and conceptual change. The MIT Press, Cambridge Mass, London, 1990.

T. Gärling, A. Böök, and E. Lindberg. Spatial orientation and wayfinding in the designed environment: A conceptual analysis and some suggestions for postoccupancy evaluation. *Journal of Architectural and Planning Research*, 3:55–64, 1986.

J. J. Gibson. *The ecological approach to visual perception*. Boston: Houghton Miain., 1979.

O. Gun, R. Woodbury, B. Peters, and M. Sheikholeslami. *Elements of Parametric Design*. Routledge, 2010.

T. Hartley, I. Trinkler, and N. Burgess. Geometric determinants of human spatial memory. *Cognition*, 94:39–75, 2004.

S. Kaplan and R. Kaplan. *Cognition and environment: functioning in an uncertain world*. New York: Praeger, 1982.

V. Kondyli, M. Bhatt, and T. Hartmann. Towards people-centred precedents for parametric design: The case of wayfinding in large-scale buildings. In *Lean & Computing in Construction Congress (LC3), Vol. 2 (CONVR)*, Heraklion, Greece, July 2017a. (to appear).

V. Kondyli, C. Schultz, and M. Bhatt. Evidence-based parametric design: Computationally generated spatial morphologies satisfying behavioural-based design constraints. In M. Y. C. K. P. F. Eliseo Clementini, Maureen Donnelly and A. Ballatore, editors, *13th International Conference on Spatial Information Theory (COSIT 2017)*, 2017b. (to appear).

D. R. Montello. *The Cambridge handbook of visuospatial thinking*, chapter Navigation, pages 257–294. Cambridge University Press, Cambridge, 2005.

R. Norton. *An Introduction to the Synthesis and Analysis of Mechanisms and Machines*. 2003.

M. O'Neill. Evaluation of a conceptual model of architectural legibility. *Environment and Behavior*, 23 (3):259–284, May 1991.

W. Rybczynski. Parametric design: What's gotten lost amid the algorithms. *The Journal of the Americal Institute of Architects*, 2013.

C. Schultz, M. Bhatt, and A. Borrmann. Bridging qualitative spatial constraints and feature-based parametric modelling: Expressing visibility and movement constraints. *Advanced Engineering Informatics*, 31:2 – 17, 2017. ISSN 1474-0346. Towards a new generation of the smart built environment.

R. Snowden, P. Thompson, and T. Troscianko. *Basic Vision. An introduction to visual perception*. Oxford University Press, Oxford, 2006.

B. Tversky. *The cambridge handbook of visuospatial thinking*, chapter Functional significance of visuospatial representations. Cambridge University Press, Cambridge, 2005.

R. Ulrich, L. Berry, X. Quan, and J. Parish. A conceptual framework for the domain of evidence-based design. *Health Environ. Res. Des. J.*, 4:95–114, 2010.

J. Weisman. Evaluating architectural legibility: Way-finding and the built environment. *Environment and Behavior*, 13(2):189–20, 1981.

G. Weiss. *Body images: Embodiment as intercorporeality*. Routledge, New York, 1999.

J. M. Wiener, C. Holscher, S. Buchner, and L. Konieczny. Gaze behaviour during space perception and spatial decision making. *sychological Research*, 76:713–729, 2012.

Using BIM Throughout the Occupancy of Residential Buildings to Benefit Homeowners: A Roadmap to Viability

Stewart Long, Haijiang Li
Cardiff University, United Kingdom
stewartwork@live.co.uk

Abstract. This paper considers how homeowners can benefit from the use of Building Information Modelling (BIM) during the occupancy phase of residential buildings, and the issues that may arise, alongside the authors' proposed solutions. Four key deliverables have been considered; economic, social and environmental benefits, and the facilitation of efficient information management. These deliverables are to be achieved through home automation, the availability of building information, virtual house viewings and big data analytics. The core issues are considered to be user accessibility, ownership and viability. A "Home BIM" cloud application has been proposed as a workable solution. The application is based on a data-rich BIM model, enhanced with occupancy data using the Internet of Things (IoT). The outputs discussed include instructing actuators for home automation, and accessible information and functions displayed via a user-friendly interface. A roadmap to delivering such an application has been presented.

1 Introduction

1.1 Scope

This paper investigates the use of building information modelling (BIM) during the occupancy of residential buildings, to deliver benefits to homeowners. The paper anticipates what issues may arise, and proposes solutions to overcome these. The term "homeowner" is used as an umbrella term throughout to describe property owners and occupants.

1.2 Background Study

1.2.1 Delivering Benefits beyond Environmental Performance

There has long been a drive toward improving the environmental performance of new homes in the UK, notably the use of SAP calculations and Code for Sustainable Homes (CfSH). In 2015 BRE launched the Home Quality Mark (HQM) which sets a precedent for home ratings by also considering the social and economic well-being of homeowners. This includes factors such as comfort, low running costs, digital connectivity, interaction with the local community and accessible home controls. It is recognised that decisions made during occupancy can help to achieve and maintain these desired outcomes. TEDDINET supports digital innovation in energy demand by covering topics including data availability and data visualisation.

1.2.2 Maintaining and Using Information about the Building after Handover

New home rating schemes generally consist of a design stage and an as-built compliance check. Post occupancy evaluations are not frequently carried out in residential buildings, and so the accuracy of building information can deteriorate. This can cause safety concerns, planning and maintenance issues, and results in significant cost and time implications for building works. Data-rich, well-maintained BIM models may be able to avert these issues by providing accurate building data in a structured, accessible manner. That in turn will facilitate the delivery of economic, social and environmental benefits. This paper proposes that BIM is currently underutilised during occupancy, and can be a valuable resource to homeowners.

1.3 Research Question

How can BIM achieve economical (A), social (B) and environmental (C) benefits for homeowners, and be used for efficient information management (D)?

2 Literature Review

2.1 Information Exchange at Handover

Eadie et al (2013) found that 3D models and COBie datasets were rarely handed over to clients and facility managers, despite the prospective financial benefits. Kofler and Kastner (2010) noted that data contained in a BIM model produced during design and construction could be used for decision-making during occupancy. A system named ThinkHome was proposed to use data such as material properties to improve building energy efficiency and comfort. The information upon which it operates was to be automated as much as possible, and a BIM model was to be used to facilitate the transfer of data between phases. Many studies have suggested the use of BIM model data to rapidly populate facility management systems. This would be particularly useful in leasehold residential buildings such as flats.

2.2 Capturing and Using Data during the Occupancy Phase

Motawa and Carter (2012) highlighted that systematic methodology is needed to monitor and control buildings to ensure that the environmental targets set out in the design phase are being met. To facilitate this BIM was specified as a means of storing and exchanging information, including automatic meter readings, supplier documents, and sensor data. Ozturk et al (2012) also acknowledged that the use of data from sensing devices and meters in a BIM environment would improve the quality of post occupancy evaluations and so reduce operational costs. Sensors are recommended for monitoring both movement and the building environment. The paper also recognises the Internet of Things (IoT) as an effective means of populating cloud databases, consolidating data from a number of interconnected devices. It is noted, however, that the data input to a BIM model should be concise and have a purpose, so as to optimise performance and prevent the storage of redundant information. Radmehr et al. (2014) suggested the use of BIM as a real time design tool. This can be applied to building works and maintenance during the occupancy phase, to aid decision-making.

2.3 Barriers to Adoption

Volk et al (2014) discovered that BIM processes were not established for existing buildings, mainly due to data uncertainties and model maintenance. The paper called for legal and organisational frameworks to consider existing buildings. McAdam (2010) recognised that there is a need to specify BIM responsibilities throughout the project. The use and status of the model including level of detail (LOD) were cited as concerns. The ownership of particular elements such as worksets was also flagged as unresolved. It was concluded that collaborative procurement would be appropriate to specify information exchanges.

3 Benefits to Homeowners

This section describes how BIM can be used to achieve the deliverables set out by the research question in section 1.3, namely via; home automation, the availability of building information, virtual house viewings and big data analytics.

3.1 Home Automation

3.1.1. Optimisation of Building Services and Lighting

To optimise usage, real time consumption data from smart meters can be analysed alongside building environment data from building energy management (BEM) systems such as sensors, as suggested by Ozturk et al. (2012) and Kofler and Kastner (2010). Data analytics can be executed using artificial intelligence (AI) for efficiency, which can be programmed to "learn" by recalling past decisions made in similar scenarios, described by Kumari et al. (2013). This can be processed within a BIM environment to form logical outcomes using semantic reasoning. BIM will allow factors such as geospatial referencing, geometry, building fabric and solar/weather conditions to be accounted for. The target output would be autonomous, pre-emptive decision-making to inform actuators on how best to regulate the building environment, so as to reduce energy consumption and improve home comfort.

3.1.2. Automated Remedial Works Recommendations

Before optimisation, it can sometimes be more cost-effective for homeowners to reduce their reliance on building services by conducting home improvements to the building fabric. BIM could be used to conduct analysis to inform such management decisions. For example building sensor data can be mapped using 3D geometry from the BIM model, to show indicative heat distribution throughout the property. This could be used to flag the cavity walls most prone to allowing heat loss, to allow the homeowner to cost-effectively target investment for reducing energy consumption. Furthermore, AI can be used to interpret the heat data, alongside building fabric data from the BIM model. Iterative remodelling – referencing a database of alternative insulation products – could be incorporated into the system to make recommendations to the homeowner. Developing this intelligent computing methodology would require investment, potentially from proprietary material suppliers. It is envisaged that the system could integrate with gbXML/IFC files from IES ERGON.

3.1.3. BIM Deliverables

Hence by monitoring and automating building services – using data from smart meters and sensors to populate BIM environments – BIM can deliver economic, social and environmental benefits to homeowners. Importantly, large volumes of data are structured and processed efficiently, producing useful and intuitive outputs for homeowners.

3.2 Availability of Building Information

Managed well, a data-rich BIM model can provide a platform to store and analyse data, and export useful information to inform homeowner decision-making during occupancy. It is important that the data contained within a model is kept current, so as to provide accurate – and therefore useful – outputs. From the model, the user (the homeowner or a nominated person) can use BIM to access and produce a suite of information to aid redesign, building works and maintenance. This has been demonstrated by three examples in Table 1.

Table 1 illustrates how all deliverables set out in section 1.3 can be achieved with the use of BIM. The benefits described are mostly cost-saving, as a result of utilising the information input to the model during the design and construction phases. The potential use of design and construction data during occupancy was noted by Kofler and Kastner (2010).

Table 1 – Using BIM to deliver benefits to homeowners during redesign, building works and maintenance

Example works	Information Required	How BIM can provide this information	Benefits to the homeowner	BIM Deliverable
Redesign of layout or architecture	2D/3D visuals, and immersive environments	3D rendering e.g. in 3DS Max or Envisioneer	Enables design options appraisal	A
		Virtual or augmented reality walkthroughs in game engines (exporting in FBX format)	Better understanding of design at early stage to achieve desired outcome	A, B
		Geometrical information for use in specialist simulation software e.g. DIALux (gbXML)	Detailed analysis to ensure home comfort, utilisation of natural light to assist in design	A, B
	Material requirements	Material scheduling and quantity take-offs e.g. using Autodesk Revit	Greater degree of cost certainty	A
Extension or modification to building	Ground conditions	Model can store topographical and geological survey data	Assists substructure design and reduces the need for excessive site investigations	A, D
	Building structure	Structural analysis to assess impact on existing structure e.g. using Autodesk Robot	Enables design optimisation to reduce material quantity, as well as temporary works planning	A, C, D
	Services routing	Construction issue drawings can be exported (.dwg or PDF). Augmented reality can identify locations of services hidden within walls	Improves safety and reduces risk of damage to equipment. Also prevents unnecessary site surveys, reducing cost and programme	A, B, D
	Programme	4D modelling for construction sequencing	Improved time certainty	A
Maintenance check for boiler	Specification and meter data	Supplier manual, install date, meter data and previous maintenance reports can be stored in the model for future reference	Readily accessible information. Can use to schedule future maintenance to improve efficiency (e.g. using YouBIM by EngWorks)	A, C, D

3.3 Virtual House Viewings

BIM model data often becomes redundant following the completion of a residential building, but it could be exported to game engines to create immersive environments. One such data exchange process between building information models and game engines such as Unity – as defined by McCabe and McPolin (2015) – is to export an FBX file from an Autodesk product, whilst ensuring that materials assigned in Revit are converted to standard materials using Autodesk 3DS Max. This could be used by homeowners to provide virtual house viewings, minimising agent fees and disruption from viewings. It could also accelerate the sales process by allowing concurrent viewings at the buyers' convenience. Distribution of this service would benefit from online platforms such as 4BIM, which allows browser viewing and screen sharing for guided viewings. The provision of virtual house viewings could therefore deliver both economic benefits and social benefits to homeowners who are looking to relocate.

3.4 Big Data Analytics

Big data – collated from widespread adoption of BIM within residential buildings – could be used to identify usage patterns and trends within local communities, and potentially on a national scale. The Internet of Things (IoT) can be used to connect to smart devices for greater data collation, providing a data pool for an all-in-one smart home user system. This could be conducted via interoperable IoT platforms such as ARTIK Cloud. Homeowners will benefit in a number of ways: from allowing the benchmarking of energy consumption to target homes for the government's Energy Company Obligation (ECO) scheme, to indicating peak times for hot water demand in apartment blocks so that facility managers can prepare accordingly. Widespread data collation from the residential market would also significantly increase the volume of data available for analysing BIM usage and behavioural patterns during occupancy, using data mining. This could contribute to research and be used to direct the development of future BIM applications. An easily distributable application would allow new technologies to be trialled, refined and validated in real world environments. It is noted that sharing data is a prerequisite to these benefits; security risk is discussed in section 5.2.3.

4 Case Study: North West Bicester Eco-Town

North West Bicester is a pioneering eco-town currently under development with all homes built to Level 5 of CfSH and many sustainable features that make it a zero net carbon development. Homeowners can influence their carbon footprint and target cost-savings by observing energy consumption charts – split into night, morning, afternoon and evening – on real time information systems installed in each home (A2Dominion 2015).

Another feature of these systems is the integration of local transport information including buses, trains and cycle routes (A2Dominion 2015). This provides interaction with the local community: a social benefit considered by the HQM scheme, as discussed in section 1.2.1.

This case study demonstrates the potential for technology to deliver economic (bill savings), social (interaction with community) and environmental (analysis of energy efficiency during occupancy) benefits to homeowners. The real time information systems are an efficient information management tool, providing a user-friendly interface for quick and easy interpretation of energy usage data and other beneficial information.

5 Anticipated Problems and Proposed Solutions

5.1 User Accessibility: Developing a "Home BIM" Application

5.1.1. The User

A key consideration in planning how BIM can be used during the occupancy phase of a residential building is the user. Specialist BIM technicians may need to be appointed to manage the model, but the day-to-day user will be untrained homeowners. Hence this paper recommends the development of an out of the box "Home BIM" application that acts as a graphical user interface (GUI) between the homeowner and the technical BIM environment. Home BIM should automatically retrieve information and functionality from the BIM model using an application programming interface (API), to output useful information to an intuitive and navigable GUI. This will ensure that outputs are communicated effectively, allowing the homeowner to realise the benefits discussed in section 3. The real time information systems – described in section 4 will indicate how homeowners interact with home technology systems.

5.1.2. Content

The content of Home BIM should be defined by considering the desired outputs that will benefit homeowners. Figure 1 shows example modules that are accessed from a tray at the bottom of the screenshots (namely energy, virtual home, whole building tools, maintenance, community and building services). These modules will categorise a suite of outputs (information and functions) that utilise BIM capabilities. One example is solar and shading analysis within the 'Virtual home' module. Solar analysis may have been considered by the architect, but additional value can be attained by processing real time weather data into the model during occupancy, so that the homeowner can view daylight hours. The 'Home redesign suite' feature would allow homeowners to strategically manage the redesign of areas within a virtual world, to inform options appraisals and automatically produce materials schedules to improve cost certainty. A 'Building Services' module could provide existing services information to the user, as highlighted as a potential benefit in Table 1.

Hence Home BIM can enable homeowners to benefit from elements of BIM models that may otherwise become redundant after handover. As well as predefined modules, there is scope to allow third party add-ins to deliver further opportunities, using interoperable data formats.

5.1.3. User Interface

The GUI is critical to the effectiveness of Home BIM, in order to allow homeowners to navigate and utilise the application. Inspiration can be drawn from the across the industry: from the real time information systems used at North West Bicester – discussed in section 4 – to digital media companies who develop residential marketing material. By analysing similar systems and evaluating their effectiveness, indicative screenshots of a GUI for Home BIM on a tablet device have been produced, and are illustrated in figure 1 and figure 2. It is proposed that the application will launch from an initial home screen (figure 1) and users will enter into different modules from the bottom tray. Homeowners will follow a logical touchscreen selection process to navigate to the output required (figure 2). Basic navigation controls (settings, home screen and back) are included to the right. For ease of access a search bar and list of favourite or recent items can be incorporated into the home screen.

Figure 1 – Proposed home screen for the Home BIM application

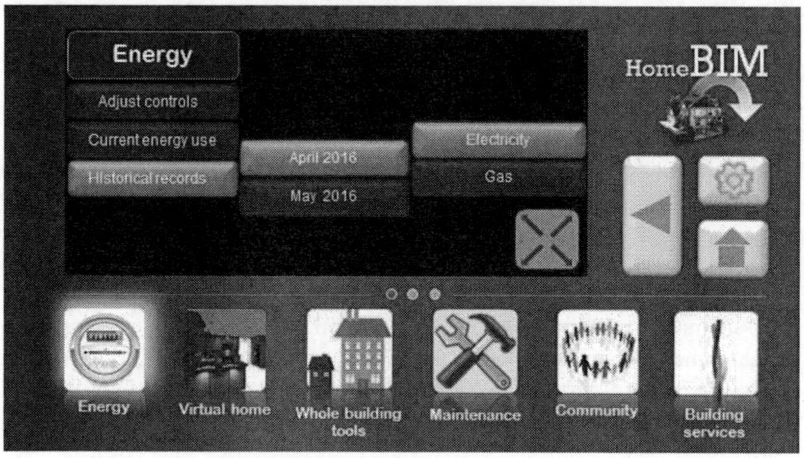

Figure 2 – Navigation through the Home BIM application

5.2 Ownership

5.2.1. Contractual Ownership

At building handover, numerous parties will have contributed to the development of a BIM model. Not all BIM elements will be relevant for decision-making during occupancy, so the homeowner's information requirements must be defined, as well as the terms under which the transfer of ownership and licencing of intellectual property will occur. This can be arranged using alliancing contracts, collateral warranties and contractual clauses. Where proprietary BIM objects are used in design but not shared this should be logged and, where appropriate, replaced with similar publically available objects from the NBS National BIM Library. Refurbishment projects may utilise data from an existing Asset Information Model (AIM).

5.2.2. Maintenance

Homeowners will need to ensure that the BIM model remains accurate and current following any redesign, building works or maintenance. As discussed this is likely to require the appointment of specialist BIM technicians. All parties who contribute to the model must be assigned accountability for their edits, as any errors may reduce the effectiveness of the system, result in rework, or cause technical issues such as file corruption. The NBS BIM Toolkit can be used to assign responsibilities and manage project information requirements.

5.2.3. Security Risk

The BIM model will be accessed and edited by a number of parties, even after building handover. Therefore the security of information will be a key concern to many: the homeowner in order to maintain personal privacy and the integrity of the model data, and organisations that use proprietary objects and analysis tools. PAS 1192-5:2015 – "Specification for security-minded building information modelling, digital built environments and smart asset management" – has been produced to address security threats during information exchanges. The specification directs protocols to secure information and instil confidence. It was fast-tracked as a PAS (rather than a British Standard) as the security threat to digital information exchanges has been recognised as a pressing industrywide issue.

5.3 Viability

In order to make Home BIM a viable proposition, this section of the paper considers the technical requirements of such a system. A business case would need to be put forward for the development of Home BIM to prove feasibility, but this is outside of this paper's remit.

5.3.1. Information Exchanges Using Model View Definitions

Table 1 outlined the information required for some example jobs during occupancy. Not all data stored in a BIM model will be applicable to every job or user – due to redundancy or confidentially – and so it is important to define data exchange requirements. Ramaji and Memari (2015) noted the benefit of creating exchange modules to specify the required information in plain terms. An example of how this can be applied to a specific job during the occupancy phase is show in Table 2, taking a building extension as an example.

Table 2 – Example exchange model for a building extension

Type	BIM model, PDF or DWG documents
Project Stage	Occupancy (building modification)
Exchange Disciplines	Designer, Contractor, Client (homeowner)
Description	The objective is to provide existing structural and building services information to the designer and contractor, to facilitate the design and construction of a building extension. Structural drawings and building services schematics will be exported directly from the model.

These exchange modules can then be used to determine the IFC elements needed to develop Model View Definitions (MVDs). An MVD is a legal subset of the IFC schema – encoded in mvdXML in IFC2x3 or IFC4 – that is used to define and validate data during specific information exchanges. When creating MVDs, guidance should be sought from ISO 16739:2013 "IFC for data sharing in the construction and facility management industries", ISO 29481: the Information Delivery Manual (IDM) and ISO 12006-3, which includes the International Framework for Dictionaries (IFD). Figure 10 shows how IFC information exchanges can be developed and refined for MVDs.

Figure 10 – The process of developing IFC data exchange requirements (See et al. 2011)

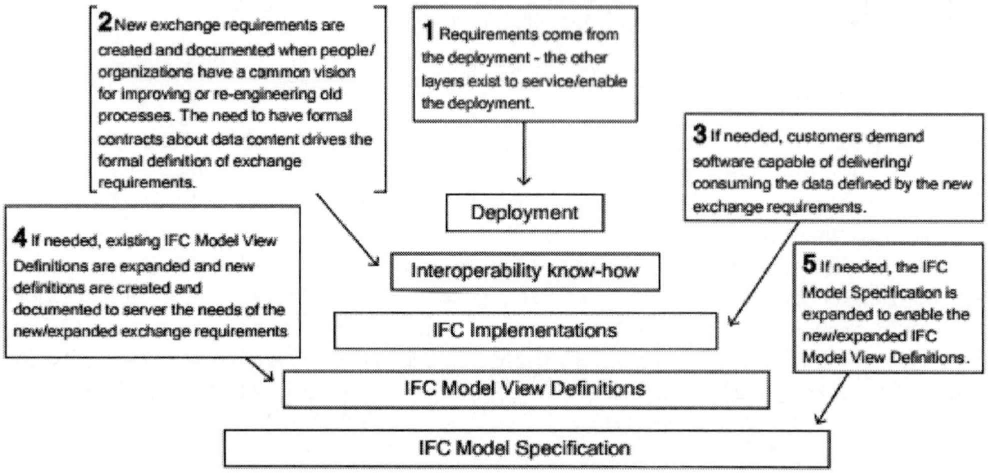

MVDs will enable effective information exchanges for the Home BIM system, to improve outputs and user experience. Refining MVDs will be an iterative process as Home BIM usage statistics and feedback is received, both from homeowners and technical consultants.

5.3.2. IT Infrastructure

It is important that Home BIM is easily distributable, without the need for homeowners to invest in complex, costly IT systems. It would also be beneficial for the homeowner to be able to access the information at any time from any device. Therefore it is proposed that Home BIM should be developed as a software as a service (SaaS) cloud application, providing a sophisticated service that does not require substantial memory or processing power in the host device. The BIM environment would be accessed and modified or exported from the cloud by specialists. Internet access is critical for functionality, data exchanges and updates.

6 Roadmap

6.1 The Current Situation

BIM use by homeowners during occupancy is very rare, partly due to lack of awareness of BIM and its potential benefits, and also due to training requirements. Commercial facility managers are using BIM, but not to the extent that it is utilised in design and construction.

6.2 Moving Forward: The Next Steps

Guidance on BIM for residential building occupancy is required, potentially developing on the content of ISO 16739:2013. Dedicated MVDs – specific to residential occupancy – are needed. A framework of responsibilities should also be defined, using the NBS BIM Toolkit, and considering the contractual impacts between stakeholders. And finally the ontology for an out of the box Home BIM cloud application should be defined.

6.3 Long Term Visions

BIM could one day be a standard feature utilised during the occupancy of all residential buildings, potentially forming the basis of home user guides (HUGs) and operation and maintenance (O&M) manuals. Further benefits, beyond those described in this paper, can be realised as technology develops and is trialled. Procuring BIM models for residential buildings is likely to begin in complex, high-rise buildings, but later spread to standard housing as the industry becomes more familiar with the process. As well as new build homes, technologies such as point cloud scanning and structure-from-motion may facilitate the use of Home BIM in existing housing stock. The challenge will be making this cost effective.

7 Conclusions

This paper shows that BIM can be used during residential occupancy building to deliver a range of benefits to homeowners. This was demonstrated by investigating home automation, the improved availability of building information, virtual house viewings and big data analytics. User accessibility, ownership and viability were key concerns. This paper called for guidance specific to residential occupancy for the creation of dedicated MVDs and a framework of BIM responsibilities. The paper also proposed the development of a Home BIM cloud application to provide a GUI between homeowners and the technical BIM environment.

References

A2Dominion (2015). Construction begins on the UK's first eco town [online], http://nwbicester.co.uk/2014/01/construction-begins-on-the-uks-first-eco-town, accessed April 2017.

Backes, D., Ramirez, C., Thomson, C., Bordbar, N., O'Brien, B., Kooner, K., Ghose, A., Malki-Epshtein, L. and Boehm, J. (2012). A "green" BIM for UCL's Chadwick Building: Phase 1 Summer 2012 [online], http://www.ucl.ac.uk/3dim/bim/green_bim/phase_1, accessed: April 2017.

Davis, D., Karlshoj, J. and See, R. (2011). An Integrated Process for Delivering IFC Based Data Exchange. United Kingdom: BuildingSMART UK

Eadie, R., Browne, M., Odeyinka, H., McKeown, C. and McNiff, S. (2013). BIM implementation throughout the UK construction project lifecycle: An analysis. Automation in Construction 36, pp. 145-151.

Kofler, M. J. and Kastner, W. (2010). A knowledge Base for Energy-Efficient Smart Homes. Energy Conference and Exhibition (EnergyCon), 2010 IEEE International. Manama, 18-22 December, 2010. Vienna, Automation Systems Group, pp. 85-90.

Kumari, S., Abhushek, R. and Panda, B. S. (2013). Intelligent Computing Relating to Cloud Computing. International Journal of Mechnical Engineerig and Computer Applications(IJMCA), 1(1).

McAdam, B. (2010). Building information modelling: the UK legal context. Bingley: Emerald Group Publishing Limited.

McCabe, A. and McPolin, D. (2015). Virtual reality: immersed in the structural world. The Structural Engineer 93(3), pp. 20-23.

Motawa, I. and Carter, K. (2012). Sustainable BIM-based Evaluation of Buildings. Procedia – Social and Behavioural Sciences 74(0), pp. 419-428

Ozturk, Z., Arayici, Y. and Coates, S. P. (2012). Post occupancy evaluation (POE) in residential buildings utilizing BIM and sensing devices: Salford energy house example. In: Retrofit 2012. Greater Manchester, 24-26 January 2012. Salford, University of Salford.

Ramaji, I. J. and Memari, A. M. (2015). Information Exchange Standardization for BIM Application to Multi-Story Modular Residential Buildings. AEI 2015. Washington, ASCE, pp. 13-24.

Volk, R., Stengel, J. and Schultmann, F. (2014). Building Information Modeling (BIM) for existing buildings – Literature review and future needs. Automation in Construction 38, pp. 109-127.

Application of global sensitivity analysis methods in geotechnical problems

Mahmoudi E, Hölter R, König M, Schanz T
Ruhr-Universität Bochum, Germany
Elham.Mahmoudi@rub.de

Abstract. In general, the remarkable amount of uncertainties involved in the material parameters is considered as an explicit feature of any geotechnical problems, due to their geological origin. Therefore, in the context of model calibration and validation, conducting a sensitivity analysis is substantial as the first step. It identifies key input factors that have the most contribution to the uncertainty of the model output. This study employs three commonly used sensitivity analysis methods on a sophisticated geotechnical problem. The simulation of the excavation and operation of a solution-mined cavity in the rock salt, used as compressed air energy deals with highly non-linear phenomena, and includes many constitutive parameters as input. Sensitivity measures of different variables involved in the mechanical response of the cavern are computed by different global sensitivity methods, namely Sobol′/Saltelli, Random Balance Design, and Elementary Effect (Morris) method. An interpretation of the sensitivity indices provided by different methods is presented through a comparative study. The obtained results reveal that the applied methods provide identical parameter importance rankings, although not all of them are able to present the same information about the system behaviour.

1. Introduction

A crucial aspect in geotechnical engineering is providing an accurate prediction of the serviceability, the stability and soil-structures interaction behaviour. To accomplish this, one needs to identify the constitutive geo-mechanical properties of the geomaterials precisely. For many decades, researchers developed measurement techniques, analytical and numerical analysis methods to infer and simulate the constitutive behaviour of geological materials. However, independent from the accuracy level of the applied methodology, the properties of geomaterials, as a natural heterogeneous material, are associated with a significant amount of uncertainties. Despite the inherent randomness of soil properties (also known as aleatoric uncertainty), there is another category of uncertainty called as epistemic uncertainty. The latter one is mostly due to the lack of available knowledge about the natural phenomena. In geotechnical applications, the epistemic uncertainties mainly result from the existing uncertainties in the experimental and in-situ investigation and their interpretation for estimating the input factors. Thereupon, epistemic uncertainty can be reduced or even omitted by conducting an adequate amount of informative measurements and explorations. In the following, model calibration methods, either deterministic or probabilistic ones can provide an accurate assignment of the geomaterial properties.

Generally, the response of a system is not affected equally by all the involved factors. On the other hand, reducing the associated uncertainty in some input parameters may decrease noticeably the uncertainty measures in the model response, compared to the others. Hence, identifying those dominating input variables enables an effective selection of the measurement design. In this regard, the Sensitivity Analysis (SA) can be employed to detect the key input factors which have the greatest impact on the model output variation. In practice, two main categories of SA methods can be distinguished, the local SA category and the global one. In the local approach, the effect of a small variation of a single input parameter on the model output is investigated, while all the other factors are fixed. This approach also is known as one at a time and involves partial derivatives. The local methods can be considered as the historically first attempts to conduct SA and they provided valuable results. In general, numerical implementation of differential analysis and the demanding computational effort for local methods is affordable, hence they will be effective, specifically in the analysis of large systems. For a review of different local SA methods, see Cacuci, et al., (2003). However, calculating derivations around a base point in the space of an individual input factor makes this methodology model-dependent. Therefore, when the system deals with non-linear/ non-monotonic models, the local approach of SA may not provide a reliable importance ranking of the input factors. In this regard, the derivatives should be substituted with an exploration of the entire input parameter space. To accomplish this, the second category of sensitivity analysis methods, i.e., "Global" one are developed. The global methods consider the entire variable space of inputs to estimate their impacts on the model responses. With the advancement of computational capabilities, comprehensive numerical approaches are increasingly used for simulating different geotechnical problems. These sophisticated simulation models of underground structures are supposed to model coupled and highly nonlinear phenomena involved in the geomaterials behaviour. On this subject, the global sensitivity analyses techniques can be considered as a proper alternative for such models. In the last five decades, a diverse range of SA techniques have been developed in different scientific disciplines. Thereupon, for the choice of an appropriate SA method, among all the available techniques, a non-expert SA operator (designer, who has a primary knowledge about the existing variety of methods), may be confused or even misled. In this regard, some attributes of the model of interest can be considered as key features to facilitate the choice of the proper method. In the following, in addition to introducing some common global SA methods, a number of general fundamental aspects of employing an appropriate method, considering system features are discussed.

In this study, three alternative global SA methods, namely, Random Balance Design (RBD), Sobol′/Saltelli, and Elementary Effect (Morris) are introduced and applied to a geotechnical task solved by a finite element model. Here, the response of a rock salt cavity, employed as a compressed air energy storage is investigated. The rock salt formation, as a porous media with low permeability and creep features, has been used as host rock of the hydrocarbon storage for decades. Nowadays there is a new trend to use them as the storage for the excess electrical energy produced by renewable resources in the form of compressed air or Hydrogen (Mahmoudi et al., 2016a). Consideration of the uncertainty in the mechanical properties of such a huge structure (the storage volume may reach to 1 million m^3), which is extended vertically downward more than hundred meters from the ground level is substantial (Mahmoudi et al. 2016b). Here, the stress state around the cavity is regarded as the interested model output. Firstly, a deterministic model of a typical compressed air storage in rock salt is generated. In the following, the performance of different SA techniques is compared in the aspect of required computational effort and result conformity. Furthermore, provided sensitivity indices by different methods are used to achieve a better understanding of the system behaviour, in the aspect of the probable interaction and/or non-linearity.

2. Global sensitivity analysis

In general, global SA techniques are developed to detect the most influential set of parameters which dominate the system output and are precedence to guide any additional measurement or observation efforts. Moreover, global SA may object to detect ineffective input variables. Hence, it enables the designer to fix their values based on a simplified knowledge and reduce the model complexity for any further deterministic or probabilistic investigation. Also, global SA can be applied in the subject of optimum experimental design, as conducted by the authors to provide an optimum measurement design for a loading test set-up (Hölter et al. (2015)).

As mentioned previously, there are several well-developed global SA techniques, which can evaluate the uncertain input factors and rank them using different statistical measures. Since these methods have their own definition of "importance and/or significance", their obtained importance ranking may disapprove each other and lead to confused or inconclusive results, subsequently (Rocquigny et al. 2008). Thereupon, the term of "important factor" for the model of interest should be predefined. A so-called setting can provide such a definition (for a general review on the different settings, the reader is referred to Saltelli et al. (2008)). Among the others, two common settings are: *i)* The Factor Prioritization setting: it is defined to detect a factor which enforced the greatest reduction in the output variance when its true value is identified. This setting can detect and rank those factors which have the largest share in the output's uncertainty and deserve the most accurate identification plan, *ii)* The Factor Fixing setting: it can detect non-influential factors. Fixing such factors at any given value over their range of variability makes no significant reduction in the output variance. This setting is a proper choice to simplify the model of interest when it is dealing with many input variables.

2.1 Variance-based methodology

In general, Variance-based (VB) methods estimates the output variance and the contribution of the uncertainty of each individual input factor and their probable interaction in this variance. VB methods are independent from linearity, monotonicity, additivity, etc. (i.e., model-independent), and they can evaluate the interaction effects among the input factors. Variance-Based methods (VB) for SA were first employed by chemists in the early 1970s (Cukier et al., 1973). Later, Sobol′ (1993) developed the work of them to calculate the sensitivity measures, using a Monte Carlo-based implementation. A review of different VB methods with their recent developments can be found in Saltelli et al. (2008). In the following, the methodology of analysis of variance based on variance decomposition is briefly presented.

Let us consider a generic model of $Y = f\,(X_i), \forall i = 1, \dots, k$, where k is the number of input parameters, and the factor prioritization setting is adopted. In this regard, parameter X_i is fixed at $\grave{x}_i$ and the conditional variance of model $V_{X\sim i}(Y|X_i = \grave{x}_i)$ is evaluated. The notation V is the variance value, and $X\sim i$ is the vector of all input variables but X_i. The conditional variance may strongly depend on the assigned value for $\grave{x}_i$. To generalise this measure, one can take the average and the variance of it over all possible $\grave{x}_i$, denoting by $E_{X_i}(V_{X\sim i}(Y|X_i = \grave{x}_i))$ and $V_{X_i}\,(E_{X\sim i}(Y|X_i = \grave{x}_i)$, respectively. Here, it should be mentioned that $V_{X_i}\,(E_{X\sim i}(Y|X_i) + E_{X_i}\left(V_{X\sim i}(Y|X_i)\right)$=1. Normalizing the term of $V_{X_i}\,(E_{X\sim i}(Y|X_i)$ on model variance, provides the first order sensitivity index as follows,

$$S_i = \frac{V_{X_i}(E_{X\sim i}(Y|X_i = \grave{x}_i)}{V(Y)}.$$

S_i is known as first order effect of X_i on $V(Y)$. A high value of S_i, and hence higher $V_{X_i}(E_{X\sim i}(Y|X_i = \grave{x}_i)$ indicates an important input variable. An important factor here denotes a variable which decreasing its variance will reduce the uncertainty of model output most. Hence, in the concept of model's uncertainty reduction, this parameter has the priority to be identified. For non-additive models or models with interaction effect between input parameters where $\sum_{i=1}^{k} S_i < 1$, the higher order of sensitivity indices due to interaction between X_i and the other parameters, is also involved in the variance of output. In this regard, another sensitivity index denoted as S_{Ti} is presented,

$$S_{Ti} = 1 - \frac{V(E(Y|X_i = \grave{x}_i)}{V(Y)} = \frac{E(V(Y|X_i = \grave{x}_i)}{V(Y)}.$$

The term of $E(V_{x\sim i}(Y|X_i = \acute{x}_i))$ indicates the average of the remaining variance of *Y*, when the X_i is fixed, and is known as residual term. S_{Ti} covers a full set of terms that consist parameter X_i. Recalling the definition of the factor fixing setting, S_{Ti} can be contemplated as an index for this setting. The present study employed a Monte Carlo based computational strategy proposed by Saltelli et al. (2002). This methodology which is referred to as Sobol′/Saltelli method in this paper, can evaluate both sensitivity indices forcing $N(k+2)$ model runs. *N* is the required number of random samples in Monte Carlo simulation and should be chosen based on a convergence analysis. Although, the proposed strategy by Saltelli et al. (2002) drastically reduce the crude Monte Carlo (where kN^2 model evaluations was needed) initially proposed by Sobol′(1993), still is not affordable for models that their execution is not computationally cheap and many input parameters are involved. To address this issue, one can firstly conduct a qualitative approach as screening to freeze some of non-influential parameters and subsequently apply the Sobol′/Saltelli method on the reduced number of parameters. However, in conducting process of VB methods on expensive models, one can employ surrogate modelling techniques, which drastically reduce the regarded computational time (Khaledi et al. (2014)). It should be stated that the first order and the total effect sensitivity indices provide additional results about the model of interest and input parameters. As stated previously, $\sum_{i=1}^{k} S_i = 1$ can reveal the additivity of model, and any difference between S_{Ti} and S_i signifies the existence of interaction effects between X_i and the other parameters.

2.2 Random Balance Design

One of the first well-designed methods for conducting SA, which could explore the entire input space for monotonic and non-monotonic models was Fourier Amplitude Sensitivity Test (FAST), (Saltelli et al.1999). The core feature of FAST is exploring the multi-dimensional space of the input factors by a suitably defined search-curve. FAST method computes the main effect contribution of each input factor to the variance of the output, it can be considered same as the S_i measure in Sobol' method. Recalling the generic model of $Y = f\ (X_i), \forall i = 1, \dots, k$, the factor values are sampled in *N* sample points from a periodic curve exploring the space of a *k*-dimensional cube, with a different frequency ω_i assigned to each factor. The frequencies should be selected such that they are free of interferences up to a given order of higher harmonies, *M*. Afterwards, the Fourier spectrum is calculated on the model output at each sample point for the frequency of ω_i. The parametric curve is defined as,

$$X_i(s_j) = G_i(\sin \omega_i s_j), \qquad \forall i = 1, \dots k;\ \forall j = 1, \dots, N$$

where s_j is a scalar variable varying over the range $-\Pi < s_j < +\Pi$, and sampled over its range using *N* sample points. G_i is the transformation function which is chosen according to the desired probability density function of the input parameter of X_i, and ω_i are the frequencies, associated with each factor. Saltelli et al. (1999) proposed the following transformation to provide a uniformly distributed sample for the factors

$$X_i = \frac{1}{2} + \frac{1}{\Pi}\sin^{-1}\sin(\omega_i s_j),$$

which is a set of straight lines oscillating in the range of [0-1], while $-\pi < s_j < +\pi$. The classic FAST method forces a complex algorithm to set all the frequencies free of interferences (Tarantola at al., 2006). In this regard, Tarantola et al. simplified the method and proposed RBD. In this method, the input space is explored using an arbitrary same frequency ω for all input factors. Although this assumption avoids the complex calculation of different frequencies involved in original FAST method, the generated curves do not cover the entire input space. This drawback is addressed by employing random permutation of sample points to assure a full coverage of the input space. Then, the sample points are ranked with respect to X_i and the associated evaluated model outputs are re-ordered, subsequently. Then, the frequency ω and its higher harmonies (i.e., 2ω, 3ω, ..., $M\omega$) will be applied to calculate the Fourier spectrum on the model output $F(\omega)$. In the following, the first-order sensitivity index is evaluated as

$$S_i = \frac{1}{V_Y}(\tilde{V}_{X_i} = \sum_{l=1}^{M} F(\omega)|_{\omega=l}).$$

Afterward, the aforementioned ranking process is repeated for each X_i, using the same initially N sampled points. Due to the use of random permutation, the calculation cost of this method is decreased to N model evaluations. For more details the reader is referred to Tarantola at al. (2006). However, the RBD method merely computes the first-order term, therefore it just able to decompose the 100% of output variance in the case of additive models. In this regard, one may use $\sum_{i=1}^{k} S_i$ to identify whether the model is additive or non-additive. If the sum is noticeably smaller than 1, one should employ another algorithm to compute probable non-linearity/interactions. An advantage of RBD is that it is relatively easy to implement. Also, the sample size N, independent of the number of factors, makes it an affordable technique even for computationally expensive models.

2.3 Elementary Effect (Morris) method

The main idea of screening, which is exploring the model behaviour based on a discretising of the input space, is originated from the local SA techniques. These methods can be adapted to the complex model with tens of input parameters to identify the non-influential factors with a relatively small number of model runs. Morris (1991) presented the Elementary Effect as a global SA method. This method is referred to as Morris method hereafter. The method of Morris allows to identify inputs having negligible effects, and inputs that express large non-linear and/or interaction effects. Based on the proposed technique by Morris, each parameter's range is normalized and discretized, therefore the parameter space of the model is converted to a k-dimensional unit cube. In order to calculate the Elementary Effect of the ith parameter EE_i, ($\forall i$=1,2, ..., k) for a given point in the grid $X = (X_1, \ldots, X_i, \ldots, X_k)$, Δ is added to the ith input parameter in a random order. Hereby, Δ is an arbitrary increment and EE_i is calculated by

$$EE_i = \frac{Y(X_1, \ldots, X_i + e_i\Delta, \ldots, X_k)}{\Delta},$$

here e_i is a unit vector in direction i, which is selected randomly. To compute EE_i for k parameters, Morris proposed an efficient methodology which crosses a trajectory of (k+1) points in the normalized parameter space. Each trajectory provides one EE for each input parameter and by considering r trajectories ($r \approx$10-500), the total number of required model evaluation is $r(k+1)$. Now there is a collection of r times EEs for each parameter. The mean and the standard deviation of EEs denoted as μ and σ, respectively, are calculated as

$$\mu_i = \frac{1}{r}\sum_{j=1}^{r} EE_i^j, \qquad \sigma_i = \sqrt{\frac{1}{r-1}\sum_{j=1}^{r}(EE_i^j - \mu)^2},$$

μ_i and σ_i are considered as the sensitivity indices. μ represents the average effect of each parameter over the parameter space, and σ can notice the existence of any interaction between parameters and/or non-linearity of the model. Also, μ_i may provide information about the sign of the input's effect on the system behaviour, which helps to realise the nature of the problem.

Nevertheless, different signs of EE_i, may lead to significant changes in their mean value μ, and an imprecise parameter ranking, subsequently. In this regard, Compolongo et al. (2007) suggested to use the mean of absolute Elementary Effect indices $|EE_i|$, denoted as μ^*. The smaller μ^* of an input, identifies a less contribution to the output uncertainty. This measure is suitable for the factor fixing setting. Moreover, as Saltelli et al. (2008) mentioned, a lower value of σ, which is due to similar values of the Elementary Effects, reveals that the effect of X_i is almost independent of the values taken by the other factors. Therefore, it can be used as an identification measure to detect the interaction/non-linearity effects between input factors.

2.4 Choose a proper SA method

As a conclusion of all introduced methods, one may provide a primary guideline to choose an appropriate method. Fig.1 depicts such a decision tree which leads to the most appropriate technique based on the system features as model complexity, demanding computational costs and the dimension of the input space. Based on illustrated graph in Fig.1, one should firstly consider the complexity of the model, the local approach is the best choice for linear systems, for the others, global techniques must be employed. At the further steps, the number of involved parameters and the regarded computational costs in a single model evaluation, are decisive features. In general, using screening methods for the models with a high number of input parameters and computationally expensive ones is recommended. Also, one may use the grouping techniques as recommended in Saltelli et al. (2008) to shrink input space. Afterward, one may fix a set of non-influential inputs and further evaluates the VB sensitivity measures suggested by Sobol′.

Nevertheless, in the following, we applied all three techniques on the same rock salt storage cavern model to compare their outcomes' conformity and abilities to provide additional information about the model response.

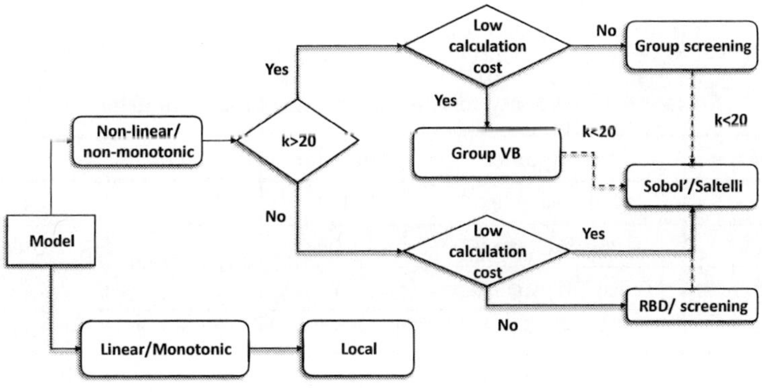

Figure 1: Diagram for the choice of a proper sensitivity analysis method

3. Numerical example

A typical salt cavern with a simplified geometry is modelled using a finite element model. Since the cavern has a cylindrical shape, only half of the geometry has been simulated. The axisymmetrical model with a height of 800m and a width of 300m is shown in Fig.1. This figure, also demonstrates the geometry of the modelled cavern and the applied boundary conditions, in addition to the discretised finite element mesh. A detailed description of the simulated excavation and operation process was given in Mahmoudi et al (2016b). To guarantee the stability and serviceability of the cavity, dilatant zones caused by specific stress state in rock salt should be avoided. The dilatant behaviour is defined by the beginning of the irreversible volumetric expansion, and may initiate the damage progress and leads to long-time failure (Cristescu and Hunsche, 1998). In this regard, the stress state of the rock salt around the cavern is considered as the interested model output. In this study, the level of one-third of cavern's height from its bottom (point B in Fig.2), is treated as a benchmark region for any observations. The finite element model is constituted based on an elasto-viscoplastic creep material model, presented in Mahmoudi et al. (2016a). Nine constitutive parameters are regarded as the uncertain parameters. Tab.1 represents the definition and the assumed statistical measures of these uncertain parameters. It also should be mentioned that all the regarded uncertain parameters are assumed to follow a Gaussian probability distribution.

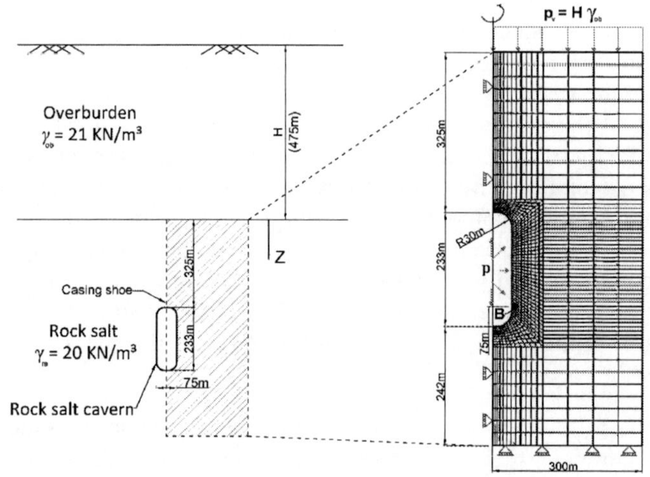

Figure 2: Representative stratigraphy of salt deposit (left), geometry, boundary conditions, and mesh discretization of the salt cavern model (right)

Table 1: Uncertainty representation of material parameters

Parameter	Description	Dimension	Mean	STD
E	Elastic modulus	[GPa]	22	3.30
ν	Poisson Ratio	[-]	0.25	0.0125
n	Transition parameter	[-]	3	0.45
N	Flow exponent	[-]	3	0.45
μ	Fluidity parameter	[s^{-1}]	0.58e-11	0.58e-12
a_1	Hardening parameter	[$MPa^{(2-n)}$]	0.4e-4	0.4e-5
η	Hardening parameter	[-]	0.8	0.08
η_M^*	Maxwell coefficient	[MPa.s]	1.75e12	2.625e11
γ	Ultimate parameter	[-]	0.095	0.0095

4. Results

The three aforementioned SA techniques in Sect. 2 are applied to the model introduced in Sect.3. The obtained results and remarks are presented in the following.

4.1 Convergence analysis

As mentioned previously, the required number of model evaluations in the Monte Carlo based approach proposed by Saltelli can be adjusted within a convergence analysis. To conduct a convergence analysis, firstly R replicas (in this study R=50) of a base sample of dimension N should be generated. Then the corresponding sensitivity measures for each replica is evaluated. In this step, the statistical measures of the indices (namely, mean and coefficient of variation) are evaluated. These steps are repeated for various sample size (N) till its coefficient of variation (COV) converges. Fig.3 depicts the convergence of the S_{Ti} regarding the required number of samples (N) for 6 out of 9 input parameters. For accurate estimations of the sensitivity measures, we selected N=1500, and subsequently the required number of model evaluation is 22000.

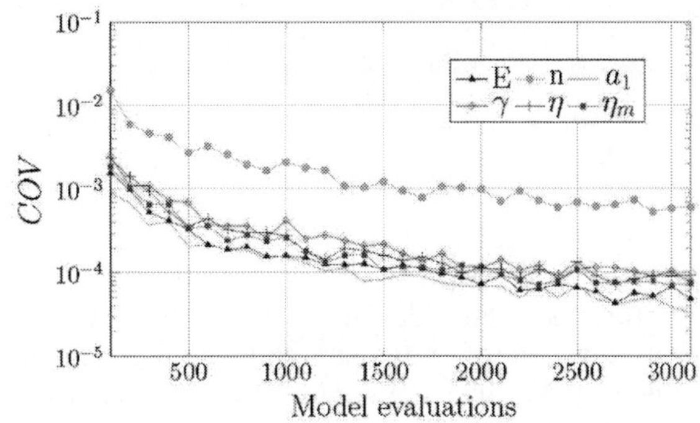

Figure 3: Monitoring the convergence of the S_{Ti} index vs. number of samples

4.2 The comparative study

The calculated first order indices S_i for different constitutive parameters by Sobol′/Saltelli and RBD methods are shown in the Fig.4. The results are mostly identical, while the RBD method merely needs about 500-1000 model evaluations compared to the 22000 required ones in Sobol′/Saltelli's technique. The other comparison is between the calculated sensitivity indices by Morris and Sobol′/Saltelli methods. Fig.5 illustrates the result of S_{Ti} and μ^* in left and right side, respectively. Based on the gained results, the importance ranking of input parameters obtained by Morris method is more obvious than S_{Ti}.In this study, Morris method enforced 3000 model evaluations (r=300, but could be chosen less). Although the scale of provided SA measures is different, but the obtained ranking is mostly same. One may conclude that the three input parameters of Poisson ratio $\boldsymbol{v}$, the flow exponent $\boldsymbol{N}$, and the fluidity parameter $\boldsymbol{\mu}$ have the least contributions in the stress state of point B in Fig.2 and can be treated as fixed values for further investigations. The authors used such results in Mahmoudi et al. (2016a) to reduce the input space's dimension to perform a reliability analysis.

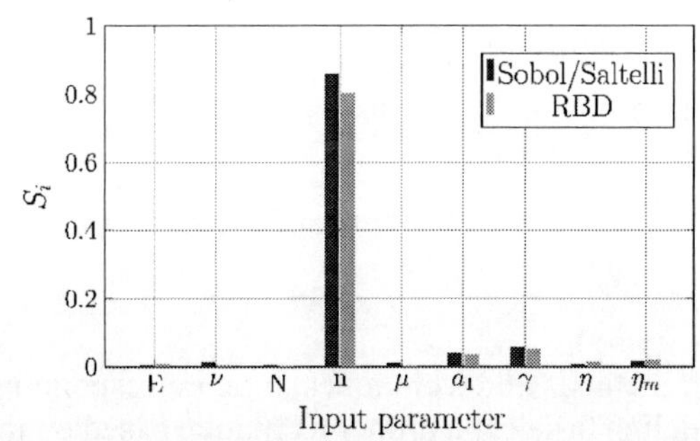

Figure 4: Comparison between the RBD and the Sobol′/Saltelli methods

4.3 Detecting non-linearity and interaction effects

As mentioned in Sect.3, the Morris and Sobol′/Saltelli methods, are both able to provide some more additional information about the model features.

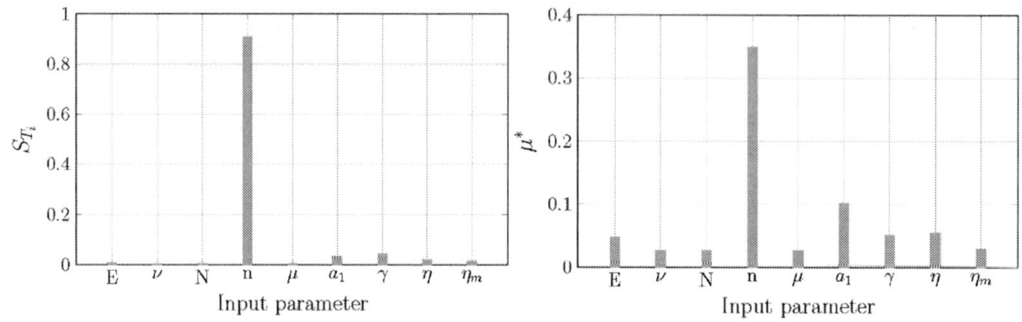

Figure 5: Comparison between the obtained S_{Ti} and the μ^* indices in point B as displayed in Fig.2

For instance, Fig.6 (left) displays results of five conducted SA in different points around the benchmark level in the frame of a cross plot of $\sigma - \mu$. Based on the obtained results, transition parameter ***n*** shows the most standard deviation, which indicates the existence of non-linearity/interaction effects between this parameter and the others. In addition, the almost zero effect of the parameters ***ν***, ***N***, and ***μ***, which already have been identified as the non-influential ones is clearly shown, also their regarded σ is negligible. Additional information which can be extracted from such a graph is the sign of the input parameter's effect on the model output. As shown in Fig.6 (left), ***n*** has a negative effect on the stress state of the cavern's wall. This is justified based on the definition of this parameter, which assigns the dilatancy boundary (For more details see Mahmoudi et al. (2016a)). Moreover, on the right side of Fig.6 the obtained S_i as a function of the $S_{Ti} - S_i$ is depicted. According to that, one can identify the ratio between the first-order effect and the interaction effects, as it shows a large interaction effects for parameter ***n***. Also, comparing the graphs in Fig.6 enables the designer to distinguish the non-linearity and interaction effects involved in the model, since the right one just reveals the interaction effects and the left one includes both. For example, parameters ***n*** and ***a₁*** show the same interaction effects but ***n*** has a higher non-linear effect.

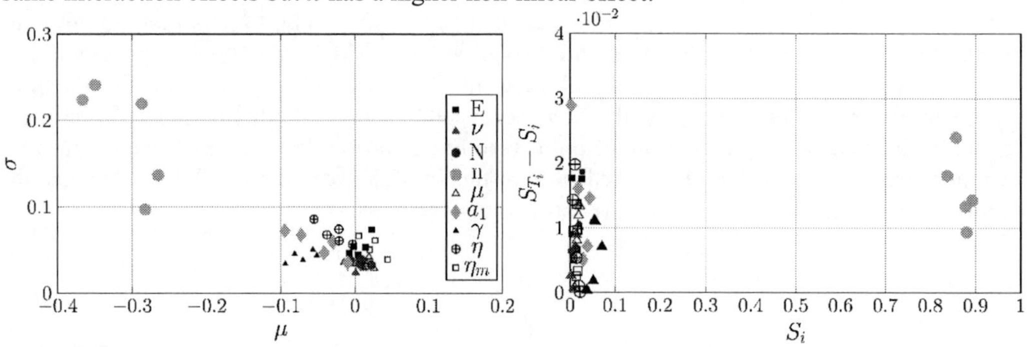

Figure 6: Standard deviation of *EE* vs. μ^* (left), and first-order (S_i) index vs. $S_{Ti} - S_i$ (right)

5. Conclusion

In this study, different SA methods and techniques, their corresponding results and settings are briefly introduced. A guideline to select a proper technique based on the attributes of the model including complexity, computational costs and the number of parameters involved is presented.

A decision tree introduced to guide the user for selecting the most appropriate technique among the others. Since the expensive SA methods as Sobol′/Saltelli provide measures to have a better understanding of the system behaviour, sometimes the designer may afford the expensive methods to achieve such a sophisticated knowledge. In the following, three different global SA methods are applied on a geotechnical model, namely an underground energy storage in rock salt. The specific level and huge geometry of such an underground structure confront the design process with a significant amount of uncertainties. Hence, to reduce the involved uncertainties through model calibration or further observations, conducting SA techniques is a proper approach. The performance of different methods and the conformity of the provided results are discussed. The study reveals that the applied SA methods assign same parameter importance rankings in the considered simulation model. It can be concluded that the RBD, which requires generally less computational effort rather than Sobol′/Saltelli technique, provides a suitable alternative for S_i. Moreover, the comparative study demonstrated that Morris method can offer a suitable alternative for the S_{Ti} as a VB index. It also can detect the positive/negative effects of parameters and nonlinearity and/or interaction effects.

Acknowledgement

The Authors would like to gratefully acknowledge the support of the German Research Foundation (DFG) through the Collaborative Research Center (SFB 837).

References

Cacuci, D. (2003). *Sensitivity and uncertainty analysis.* 1st ed. Boca Raton, Fla.: Chapman & Hall/CRC.

Campolongo, F., Cariboni, J. and Saltelli, A. (2007). An effective screening design for sensitivity analysis of large models. *Environmental Modelling & Software*, 22(10), pp.1509-1518.

Cristescu, N. and Hunsche, U. (1998). *Time effects in rock mechanics.* 1st ed. Chichester: Wiley.

Cukier, R. I., Fortuin, C. M., Schuler, K. E., Petschek, A. G. and Schaibly, J. H. (1973). Study of the sensitivity of coupled reaction systems to uncertainties in rate coefficients, Chem. Phys., 59(8), pp. 3873–3878.

Hoelter, R., Mahmoudi, E. and Schanz, T. (2015). Optimal sensor location for parameter identification in soft clay. In: *AIP Conference Proceedings.*

Khaledi, K., Mahmoudi, E., Datcheva, M., König, D. and Schanz, T. (2016). Sensitivity analysis and parameter identification of a time dependent constitutive model for rock salt. *Journal of Computational and Applied Mathematics*, 293, pp.128-138.

Khaledi, K., Miro, S., König, M. and Schanz, T. (2014). Robust and reliable metamodels for mechanized tunnel simulations. *Computers and Geotechnics*, 61, pp.1-12.

Mahmoudi, E., Khaledi, K., Miro, S., König, D. and Schanz, T. (2016a). Probabilistic Analysis of a Rock Salt Cavern with Application to Energy Storage Systems. *Rock Mechanics and Rock Engineering*, 50(1), pp.139-157.

Mahmoudi, E., Khaledi, K., von Blumenthal, A., König, D. and Schanz, T. (2016b). Concept for an integral approach to explore the behavior of rock salt caverns under thermo-mechanical cyclic loading in energy storage systems. *Environmental Earth Sciences*, 75(14).

Morris, M. D. (1991). Technometrics: Factorial Sampling Plans for Preliminary Computational Experiments, Taylor & Francis, Ltd.

Rocquigny, E., Devictor, N. and Tarantola, S. (2008). *Uncertainty in industrial practice.* England: J. Wiley.

Saltelli, A., Tarantola, S. and Chan, K. (1999). A Quantitative Model-Independent Method for Global Sensitivity Analysis of Model Output. *Technometrics*, 41(1), p.39.

Saltelli, A. (2002). Making best use of model evaluations to compute sensitivity indices. *Computer Physics Communications*, 145(2), pp.280-297.

Saltelli, A., Ratto, M., Andres, T., Campolongo, F., Cariboni, J., Gatelli, D., Saisana, M. and Tarantola, S. (2008). Global sensitivity analysis: the primer, John Wiley & Sons.

Sobol', I. M. (1993). Sensitivity estimates for nonlinear mathematical models, Mathematical Modelling and Computational Experiment 1, 407{414. English translation of russian original paper Sobol' (1990).

Tarantola, S., Gatelli, D. and Mara, T. (2006). Random balance designs for the estimation of first order global sensitivity indices. *Reliability Engineering & System Safety*, 91(6), pp.717-727.

IFC-based Modeling and Management of Design Options

Hannah Mattern, Markus König
Ruhr University Bochum, Germany
Hanah.Mattern@ruhr-uni-bochum.de

Abstract. The design of a building represents a gradual process with continuously increasing level of detail. Due to complex and dynamic boundary conditions, building design might be subject to modifications and adaptions. To find the optimum solution for the client, possible design options need to be analyzed concerning project-specific requirements. Thus, the investigation and comparison of evolving design options represents an important process in the design of buildings. Early planning phases are frequently subject to changes which may show a decisive influence on the total project course. Considering the generation of design options, complex interdependencies between building elements and structure need to be considered. Modifications may refer to building topology, geometric details or semantic aspects. Traditional approaches base on a manual creation of design options (e.g., providing 2D drawings for possible design options), which represents a time-consuming and error-prone approach. In contrast, the BIM methodology offers new prospects to optimize planning and construction processes due to model-based collaboration between different domains. As BIM models offer rich information concerning geometry and semantics, they are highly applicable for various analysis and simulation tasks and thus, suitable for analyzing design options. To support a consistent exchange of BIM-related data between different project participants and software applications, the use of a neutral and open data format is essential. In this context, Industry Foundation Classes (IFC) represent a standardized format covering a wide range of applications. The application of Graph Data Models is introduced to represent building information as well as design options within one consistent model. Following this approach, architects, designers, contractors and clients are provided with a comprehensible description of design options.

1. Introduction

BIM models cover a wide range of structured information including both semantics and geometry. As the design process is split into planning domains with different software tools, the use of an open data format represents a prerequisite for successful project collaboration. The planning process is determined by a high number of project participants with partly contradicting interests. In the continuously evolving planning process, frequent changes and modifications lead to the investigation of multiple design options, especially at early phases. In this context, complex relationships between building objects need to be considered. Focusing on the management of design options based on an open data format, IFC are limited to the representation of *explicit* design options. Thus, a comparison of alternative designs requires the creation of independent building models. This methodology causes different identifiers for the same object. Furthermore, the use of separate models leads to a high amount of redundant data, which gradually increases with the number of possible design options. By integrating possible options within one consistent model, analysis and simulation tasks become easier as results are directly compared.

This paper is structured as follows. First, possible modifications that might appear in early planning phases are classified into different categories. These so-called "option classes" are described concerning affected elements, occurrence in the planning phase and effect on overall building structure. Exemplary modifications leading to the single option classes are given. Subsequently, the structure and content of the IFC4 data model are analyzed concerning entities that might be affected by the described option classes. General ideas on extending the IFC data model to implement design options are presented. First approaches are described based on two examples focusing on structural options.

2. Methodology

Focusing on model-based planning and construction, concepts for an efficient management of design options are missing. In consequence, this project aims at deriving and managing different options in one consistent data model provided in the IFC format.

Consistency is achieved by using object identifiers that remain constant through the whole planning process. Following an object-oriented approach, an explicit building model is generated by choosing all objects related to the selected design option. To cover the effect of changes during early planning stages, a formal description of objects and relationships which might be subject to modifications is required. The creation of redundant information is prevented by modeling differences between design options exclusively. Objects which are part of various design options are instantiated only once. This approach also avoids the use of multiple identifiers referring to the same object. To describe different design options within one model, the IFC schema needs to be expanded by relationship objects supporting alternative designs. Furthermore, the investigation of objects instantiated by IFC classes (*IfcBuilding*, *IfcWall*, *IfcMaterialLayer*) concerning possible modifications led to the definition of classes describing different categories of design options. The defined classes comprise *Structural*, *Functional* and *Product* Options, which differ concerning

- the effect on other elements,
- the effect on overall building structure and
- the appearance during the planning process.

To structure the resulting building model comprising different options, the application of a graph data model is proposed. Thus, the overall concept consists of the following work steps:

1) Implement graph-based representation of IFC model.
2) Define classes and relationships to implement design options.
3) Develop graph transformation rules to extract and combine options.

After a brief introduction to IFC-based version and change management, first examples of using Graph Data Models (GDM) for representing options in a logical and transparent structure are given.

3. Related Work

Regarding a model-based planning process, several approaches to perform version management have been made. Concerning the versioning of IFC models, Nour and Beucke (2008), Richter and Beucke (2008), Weise (2006) and van Berlo *et al.* (2012) concentrate on object based strategies. In contrast, Koch and Firmenich (2011) as well as Jaly-Zada *et al.* (2015) focus on change oriented versioning. However, concentrating on the generation of design options, BIM servers used for project collaboration do not offer applicable methods (Beetz *et al.*, 2011). Currently, the focus lies on analyzing BIM models rather than efficiently comparing and investigating design options (Lee *et al.*, 2012). Well-known BIM tools partly cover the generation of alternative designs, but require the creation of separate models for each option (Autodesk Revit 2017). Other tools are limited to the detection of geometric changes between single models

(ArchiCAD 18) or the documentation of added, missing and changed elements (Allplan, Niedermaier and Bäck 2014). Modeling tools rather focus on tracking modifications but do not support an automated generation of designs resulting from the detected modifications. One drawback of using separate models representing design options is the creation of redundant data. Elements which are contained in more than one model are provided repetitively. The amount of redundant data gradually increases with the number of design options as more models need to be managed. Furthermore, the use of different identifiers referring to a specific object results in inconsistency between the models and complicates analysis and simulation tasks. To enable an efficient comparison and analysis of various design options, the use of a consistent BIM model is inevitable. Objects need to be tracked though the whole planning phase by unique and traceable identifiers.

3.1 Graph Data Models

Graph Data Models (GDM) represent a well-established approach to describe complex systems with a large number of highly interdependent elements (Boccaletti *et al.*, 2006). As BIM models consist of a high number of objects and complex relationships, the application of GDM for analyzing building information is of special importance. For managing design options within a consistent BIM model, the applied data model needs to be highly flexible. Isaac *et al.* (2013) provide a system model of the building and use graphs to represent the topology of the project. Khalili and Chua (2015) use weighted graph principles for implementing an IFC-based algorithm for automatic deduction of topological relationships. Tauscher *et al.* (2016) generate directed graphs that serve as semantic data pools facilitating generic queries. In Langenhan *et al.* (2013), the topology of spatial configurations is extracted from BIM models and represented as graphs. Skandhakumar *et al.* (2016) introduce how graph theory can be utilised as a representation language of BIM models and security related functions. Van Treeck and Rank (2007) identify different subgraphs to represent a BIM model for performing building energy simulations.

GDM might be applied for different purposes in the context of construction projects. According to Isaac *et al.* (2013), graph-based models provide an integrated representation of information on different project aspects (such as requirements, design and construction planning) in a single model. Furthermore, they allow modifying and updating data through the application of graph transformation rules. Consequently, graph-based models are applicable for representing the dynamic planning process in which new types of elements and relationships are added over time. Subsequently, GDM might be used for analyzing the project topology through the application of graph theoretic algorithms. Regarding the promising features of transparency and comprehensibility, GDM are proposed to describe various design options which are combined in a comprehensive model. The following section provides a brief overview on the basic approach of transferring an IFC model to a GDM.

4. From IFC Model to Graph Data Model (GDM)

The IFC model consists of objects representing physical and non-physical elements describing a building. According to the IFC4 schema, objectified relationships are the preferred way to handle relationships among objects. This opens the possibility to later handle relationship specific behaviour (buildingSMART, 2013) and represents a sound possibility to introduce design options in a model. When transferring an IFC model to a GDM, project elements are translated into nodes (N) while relationships between objects are implemented as links (L) between elements. Thus, a Graph $G = (N, L)$ comprises two sets N and L, such that $N \neq \mathbf{0}$ while L is a set of element pairs of N (Isaac *et al.*, 2013). Adding further information is realized by adding weighted links to the graph. Integrating disparate aspects as building program or design in the graph-based model is facilitated by the fact that relationships between elements belonging to different aspects are defined as simple links between nodes (Isaac *et al.*, 2013). To reduce the amount of data and resulting complexity of the derived GDM, information on project elements and their relationships used to define the graph-based model, might be linked to external databases.

Explicit design options are created by choosing all objects belonging to the respective option. The selection process is based on the GDM covering all possible options. Due to the flexible structure of GDM, changes and modifications are possible during the complete planning process by the definition and application of graph transformation rules.

The described concept is implemented using Neo4j which is an open source NoSQL graph database implemented in Java and Scala. Database requests are handled using CYPHER, a declarative, SQL-inspired language for describing patterns in graphs visually using an ASCII-art syntax (Neo4j Graph Database, 2017). CYPHER allows selecting, inserting, updating or deleting objects from the graph database.

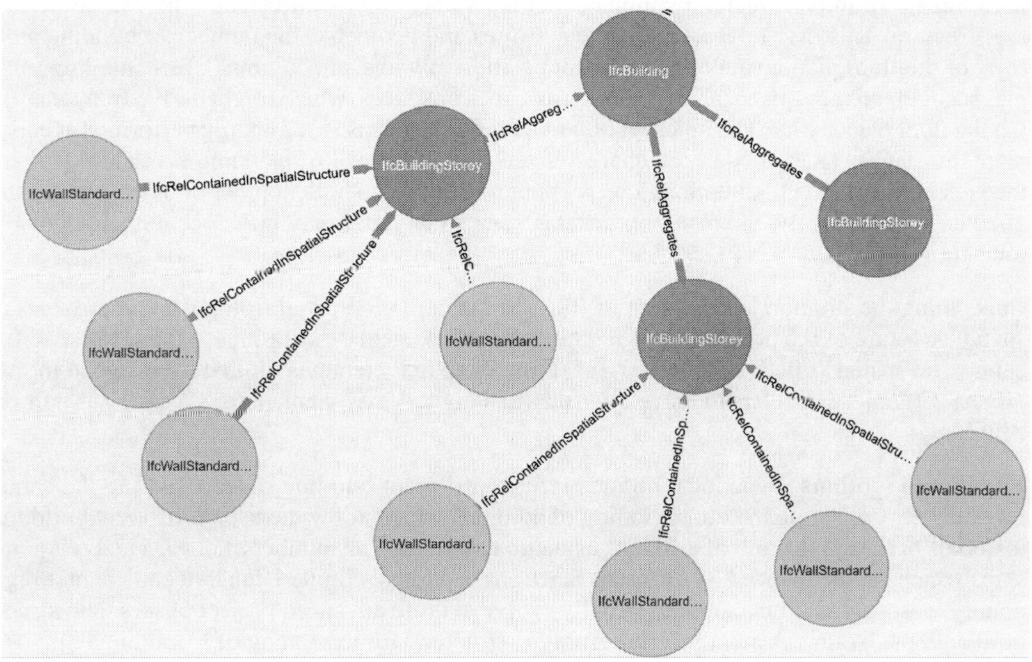

Figure 1: Graph-based representation of a simple building
(small selection with building, storeys and walls)

5. IFC-based Management of Design Options

IFC 4 Add 2 considers revision control as marking objects with a "change action" that indicates whether the object was added, modified, deleted, or has no change. A comparison is conducted when a project is retrieved at a predefined revision sequence and the state of objects is merged when combining the model with existing data. However, performing revision control with IFC 4 Add 2 is only possible if an object's GUID is not modified. This might cause problems in case of editing and revising a model with different software tools (buildingSMART, 2013).

5.1 Definition of Option Classes

The following section gives a brief overview on different categories of design options which need to be represented and managed by GDM. Furthermore, the categories may help the user to understand the effect of design option when investigating multiple alternatives within one model. Modifications which rely on geometric details exclusively are not considered as separate design options (e.g., changing the thickness of a wall). To enable geometric changes, the application of parametric modelling techniques is recommended.

Structural Options: Structural options comprise modifications influencing the overall building structure. This may refer to exterior enclosures and geometry, the number of building storeys, or the floor plan layout (e.g., different position of walls and columns). Structural options may also refer to non-physical objects such as zones or spaces, which might derive from changing the floor plan layout. The investigation of structural options is commonly performed at early planning stages. Thus, models are characterized by a low level of planning precision. Due to the generation of structural options at early planning phases, a high number of objects might be affected. Consequently, the resulting designs vary widely and may influence numerous planning domains.

Concerning the structure and content of IFC, the concept of "Spatial Composition" provides a spatial structure of the project by aggregating spatial elements. According to the IFC4 specification, the spatial structure is a hierarchical tree of spatial elements ultimately assigned to the project. Composition refers to the relationship to a higher-level element (e.g. a storey as part of a building).

Functional Options: Functional options refer to different building objects sharing the same function, e.g., material and dimensioning of columns which allow the use of different building materials or the application of different insulation systems. The number of objects and relationships which can be realized by different functional options is limited due to technical and regulatory reasons. Functional options usually evolve at more advanced project phases than structural options. Examples mainly derive from the structural dimensioning of a building (e.g., using a column instead of installing a load-bearing wall). Concerning the scope of IFC4, *IfcStructuralConnection* might be subject to functional options as this superclass of entities represents structural supports or connecting elements (nodes).

Product Options: Replacing one object by another similar object or changing attributes of a single object represents the simplest form of creating design options. Product options have no influence on other building elements (e.g., windows with different glass types). In most cases, numerous objects of the same type are affected by the creation of a product option (e.g., all windows of a certain size). Instead of examining complex interactions between affected objects, the classification of objects which are frequently subject to alternative designs is required. Focusing on product options, elements of building services are of special importance. The generation of product options requires a higher level of planning precision, which is observed at more advanced planning phases.

Product Options may refer to physical instances of the superclass *IfcElement*. As elements of the building services are frequently subject to changes, instances of *IfcDistributionElement* need to be covered by product options. Thus, elements related to building services (esp. heating, cooling and ventilation systems as well as sanitary and electrical installations) are of special importance.

5.2 Realization of Option Classes in IFC

In the following, the scope and content of IFC4 is examined concerning the applicability and technical feasibility to implement the above described categories. The general idea comprises implementing options by adding or expanding classes to the existing IFC EXPRESS data model using the STEP physical file format. Subsequently, examples of structural options serve to illustrate the development of new entities and relationships.

Objects: The IFC4 schema comprises seven fundamental entity types, which are all derived from *IfcObject*. In the context of design options, entities of the type "product" are important. A "product" represents a "physical object (manufactured, supplied or created) for incorporation into a project, which may be physically existing or tangible. Products may be defined by shape representations and have a location in the coordinate space" (buildingSMART, 2013). When transferring the developed option classes to the IFC schema, entities of type "product" might be affected by structural, functional as well product options. In addition, products might also be responsible for the development of new options (e.g., adding one storey results in a new structural option).

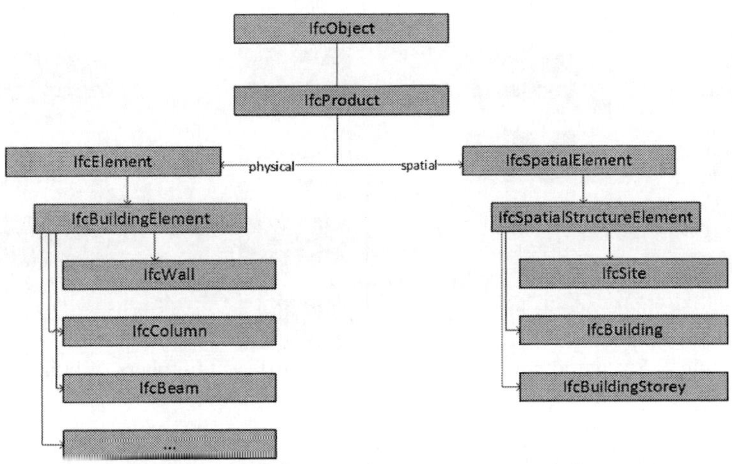

Figure 2: Entities subject to design options

Relationships: The IFC4 schema covers six fundamental relationship types, which are all derived from *IfcRelationship*. The concept of "decomposition" is proposed to indicate the existence of different design options that refer to entities of the type "object". According to the IFC specification, a decomposition "defines the general concept of elements being composed or decomposed. The decomposition relationship denotes a whole/part hierarchy with the ability to navigate from the whole (the composition) to the parts and vice versa."

The following section contains examples to illustrate the concept and provides first developments of new IFC entities for managing structural options.

6. Examples

Figure 3 shows a graph covering two instances of a structural option deriving from two different approaches to structure the site. Another option results from considering different number of storeys. Figure 4 depicts two possible floor plan layouts for a given building storey. Wall 3 is of special importance as this building element is used in two options.

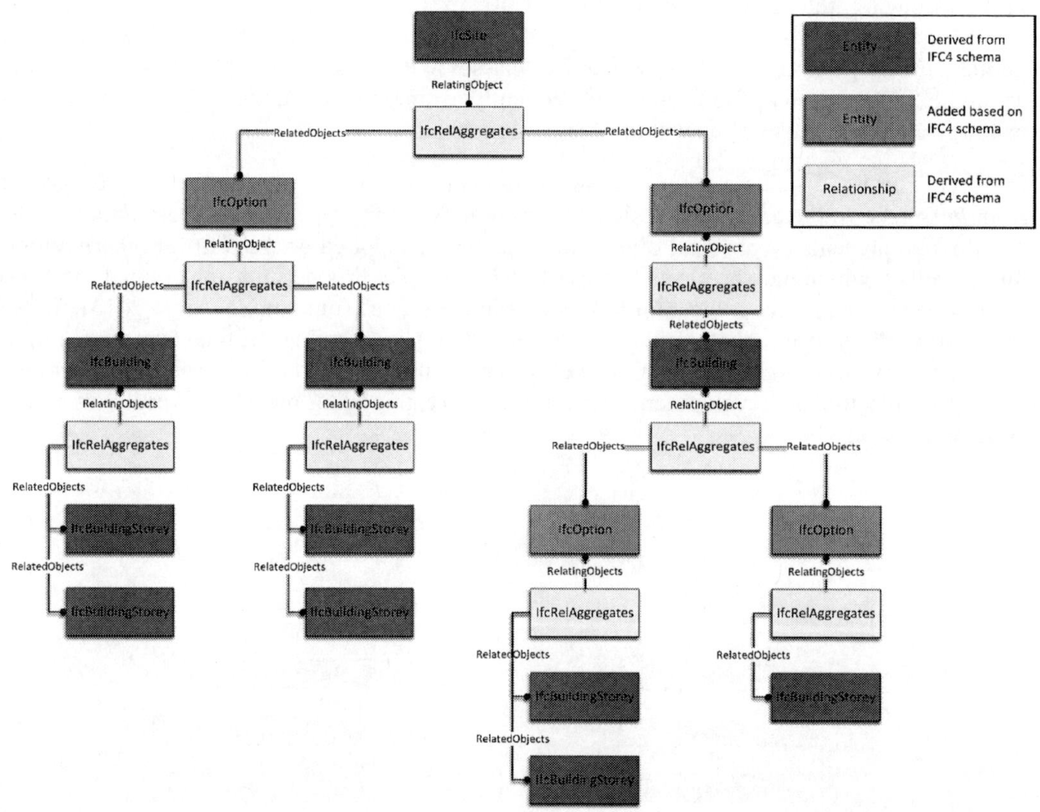

Figure 3: Example 1: Structural options in the context of different numbers of buildings and building storeys

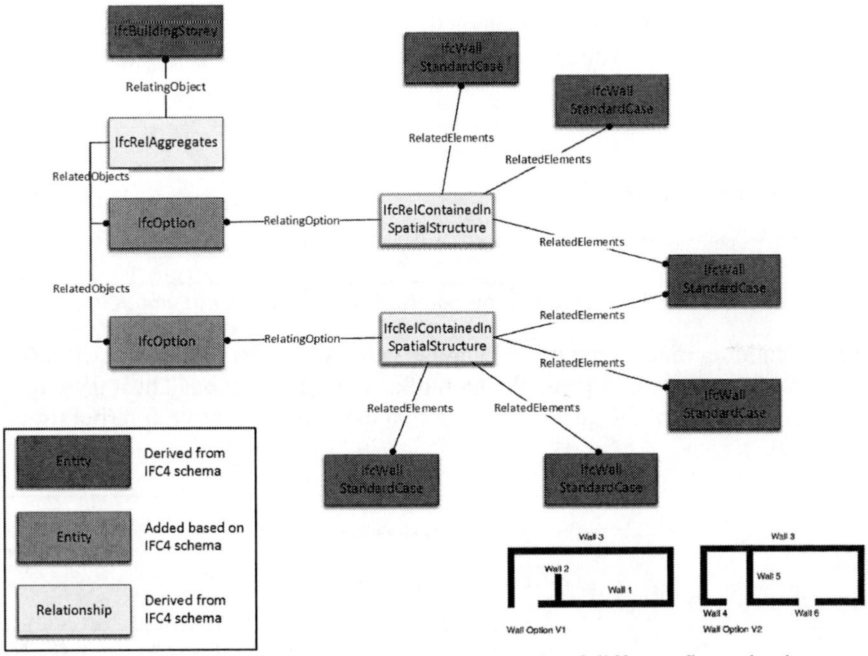

Figure 4: Example 2: Structural options in the context of different floor plan layouts

6.1 Development and Expansion of IFC Entities

The existing IFC4 schema was expanded by the new entity *IfcOption* (see Figure 5). As *IfcOption* represents a subtype of *IfcObject*, elements that might be subject to design changes are covered (see Figure 2).

```
ENTITY IfcOption
       SUBTYPE OF IfcObject;
              OptionType             : OPTIONAL IfcOptionType;
       INVERSE
              isPartOf SET [0;1] IfcRelAggregates FOR RelatedObjects;
              hasPhysicalOptions SET [0;1] OF IfcRelAggregates FOR RelatingObjects;
              hasSpatialOptions SET [0;1] OF IfcRelContainedInSpatialStructure FOR RelatingObjects;
END_ENTITY;
```

Figure 5: Modified EXPRESS Specification of *IfcOption*

To enable the assignment of the above described option classes, *IfcOptionTypeEnum* is introduced.

```
TYPE IfcOptionTypeEnum = ENUMERATION OF (
       STRUCTURAL,
       FUNCTIONAL,
       PRODUCT);
END_TYPE;
```

Figure 6: EXPRESS Specification of *IfcOptionTypeEnum* to assign option classes

Example 1 (Figure 3) contains options derived from combining spatial elements (site, building and building storey). The creation of different options is possible by using *IfcRelAggregates*.

Example 2 (Figure 4) comprises options referring to both spatial and physical objects. According to IFC4, the combination of building storey and wall is realized by *IfcRelContainedInSpa-*

tialStructure. To enable the management of different options, the existing schema was expanded according to Figure 7. Thus, objects that are part of different design options are provided only once.

```
ENTITY IfcRelContainedInSpatialStructure
	SUBTYPE OF IfcRelConnects;
		RelatedElements		: SET [1:?] OF IfcProduct;
		RelatingStructure	: IfcSpatialElement;
		RelatingOption		: IfcOption;

	WHERE
		WR31			: SIZEOF(QUERY(temp <* RelatedElements | 'IFCPRODUCTEXTENSION.IFCSPATIALSTRUCTUREELEMENT' IN TYPEOF(temp))) = 0;

END_ENTITY;
```

Figure 7: EXPRESS Specification of modified *IfcRelContainedInSpatialStructure*

To structure a building model with more than one entity of *IfcOption*, the use of *IfcGroup* is proposed. *IfcGroup* represents a generalization of any arbitrary group. Thus, the entity contains a logical collection of objects without position or shape representation (buildingSMART, 2013).

```
ENTITY IfcGroup
	SUPERTYPE OF(ONEOF(IfcAsset, IfcInventory, IfcStructuralLoadGroup, IfcStructuralResultGroup, IfcSystem, IfcOption))
	SUBTYPE OF IfcObject;
	INVERSE
		IsGroupedBy		: SET OF IfcRelAssignsToGroup FOR RelatingGroup;
END_ENTITY;
```

Figure 8: EXPRESS Specification of modified *IfcGroup*

7. Conclusion

The objective of this work is managing design options without creating redundant data. As different options are integrated within a consistent BIM model, the use of inconsistent identifiers is avoided. The developed concept is based on the structure and scope of IFC4 offering a wide application range. Graph Data Models (GDM) are proposed as transparent approach to describe the resulting models. Option classes are introduced to structure and categorize the complex possibilities of design options, which might appear at early planning phases. An expansion of the IFC schema comprising entities and relationships is presented. Next steps comprise the development of graph transition rules to derive explicit options from the overall model. The described option classes might lead to complex GDMs. To support the user by understanding different design options, the creation of sub-models is proposed. Due to complex interdependencies and restrictions, the creation of invalid combinations needs to be avoided. In this context, the relations between building elements are of special importance. Connections must only be established in valid options. Thus, possible combinations need to be examined and formally described. Furthermore, the combination of design options which are provided at different levels of detail need to be analyzed.

References

Beetz, J., Berlo, L., Laat, R. and Bonsma, P. (2011), "Advances in the development and application of an open source model server for building information", In: Morand, P. (Ed.), Proceedings of the 28th International Conference of CIB W78, France, 2011, pp. 1–7.

Boccaletti, S., Latora, V., Moreno, Y., Chavez, M. and Hwang, D.U. (2006), "Complex networks: Structure and dynamics", Physics Reports, Vol. 424 No. 4–5, pp. 175–308.

buildingSMART (2013), "IFC4 Official Release. Industry Foundation Classes Release 4", available at: http://www.buildingsmart-tech.org/ifc/IFC4/final/html/, accessed 30 May 2017.

Isaac, S., Sadeghpour, F. and Navon, R. (2013), "Analyzing Building Information Using Graph Theory", In: Proceedings of the 30th International Symposium on Automation and Robotics in Construction, Montréal, Canada, pp. 1013–1020.

Jaly-Zada, A., Koch, C. and Tizani, W. (2015), "IFC Extensions for design change management", In: Proceedings of the 32nd CIB W78 Conference 2015, Eindhoven, The Netherlands, October 27-29.

Khalili, A. and Chua, D.K.H. (2015), "IFC-Based Graph Data Model for Topological Queries on Building Elements", Journal of Computing in Civil Engineering, Vol. 29 No. 3, p. 4014046.

Koch, C. and Firmenich, B. (2011), "An approach to distributed building modeling on the basis of versions and changes", Advanced Engineering Informatics, Vol. 25 No. 2, pp. 297–310.

Langenhan, C., Weber, M., Liwicki, M., Petzold, F. and Dengel, A. (2013), "Graph-based retrieval of building information models for supporting the early design stages", Advanced Engineering Informatics, Vol. 27 No. 4, pp. 413–426.

Lee, S.-I., Bae, J.-S. and Cho, Y.S. (2012), "Efficiency analysis of Set-based Design with structural building information modeling (S-BIM) on high-rise building structures", Automation in Construction, Vol. 23, pp. 20–32.

"Neo4j Graph Database" (2017), available at: https://neo4j.com/developer/graph-database/, accessed 30 May 2017.

Niedermaier, A. and Bäck, R. (2014), Allplan BIM Compendium: *Theory and Practice,* 1st ed.

Nour, M. and Beucke, K. (2008), "An open platform for processing IFC model versions", Tsinghua Science and Technology, Vol. 13 No. S1, pp. 126–131.

Richter, T. and Beucke, K. (2008), "A concept for Utilizing Versioned Object Models in Engineering Applications", In: Proceedings of the Twelfth International Conference on Computing in Civil and Building Engineering, Tsinghua University Beijing, China.

Skandhakumar, N., Salim, F., Reid, J., Drogemuller, R. and Dawson, E. (2016), "Graph theory based representation of building information models for access control applications", Automation in Construction, Vol. 68, pp. 44–51.

Tauscher, E., Bargstädt, H.-J. and Smarsly, K. (2016), "Generic BIM queries based on the IFC object model using graph theory", In: Proceedings of the 16th International Conference on Computing in Civil and Building Engineering (ICCCBE), Osaka, Japan.

van Berlo, Beetz, J., Bos, P., Hendriks, H. and van Tongeren, R. (2012), "Collaborative engineering with IFC: new insights and technology", In: Proceedings of the 9th European Conference on Product and Process Modelling, Reykjavik, Iceland, July 25-27.

van Treeck, C. and Rank, E. (2007), "Dimensional reduction of 3D building models using graph theory and its application in building energy simulation", Engineering with Computers, Vol. 23 No. 2, pp. 109–122.

Weise, M. (2006), "Ein Ansatz zur Abbildung von Änderungen in der modell-basierten Objektplanung. An approach for the representation of changes in model-based design", Dissertation, TU Dresden, Dresden, Germany, 2006.

Case Study on Preventative Maintenance for Asphalt Pavements

Dominic J. Michels[1], Brian K. Wood[2], Gabriel Dadi[1], Timothy R.B. Taylor[1]
1-University of Kentucky, United States; 2-Plantmix Asphalt Industry of Kentucky, United States
tim.taylor@uky.edu

Abstract. The U.S. highway industry has seen increasing use over time of preventative maintenance treatments on its asphalt pavements. Performance of the most prevalent treatments employed by the state DOT in the case study – Thin Asphalt Overlay (Thinlay) and Microsurfacing – has yet to be examined in-depth in-situ analysis. This paper describes the data collection process to find the Pavement Condition Index (PCI) of each preventative maintenance site in the state from the last 10 years. With PCI from each site, deterioration curves were generated for each treatment – providing the estimated life extension benefit of each. The analysis then converted life extension to annualized costs to determine which product was more cost effective. Cost effectiveness would be the definitive metric in determining which product is of higher quality.

1. Introduction

In recent years, the paving industry has seen Microsurfacing, Thinlay, and other preventative maintenance treatments being increasingly applied to asphalt pavements. Lemer (2004) found that the perceived value of preventative maintenance of roadway pavements was recognized by State Transportation Agencies in addressing transportation infrastructure system preservation. The United States Federal Highway Administration (FHWA) defines preventative maintenance as “a planned strategy of cost effective treatments to an existing roadway system and its appurtenances that preserves the system, retards future deterioration, and maintains or improves the functional condition of the system (without significantly increasing the structural capacity)” (FHWA 2005). Rajagopal (2010) examined the effectiveness of Microsurfacing on pavement rehabilitation and found that the method can be effective when applied to pavements that have experienced only minor detrition. Peshkin et al. (2004) examined the optimal timing of pavement preventative maintenance methodologies and stated that, “proper analysis of data identifies the optimal time to apply [preventative maintenance] treatments” (p. 63) and noted that future research is needed to develop optimal timing on preventative maintenance and that additional in-situ investigations of preventative maintenance technologies are needed to develop a better understanding of the performance of the methodology. The current work extends this previous research by investigating the performance of these preventative maintenance treatments in terms of life-cycle economics. To perform this investigation, data on all preventative maintenance projects in the state over the previous 10 years was compiled. The projects span a large variety of traffic conditions, age, and pre-existing surface age. With the large variety of conditions represented, some general conclusions can be made about the different paving materials.

2. Product Descriptions

Although both products are used in preventative maintenance applications, they have very different properties and construction practices. These properties range from the gradation of the mix to the simple thickness of the mat. Figure 2.1 below illustrates some of these differences.

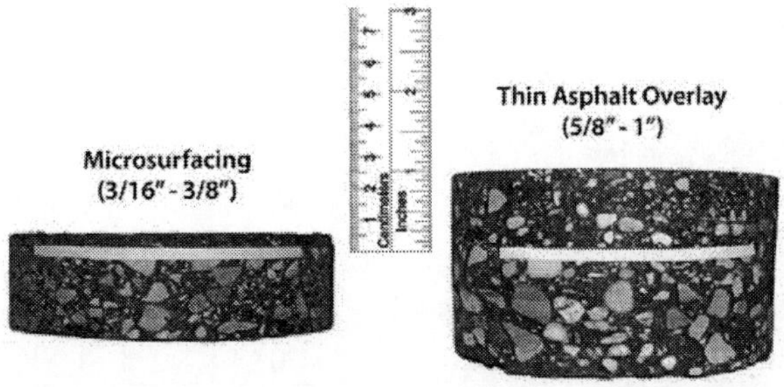

Figure 2.1: Microsurfacing/Thinlay Profiles (Plantmix Asphalt Industry of Kentucky)

Thinlay is typically applied between 5/8" to 1" of thickness, compared to Microsurfacing which is between 3/16" and 3/8" thick. During construction, a Thinlay is applied in the same manner as any HMA overlay. There are no specialized materials or equipment required by the contractor. When applying Microsurfacing, a polymer modified emulsion is mixed on site with the aggregate at the paver. A nozzle on the paver sprays water onto to the surface ahead of the material in order to improve bonding. Additionally, in many instances, a road will be crack sealed before Microsurfacing is applied in order to retard crack propagation through the new surface.

3. Establishing an Evaluation Method

A number of different rating systems and evaluation methods exist for quantifying pavement conditions. Two prevalent methods were examined and compared. These are the PASER and PAVER systems, which utilize two very different procedures for collecting data and assigning a condition number to the pavement in question.

PASER is a more simplified method of surveying pavement condition. It involves examining pavement distresses from a general viewpoint as opposed to physically measuring cracks and deformations. There are rating categories for this system that range from 1 (failed pavement) to 10 (excellent pavement). The rating selected by the evaluator depends upon variables such as crack spacing, crack width, patching, crack spalling, and the density of fatigue cracking. The PASER manual provides pictures and descriptions of all the distress types and varying severity levels (Transportation Information Center 2002).

PAVER is a more involved system than PASER, with the evaluator obtaining detailed distress measurements as opposed to PASER. This system provides a PCI (Pavement Condition Index) that ranges from 0 (failed pavement) to 100 (excellent pavement). The use of this method was examined within ASTM D6433, Standard Practice for Roads and Parking Lots Pavement Condition Index Surveys. Using this standard, the evaluator selects a number of random sample units (typically 2500 ± 1000 square feet), and measures all of the distresses in those units. Through an iterative calculation, these measurements are used to determine the final PCI of the pavement (ASTM 2007).

After comparing these two systems, it was determined that ASTM D6433 would provide stronger, less biased data for this particular study. The need to accurately monitor pavement condition trends for industry research suggests that a more involved system than PASER is required. After reaching this conclusion, preparation began to undergo pavement evaluations according to the ASTM method.

4. ASTM D6433 Procedure

Required Equipment:

- Surveyor's Wheel
- 6.5 Foot Level
- Folding Ruler
- PAVER Distress Identification Manual
- Data Sheets with Storage Clipboard

The data collection for the project began with a windshield survey performed by driving the roadway in question. This practice helps to determine the consistency of the roadway and to check if there are any significant areas of unrepresentative distresses. When beginning to evaluate a pavement, random sample units must first be selected, which are then known to be consistent with the general roadway condition by performing the windshield observations. These units can range in area from 1500 to 3500 square feet. When in the field, a starting point is randomly selected, and the desired length of the unit is measured along with the width. Next, the evaluator can begin measuring distresses using the surveyor's wheel. Some distresses are measured as linear feet, and others as square feet. Table 4.1 summarizes the distress types defined by PAVER.

Table 4.1: PAVER Distress Types (continued)

Distress Type	**Measurement Type**
Alligator Cracking	Area
Bleeding	Area
Block Cracking	Area
Bumps and Sag	Length
Corrugation	Area
Depression	Area
Edge Cracking	Length
Joint Reflection Cracking	Length
Lane/Shoulder Drop-off	Length
Longitudinal and Transverse Cracking	Length
Patching	Area
Polished Aggregate	Area
Potholes	Count
Railroad Crossing	Area
Rutting	Area

Shoving	Area
Slippage Cracking	Area
Swell	Area
Raveling	Area
Weathering	Area

Distress measurements are quantified by both the numerical component as well as the severity level, which can be Low, Medium, or High. For example, severity level in longitudinal and transverse cracking is determined by crack width, spalling, and crack sealing condition. After determining both components, the evaluator records the measurement on the data sheet for that sample unit.

Once the desired number of sample units is gathered, the field work for that pavement section is complete, and the PCI calculation is performed. First, the density for each distress type is calculated as a percentage by dividing the measurement by the sample unit area. Using the density and the severity level, a deduct value is determined for that distress by consulting the deduct value curves provided by ASTM.

After assigning each distress type a deduct value, an iterative process is used to calculate the maximum CDV (Corrected Deduct Value). This is described as follows:

1) If either one or zero deduct values are greater than two, then the sum of the deduct values is used as the max CDV. Otherwise, the iterative process must be used.
2) List the deduct values in descending order.
3) Calculate m, the allowable number of deducts (do not round m to a whole number).
   a. $m = 1 + \left(\frac{9}{98}\right)(100 - HDV) \leq 10 \; (Eq. 1)$
   b. HDV = highest individual deduct value
4) Reduce the number of individual deduct values to the m largest deduct values, including the fraction. For example, if there are 8 deduct values, but m = 6.4, then only use the 6 highest deduct values along with 0.4 of the 7th. If the number of deduct values is less than m, use all of the deduct values.
5) With the usable deduct values recorded depending on m, complete the iterative process of reducing the smallest value greater than 2.0 to 2.0 and summing the deduct values.
6) Record q as the number of deduct values with a value greater than 2.0.
7) The correction curves, as shown below, are then used to find the CDV (corrected deduct value) using q and the total sum of DV's as variables.
8) Repeat this process until q=1.
9) Take the largest of the CDV's as the max CDV.
10) PCI is then calculated as 100 – max CDV.

Once a PCI is calculated for each sample unit in the section, an area weighted average is calculated in order to determine the final PCI of the pavement.

5. List of Pavement Sites and Raw Data

To properly draw any conclusions from the set of data, a sufficient number of both Microsurfacing and Thinlay sites would need to be evaluated. By examining state bidding information, the recent history of these products within the state provided a total of 42 different sites to evaluate, including 26 Microsurfacing, 15 Thinlay, and 1 Chip Seal. These sites represent a multitude of different ages, traffic conditions, geographic distribution, and pre-surfacing conditions.

Using the previously described methods of analysis under ASTM D6433, the sites were systematically evaluated through the months of June, July, and August of 2016. There were a total of 145 sample units surveyed, which correlates to an average of about 3.5 per site, and totals 342,637 square feet. Ovcr all 42 sites, approximately 1600 photos were taken and entered into a database. Using the PCI calculation process, each sample unit was assigned a value and all of the units in a site were averaged by area to find a final PCI. This information is summarized in Table 5.1 below.

Table 5.1: Summary of PCI Data (continued)

Date Visited	County	Surface Age	Let Year	Route Type	Treatment	PCI
6/17/2016	A	2014	2013	State	Thinlay	98.0
7/19/2016	B	2013	2013	State	Thinlay	97.9
7/19/2016	C	2015	2015	US	Thinlay	95.3
6/17/2016	D	2016	2015	State	Thinlay	93.9
7/2/2016	E	2016	2015	State	Chip Seal (Pre-Condition)	92.2
6/16/2016	F	2013	2013	US	Thinlay	91.7
6/15/2016	G	2014	2014	State	Thinlay	91.7
6/14/2016	H	2013	2012	US	Thinlay	91.5
7/20/2016	I	2015	2015	State	Micro	91.4
6/8/2016	J	2014	2014	US	Cape Seal	90.6
6/16/2016	K	2012	2012	State	Thinlay	90.5
6/8/2016	J	2014	2014	US	Double Micro	90.3
6/8/2016	J	2014	2014	US	Thinlay	90.3
6/15/2016	G	2014	2014	State	Thinlay	88.9
7/22/2016	L	2014	2013	State	Thinlay	88.5
7/7/2016	M	2015	2015	State	Thinlay	87.8
6/8/2016	J	2014	2014	US	Micro	87.7
7/20/2016	I	2015	2015	State	Micro	86.7
6/14/2016	G	2011	2011	State	Micro	86.5
6/8/2016	J	2014	2014	US	Crack Seal	74.3
7/7/2016	N	2015	2015	State	Micro	74.2
6/14/2016	O	2011	2011	State	Micro	74.1
6/8/2016	J	2014	2014	US	Control	72.8
7/21/2016	P	2013	2012	State	Thinlay	72.7
6/29/2016	Q	2015	2015	State	Micro	71.3
6/16/2016	K	2016	2015	US	Micro (Pre-Condition)	69.6
6/16/2016	R	2016	2015	US	Micro (Pre-Condition)	67.1
7/21/2016	S	2015	2015	US	Micro	64.3
7/20/2016	T	2011	2011	US	Micro	62.4
7/21/2016	U	2011/2007	2007	State	Thinlay	61.7
7/20/2016	V	2016	2015	State	Thinlay (Pre-Condition)	61.1
6/16/2016	W	2016	2015	US	Micro (Pre-Condition)	60.6
7/7/2016	X	2015	2015	State	Micro	60.1

6/23/2016	Y	2015	2015	US	Micro	59.4
6/24/2016	Z	2015	2015	State	Micro	58.6
7/21/2016	P	2016	2015	State	Thinlay (Pre-Condition)	56.9
6/29/2016	AA	2015	2015	US	Micro	58.0
7/20/2016	BB	2012	2012	US	Micro	56.7
6/15/2016	CC	2012	2012	Parkway	Micro	55.1
7/22/2016	DD	2007	2007	State	Thinlay	55.1
7/6/2016	EE	2015	2015	State	Micro	54.3
7/6/2016	FF	2013	2012	State	Micro	54.2
7/6/2016	GG	2014	2013	State	Micro	52.6
6/30/2016	HH	2013	2012	US	Micro	52.4
7/19/2016	II	2015	2015	State	Micro	52.0
6/16/2016	JJ	2016	2015	US	Micro (Pre-Condition)	51.4
6/24/2016	KK	2010	2010	US	Micro	39.1
6/23/2016	LL	2010	2010	State	Micro	37.4
7/7/2016	X	2012	2012	State	Micro	33.0
7/1/2016	MM	2008	2008	Parkway	Micro	24.8
8/10/2016	R	2016	2015	US	Micro	63.9
8/10/2016	JJ	2016	2015	US	Micro	68.4

When scanning the raw data, it becomes quickly apparent that the Microsurfacing PCIs trend to the bottom of the list, while the Thinlay numbers trend to the top.

In addition to PCI data collected on Microsurfacing and Thinlay, some pre-condition data was recorded for sites soon to be treated. These included those in the counties of R, JJ, K, W, V, and P.

The sites in counties JJ, W, and V contained alligator cracking, indicating structural issues. These observations may suggest that these are not ideal preventative maintenance candidates, since significant damage to the pavement cross section has already occurred. Counties R, W, P, and JJ contained rutting along the wheel paths. While it was all low severity rutting under ½" maximum depth, it further counts against these sites as viable candidates.

Very shortly after Microsurfacing was applied to the county R and JJ precondition sites, the opportunity was taken to observe how Microsurfacing was performing early in its life. Since R County exhibited rutting and JJ County exhibited rutting/alligator cracking before treatment, the observations yielded results about how distresses reflect through Microsurfacing. Both the sites showed that the rutting had immediately reflected through after construction, providing concrete evidence that Microsurfacing struggles to fill ruts when applied. The alligator cracking encountered at JJ County in the pre-condition state had not reflected through that early in the treatment's life.

6. Statistical Analysis of Raw Data and the Prediction Model

The raw data of PCI for each pavement product must be analysed statistically in order to justify any valid conclusions on cost of ownership. SAS version 9.4 was the chosen software. The sample sizes were 26 Microsurfacing sites and 15 Thinlay sites. In addition, an alpha of 0.05 was chosen a priori for significance tests and confidence intervals. Multiple linear regression was chosen as the mechanic for defining a PCI prediction model for each treatment. Through backwards selection (removing the least significant factor in each run), Age and

Treatment Type Indicator (0 for Microsurfacing, 1 for Thinlay) were found to be the only significant predictors, as shown in the results below:

Table 6.1: Optimized PCI Prediction Model

Parameter Estimates								
Variable	Label	DF	Parameter Estimate	Standard Error	t Value	Pr > |t|	95% Confidence Limits	
Intercept	Intercept	1	71.08939	3.26886	21.75	<.0001	64.47194	77.70684
Age	Age	1	-4.07303	0.85809	-4.75	<.0001	-5.81014	-2.33593
TypeInd	TypeInd	1	27.42422	4.03612	6.79	<.0001	19.25351	35.59492

As seen in Table 6.1, the only variables that remained significant in predicting PCI were Age and the Treatment Type, with p values less than 0.0001. As Age increases by 1 year, PCI decreases on average by 4.07 when holding the Treatment Type constant. Thinlay sites (TypeInd of 1) increase the PCI by 27.42 when holding Age constant. Generally speaking, these results indicate that the slope of PCI vs. Age does not change between Thinlay and Microsurfacing. However, the intercept changes by 27.42 PCI. This could be indicating that Microsurfacing generally starts its life at a much lower PCI than Thinlay and then deteriorates at the same rate afterwards.

The final model for predicting PCI based on Age and Treatment Type is as follows:

$$PCI = 71.09 - 4.07 * Age + 27.42 * TypeInd \; (Eq. 2)$$

The R Squared value for this model is 0.6248, meaning that it is accounting for the majority of the variance in PCI (62.48%) and should be considered an acceptable value.

A second multiple linear regression was run that included the distress densities and the treatment type indicator. Theoretically, if all distresses are held constant between two pavements, then the PCI found during the survey should be exactly the same. With Treatment Type added as a variable to the model of significant distresses, the analysis found that PCI increases by 6.6 when considering Thinlay sites. Obviously, this is not a true statement and the PCI value of 6.64 represents error in the data collection in favor of Thinlay.

To determine the life extension benefit of each product, a PCI trigger of 55 was chosen (the fair/poor rating border per ASTM D6433). Theoretically, this PCI is when another pavement treatment would be needed in order to maintain an acceptable driving surface.

With the PCI threshold chosen, the model equation is used to calculate Microsurfacing's life extension:

$$PCI = 71.09 - 4.07 * Age \; (Eq. 3)$$

$$55 = 71.09 - 4.07 * Micro\ Life\ Extension$$

$$Microsurfacing\ Life\ Extension = 4.0\ years$$

For the Thinlay life extension, 6.64 will be added to the PCI threshold of 55 to account for the data collection error – resulting in a Thinlay PCI threshold of 61.64. The life extension calculation is then as follows:

$$PCI = 98.51 - 4.07 * Age\ (Eq.4)$$

$$61.64 = 98.51 - 4.07 * Thinlay\ Life\ Extension$$

$$Thinlay\ Life\ Extension = 9.1\ years$$

Ultimately, Thinlay is shows to provide more than double the life extension than that of Microsurfacing. It is important to note that this data is only applicable to the maintenance projects included in the case study at the time of data collection. These numbers should not be extrapolated to use of these treatments in other regions.

These models are represented graphically in this figure showing the raw data and the trendlines:

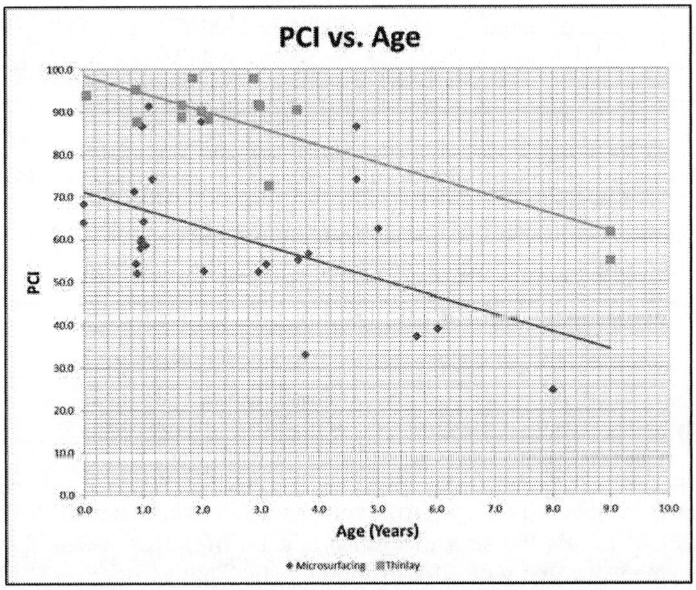

Figure 6.1: PCI vs. Age with Prediction Model

7. Cost of Ownership Comparison

Though Thinlay has been shown to provide more life extension than Microsurfacing, the question arises of which one provides more cost benefit? The first step is to determine the unit price of each product. This was accomplished by compiling prices and quantities from the bid tab for each project, available from the state DOT. Microsurfacing was simpler due to the fact that it is bid as dollars per square yard.

Averaging the unit prices from the state bid tabs provides a unit price of $2.40 per square yard for Microsurfacing.

Calculating the unit price for Thinlay involved some extra steps, since it is bid as dollars per ton. In alternate bid jobs, it was a simple step of multiplying the quantity in tons by the cost per ton to find total dollars. The total dollars was then divided by the quantity in square yards to find dollars per square yard. On non-alternate bid jobs where square yardage is not given, a common conversion factor of 110 pounds per SY-Inch was used to convert from the tonnage quantity to square yards. First, the tonnage was divided by the conversion factor to find SY-Inch, which was then divided by the pavement thickness (5/8") to find the square yards.

By averaging the unit prices for Thinlay bid tabs, we find that Thinlay has an average cost of $2.63 per square yard.

Next, the dollars per square yard value was annualized for each product at the chosen PCI threshold of 55 by dividing the average unit cost by the age associated with the threshold. The annualized unit cost was then converted to annualized dollars per lane mile assuming 12' wide lanes. The annualized costs are shown below in Table 10.3.

Table 7.1: Annualized Costs at PCI = 55

Treatment Type	Extended Life	Annualized Cost/SY		Annualized Cost/Ln. Mile	
Microsurfacing	4.0	$	0.60	$	4,224.00
Thinlay	9.1	$	0.29	$	2,041.60

Based on this simple analysis, it is apparent that Thinlay is more cost effective than Microsurfacing, despite having a higher up-front cost. Thinlay begins at being $0.23/SY more expensive than Microsurfacing, though becomes less than half the cost of Microsurfacing over the life extension of each product. As the threshold point lowers, the difference in cost for the products begins to slightly narrow. However, delaying the treatment to a point where the pavement begins to fail is contradictory to the primary purpose of preventative maintenance itself.

8. Conclusions

The statistical results showed that there is a significant difference in PCI performance between Microsurfacing and Thinlay. However, the difference is not in the slope of PCI vs. Age but in the PCI towards the start of each product's life. This means that in the projects investigated pavements treated with Microsurfacing and Thinlay degraded at the same rate. It is suspected that Microsurfacing is more sensitive to the existing conditions of the pavement in which it is applied. This concept was demonstrated when comparing the pre-condition distresses to the distresses after Microsurfacing was applied. The rutting encountered in those sites immediately reflected through the treatment – indicating that Microsurfacing does not provide the structure necessary to fill ruts. The alligator cracking encountered at JJ County did not reflect through immediately. However, it should be noted that preventive maintenance should not be used to correct structural damage – such as alligator cracking – in pavements. This position is supported by an FHWA document stating that preventative maintenance is not designed to address deficiencies in the pavement structure (FHWA 2004). This investigation suggests that economic performance of preventative maintenance treatments is dependent upon the condition of the pavement and are not appropriate for pavements which require more extensive rehabilitation or reconstruction.

8.1 Limitations of the Research

While this paper provided a number of valid and interesting conclusions, there were some limitations and imperfections in the methodology. The major limitation was that pre-condition data could not be found for the roadway before the treatment was applied – with the exception of six sites. The PCI of the previous surface is a major factor in predicting how the PCI will progress in the new surface. As previously mentioned, the data represents how preventive maintenance is likely performing under the current conditions in the state.

As pavement practitioners are aware, pavements do not deteriorate linearly over their lifespan. As the roadway ages, PCI deterioration typically accelerates until the pavement reaches the "failed" status. However, this paper presented the PCI prediction model using multiple linear regression. Since multiple pavement sites were used to construct the PCI vs. Age graphs, the statistical spread was higher than what would be seen in data collected on a single pavement site over time. Therefore, a precise non-linear model was difficult to fit to this project data in terms of statistical quality. Multiple linear regression provided a means of extracting useful results from the data analysis.

Lastly, the data collected does not account for construction quality – which can drastically affect the PCI at the start of a pavement's life cycle. A number of different contractors worked on the sites examined in this study. Paving methodology and quality control could certainly vary between them. Ideally, testing and QA/QC data would be added as a factor in the multiple linear regression model but this data was not available for the current investigation.

References

ASTM. (2007). Standard Practice for Roads and Parking Lots Pavement Condition Index Surveys. D6433, ASTM International, West Conshohocken, PA.

FHWA. (2005). Pavement Preservation Definitions. https://www.fhwa.dot.gov/pavement/preservation/091205.cfm. Accessed April 2017.

FHWA. (2004). Preventive Maintenance Eligibility. https://www.fhwa.dot.gov/preservation/100804.cfm. Accessed April 2017.

Lemer, A., (2004). Public benefits of highway system preservation and maintenance NCHRP Synthesis 330.

Peshkin, D., Zimmerman, K., and Hoerner. (2004). Optimal timing of pavement preventative maintenance treatment applications. NCHRP Report 523. DOI 10.17226/13772.

Rajagopal, A. (2010). Effectiveness of chip sealing and microsurfacing on pavement serviceability and life. FHWA/OH-2010/8.

Transportation Information Center. (2002). PASER Asphalt Roads Manual. Wisconsin Transportation Information Center, Madison, WI.

Parametric information modelling of mechanised tunnelling projects for multi-level decision support

Jelena Ninic, Christian Koch and Walid Tizani
University of Nottingham, United Kingdom
jelena.ninic@nottingham.ac.uk

Abstract. This paper presents a concept for parametric modelling of mechanized tunnelling within a state of the art design environment, as a basis for the design assessment on different levels of details (LoDs). To this end, a parametric representation of each system component (soil with excavation, tunnel lining with grouting, Tunnel Boring Machine (TBM) and buildings) is developed in the information model for three LoDs (high, medium and low) and used for the automated generation of the numerical models of the tunnel construction process and soil-structure interaction. The platform enables a flexible, user-friendly generation of the tunnel structure for arbitrary alignments based on predefined structural families for each component, supporting the design process and at the same time providing an insight into stability and safety of the design. This model, with selected optimal LoDs for each component w.r.t. the objective of the analysis, is used for efficient design and process optimisation in mechanized tunnelling. Efficiency and accuracy are further demonstrated through error-free exchange of information between Building Information Modelling (BIM) and the numerical simulation and with significantly reduced computational effort. The results reveal that this approach is a major step towards the sensible modelling and numerical analysis of complex tunnelling project information at the early design stages.

1. Introduction

With increasing urbanisation and mobility, the need for underground tunnel facilities becomes evident. The efficient and safe design and construction of mechanised tunnels involves complex data management incorporating information not only about the tunnel structure, but also about the existing built infrastructure, the ground and the boring machine. In early design phases, crucial decisions have to be made, for example, on the alignment of the tunnel track in order to minimise the risks of settlement induced damages to existing buildings. This task can now be supported by sophisticated, process-oriented finite element (FE) analysis. However, the required FE models are characterised by a high degree of detail at high costs of preparation and computational effort preventing them from being readily applied during what-if scenario analyses at early design stages.

The appraisal of different design alternatives is essential for ensuring optimal designs. Assessing the effects of various alternatives for tunnelling projects on the surrounding environment is a multi-disciplinary and complex problem. The current state of the art process is cumbersome and requires significant computing resources and time (sophisticated simulations including all details can take days or weeks to complete). This often leads to sub-optimal solutions and could possibly result in a solution that is not ideal in terms of its effect on the existing infrastructure. However, in the conceptual phase, a designer often only needs approximate estimations for many different scenarios, e.g. tunnel track alternatives. To ensure a seamless workflow, the computation time should be minimised. If preliminary analysis (with consideration of uncertainties) indicates the potential for hazards, a more detailed evaluation of the model is required.

BIM has gained increasing attention in complex infrastructure projects, simplifying the planning and analysis and increasing productivity in design and construction. In tunnelling applications, the BIM concept has been used to create a tunnel information modelling framework that creates and interlinks a ground model, a tunnel lining model, a tunnel boring machine model and built environment model (Koch, et al., 2015). Furthermore, a multi-level information representation of the built environment has been developed to support planning and analysis tasks by (Borrmann, et al., 2014). On the other hand, in current engineering practice, the proof of tunnel design is often carried out by employing numerical simulations (Meschke, et al., 2013; Do, et al., 2014; Ninic & Meschke, 2015). These models are usually generated based on design documents and reports. Even if the underlying information needed for numerical analysis is stored in a BIM, the translation from an information model to a computational model is still dominated by manual work. Such an approach therefore incurs significant work carried out by experts, and is furthermore susceptible to human error. Hence, it is evident that an automated link between information management (in the form of a BIM) and numerical analysis is necessary. Such a link will enable the continuous, error-free exchange of information between BIM and numerical simulation from the design stages of a project over the construction phase to operation. In the field of structural analysis, the link between information and numerical modelling has been addressed recently in (Nawari & Kuenstle, 2015; Svoboda, et al., 2014; Breitenberger, et al., 2015) where FE methods and Isogeometric Analysis (IGA) are applied for the assessment of the structural behaviour. In tunnelling application, the first attempt of linking BIM and structural assessment by means of numerical modelling is presented in (Meschke, et al., 2014; Ninic, et al., 2017; Alsahly, et al., 2016), where data obtained from a Tunnel Information Model (TIM) (Amann, et al., 2013) is used for the automated generation of a numerical model for a real-world tunnelling project, the Wehrhahn metro line in Dusseldorf (WHL).

In this paper, a concept for parametric modelling of shield bored tunnelling projects - called "SATBIM" - is presented. This forms the basis for multi-level structural analysis of the settlement behaviour (Ninić & Koch, 2017). To this end, parametric representations for each of the system components (tunnel lining with grouting, soil with excavation, existing buildings, and tunnel boring machine (TBM)) are developed for three different levels of details (LOD). Figure 1 depicts the multi-level approach for the system components building and tunnel lining.

This parametric information model is then used to automatically generate numerical models to simulate the tunnel construction process taking into account appropriate levels of detail per component and design objective. The proposed concept is implemented within Autodesk Revit and Dynamo and tested in a what-if scenario analysis for a small tunnelling project.

2. Methodology

2.1. Overall concept

The main idea of the SATBIM project is to dynamically generate simulation models from a multi-level information model at the required LoD for the specific problem to be solved. For example, minimising the overall risk of damage to buildings induced by tunnelling needs high LoD for structures and topology of the soil, however for the lining structure and its installation process, a lower LoD is sufficient to achieve high accuracy of the solution (see Fig. 1, red arrows). On the other hand, estimating stresses in the tunnel structure needs low LoD for buildings and high LoD for lining and its installation process, while surface topology of the soil is not crucial for the accuracy of the results (see Fig. 1, black arrows).

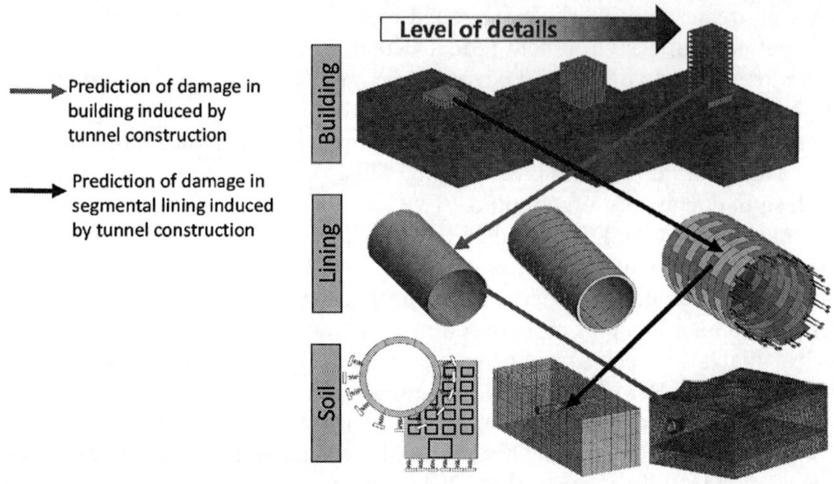

Figure 1: Alternatives for selection of LoDs for individual components based on the objective of the analysis

2.2. Parametric multi-level information and numerical modelling

This section presents a comprehensive concept for incorporating multi-scale representations into building information models, with a particular focus on the geometric-semantic modelling of shield tunnels, in a form suitable for direct application of the model for further numerical analysis.

The shield-supported tunnel advance beneath the groundwater table in soft soil requires permanent support of the surrounding underground to prevent the groundwater from flowing into the construction site. A realistic model to be applied during construction and in the design phase needs to represent all components of the tunnelling process relevant for the prognosis of the response of the surrounding soil during excavation. These components include:

- the segmental lining with the support measures applied at the tunnel face and at the tail void,
- the underground soil,
- the TBM and the hydraulic jacks,
- the existing infrastructure (e.g. buildings).

For each component three LoDs are defined: low (LoD 1), medium (LoD 2) and high (LoD 3). In general, in the lowest level of detail, non-volumetric representation of the component is assumed, since in the corresponding numerical model, components are not represented with structural models but instead with the analytical or empirical models assigned through a set of boundary conditions. On the medium LoD, for each component, a volumetric representation is established, where the component is "occupying" the exact volume; however the geometry is simplified, i.e. approximated. Finally, the highest LoD includes more detail about the actual geometry of the component. However, components such as TBM still do not include details of the machinery and the equipment inside the shield, and therefore, an even higher representation (LoD 4) could be introduced as an extension.

For each component, on each level of detail, an entity type or family for the corresponding component is defined. In order to keep consistency between different LoD, parametric consistency between families is defined as shown in Fig. 2. The full set of parameters defining a component is needed for definition of the highest LoD (LoD 3), while only a subset of the same list is used for definition of medium and lower LoD (LoD 2, LoD 1), respectively.

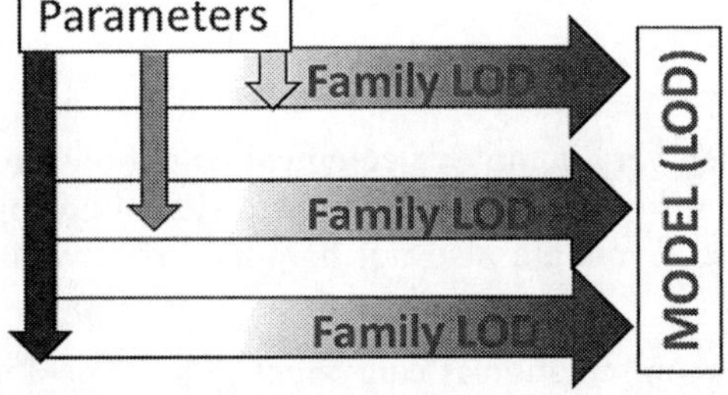

Figure 2: Multi-level representation of geometry: parameter consistency between different LoDs for individual components.

2.2.1. Tunnel lining model

Each tunnel project has special tunnel lining requirements, depending on the diameter, the soil conditions and the routing, so that a safe and durable tunnel structure can be produced in order to withstand demanding use for up to 100 years. The geometry of the entire ring and its individual segments as well as the arrangement of the joints and their sealing must be designed such that the can be easily moulded for the designed tunnel alignment. When using universal rings, the designed alignment of the tunnel is formed by adjusting the rotations of the standardised rings to follow a certain curvature.

Based on a given alignment (e.g. a 3D curve), the following parameters are needed to create the tunnel lining structure at LoD 1: *Lining ring length* and *Lining outer radius* (Fig. 3a). Following this, parameters specifying the inner radius, the taper, and the material are added to build the lining model at LoD 2. If the number of *Lining segments* per ring is defined, a LoD 3 representation can be generated (Fig. 3a).

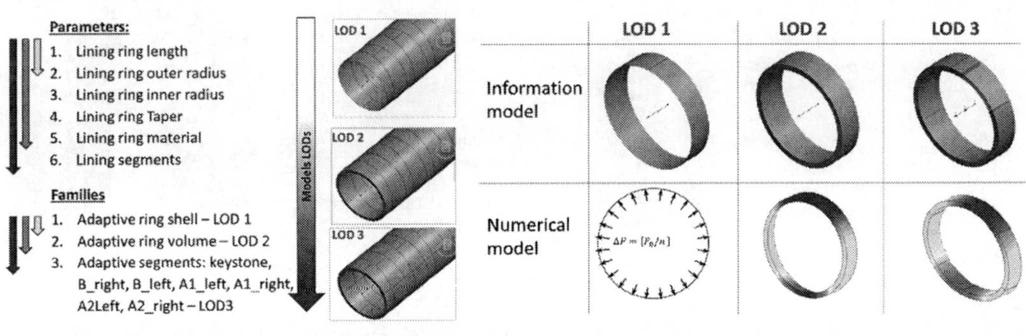

Figure 3: Multi-level tunnel lining modelling. (a) Information model: Parameters, families and models. (b) Mapping information model to numerical model

Figure 3b illustrates the mapping at different LoDs of the information model to the corresponding numerical models. While on LoD 1, the numerical representation is based on a 2D plain strain model on LoD 2 the lining tube is modelled by means of volume elements per ring that can be activated in the course of the simulation advance (Fig. 3b). In order to account for the reduced stiffness of the tunnel lining due to the presence of joints and for the segment-wise installation of the tunnel lining, a model for longitudinal and ring joints is used in the LoD 3 numerical model (Fig. 3b).

2.2.2. Soil model

In tunnelling projects, often very complex geological conditions are met. It is very common that the tunnel construction is conducted through the different geological layers and under the water level, and that those layers are also not homogeneous, which adds a vast amount of uncertainty to the project.

The highest LoD for soil representation is equivalent to a 3D geological model consisting of geotechnical layers represented with a single or multiple geometric volume and material descriptions for each corresponding layer (Fig. 4a). If such a detailed 3D geological model is not available, but only an estimation about the geometry and composition of the soil, for the medium level of detail (LoD 2), a rectangular bounding box, representing a substitute soil volume, is defined. This bounding box is used to delimit the simulation model and is chosen large enough so that the model boundaries do not affect the simulation results while being small enough to not unnecessarily expand the complexity of the model. The size of the bounding box depends on the tunnel alignment, the overburden and the excavation radius. Finally, if there is no information of the geometry of the soil layers, and only rough information about the material through which the tunnel will be constructed, on the lowest LoD the soil is represented with no geometry but only parametrically assigned elastic material parameter values (LoD 1).

Figure 4b depicts the mapping of the information model to the numerical model of the soil. On LoD 1, the soil is represented using a linear elastic subgrade reaction model (Vesic, 1963; Kolymbas, 1998). On LoD 2 and LoD 3, a structural FE model including geometry and a two-phase fully saturated material description (Nagel & Meschke, 2010) is used (Fig. 4b).

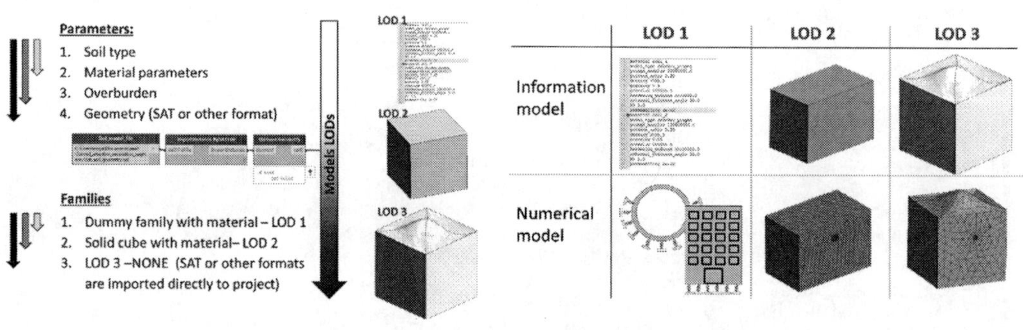

(a) (b)

Figure 4: Multi-level soil modelling. (a) Information model: Parameters, families and models. (b) Mapping information model to numerical model

2.2.3. Built environment model

Existing buildings can be represented by the equivalent load of the dead weight, using substitute models or using detailed structural models (Fig. 5). For the lowest LoD (LoD 1), only a surface representation of the building is adopted, representing the footprint area. This model corresponds to a numerical model where the building is represented by the equivalent surface dead load of the building. On LoD 2, a building is represented with the volume occupied by the building, and parameters define the number of floors, the floor height, etc. Finally, for LoD 3, dedicated floor slabs and columns are generated based on the complete set of parameters.

Figure 5b illustrates the mapping of the information model to the numerical model of a building. On LoD 1, buildings are substituted with a dead load derived from the building weight acting on the soil surface, neglecting soil-structure interaction and building stiffness. On LoD 2, buildings are considered by means of reduced models with a substitute elastic stiffness E, height H and weight ρ (Schindler & Mark, 2013). Full structural frame models are used on LoD 3, modelling columns and floor slabs with isotropic volume hexahedra kinematic linear elements.

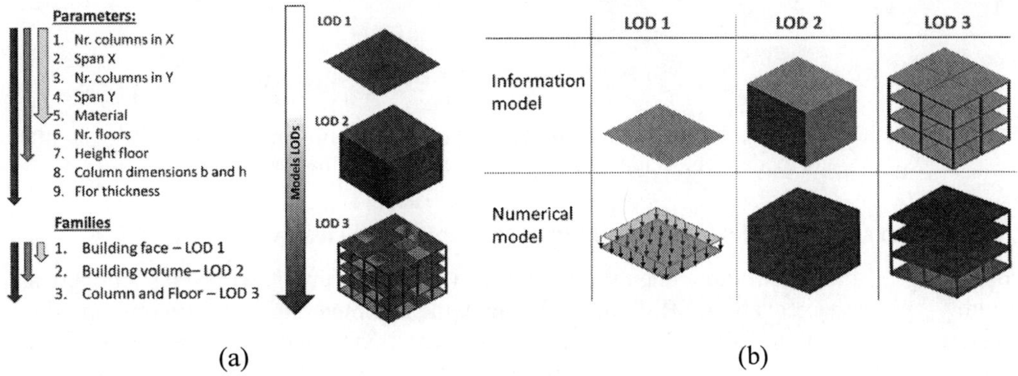

Figure 5: Multi-level building modelling: (a) Information model: Parameters, families and models. (b) Mapping information model to numerical model

2.2.4. Tunnel boring machine model

The TBM can be represented by the outer shell of the shield, using a simplified volumetric model or a more detailed volumetric model of the shield (Fig. 6). For LoD 1, only a surface representation of the TBM is adopted, representing the outer surface of the shield. This model corresponds to a numerical model where the TBM is represented exactly as a set of boundary conditions limiting the deformation of the soil to the respective shield outer shell coordinates. On LoD 2, the TBM is represented with a shield volume considering the thickness of the shield, tapered geometry and material. In the equivalent numerical model, this volume is used to represent the TBM as a deformable body moving through the soil and interacting with the ground through surface-to-surface contact. Finally, on LoD 3, details of the TBM such as hydraulic jacks and shield wall (for abutment of hydraulic jacks) are modelled. This is used in the numerical representation for modelling of the TBM advance, which is pushed forward by elongation of hydraulic jacks. An automatic steering algorithm controls the individual jack thrusts to keep the TBM within the designed alignment and avoid drift off-course.

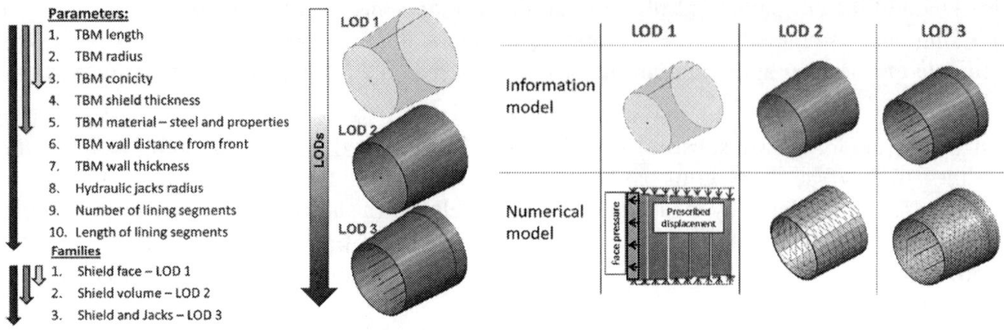

(a) (b)

Figure 6: Multi-level tunnel boring machine modelling: (a) Information model: Parameters, families and models. (b) Mapping information model to numerical model

2.3. Integrated multi-level tunnel information and numerical model

Combining all individual components on selected the LoDs (lining with its alignment and grouting, soil with excavation, TBM, and buildings), the complete tunnel information model is generated as shown in Figure 7. For each component, individual local parameters (LoD, geometrical and material parameters) are defined. On the other hand, there are also global parameters that are shared by multiple components such as ring length, excavation radius, number of steps/slices, overburden, etc. These local parameters are keeping the consistency of the global model.

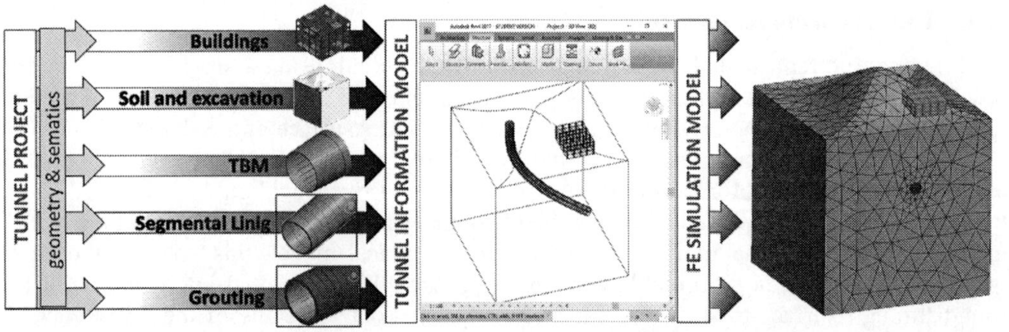

(a) (b) (c)

Figure 7: Multi-level tunnel information and numerical modelling. (a) Combining sub-models based on local and global parameters. (b) Integrated tunnel information model. (c) Generated numerical model.

The simulation model for tunnelling is generated based on geometry and semantics from the design model exported by means of custom Dynamo nodes. The geometry of all individual components is exported in ACIS format, while the model semantics are exported to text files for each component separately, containing the local parameters, together with one main file containing the global parameters. Our newly developed tool "SatBimModeller" with a high degree of automation reads the geometry and semantic data, generates numerical model, setups and then executes the simulation model and post-processes the results for visualisation in the design tool.

3. Workflow and implementation

The multi-level information model for tunnelling is developed using the industry-standard tools Revit and Dynamo (AUTODESK, 2017), allowing for consistent parametric modelling on different LoDs. For each tunnel component and on each LoD, a so-called "Revit family" for the corresponding component is created. A family in Revit is a class with parametric definitions and constraints, allowing to define specific family attributes on individual family instances (Revit objects). In order to keep consistency between different LoDs, in SATBIM parametric consistency between families is defined as shown in Figure 2 and as introduced in Section 2.2. The full set of parameters defining a component is needed for the definition on the highest LoD, while only a subset of the parameter list is used on lower LoDs. This way of handling parameters allows for automated preservation of the consistency of the multi-scale model.

For each model component on each LoD, a corresponding numerical model has been developed using the pre/post processor GiD (2017) and the open source Finite Element simulation software KRATOS (2017). The generation of the complete structural model, consistency between individual components, simulation scripts and visualisation features are handled by our newly developed software called "SatBimModeller". All details about the newly developed modeller can be found in (Ninic, et al., 2017).

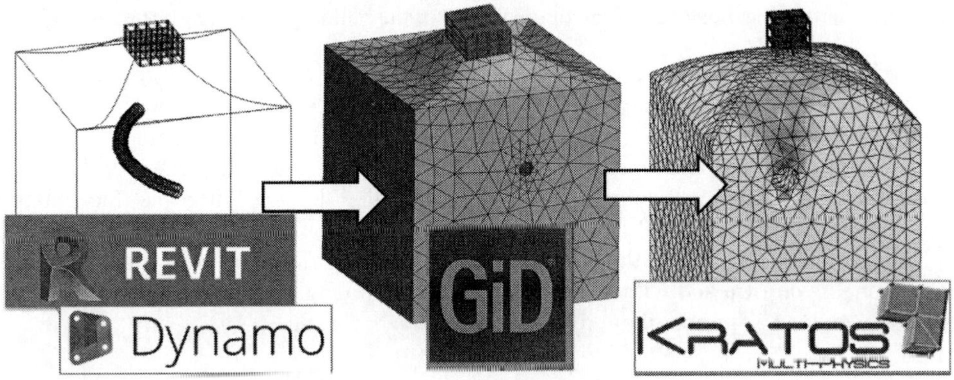

Figure 8: Workflow and implementation of the SATBIM framework

4. Example

The SATBIM platform has been successfully applied for the generation of information and numerical models and for the visualisation of structural assessment. Depending on the design scenario, the optimal LoD of each individual component is selected, leading to robust and computationally efficient numerical assessment (see Figure 9). Knowledge about the optimal building LoD for the scenario of shield tunnelling in vicinity of existing infrastructure from the previous studies conducted based on the SATBIM concept is applied to further optimise the size of the model without reducing the accuracy of the solution. To this end, in the first case, all buildings are modelled on the highest LoD, while in the second case, only buildings with high sensitivity to LoD are modelled with high accuracy, while the rest is modelled with LoD 2, which significantly reduces the size of the problem (see Figure 10).

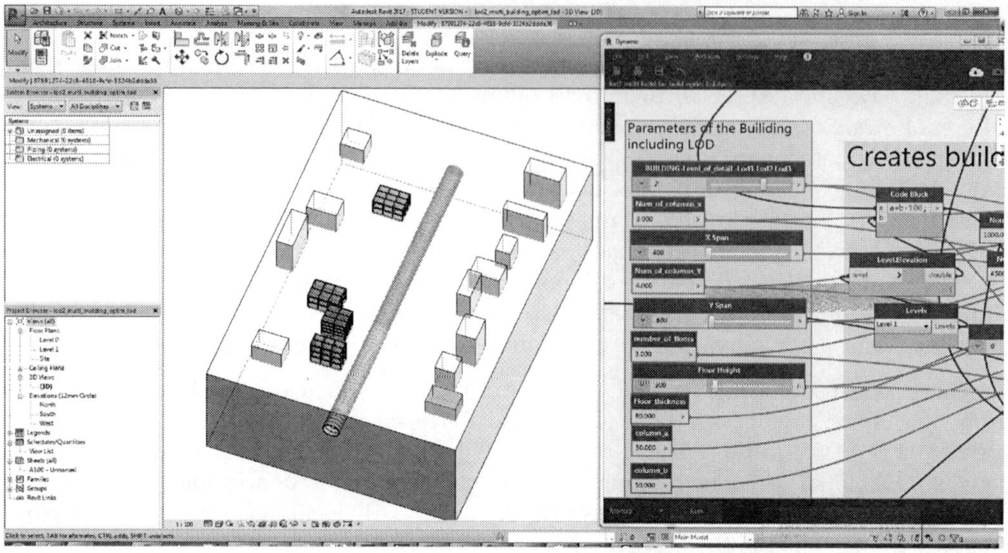

Figure 9: Parametric information model for a 200 m long tunnel section used for the generation of a large-scale simulation. Selection of the optimal LoD of the building in Dynamo user interface.

In both models, LoD 2 is selected for the representation of the tunnel lining structure and the TBM. This model accounts for the shield as a deformable body moving through the soil and interacting with the ground through surface-to-surface contact. The tunnel advance is modelled by means of deactivation of soil elements and installation of the lining rings and grouting elements. Tunnelling-induced deformations are controlled by applying the face support pressure and the grouting pressure at the tunnel face and in the steering gap, respectively. The Mohr Coulomb model is used as the constitutive relation for effective stress and strain in the soil. The tunnel is constructed with 80 lining rings of 2.5m length and 10m excavation radius are excavated under 17.5m of soil overburden.

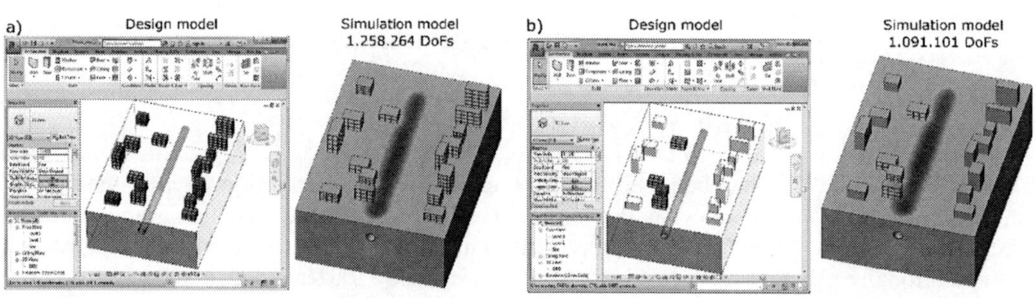

(a) (b)

Figure 10: Information (design) and simulation model for a more than 200m long tunnel section used for the generation of a numerical simulation and results of FE simulation generated using "SatBimModeller" for a) Model 1: highest LoD for representation of the infrastructure and b) Model 2: optimised LoD for representation of the infrastructure.

Considering a spatial discretization of all components (soil, lining, TBM and buildings) the models are finally described with 1,258,264 and 1,091,101 Degrees of Freedom (DoFs) for Model 1- high (LoD3) and Model 2- optimised (LoD2 and LoD3) representation of buildings, respectively. The model size strongly influences the computational costs as shown in Table 1, where the individual as well as the total time for the solution are listed.

Table 1: Runtime for the solution steps of Model 1 and Model 2 from the Figure10.

Computational costs	Model 1	Model 2
Conditioning time per step[s]	4.2	3.6
Assembly time per step [s]	26.2	19.8
Solve time per step [s]	281.7	244.2
I/O time per step [s]	4.0	3.6
Total time [min]	2916	2410

Although the size of the model and consequently the computational costs differ significantly, the final output of the numerical analysis is identical for Models 1 and 2 as shown in Figure 10. This is due to fact that the complexity of the model is optimised without affecting the important, i.e. the influencing features of the model w.r.t. the objective of our analysis, which in this case is tunnelling-induced settlements and interaction with existing buildings.

5. Conclusions

This paper proposes a novel concept of parametric information modelling for multi-level decision support for mechanised tunnelling projects: SATBIM is an integrated, open-source platform for information modelling, structural analysis and visualisation. Within this platform, industry-standard tools (Autodesk Revit and Dynamo) are employed for the design of the tunnel structure and the surrounding infrastructure with consideration of LoDs for all system components. Based on the multi-level, parametric BIM, multi-level numerical models are developed for each component, considering proper geometric as well as material representation, interfaces and the representation of the construction process. The numerical models are then fully automatically instantiated and executed based on the BIM. Finally, the simulation outputs are read back and visualised within Revit.

SATBIM enables efficient design and assessment of design alternatives reducing the modelling efforts and commutation time by: (i) minimisation of the efforts needed for model generation; (ii) representation on different LoDs leading to computationally efficient simulations; and (iii) effective visualisation of the simulation results. This efficiency is demonstrated in the numerical example presented in this paper. Applying the optimal LoDs of the components in the information models and automatically generating corresponding numerical simulations, the computational efforts are significantly reduced without affecting the accuracy of the assessment. The efficiency of this framework will be further improved by: i) on-demand analysis based on analytical and empirical solutions for structural response to tunnelling; and ii) integration of Iso-Geometric Analysis and making a direct use of the B-rep geometries generated in the BIM for definition of numerical models. The SATBIM toolkit will be made available as open source software together with tutorials, a complete manual, and a number of benchmark example at Github repository: https: //github.com/satbim.

Acknowledgement

This project has received funding from the European Union's Horizon 2020 research and innovation programme under the Marie Sklodowska-Curie grant agreement No 702874. This support is gratefully acknowledged.

References

Alsahly, A., Gall, V.E., Marwan, A., Ninic, J., Meschke, G., Vonthron, A., M., Koenig. (2016). From Building Information Modeling to Real time Simulation in Mechanized tunneling. Proceedings of the World Tunneling Congress 2016. San Francisco.

Amann, J., Borrmann, A., Hegemann, F., Jubierre, J., Flurl, M., Koch, C., Koenig, M. (2103). A refined product model for shield tunnels based on a generalized approach for alignment representation. Proc. of the 1st International Conference on Civil and Building Engineering Informatics.

AUTODESK. Autodesk Revit. (2017). http://www.autodesk.co.uk/products/revit-family/.

Borrmann, A., M. Flurl, J.R. Jubierre, R.P. Mundani, and E. Rank. (2014). Synchronous collaborative tunnel design based on consistency-preserving multi-scale models. Advanced Engineering Informatics, 2014, pp. 499 - 517.

Breitenberger, M., A. Apostolatos, B. Philipp, R. Wuechner, and K.U. Bletzinger (2015). Analysis in computer aided design: Nonlinear isogeometric B-Rep analysis of shell structures. Computer Methods in Applied Mechanics and Engineering 284, pp. 401-457.

CIMNE, International Center for Numerical Methods in Engineering (2017). GiD: the personal pre- and postprocessor. . http://www.gidhome.com/.

CIMNE, International Center for Numerical Methods in Engineering (2017). Kratos Multi-physics. http://www.cimne.com/kratos/.

Do, N., D. Dias, P. Oreste, and Djeran-Maigre I. (2014). Three-dimensional numerical simulation for mechanized tunnelling in soft ground: the influence of the joint pattern. Acta Geotechnica 9, no. 4, pp. 673-694.

Koch, C., F. Hegemann, and M. König (2015). Tunnel information modelling to support interactions in mechanized tunneling. Proc. of the 32nd CIB-W78 Conference on Information Technology in Construction. Eindhoven, The Netherlands.

Kolymbas, D. (1998). Geotechnik - Tunnelbau und Tunnelmechanik. Springer.

Meschke, G., J. Ninic, J. Stascheit, and A. Alsahly (2013). Parallelized computational modeling of pile-soil interactions in mechanized tunneling. Engineering Structures 47, pp. 35-44.

Meschke, G., S. Freitag, A. Alsahly, J. Ninic, Schindler S., and C. Koch (2014). Numerical Simulation in Mechanized Tunneling in Urban Environments in the Framework of a Tunnel Information Model. Bauingenieur 89, no. 11, pp. 457-466.

Nagel, F., and G. Meschke (2010). An elasto-plastic three phase model for partially saturated soil for the finite element simulation of compressed air support in tunnelling. International Journal for Numerical and Analytical Methods in Geomechanics 34, pp. 605-625.

Nawari, N., and M. Kuenstle (2015). Building Information Modeling: Framework for Structural Design. 978-1-4822-4043-6 vols. CRC Press.

Ninić, J., and C. Koch (2017). Parametric multi-level tunnel modelling for design support and numerical analysis. EURO:TUN 2017 - IV International Conference on Computational Methods in Tunneling and Subsurface Engineering. Innsbruck, Austria, pp.169-176.

Ninic, J., and G. Meschke (2015). Model update and real-time steering of tunnel boring machines using simulation-based meta models. Tunnelling and Underground Space Technology 45, pp. 138-152.

Ninic, J., S. Freitag, and G. Meschke (2017). A hybrid finite element and surrogate modelling approach for simulation and monitoring supported TBM steering. Tunnelling and Underground Space Technology 63, pp. 12-28.

Schindler, S., and P. Mark (2013). Evaluation of building stiffness in the risk-assessment of structures affected by settlements. Proceedings of Third International Conference on Computational Methods in Tunneling and Subsurface Engineering. Bochum: Ruhr University Bochum.

Svoboda, L., J. Novak, L. Kurilla, and J. Zeman (2014). A framework for integrated design of algorithmic architectural forms. Advances in Engineering Software 72, pp. 109 - 118.

Vesic, A. B. (1963). "Beams on Elastic Subgrade and the Winkler's Hypothesis." Proceedings of 5th International Conference of Soil Mechanics.

Ninić, J., C. Koch, J. Stascheit (2017). An integrated platform for design and numerical analysis of shield tunnelling processes on different levels of detail. Advances in Engineering Software. DOI: 10.1016/j.advengsoft.2017.05.012.

Computer Technology for Serious Games in Education: A Literature Review

Carlos A. Osorio-Sandoval, Christian Koch, Walid Tizani
University of Nottingham, UK
carlos.osoriosandoval@nottingham.ac.uk

Abstract. Serious games are games which purpose differs from entertainment. The quick development of computer and gaming technology has brought attention to them, but a current state-of-the-art on its application had not been addressed in literature. In this paper, we identified trends in the application of computer and gaming technology in serious games for education. Game engines, augmented reality, virtual reality, mobile devices and building information modelling are the trending technologies used by researchers and developers in the field. Some insights on the way in which these technologies are being implemented are provided. We found that by applying these technologies it is possible to achieve some of the characteristics that stakeholders look for in serious games for education: immersion, ubiquity, high quality graphics, interoperability and quick game content development.

1. Introduction

It has been difficult for researchers to define games, or even to list the conditions that a system or an object must meet to be considered a game. Although several attempts have been made, there is neither a definition, nor a single necessary or sufficient condition in literature that satisfies everyone. In fact, the idea of "family resemblance" developed by Wittgenstein (1958) was originally explained using games as an example. By examining different types of games, we see a complicated network of similarities overlapping and crisscrossing: sometimes overall similarities, sometimes similarities of detail (Wittgenstein, 1958). There is no essence among them (Mayer, et al., 2016) and they seem to share no single characteristic (Duke, 1974).

For example, voluntarism is an aspect of games recognized by many of the most cited authors that have attempted to describe them (Huizinga, 1949; Suits, 1978), yet, when talking about games for educational purposes, Becker (2010) points out that in any formal education setting the tasks that learners are given to do are typically not voluntary.

Despite this debate, it is true that we recognize a game when we see it (Crookall, 2010), and that even children learn what games are fairly easily (Mayer, et al., 2016).

Even though serious games are a more specific kind of games, the above disagreement concerning both its definition and characteristics remains the same. The only boundary that appears to be true amongst the various researchers and developers that address serious games seems to be that its purposes differ from entertainment. Nevertheless, according to Sawyer (2008), there are at least 13 other terms used to refer to these games.

Regardless, the field of serious games has been growing rapidly, and drawing attention of several stakeholders from a broad spectrum of areas. Laamarti, et al. (2014) carried out a survey of published articles related to serious games using online archives from 1995 to 2013 and found out an exponential growth in the number of research papers published in the field with more than 1200 articles in 2013 alone. Current figures continue to rise with more than 2000 articles published in 2016 (De Lope & Medina-Medina, 2016).

Several attempts to classify serious games have been made in recent years. A wide variety of taxonomy proposals can be found in the literature (Kirriemuir & Mcfarlane, 2004; Sawyer, 2008; Botte, et al., 2009; Djaouti, et al., 2011; Boughzala, et al., 2013; Laamarti, et al., 2014), but more often than not, stakeholders use one that fits only their own audience (Kirriemuir & Mcfarlane, 2004), leaving out other instances that would be considered serious games by others.

Serious games are claimed to have positive impacts on the players' development of several different skills (Susi, et al., 2007). They enhance the standard formal teaching methods in a laboratory environment to test and reinforce the relevance of theories to practice (Nassar, 2003). Furthermore, they provide a mechanism for active learning that results in longer-term recall, synthesis, and problem-solving skills than learning by hearing, reading, or watching (Korman & Johnston, 2010). They can be applied to a broad spectrum of application areas, e.g. military, government, educational, corporate, and healthcare (Backlund, et al., 2007).

In an effort to cover an identified gap in knowledge and experience between the graduate engineer and the real world construction engineer, serious games have been used in construction management education since the late 60's. Most of these games, however, are text based and their developments have not kept pace with the substantial increase in microcomputers power and advances in graphics and video technologies (Al-Jibouri & Mawdesley, 2001)

Using computers for playing games is something relatively new, given that one of the first games of this kind was built in 1950 (Bateman, 2014), and that the first paper on computer chess was published the same year (Shannon, 1950).

The quick development of computer and gaming technology has brought even more attention to serious games' developers, but a current state-of-the-art on its application has not been addressed in literature yet.

Although serious games for construction management education are the main interest of the authors of this paper, we will review serious games for education in a broader sense in order to identify the technologies that are being used by researchers and developers in the serious games domain.

2. Objective and methodology

In this paper, we will present a literature review on serious games for education with focus on the trends in computer and gaming technology application. Although serious games will be addressed, we have no intention on classifying or defining them. Our aim is to answer the question: *How is computer and gaming technology being used in the context of serious games for education?*

To achieve our objective, we will:

- Identify base literature by using selected keywords ("serious game(s)", "game-based", "gamification", "edutainment", "game(s) for learning/training/teaching", and "simulation game(s)").
- Identify secondary literature by searching for base literature paper's references.
- Identify the technology elements employed by the serious game's developer.
- Synthesize amassed knowledge and provide a description of the state of the art in the area.

3. Results

3.1. Trends in application of technology

The base literature was identified by searching in the Scopus database using the selected keywords ("serious game(s)", "game-based", "gamification", "edutainment", "game(s) for learning" "game(s) for training", "game(s) for teaching", and "simulation game(s)"), which resulted in 12,790 hits.

The results were filtered by including the keyword "education" to the search results, which narrowed the literature to 1,950 hits.

The technologies to review were identified by analysing the keywords of the remaining papers in the search results. Virtual reality, mobile devices, augmented reality and game engines were the keywords with more hits within the filtered papers.

The authors decided to include Building Information Modelling (BIM) in this review even when the number of papers found through our first search was not significant, because there is an increasing interest in this technology within our field of work, and in its applications in serious games.

In this review, we included papers describing a game targeted at teaching an identifiable subject, which must fall in an identifiable field of education. In addition, the included papers must describe how at least one of the selected technologies was implemented. We excluded book chapters, papers written in languages other than English and papers with restricted access.

After applying these criteria, backward and forward snowballing techniques were used to increment the number of papers reviewed.

Table 1 shows our identified trends in application of technology and the number of papers included in this review.

Table 1: Trends in application of technology.

Keyword	Papers
Virtual reality	21
Mobile devices	8
Augmented reality	6
Game engine	8
Building Information Modelling	4

It should be noted that some papers included more than one of these technologies, which means that they could be included more than once.

We used the UNESCO's International Standard Classification of Education (ISCE) (2011) to identify the targeted field of education of the games described in the included papers. The bellow paragraph shows the number of papers found for each of the nine broad groups of the ISCE written in italics along with the number of papers for the specific field of education in brackets.

General programmes: 4 (basic programmes: 2, literacy and numeracy: 2); *Education: 0*; *Humanities and arts: 5* (arts: 2, humanities: 3); *Social sciences, business and law: 2* (business and administration: 2); *Sciences: 5* (life sciences: 2, physical sciences: 2, mathematics and statistics: 1); *Engineering, manufacturing and construction: 7* (engineering and engineering trades: 1, architecture and building: 6); *Agriculture: 0*; *Health and welfare: 4* (health: 4); *Services: 6* (personal services: 1, environmental protection: 1, security services: 4); *Not known or unspecified: 0.*

3.2. Game Engines

At the centre of almost every modern game, be it a serious game or a game for entertainment, lies a game engine of some sort, providing the complex technology base that the game is built upon (Anderson, et al., 2013).

Game engines are commonly implemented as an integrated collection of modules, with differing functionalities. Analysis of a range of current game engines suggests the following modules are common: graphics module, responsible for the generation of the 2D/3D graphics; physics module, which ensures that objects behave according to physical laws; collision detection module, used to ensure that certain actions occur when two objects collide; input/output module, which provides tools that allow the user to communicate and interact with the game; sound module; artificial intelligence module, often used to create non playing characters that interact intelligently with the player; and network module, responsible for the multiplayer implementation of the game (Petridis, et al., 2010).

Several commercial off-the-shelf (COTS) game engines have been used by serious game developers in an effort to deliver their products faster, cheaper, and taking advantage of the available resources that game engines have regardless of their programming experience. However, many developers have found that their projects require different features than those available in the COTS game engines, thus, they end up designing their own.

Of the 21 papers included in this review which describe serious games developed using game engines, 12 selected Unity (May, et al., 2012; Ayer, et al., 2014; Da Silva, et al., 2014; Dib & Adamo-Villani, 2014; García Hernández, et al., 2014; Tobar-Muñoz, et al., 2014; Boada, et al., 2015; Escudeiro, et al., 2015; Wu & Kaushik, 2015; Bhagat, et al., 2016; Monteiro de Lima, et al., 2016; Hu, et al., 2016). Amongst the reasons for choosing Unity over other game engines, we found that functionality, multiplatform deployment, availability at no cost and capability of interfacing with major 3D tools and file formats were the most relevant.

Other COTS game engines used in literature were Soruce (Backlund, et al., 2007), Unreal (Gatzidis, et al., 2009), Delta3d (Koepnick, et al., 2009), XNA Studio (Birchall & Gatzidis, 2011), Torque 3D (Lin, et al., 2011) and Sprite (Jones, et al., 2016). Tool support, easy to use interface, specific built-in features, character animation, compatibility with model formats, low development cost and specific platform deployment were amongst the characteristics that game developers were after when choosing these game engines.

We found 3 papers describing a game developed using a specially designed game engine. The Termite engine (Shabalina, et al., 2010) is an engine for mobile devices that includes a renderer that displays 2D graphics and animations, a user interface, a resource and an audio manager; the BIM-Game engine (Rüppel & Schatz, 2011) is comparable to a usual game engine with the ability to process BIM data; the engine used by Wei & Hiung (2012), which was not named, is an engine for mobile devices and includes multi-touch recognition, image display, animation rendering, string display, sound, collision detection and scrolling.

3.3. Augmented Reality

The term augmented reality (AR) refers to any case in which an otherwise real environment is enhanced by means of virtual objects (Milgram & Kishino, 1994). Contrary to virtual reality, AR allows the user to see the real world, thus, supplementing reality, rather than completely replacing it (Azuma, 1997). According to Azuma (1997), AR is technology that has three key requirements: it combines real and virtual content, it is interactive in real time, and it is registered in 3D.

Since the late '90s, AR technologies have been used in games (Jebara, et al., 1997; Ohshima, et al., 1998; Ohshima, et al., 1999) and education (Billinghurst, 2002; Shelton, 2002). In recent times, the use of AR has increased in both fields.

In Table 2, a list of papers describing serious games in which AR technologies are applied can be found:

Table 2: Augmented reality in serious games.

Reference	Game name	Description of AR technology usage
Berry, et al. (2006)	Music Table	Players place specially marked objects on a tabletop, an overhead camera feeds video to software based on ARToolKit, which searches the camera images for the special marks and places a computer generated, animated 3D model at a corresponding position mixing it with the original video image.
Jung & Lee (2008)	Hangeul Learning System	Using a web camera to capture markers placed by the users, the system displays a corresponding text, image or 3D object using the pattern matching part of ARToolKit.
Irawati, et al. (2008)	Domino Effect Simulation	The user wears a head mounted display with a camera attached. The users sees a real Lego base and a virtual domino arrangement aligned using markers on the real base. The user interacts with the dominoes by pushing a paddle with an AR fiducial marker attached to track its position and orientation.
Lee & Lee (2008)	Ria's Math Play	Using dice, player pieces, and a board with multiple markers, the system displays virtual images using a camera and the pattern matching part of ARToolKit.
Campos & Pessanha (2011)	*No game name given*	Players place game pieces with AR markers in a wooden board with a fixed camera, which processes the real time video information and displays 3D models of animals.
Boletsis & McCallum (2013)	The Table Mystery	Players use a tablet to scan a periodic table, in which the chemical elements are used as AR markers, and see 3D clues.
Ayer, et al. (2014; 2016)	ecoCampus	Users hold up a mobile computing device to view a fiducial marker hung on an existing wall, the system displays a virtual full-scale mock-up of a wall designed by them previously.
Tobar-Muñoz, et al. (2014)	Gremlings in my mirror	The interaction with the game is through defined markers. An AR interaction framework was built over NyARToolKit and Unity for implementation of the proposed interaction types.

3.4. Virtual Reality

Conventionally, a Virtual Reality (VR) environment is one in which the participant-observer is totally immersed in, and able to interact with, a completely synthetic world, which may mimic the properties of some real-world environments, existing or fictional, or exceed the bounds of physical reality by creating a world in which the physical laws ordinarily governing space, time, mechanics, material properties, etc. no longer hold (Milgram & Kishino, 1994).

The first application of VR was flight simulation conducted by NASA. Since then, VR has been applied to simulator training in several fields, games for the entertainment industry, architectural walk troughs, medical imaging, modelling of historical sites and education, amongst others (Bell & Fogler, 1995).

In the following table, a list of papers describing serious games in which VR technologies are applied can be found:

Table 3: Virtual reality in serious games.

Reference	Game name	Description of VR technology usage
Cai, et al. (2006)	Bio-X games	Protein backbone structures were modelled and mapped into playgrounds. Characters were designed and animated using physical modelling techniques, a motion capturing system and the Maya software. For 3D immersive visualization, VR stereographic viewing was applied. A cyberglove, a 3D WAN and a mouse were used to interact with the VR environment.
Irawati, et al. (2008)	Domino Effect Simulation	The user can see the virtual world, consisting of a set of rigid objects arranged with a specific configuration so that the movement of one object can trigger the movement of the object nearby, through a desktop, an immersive display (CAVE-like) environment, and a video-see through Head Mounted Display. To interact with the system, the user can use a haptic device which provides a haptic force feedback
Qin, et al. (2010)	Stopping the Fountains	Players use a haptic input device to manipulate surgical tools in a 3D virtual environment. The authors simulated the feeling of touch for contacts between virtual instruments and tissues using the Haptic Library API in the OpenHaptics toolkit.
Jacobson (2011)	Gates of Horus	Players navigate a virtual environment in an immersive display, consisting of an all-digital partial-dome display, by using a device with an internal gyroscope that allows the user to rotate view in the game by rotating the device.
Bhagat, et al. (2016)	Real-world firing range	Users interact with a VR firing range, displayed on a screen, by using a simulation T91 riffle gun with a recoil effect device and an invisible laser infrared emitter source on the muzzle, which emits a spot on the screen that is detected through a web cam and transformed into a simulated bullet impact point.
Monteiro de Lima, et al. (2016)	DocTraining	Users interact with a virtual environment using Google Cardboard immersion glasses and a smartphone with gyroscope, which allows head tracking, meaning that users must move their heads to see different images in the virtual environment.

3.5. Mobile Devices

Recent developments in communications and wireless technologies have resulted in mobile devices becoming widely available, more convenient, and less expensive (Wu, et al., 2012). Mobile devices are used daily for communication, entertainment and learning, and the development and usage of its software applications has been on the rise for the last decade.

In the following table, a list of papers describing serious games developed for mobile devices can be found:

Table 4: Mobile devices in serious games.

Reference	Game name	Description of mobile device usage
Shabalina, et al. (2010)	The Termite Planet	The game was designed using a special game engine for mobile devices. It is meant to be played in mobile phones.
Wei & Hiung (2012)	Hamster Circuit	Two versions of this game were developed, one for iPad and one for iPhone, to be played anytime and anywhere.
Harriehausen-Mühlbauer (2012)	Quiz Lounge	Originally developed for Blackberry devices, but ported into other platforms, the game is intended to be played anywhere, anytime.
Boletsis & McCallum (2013)	The Table Mystery	Players use a tablet to scan a periodic table, in which the chemical elements are used as AR markers, and see 3D clues. The game must be played in a determined place, where the periodic table with the markers is.
Ayer, et al. (2014; 2016)	ecoCampus	Users hold up a mobile device to view a fiducial marker hung on a wall, the system displays a virtual full-scale mock-up of a wall designed by them previously. The game must be played in a determined place, where the wall with the fiducial marker is.
Tobar-Muñoz, et al. (2014)	Gremlings in my mirror	This game is designed to be played as an AR game which is displayed in a mobile device pointing towards a marker-referenced map.
Monteiro de Lima, et al. (2016)	DocTraining	This game can be played in smartphones or tablets anywhere. In addition, a smartphone with a gyroscope can be used alongside with Google Cardboard immersion glasses to play in a VR environment.
Jones, et al. (2016)	Taffy Town	This game is meant to run on the iPad and iPad Mini mobile devices. It was developed using Apple's XCode IDE, iOS Software Development Kit, and 2D game engine and framework Sprite Kit.

3.6. Building Information Modelling

The presentation of building information as game content enjoys an increasing interest from various fields throughout the civil-engineering sector. The application of serious games or virtual reality visualisations for clients are just two examples (Wagner & Rüppel, 2016).

Building Information Modelling (BIM) provides a rich source of building data and is an ideal basis for constructing realistic virtual environments. However, a significant amount of work is involved in transforming these models into something that is both human navigable and human interactive within the virtual environment (Bille, et al., 2014).

Table 5 shows a list of papers describing serious games developed using BIM technologies:

Table 5: Building Information Modelling in serious games.

Reference	Game name	Description of BIM usage
Rüppel & Schatz (2011)	Serious Human Rescue Game	BIM models serve as a basis for the virtual world in which players guide their avatars. They used the BIM-game engine, which supports IFC and uses Autodesk Revit API to process BIM data.
Yan, et al. (2011)	BIM-Game	It allows the access of BIM information in real time and feed the data to game play. Designers play games with their BIM models, integrating

		characters, graphics, audio, physics, artificial intelligence and game strategies to evaluate the design.
Dib & Adamo-Villani (2014)	Sustainability Challenge	The platform for the game is based on Autodesk Revit, Maya and the Unity game engine
Wu & Kaushik (2015)	*No game name given*	BIM models authored in Autodesk Revit and exported as FBX files are processed in Autodesk 3ds Max and imported new assets to the Unity game engine.

4. Conclusions

In this paper, we presented a literature review on serious games for education with focus on computer and gaming technology application.

Although serious games for construction management education are the main interest of the authors of this paper, we reviewed serious games for education in a broader sense in order to identify the technologies that are being used by researchers and developers in the serious games domain.

We identified game engines, augmented reality, virtual reality, mobile devices and building information modelling as the trending technologies used by researchers and developers in the field. Often, these technologies are applied together to take advantage of the value that each one brings to the serious game.

We reviewed papers describing serious games for almost all fields of education, according to UNESCO's International Standard Classification of Education (2011). This suggests that there are stakeholders from many backgrounds and with very different objectives interested in developing, researching, playing and teaching with serious games.

However, we found that there are some common characteristics that stakeholders are looking for when applying the identified technologies into their serious games, which are immersion, ubiquity, high quality graphics, interoperability and quick game content development.

Game engines provide a way to achieve these characteristics, as many of them offer multiplatform deployment, which may result in ubiquitous games that can be played in mobile devices at any time and place. AR and VR technologies are often compatible with game engines, which may help achieving immersion. Compatibility between game engines and BIM models would help developing game content faster and brings the possibility of using real world-based game scenarios able to take advantage of all the information contained in them.

References

Abt, C. C., 1966. Games for learning. Occasional Paper No. 7. *Cambridge Mass.: Educational Services, Incorporated.*

Al-Jibouri, S. H. & Mawdesley, M. J., 2001. Design and experience with a computer game for teaching construction project planning and control. *Engineering, Construction and Architectural Management,* 8(5-6), pp. 418-427.

Anderson, E. F. et al., 2013. Choosing the infrastructure for entertainment and serious games - A whiteroom benchmarck for game engine selection. *5th International Conference on Games and Virtual Worlds for Serious Applications (VS-GAMES)*, 11-13 September, pp. 1-8.

Ayer, S. K., Messner, J. I. & Anumba, C. J., 2014. Development of ecoCampus: A prototype system for sustainable building design education. *Journal of Information Technology in Construction,* Volume 19, pp. 520-533.

Ayer, S. K., Messner, J. I. & Anumba, C. J., 2016. Augmented reality gaming in sustainable design education. *Journal of Architectural Engineering,* 22(1), p. 04015012.

Azuma, R. T., 1997. A survey of augmented reality. *Presence: Teleoperators and virtual environments,* 6(4), pp. 355-385.

Bäck, A., 2008. The paper world of Bernard Suits. *Journal of the Philosophy of Sport,* 35(2), pp. 156-174.

Backlund, P. et al., 2007. Sidh - A game based firefighter training simulation. *11th International Conference Information Visualization IV'07*, pp. 899-907.

Bateman, C., 2014. Meet Bertie the Brain, the world's first arcade game, built in Toronto. *Retrieved December 2016, from http://spacing.ca/toronto/2014/08/13/meet-bertie-brain-worlds-first-arcade-game-built-toronto/.*

Becker, K., 2010. Distinctions between games and learning: A review of current literature. *Gaming and Cognition: Theories and Perspectives from Learning Sciences,* pp. 22-51.

Bell, J. T. & Fogler, H. S., 1995. Low-cost virtual reality and its application to chemical engineering-part two. *Computing and Systems Technology Division Communications,* 18(2), pp. 12-28.

Berne, E., 1964. *Games People Play - The Basic Hand Book of Transactional Analysis.* New York: Ballantine Books.

Berry, R. et al., 2006. Tunes on the table. *Multimedia Systems,* 11(3), pp. 280-289.

Bhagat, K. K., Liou, W.-K. & Chang, C.-Y., 2016. A cost-effective interactive 3D visrtual reality system applied to military live firing fighting. *Virtual Reality,* 20(2), pp. 127-140.

Bille, R., Smith, S. P., Maund, K. & Brewer, G., 2014. Extending building information models into game engines. *Proceedings of the 2014 Conference on Interactive Entertainment*, December, pp. 1-8.

Billinghurst, M., 2002. Augmented reality in education. *New horizons for learning ,* Volume 12.

Birchall, J. & Gatzidis, C., 2011. Elemental: An insight into the development and evaluation of a secondary education chemistry game using XNA. *Third International Conference on Games and Virtual Worlds for Serious Applications,* pp. 32-39.

Boada, I. et al., 2015. Using a serious game to complement CPR instruction in a nurse faculty. *Computer Methods and Programs in Biomedicine,* 122(2), pp. 282-291.

Boletsis, C. & McCallum, S., 2013. The Table Mystery: An augmented reality collaborative game for chemistry education. *International Conference on Serious Games Development and Applications,* pp. 86-95.

Botte, B., Matera, C. & Sponsiello, M., 2009. Serious Games between simulation and game. A proposal of taxonomy. *Journal of e-Learning and Knowledge Society,* 5(2), pp. 11-21.

Boughzala, I., Bououd, I. & Michel, H., 2013. Characterization and evaluation of serious games: A perspective of their use in higher education. *46th Hawaii International Conference on System Sciences (HICSS)*, January, pp. 844-852.

Cai, Y. et al., 2006. Bio-edutainment: Learning life science through X gaming. *Computers & Graphics,* 30(1), pp. 3-9.

Campos, P. & Pessanha, S., 2011. Designing augmented reality tangible interfaces for kindergarten children. *Virtual and Mixed Reality New Trends,* pp. 12-19.

Crookall, D., 2010. Serious games, debriefing, and simulation/gaming as a discipline. *Simulation & Gaming,* 41(6), pp. 898-920.

Da Silva, C. C., Da silva Filho, A. G., Monteiro, J. S. & Dos Sandos, W. P., 2014. Developing 3D human-computer interfaces and serious games for health education in the brazilian countryside using participatory design and popular education. *International Conference on Systems, Man, and Cybernetics,* pp. 2971-2976.

De Lope, R. P. & Medina-Medina, N., 2016. Using UML to model educational games. *8th International Conference on Games and Virtual Worlds for Serious Applications (VS-Games)*, October, pp. 1-4.

Dib, H. & Adamo-Villani, N., 2014. Serious sustainability challenge game to promote teaching and learning of building sustainability. *Journal of Computing in Civil Engineering,* 28(5), p. A4014007.

Djaouti, D., Alvarez, J. & Jessel, J. P., 2011. Classifying serious games: The G/P/S model. In: P. Felicia, ed. *Handbook of research on improving learning and motivation through educational games: Multidisciplinary approaches.* Hershey PA: IGI Global, pp. 118-136.

Djaouti, D., Alvarez, J., Jessel, J. P. & Rampnoux, O., 2011. Origins of serious games. In: *Serious Games and Edutainment Applications.* London: Springer, pp. 25-43.

Duke, R. D., 1974. *Gaming: The future's language.* 1st ed. New York: Sage Publications, Inc..

Escudeiro, P. et al., 2015. Real time bidirectional translator of Portuguese sign language. *WEBIST,* pp. 203-213.

García Hernández, R. J. et al., 2014. E-cecilia: Implementation of a music game. *CoSECivi,* pp. 66-77.

Gatzidis, C. et al., 2009. Towards the development of an interactive 3D coach training serious game. *Conference in Games and Virtual Worlds for Serious Applications,* pp. 186-189.

Harriehausen-Mühlbauer, B., 2012. Quiz lounge - Game-based learning on mobile devices. *Systemics, Cybernetics and Informatics,* 11(6), pp. 82-87.

Huizinga, J., 1949. *Homo Ludens: A study in the play-element in culture.* London: Routledge & Kegan Paul.

Hu, X., Su, R. & He, L., 2016. The design and implementation of the 3D educational game based on VR headsets. *International Symposium on Educatioanl Technology,* pp. 53-56.

Irawati, S., Hong, S., Kim, J. & Ko, H., 2008. 3D edutainment environment: Learning physics through VR/AR experiences. *Proceedings of the 2008 International Conference on Advances in Computer Entertainment Technology,* pp. 21-24.

Jacobson, J., 2011. Digital dome versus desktop display in an educational game: Gates of Horus. *International Journal of Gaming and Computer-Mediated Simulations,* 3(1), pp. 13-32.

Jebara, T. et al., 1997. Stochasticks: Augmenting the billiards experience with probabilistic vision and weareable computers. *First International Symposium on Wereable Computers,* pp. 138-145.

Jones, J. R., Balci, O. & Norton, A., 2016. A cloud software system for cisualization of game-based learning data collected on mobile devices. *Proceedings of the 2015 Winter Simulation Conference,* pp. 1080-1090.

Jung, J. W. & Lee, J. W., 2008. Hangeul learning system. *International Conference on Technologies for E-Learning and Digital Entertainment,* pp. 126-134.

Kirriemuir, J. & Mcfarlane, A., 2004. Literature review in games and learning. *A NESTA Futurelab Research report - report 8.*

Koepnick, S., Norpchen, D., Sherman, W. R. & Coming, D. S., 2009. Immersive traning for two-person radiological surveys. *2009 IEEE Virtual Reality Conference*, pp. 171-174.

Korman, T. & Johnston, H., 2010. Enhancing construction management education though the use of a virtual construction company simulation system. *The 2nd International Symposium on Engineering Education and Educational Technologies: EEET.*

Laamarti, F., Eid, M. & El Saddik, A., 2014. An overview of serious games. *International Journal of Computer Games Technology,* p. 15.

Lee, H. S. & Lee, J. W., 2008. Mathematical education game based on augmented reality. *International Conference on Technologies for E-Learning and Digital Entertainment,* pp. 442-450.

Lin, K. Y., Son, J. W. & Rojas, E. M., 2011. A pilot study of a 3D game environment for construction safety education. *Journal of Information Technology in Construction,* 16(5), pp. 69-83.

Mayer, I., Warmelink, H. & Zhou, Q., 2016. A frame-reflective discourse analysis of serious games. *British Journal of Educational Technology,* 2(342-357), p. 47.

May, M., Holzer, F. & Otto, F., 2012. eLearning in facility management by serious games. *International Conference on e-Learning,* pp. 294-304.

Milgram, P. & Kishino, F., 1994. A taxonomy of mixed reality visual displays. *IEICE TRANSACTIONS on Information and Systems,* 77(12), pp. 1321-1329.

Mohamed, Y. & Ali, M., 2013. Development of a distributed construction project management game with cots in the loop. *Proceedings of the 2013 Winter Simulation Conference,* pp. 3145-3156.

Monteiro de Lima, R. et al., 2016. A 3D serious game for medical students training in clinical cases. *International Conference on Serious Games Applications for Health (SeGAH),* pp. 1-9.

Nassar, K., 2003. Construction contracts in a competitive market: C³M, a simulation game. *Engineering, Construction and Architectural Management,* 10(3), pp. 172-178.

Ohshima, T., Satoh, K., Yamamoto, H. & Tamura, H., 1998. Ar2 hockey: A case study of collaborative augmented reality. *VRAIS'98: Proceedings of the Virtual Reality Annual International Symposium, IEEE Computer Society, Washington, DC, USA s. 268.*

Ohshima, T., Satoh, K., Yamamoto, H. & Tamura, H., 1999. RV-Border Guards: A multi-player mixed reality entertainment. *Trans. Virtual Reality Soc. Japan,* 4(4), pp. 699-705.

Petridis, P., Dunwell, I., De Freitas, S. & Panzoli, D., 2010. An engine selection methodology for high fidelity serious games. *2010 Second International Conference on Games and Virtual Worlds for Serious Applications*, March, pp. 27-34.

Qin, J., Chui, Y. P. & Pang, W. M., 2010. Learning blood management in orthopedic surgery through gameplay. *IEEE Computer Graphics and Applications,* 30(2), pp. 45-57.

Rapoport, A., 1960. *Fights, Games, and Debates.* Ann Arbor: University of Michigan Press.

Rowe, M. W., 1992. The definition of game. *Philosophy,* 67(262), pp. 467-479.

Rüppel, U. & Schatz, K., 2011. Designing a BIM-based serious game for fire safety evacuation simulations. *Advanced Engineering Informatics,* 25(4), pp. 600-611.

Sawyer, B., 2008. Serious games taxonomy. *Retrieved December 2016, from https://thedigitalentertainmentalliance.files.wordpress.com/2011/08/serious-games-taxonomy.pdf.*

Shabalina, O. et al., 2010. Mobile learning games for primary education. *Proceedings of the 4th European Conference on Games-Based Learning: ECGBL2010,* pp. 350-359.

Shannon, C. E., 1950. Programming a computer for playing chess. *Philosophical Magazine,* Volume 41, pp. 256-275.

Shelton, B. E., 2002. Augmented reality in education. *New horizons for learning* , 9(1).

Suits, B., 1967. What is a game?. *Philosophy of Science,* 34(2), pp. 148-156.

Suits, B. H., 1978. *The Grasshopper: Games, Life and Utopia.* Toronto: University of Toronto Press.

Susi, T., Johannesson, M. & Backlund, P., 2007. *Serious games - An overview,* Technical Report HS-IKI-TR-07-001: University of Skövde, Sweden.

Tobar-Muñoz, H., Fabregat, R. & Baldiris, S., 2014. Using a videogame with augmented reality for an inclusive logical skills learning session. *International Symposium on Computers and Education (SIIE),* pp. 189-194.

UNESCO Institute for Statistics, 2011. *International Standard Classification of Education ISCE 2011.* [Online] Available at: http://www.uis.unesco.org/Education/Documents/isced-2011-en.pdf [Accessed 9 February 2017].

Wagner, A. & Rüppel, U., 2016. Generation of serious games environments from BIM for a virtual reality crisis-management system. *Proceedings of the 11th European Conference on Product and Process Modelling*, 07-09 September.

Wei, C. M. & Hiung, L. H., 2012. Mobile educational game: Hamster Circuit. *4th International Conference on Intelligent and Advanced Systems,* pp. 811-813.

Wittgenstein, L., 1958. *Philosophical Investigations.* 3rd ed. Oxford: Basil Blackwell Ltd.

Wu, W. H. et al., 2012. Review of trends from mobile learning studies: A meta-analysis.. *Computers & Education,* 59(2), pp. 817-827.

Wu, W. & Kaushik, I., 2015. A BIM-based educational gaming prototype for undergraduate research and education in design for sustainable aging. *Proceedings of the 2015 Winter Simulation Conference*, December, pp. 1091-1102.

Yan, W., Culp, C. & Graf, R., 2011. Integrating BIM and gaming for real-time interactive architectural visualization. *Automation in Construction,* 20(4), pp. 446-458.

Towards an adaptive framework for customized civil engineering platforms

Michael Polter, Raimar Scherer
Technische Universität Dresden, Germany
Michael.Polter@tu-dresden.de

Abstract. Monolithic software tools still dominate the everyday work of civil engineers. Complex, collaborative workflows demand repeated input and data exchange operations. Furthermore, the accuracy of computation results often is still restricted by the limitation of desktop PCs. We introduce the BIMgrid, a work in progress to develop an innovative, adaptive framework for the implementation of customized civil engineering applications. It is a tool for software developers, which allows the flexible extension of existing applications and platforms with various functionality and their customization to the specific needs of engineering companies. We illustrate the architecture of the BIMgrid, the interface concepts for the integration of external tools and the utilization of their functionality by third party applications. We also present our reference implementation, which not only demonstrates the utilization of the framework but also can be used as a blueprint for the creation of a customized tool and hardware adaptation platform.

1. Introduction

Nowadays, engineers are faced with a large number of different computation and collaboration tools as well as database implementations, which have to be utilized in combination to solve complex, cross-domain tasks. Often this involves much effort in data management and manual input, especially when collaboration with external partners results in multiple iteration loops. Although some integration solutions for the connection of tools and workflow automation emerge, in general they miss a certain flexibility regarding to the established practice in companies. Usually users get tied to the products of a vendor and if they don't provide a specific feature or a single tool exceeds the capabilities of the local machine, a manual switch between applications is again inevitable. With the upcoming hype of cloud computing, big vendors increasingly offer integrated solutions that completely outsource the engineer's workstation to the cloud. However, these pay-per-use products don't consider the investments of companies in hard- and software which were made so far and tend to cause running costs that are difficult to control. In addition, they come along with problems in data security and privacy. In 2010 over 90 % of SMEs (small and medium-sized enterprises) in construction industry did not have a powerful IT infrastructure (Kumar and Cheng, 2010). Even though this percentage may have been decreased, the problem of optimal resource usage is still present. Studies show that in SMEs available resources often are not used to their capacity with idle times up to 95 % (Klitz, 2004). Existing middleware for the connection of computers to a private grid are generally designed for big data centers. They are mostly limited to UNIX-based networks, rarely offer a graphical user interface and hence are inappropriate for a direct application in engineering offices.

The development of software solutions from the scratch, which address all the aforementioned problems, usually exceeds the financial capabilities of SMEs. In this paper, we introduce the BIMgrid, a framework for the customized connection of applications, integrated data management as well as combined utilization of private grid and public cloud computing power. We also present our reference implementation, called the BIMgrid Core, which provides a stub for software developers to implement a platform or enhance existing applications, customized to the specific needs and practices of a civil engineering company. Our concept provides interfaces for the transparent integration of tools and technologies from different functional domains like computation, data management, workflow scheduling and hardware infrastructure. The overall aim is to support engineers in the automation of complex workflows, the efficient management of potential big amounts of data and the provision of a shared platform to ease the data exchange between project partners while preserving the investments of a company.

This paper is structured as follows. In the subsequent section we briefly discuss the state of the art in integration approaches as well as other related research and compare them with our work. In section 3 we present our approach. We first propose the idea and architecture of the BIMgrid framework in section 3.1 and then take a deeper look into our reference implementation to clarify the concept and illustrate its intended application by software developers in section 3.2. In the end, section 4 concludes the paper and gives an outlook on future work.

2. Related Work

The SaaS (software as a service) principle describes the access to software with web services and hence represents the basis for a centralized use of distributed high capacity hardware at low cost (Chuang, Lee and Wu, 2011). In this context, Cheng et al. propose a SaaS-based framework for the connection of civil engineering applications with the web service technology (Cheng et al., 2010). Though we also follow this principle, our concept additionally considers workflow management and the flexible selection of the target hardware, instead of linking-up applications directly.

The ONELAB (Open Numerical Engineering LABoratory) also aims on the integration of different tools like mesh generators and numerical solvers through the provision of an open source interface toolkit (Geuzaine et al., 2013). It allows the execution of workflows involving multiple tools under a uniform user interface as well as the integration of distributed hardware through TCP/IP socket communication. But in contrast to our approach, the ONELAB does neither provide an intelligent workflow orchestration nor integrated data management capabilities.

Commercial software vendors also increasingly offer solutions to seamlessly connect applications in "customized platforms", including data management and workflow processing capabilities. The ANSYS workbench[1] allows the integration of solvers and CAD (computer aided design) software and the management of the corresponding models. Change propagation, model import from popular CAD vendors and script-based workflow automation are supported. Though ANSYS offers a cloud migrated version of some tools, the original workbench is tied to a single workstation, provides no on-demand access to distributed resources and hence is limited to sequential workflow processing. The integration of grid and on demand extension with cloud resources make the BIMgrid more flexible and also allow the parallel execution of tasks, which is a huge advantage especially for parametric studies.

The mOSAIC approach follows the principle to build customized applications for different computation infrastructure (Cretella, Di Martino and Stankovski, 2012). Semantic OWL (Web Ontology Language)-formalized application descriptions are used to pick components from a pool and to integrate them in the final application. The aim is also to select suitable computation resources for a given task. Unlike our approach, for each computation infrastructure mOSAIC generates a new static application instance which has to be deployed while the BIMgrid aims on dynamic hardware selection for each task.

[1] http://www.cadfem.de/produkte/ansys/ansys-workbench.html

Alonso et al. focus on the combined utilization of local hardware for parallel execution of 3D dynamic analyses of large dimension buildings (Alonso, Hernández and Moltò, 2008). Their proposed application is based on the GMarte software abstraction layer, which they use to couple a parallel simulator with a local grid infrastructure. Just like the BIMgrid, the application includes capabilities of the hardware nodes in the scheduling process. However, dependencies between jobs are not considered, which may result in communication overhead and ineffective hardware use in case of complex workflows with multiple post processing steps. Also the application is limited to the domain of structural 3D analysis.

To date, no integrated solution is known to the authors that covers and combines all functional areas of the BIMgrid.

3. The BIMgrid

In this section we give an overview about the BIMgrid framework and our prototype implementation. The framework conception is technology independent and can be implemented in an arbitrary programming language. In the following, we refer to the role of the "developer" as the person, who instantiates the BIMgrid framework and adapts it to the envisaged area of application. In section 2.2 we describe our exemplary BIMgrid instantiation prototype that we refer to as the BIMgrid Core. It demonstrates the flexibility of the concept and at the same time represents a core implementation that can be directly used and extended by developers. Both, the framework and the prototype, are subject of continuous development and hence this paper can be seen as a snapshot of our research.

3.1 BIMgrid Framework

The BIMgrid framework represents a reference concept for the implementation of an integrated software platform, which is tailored to established working processes as well as to technical conditions of a company, without the need to develop an new software product from the scratch. It can also be recognized as a blueprint for an adapter, which encapsulates miscellaneous technologies (like solvers, databases, infrastructure, workflow specifications) and provides them to external applications through a uniform interface. Therefore the BIMgrid is designed as a layered, component-based architecture with three types of layers (Fig. 1). The *Core Layer* contains fixed, domain independent components for the orchestration of data and control flows between all other framework components and the internal management logic. The two *External Layers* include 3rd party software, which extends the platform with various desired functionality. They, for example, contain solver kernels for performing calculations, database implementations but also applications that themselves use the BIMgrid features. *Interface Layers*, we also refer to them as adapter layers, contain all kinds of elements that link the external and the core components together. The Interface Layers generally have to be implemented by the developer, unless they cannot be integrated through existing libraries or software solutions. The elements of the framework and their tasks in platform implementations are described in the following.

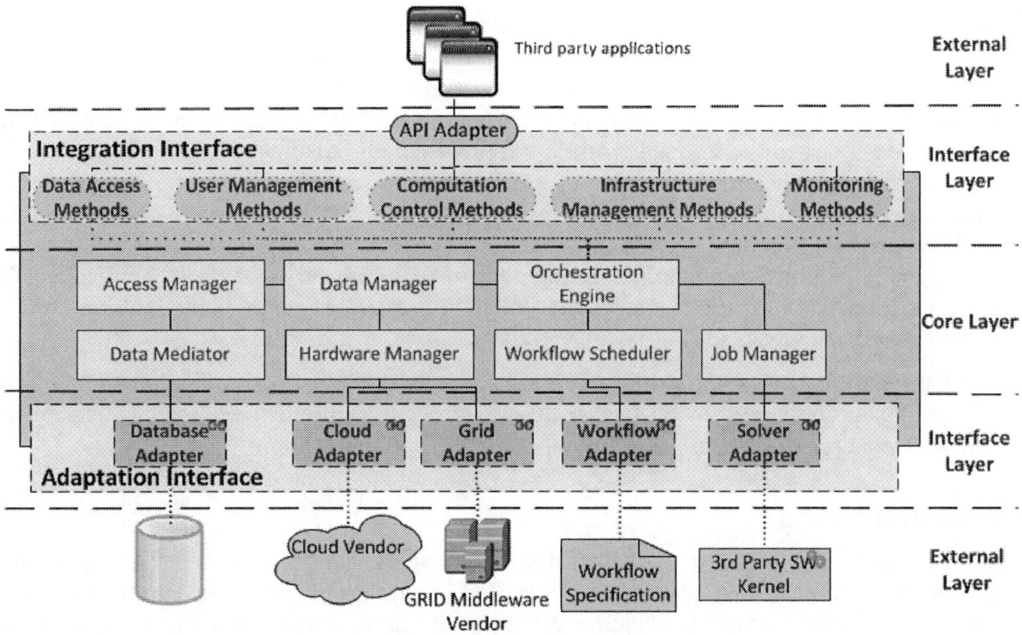

Figure 1: BIMgrid framework

The *Core Layer* is arranged between the adapter layers and represents the "glue code" between functional components and applications, which use them through the BIMgrid. The *Orchestration Engine* orchestrates all control and data flows between the components. It is the central core component and itself consists of several sub components. The Orchestration Engine provides a set of predefined interfaces (further details in section 2.2) which are mapped to external applications in the integration interface, to provide the capabilities of the BIMgrid to third party software. The *Hardware Manager* provides the implemented BIMgrid platform with access to the hardware infrastructure (grid nodes, cloud images). The *Data Manager* represents a uniform interface for the other core components to access persisted data in the constructs of the implementation programming language. Further, it manages information on where specific data (e.g. temporary intermediate results of a specific computation job) is located within the database or throughout the hardware, which is connected to the platform. Therefore it uses methods of the Hardware Manager. The *Data Mediator* encapsulates the database access and transforms data between vendor specific representations and data constructs of the programming language, used for the implementation of the BIMgrid platform. If multiple data sources are integrated, the Data Mediator also connects them through the orchestration of complex requests of the Data. The *Access Manager* controls the data access according to the rights management implementation chosen by the developer. The *Job Manager* creates and manages abstract computation job descriptions. They, for example, contain input parameters and information about the solver that executes the job. Submitted workflows have to be interpreted and the jobs mapped spatially and temporally to computation nodes, according to their relations and potential further preferences of the user. This task is realized by the *Workflow Scheduler*.

The *Adaptation Interface* represents one of the two *Interface Layers* and contains the adapters, which generally have to be implemented by the developer to integrate the capabilities of external components into a BIMgrid implementation. The *Database Adapter* is responsible for the translation of the Data Manager's and Data Mediator's requests to the syntax of the database. The *Cloud Adapter* handles the mapping between the vendor specific API (application programming interface) and the programming language used for the BIMgrid implementation. The same does the *Grid Adapter* for the integrated grid middleware. The *Workflow Adapter* provides a concept mapping for the conversions of the used workflow language constructs to the internal workflow representation. Abstract job descriptions of the Job Manager are translated into solver specific input formats by the *Solver Adapter*. The second *Interface Layer* contains the *Integration Interface* that, contrary to the Adaptation Interface, provides functions for the integration of the BIMgrid into third party applications, from complex platforms to simple user interfaces. According to the area of application for which the framework is implemented, the integration interface implementation can contain different functional areas (see Fig. 1).

Since the *External Layers* comprise third party software that must not be implemented by the developer, they don't need to be further described here. In the next section, we clarify the framework concept with examples from our reference implementation.

3.2 BIMgrid Core

Our example implementation of the BIMgrid framework can also be seen as a reference implementation that can be adapted and extended by the developer according to his needs. Depending on which area of application is envisaged, the functional range of the framework implementation can differ significantly. In this section we describe our reference implementation that is customized to the automatization and parallelization of a huge number of computations. Therefore we focused on the use of the computation infrastructure and the management of huge amounts of data. Figure 2 shows the schematic representation of the BIMgrid Core, which is described in the following. The core components are all implemented in Java. They are application independent and can be used directly by developers as starting point for their implementation. Just like the BIMgrid framework, the BIMgrid Core is also a work in progress and not all conceptual parts are implemented yet.

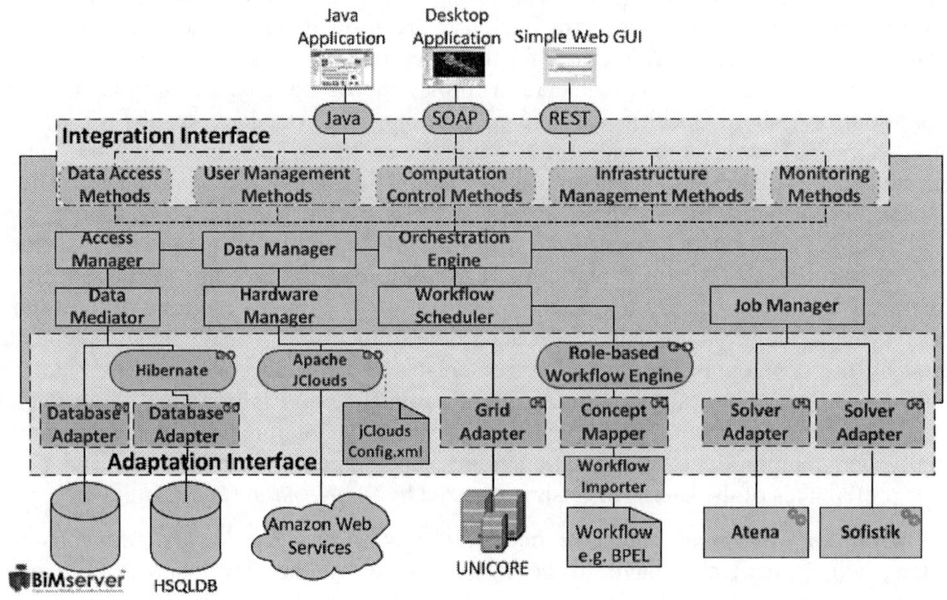

Figure 2: BIMgrid Core

Integration Interface

Different applications are compatible with different interface technologies. Since the BIMgrid Core is implemented in Java, it can be directly integrated into external Java applications by using its Java methods. This way, no adaptation to a specific message format is needed and hence this is the most performant variant. However, in most cases external applications won't provide an API that is compatible with the BIMgrid from the scratch. The developer has to implement an adapter to match the APIs. A widely used communication protocol is the SOAP (Simple Object Access Protocol). The BIMgrid Core provides a SOAP adapter and hence is able to communicate with corresponding desktop as well as web applications. Not every use case prescribes a complex legacy application. It is also possible to use the BIMgrid for simple applications, e.g. if only the existing hardware infrastructure shall be connected to parallelize a huge amount of jobs. In this case, the developer can create a browser-based web interface that only provides functionality for up-/download of files, starting as well as interrupting of jobs and status requests. For realizing such plain browser-based applications, a REST (Representational State Transfer) interface is a suitable solution, because it calls the methods of the BIMgrid over predefined, fixed URLs (Uniform Resource Locators). This communication protocol gets along without complex message preparation and thus is also suitable for applications on mobile devices. The enumeration of each single method of the integration interface would go beyond the scope of this paper. However, a detailed API description is available to the developer. Therefore only groups of API functions are enumerated in the following:

- Data Access: request and filter operations for upload and download of artifacts such as model files, computation results or monitoring logs.
- User Management: methods for registration, login and all functionality concerning rights management such as role definition and assignment.
- Computation Control: for starting, interrupting and aborting jobs.
- Infrastructure management: a high level abstraction from the management of the computation infrastructure, e.g. for disabling of corrupted grid nodes or the definition of additional cloud image templates (virtual machines). Since the capabilities and provided interfaces of adapted grid middlewares or cloud vendors can differ significantly, usually not all necessary functions to manage a computation infrastructure can be provided by the BIMgrid API. The range of functionality essentially depends on the implementation of the middleware adapter.
- Monitoring: allows requests of status information for running jobs as well as the computation infrastructure, e.g. available grid nodes or utilization of cloud capacity.

This flexible adapter principle allows the functional extension of complex legacy applications on servers, the automatization of workflows for desktop applications as well as the usage and monitoring of complex IT infrastructures, even from mobile devices. Currently, the prototype contains an implementation of the Java and SOAP API, which both are continuously developed with the increasing functional range of the BIMgrid core.

Adaptation Interface

Exchangeable components as well as computation infrastructure can be integrated through implementation of the corresponding adapters, which are, except in case of the cloud vendor, represented by java classes. We divided the Java Adaptation Interface further into three layers to enhance the flexibility in customization of the platform behavior: (I) Java Interface, (II) abstract adapter Java class and (III) adapter implementation Java class. On top, the interfaces provide the signatures of the methods, which are mandatory to be implemented. The abstract adapter class implements the interface and provides default implementations for some of the methods. The adapter implementation class must be implemented by the developer and inherits from the abstract adapter class. This way the developer can decide whether to use the default behavior of the adapter or to overwrite it with functionality of the adapted component. In the following, we give a brief overview about the adapter components.

The *Solver Adapter* is the most important component, because it is responsible for the integration of the computation capabilities into the BIMgrid. Since Microsoft Windows is still dominating in civil engineering companies, our solver API is tailored to this operating system, though in principle the framework isn't tied to a specific operating system. Hence, currently it is possible to integrate each software that runs on Microsoft Windows and can be controlled via command line. In the *Solver Adapter* we specify the command scheme for the command line execution, the necessary input parameters and the file structure, which is needed by the solver kernel to operate. The Hardware Manager then creates batch files for the computation jobs and distributes them on the computation infrastructure. In our prototype we integrated the Atena[2] solver for nonlinear analyses and the FEM (Finite Element Method) solver Sofistik[3].

The *Grid Adapter* encapsulates third-party grid middleware, which is used to combine local hardware infrastructure to a private grid. It contains methods for job management, data access and status requests. Further, it offers interfaces for discovering the capabilities of the grid nodes, which are used in the workflow scheduling algorithm. Since not each grid middleware provides such information, the corresponding method bodies can also be left empty and the scheduling algorithm will switch to an alternate version. In our core implementation we adapt the UNICORE middleware[4] which already provides a Java API. So the adapter implementation only forwards the methods of the UNICORE API to the corresponding methods of the Hardware Manager.

The *Database Adapter* provides abstraction interfaces for the common features of database implementations like a generic request API, data management methods and conversions into internal Java-based data structures. It is based on the Hibernate Framework[5] and hence compatible with a huge number of database implementations with only minor code changes. We provide a default adapter for the Hyper SQL Database[6].

Within the BIMgrid Core, the *Cloud Adapter* represents a special case, because it is implemented through the *Apache jClouds*[7] library. It provides a whole abstraction layer for features like authentication, resource management and job control for common cloud vendors. In most cases, the developer only has to adjust the configuration file with vendor specific properties like login credentials, SSL certificates or resource locators. If very vendor specific features are requested, jClouds also provides access to the native API of the vendor. However, in this case they have to be provided in a Java class. Exemplary we implemented a connection to Amazon Web Services (AWS).

In the current stage of development, the workflow is generated by an internal workflow scheduler component, based on basic temporal relations between jobs, which can be specified at input model upload. However, from our point of view it is crucial to give the user leeway for the definition of customized workflows. Our colleagues from the chair of software

[2] http://www.cervenka.cz/products/atena/
[3] http://www.sofistik.com/
[4] https://www.unicore.eu/
[5] http://hibernate.org/
[6] http://hsqldb.org/
[7] https://jclouds.apache.org/

technology developed an adaptive workflow engine we simply refer to as the "Role-Based Workflow Engine". Since this engine exactly matches our plugin concept, we are going to integrate it into the BIMgrid Core as a fixed component. It provides interface descriptions that developers use to implement adapters for different workflow languages. These so-called *Concept Mappers* (see fig. 2) describe the mappings, which have to be provided and hence correspond to adapter components in the framework. The engine also allows mashing up different domain concepts for the design of unique process definitions beyond the restrictions of a single workflow language and hence customized to the needs of the engineer. The Role-Based Workflow Engine provides default Concept Mappers for BPEL (Business Process Execution Language) and JPDL (jBPM Process Definition Language). For a more detailed description of the Role-based Workflow Engine we refer to Richly and Goetz (2010).

Infrastructure Integration

In contrast to the most commercially developed engineering platforms, which are nowadays usually directly hosted in the cloud, the BIMgrid framework envisages the transparent utilization of the already existing IT infrastructure of a company and hence provides a much more cost-effective business model. As described in the former section, the access interface to the local computing grid is provided by the grid middleware adapter whereas the APIs of cloud vendors are encapsulated in the jClouds library. Different infrastructure configurations are summarized in so-called *computation engines*, which are defined in the configuration file of the platform. A computation engine includes the specification of:

- Adapter class of the solver kernels (specifying the computation software provided by the engine)
- Adapter class of the middleware to be used (specifying whether the engine provides grid / cloud or combined computation resources)
- Upper limit of parallel tasks per user (to prevent the exclusive utilization of the platform capacity by a single user in collaborative scenarios)

In the next iteration of the BIMgrid Core, the task limit will be specified dynamically, based on the current utilization of the platform. In our prototype web interface the user selects the engine for his computation task from a dropdown list. For example, an engine called "private grid – Sofistik" processes the submitted jobs with the Sofistik solver in the private company grid. More resource demanding structural analyses could be performed by the "cloud – Atena" engine, where the platform instantiates pre-defined cloud images, which contain the Atena solver, and submits the jobs to the Amazon Web Services image instances.

We also envisage enhancing the prototype with a capability for the definition of scheduling policies in the configuration file to adapt the scheduling algorithm to the user's needs. For example, the definition of cost limits for cloud usage or the change between deadline-based and lowest-cost policies will provide more flexibility. Based on these policies, a completely automated engine selection is envisaged. However, manual selection of the engine will always be possible to grant the user absolute data sovereignty. Especially when processing sensible data some would like to restrict the computation to the private grid.

Data Management

The IFC (Industry Foundation Classes) standard becomes more and more important for civil engineering projects and therefore is increasingly supported by software vendors as input and output format. This allows the usage and dynamic enhancement of IFC models throughout the building life cycle. Common software products indeed increasingly allow import of IFC files, but lack of efficient file and revision management. The BIMserver (Beetz et al., 2010) provides a suitable solution for IFC based data management. Since it is executed in a web service container and provides a Java API, it can be integrated into the BIMgrid architecture without performance losses and thus transparently extend the functionality with a variety of IFC management methods, including versioning and revision management.

The BIMgrid Core integrates the BIMserver with the internal database to a federative database system and organizes IFC files together with vendor specific data formats in projects. Through the web service interfaces, the project artifacts can be directly provided to project partners, even across companies. Just like the BIMgrid Core integrates the BIMserver in its data management, a platform developer may integrate the combined data management of the BIMgrid into his platform and combine the variety of features with his own capabilities.

A role-based rights management allows a flexible regulation of data access with "Project Leader" being the only pre-defined role. The "Project Leader" is able to define further roles and to assign them to registered users. For each role, he defines access rights according to the CRUD principle (create, read, update delete) for a specific scope. Computations in the BIMgrid are organized in projects, which represent the root of the graph and have one or multiple jobs assigned. A job represents a collection of associated computations (tasks), e.g. in parametric studies. Data artifacts can either be assigned to a hierarchy level manually (e.g. IFC files to a specific project) or are automatically assigned to the organizational unit that creates them (e.g. output files of a task are automatically belong to this task). Scopes can be defined on project or job basis and always include subordinate hierarchy levels. This concept allows a granular access management without enforcing restrictions to the developer. If an integration of a BIMgrid implementation into a third party platform is envisaged, the access management can also be completely delegated to this platform.

In the next section, we draw conclusions and take a look on our next research and development steps.

4. Conclusions and Future Work

In small and medium-sized civil engineering companies, the available IT infrastructure is usually not used to its capacity. Working processes are still predominantly spread among dedicated, monolithic tools without a shared data basis while upcoming cloud solutions provide more flexibility, but come along with running costs and data security issues. The development of customized, integrated software solutions is in general unaffordable for SMEs. In this paper, we introduced the BIMgrid framework for software developers, which allows the flexible extension of existing applications and platforms with various functionality and hence their customization to the needs of engineers. The framework Core and Interface layers can be implemented in an arbitrary programming language and reused in different applications.

We also presented our reference implementation, called the BIMgrid Core, to illustrate the flexibility and application of the framework. Its main features are the transparent integration of private grid and public cloud resources, the capability to define customized workflows with different workflow languages and to process them under utilization of a variety of solvers and applications which can be controlled via command line scripts. Finally, combined data management capabilities are provided, including the IFC standard and based on a federative database system. An extensive API, composed of Java, SOAP and REST interfaces, allows the integration of the BIMgrid Core functionality into complex legacy systems or the utilization of selected features by third party applications. Developers can directly extend the BIMgrid Core to customized applications, without the need to implement the Core layer themselves. They can also utilize our already implemented "off-the-shelf" adapters for third party applications like HSQL database, UNICORE grid middleware, Amazon Web Services and a continuously increasing number of computation kernels. This way, customized applications can be reassembled cost-effectively and time-saving from existing functional components instead of being developed from the scratch.

One of our next research steps will be refinement of the BIMgrid Core's internal scheduling algorithm to better consider the combination of job dependencies and capabilities of hardware nodes in the private grid as well as predefined cloud images to improve job distribution. Furthermore, the extension of the functional range through the integration of new solvers is planned. Next, we want to add capabilities for thermal computations with the EnergyPlus solver. We also always work on the improvement of the default behavior of the adapter classes to ease the application of the BIMgrid Core for developers.

Acknowledgements

This research has been funded by the European Union as part of the project HESMOS (Grant No. 26088).

References

Alonso, J. M., Hernández, V., Moltó, G. (2008). A high-throughput application for the dynamic analysis of structures on a Grid environment, Advances in Engineering Software 39(10), pp. 839–848.

Beetz, J., van Berlo, L., de Laat, R., van den Helm, P. (2010). bimserver.org – An Open Source IFC Model Server, In: Proceedings of the 27th CIB W78, 2010, Cairo, Egypt.

Cheng, J. C., Law, K. H., Bjornsson, H., Jones, A., Sriram, R. (2010). A service oriented framework for construction supply chain integration, Automation in construction 19(2), pp. 245–260.

Chuang, T.-H., Lee, B.-C. & Wu, I.-C. (2011). Applying cloud computing technology to BIM visualization and manipulation. In: 28th International Symposium on Automation and Robotics in Construction. 201, pp. 144–149.

Cretella, G., Di Martino, B., Stankovski, V. (2012). Using the mOSAIC's semantic engine to design and develop civil engineering cloud applications. In: Proceedings of the 14th International Conference on Information Integration and Web-based Applications & Services, ACM, 2012, pp. 378–386.

Geuzaine, C., Henrotte, F., Remacle, J. F., Marchandise, E., Sabariego, R. (2013). ONELAB: Open Numerical Engineering LABoratory, In: Proceedings of the 11th Colloque National en Calcul des Structures, 2013, Giens, France.

Klitz, M. (2004). Grids – Beschreibung des Grid-Gedankens und Abgrenzungen. TU Kaiserslautern, Kaiserslautern, Germany.

Kumar, B., Cheng, J. C. P., McGibbney, L. (2010). Cloud computing and its implications for construction IT. In: Proceedings of the International Conference on Computing in Civil and Building Engineering, 2010, Nottingham, United Kingdom.

Richly, S., Goetz, S. (2010). Role-Based Multi-Purpose Workflow Engine Architecture. In: Proceedings of the 5th Workshop on Technologies for Context-Aware Business Process Management, 2010, Madeira, Portugal.

Deep Neural Network Architectures for Component-Based Machine Learning Model in Building Energy Predictions

Sundaravelpandian Singaravel[1], Philipp Geyer[1], Johan Suykens[2]
[1]Architectural Engineering Division, KU Leuven, Belgium
[2]ESAT-STADIUS, KU Leuven, Belgium
sundar.singaravel@kuleuven.be

Abstract. Artificial Neural Networks (ANN) are a universal approximator for any non-linear function. However, ANN approximation strongly depends on the architecture, i.e. the structure of the neurons and the training methods. This paper evaluates ANN architectures to model components that represent a building for its energy prediction. ANN architectures evaluated are one-hidden layer neural network (NN), deep NN and stacked autoencoder deep NN. The performance of these ANN architectures is assessed against Random Forest models. Results indicate that ANN methods increase the performance in percentage of coefficient of determination (R^2) between 0.57% to 9.65% compared to Random Forest models. Within ANN architectures evaluated, deep NN architectures performed better for most cases.

1 Introduction

Energy performance analysis is becoming an important element within a building design process. The need for having accurate prediction is raising with stringent sustainability requirements and use of energy analysis by various stakeholders. Limitations of current modelling practices are (1) presence of performance- and prediction gaps (Singaravel & Geyer, 2016) (2) detailed simulations are time-consuming and requires a lot of as-built information which is typically not available during design stages.

Developing buildings that are energy-efficient throughout its lifecycle, requires it to be designed and operated with energy-efficiency as an outcome. Building performance evaluation plays a major role in keeping it energy-efficient throughout its lifecycle. Performance is evaluated through Building Energy Models (BEM) during its design and typically through data models during the operational stage (ASHRAE, 2013). The shift from BEM to data models makes it hard to compare the results generated during design and operational stages of a building. Hence, having models that can be used throughout a building's lifecycle can be beneficial. Challenge with data collected during the operational stage is that the data can be noisy which could affect the performance of the models.

Machine learning models (MLMs) can capture interactions observed within detailed simulation models with simple input structure (Horsey, et al., 2016). High calculation speed together with high accuracy makes it an ideal alternative for detailed simulations in certain phases of design. Typical methodology to develop MLM for energy prediction is to have a single model with representative inputs. Limitations of this approach are (1) the inability to quantify the reason for a prediction and (2) the validity restricted to the dataset used to develop it. These limitations are overcome through component-based MLM approach, which gives the ability to quantify the reason for a prediction and increases the reusability of MLMs in a new situation (Singaravel, et al., 2017).

Machine learning (ML) algorithms available ranges from simple curve fitting models to more complex models like Artificial Neural Network (ANN). In this paper, ANN architectures are evaluated as a potential method for working with hourly non-linear data generated from detailed BEM; as ANN offers the following benefits over other ML algorithms:

- Performance increase with the addition of more training data, while traditional ML algorithms performance remains constant after a certain amount of data. Changing the architecture of the neural network (NN) model enables learning on additional data (Ng, 2016)
- Highly flexible architecture
- Indirectly identify complex connections between independent and dependent variables (Tu, 1996)
- Ability to identify all possible interactions within the data (Tu, 1996)
- Ability to be developed using various optimisation algorithms (Tu, 1996)

The objective of the paper is (1) to present the developed ANN architectures for further improving the performance of the current component-based MLM (2) identify characteristics of ANN architecture that results in good generalisation (3) evaluate the performance of the developed ANN on noisy data as they are present in measured data.

2 Description of the current component-based MLM

A component-based MLM has been developed with data from BEM of a simple box building with climate data from Amsterdam, Brussels and Paris with 0% and 100% occupancy. The simple box building is modelled in IES VE (Integrated Environmental Solutions Virtual Environment) software. The data used for developing the current MLM's are generated through simulations; MLM can also be developed with monitoring data (if available). Figure 1 shows the structure of developed component-based MLM. The model gives a transient response of heat flows corresponding to the component. These heat flows are aggregated at heating and cooling set-points to predict the heating and cooling energy demand (Singaravel, et al., 2017).

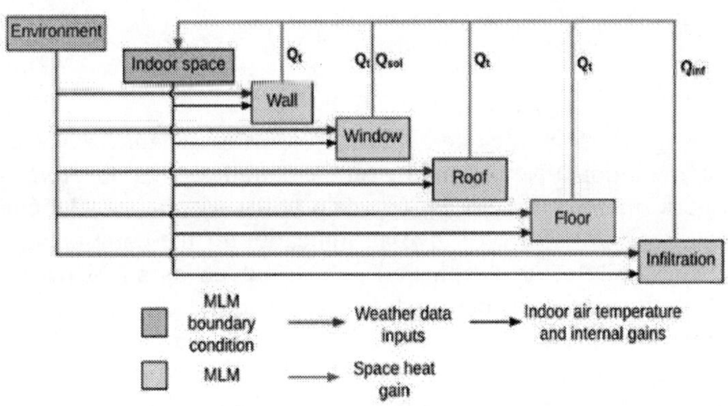

Figure 1Model structure of the component-based MLM (Singaravel, et al., 2017)

The random forest algorithm is used to develop all the components as it performed best for the majority of the components cross-validation dataset (Singaravel, et al., 2017). Furthermore, this model was evaluated for generalisation with data from London with three occupancy schedules, which are 100% occupancy (referred as London 100 in Table 1), 0% occupancy (referred as London 0 in Table 1) and 100% occupancy between 8:00 to 18:00. The cooling energy case for occupancy between 8:00 to 18:00 did not generalise well, as effects of thermal mass were not captured within the training data (Singaravel, et al., 2017). Since the data used for this paper does not incorporate the effect of thermal mass corresponding to occupancy between 8:00 to 18:00; this generalisation case is not used to evaluate ANN architectures performance in this paper. The component level performance i.e. coefficient of determination (R^2) is given in Table 1:

Table 1 Performance (i.e. R^2) of Random Forest models on test data (Singaravel, et al., 2017)

Components	London 0	London 100
Wall - gains and losses	0.8681	0.8407
Window - gains and losses	0.9545	0.9380
Window - Solar gain	0.9546	0.9540
Roof - gains and losses	0.8517	0.8708
Floor - gains and losses	0.8488	0.8538
Infiltration - gains and losses	0.9909	0.9870

In the following section, the performance of the developed component-based MLM using random forest algorithm is compared with ANN models. This comparison will highlight the need for developing MLM using more complex algorithms, to achieve high performance on test data. High performance on test data is important because it will reduce the effect of accumulated error occurring across the components.

3 Methodology

ANN architectures range from simple one-hidden layer NN to dynamic ANN architectures like recurrent NN and convolution NN. Depending on the complexity of the ANN architecture the training time and performance of ANN on test data will vary. Hence, the complexity of the selected architectures in this paper will give an indication of the complexity required model such systems. The ANN architectures evaluated are one-hidden layer NN, deep NN and stacked autoencoder deep NN. Within the selected architectures, one-hidden layer NN is a simple model structure, while other architectures are more complex model structure. These networks are developed using MATLAB's neural network toolbox. The performance measure is the fit, expressed by R^2, for the independent case London that is not included in the training data and acts as test data.

3.1 Description of ANN architectures evaluated

Fours different architectures are evaluated in the paper: A traditional one-hidden layer NN, one deep NN and two architectures of stacked autoencoder deep NN.

One-hidden layer NN is a simple NN architecture with consists of an input layer, one hidden layer and an output layer (see Table 2). The activation function used in the hidden and output layers are a sigmoid and a linear activation. Deep NN is similar to the one-hidden layer NN, except for the number of hidden layers. The deep NN architecture evaluated for this paper consists of an input layer, two hidden layers and output layer. Activation functions evaluated are same as the one-hidden layer NN. These ANN architectures are trained using 'Bayesian regularization backpropagation' method. Regularization of ANN is performed to reduce generalisation error rather than its training error (Goodfellow, et al., 2016). Resulting in ANN models that perform well on new or unseen data. Bayesian regularization backpropagation method applies regularization through Bayesian inference and requires no cross-validation data during the training process (MacKay, 1995).

Autoencoders consist of an encoder and a decoder, which attempts to replicate the input into an output mirroring the input data (Goodfellow, et al., 2016). Sparse autoencoder is used to develop the NN architecture. This autoencoder can identify interesting relationships within the data and extract good representations (or features extraction) of the data resulting in good performing deep NN (Vincent, et al., 2010). Features extraction means a representation of most relevant information from the input data in a high or low dimensional space. An example of such a feature is an automatically extracted climate representation that consists of interactions between ambient temperature, solar radiation and relative humidity.

Stacked autoencoder deep neural network is developed with two different architectures (see Table 3) in this paper. Since, the use of autoencoder as part of the NN is to extract interesting structures (i.e. feature extraction). Decoders are omitted as the reconstruction of input data is not important. The training process of stacked autoencoder deep NN is a two-step process. The first step is a pre-training process, where all the layers are trained separately. Pre-training is followed by initializing the network with the weights obtained from pre-training and training the complete network called fine-tuning. Pre-training is performed using scaled conjugate gradient backpropagation, and fine-tuning is done using Bayesian regularization backpropagation.

The first architecture consists of an input layer, an encoder layer, one-hidden layer and an output layer. The hidden and output layers together are referred as regression layer. In this architecture, the features learnt by the encoder are inputted to the regression layer for obtaining the final prediction. In the second architecture, two encoders together with a regression layer are used to construct the ANN. The encoder layer uses saturating linear activation function.

Table 2 Architecture of one-hidden layer and deep NN

One-hidden layer NN	Deep NN
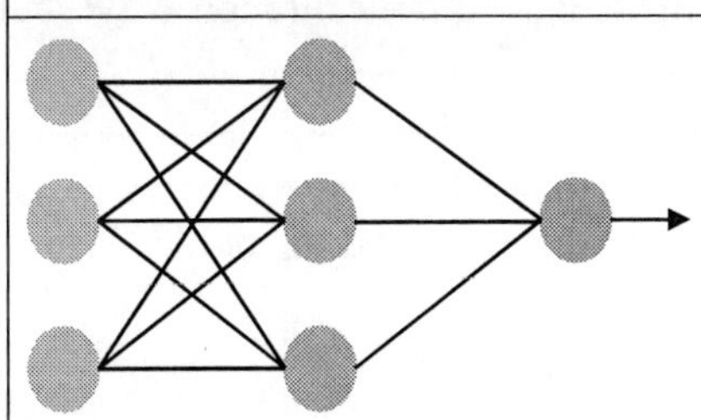	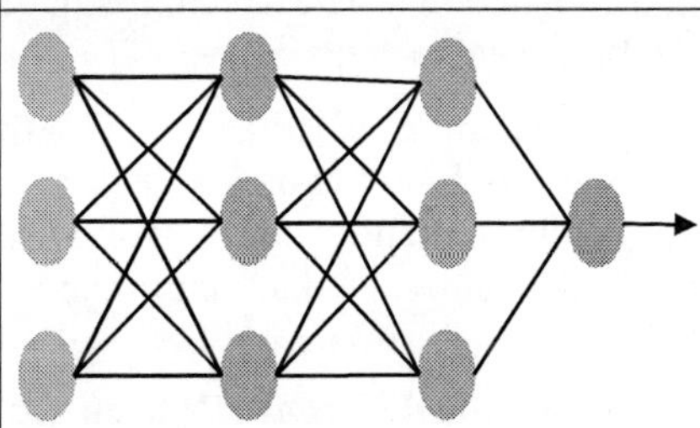
Number of hidden layer: **1** Hidden layer activation: **Sigmoid** Output layer activation: **Linear**	Number of hidden layer: **2** Hidden layer activation: **Sigmoid** Output layer activation: **Linear**

Table 3 Architecture of stacked autoencoder deep NN

Stacked autoencoder deep NN architecture 1	Stacked autoencoder deep NN architecture 2
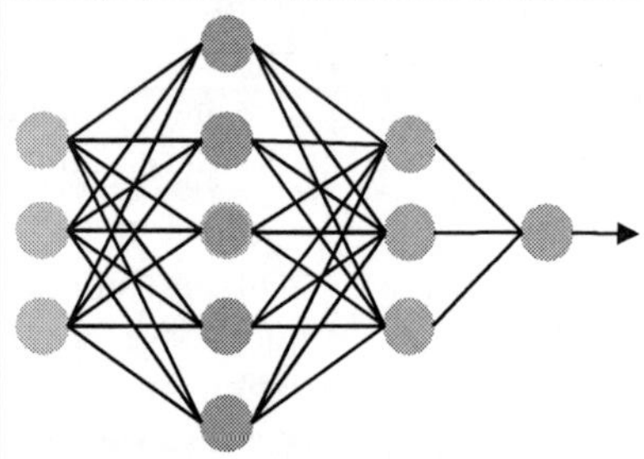	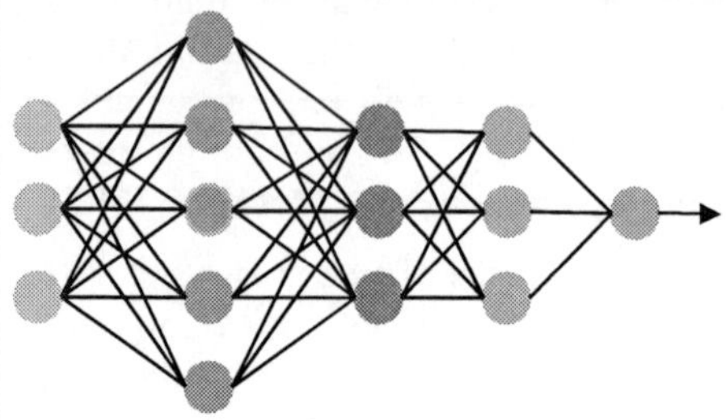
One Encoder is present 1st encoder layer activation: **Saturating linear** Sparsity proportion: 0.10 2nd hidden layer activation: **Sigmoid** Output layer activation: **Linear**	**Two** Encoder layers are present 1st & 2nd encoder layer activation: **Saturating linear** Sparsity proportion: 0.10 3rd hidden layer activation: **Sigmoid** Output layer activation: **Linear**

3.2 Identifying required hidden units in each NN layer

Development of the one-hidden layer and deep NN

The required number of hidden units in the respective layer are identified based on the mean squared error (MSE) on test data (i.e. data from London BEM model). The model configuration with the lowest MSE is selected.

Development of stacked autoencoder deep NN

Architecture 1: The same number of hidden units obtained for the one-hidden layer NN is used for the hidden layer of the stacked autoencoder deep NN. In this section, the number of hidden units for the encoder layer is selected using unsupervised learning; that is the autoencoder's ability to reconstruct both training and test data with low MSE. This layer is stacked together with the regression layer to form a deep architecture. The stacked model is trained together for obtaining the final model. The development of the final model is done through a layer-wise pre-training and fine-tuning steps.

Architecture 2: The number of hidden units for the hidden layer and first encoder layer are selected based on the results from the previous steps. The value of hidden units for the second encoder layer is the centre of hidden units between the first encoder layer and the hidden layer. All the layers are stacked and trained to obtain the final model.

3.3 Evaluation of the different NN architectures

The performance of the developed ANN models is evaluated against the R^2 of random forest models on test data (without noise). A white Gaussian noise is added to ambient temperature, global radiation, wind speed, wind direction, solar azimuth and solar altitude. The performance of the ANN models with noisy inputs is evaluated against the R^2 of ANN models with no-noise inputs.

4 Results

4.1 Identification of required hidden units

The number of hidden units corresponding to the lowest MSE on test data is used in the ANN architecture. Figure 2 shows the MSE for different hidden units of one-hidden layer NN (top left), deep NN (top right) and autoencoder layer (bottom) on training and test data of wall component. It can be noted from the figure that one-hidden layer NN with 15 hidden units has the lowest MSE. Hence, it has been selected for further evaluation. Similar, process is repeated for other ANN architectures and components. Table 4 shows the number of hidden units selected in each layer of an ANN architecture for each component.

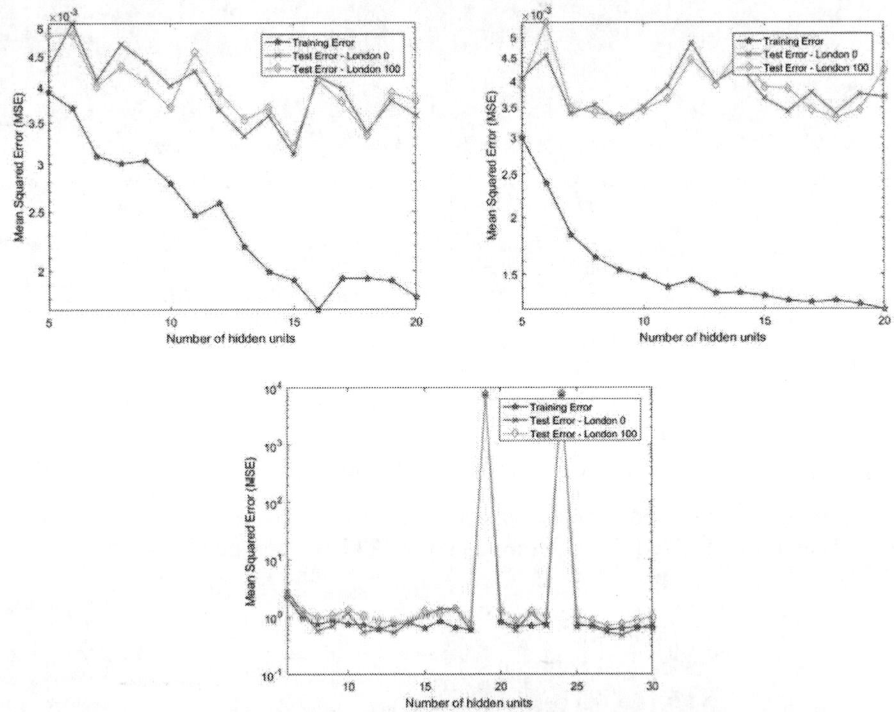

Figure 2 Identification of hidden units one-hidden layer NN (top left), deep NN (top right) and autoencoder layer (bottom) for wall component

Table 4 Number of hidden units per layer

	One-hidden layer NN	**Deep NN**	**Stacked Autoencoder Deep NN 1**	**Stacked Autoencoder Deep NN 2**
Wall	[15]	[9 , 9]	[26 , 15]	[26 , 21 , 15]
Window- Conduction	[15]	[5 , 5]	[21 , 15]	[21 , 18 , 15]
Window- Solar gain	[16]	[12 , 12]	[21 , 16]	[21 , 19 , 16]
Roof	[17]	[8 , 8]	[25 , 17]	[25 , 21 , 17]
Floor	[14]	[12 , 12]	[18 , 14]	[18 , 16 , 14]
Infiltration	[9]	[5 , 5]	[23 , 9]	[23 , 16 , 9]

4.2 Performance of different ANN architecture on test data

Figure 3 shows the test data performance improvement of ANN models compared to the random forest model.

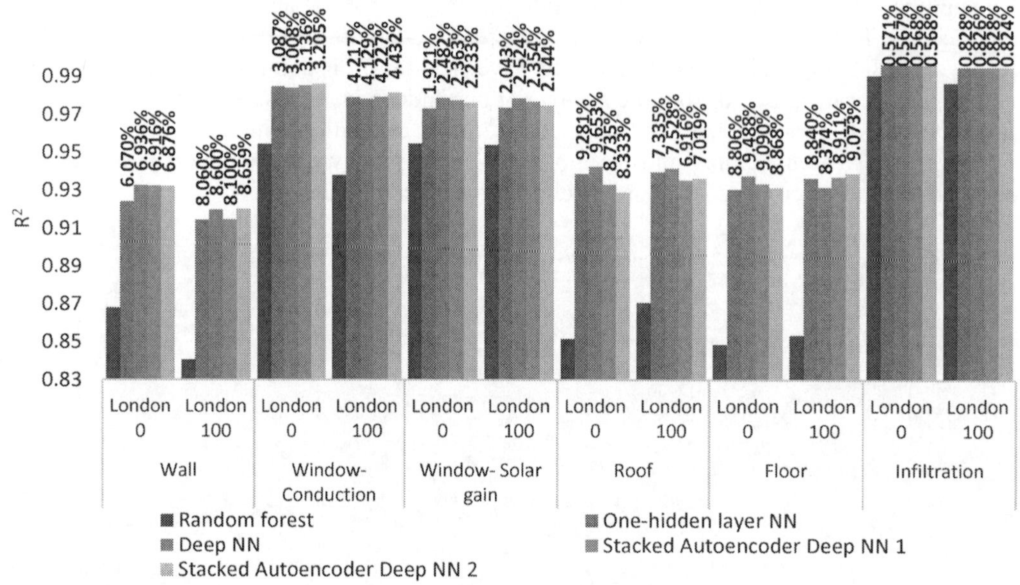

Figure 3 R^2 for different ANN architectures compared to random forest models

4.3 Performance of different ANN architecture on noisy test data

Figure 4 shows the performance decrease when ANN models are inputted with noisy data. White Gaussian noise is added through the `awgn()` MATLAB command.

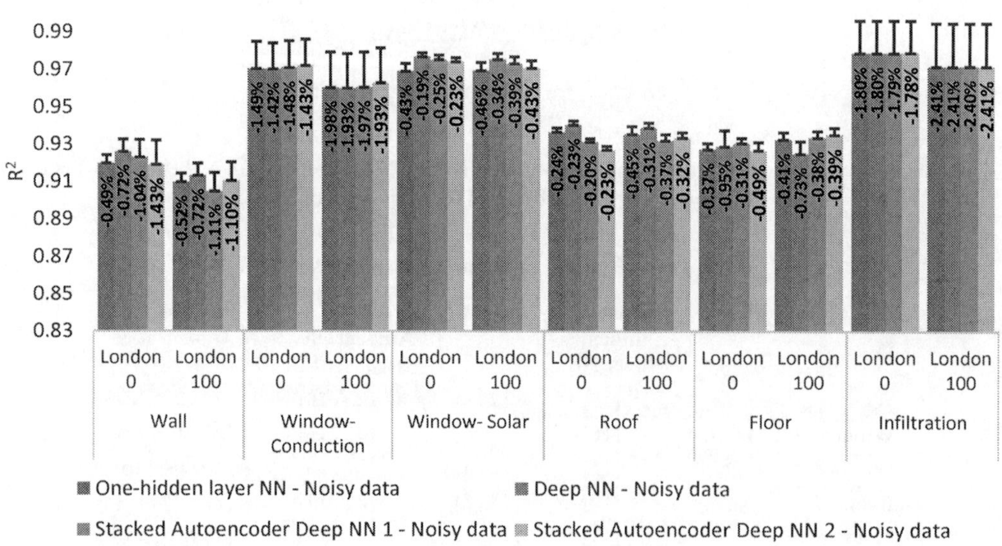

Figure 4 R^2 for different ANN architectures with no-noise (error bars) and noisy data. Percentage is reduction in performance in percentage of R^2

5 Conclusion

Results indicate that ANN, in general, performs better than random forest models. The performance increase in percentage of R^2 ranges between 0.57% to 9.65% (see Figure 3). The performance can be further improved by optimising the structure of ANN through grid search or other optimisation techniques. The increase in performance will result in a reduction in accumulated error within the component-based model.

The performance of the ANN models is not affected a lot when noisy input data is used (see Figure 4). The performance reduction (compared to models without noisy data) in percentage of R^2 ranges between 0.19% to 2.36%. Implying that it would be possible to develop models that can be applied throughout the life-cycle of a building. Noisy input data from smart building contexts can be used to train such neural networks in a component-based approach. Furthermore, the addition of de-noising layer into the ANN architecture is expected to increase the robustness of these models.

Results also indicate that approaches with feature extraction, such as deep NN architectures and stacked autoencoders, perform better than one-hidden layer NN in most cases. For the given case, the performance increase is marginal. However, more complex cases will have a larger dataset and with more features (i.e. input parameters). In this situation, performance improvements of feature extraction are expected to become prominent resulting in better performance. This is achieved by taking the inputs into a higher dimensional input space, by having the number of hidden units greater than the number of features or inputs. Therefore, architectures capable of feature extraction, such as Deep NN, will be used for the component-based method in future.

Finally, the flexibility offered by ANN's makes it a suitable machine learning method to handle a large quantity of real-world and simulated data for energy performance evaluation. However, development of good NN models is a time-consuming process. This effort is quantified based on the extent to which these models can generalise in the evaluation of building energy performance. The limitations of model generalisation are to be researched further.

Acknowledgements

The research is funded by STG-14-00346 at KUL. The authors acknowledge the support of ERC AdG A-DATADRIVE-B (290923), KUL: GOA/10/09 MaNet, CoE PFV/10/002 (OPTEC), BIL12/11T; FWO: G.0377.12, G.088114N, G0A4917N; IUAPP7/19 DYSCO.

References

ASHRAE, 2013. *2013 ASHRAE Handbook - Fundamentals.* Atlanta: ASHRAE.

Goodfellow, I., Bengio, Y. & Courville, A., 2016. *Deep Learning.* Cambridge, Massachusetts; London, England : MIT Press.

Horsey, H., Fleming, K., Ball, B. & Long, N., 2016. *Achieving Actionable Results from Available Inputs: Metamodels Take Building Energy Simulations One Step Further.* Golden, CO (United States)), National Renewable Energy Laboratory (NREL).

MacKay, D. J., 1995. Probable networks and plausible predictions—a review of practical Bayesian methods for supervised neural networks. *Network: Computation in Neural Systems,* Volume 6(3), pp. 469-505.

Ng, A., 2016. *Machine Learning Yearning.* Draft - Version 0.5 ed. : .

Singaravel, S. & Geyer, P., 2016. *Simplifying Building Energy Performance Models to support an Integrated Design workflow.* Kraków, EG-ICE .

Singaravel, S., Geyer, P. & Suykens, J., 2017. *Component-Based Machine Learning Modelling Approach For Design (In review).* San Francisco, IBPSA.

Tu, J. V., 1996. Advantages and disadvantages of using artificial neural networks versus logistic regression for predicting medical outcomes. *Journal of clinical epidemiology,* 49(11), pp. pp.1225-1231.

Vincent, P. et al., 2010. Stacked denoising autoencoders: Learning useful representations in a deep network with a local denoising criterion. *Journal of Machine Learning Research,* Volume 11, pp. 3371-3408.

IFC-based modeling of cyber-physical systems in civil engineering

Kay Smarsly, Michael Theiler and Kosmas Dragos
Bauhaus University Weimar, Germany
kay.smarsly@uni-weimar.de

Abstract. The term "cyber-physical system" (CPS) refers to a new generation of engineering systems integrating computing, networking, and physical processes. Traditional building information, such as geometry, material or cost, can be represented based on the Industry Foundation Classes (IFC), an open standard used for building information modeling (BIM). However, information representing cyber-physical systems cannot be fully described with the IFC standard. Focusing on CPS applications in structural health monitoring and control, this paper presents an extension of the current IFC schema, enabling BIM-based modeling of cyber-physical systems in compliance with the IFC standard. BIM-based, IFC-compliant CPS modeling facilitates the design process, the documentation, and the information exchange of cyber-physical systems. In this study, a semantic model is developed, serving as a technology-independent metamodel to formally describe cyber-physical systems deployed in structural health monitoring and control applications. Supporting BIM-based, IFC-compliant modeling of cyber-physical systems, the semantic model is mapped into the IFC schema. Validating the BIM-based CPS modeling approach proposed herein, a CPS prototype for structural health monitoring and control is designed, implemented, and tested in laboratory experiments.

1. Introduction

The incorporation of quasi-automated self-regulating optimization technologies in engineering, leveraging features from the fields of embedded systems and the Internet of Things, has been gaining increasing attention in an attempt to enhance the efficiency and the sustainability of engineering applications (Smarsly et al., 2013). In this context, cyber-physical systems have been introduced as an approach to merge the digital and the real world, integrating physical processes with computational and networking processes (Sanfelice, 2016). Examples include smart structures instrumented with active or semi-active tuned mass dampers (Casciati & Chen, 2012) or wind turbines instrumented with intelligent monitoring and control systems that are online accessible through cyber infrastructures (Smarsly & Hartmann, 2009a, 2009b; Smarsly et al., 2012).

In many engineering applications, the inherent dynamic physical processes are optimized utilizing information obtained by computational models created to describe the physical processes (Bilek et al., 2003; Smarsly, 2013). Computational models are typically based on data collected from the physical processes (data-driven models) and/or on the principles characterizing the physical processes (physics-based models). Moreover, by integrating additional physical elements (e.g. actuators) or virtual elements (software) into the physical processes, computational models are extended to computational processes that facilitate the automated control of physical processes or automated decision making (Legatiuk et al., 2017). The application of cyber-physical systems has been widespread in several engineering fields, such as civil engineering (Huang et al., 2010), construction (Yuan et al., 2016), aerospace engineering (Atkins & Bradley, 2013), and aviation (Sampigethaya & Poovendran, 2013).

From a civil engineering perspective, cyber-physical systems are predominantly associated with computer-aided monitoring and control of structural systems, falling essentially within the scope of structural health monitoring (SHM) and control (Bhuiyan et al, 2016). Here, owing to the automation intrinsic to cyber-physical system (CPS) operation, the requirement of high levels of intelligence in the computational and networking processes comes to the forefront. It can be, therefore, argued that cyber-physical systems in civil engineering primarily concern wireless SHM systems comprising "smart" wireless sensor nodes, i.e. sensor nodes with enhanced intelligence levels able to automatically execute SHM tasks (Hackmann et al., 2014). A CPS in civil engineering is composed of two subsystems, (i) the physical subsystem, which is the structure itself, and (ii) the computational subsystem, which is the monitoring and control system including the networking processes. The physical processes encompass the responses of the physical subsystem under dynamic actions, while the computational processes include collecting structural response data through the SHM system and managing the actuators or software elements for structural control and decision making (control elements). Finally, the networking processes are primarily associated with the communication between the SHM system and control elements.

Despite the increasing adoption of cyber-physical systems in structural health monitoring and control applications, research that investigates modeling methodologies for model-based representation of cyber-physical systems is very limited. There is a clear lack of modeling approaches facilitating a precise model-based representation of information relevant to a CPS, such as information on the sensor node design, information on the algorithms embedded into the sensor nodes, information on the configuration and topology of the sensor network, or information about the overall monitoring and control strategies ("CPS-related information"). However, a clear representation of CPS-related information is critical to assessing the CPS performance on a sound mathematical basis in order to ensure a high monitoring/control quality of the CPS. This study aims to resolve this major modeling bottleneck by advancing a metamodeling approach proposed for cyber-physical systems. Since the Industry Foundation Classes (IFC) are a widely-used, open standard for digital modeling of building information ("building information modeling", BIM), this study builds upon the IFC standard to represent CPS-related information. Although the IFC schema allows representing a plethora of building information, it is not possible to represent CPS-related information with the IFC schema. To overcome this drawback, extensible IFC constructs, such as proxy entities and user-defined property sets may be used, as proposed by Delgado et al. (2016). However, using these extensible constructs, being unspecific and non-standard, may cause a semantic loss of information. To avoid a semantic loss of information, in this study an extension of the IFC schema is proposed that allows representing CPS-related information not included in the current version of the standardized IFC schema. As a result, in contrast to approaches combining different ontologies and metamodels with self-defined semantic models (Jeong et al., 2017), all information needed for a well-defined representation of cyber-physical systems is contained in a single building information model based on an extended IFC schema.

This paper is organized as follows. First, a semantic model is developed, serving as a technology-independent metamodel to formally describe cyber-physical systems deployed in structural health monitoring and control applications. Then, the semantic model is mapped into the IFC schema, facilitating BIM-based modeling of cyber-physical systems. To validate the proposed BIM-based modeling approach in laboratory experiments, a CPS prototype is designed and implemented for structural health monitoring.

2. A semantic model for cyber-physical systems

The semantic model, representing a metamodel for modeling cyber-physical systems, is proposed to describe cyber-physical systems deployed in structural health monitoring and control applications. The semantic model allows representing the physical, computational, and networking subsystem of a CPS, where the networking subsystems are considered semantic parts of the computational subsystems. Figure 1 shows an extract of the semantic model proposed in this study, illustrating the physical and the computational subsystem of a CPS. The computational subsystem, i.e. the structural health monitoring and control system, is composed of one or more sensor networks and a computer system, which includes processes and, optionally, additional resources required for data management and data analysis. A sensor network, characterized by a topology, is composed of a number of nodes that can be classified into two categories or generic types, sensor nodes and base stations. As can be seen from Figure 1, nodes of both categories require a power unit, a communication unit, a node specification, and a semantic reference to the structural components being monitored or controlled. In addition, each node category, sensor nodes and base stations, includes processes, e.g. for on-board data analysis of the structural system. Resources of a node may include, e.g., flash memory for temporary data storage. Usually, a sensor node has sensors and actuators attached. However, if a sensor node deployed in a sensor network is designed solely for forwarding messages of other sensor nodes without sensing or actuating, there is no need to attach sensors or actuators to the sensor node. Both sensors and actuators, as illustrated in Figure 1, are therefore considered optional elements of a sensor node.

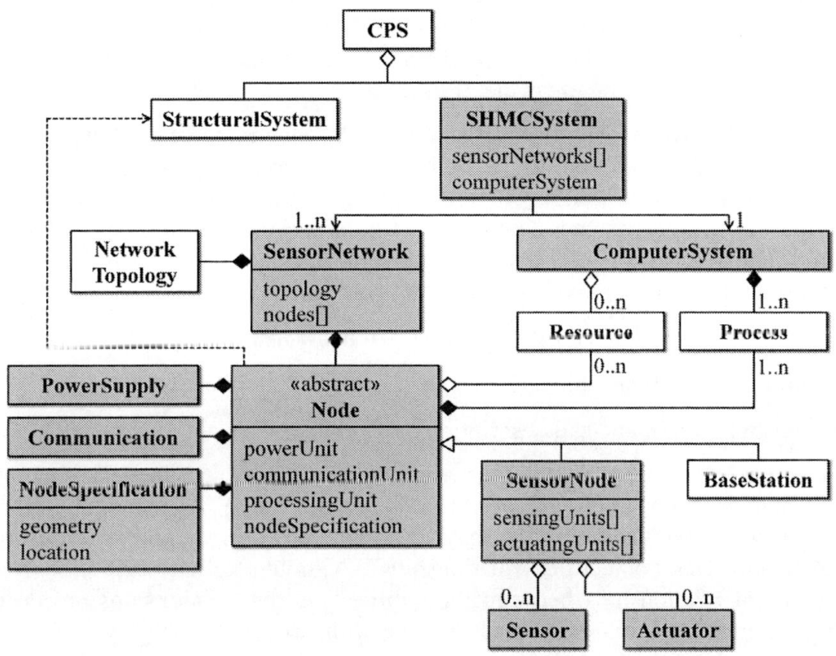

Figure 1: Extract of the semantic model for cyber-physical systems deployed in structural health monitoring and control applications.

Regarding the IFC representation of the CPS semantic model, it should be noted that the physical subsystem or, more precisely, the structural system can be described with the existing IFC standard using traditional building information. However, the mapping capabilities of the current IFC standard are not sufficient for modeling CPS-related information (Smarsly & Tauscher, 2016). Hence, a conceptual approach towards modeling CPS-related information through an IFC schema extension is introduced. In the following sections, the IFC mapping of a distinct subset of the CPS semantic model, which is plotted as gray-colored elements in Figure 1, is illustratively demonstrated. While further IFC mapping aspects, such as mapping of the network topology or mapping of processes and resources of sensor nodes and computer systems, fall beyond the scope of this paper, the following sections emphasize the focus on extending the IFC with the subset of the CPS semantic model containing CPS-related information about

1. the aggregation of sensor node subcomponents into ***sensor nodes*** (such as sensors, actuators, communication unit, power supply unit),
2. the grouping of sensor nodes to a ***sensor network***, and, finally,
3. the composition of sensor networks and computer systems to a ***structural health monitoring and control system*** being part of a CPS.

3. Extending the IFC schema with semantic CPS information

Building information modeling (BIM) provides information and tools for planning, designing, constructing, and managing buildings and civil infrastructure (BuildingSMART, 2017). BIM is usually based on a 3D geometric model supplemented by semantic information pertinent to the represented elements, while the IFC serves as an open, non-proprietary standard for documenting and exchanging BIM models (ISO 16739, 2013). With the IFC, a standard for comprehensive semantic building models has been established representing building information in all phases of the life cycle of the building.

The IFC schema follows an object-oriented approach, containing several classes, serving as "templates", hereinafter referred to as entities, to describe building-related information. Inheritance mechanisms are used to generalize the semantic meaning and the implementation of the entities to the furthest possible extent. Representing the most abstract fundamental entity, a root entity in the IFC schema, named *IfcRoot*, is used as a basis for other entities. Therefore, the *IfcRoot* entity provides capabilities for

- the identification of an entity by a globa ique identifier,
- the definition of ownership and change information of an entity, and
- the attribution of name and description of an entity.

Furthermore, the IFC schema captures general constructs of object models, such as objects, properties, and relationships: *Objects* describe any "thing" semantically represented, *properties* cover all characteristics that may be assigned to objects, and *relationships* among objects are mapped as "objectified relationships", without explicit attributions that would directly represent relationships between the entities, i.e. the relationships are described by relationship objects that point to all objects related with each other.

3.1 Existing capabilities for extending the IFC schema

In this subsection, the existing capabilities for extending the IFC standard are discussed with respect to mapping CPS-related information into the IFC schema. In this direction, the following discussion concerns leveraging extensible constructs already included in the current IFC schema, (i) proxy elements, (ii) object type definitions, and (iii) property sets.

Proxy elements are either placeholders without a predefined connotation or containers used to wrap objects. Consequently, using proxy elements for mapping CPS-related information (which are considered "non-standard" IFC objects) into the IFC schema may result in a semantic loss of information. Thus, for a semantically well-defined representation of non-standard IFC objects, proxy elements are not suitable.

Object type definitions provide a concept to semantically differentiate objects without the need for additional entities that are derived from more general entities. Therefore, several IFC entities provide an attribute to further differentiate the object type. For example, a sensor represented in the IFC schema by the entity *IfcSensor* can be associated with the predefined type *WINDSENSOR* indicating that this sensor is used for sensing the airflow speed and direction. If no appropriate enumerator is available for denoting the object type, custom values may be used to define the object type. Since object types may be assigned with any alphanumeric value, some convention is required to render the information computer-interpretable. Therefore, using non-standard, user-defined object type definitions for mapping CPS-related information into the IFC schema may be problematic and error-prone.

Property sets, representing a generic approach towards describing object properties based on key-value pairs, allow attaching additional data to IFC entities. For property sets, predefined keys (and corresponding data types for the values) are defined in the IFC standard, while user-defined key-value pairs may be part of an IFC model instance as well. However, similar to user-defined object type definitions, non-standard IFC properties may be problematic for mapping CPS-related information into the IFC schema due to their indefinite keywords.

In summary, CPS-related information can partially be represented with proxy elements, object type definitions, and property sets. However, such partial representation of CPS-related information may cause a semantic loss of information. Consequently, an explicit IFC extension is introduced in the following subsection for mapping CPS-related information into the IFC schema in a standardized manner.

3.2 CPS-related extension of the IFC schema

The IFC extension proposed in this study comprises a definition of new entities and a specification of attributes relevant to the CPS-related information to be mapped. An extract of the IFC schema extension is presented in Figure 2. Exemplarily, three entities added to the IFC schema are illuminated in more detail. These entities, in Figure 2 gray-colored, are sensor nodes (*IfcSensorNode*), sensor networks (*IfcSensorNetwork*), and structural health monitoring and control systems (*IfcMonitoringControlSystem*) within a CPS. The entities are integrated into the inheritance tree of the existing IFC schema according to their semantic meaning.

Sensor nodes

As can be seen from Figure 2, sensor nodes, represented by *IfcSensorNode* entities, are considered objects (*IfcObject*) or, more precisely, products (*IfcProduct*). A product according to the IFC standard is an abstract representation of any object that appears in a geometric or spatial context. Thus, the *IfcProduct* entity is assigned with a geometric representation and a location. Furthermore, references to other *IfcProduct* entities may be mapped, such as the relation between a sensor node and the structural elements being monitored. Taking a closer look at the IFC inheritance tree, a sensor node is an AEC (architecture, engineering, and construction) product, represented by the abstract entity *IfcElement*. Among other functionalities, an *IfcElement* entity may be connected to other IFC elements, e.g. to logically represent the network connection between sensor nodes.

A sensor node is an element of a distributed system, represented by the entity *IfcDistributionElement*. Distributed elements may be assigned with a port (*IfcPort*) via the objectified relationship *IfcRelConnectsPortToElement*. A port provides means for an element to connect to other elements. Therewith, a physical representation of a connection, such as a tethered connection, can be mapped. With the subtype *IfcDistributionPort*, the flow direction of the port is mapped, indicating whether a port is a sink, a source, or both. Since sensor nodes are used to control other elements of a distributed system, the entity *IfcDistributionControlElement* is used as base entity for the *IfcSensorNode* entity.

As introduced in the CPS semantic model, a sensor node integrates several components (sensors, actuators, and other resources). Therefore, inherited from the abstract *IfcObjectDefinition* entity shown in Figure 2, an aggregation between a sensor node and the sensor node components is represented using the objectified *IfcRelAggregates* relationship entity. In particular, sensors represented by the entity *IfcSensor* and actuators represented by the entity *IfcActuator* may be part of a sensor node.

Through object type definitions, *IfcSensor* entities may be specialized to specific sensor types. However, the current IFC schema does not provide predefined enumerators to describe all sensor types typically deployed in cyber-physical systems. Therefore, additional enumerators are added to the IFC schema, e.g. for representing sensor information related to accelerometers and stain gauges. Furthermore, additional predefined property sets are added to the sensor types that are not available in the current IFC schema. Besides sensors and actuators, other *IfcProduct* entities for the power supply and the communication unit are part of a sensor node. For example, a battery is represented by the entity *IfcElectricFlowStorageDevice* (predefined object type: *BATTERY*) and an antenna is represented using the entity *IfcCommunicationsAppliance* (predefined object type: *ANTENNA*).

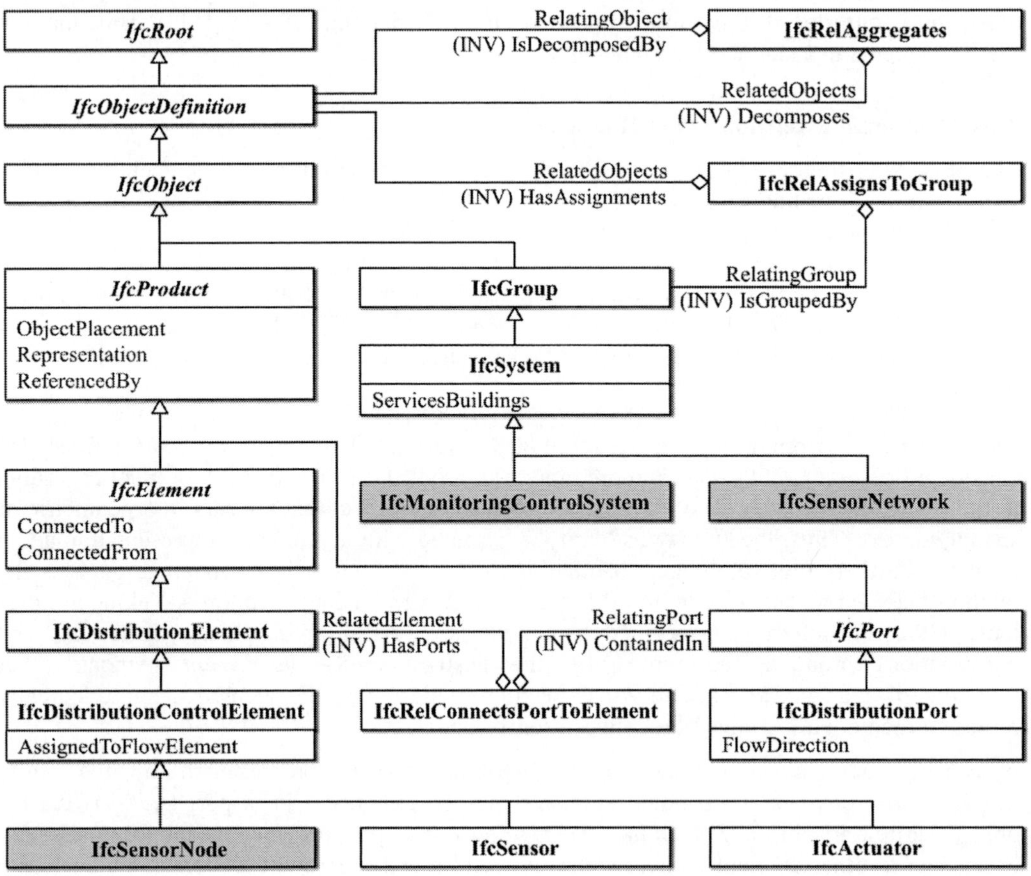

Figure 2: Extract of the CPS-related extension of the IFC schema with new IFC entities gray-colored.

Sensor networks

A sensor network (*IfcSensorNetwork*), according to the CPS semantic model, is a collection of nodes, e.g. sensor nodes and base stations. In this sense, a sensor network is a distinct aggregation of nodes under topological, non-geometrical grouping aspects represented in the IFC schema through the *IfcGroup* entity, as illustrated in Figure 2. Furthermore, a sensor network shows characteristics of a system (*IfcSystem*), which is a subtype of a group. A system is an organized combination of related parts, composed for a common purpose to provide a certain service. Here, the system's grouping aspect derived from the *IfcGroup* entity can be interpreted as a functionally related aggregation of the nodes assembled in the system. The relation between the sensor nodes and the sensor network is mapped by an *IfcRelAssignsToGroup* relationship object. Last but not least, an *IfcSystem* entity assigns the system to spatial structure entities, such as sites, buildings, stories, spaces, or spatial zones.

Structural health monitoring and control systems

A structural health monitoring and control system (*IfcMonitoringControlSystem*), being part of a CPS, is a functionally related aggregation of entities. Here, the SHM and control system is grouped by the sensor network(s) it includes and the computer system. In the IFC schema, a computer device may be represented with the entity *IfcCommunicationsAppliance* (predefined object type: *COMPUTER*), while a sensor network is represented with the entity *IfcSensor-Network*.

In this study, a schema file representing the IFC schema extension is developed based on the EXPRESS standard (ISO 10303-11, 2004). EXPRESS is a data modeling language for product data related to a specific domain of interest, e.g. for the automotive, the aeronautic, or the building industry. The proposed schema file as well as the IFC model instance developed in the following sections, based on the extended IFC schema, are formally verified using professional checking tools (Apstex, 2017). The checking tools applied for verification are also used for the official certification of IFC interfaces of commercial BIM software tools (b-Cert, 2017).

4. BIM-based modeling and implementation of a cyber-physical system

To validate the BIM-based CPS modeling approach in laboratory experiments, a CPS prototype is designed and implemented for structural health monitoring and control. The CPS prototype consists of a four-story laboratory shear frame structure equipped with a wireless structural health monitoring and control system. The SHM and control system is composed of wireless sensor nodes capable of local data processing and automated decision making with respect to damage ("virtual actuation"). As shown in Figure 3, each story of the structure is a rectangular 300 mm × 200 mm (length × width) aluminum plate fixed to four aluminum columns of 20 mm × 2 mm rectangular cross sections. The weak sides of the column cross sections (i.e. the shorter sides) are aligned with the length of the plate. The height of each story is 300 mm.

The BIM-based model of the CPS prototype, shown in Figure 3, consists of the structural system and the structural health monitoring and control system (i.e. wireless sensor nodes). Clearly, modeling the CPS prototype with conventional IFC-compliant BIM software tools would not be possible, because the proposed CPS-related extension of the IFC schema is not fully supported by conventional BIM software tools – only the structural system can be modeled with conventional BIM software tools. Therefore, upon BIM-based modeling of the structural system, the IFC model instance of the structural system is exported as an IFC file. In the IFC file, specific CPS-related information about the structural health monitoring and control system, which cannot be modeled using conventional BIM software tools, is added, achieving a full BIM model of the CPS prototype. The IFC file can advantageously be used to document and to archive CPS-related information in compliance with the IFC standard.

Upon BIM-based modeling, the CPS prototype is physically implemented to validate the proposed IFC extension in laboratory experiments (Figure 4). The wireless sensor nodes of the CPS prototype are of type Oracle SunSPOT (Oracle, 2010). The SunSPOT sensor nodes are equipped with a Java-programmable 400 MHz ARM microprocessor, 512 kB RAM, and 4 MB flash memory. Wireless communication is achieved via an IEEE 802.15.4 radio transceiver using the ZigBee protocol. The sensing board includes a digital output accelerometer, a temperature sensor, and a light sensor. The accelerometer used in this study is of type MMA7455L, and it is able to sample up to 250 Hz, with selectable measurement ranges of ±2 g, ±6 g, or ±8 g.

Figure 3: BIM-based model of the CPS prototype.

Figure 4: Physical implementation of the CPS prototype.

Automated damage detection is implemented into the sensor nodes. The automated damage detection involves local data processing and information exchange among the sensor nodes for extracting the mode shapes of the test structure through frequency domain decomposition (Brincker et al., 2000). Local data processing essentially comprises collecting acceleration response measurements and transforming the collected data into the frequency domain via a fast Fourier transform algorithm embedded into the sensor nodes. For details on the embedded damage detection approach, the interested reader is referred to Smarsly & Law (2013) and Smarsly & Petryna (2014). Two laboratory tests are performed on the CPS prototype, one with the initial structural state of the structure and one after introducing damage to the structure by loosening the column-to-plate connections on one side of the structure. The damage is reflected on the Fourier transforms of acceleration response data, as calculated by the wireless sensor nodes deployed (Figure 5). From Figure 5, it is clear that the introduced damage results in a migration of the peaks in the Fourier spectrum towards lower frequencies, i.e. the structure becomes more flexible in the damaged state. In the damaged state, the frequency is notably lower than in the undamaged structural state, while low deviations are also observed in the corresponding mode shape. As a result of the differences in the identified fundamental frequency and the extracted mode shape, the sensor nodes, through its "virtual" actuators, transmit a damage detection alert signal to the base station.

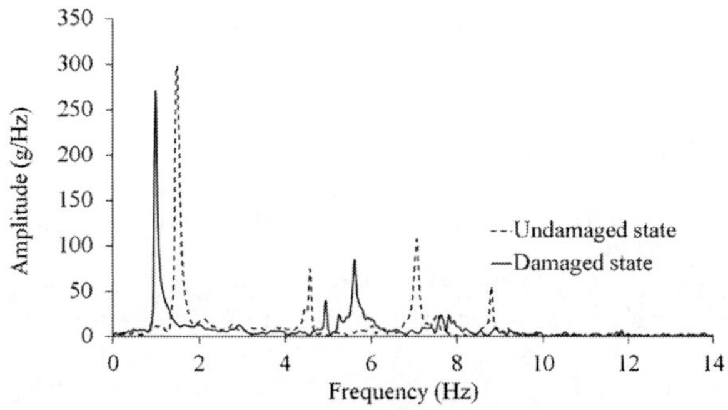

Figure 5. Comparison between Fourier spectra of the initial structural state and the damaged structural state for story 3.

5. Summary and conclusions

In this study, a novel BIM-based modeling approach for cyber-physical systems has been presented and validated in laboratory experiments. Focusing on CPS applications for structural health monitoring and control, an extension of the current IFC schema has been proposed to represent CPS-related information, enabling BIM-based modeling of cyber-physical systems in compliance with the IFC standard. The IFC schema extension has been developed based on a CPS semantic model, which serves as a technology-independent metamodel to formally describe cyber-physical systems deployed in structural health monitoring and control applications. To validate the BIM-based CPS modeling approach, a CPS prototype has been designed, implemented and tested in laboratory experiments. As a result, it is concluded that BIM-based CPS modeling in compliance with the IFC standard facilitates the design process, the documentation, and the information exchange of cyber-physical systems.

Acknowledgments

The authors would like to gratefully acknowledge the financial support provided by the German Research Foundation (DFG) through grant numbers SM 281/7-1 and GRK 1462. Any opinions, findings, conclusions, or recommendations expressed in this paper are solely those of the authors and do not necessarily reflect the views of DFG or any other organizations and collaborators.

References

Apstex (2017). IFC Tools Project. Online: http://www.apstex.com, accessed: 2017-04-12.

Atkins, E.M. & Bradley, J.M. (2013). Aerospace cyber-physical systems education. In: The American Institute of Aeronautics and Astronautics Infotech Aerospace Conference, 2013, Boston, MA, USA.

b-Cert (2017). The official platform for the buildingSMART IFC4 certification. Online: http://www.b-cert.org, accessed: 2017-04-12.

Bhuiyan, M. Z. A., Wu, J., Wang, G., Cao, J. & Jiang, W. (2016). Sensing and Decision Making in Cyber-Physical Systems: The Case of Structural Event Monitoring, IEEE Transactions on Industrial Informatics 12(6), pp. 2103-2114.

Bilek, J., Mittrup, I., Smarsly, K. & Hartmann, D. (2003). Agent-based Concepts for the Holistic Modeling of Concurrent Processes in Structural Engineering. In: Proc. of the 10th ISPE International Conference on Concurrent Engineering: Research and Applications. Madeira, Portugal, July 26, 2003.

Brincker, R., Andersen, P. & Zhang, L. (2000). Modal identification from ambient responses using frequency domain decomposition". In: Proc. of the 18th International Modal Analysis Conference. San Antonio, TX, USA, 07/02/2000.

BuildingSMART (2017). IFC Infrastructure Room. Online: http://www.buildingsmart-tech.org/infrastructure, accessed: 2017-04-12.

Casciati, S. & Chen, Z. C. (2012). An active mass damper system for structural control using real-time wireless sensors, Structural Control and Health Monitoring 19(8), pp. 758-767.

Delgado, J. M. D., Butler, L. J., Gibbons, N., Brilakis, I., Elshafie, M. Z. E. B. & Middleton, C. (2016). Management of structural monitoring data of bridges using BIM. Proceedings of the Institution of Civil Engineers – Bridge Engineering (to appear).

Dragos, K. & Smarsly, K. (2015). A Comparative Review of Wireless Sensor Nodes for Structural Health Monitoring. In: Proc. of the 7th International Conference on Structural Health Monitoring of Intelligent Infrastructure. Turin, Italy, 07/01/2015.

Hackmann, G., Guo, W., Yan, G., Sun, Z., Lu, C. & Dyke, S. (2014). Cyber-physical co-design of distributed structural health monitoring with wireless sensor networks, IEEE Transactions on Parallel and Distributed Systems 25(1), pp. 63-72.

Huang, H.-M., Tidwell, T., Gill, C., Lu, C., Gao, X. & Dyke, S. (2010). Cyber-physical systems for real-time hybrid structural testing: A case study. In: Proc. of the International Conference on Cyber-Physical Systems. Stockholm, Sweden, 04/14/2014.

ISO 10303-11 (2004). Industrial automation systems and integration - Product data representation and exchange – Part 11: Description methods: The EXPRESS language reference manual.

ISO 16739 (2013). Industry Foundation Classes (IFC) for data sharing in the construction and facility managem. industries.

Jeong, S., Hou, R., Lynch J. P., Sohn, H. & Law, K. H. (2017). An information modeling framework for bridge monitoring. Advances in Engineering Software (to appear).

Legatiuk, D., Dragos, K. & Smarsly, K. (2017). Modeling and evaluation of cyber-physical systems in civil engineering. In: Proc. of the 88th Annual Meeting of the International Association of Applied Mathematics and Mechanics, March 6, 2017, Weimar, Germany.

Oracle Corp. (2010). Sun SPOT eDEMO Technical Datasheet, 8th edition. Sun Labs,Santa Clara, CA, USA, 2010.

Sampigethaya, C. & Poovendran, R. (2013). Aviation Cyber–Physical Systems: Foundations for Future Aircraft and Air Transport, Proc. of the IEEE 101(8), pp. 1834-1855.

Sanfelice, R. G. (2016). Analysis and design of cyber-physical systems: a hybrid control systems approach. In: Rawat D.B. and Rodriguez J.J.P.C. (eds.). Cyber-physical systems: From theory to practice, Boca Raton, FL, USA: CRC Press (Taylor & Francis Group), pp. 3-31.

Smarsly, K. (2013). Agricultural ecosystem monitoring based on autonomous sensor systems. In: Center for Spatial Information Science and Systems, George Mason University. In: Proc. of the Second International Conference on Agro-Geoinformatics 2013. Fairfax, VA, USA, August 12, 2013.

Smarsly, K. & Hartmann, D. (2009a). Multi-scale monitoring of wind energy plants based on agent technology. In: Proc. of the 7th International Workshop on Structural Health Monitoring. Stanford, CA, USA, 09/09/2009.

Smarsly, K. & Hartmann, D. (2009b). Real-time monitoring of wind energy converters based on software agents. In: Proc. of the 18th International Conference on the Applications of Computer Science and Mathematics in Architecture and Civil Engineering. Weimar, Germany, 07/07/2009.

Smarsly, K., Hartmann, D. & Law, K. H. (2012). Structural Health Monitoring of Wind Turbines Observed by Autonomous Software Components – 2nd Level Monitoring. In: Proc. of the International Conference on Computing in Civil and Building Engineering. Moscow, Russia, 06/27/2012.

Smarsly, K., Hartmann, D. & Law, K. H. (2013). A Computational Framework for Life-Cycle Management of Wind Turbines incorporating Structural Health Monitoring. Structural Health Monitoring – An International Journal, 12(4), pp. 359-376

Smarsly, K. & Law, K. H. (2013). Advanced Structural Health Monitoring based on Multi-Agent Technology. In: Zander, J. & Mostermann, P. (eds.). Computation for Humanity: Information Technology to Advance Society. Pp. 95-126. Boca Raton, FL, USA: CRC Press – Taylor & Francis Group, LLC.

Smarsly, K., Law, K. H. & Hartmann, D. (2012). Towards Life-Cycle Management of Wind Turbines based on Structural Health Monitoring. In: Proc. of the 1st International Conference on Performance-Based Life-Cycle Structural Engineering. Hong Kong, China, 12/05/2012.

Smarsly, K., Lehner, K. & Hartmann, D. (2007). Structural Health Monitoring based on Artificial Intelligence Techniques. In: Proc. of the Intern. Workshop on Computing in Civil Engineering. Pittsburgh, PA, USA, 07/24/2007.

Smarsly, K. & Petryna, Y. (2014). A Decentralized Approach towards Autonomous Fault Detection in Wireless Structural Health Monitoring Systems. In: Proc. of the 7th European Workshop on Structural Health Monitoring. Nantes, France, 07/08/2014.

Smarsly, K. & Tauscher, E. (2016). Monitoring information modeling for semantic mapping of structural health monitoring systems. In: Proc. of the 16th International Conference on Computing in Civil and Building Engineering. Osaka, Japan, 07/06/2016.

Yuan, X., Anumba, C. J. & Parfitt, M. K. (2016). Cyber-physical systems for temporary structure monitoring, Automation in Construction 66(2016), pp. 1-14.

Improving infrastructure-asset management through reasoning that is compatible with mental models of engineers

Ian F.C. Smith
EPFL, Switzerland
Ian.Smith@epfl.ch

Abstract. Infrastructure asset-management decision making is improved when there is accurate knowledge of real behaviour. Site inspection, sensing and judicious model-based data-interpretation improves knowledge of real behaviour. This knowledge may reveal previously unknown reserve capacity, especially when the critical limit state occurs under nominally elastic stresses (for example, deflection and fatigue). Good data-interpretation techniques need to be accurate, robust with respect to unknown aspects of uncertainty and understandable by practising engineers. This paper focuses principally on this third requirement. Since information related to structural behaviour may become available gradually over periods of several years, bridge engineers need to employ methods that are easy to understand while accommodating essential aspects such as model uncertainty. An interactive approach called error-domain model falsification is described in this paper. Several aspects of this approach make it more understandable to practising engineers compared with Bayesian model updating. A case study is used to illustrate important aspects.

1. Introduction

A recent report by the World Economic Forum (WEF, 2014) stated that infrastructure demand exceeds supply (existing structures plus new construction) by $1 trillion per year and this gap is increasing each year. It is not likely that over the long term it will be possible to reduce demand. It is equally unlikely that the rate of supply of new construction will be able to increase so much as to make up this difference. The only viable solution is to manage existing infrastructure more efficiently, including repair, retrofit and improvement, so that needs for complete replacement are minimized, thus creating the situation where most infrastructure elements last indefinitely.

Fortunately, there is usually reserve capacity in infrastructure at levels much above the codified safety and serviceability requirements. Adding reserve capacity during design is justifiable due to the high-risks involved, particularly within contexts of incomplete knowledge of conditions on constructions sites. The challenge is that once an infrastructure element, such as a bridge, has passed the construction stage, this reserve capacity is unknown. Also, behavior models used during design are usually so conservative that they provide poor support for estimating reserve capacity.

Measurement of behavior has much potential to improve asset management. Through identifying good behavior models, future management challenges - such as evaluating the effects of load increases, bridge widening, adding cycling lanes, vehicle damage and deterioration - are supported so that actions can be optimized. However, interpreting measurement data is hard since there is much uncertainty from many sources. While there are entire journals, yearly conferences and books that present results from research into structural health monitoring, for example (Catbas et al, 2013) , most provide proposals for damage detection; very few deal with the special context of infrastructure asset management where reserve capacity is of interest.

This paper describes a data-interpretation methodology called Error Domain Model Falsification (EDMF) that is intended to be used to interpret data taken from measurement of large infrastructure elements for the purposes of asset management. A case study of a bridge in Switzerland is used to illustrate the approach. Finally, EDMF is compared with Bayesian model updating in terms of accuracy, precision, computational expense, understandability for practitioners and finally, ease of modification.

2. Model Falsification Reasoning

Structural identification is an exercise in diagnosis since behavior is inferred from measurements. In scientific fields when measurements are used to falsify a theory (behavior model), this is considered to be strong science (Popper, 2002). Measurements that are used only to validate a theory involves a weaker science than falsification since there is a chance that other measurements could falsify the theory. The development of EDMF is supported by this hypothesis. A summary of the evolution and use of EDMF on full-scale systems is provided in Smith (2016)

EDMF begins with a site visit, see Figure 1. Then a sensitivity study is used to determine which of the model parameters requiring identification provide the most variation in the behavior of interest. This sensitivity study helps determine the best model class. Ranges in values of the model parameters are then fixed using engineering judgement and contextual knowledge. Sampling of parameter values in these ranges are used to generate model instances that are used to provide predictions at measurement locations.

Falsification of model instances occurs when the difference between measurements and predictions fall outside of threshold values that are determined by combining modelling and measurement uncertainties. Falsification can occur at *any* one measurement location. An expected identifiability is fixed, say at 95%, so that thresholds can be quantified. Since there are usually a small number of measurements, a correction for non-infinite measurements is applied (Sidak, 1967). This is analogous to the revised normal distribution that is provided by the Student t-distribution.

The candidate model set (CMS) is obtained by collecting model instances that are not falsified. While these models were determined by combining estimated probabilities of measurement and modelling uncertainties, once in the CMS all models are assumed to be equally probable. Knowledge of uncertainty distributions is usually so poor that any other assumption is not justified.

The CMS is then used for asset management through evaluation of reserve capacity and predictions of repair, retrofit and improvement scenarios. Such predictions do not usually involve cases where interpolations are made between measurement points. This activity requires extrapolations and therefore, it is essential to ensure that the CMS includes at least one model instance that is a good representation of real behavior.

Identification of the right model class using measurements is a core challenge in every field of experimental science. While this methodology cannot guarantee that the right model class has been chosen (thus helping to ensure that the CMS includes the right model instance) EDMF provides important support for this challenge. When the CMS is empty, the entire model class is falsified. Experience on tens of full scale structures has shown that this is a common occurrence when simple design-based model classes are used. Structural evaluations are iterative activities of observation, measurement and data interpretation and EDMF has been shown to provide support in a compatible framework (Pasquier and Smith, 2016)

When a model class is falsified, there are several options available to the engineer. In the flow chart, Figure 1, a new model class can be tried. Finding a new model-class possibility should be verified by a site visit. For example if the new model class involves a model of rolling support that has sliding resistance due to aging, there should be visible evidence of such behavior. Other options include examining the measurements for outliers and making more measurements. For example when one measurement is responsible for falsifying a majority of the initial model set, it should be evaluated as a possible outlier. More information and cases studies are provided in (Pasquier and Smith, 2016).

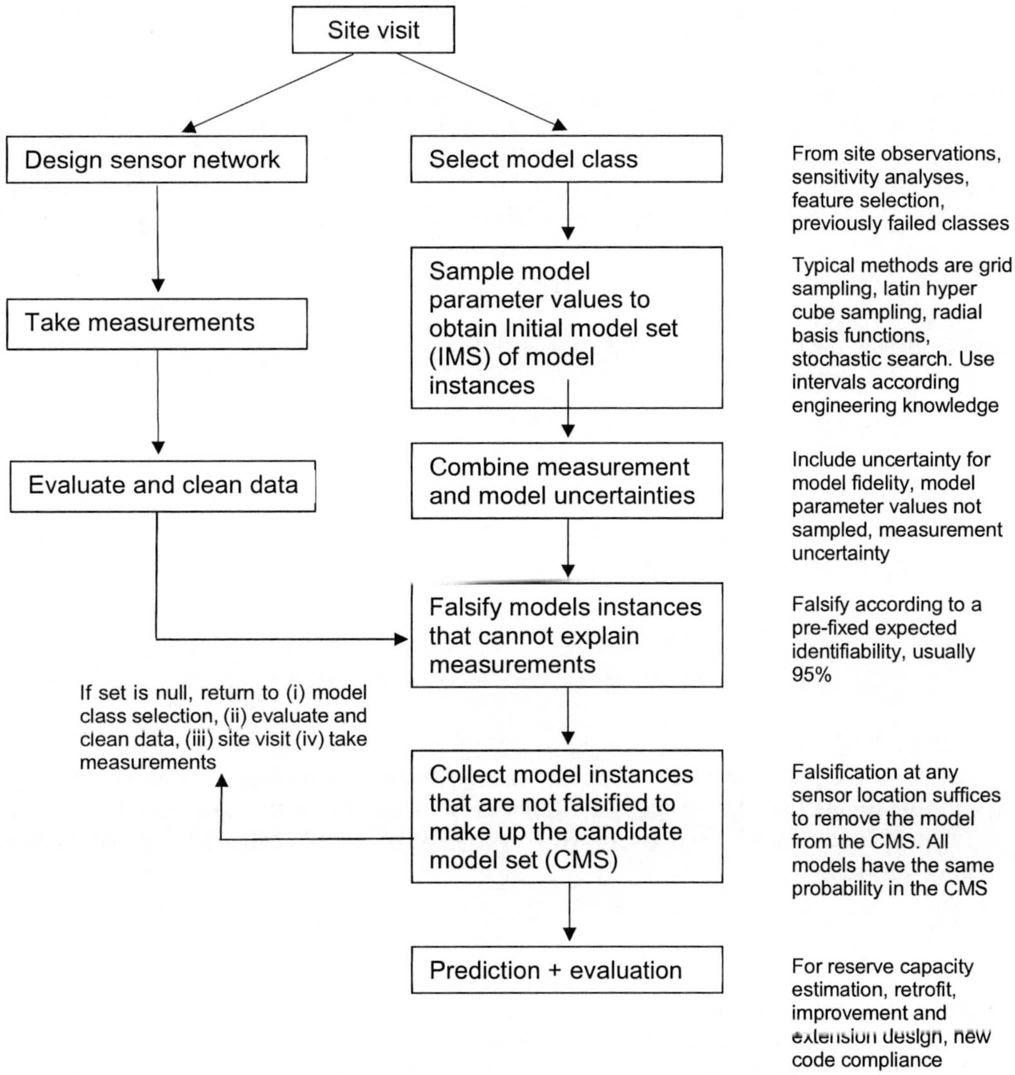

Figure 1 A flow chart of the EDMF methodology with additional comments on the right. These comments refer to activities on the right side of the flowchart. This flowchart is relevant equally for static load tests, dynamic testing and for continuous measurement.

A mathematical representation of model falsification has been developed by (Pasquier and Smith, 2016). Fixing the initial model set as $\mathbf{\Omega}$, model instances in this set having parameter-value vectors, $\boldsymbol{\theta}$, a finite number of measurements, n_m, the candidate model set $\boldsymbol{\Omega}''$ after falsification is

$$\boldsymbol{\Omega}'' = \{\boldsymbol{\theta} \in \boldsymbol{\Omega} | \forall i: \Pr(u_{i,low} \leq g_i(\boldsymbol{\theta}) - y_i \leq u_{i,high}) \leq \phi^{1/n_m}\} \quad (1)$$

where Pr is probability, $u_{i,low}, u_{i,high}$ are threshold bounds, $g_i(\boldsymbol{\theta})$ is the model instance prediction at measurement position i, y_i is the measurement at i and ϕ is the expected identifiability, sometimes referred to as the probability of identification which is usually taken to be 95%. The threshold bounds are defined such that

$$\forall i: \quad \phi^{1/n_m} = \int_{u_{i,low}}^{u_{i,high}} f_{U_{c,i}}(u_{c,i}) du_{c,i} \quad (2)$$

Where $U_{c,i}$is the combined measurement and modelling uncertainty and $f_{U_{c,i}}(u_{c,i})$ is its distribution function. All models that are falsified using Equation 1 are assigned a probability

$$\Pr(\boldsymbol{\theta} \notin \boldsymbol{\Omega}'') = 0 \quad (3)$$

and models in the CMS have a constant probability

$$\Pr(\boldsymbol{\theta} \in \boldsymbol{\Omega}'') = \frac{1}{\int_{\boldsymbol{\theta} \in \boldsymbol{\Omega}} d\boldsymbol{\theta}} \quad (4)$$

Predictions are made using the instances of the CMS with the modelling uncertainty, $U_{model,j}$. At measurement location n_q the prediction of a quantity Q_j is defined using the improved knowledge of parameter values θ" as follows:

$$Q_j = g_j(\boldsymbol{\theta}'') + U_{model,j} \quad \forall j \in \{1, \dots, n_q\} \quad (5)$$

3. Case Study

To illustrate the EDMF approach, the Aarwangen Bridge, Switzerland, a tubular steel-concrete composite bridge having two spans of 48m with welded tubular steel trusses connected to an 8m-wide concrete deck is used. Every week over 2,500 trucks averaging 18 tons take the bridge in both directions.

Shortly after construction, six static load tests, involving two trucks in three configurations were carried out. A site visit confirmed that the as-built bridge conformed to the drawings and that no significant variation in dimensions were observed. Since the bridge was just built, no deterioration was present. The measurement system was configured using engineering experience without a comparative numerical study of criteria such as the value of information and practical considerations. Eighteen strain gauges, placed on diagonals as well as upper and lower truss chords, recorded strains.

Following the site visit, a 3-D finite-element model was built and a sensitivity study showed that several uncertain parameter values had an important influence on the response of the structure. These were identified to be the Young's Modulus of the concrete and the pavement, the rotational stiffness of the truss connections, and the longitudinal stiffness of the expansion joints at the ends of the bridge. Engineering judgment was used to define the range of possible values of these parameters. Sampling combinations of values of these parameters resulted in an initial model set (IMS) of 15,625 model instances. Falsification thresholds were computed at a 95% expected identifiability by combining 14 uncertainty sources using Monte Carlo sampling.

Error domain model falsification involves determining which residuals (model-prediction values – measurements) fall within the thresholds at all measurement locations for all load cases. After cleaning the data for outliers, malfunctioning strain gauges and redundant information, 15,556 model instances were falsified leading to a population of 69 instances in the candidate-model set (CMS).

Fatigue of the tubular truss chord connections is the critical limit state. After measurements, data-interpretation using EDMF and prediction, the CMS resulted in an average of 80% reduction in the uncertainty associated with remaining fatigue life and furthermore, compared with the design stage calculations, fatigue lives at critical connections were increased by an average of 88%. Finally, uncertain misevaluations were evaluated using a sensitivity study. Misevaluations of up to 50% of uncertainties resulted in only a marginal change to these improvements. For the worst case (most severe model instance) the remaining fatigue life increased from 259 to 441 years.

This study has resulted in a very comfortable reserve capacity for load increases that are expected in the future. Asset managers have been able to unlock reserve capacity through measurements. Rather than having to use design calculations, engineers can now use information that corresponds to real behaviour. Further details are available in (Pasquier et al, 2014 and 2016)

4. Comparison of EDMF with Traditional Applications of Bayesian Model Updating

Most applications of Bayesian model updating involve the assumptions of zero-mean, independent Gaussian uncertainty distributions. Many important sources of uncertainty in civil infrastructure do not have zero means, they are not independent and their forms are not Gaussian. This creates a situation where traditional applications of Bayesian model updating results in biased identification and prediction and this weakness has been illustrated in a recent study. (Pasquier and Smith, 2015)

Compatibility with mental models of engineers A modified version of Bayesian model updating has been shown to provide similar results as EDMF (Pai and Smith, 2017). While these modifications have increased robustness to unknown values of correlation between measurement locations, Bayesian model updating remains difficult to understand and difficult to modify for practising engineers. Practising engineers are generally not happy to use conditional probabilities since they have difficulty mapping their domain knowledge to the components required by Bayesian updating. The practical advantages of EDMF are a logical engineering starting point, ease of understanding and ease of modification. These advantages are due to a close correspondence of mental models of the identification task. Engineers understand the idea of falsification because ruling out possibilities is part of their set of decision-making strategies. This has been verified repeatedly with practitioners over the past five years.

Multi-criteria comparison A comparison of EDMF, traditional Bayesian model updating and modified Bayesian model updating according to several aspects is presented in Table 1. Modified Bayesian model updating uses the same conditional probability formula as is used with traditional Bayesian model updating. However, as with EDMF, uniform probability distributions are used. This makes the modified Bayesian formulation just as robust as EDMF when correlations between predictions at measurement locations are unknown. However, changes in information as not done as transparently as with EDMF and there are more situations where a complete recalculation is necessary.

Table 1 Comparison of three data-interpretation strategies

	EDMF	Traditional Bayesian model updating	Modified Bayesian model updating
Input	Measurements Model class Max/min values of model parameters, measurements and model uncertainty Reliability of identification	Measurements Model class Prior probabilities Likelihood functions for each measurement location	Measurements Model class Max/min values of model parameters, measurements and model uncertainty Reliability of identification
Output	Candidate model set	Multivariate probability distribution functions	Multivariate probability distribution functions
Modifications	Changes to variable ranges and uncertainties made explicity	Changes require transformation	Changes to variable ranges and uncertainties made explicity
Strengths	Engineering knowledge directly related to input Robust extrapolation with systematic uncertainty Complete falsification helps find right model class Changes to uncertainties do not lead to re-execution	Computation times generally less than for EDMF Accurate when all distributions and all correlations are known and when there are no systematic uncertainties	Robust extrapolation with systematic uncertainty Computation times generally less than for EDMF Wrong model class leads to no starting point
Weaknesses	Sensitive to outliers Computation time	Not understood by practitioners Most changes require re-execution	Not understood by practitioners Most changes require re-execution
Comments	Adaptive sampling and surrogate modelling under development	Extrapolation may be inaccurate	

Finally, conditional probabilities are not understood by practising engineers. This means that often Bayesian data-interpretation is out-sourced to consultants while the engineers who are responsible for the structure treat the calculation algorithms as black boxes. Since data may have to be reinterpreted several times over the lives of civil infrastructure, this situation is not optimal. Engineers who are responsible for asset management need to understand how data is interpreted so they can introduce changes themselves. EDMF provides a strategy that engineers can understand since it corresponds more closely to their mental models of data interpretation and asset management,

5. Conclusions

EDMF is a methodology for measurement data interpretation that is more robust with respect to inaccurate modelling assumptions than traditional proposals and it is compatible with the knowledge and needs of civil-infrastructure asset managers. As a result, making changes in light of new information is less likely to result in inappropriate decisions.

6. Acknowledgements

The work described in this paper was supported by the Swiss National Science Foundation under contract 200020_169026 and by the Singapore-ETH Centre (SEC). The SEC was established as a collaboration between ETH Zurich and National Research Foundation (NRF) Singapore (FI 370074011-370074016) under the auspices of the NRF's Campus for Research Excellence and Technological Enterprise (CREATE) program.

References

Çatbas, F. N , Kijewski-Correa, T., and Aktan, A. E. (eds) (2013). Structural Identification of Constructed Systems. Reston, VA: American Society of Civil Engineers, 248p

Pai, S.G.S. and Smith, I.F.C (2017) "Comparing Three Methodologies for System Identification and Prediction". Proceedings 14th International Probabilistic Workshop, Ghent, Springer International Publishing, Switzerland. DOI: 10.1007/978-3-319-47886-9_6, pp 81-95,

Pasquier, R. and Smith, I.F.C. (2015) "Robust system identification and model predictions in the presence of systematic uncertainty" Advanced Engineering Informatics, 29 (4), 1096-1109 doi:10.1016/j.aei.2015.07.007

Pasquier R. and Smith I. F. C. (2016) "Iterative structural identification framework for evaluation of existing structures", Engineering Structures, 106, 179-194. 10.1016/j.engstruct.2015.09.039

Pasquier, R., Goulet, J., Acevedo, C., and Smith, I.F.C. (2014) "Improving Fatigue Evaluations of Structures Using In-Service Behavior Measurement Data" J. Bridge Eng., 19(11), 04014045

Pasquier, R., D'Angelo, L., Goulet, J., Acevedo, C., Nussbaumer, A. and Smith, I.F.C: (2016). "Measurement, Data Interpretation, and Uncertainty Propagation for Fatigue Assessments of Structures." Journal of Bridge Engineering, 10.1061/(ASCE)BE.1943-5592.0000861,04015087

Popper, K.R. (2002) The logic of scientific discovery, 3rd ed. New York, Routledge.

Sidak, Z. (1967) "Rectangular confidence regions for the means of multivariate normal distributions" Journal of the American Statistical Association, Vol 62, 626-633.

Smith, I.F.C. (2016) "Studies of sensor data interpretation for asset management of the built environment" Frontiers in Built Environment, 2:8. doi: 10.3389/fbuil.2016.00008

WEF (2014) Report to the World Economic Forum, Boston Consulting Group

Framework for shared visualization and real-time information flow to the construction site

Ranjith K. Soman, David Birch, Jennifer K Whyte
Imperial College London, United Kingdom
ranjithks17@imperial.ac.uk

Abstract: The aim of this paper is to develop a framework for shared visualization between design office and construction office using augmented reality as a platform with a focus on the security of Building Information Model. The current paper is part of an ongoing study aimed at creating a real-time bi-directional information flow between the construction office and site and focuses on a shared visualisation context. A framework architecture for enabling shared visualisation with a stress on the security of Building Information Model is discussed. A prototype application based on the framework was deployed on an Android device in a controlled environment for testing. The application augmented Building Information objects dynamically to the real-world without any latency. Salient features of the prototype include dynamic loading of Building Information content during the runtime, data encapsulation based on user privileges, deployability on portable low-end computing devices etc. Using shared visualization would empower the construction engineers with real-time models updates with access to many near-optimal management solutions. This enables the engineers to narrow in on the best solution under given constraints

1. Introduction

The global construction industry accounted for approximately 11 % of the global GDP in 2011 and is predicted to increase to more than 13.2 % by 2020 (Roumeliotis, 2011). The major contribution to these sums comes from complex infrastructure projects with numerous interdependencies. Despite being large and complex, many of these projects are still managed with traditional construction management practices (creating a centralized baseline plan for decentralized construction execution and monitoring the same in a centralized manner). This results in cost overruns and schedule delays. Building on the advances in the computing and visualization domains, the construction industry is moving towards more agile project management practices to improve the performance and efficiency (Levitt, 2011; Whyte & Levitt, 2011). Our paper discusses a subsystem for such an agile project management practice by enabling shared visualization of the project model (designed and as-built) between different design teams and engineers at the construction site using virtual reality (VR) / augmented reality (AR) stressing on the security of the Building Information Model.

Applications of AR have helped in improving the performance of AEC domains in areas such as as-built and as-planned project status management, pre-empting work package schedule disputes, enhancing collaboration etc. (Behzadan, Dong, & Kamat, 2015; Kamat et al., 2011; Rankohi & Waugh, 2013). With advancements in mobile computing and the and availability of sensing and positioning systems in smaller devices, AR has shifted from bulky computers to smartphones and tablets (Bae, White, Golparvar-Fard, Pan, & Sun, 2015; Kodeboyina & Varghese, 2016).Construction researchers are using AR as a platform to visualize Building Information Data (Behzadan et al., 2015; Golparvar-Fard, Peña-Mora, & Savarese, 2009; Kopsida & Brilakis, 2016). Mobile based AR systems retrieve parts of Building Information Models stored in clouds for visualization rather than storing the model on the AR device. However, there are inherent risks in using central Building Information Modelling server pertaining to security of the model (Mahamadu, Mahdjoubi, & Booth, 2013). With infrastructure sector moving in the direction of digital transformation(Kemp et al., 2017) with an increase in use and dependence on information and communication technologies, there is a need to address the inherent vulnerability issues as stated in PAS 1192-5:2015 standards(BSI, 2015). However, there aren't many studies addressing this issue. The current study makes an attempt to address this vulnerability by exploring the potential of AR in increasing the security of digital built assets within the built environment.

Hence, the aim of this paper is to develop a framework for shared visualization between design office and construction office using AR as a platform with a focus on the security of Building Information Model. The remainder of this paper is divided into 4 sections. Section 2 describes how this paper fits into the overall framework on the bi-directional informational flow between the construction site and office (Ph.D. work in initial stages at Imperial College London). Section 3 describes the prototype in development and section 4 gives a glimpse into the early prototype. Section 5 states the conclusions from the early prototype study and gives directions for the further work in this area.

2. Framework

The framework for shared visualization between construction office and construction site is shown in Figure 1.The current framework forms a subset of the integrated framework on interactive visualisation and data acquisition proposed by Soman & Whyte (2017).

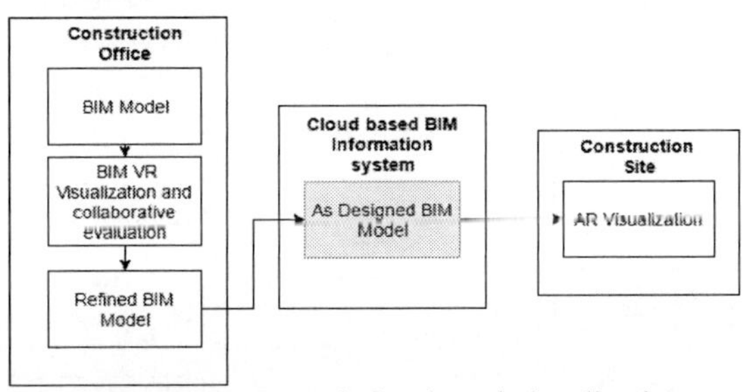

Figure 1: Framework for shared visualization between construction office and construction site

At the construction office, Building Information Models are made and visualized in a VR environment for verification. Once the model is ready, it is uploaded into a secure server. Models can be accessed by users with correct privileges in real time from then on. Further changes in the model can be uploaded to server from time to time which will be reflected in the devices used by the users in real time. The next section describes the architecture of the framework in detail.

3. Framework Architecture

The shared visualization part of the framework was focussed on the early prototype development. The aim of this prototype is to visualize a model in the real world dynamically. This is achieved using a cloud server for holding the latest model and marker based tracking on an Android phone for displaying the model augmented over the real world. The current prototype is built on top of the low-cost AR framework created by Kodeboyina & Varghese (2016). The application is built on top of a commercial game engine and the Android platform was chosen as target build due to its developer-friendly API and its wide availability due to its economy.

Almost all the commercial Building Information Modelling suites have a workflow to export their models to a game engine. The model is packaged into a game engine 'asset', the format for a 3D object in the game engine environment. The current frameworks using AR build the asset directly into packages and hard code them into the mobile application (Kodeboyina & Varghese, 2016) this makes change impossible. However, this method wouldn't suit construction as the models are frequently amended based on change orders. Hence, every time a model is updated, the application containing the model should be updated. Also, it should be noted that the Building Information Models are packaged into the mobile application and stored on the portable device. This approach increases the size of the application. Furthermore, the model is in the phone memory and the security of the data is limited to the security of the phone.

The current prototype uses a dynamic method to load the model on the portable device at run time. The model is downloaded and cached on the portable device during the runtime. Once the application on the device closes, the model and related data are deleted. This makes the application light (i.e. reduces the install size of the application) as well as making the model secure. The model stored on a server can be encrypted and access may be controlled. This is made possible by packaging the asset into a bundle and the uploading it into the cloud platform and downloading during the runtime.

The current prototype has three components as shown in Figure 2.

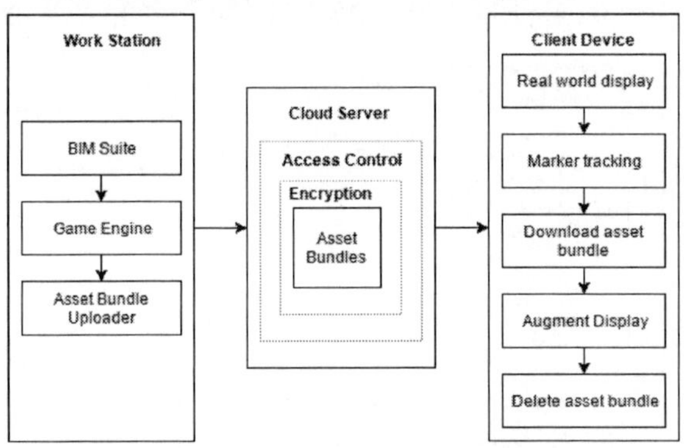

Figure 2: Prototype architecture

1. Workstation – This is the computer used for content creation. It has BIM package and game engine installed in it. The 3D model is imported into the game engine and attached with the marker. The 3D content is classified and packaged according to its use. This helps in assigning the 3D content to the respective work groups (structural, architecture, MEP etc. and the level of details). These packages are then built into multiple asset bundles. For example, all the 3D content and data pertaining to structural elements are built into a structural asset bundle. Only users having access to structural elements would be able to download this asset bundle. Once the asset bundle is built, it is then uploaded to the cloud server. There is an option for the device to view the contents in VR without attaching the model to a marker. This is enabled through VR rendering capability of the game engine chosen. It can be used to visualize the model in VR for design checking and iterations.

2. Cloud server – The cloud server is a web application with encrypted storage and access control. It is easier to secure a web cloud server rather than securing every device which needs to access the model. The Web application is built on REST API and OAuth 2.0 framework. The REST API offers visibility, reliability, and scalability

as well as a clear separation between a cloud and a server. This increases the security of the models stored in the server. OAuth 2.0 offers simple yet secure authentication to the secure storage. It makes the user use their existing company logins and need not create separate logins making the server integrated to the company's authentication workflows.

3. Client device – It is essentially a portable Android device with a camera. The application is built on the Android platform. Users must enter their credentials to log into the server. The server will allow downloading asset bundles permitted for the user. Once logged in, the camera shows the background video on the screen. Videos frames are searched for a visual marker. Once the tracking algorithm determines a marker in a frame, the asset bundle is requested from the server using the user's credentials. If the user has access, asset bundles allocated to his credentials will be downloaded. These assets would then be overlaid on the background frame at a position relative to the marker. Once the assets are loaded, even if you remove the marker, the asset would stay in the 3D space. When the user exits the application, the downloaded model would be deleted from the phones memory.

The next section describes the features and the implementation of an early prototype based on the framework explained.

4. Prototype Implementation

The early prototype was created using Unity3D game engine coupled with Vuforia SDK and Google Drive API (to enable REST and OAuth capabilities). Unity 3D was used for the creating the environment, projecting the Building Information components onto the 3D space etc. It was also used to package assets according to work package and upload them to the server. Vuforia SDK was used for marker-based tracking and augmented visualization of contents on the 3D space. Google drive API was used for secured storage with OATH2.0 security. For VR, Cardboard SDK was used. The application was so created that the Building Information contents were downloaded only during the runtime and destroyed once the application has exited the program. This is illustrated in Figure 4. Figure 4 (A) shows the scene during initialisation. Please note the play button (marked by a red oval) is not highlighted. The blue oval shows two assets (AR camera and Image target) loaded into the scene during this time. Figure 4 (B) displays the assets loaded into the scene during runtime. Please note the play button in the ON state as marked by red oval shape. The blue oval shows that an extra asset (bookshelf) loaded onto the scene during the runtime. Loading the asset during the runtime increases the security of the Building Information Model. It is not stored locally beyond the life of the application runtime. Also, as the model is stored on the server, it is easier to deploy revisions without changing the base application

Figure 3 illustrates the data encapsulation concept in the application. There is an asset TV set loaded onto the scene in Figure 3 in addition to the assets shown in Figure 4(B).This is because the user privileges when the application is run in Figure 3is higher than that of Figure 4(B). The same concept can be used extensively to hide and show various aspects of Building Information Model based on the privileges of the user. This concept increases the Building Information Model security to the next level where the information is given to the user on a 'need to know' basis.

Figure 3 : Screen shot illustrating the data encapsulation based on user privileges.

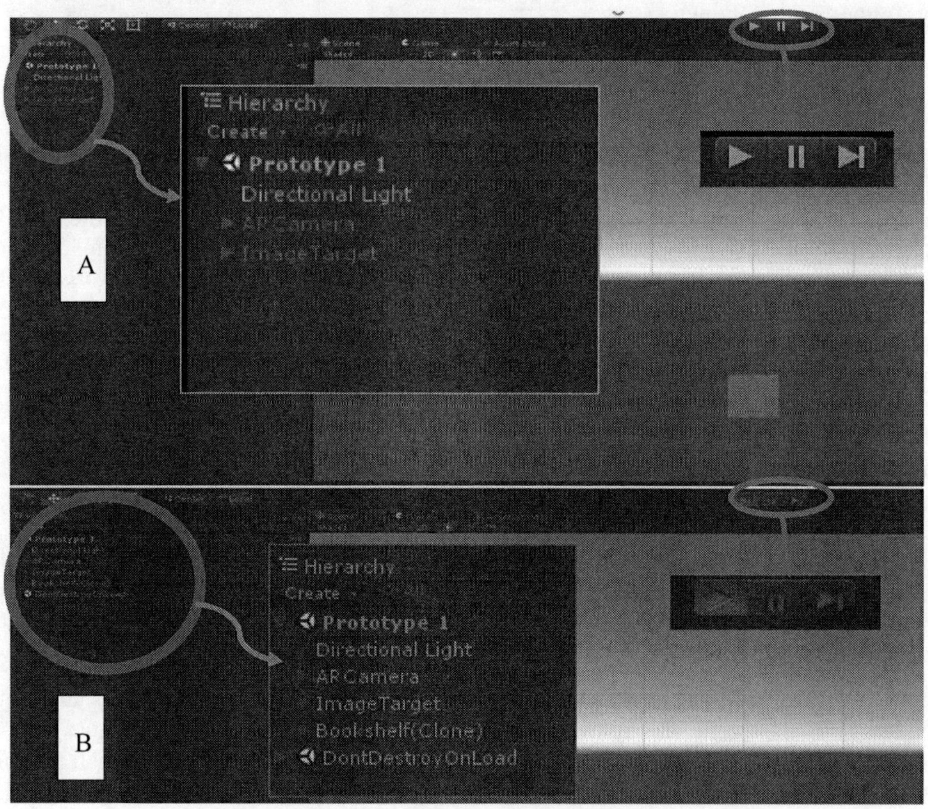

Figure 4: Screenshot illustrating the loading of BIM content during runtime
(A) Scene during initialisation (B) Scene during runtime

Figure 5 shows the photos of the implementation of the prototype on an Android device. Users need to enter their username, password, and role to access the server (Figure (A)). Once the user obtains access to the server, the assets that are accessible to their role would be

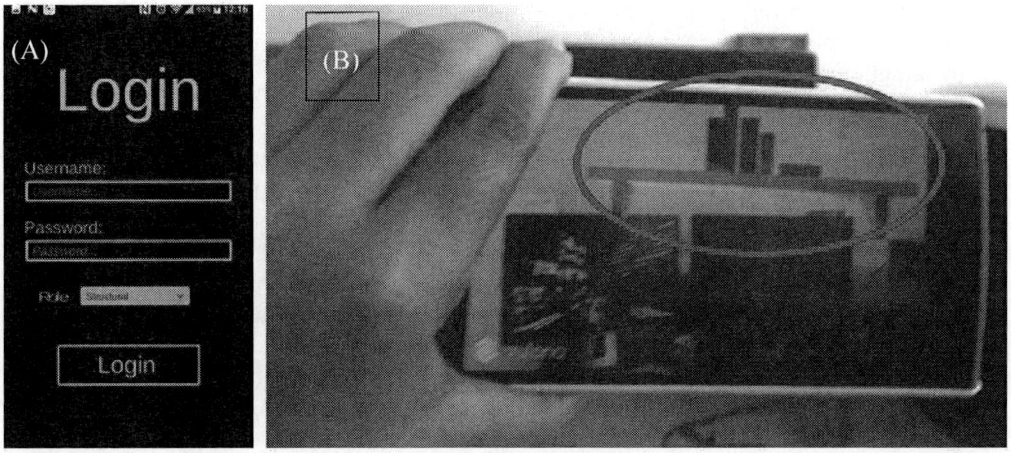

Figure 5 : Photos of the (A) login page and (B) augmentation of 3D content on the real world

downloaded and displayed during the runtime. Augmentation of a book shelf on the real world is shown in Figure (B).

5. Conclusions and Further Work

A framework for shared visualization between design office and construction office using AR as a platform with a focus on the security of Building Information Model is presented in this paper. The framework is tested through the development of a prototype application for augmented visualisation of BIM model. The prototype application was developed with the security of the Building Information Model as the prime focus and the results of the implementation are presented in this paper. The application presented in this paper is a significant improvement on the application mentioned in Kodeboyina & Varghese, 2016 .The improvement is achieved by dynamic loading of building information model in the application as opposed to hard coding the model in the application.

The prototype uses a dynamic method to load Building Information objects onto the real world during the runtime thereby increasing the security of the model. In addition, it provides authentication and layered user privileges to encapsulate the data and release it on a need to know basis. This increases the security of the model as well as making the application less bulky enabling portable low-end computing devices to run it smoothly. It is enabled by breaking up of large models into smaller work group components and downloaded when the need arises during the runtime. The prototype was deployed on a low cost portable Android device in a controlled environment for testing and the application augmented Building Information object dynamically to the real-world without any latency. The observations from the prototype implementations lead points that the modern smart devices have the capability to render virtual models into the real world and the embedded sensors are accurate enough to do the tracking in an efficient manner. This opens the doors to low-end computing and highly accessible AR devices which can be used at the construction site for visualization of Building Information Models. The high accessibility enables engineers and site personnel in the industry to take ownership of latest technology and experiment with it in their roles, leading to a proliferation of related innovation. Also, the proposed framework addresses the inherent vulnerability issues as stated in PAS 1192-5:2015 standards, occurring while infrastructure sector moves towards digital transformation, to an extent. Hence it provides a roadmap for implementation of a secure central Building Information Model. This is critical as Building Information Modelling is becoming a necessary requirement in several countries and projects are moving towards a central Building Information Model.

Further work to be done includes, deploying the application on a real construction site and collecting the feedback from the construction site experience to improve the prototype. A construction site implementation of the prototype is planned in collaboration with industry partner of the Centre for Systems Engineering and Innovation. It is necessary to integrate user interfaces for interaction with the models which is yet to be implemented. Work needs to be done on automation of the workflows for creation and uploading of Building Information bundle packages. Long-term objectives include creating a framework for bidirectional real-time information flow between the construction site and office(as shown in Figure 6) using VR/AR and the Internet of Things and studying the data utilization patterns.

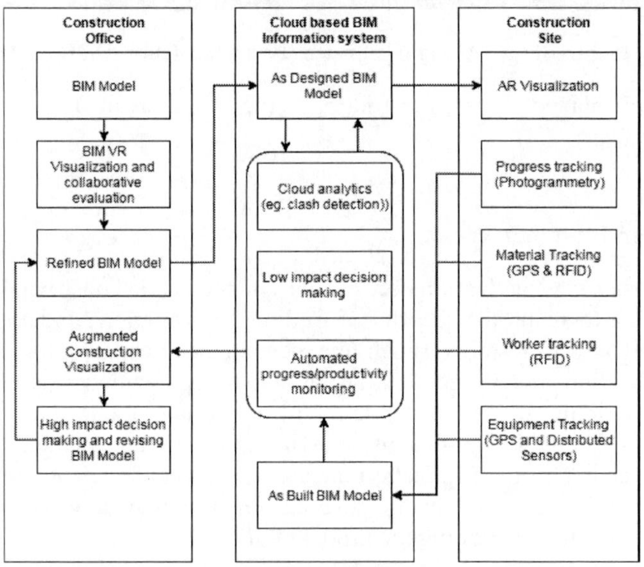

Figure 6 : Frame work for interactive visualisation
and automated data acquisition (Soman & Whyte, 2017)

The current paper presents a roadmap to the research community on how to use augmented reality as a platform for secure and shared visualisation of building information model on a construction site. Further research should be conducted in this area to study the implications of the current framework on issues such as health and safety issues, ideal data formats for efficient data transfers, interoperability, and integration with existing workflows etc.

6. Acknowledgement

The current paper is part of the Ph.D. study (started on 14/02/2017) at the Centre for Systems Engineering and Innovation at Imperial College London. The study is co-sponsored through a Skempton Scholarship and a studentship from Bentley Systems.

References

Bae, H., White, J., Golparvar-Fard, M., Pan, Y., & Sun, Y. (2015). Fast and scalable 3D cyber-physical modeling for high-precision mobile augmented reality systems. *Personal and Ubiquitous Computing, 19*(8), 1275–1294. https://doi.org/10.1007/s00779-015-0892-6

Behzadan, A. H., Dong, S., & Kamat, V. R. (2015). Augmented reality visualization: A review of civil infrastructure system applications. *Advanced Engineering Informatics, 29*(2), 252–267. https://doi.org/10.1016/j.aei.2015.03.005

BSI. (2015). PAS 1192-5-2015: Specification for security-minded building information modelling, digital built environments and smart asset management. *British Standards Institution (BSI)*.

Golparvar-Fard, M., Peña-Mora, F., & Savarese, S. (2009). D4AR–a 4-dimensional augmented reality model for automating construction progress monitoring data collection, processing and communication. In *Journal of information technology in construction* (Vol. 14, pp. 129–153).

Kamat, V. R., Martinez, J. C., Fischer, M., Golparvar-Fard, M., Peña-Mora, F., & Savarese, S. (2011). Research in Visualization Techniques for Field Construction. *Journal of Construction Engineering and Management, 137*(10), 853–862. https://doi.org/10.1061/(ASCE)CO.1943-7862.0000262

Kemp, A., Enzer, M., Schooling, J., Whyte, J., Colvin, S., Agnew, R., ... Chambers, P. (2017). *State Of The Nation 2017 : Digital Transformation.* London. Retrieved from https://www.ice.org.uk/getattachment/media-and-policy/policy/state-of-the-nation-2017-digital-transformation/state-of-the-nation-2017-digital-transformation.pdf.aspx

Kodeboyina, S. M., & Varghese, K. (2016). Low Cost Augmented Reality Framework for Construction Applications. In *Proceedings of 33rd ISARC.*

Kopsida, M., & Brilakis, I. (2016). Markerless BIM Registration for Mobile Augmented Reality Based Inspection, (July), 1–7.

Levitt, R. E. (2011). Towards project management 2.0. *Engineering Project Organization Journal, 1*(3), 197–210. https://doi.org/10.1080/21573727.2011.609558

Mahamadu, A.-M., Mahdjoubi, L., & Booth, C. (2013). Challenges to BIM-Cloud Integration: Implication of Security Issues on Secure Collaboration. In *2013 IEEE 5th International Conference on Cloud Computing Technology and Science* (Vol. 2, pp. 209–214). IEEE. https://doi.org/10.1109/CloudCom.2013.127

Rankohi, S., & Waugh, L. (2013). Review and analysis of augmented reality literature for construction industry. *Visualization in Engineering, 1*(2005), 1–18.

Roumeliotis, G. (2011). Global construction growth to outpace GDP this decade - PwC. Retrieved January 31, 2017, from http://in.reuters.com/article/idINIndia-55293920110303

Soman, R. K., & Whyte, J. K. (2017). A FRAMEWORK FOR CLOUD-BASED VIRTUAL AND AUGMENTED REALITY USING REAL-TIME INFORMATION FOR CONSTRUCTION PROGRESS MONITORING. In *Proc. Lean & Computing in Construction Congress (LC3)* (Vol. 1). Heraklion, Greece.

Whyte, J., & Levitt, R. (2011). *Information Management and the Management of Projects. The Oxford Handbook of Project Management.* Oxford University Press. https://doi.org/10.1093/oxfordhb/9780199563142.003.0016

A Graph-Based Generative Method for Supporting Bridge Design

Ślusarczyk, E. Grabska, B. Strug,
Jagiellonian University, Poland
barbara.strug@uj.edu.pl

Abstract. This paper deals with a CAD tool supporting the conceptual phase of the bridge design process. Design drawings are created on the monitor screen by arranging elements of a visual language. It is possible to define visual design patterns, which are added to the visual language vocabulary. Both design drawings and the visual patterns are represented by graph-based data structures which are obtained automatically. The graph rules, which make it possible to replace subgraphs corresponding to visual patterns by subgraphs representing other patterns, are defined. By substituting selected subgraphs in the internal graph representations of drawings by other subgraphs in the possible way, the proposed system generates graph structures representing innovative bridge designs.

1. Introduction

Nowadays CAD systems facilitate an integration of various phases and aspects of engineering processes (Pahl & Beitz, 1996). CAD software is widely used to support the process of generating design drawings and product models. However CAD systems still lack generative methods to easily generate classes of similar design variants. For example models of bridges often have similar structures but differ in sizes or fitting to varying environmental conditions (Chung & Wang, 2014; Pipinato, 2015). For many years structures of design objects have been represented and generated using graphs and graph transformations (Rozenberg, 1999; Vilgertshofer & Borrmann, 2016).

This paper deals with the problem of the conceptual phase of bridge design in the unified graphical environment delivered by the system called *GraphTool*, which supports graph transformations (Ryszka & Grabska, 2013). This new software provides graphical editors for defining different types of graphs and graph transformation rules. Graph structures, which can be transformed using graph rules, are used as internal representations of bridge designs.

The designer generates drawings of bridges by arranging elements of the visual language. The vocabulary of this language is composed of visual primitives and visual relations between them. Bridge drawing parts can be considered as visual design patterns (Alexander, 1977), which are generated with basic elements of the language vocabulary, and added to this vocabulary. Then, elements of the extended vocabulary can be used to create design drawings.

One of the challenges of CAD systems is to automatically transform design drawings on the monitor screen into appropriate graph-based date structures (Strug et al., 2016). In the presented approach both topological structures and semantic properties (geometrical parameters, materials, environment aspects) of bridges are represented by composition graphs (CP-graphs) and their attributes, respectively (Borkowski & Grabska, 1995). A CP-graph is a labelled and attributed graph, where nodes represent components of artefacts and are labelled by names of components they represent. To each node a number of bonds expressing potential connections between components is assigned. Bonds are connected by edges representing relations between components and labelled by the relation names. Moreover nodes have attributes specifying properties of components assigned to them. Both whole design drawings generated by the designer and the visual patterns are automatically transformed into the corresponding CP-graphs. Nodes of these graphs represent visual primitives corresponding to structural components of bridges, like abutments, pylons, beams, arches and different types of cables, while edges represent relations between bridge components.

CP-graphs representing bridges are modified using CP-graph transformation rules designed in *GraphTool*. By substituting selected subgraphs in the specified way *GraphTool* generates different CP-graphs representing possible bridge structures with geometry and material properties specified by graph attributes. The possibility of relating attributes of right-hand sides of CP-graph rules to attributes of their left-hand sides enables us to capture parametric modeling knowledge.

On the basis of knowledge encoded in CP-graphs the compatibility of designs with the given requirements and constraints (for example weight of components, their shapes, stiffness, bending and compression degrees) can be tested. The valid graph structures can be saved in the GraphML format and passed to the interpretation application where they are visualized and other design criteria, like distribution of stresses in the designed structure or load transmission, can be checked. The proposed generative method allows the system supporting design to automatically model alternative bridge designs, which can be easily adapted to different use case scenarios and environmental conditions.

2. Bridge Design Patterns

This section explains how visual design patterns can be used during conceptual design of bridges. Apart from a vocabulary of a visual language being a finite set of visual primitives, a finite set of rules specifying possible configurations of these primitives in space is defined. Using these elements the designer by means of a system editor creates design drawings, which represent general ideas about design solutions (Grabska et al., 2012).

Visual primitives used in designing bridges represent abutments, pylons, beams, supports, arches and different types of cables. Three relations between them are considered. Two relations represent fixed and hinged connections between components of the bridge, while the third is the join relation. The visual primitives constituting a vocabulary of the visual language used in the bridge design are depicted in Fig. 1b. Design drawings representing bridge projects are composed of these visual primitives arbitrary arranged by the designer. Fig. 1a presents different types of bridges which can be created using these primitives.

The primitives used to create drawings can be parameterized. Their sizes and positions are specified by the designer. Two bridges composed of the same visual primitives but with different values of parameters are shown in Fig. 2.

Using primitives of the visual language the visual design patterns, which represent parts of bridges, are formed. Such patterns are convenient in design when the same structure is to be repeated a number of times (Strug & Ślusarczyk, 2009). Each of these patterns consists of two pylons or two supports and beams, arches or cables connecting them. Four visual design patterns, which can be seen in bridges shown in Fig. 1a and used in creating other bridge drawings are presented in Fig. 3.

3. CP-graph Representation of Bridges

In the presented approach composition graphs (CP-graphs) are used as the internal representation of bridge designs (Borkowski & Grabska, 1995). CP-graphs are labelled and attributed graphs, which represent both topological and semantic features of bridges. Nodes of these graphs represent structural components of bridges, like abutments, pylons, beams, arches, supports and different types of cables. The type of a component represented by a node is determined by its label. Moreover nodes have attributes specifying properties of components assigned to them. To each node a number of bonds detailing connections between structural bridge components is assigned. Bonds are connected by edges representing relations between bridge components and labelled by the relation names.

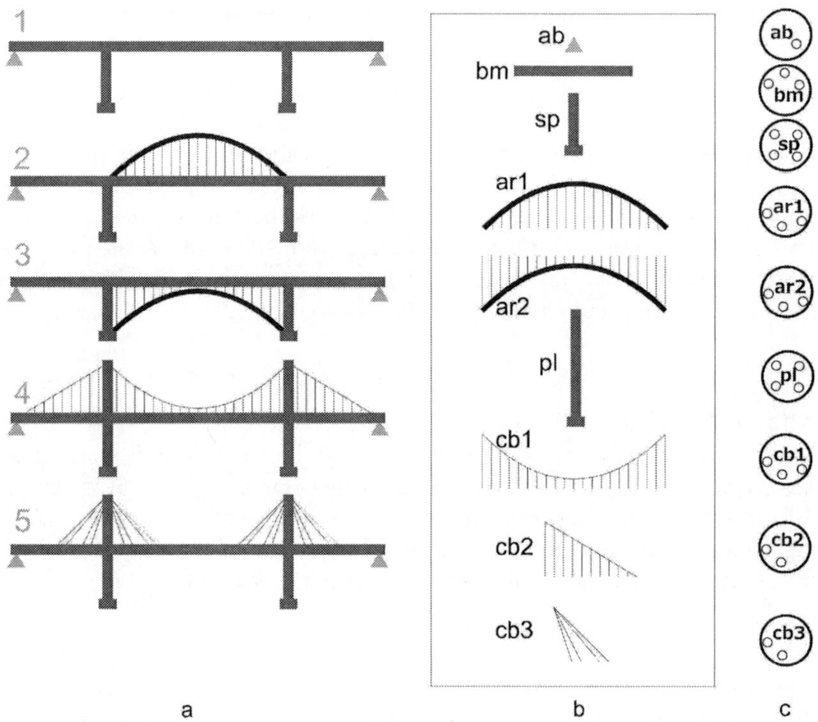

Figure 1: a) Different types of bridges, b) graphical primitives used in the drawings

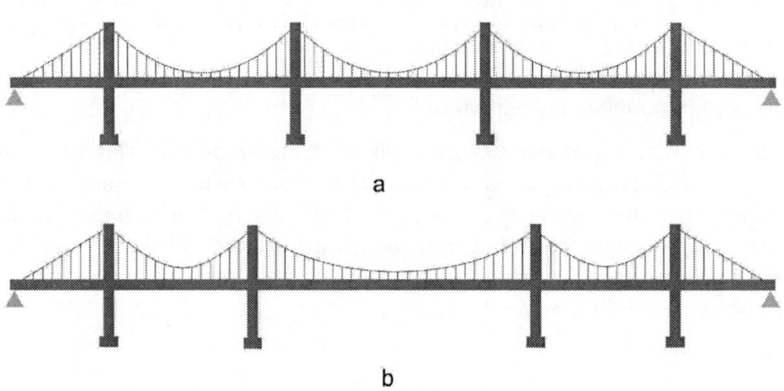

Figure 2: Two similar bridges obtained using different parameters

The formal definition of a CP-graph is as follows.

Let Σ be a finite alphabet used to label object nodes, bond nodes and edges. Let A be a nonempty, finite set of attributes. For each attribute $a \in A$, let D_a be a fixed, nonempty set of its admissible values, known as the domain of a.

A CP-graph G is a tuple $G = (V, B, E, bd, s, t, lab, atr)$, where:

1. V, B, E are pairwise disjoint finite sets, whose elements are respectively called nodes, bonds and edges,
2. $bd: V \rightarrow 2^B$ is a function assigning sets of bonds to nodes in such a way that $\forall x \in B$ $\exists! \, y \in V: x \in bd(y)$, i.e., each bond belongs to exactly one node,
3. $s, t: E \rightarrow B$ are functions assigning to edges source and target bonds, respectively, in such a way that $\forall e \in E \; \exists x, y \in V: s(e) \in bd(x) \wedge t(e) \in bd(y) \wedge x \neq y$,
4. $lab: V \cup B \cup E \rightarrow \Sigma$ is a labelling function,
5. $atr: V \cup B \cup E \rightarrow 2^A$ is an attributing function.

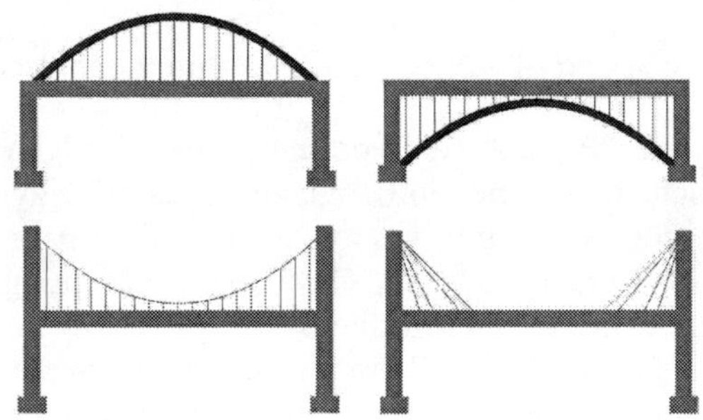

Figure 3: Visual design patterns representing parts of bridges

Let us consider the bridge and its CP-graph representation shown in Figs. 4a and 4b. The bridge is composed of the following prototypical parts: an abutment, a beam, a pylon, a cable1 and a cable2. The CP-graph nodes representing these parts are labeled as *ab*, *bm*, *pl*, *cb1* and *cb2*, respectively. Bonds assigned to nodes are drawn as small circles. The edge labels *fx* and *hn* denote fixed and hinged connections between components of the bridge. The edge label *jn* denotes the join relation.

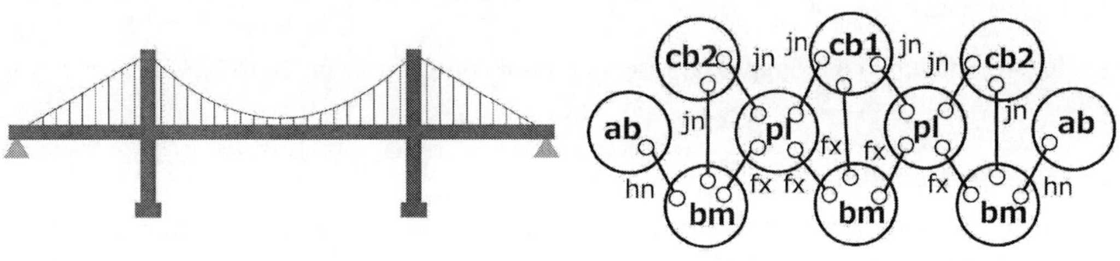

a b

Figure 4: A bridge and a CP-graph representing it

Bonds of CP-graph nodes, which are not engaged are called free and represent places on components where other components can be attached. Each free bond of a node signals a potential connection of a node with other nodes. Free bonds play also an important role in CP-graph modifications, as subgraphs with the same number of free bonds can easily replace each other with the constant embedding in the rest part of the CP-graph.

A part of a bridge from Fig. 4 and a subCP-graph representing it are shown in Fig. 5. Free bonds numbered 1 and 2 assigned to the node labelled *pl* correspond to parts of a pylon where cables and pylons can be attached to lengthen the bridge.

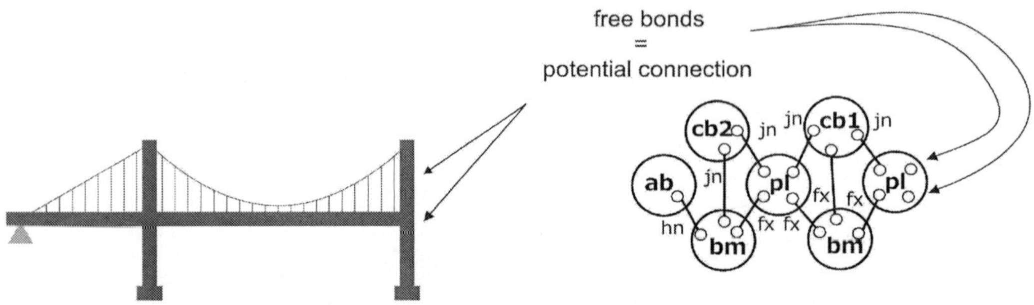

Figure 5: A part of a bridge and a CP-graph representing it

It is worth noticing that one CP-graph can represent several bridge models depending on the graphical primitives, which are assigned to CP-graph nodes by a given interpretation, and the transformations specified for these primitives by values of their parameters, which are treated as attributes assigned to CP-graph nodes. A CP-graph representing a topology of potential bridges is shown in Fig. 7a, while both bridge drawings shown in Fig. 2 and the drawings presented in Fig. 7b correspond to this CP-graph. The drawings are obtained using the same set of primitives, to which different transformations specified by parameter values were used.

CP-graphs representing visual bridge patterns shown in Fig. 2 are presented in Fig. 6.

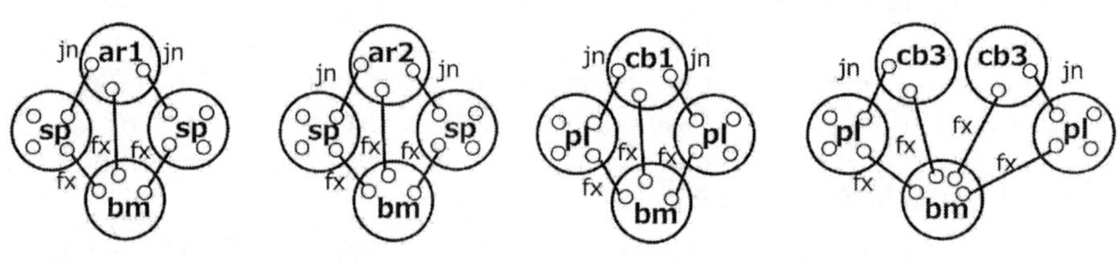

Figure 6: CP-graphs representing visual bridge patterns from Fig. 2.

4. CP-graph Modification Rules

When the designer generates a bridge drawing by means of a system editor its internal representation in the form of a CP-graph is automatically created. Inserting each visual primitive causes the new labelled node to be added to the CP-graph. Creating edges between bonds of nodes is controlled by means of label-dependent rules. CP-graph nodes with their bonds and labels, which correspond to the visual primitives shown in Fig. 1b, are presented in Fig. 1c.

A given CP-graph representing a drawing of a bridge can be modified using CP-graph transformation rules defined using *GraphTool*. These rules enable the system to replace CP-graph subgraphs corresponding to visual patterns by subgraphs representing other visual patterns. By substituting selected subgraphs in the internal CP-graph representations of drawings by other subgraphs in the specified way, the proposed system generates graph structures representing innovative bridge designs.

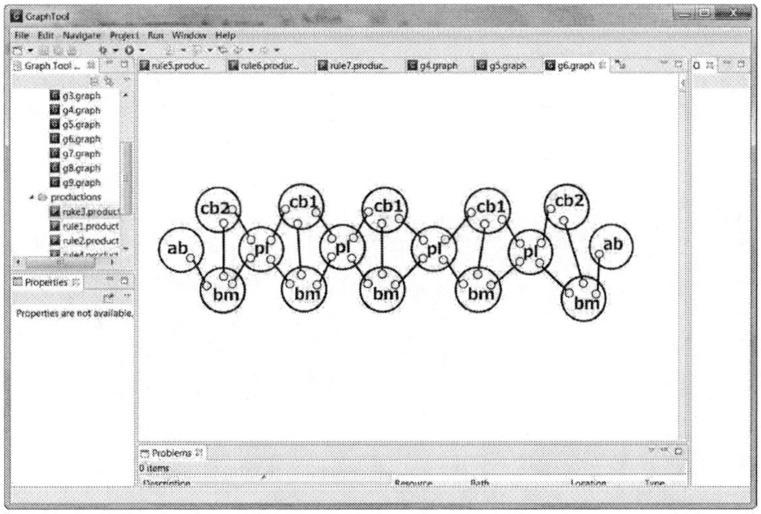

a

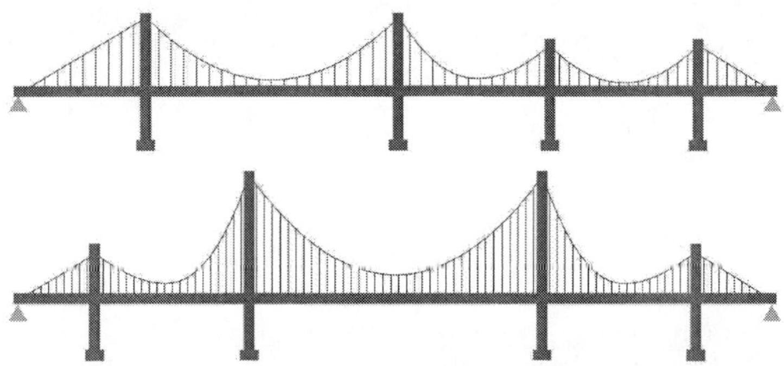

b

Figure 7: a) A CP-graph representing potential bridges, b) two different bridges corresponding to this CP-graph

A CP-graph transformation rule is of the form $p = (l, r, sr)$, where l and r are attributed CP-graphs with the same number of ordered free bonds and sr is a set of functions specifying the way in which attributes assigned to nodes of l are transferred to the attributes assigned to nodes of r. Each attribute has a set of possible values, which are established during the rule application. The application of the rule p to a CP-graph G consists in substituting r for a CP-graph being an isomorphic image of l in G, replacing free bonds of the CP-graph being removed with the corresponding free bonds of r, and specifying values of attributes assigned to elements of r according to functions of sr.

Both sides of each transformation rule contain CP-graphs representing visual bridge patterns, where the left-hand side one can be substituted by the right-hand side one in a given CP-graph representing the whole bridge. The transformation rules allow only substituting subgraphs containing nodes corresponding to two pylons by other subgraphs also containing two such nodes, and subgraphs containing nodes corresponding to two supports by other subgraphs containing two such nodes. The rule application does not change the values of attributes of isomorphic nodes of the left and right-hand sides. Only for new nodes of right-hand sides values of attributes are specified.

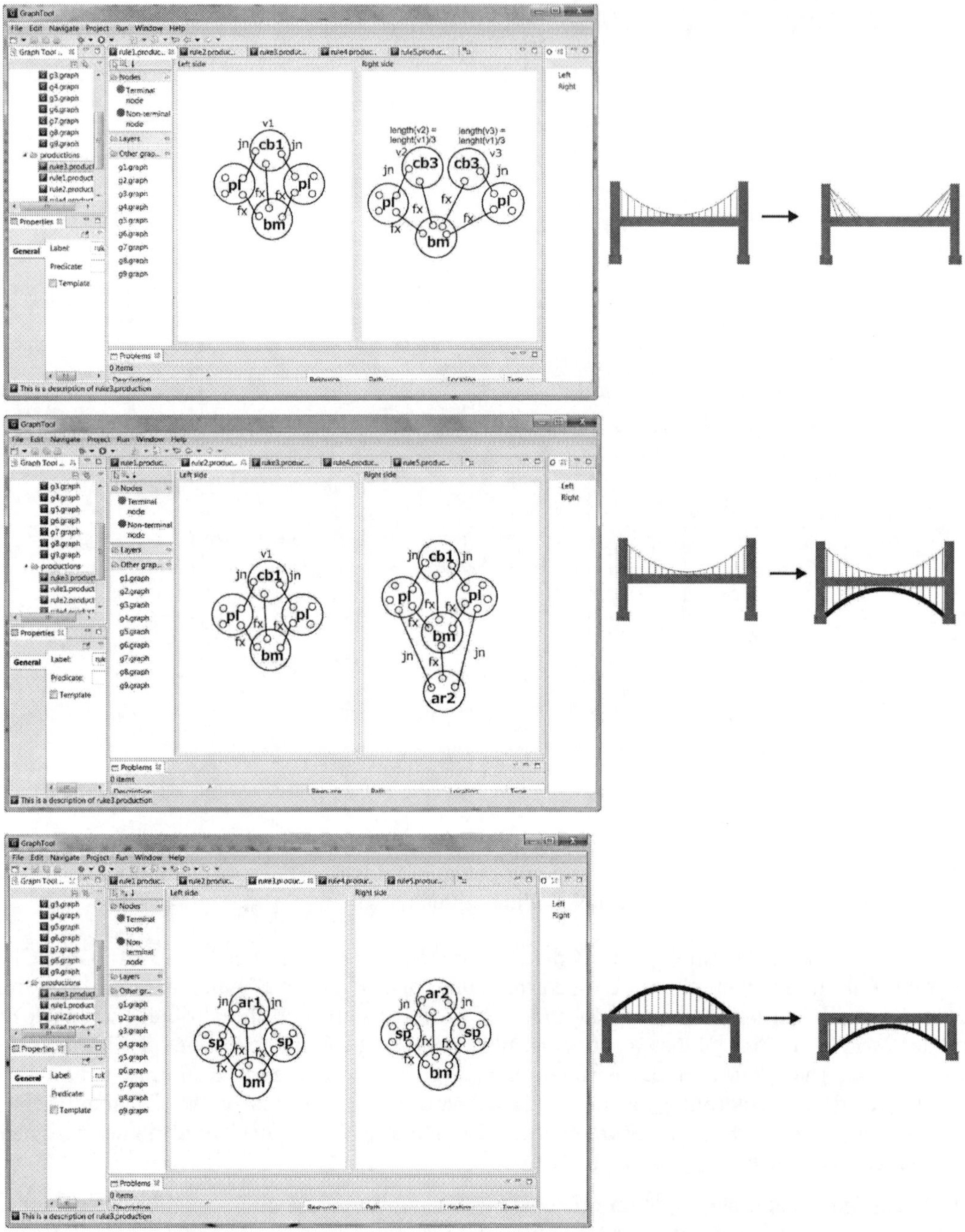

Figure 8: CP-graph transformation rules and the corresponding modifications of bridges

In Fig. 8 examples of CP-graph transformation rules, which allow generating representations of bridges of different types, are shown. To all nodes of both sides of rules the attribute *length,* which specifies the length of the corresponding bridge fragments, is assigned. Additionally to nodes labelled *pl* and *ab* the attribute *position*, which specifies the location of pylons and abutments, respectively, is assigned. During the rule application it is assumed that its left-hand side has the same value of attributes as where assigned the corresponding subgraph of the CP-graph obtained while the designer created the bridge model. The replacement of visual patterns corresponding to replacing CP-graph subgraphs by the rules is shown near the rules. As the result of applying the first rule the bridge drawing number 4 from Fig. 1a is transformed into the drawing shown in Fig. 9a. The value of the attribute *length* of both nodes labelled *cb3* on the rule right-hand side is set to one third of the value of the same attribute assigned to node *v1* of the rule left-hand side. The third allows transforming the bridge number 2 to bridge number 3 in Fig. 1a. The result of applying two times the second rule to the CP-graph from Fig. 7a leads to the CP-graph representing the bridge drawing from Fig. 9b.

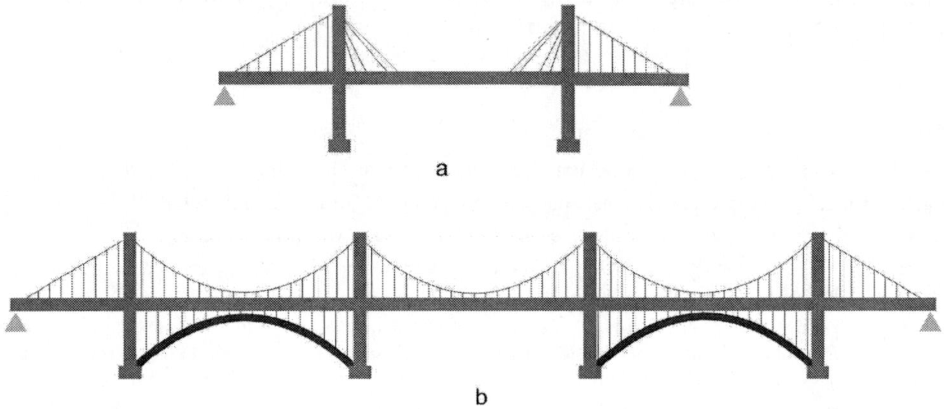

Figure 9: New bridges obtained using CP-graph transformation rules on their CP-graph representations

GraphTool is an Integrated Development Environment dedicated to create graph grammars. It provides the user with tools necessary to define graphs, and graph transformation rules. By replacing CP-graph subgraphs in the way specified in transformation rules the *GraphTool* generates different CP-graphs representing possible bridge structures with geometry and material properties specified by graph attributes. *GraphTool* is implemented in the Java language as a plugin for the Eclipse framework, and is based on the EMF library (Eclipse Modeling Framework).

GraphTool, which is used to define CP-graph transformation rules, gives the designer the possibility to replace subgraphs by the ones which only differ in the attribute values. Therefore the structure, topology, materials used and appearance of generated models can be adjusted to a profile of a river valley or a road that should be traversed by the bridge. Generating alternative bridge designs is possible by scaling and adjusting the dimensions or shapes of the bridge elements, which is performed by changing values of attributes assigned to CP-graph nodes. For example changing positions of pylons and lengths of beams is performed by changing the way of assigning attribute values in CP-graph transformation rules. The possibility of relating attributes of right-hand sides of CP-graph rules to attributes of their left-hand sides enables us to capture parametric modeling knowledge.

5. Conclusions

Conceptual design can be characterized by experimentation. The experimentation in conceptual CAD tasks recently entails the generation and visualization of models and their evaluation. This paper has investigated supporting experimentation on the example of the conceptual phase of the bridge design process aided by the CAD-like system in the unified graphical environment. This system is equipped with a visual editor for creating preliminary bridge designs with the use of the visual language and *GraphTool* supporting graph transformations. Graph structures used as internal representations of bridge designs are obtained automatically and can be transformed using graph rules. The presented CAD-like system enables the designer to experiment with his/her own design by automatic generation of new design solutions on the basis of visual patterns being selected bridge design parts.

The next steps of our research are to investigate more internal mechanisms of CAD systems, for instance such as an ability to learn and evaluation mechanism.

References

Pahl, G., Beitz, W. (1996). Engineering Design: A Systematic Approach, Springer.

Chung, C., Wang, S. (2014). Computational Analysis and Design of Bridge Structures, CRC Press.

Pipinato, A. (Ed.) (2015). Innovative Bridge Design Handbook, Butterworth-Heinemann.

Rozenberg, G. (1999). Handbook of Graph Grammars and Computing by Graph Transformations, vol.2 Applications, Languages and Tools, World Scientific, London.

Vilgertshofer, S., Borrmann, A. (2016). A Graph Transformation Based Method for the Semi-Automatic Generation of Parametric Models of Shield Tunnels, In: Ślusarczyk, G. et al. (Eds.) Proc. of the 23rd International Workshop on Intelligent Computing in Engineering, EG-ICE 2016, Kraków, pp. 95-104.

Ryszka, I., Grabska, E. (2013). GraphTool - a new System of Graph Generation, ADVCOMP 2013, The Seventh International Conference on Advanced Engineering Computing and Applications in Sciences, ISBN: 978-1-61208-290-5, pp. 79-83.

Alexander, Ch. (1977). A Pattern language, Towns, buildings, constructions, Oxford University Press.

Strug, B., Ślusarczyk, G., Grabska, E. (2016). Design Patterns in Generation of Artefacts in Required Styles, In: Soddu, C., Colabella, E. (Eds.), Proc. of the 19th Generative Art Conference, GA2016, Florence, pp. 71-78.

Borkowski, A., Grabska, E. (1995). Representing designs by composite graphs, In: Smith, I. (Ed.), Proc. of the IABSE Colloquium on Knowledge Support Systems in Civil Engineering, Bergamo, March 1995, IABSE Reports 72, pp. 27-36.

Grabska, E., Łachwa, A., Ślusarczyk, G. (2012). New visual languages supporting design of multi-storey buildings, Advanced Engineering Informatics, 26, pp. 681-690.

Strug, B., Ślusarczyk, G. (2009). Reasoning about designs through frequent patterns mining, Advanced Engineering Informatics, 4, pp. 361-369.

Natural Language Controlled Parametric Design

Lucian-Constantin UNGUREANU, Timo HARTMANN
Technical University of Berlin, Germany
l.ungureanu@tu-berlin.de

Abstract. The aim of this paper is to propose a flipped approach of human-computer interaction. Taking into account the challenging social and physical context the civil products need to be created, the practitioners rely on finding creative ways to solve the daily issues. Integrated Collaborative Engineering (ICE) provides the framework which allows the practitioners to focus mainly on the creative part of the design. The current progress in the field of technology provides the tools are needed (hardware and software), but, paradoxically, due to technological advancements, these tools become more and more intricate. Consequently, the practitioners need to stay up-to-date and most of the times, only using a limited amount of software capabilities. Thus, instead of asking the practitioners to familiarise with software formalism, the authors propose the use of natural language for human-machine interaction. This paper focuses on features extraction out of natural language aiming to control the parametric design. This paper proposes a framework to achieve this, and at the same time investigate the requirements needed to create an ontology towards controlling the parametric design using natural language. Finally, the paper draws future research directions, as well the main concerns and limitations.

1. Introduction

The main process which aims at testing and implementing different design perspectives is the Integrated Collaborative Engineering (ICE). The objective of ICE is to provide the practitioners with a way to focus on the creative side of the design when it comes to providing solutions to issues and design questions, and this process should involve all actors. The current practice of collaborative design process requires the use of the generated 3D models to visualize the design, also as input for the multi-physics simulations required. Generating, implementing, and testing a limited number of options consumes more than 50% of the current design time (*Gane and Haymaker, 2009*). In a perfect scenario, the changes will be applied and assessed in real time during the collaboration workshops, ending with a suitable solution agreed by all parties. However, often the participants do not have the skills to handle the tools and not enough knowledge about specific software formalism. In reality, most of the collaborative design meetings end with a possible range of options and alternatives which will be later on implemented by the designers and discussed during a follow-up meeting. This leads to a fragmented and repetitive process, and the main factors are highlighting an insufficient development of the tools. Thus, the creative side of design exploration is limited and restricted.

Parametric design and engineering (PDE) offer the opportunity to expand the design explorations side. PDE allows for a hierarchical and logical decomposition of the product, considering the interfaces between elements and data in order to create a highly automated routine and a minimum number of parameters to control the whole systems. This number of parameters is user defined. Each parametric model is created with a specific purpose in mind. For most of the users, which are going to use a parametric model, the main idea follows the black-box principle. The user knows the parameters he can control in order to achieve a specific output, being also aware of all the capabilities and limitations. The advanced users can actually modify the black box content by actually updating a specific parametric model.

As highlighted above, the main issue regarding the use of the software is related to differences in the languages used. As human beings, we are using natural language. On the other hand, the software is using a formalized language. Nowadays, the most common interaction of the user with the software is through the graphical user interface which is a manual step to translate the knowledge created using the natural language to the machine readable language/format. The manual translation process is user driven and uses the user understanding and his knowledge of the software formalism.

An innovative approach is required to make better use the existing knowledge, and this can be achieved by flipping the approach: instead of asking the practitioners to get familiar with a specific software formalism, we can train machines to make a better use of natural language. In order to do this, it is required to represent the knowledge in a such a way to allow the machines to grasp the human meaning of the things. Most of the efforts regarding the development of knowledge representations in the civil engineering field (or ontological categories) focus on software interoperability issues, linking across domains, logical inference and proofs (Pauwels et al., 2016), or towards a formal representation of domain knowledge. These efforts are not oriented towards the use of natural language. One might ask *"Why do we need to represent everything in natural language?"* and for this, we can quote *Sowa (2000)* who said that "*...natural language is the ultimate knowledge representation language...*".

Sowa (2000) pointed out, following the philosophical view of Pierce and Whitehead, that the "*intention*" defines the way an entity is classified, and the "*purpose*" determines the domain including the ontological categories and the granularity. The aim of this research is to identify the requirements to control parametric design using natural language. Parametric design is an abstract representation which takes different forms, but its main scope is to provide a holistic approach. It takes into account the interdependencies between system components. The paper is structured as follows: the next section introduces the proposed framework for natural language controlled parametric design followed by the section which identifies the requirements for defining the ontological categories needed to fulfill the purpose of the framework.

2. Proposed Framework - "Intention" & "Purpose"

As mentioned earlier, most of the efforts regarding knowledge representation and definition of ontological categories in the field of civil engineering are not oriented towards the use of natural language. Besides the use of ontological categories for a domain, including the relations between these, there is not a structured way to represent communication knowledge of the civil engineering domain. Knowledge exchange in civil engineering field is done using natural language communication. The use of natural language to communicate effectively in a specific domain creates what *Rambow (1990)* and *Kittredge et al. (1991)* coined as *domain communication knowledge*. In addition, domain communication knowledge has two levels: (i) formal and (ii) informal. Means such as textbooks, reports, and standards represent the means to create the *formal communication knowledge of the domain*. In contrast, meetings, emails, mails, phone calls, represent the major communication means of the civil engineering field and in all the cases the professionals are making use of natural language. This creates the third dimension called i*nformal communication knowledge of the domain*. Fig.1 present a hierarchical view of the domain knowledge. In short, the informal communication knowledge of the domain includes the formal communication knowledge, which in addition includes the domain knowledge. From its earliest beginning the industry used natural language for communication, and by this, the field possesses an enormous amount of background knowledge, and this knowledge pool increases every day.

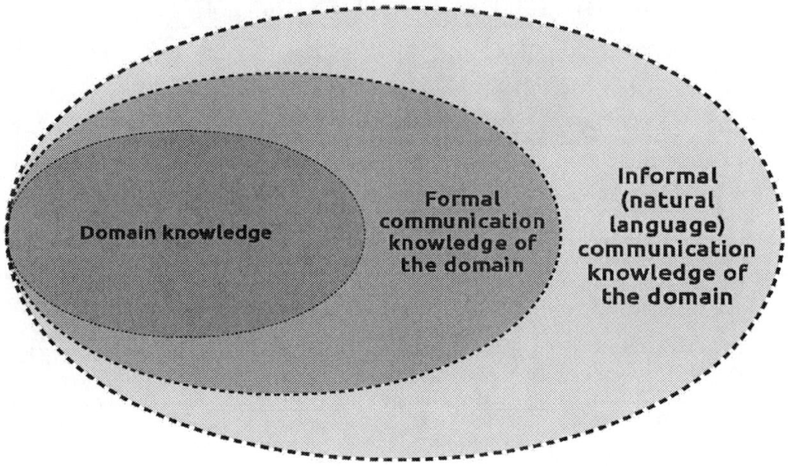

Figure 1: The hierarchical view of domain knowledge

As "*intention*", this paper investigates the use of natural language processing in combination with parametric design for the "*purpose*" to support the collaborative design process. For this, there are two possible directions to be followed: command-like input (the user specify exactly to the agent what actions need to do) and features extraction. In the last case, the agent listens to the discussions, conversations, dialogues and extracts specific features which will be used to manipulate the design. The example below shows an example of feature extraction.

Conversation:*The length of the bridge must be changed to 280 meters*

Feature extracted: *bridge_ length = 280m; action: "change"*

This paper focuses on features extraction out of natural language as shown in Fig.2 aiming to control the parametric design. To achieve such a high-level interaction between computers(machine) and human(natural) the development of a specific ontology is the first step (*Sowa, 2000)*. This paper aims to establish a framework for the development of ontologies to support the implementation of natural language to control the parametric design during collaborative design sessions. This study will make use the two sources of ontological categories as defined by *Sowa (2000)*: observations as a source of knowledge and reasoning as a source of existential extension of the knowledge.

Taking as example the above extract of human to human conversation: "*The length of the bridge must be changed to 280 meters*", each thing needs to be analyzed and included in the ontology. The preliminary ontological construction presented by Fig.3 was created for some of the things.

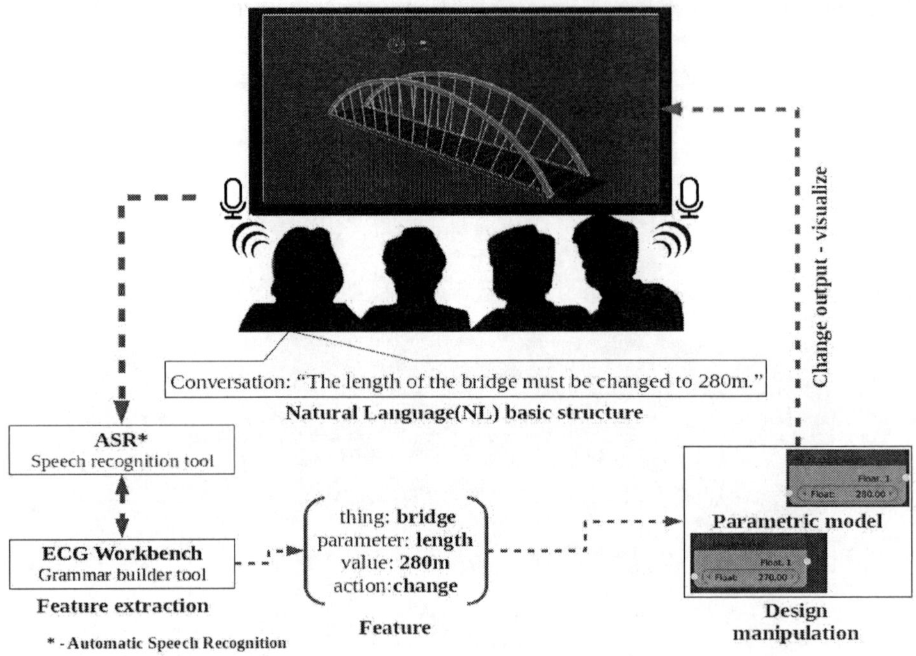

Figure 2: Framework of natural language controlled parametric design

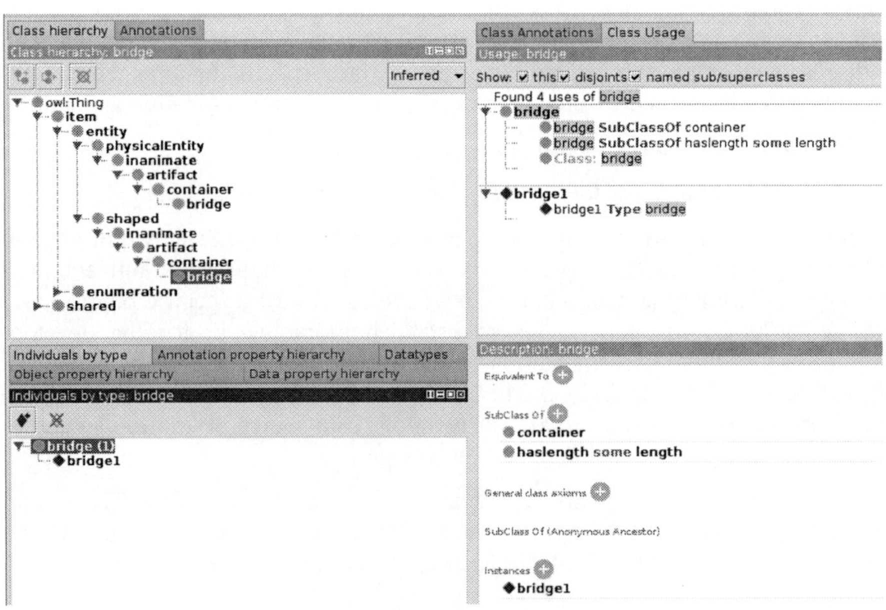

Figure 3: Ontology creation

Once the ontology is created, this is integrated into a semantic analyzer tool which makes use of a formalism called Embodied Construction Grammar(ECG) (*Feldman et al., 2009*). The same authors mention that the ECG formalism "*combines deep insights from cognitive linguistics with advanced techniques of neural computation*". Semantics, which focus on the study of meaning, allows the machines to deconstruct the communication into high-level structures, basic structures, down to the core unit. High-level structures are the section and the paragraphs; the basic structure is the sentence; the word is the core unit. These allow the machines to analyze the morphology, syntax, and semantics. Morphology deals with the word forms, syntax deal with grammar and semantics deals with meaning. Semantics still represents the biggest challenge. Explicit definition of the ontological categories, as well a good definition of the relations between these categories help the machines infer the meaning of a specific word. ECG Workbench is a tool to support grammar writing and analysis. Constructions, Schemas and Ontologies are the main components of grammar analyzer.

The Constructions contain the basic parts of speech such as nouns, verbs, adjectives, singular, plural, prepositions, etc. Each part is defined in relation with its ontology. Taking again the case of our example, the thing "*bridge*" is identified as a noun. Moreover, it is identified as a singular noun. Following the guidelines provided by the authors, the constructor created for the thing "*bridge*" is shown in the Fig.4.

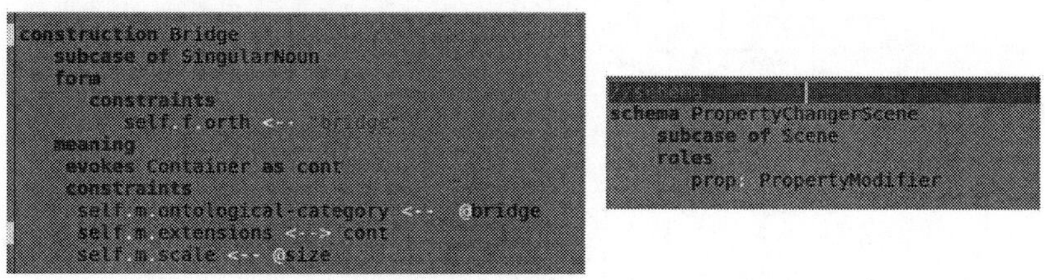

Figure 4: Example of constructors and schema

The Schema represents a set of rules, independent of linguistic construction, which are "partial representation of the neurally-based conceptual structures" (*Feldman et al., 2009*). A set of schemas is used to define the semantic in context. Based on context, a specific pattern will be followed. To exemplify again, the above example is used.

Conversation1: *...The length of the bridge must be changed to 280 meters...*

Conversation2: *...Was the length of the bridge changed to 280 meters?...*

In both cases, the context of the conversation is focused on the bridge length. Nevertheless, the meaning in the context of both propositions is clear for human beings. Schemas play an important role in helping the machines to grasp the meaning from the context in order to be able to extract the features presented bellow. Both Constructions and Schemas make extensive use of the ontologies.

Feature Conversation1: *bridge_ length = 280m; action: "change"*

Feature Conversation2: *bridge_ length = 280m; action: "check"*

To close the loop, a modeling environment which allows the use of parametric design will be employed. The purpose is to test the ontology we proposed and to extract a set of guidelines to be used when building ontology as knowledge representation of civil engineering informal communication domain. This study will focus mainly on the requirements of natural language integration during the design phase, but nevertheless, it is desired that the created ontology will represent a shared ontology to be used for other applications and during different life-cycle phases.

3. Knowledge expressed by Natural Language – a Bridge Example

As mentioned previously, the focus of this research is on the use of natural language to control the parametric design. Parametric design allows for a holistic approach. Mainly, takes the form of an abstract representation as a script following the systemic logic of product decomposition and definition components inter-relationships. Consequently, this approach allows for the use of a limited number of input parameters to control the design. The design intent defines which parameters must control the output. The input block represented in Fig. 5 contain the selected parameter expected to control the design. Based on the input values, the transformations of the system takes place inside the Parametric representation block which contains the user defined logic. As a result of the transformation process, the output node renders the expected design. Thus, a such as approach offers the advantage of reducing the amount of human knowledge required to be represented. The following offer an insight into the efforts of representing the informal communication knowledge with the purpose of controlling the parametric model presented in Fig.5

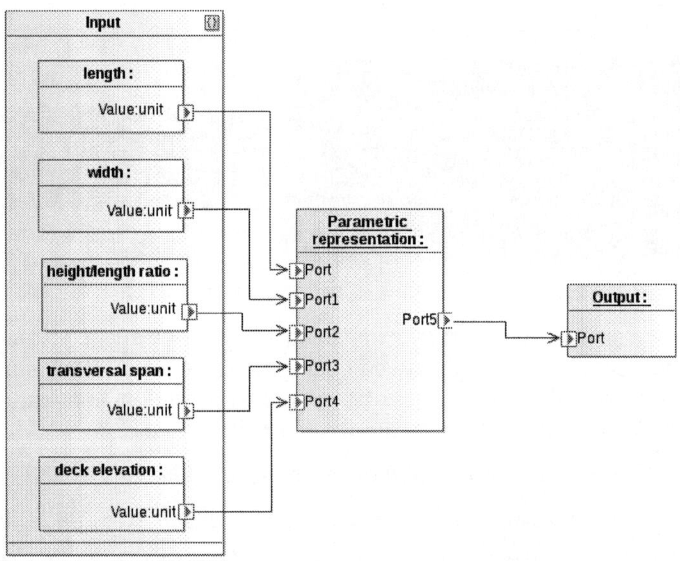

Figure 5: High-level view of the parametric model

3.1 Ontological Categories

The natural language(NL) based ontological categories proposed by the authors of ECG Workbench (*Feldman et al., 2009*) were expanded in order to include those categories related to *thing: bridge*. As presented in Fig.6, the thing: bridge can take two forms in natural language: (1) *container* as subclass of *artifact* and *physicalEntity* classes and (2) as subclass of *process*. The following two examples of NL conversations covers the both case.

(1) The bridge length need to be changed to 280m.

(2)We need to bridge that gap.

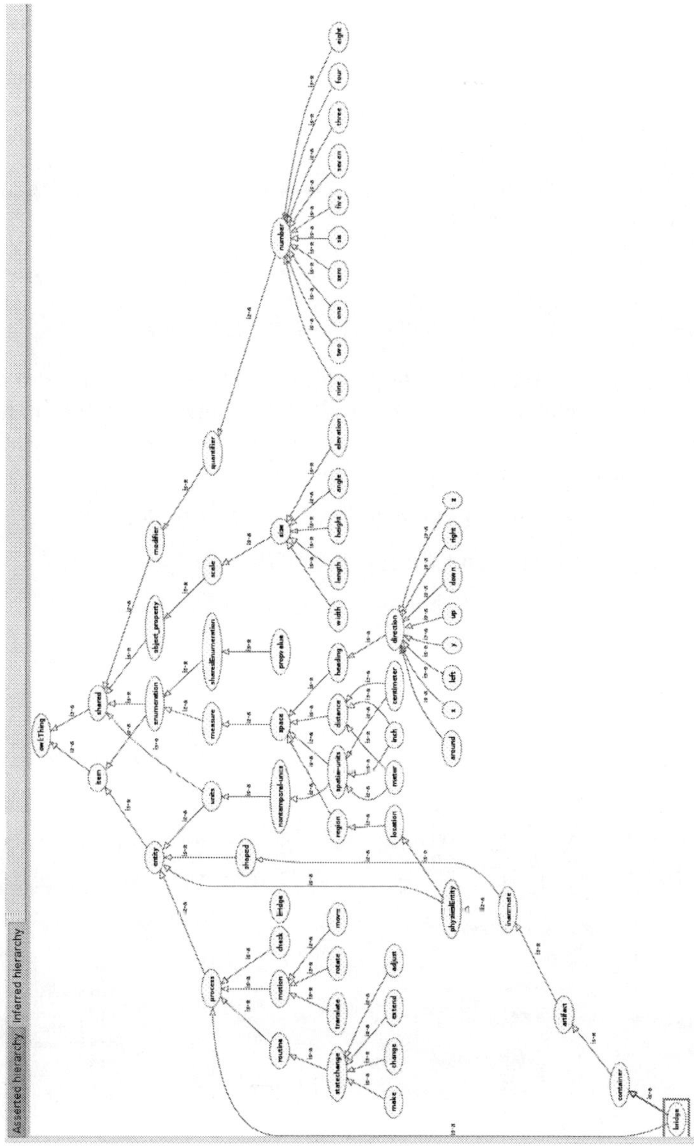

Figure 6: Ontological categories - focus on bridge

Using the grammar analyzer engine and analyzing the *thing: bridge*, the following three options are identified: (1) verb present form, (2) verb - base form and (3) noun. These three options are shown in Fig.7 Taking into account the context and using the language markers "*to*" and "*the*", the distinction between verb and noun is made as shown in Fig. 8.

Other ontological categories presented in Fig.6and defined in relation to the thing: bridge are related to its properties, such as the things related to size (length, width, height, etc.) and those related to its orientation. Moreover, these categories are defined in relations to the main parameters controlling the procedure created using parametric design as presented in Fig.7.

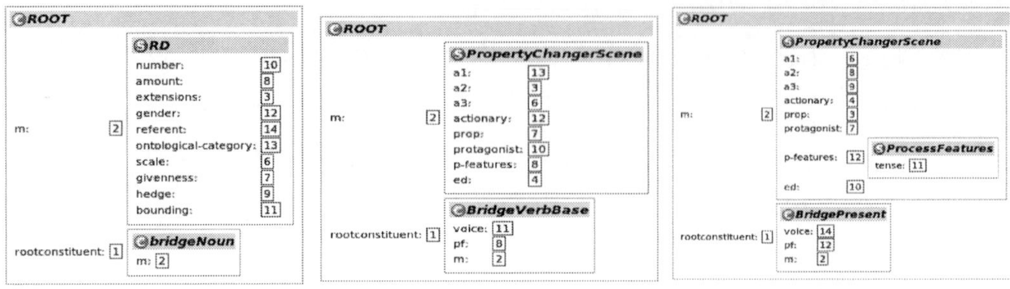

Figure 7: Thing: Bridge

In the same time, categories related to data properties such as *propValue* and the *units* related to *propValue* need to be included. One specific danger is represented by the fact that the unit related to a value is not always specified during a natural language conversation, but mainly inferred based on context. A such example is given bellow:

Human1: "*What is the width of the bridge?*"

Human2: "*It is around 20 meters*"

Human1: "*I think that we will have to change it to 25.*"

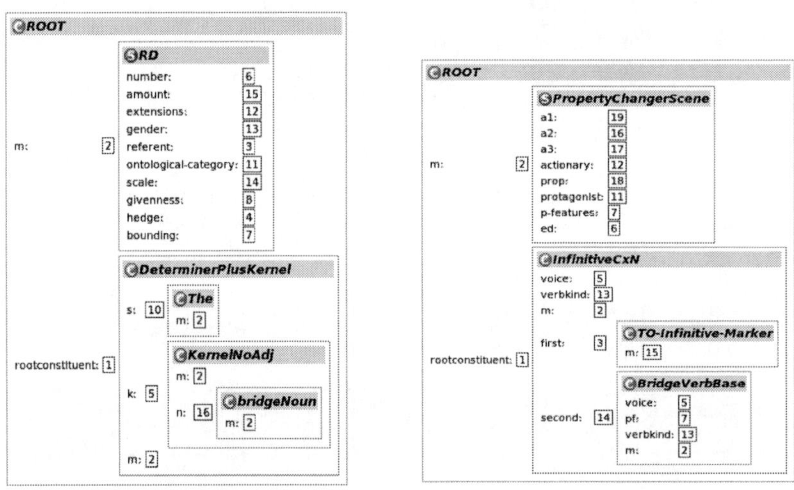

(a) the bridge (b) to bridge

Figure 8: Analysis of the thing: bridge using the language markers

3.2 Logical Relationships

Natural language allows us to represent the knowledge in a way which is natural for humans. Humans can create a context and to communicate within the context. The creation of a context can be done using different means and ways, and the humans can infer and recognize it easily. A team working on a specific project, a meeting set for a specific purpose are forms of context creation. For example, a collaborative workshop scheduled to discuss the design of a new bridge crossing the Danube river inside the city of Vienna is a created context. During the workshop, the attendees will no longer refer to it as "*the new bridge crossing the Danube river inside the city of Vienna*" but only as *the bridge*. In the same context, all the stakeholders, based on their background information, know that a bridge has a specific shape, form, materials, length, width, spatial position, etc. This process is known as inference, and it allows the use of background information. To allow the computers to replicate this process, the ontological categories are represented in a specific way which makes it possible to specify the logical relationship.

Using as starting point the categories represented in Fig.6 there are logical relationships between the concepts(things). These logical relationships can be expressed using different syntaxes. The natural language expression, "*length of the bridge*", as well the other properties, and for each property their specific value and specific unit can be represented as shown in Fig.9.

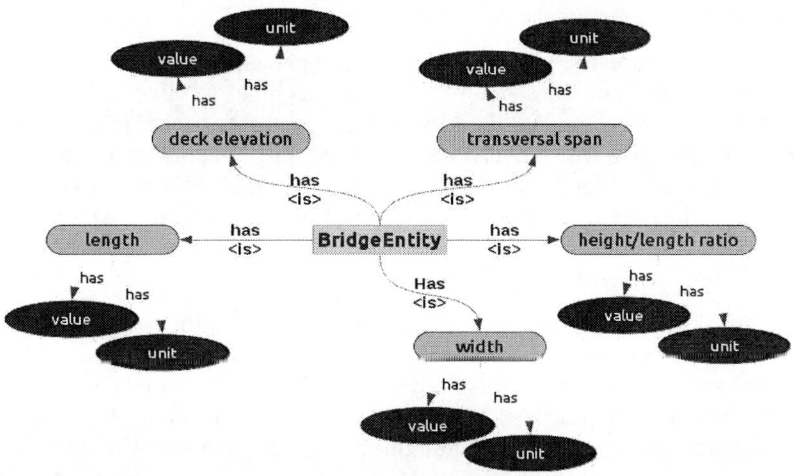

Figure 9: Bridge entity

Fig.6 shows the *thing:bridge* as artifact, as well as process. As discussed earlier there are differences between the two concepts and the humans are inferring this based on context. To allow the machines to infer this background knowledge, it is necessary to specify that these two concepts are not the same. To do this is required to indicate that the concepts defined under shaped and physicalEntity are not the same as the one defined under process. The relation is called role disjointness and is defined as presented in equation 1. When reasoning, the two concepts are now disjoint.

$$\left(shaped \wedge physicalEntity \right) \cap process = \varnothing \quad (1)$$

4. Conclusions

Nowadays, the innovations in the field of technology are reshaping all the industries, including the civil engineering. Paradoxically, one of the biggest challenges is due to the advancements of the tools used during design. Lately, the complexity of the software has increased, and often the users are using only a small part of the capabilities provides. This is because of the need for understanding and getting familiar with the software formalism. This means that the practitioners are spending a considerable amount of time on understanding the way the tools, primarily created to support the process, can be used during the process. The research team wants to flip the focus. Machines need to understand the formalism used by the practitioners in the field of civil engineering, to support the process, and at the same time to allow the professionals to focus on solving the design challenges. The approach used by the research team is to concentrate on the use of natural language to control the parametric design.

The current way this research is presented has several limitations which we see as future research directions. In practice, various development scenarios are possible when it comes to collaboratively designing and engineering a product. The example proposed over the paper might not be the one to express the reality, but rather a simplistic one to showcase the vastness of the research needed to be done in this direction. Identification of various practical scenarios, workflows, and communication and collaboration routines plays an important role regarding the possibility to setup guidelines on how to develop the parametric models. Moreover, this will help to have a better understanding of how the context creation patterns in the civil engineering field. Consequently, an ontology will never be complete and strategies regarding the continuous maintenance are needed.

A big challenge towards using natural language is represented by the enormous amount of knowledge which needs to be translated to allow the machines to infer it. The use of advanced parametric design reduces the numbers of things required to be inferred by machines. Although this an advantage which overcomes the need for high computational power required by reasoner engines, the logic embedded into the parametric definition constraints design options. The use of speech recognition tools represent set another challenge. Punctuation plays an important role on meaning demarcation, and currently, the speech recognition tools do not extract it directly out of conversations.

The previous ontologies developed by the practitioners mainly focused on the representation of the knowledge associated to the civil engineering domain. Mainly focused on technical aspects, the link showing the use of this knowledge on a daily basis using natural language is missing on the previous approaches. Besides the domain knowledge, an ontology meant to drive the human-computer interaction through natural language need to contain as well the vocabulary used on a daily basis in practice. Future research, using data engineering techniques, will focus on the vocabulary and patterns identification out of natural language conversations. Moreover, the context drives the semantic analysis, and future research will have to investigate the way the unstructured/informal communication creates these contexts in order to extract specific patterns.

References

Feldman, J., Dodge, E., & Bryant, J. (2009). Embodied construction grammar.

Gane, V., & Haymaker, J. (2009). Benchmarking current conceptual high-rise design processes. Journal of Architectural Engineering, 16(3), 100-111.

Kittredge, R., Korelsky, T., & Rambow, O. (1991). On the need for domain communication knowledge. Computational Intelligence, 7(4), 305-314.

Pauwels, P., Zhang, S., & Lee, Y. C. (2016). Semantic web technologies in AEC industry: A literature overview. Automation in Construction.

Rambow, O. (1990, June). Domain communication knowledge. In Fifth International Workshop on Natural Language Generation (pp. 87-94).

Sowa, J. F. (2000). Knowledge Representation: Logical. Philosophical, and Computational Foundations, Brooks/Cole, Pacific Grove.

A Case Study Application of Unmanned Aerial Systems (UAS) on Highway Construction Projects

Xi Wang, Gabriel B. Dadi, P.E., Ph.D., and Timothy R.B. Taylor, P.E., Ph.D.
University of Kentucky, United States
xi.wang@uky.edu

Abstract. Earthwork operations are often one of the major cost items on infrastructure construction projects. Precise estimates of actual earthwork volumes are important for both transportation agencies and contractors alike to ensure appropriate payments are made. Recently, unmanned aerial systems (UAS) have become popular for numerous surveying applications because they require less cost and time consumption compared with other common estimate approaches relying on drawings, equipment activity or a few survey points. In this study, UAS and digital photogrammetry technology are adopted to estimate earthwork volumes of a highway extension project. Two 3D point cloud models are generated to track the earthwork volume changes during construction. The resulting vertical and horizontal accuracy and its dependent factors including the use of ground control points are explained and discussed. The test results in this project prove the robust capabilities of UAS in earthwork volume measurement.

1. Introduction

Earthwork is engineering works created through the moving of massive quantities of soil or rock. The purpose is to reconfigure the topography of a construction site to meet the design requirements (Nunnally, 2004). As an important mission of a construction project, the earthwork operation is mainly executed in the early stage of the construction process. This means the earthwork progress controls the overall project schedule. Besides, earthwork is often one of the major cost items on most construction projects because of the long operation time and cost uncertainties caused by unstable geographical conditions and construction organization plans. It is essential to make the best possible measurement of the quantity of earthwork materials that has been excavated and placed. An accurate estimation of earthwork quantity not only enables contractors to present an accurate bid, assign construction assets reasonably, and formulate a project schedule but also helps owners make correct payments. Therefore, the selection of a proper measurement method is the prerequisite to accurate estimations and cost control.

In recent years, the surveying industry has seen significant changes with the development of modern technologies. However, the implementation of advanced survey techniques in construction is still in the early stages. According to the latest standard specifications published by the Department of Transportation (DOT) of each state, most states are predominantly using conventional methods such as tape and manual calculation methods based on the blueprints to collect data and calculate quantities for payments in the earthwork process. As shown in Figure 1, 68% of states measure the roadway excavation in its original position by taking cross sections and computing the volume by the average-end-area method. The cross-section method involves plotting cross sections of the existing and proposed levels at certain intervals across the construction site (Hintz and Vonderohe, 2011). The accuracy largely relies on the selected distance between the sections. Closer sections improve the estimation accuracy but require much longer time. A balance has to be made between accuracy and efficiency, which could result in various levels of errors. The average-end-area method is usually applied to estimate the earthwork volume involved in large and complex areas (Epps and Marion, 1990). The area is divided into a grid indicating the depth of cut or fill at each grid intersection. The method involves taking off the existing and proposed ground levels at each node of the grid. As with the cross-section method, the accuracy depends on the size of the grid which is used. Also, the average-end-area method is accurate only for commonly used straight excavations but tends to overestimate the volume.

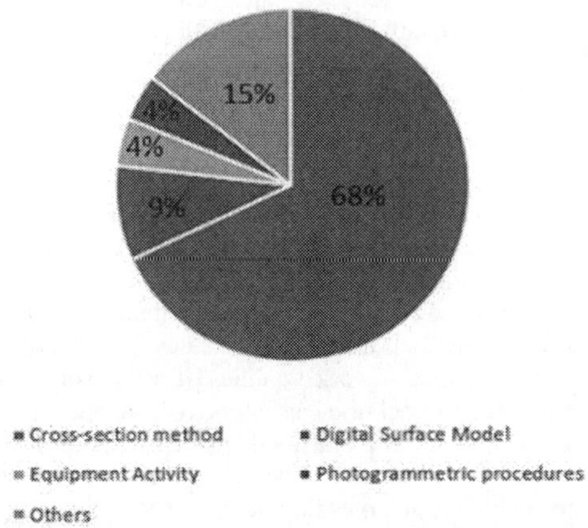

Figure 1: The Earthwork Volume Measurement Methods Applied by DOTs

The methods mentioned above are inefficient as they require a large amount of time to collect data on the site and go through a tedious quantity calculation process (Yanalak 2005). Although some Departments have started to use software products such as AutoCAD to make their work easier and faster, the fundamentals of manual methods are still used to find the quantities of earthwork while applying a software. Therefore, it is imperative to upgrade the current practices of data acquisition and computation methods. In this paper, the unmanned aerial systems (UAS) is introduced to estimate the earthwork volume with the cooperation of digital photogrammetry. The UAS, or colloquially drones, are remotely controlled aircraft equipped with various sensors such as cameras, Global Positioning System (GPS), or other communication devices. The developed GPS technology enable the UASs to provide accurate geo-referenced visual assets. With the cooperation of digital photogrammetry, a well-established technology for obtaining three-dimension (3D) geometric information for real-world objects from single or multiple photographs, a geo-referenced three-dimensional (3D) model is generated for survey applications.

With the improvement and wide applications of the UAS in recent years, it has become attractive for various surveying applications in civil engineering. Metni and Hamel (2007) described the dynamics of an UAS for monitoring of structures and maintenance of bridges; Morgenthal and Hallermann (2014) discussed the use of a UAS for inspection of critical structural components and hot spots that are hard to reach. Rathinam et al (2008) addressed the problem of monitoring some such civil systems such as oil-gas pipelines using an autonomous UAS based on visual feedback. In construction, Sibert and Teizer (2014) evaluated the performance of the application of the UAS in surveying earthwork projects. They developed a performance model for estimating the position error and conducted tests in several realistic construction environments. Hugenholtz et al. (2014) quantified the accuracies of an in-house developed UAS through a stockpile volumetric survey. However, research conducted on UAS and photogrammetry applications is still in its infancy, especially in the earthwork volume measurement application. As an emerging technology in construction, it requires much practice to reveal various possibilities in operations and prove its feasibility. This paper gives a thorough analysis of the potential use of the UAS and digital photogrammetry technology in estimating earthwork volume of a highway extension project with respect to the accuracy and efficiency. First, the image acquisition plan, the key to obtaining high accuracy results in the process of modeling, is discussed because it directly determines the overlap rate between images. Second, a detailed description concerning the 3D point cloud models generation process in photogrammetry software is presented. In this project, two geo-referenced 3D point cloud models are created to identify the volume changes of the earthwork between two stages of the construction process. After the model establishment, the ground control points (GCPs) are introduced to perform an absolute accuracy test and adjustment. The error analysis is conducted through the comparisons between the actual and computed coordinates of GCPs. As a result, the positional error of each GCP in both vertical and horizontal directions can be identified. Last, the processing parameters, which may potentially have a major influence on the accuracy, are briefly reviewed.

2. Image Acquisition Planning

As introduced earlier, the UAS is used to capture images of the construction site, and the earthwork volume will be measured in a 3D point cloud model generated by a photogrammetry software. Photogrammetry is a technique of image processing to interpret the shape and location of an object from single or multiple photos of that object. (Luhmann et al. 2014). The fundamental principle of photogrammetry is triangulation. By taking photos from at least two different positions, so-called "rays of sight" can be developed from each camera to points on the object. The 3D coordinates of the points of interest are produced by the intersection of these rays, as shown in Figure 2.

Figure 2: Principle of Triangulation (Luhmann et al. 2014)

In the modeling process, the photogrammetry software will automatically find thousands of common points between images. When two or multiple points on different images are found to be the same, they match and referred to as a 3D point. In other words, a high overlap between two images will help the photogrammetry capture adequate matching of features for the creation of a single contiguous model. In most cases, the recommended overlap for most cases is at least 75% frontal overlap (with respect to the flight direction) and at least 60% side overlap (between flying tracks). The UAS used for image acquisition in this study is the DJI Inspire 1. This UAS has a maximum takeoff weight of 7.71lbs and maximum wind resistance up to 10m/s. The maximum flight time is approximately 18 minutes. It is equipped with a 20mm lens, and the stock camera has 4096 × 2160 resolution for still images (DJI 2017). Pix4Dmapper photogrammetry software is selected to process images and generate 3D point cloud model of the site. The UAS can perform manual or autonomous flight missions on the site under the control of Pix4D mobile applications. The UAS can fly automatically based on the designed parameters and flight paths. It is a flight planning tool for the autonomous flights of UAVs based on the user-defined area, boundaries or flight purposes. In this case, the project is a highway extension construction. No large vertical objects such as buildings and power towers will be modeled and calculated. Also, the project does not include forest, snow, lakes, agricultural fields that are difficult to reconstruct. Therefore, this study applies the grid pattern plan to capture images of the site. Due to the size of area, multiple grid flight plans are applied in order to avoid inadequate missing information. Also, enough overlap between each flight mission is necessary, as shown in Figure 3. Besides, flight missions should be conducted under the same conditions such as same flight heights, sun direction, and weather conditions because all images could have the same level of detail which helps facilitates points matching between images (Wang X, et al. 2017).

Figure 3: Grid Flight Plans of the Construction Project

3. Image Processing

The completion of image processing in photogrammetry normally requires three steps: initial processing, point cloud generation, and DSM or Orthomosaic generation. When starting initial processing, the photogrammetry software first identifies and measures conjugate points in the overlapping photographs (Schenk, 1997). From this initial matches, the software runs an Automatic Aerial Triangulation (AAT) and Bundle Block Adjustment (BBA). The AAT represents the mathematical process of establishing accurate relationships between the individual image coordinate systems and a defined datum and projection on the ground (Tang et al., 1997). The main objective is to ensure that each model can be oriented accurately as required. The Bundle Adjustment is the program that processes the photographic measurements to produce the final three-dimensional coordinates of all the measured points (Luhmann et al. 2014). These two methods allow the software to automatically process with or without camera positions and exterior orientations. To be more specific, by initial processing, the software produces a 3D model made of 3D points called Automatic Tie Points. Each tie point's corresponding 2D points are automatically detected in images and used to compute 3D position. Each image is processed based on the estimation of camera position when the image is acquired, which is the calibration process. Sometimes calibration in the initial process is not precise, which adds errors and noises in the 3D model such as double point layers or missing areas.

Inadequate overlap between images, reflective surface, and invisibility of vertical facades are common reasons of imprecise calibration. In this project, no buildings block the area of interest in the earthwork stage. Also, no reflective surface such as water or sand on the construction site. It is challenging to re-construct such surface because of a deficiency of visual contents. The increase of image overlaps and adding tie points manually are effective methods to improve the accuracy of calibration.

The initial process creates a model, called a rayCloud model, which is only composed of tie points. The processing time is short, so it helps users preliminarily visualize the different elements of the reconstruction and verify the accuracy of the model. However, it is not suitable for visualization and accurate measurements. For further usages and modifications, a point cloud model should be created after, the second step, point cloud densification. A point cloud is a set of data points in a three-dimensional coordinate system, and each point is defined by X, Y, and Z coordinates. The point cloud is normally used to represent the external surface of an object. It is also applied in quality inspection, multitude of visualization, and animation, etc. For more realistic visual operations, the triangle mesh should be generated. Although triangle mesh model is optimal for visualization, it is infeasible for detailed modifications on a small scale. Therefore, most operations are performed on the point cloud level.

In photogrammetry, the volume of an object is computed using the Digital Surface Model (DSM). The DSM represents the elevations of the reflective surfaces of features elevated above the Bare Earth (Hirt et al, 2010). When measuring a volume in the model, users should draw the base surface of the volume by making the vertices of the base. A manual tie point is associated with each vertex of the volume. The photogrammetry software creates the base taking into consideration the altitude, and then it projects a grid with Ground Sampling Distance (GSD) spacing on the base. The GSD is the distance between two consecutive pixel centers measured on the ground. A larger value of the image GSD leads to the less visible details. The GSD is closely associated with the flight height: high flight altitude always comes with a large GSD. For each cell of the grid, its volume is given by the equation (1) (Pix4D, 2017),

$$V = L \times W \times (Z_T - Z_B) \tag{1}$$

Where,

L = the length of the cell = GSD,

W = the width of the cell = GSD,

Z_T = the altitude of the 3D terrain,

Z_B = the altitude of the base surface of the volume.

In this project, the research team visits the construction site two times in order to identify the changes of earthwork volumes. The time interval between two visits is total 74 days. The auto grid mission flight plan by Pix4D mobile applications is adopted in this survey based on the site condition of the project. Also, the flight parameters and processing settings within the mobile application and software when creating 3D point cloud models are left to standard values in order to get a neutral and repeatable result. Important processing parameters will be discussed later to identify their influence on the measurement accuracy. After the image processing by the photogrammetry software, two 3D point cloud models of the construction site at the different stage are created based on 310 and 425 images captured by the UAV respectively, as displayed in Figure 4.

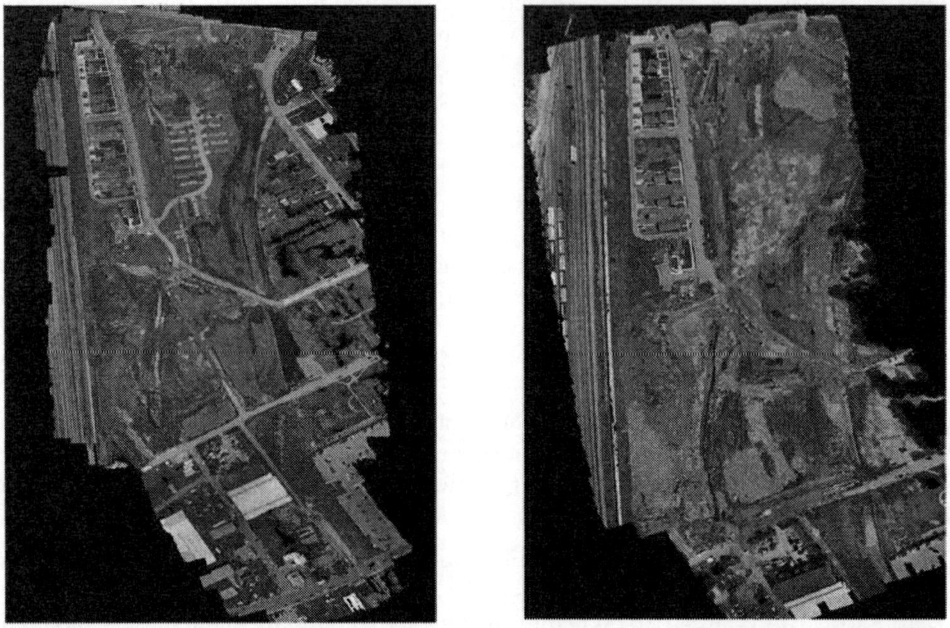

Figure 4: 3D Point Cloud Model of the Earthwork Construction of 1st Visit (left) and 2nd Visit (right)

4. Accuracy Analysis

4.1 Ground Control Points (GCPs)

In order to ensure that images are precisely positioned in relation to the Earth, images are processed with ground coordinates. Ground Control Points (GCPs) are points with known coordinates measured by highly accurate GPS units or hands in the area of interest. GCPs provide the means for orientating imagery to a ground coordinate system and have a significant impact on the quality of the derived elevation information (Wolf and DeWitt, 2000). As higher accuracy is required and user expectations increase, the need for GCPs are becoming increasingly more important. Thanks to the development of GPS technology, the collection of GCPs is now accurate, easier and more cost effective than it was in the past.

To be more specific, the photogrammetry software is capable of processing images with or without geo-locations. However, the GCPs greatly contribute to higher accuracy due to they help give the scales, orientations, and positions to the final results. The GCPs can be measured in the field with topographic methods, taken from existing geospatial data or Web Map Service (WMS) such as Google Map. Generally, GCPs should be located evenly in the area of interest to minimize the errors in scale and orientation. If GCPs are gathered at the same location, one side or the very edge of the area, the geo-reference will lose balances, which makes the GCPs unreliable or dysfunctional. Additionally, it is also recommended to place one GCP in the center of the area to further improve the quality of the reconstruction. According to some literature and guidance provided from Pix4D, a minimum number of 5 GCPs is required. Five to ten GCPs are usually adequate for large projects (Pix4D, 2017). Active construction sites may have difficulty measuring a GCP near the center; it is acceptable to omit this point if impractical. Instead, at least two additional points along the perimeter should be added. The density of GCPs not only depends on the georeferenced accuracy, but also the efficiency of collection process. Unlimited number of GCPs do not significantly contribute to accuracy improvement but require large amount of labor and time.

Figure 5: Marked GCPs in the 3D Point Cloud model of the Earthwork Site

In this project, 6 GCPs are added in the 3D point cloud model of the site; each GCPs is located at the place where is easy to identify in the model. Two models have same GCPs in order to ensure the consistency. A GPS rover is used to obtain the real coordinate of each GCP. An example of marked GCPs and their coordinates are presented in Figure 5 and Table 1.

Table 1: Coordinates of GCPs (ft)

Name	Coordinates (X, Y, Z)
GCP1	(3906793.513, 5278893.381, 952.222)
GCP2	(3906737.437, 5278945.076, 952.437)
GCP3	(3906853.023, 5278816.615, 947.889)
GCP4	(3906847.645, 5278810.920, 947.806)
GCP5	(3907452.225, 5277871.866, 935.115)
GCP6	(3907432.788, 5277846.469, 935.629)

4.2 Error Analysis

An absolute accuracy analysis is mandatory in the surveying applications. The absolute accuracy is defined by the difference between the position of features on a processed model and their true position on the Earth. Due to the calculation of earthwork volume is based on the point cloud model, the precision of point location is crucial to the result of volume computations. In this project, the computed coordinates of GCPs are compared with their actual coordinates measured by the GPS rover. In this study, EPOCH 50 GNSS is used to measure the coordinates of GCPs. Due to the precision of the selected device (3mm) in both horizontal and vertical directions, the analysis does not concern errors caused by GPS devices. The software allows direct comparisons in a table-based format. Table 2 present the difference between the computed GCPs 3D point and the original position in X, Y and Z directions by using Root Mean Square Error (RMSE). The average horizontal errors (X and Y) are 4.93cm and 3.62cm respectively, and the average height error is 2.38cm. According to some of the most cited publications (Sibert and Teizer 2014, Mesas-Carrascosa, Francisco-Javier, et al. 2016), the error is within a reasonable range in this project. In practice, no an absolute definition of "precision". Instead, the tolerance of positional accuracy always varies from the application needs or requirements.

Table 2: Positional Errors of GCPs

GCP Name	Accuracy XY/Z [m]	Error X [m]	Error Y [m]	Error Z [m]	Verified /Marked
GCP1 (3D)	0.020/ 0.020	0.075	0.020	0.014	13 / 13
GCP2 (3D)	0.020/ 0.020	-0.091	-0.011	0.010	13 / 13
GCP3 (3D)	0.020/ 0.020	0.001	-0.064	-0.033	7 / 7
GCP4 (3D)	0.020/ 0.020	0.017	-0.017	0.028	8 / 8
GCP5 (3D)	0.020/ 0.020	-0.021	0.038	0.023	8 / 8
GCP6 (3D)	0.020/ 0.020	-0.006	0.039	-0.027	8 / 8
Mean [m]		-0.004167	0.008333	0.002500	
RMS Error [m]		0.049276	0.036210	0.023768	

As introduced earlier, the number of 3D points directly decides the quality of a point cloud model. Various values of processing parameters are available to be selected depending on the requirements of visualization and accuracy. Image scale and point density are two important parameters for the 3D point cloud models creation. Image scale defines the scale of the images at which additional 3D points are calculated, and point density defines the density of the point cloud model. For example, ½ image scale means only half size images will be used to compute additional 3D points. Low point density means a 3D point is computed for every (16/image scale) pixel. These two parameters are interactive with each other and decide the point cloud densification and processing time. It is essential to choose an optimal combination to balance the model quality and efficiency. In this project, the CPU specifications of the desktop are Intel(R) Core(TM) i7-4790 CPU @ 3.60GHz, and its RAM is 32GB. The operating system is Windows 7 Professional, 64-bit. When selecting the standard values, which are ½ image scale and Medium point density, the resulting model is composed of total 40838871 points and processed using 3 hours and 12mintes. Table 3 shows the result when processing the collected images with different values.

Table 3: Evaluation of Image Scale and Point Density

	1 (Original Image Scale)	1/4 (Quarter Image Scale)
High Point Density	93532003 points, 8h:14m:50s	31136514 points, 2h:46m:34s
Low Point Density	41904150 points 4h:02m:39s	2311196 points 41m:29s

5. Results of Earthwork Volume Measurements

According to the observations, main changes of earthwork between two visits are a stockpile and a trench. In Pix4D, the base surface of the volume is created by drawing the vertices of the base, as shown in Figure 6. A manual tie point is associated with each vertex of the volume, which can be edited for accuracy improvement. Then, the software will generate the quantity of earthwork, including cut and fill volumes, and the measurement errors (Table 4).

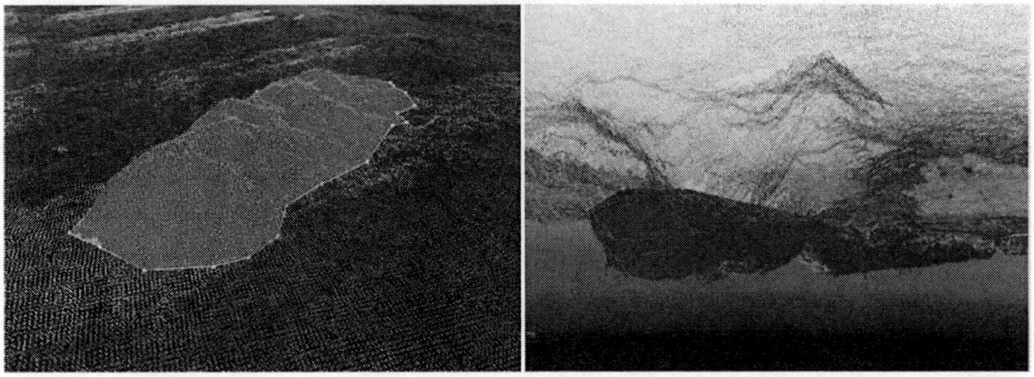

Figure 6: The Stockpile and Trench Volume in the 3D Point Cloud Model

Table 4: Volume Calculation Results (m^3)

	Stockpile	Trench
Cut Volume	81.93 ± 5.81	13.32 ± 2.05
Fill Volume	-0.01 ± 0.04	-10915.81 ± 91.70
Total Volume	81.92 ± 5.85 (6% error)	-10902.49 ± 93.75 (0.8% error)

6. Conclusion

This paper presents an implementation of UAS and photogrammetry technology in construction earthwork measurement. The authors conduct an experiment on a highway extension project in order to prove this emerging tool may help improve the accuracy and efficiency over the conventional means of earthwork quantities estimations. The major contribution of this study is to investigate the effectiveness of the emerging technology and to provide an operation reference for constructors and owners (DOTs) to upgrade current practices. Although no comparisons of the results due to the uniqueness of the project, the effectiveness of the proposed approach in this project is preliminarily validated according to some references. For instance, Siebert and Teizer (2014) compared the volumes of three earth piles computed by the automated UAV-direct geo-referenced mapping approach with the result obtained by Robotic Total Station (RTS) method. The average survey error of their experiment is around 11%. Also, the UAS photogrammetric approach is efficient, which took around 5.5 hours to complete the on and off site work when selecting standard flight and processing parameters. However, it is essential to conduct more field experiments to compare with conventional measurement methods such as cross-sections, and other advanced surveying technologies like laser scanning; The analysis should not only aim at the measurement accuracy, but also the cost, productivity, and safety. Also, potential factors such as flight height, the density of GCPs, and soil type need more definitions and discussions regarding the influence on the UAS performance. Last but not least, the applications of UAS/UAV in various aspects of construction management can be explored to prove its feasibility.

References

DJI 2017. http://www.dji.com/inspire-1/info#specs

Epps, J.W. and Corey, M.W. (1990). Cut and fill calculations by modified average-end-area method. Journal of Transportation Engineering, 116(5), pp.683-689.

Hintz, C. and Vonderohe, A. (2011). Comparison of earthwork computation methods. Transportation Research Record: Journal of the Transportation Research Board, (2215), pp.100-104.

Hirt, C., Filmer, M.S. and Featherstone, W.E. (2010). Comparison and validation of the recent freely available ASTER-GDEM ver1, SRTM ver4. 1 and GEODATA DEM-9S ver3 digital elevation models over Australia. Australian Journal of Earth Sciences, 57(3), pp.337-347.

Hugenholtz, C.H., Walker, J., Brown, O. and Myshak, S. (2014). Earthwork volumetrics with an unmanned aerial vehicle and softcopy photogrammetry. Journal of Surveying Engineering, 141(1), p.06014003.

Luhmann, T., Robson, S., Kyle, S. and Boehm, J. (2014). Close-range photogrammetry and 3D imaging. Walter de Gruyter.

Mesas-Carrascosa, F.J., Notario García, M.D., Meroño de Larriva, J.E. and García-Ferrer, A. (2016). An Analysis of the Influence of Flight Parameters in the Generation of Unmanned Aerial Vehicle (UAV) Orthomosaicks to Survey Archaeological Areas. Sensors, 16(11), p.1838.

Metni, N. and Hamel, T. (2007). A UAV for bridge inspection: Visual servoing control law with orientation limits. Automation in construction, 17(1), pp.3-10.

Morgenthal, G. and Hallermann, N. (2014). Quality assessment of unmanned aerial vehicle (UAV) based visual inspection of structures. Advances in Structural Engineering, 17(3), pp.289-302.

Nunnally, S.W. (2004). Construction methods and management. Upper Saddle River, NJ, USA: Pearson Prentice Hall.

Pix4D 2017 https://support.pix4d.com/hc/en-us#gsc.tab=0

Rathinam, S., Kim, Z.W. and Sengupta, R. (2008). Vision-based monitoring of locally linear structures using an unmanned aerial vehicle 1. Journal of Infrastructure Systems, 14(1), pp.52-63.

Schenk, T., (1997). Towards automatic aerial triangulation. ISPRS Journal of Photogrammetry and remote Sensing, 52(3), pp.110-121.

Siebert, S. and Teizer, J. (2014). Mobile 3D mapping for surveying earthwork projects using an Unmanned Aerial Vehicle (UAV) system. Automation in Construction, 41, pp.1-14.

Tang, L., Braun, J. and Debitsch, R.(1997). Automatic aerotriangulation—concept, realization and results. ISPRS journal of photogrammetry and remote sensing, 52(3), pp.122-131.

Wang, X., Al-Shabbani, Z., Sturgill, R., Kirk, A. and Dadi, G.B. (2017). Estimating Earthwork Volumes Through Use of Unmanned Aerial Systems. Transportation Research Record: Journal of the Transportation Research Board, (2630), pp.1-8.

Wolf, P.R. and B.A. DeWitt. 2000. Elements of photogrammetry with applications in GIS. Third edition. New York, McGraw-Hill.

Yanalak, M. (2005). Computing pit excavation volume. Journal of surveying engineering, 131(1), pp.15-19.

An integrated ontology-based approach for optimizing structural design at early stage with consideration of environmental impact and cost

Jisong Zhang[a,b], Haijiang Li[a,*], Yinghua Zhao[b], Guoqian Ren[a]
[a] Cardiff School of Engineering, Cardiff University, Queen's Buildings, The Parade, Cardiff, CF24 3AA, Wales UK
[b] Institute of Road and Bridge Engineering, Dalian Maritime University, Dalian, 116026, Liaoning, China
LiH@cardiff.ac.uk (Haijiang Li).

Abstract. Early stage decision-making for structural design critically influences the overall cost and environmental performance of buildings and infrastructure. However, the current approach often fails to consider the multi-perspectives of structural design, such as safety, environmental issues and cost in a comprehensive way. This paper presents a holistic approach based on knowledge processing (ontology) to facilitate a smarter decision-making process for early design stage by informing designers of the environmental impact and cost along with safety considerations. The approach can give a reasoning based quantitative understanding of how the design alternatives using different concrete materials can affect the ultimate overall performance. Embodied CO_2 and cost are both considered along with safety criteria as indicative multi-perspectives to demonstrate the novelty of the approach. A case study of a concrete structural frame is used to explain how the proposed method can be used by structural designers when taking multi performance criteria into account.

Keyword: Holistic Structural Design, Ontology, Environmental Impact, Lifecycle Cost, Multi-Criteria Decision Support

1. Introduction

A building project is chronologically composed of three main stages, namely the design, construction, and use phases. The potential for influencing environmental impact and cost performance is very high in the design stage, and decreases dramatically with the progression of time (Kohler & Moffatt, 2003). This means that a large number of building decisions are made by designers in the early phase, and this critically determines a building's ultimate performance. Structural engineers, as a key part of the design team, work alongside architects and MEP (mechanical, electrical, plumbing) engineers to ensure that buildings are strong enough to withstand all kinds of loads and actions. During the building design process, structural engineers normally pay more attention to safety and technical issues than environmental impact and cost concerns; this is because decisions related to this aspect largely hinge on the architect and client, which means that their contribution to the environmental performance is negligible (Miller & Doh, 2015). Recent years have witnessed an increased awareness of the fact that structural engineers can make significant contributions to the reduction of environmental impact and cost. However, this is only possible if they pay a great deal of attention to the sustainability and cost, because a large amount of structural material is used in structures (Wolf, et al., 2017). Additionally, attention must be paid to the various indirect benefits of structural design, such as increasing the overall net area and net height, improving lifespan, shortening the construction schedule, and reducing labor and equipment. All of these factors influence overall performance with regard to environmental impact and cost.

However, despite this growing awareness, structural engineers commonly fail to combine environmental issues and cost into a holistic structural design. This is due to the fact that, in practice, a number of barriers exist (Hou, et al., 2015). Firstly, for a structural engineer, knowledge of sustainability is fragmented and distributed in different formats. Structural engineers may experience confusion in terms of which parts of the sustainability-related context need to be considered and how environmentally efficient building material and elements can be incorporated into the design of a given structure. For example, and much the same as the layout of a concrete structure, the material choice for the structural frame includes: normal strength concrete (NSC), high-performance concrete (HPC), ultra-high performance concrete (UHPC) and the above three materials with supplementary cementitious materials (SCMs) (Woodward, 2014; Yu, et al., 2015; Zhang & Zhao, 2016). It is unclear as to how these choices will affect the environmental impact and cost performance of a whole structure. Secondly, there are insufficient regulations and sustainable tools available for structural engineers to quantify the environmental impact and the cost of the structure at early stages. BREEAM, LEED, and Australia's Green Star rating system provide more opportunities to facilitate sustainable design by marking the whole building at the later design stage. However, this is designed for decision making by architects rather than structural engineers. Thirdly, policymakers, owners, and key stakeholders are unaware of the important role that a structural engineer can play; this means that they lack financial incentives and rewards to incorporate sustainability. Under these circumstances, there is an urgent need to develop a holistic design approach to facilitate holistic structural design by informing the structural engineer the impact of their design decisions on the safety, sustainability, cost and other aspects of the building/infrastructure structure.

As one of the emerging Semantic Web technologies, ontology is widely used for knowledge sharing and reuse across different domains; it has great potential to address the problems related to holistic structural design. Ontology has many attractive features (Abanda, et al., 2013; Grzybek, et al., 2014), which include: (1) It provides a vocabulary and a framework through which to structurally model knowledge of a given domain in a format that can be processed by both machine and human. (2) It not only defines the terms in a specific domain, but also describes the relationships between these terms in various domains. (3) It provides a hierarchy of concepts in a particular domain. Because of the above advantages, it is expected that ontology could be used as a tool to develop a holistic structural design tool. However, in the field of structural design, more advanced deductive reasoning capability is required due to the existence of a large number of calculations. In order to extend the flexibility of ontology and meet the requirements of structural design, an effective and robust tool on top of ontology is needed for more specific calculation purposes. As such, semantic web rule language (SWRL) is employed in this research.

The focus of this research is to create a feasible way to help structural engineers to achieve much more comprehensive structural designs at the early design phase. The proposed approach combines sustainability and cost with safety knowledge to inform structural engineers of the environmental impact and cost performance of a structure depending on their choice of different material. Emphasis lies on the effect of structural elements and materials, which means that the non-structural elements and material are not incorporated in this work. An ontology-based decision support system is constructed to provide optimised design solutions to not only reduce embodied carbon and cost, but also to offer an alternative to structural feasibility. The structure of this paper is introduced as follows: Section 2 presents a detailed procedure for design and development of structural design ontology. A case study of a structure frame is demonstrated and validated in Section 3. Finally, Section 4 gives the main conclusions of this study.

2. Design and development of structural design ontology

In this work, three types of concrete are selected, namely NSC, HPC and UHPC. The mix proportion for NSC, HPC and UHPC are designed conforming to BS EN206-1 and available literature (Lim, et al., 2004; Larrard & Sedran, 2002; Wille & Cotulio, 2015). The embodied CO_2 footprint and cost for concrete are estimated by a simple method (Yang, et al., 2013; Gluch & Baumann, 2004; Wille & Cotulio, 2015). Table 1 presents the CO_2 footprint and cost for NSC, HPC and UHPC.

Table 1: Underlying data for CO_2 and cost assessment of NSC, HPC and UHPC

	NSC			HPC			UHPC		
	C25	C35	C45	C80	C90	C100	C160	C170	C180
CO_2 (kg CO_2 /m^3)	249	286	324	264	297	330	462	491	519
Cost ($US/m^3)	87	95	103	242	260	279	465	487	510

The developed ontology system consists of four essential segments: knowledge base, ontology management system, rules editor and query interface. The knowledge base is the crucial component since the ontology and structural design knowledge are saved in the form of an OWL file. Protégé-OWL 5.1 is employed as the ontology management system providing ontology and rule editing, SWRLTab plug-ins, reasoners and other functions are required for prototype system development. The query interface is a platform used by a structural engineer to interact with the knowledge management system. The workflow can be explained as follows: (1) The knowledge engineer converts the structural design, sustainability and cost knowledge into ontology and SWRL rules; (2) Knowledge base stores the ontology and SWRL rules that are edited through Protégé main interface and SWRLTab. (3) The rule engine in ontology management system runs the SWRL rules and generates new facts for the knowledge base; (4) The end user (e.g., structural engineer) obtains possible results by inputting the design demands from SQWRL query interface (SQWRLQueryTab). More details of the system are shown in Figure 1.

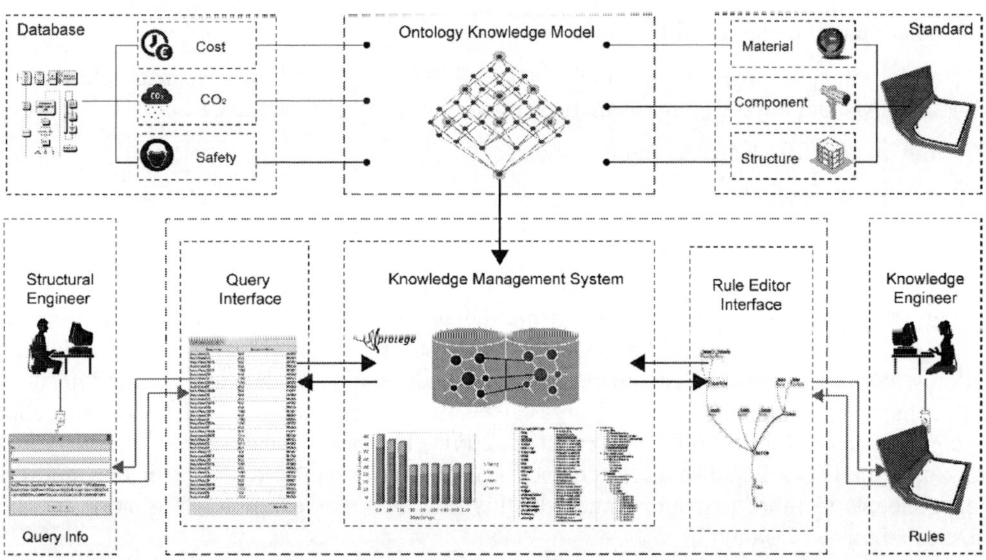

Figure 1: The developed ontology framework

From the previous literatures, many methodologies can be used for ontology development (Breitman, et al., 2007; Sure, et al., 2009; Noy & McGuinness, 2001), such as Uschold and King, Grüninger and Fox, Methontology, KACTUS and Ontology Development 101. Each methodology has its advantages and drawbacks. In this work, Ontology Development 101 is chosen because of the following reasons: (1) It is easy to use for beginners with no former experience of ontology development. (2) It provides guidance on how to implement the ontology step-by-step in the Protégé software environment. (3) It is suitable for development by reusing existing ontologies. Therefore, the following steps are used to construct the structural design ontology:

Step 1. Determine the domain and scope of the ontology

The domain and scope of the ontology can be identified by listing some basic questions (BQ) and competency questions (CQ). Asking these questions early and in easily understood language will test whether there is enough information in the ontology as it stands. For example:

BQ: What is the purpose of building this ontology?

A: To inform structural engineers of different choices and give them a quantitative understanding of how these choices will affect the ultimate environmental impact and cost performance of a building structure.

BQ: What is the domain of the ontology?

A: Structural design, sustainability and cost.

BQ: Who is the user of the developed ontology?

A: Structural engineers

CQ: What is the structure form?

A: Concrete structural frame.

CQ: What type of structural elements will be covered in this study?

A: Flat, beam, column and footing.

CQ: What kind of concrete will be used in this study?

A: Normal strength concrete with and without SCMs, high performance concrete with and without SCMs and ultra-high performance concrete with and without SCMs.

CQ: How to quantify the sustainability and cost?

A: Embodied CO_2 and $US.

Step 2. Consider reusing existing ontologies

It is worth considering reusing existing ontologies or extending existing sources for a particular domain when building a new ontology. From the available literature, there are many reusable ontologies. For example, BuildingSMART has constructed an IFC framework which, for building design, is seen as an established standard under which models of building information can be shared and exchanged so that design can be made more effective, with follow-on benefits for construction and operation (Roussey, et al., 2011). Therefore, the developed ontology in this work uses the IFC schema as a reference by adding more specific relationships or modifying their concepts to more readable names. In this ontology, for example, "Column" has been substituted for "ifcColumn".

Step 3. Enumerate important terms in the ontology

Initially, it is essential to generate an inclusive inventory of the entirety of terms that associated with the sustainability, cost and structural design in this step. As introduced previously, the underlying data of the CO_2 footprint and cost for NSC, HPC and UHPC are calculated based on the BS EN206-1, ICE database and reference papers, which are shown in Tables 1. Taking C35 as an example, 1 m^3 of C35 concrete comprised: 300 kg of cement, 1,915 kg of aggregate, and 165 kg of water. The value of embodied CO_2 for cement (Portland cement, CEM I 32.5), aggregate and water are 0.93,0.005, and 0.0003 kg CO_2 per kg material (Muller, et al., 2014; Leese & Casey, 2015), respectively. Therefore, the total embodied CO_2 of C35 can be obtained by:

$$CO_{2\text{-}M} = \sum_{i=1}^{n} W_i \times CO_{2-i} = 300\times0.93+1915\times0.004+165\times0.0003=286 \text{ kg } CO_2/m^3$$

Furthermore, on the whole building level, the building consists of a structural frame, mechanical system, electrical system, plumbing system, internal partition, external wall, windows and doors. Since the purpose of developing the ontology is for structural design, only the structural frame is considered in the ontology.

Step 4. Define the classes and the class hierarchy

Defining the classes and properties of them is the primary stage in the ontology-design development. A top-down establishment is constructed, which commences with the definition of the most general classes and subsequent specialization of the classes. Starting with a super-class in which building, building element and material are all combined, this super-class is broken down first into classes and then into sub- classes. The latter are very specific as to what may be included in them. The building element class contains non-structural elements and structural elements sub-classes. The latter contains slabs, beams, columns and footing sub-classes.

Step 5. Define the properties of classes

Defining the properties of the concepts and developing the class hierarchy are sometimes intertwined. Normally, the definition of the class is first established and then the properties of the class are described. In terms of the properties, object property, data-type property and annotation property are mainly three types of properties. Relationships between classes are defined by the object property. An example would be: hasConcrete, and isConcreteOf. Characteristics of instances of each class are defined by the data-type property, and this applies to both quantity and quality. The sort of value types found here include such things as: Number; String; Enumerated; and Boolean. As a simple example, we will take a slab made of the type of concrete classified as "C25." This can be represented in the ontology as: an instance of the slab class where "C25" is the data-type property. Further data values such as volume, reinforcement, cost and CO_2 can then be added. Furthermore, the function of the annotation property is to clarify the data and explanation by inputting a comment on some elements of the ontology wherever it is needed.

Step 6. Create instances

Within classes, individual instances have their own hierarchical place, and the process of defining each individual instance within a class will involve these steps: (1) Choose a class; (2) Locate an instance for this class; and (3) Populate the values of that specific instance. To take one example: the class, Beams, has individual instances from C25 to C180, and each of these represents one specific beam. It will be necessary to enter data-type properties manually in some cases, but in the case of others, specific values are not given because SWRL rules deduct them. For example, the span and load of a slab is manually input and regarded as initial facets, while the cross-sectional area, volume, weight and reinforcement are calculated automatically based on the SWRL rules and initial facets, which are regarded as inferred facets. Similarly, embodied CO_2 and cost values appeared in Tables 1 is presented in the form of data-type properties for the different level types of concrete. There are mainly five data-types that describe the types of values that can define the properties: string, number, boolean, enumeration, and instance-type. For example, concrete strength "fck" can have a value type of "Float", and can be quantified by using figures such as 25, 80 or 160 MPa (number data-type). Since the structural design work is a quantitative calculation process, most data-types used in this ontology are number.

Step 7. Define SWRL rules

Since the ontology only provides the structure and relations among different parts, an SWRL rule extending the ontology's flexibility is there to meet the structural calculations' requirements. SWRL is the reasoning function in the ontology in question, creating an interoperability –between rules and ontology (both semantic and inferential). A set of SWRL rules related to the structural design were extracted from Eurocode 2 and were incorporated into the development ontology for specific applications.

Step 8. Define SQWRL rules

Querying OWL ontology is done by means of Semantic Query-Enhanced Web Rule Language (SQWRL), which is a language based on SWRL. Design solutions that work can be obtained by structural engineers from SQWRLQueryTab when the design requirements are input through the Protégé query interface as SQWRL queries.

3. Case study

In this section, a case study of a concrete structural frame is used to explain how the proposed method can be used by structural designers when taking multi performance criteria into account. The framed structure is a 5-story, 3780 m^2 rectangular office building with a regular column grid of 6 m × 6 m. The overall length and width of the building is 18 m (3 × 6 m) and 42 m (7 × 6 m). The layout of the building is shown in Figure 2. The objective is to compare and select the minimum embodied CO_2 and cost of the whole structural frame.

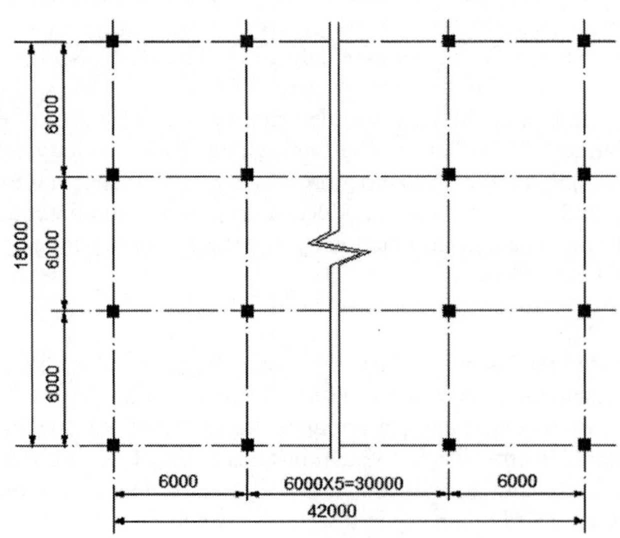

Fig.2 Layout of the structure frame

The structural frame consists of slabs, beams, columns and footings. Each of these structural elements will be calculated based on the design code which has been transformed into the semantic rules in the ontology. Each concrete class (i.e., NSC, HPC and UHPC) ranging from C25 to C180, are selected to calculate the cross-sectional area and reinforcement of these structural elements (except the footing) in the system. The footing only considers the C25 concrete since there is no need to have higher compressive strength in the foundation. After calculating the required cross-sectional area and reinforcement, the volume of the concrete and the weight of the reinforcement of the structural elements is obtained, which is further converted to the CO_2 and cost by multiplying the CO_2 and cost per unit. The structural frame sums these values from each structural element and provides the total CO_2 and cost. After comparing the alternatives, the structural frame that have the least embodied carbon is recognised as the most sustainable design solution and the one with minimum cost is considered as the most cost-efficient alternatives.

Taking the slab calculation as an example, the span and load of a slab is manually input and regarded as initial facets, while the cross-sectional area, volume, reinforcement, weight, CO_2 and cost are calculated automatically based on the SWRL rules and initial facets, which are regarded as inferred facets. Similarity, the SWRL rules for beams, columns and footings' calculations are based on the basic equations in the design code. Afterwards, the total CO_2 and cost of the structural frame can be calculated by summing the values obtained from these structural elements. The SWRL rules implemented for the slab, beam, column and footing, together with the structural frame, are shown in Table 2.

Table 2: SWRL rules for slab calculation

Rule 1	Determine the load and combination of action on the slab: p=1.35×Gk +1.5×Qk
	Slab(?S)^Gk(?S,?SGk) ^Qk(?S,?SQk)^swrlb:multiply(?x, 1.35, ?SGk) ^swrlb:multiply(?y, 1.5, ?SQk) ^swrlb:add(?Sp, ?x,?y)->p(?S? Sp)
Rule 2	Determine the design moments (M) on the slab: $M=0.125pl^2$
	Slab(?S)^p(?S,?Sp) ^length(?S,?Sl)^swrlb:multiply(?SM, 0.125, ?Sp, ?Sl,?Sl)->M(?S,?SM)
Rule 3	Determine the thickness (h) of the slab: $h=(\frac{M}{k\times b\times f_{ck}})^{0.5}$
	Slab(?S)^M(?S,?SM) ^k(?S,?Sk)^ b(?S,?Sb)^ hasConcrete(?S,?Con) ^Concrete(?Con) ^fck(?Con,?Confck)^ swrlb:multiply(?x, ?Sk, ?Sb, ?Confck) ^swrlb:divide(?y, ?SM, ?x)^swrlb:sqrt(?Sh, ?y) ->h(?S,?Sh)
Rule 4	Calculating the required reinforcement of the slab: $As=\frac{M}{0.9\times h\times f_{yd}}$
	Slab(?S)^M(?S,?SM) ^h(?S,?Sh) ^ hasReinforcement (?S,?RF)^Reinforcement(?RF)^fyd(?RF,?RFfyd)^ swrlb:multiply(?x,0.9, ?Sh, ?RFfyd) ^ swrlb:divide(?SAs, ?SM, ?x) ->As(?S,?SAs)
Rule 5	Calculating the volume of the slab: Volume=Ac×h
	Slab(?S) ^ Ac(?S,?SAc) ^ h(?S,?Sh) ^ swrlb:multiply(?SV, ?Sac, ?Sh) -> Volume (?S,?SV)
Rule 6	Calculating the weight of the slab: Weight=Volume×Density
	Slab(?S) ^ Volume((?S,?SV) ^ hasConcrete(?S,?Con) ^Concrete(?Con) ^ Density(?Con,?ConD) ^ swrlb:multiply(?SW, ?SV, ?ConD) -> weight (?S,?SW)
Rule 7	Calculating the weight of reinforcement of the slab: $Weight=\frac{D}{2}\times\frac{D}{2}\times 3.14\times Length\times 78.5\times Nbar$
	Slab(?S) Nbar(?S,?SNbar) ^ hasReinforcement(?S,?RF)^Reinforcement(?RF) ^Diameter(?RF,?RFD) ^ SLength(?RF,?RFSL) ^ swrlb:multiply(?SRFW, 0.25, ?RFD, ?RFD,3.14, ?RFL,78.5, ?SNbar)-> Weight(?S,? SRFW)
Rule 8	Calculating the total CO2 of the slab: Slab CO2= Volume of slab×CO2 per unit+ Weight of reinforcement×CO2 per unit
	Slab(?S) ^ Volume (?S,?SV) ^ hasConcrete(?S,?Con) ^Concrete(?Con) ^ SCO2(?Con,?ConCO2) ^ Weight(?S,? SRFW) ^ hasReinforcement(?S,?RF)^Reinforcement(?RF) ^RF CO2(?RF,?RFCO2) ^ swrlb:multiply(?x, ?SV, ?ConCO2) ^ swrlb:multiply(?y, ? SRFW, ? RFCO2) ^swrlb:add(?SCO2, ?x,?y)->SlabCO2(?S?,SCO2)
Rule 9	Calculating the total cost of the slab: Weight=Volume×Density
	Slab(?S) ^ Volume (?S,?SV) ^ hasConcrete(?S,?Con) ^Concrete(?Con) ^ UnitCost(?Con,?ConUC) ^ Weight(?S,? SRFW) ^ hasReinforcement(?S,?RF)^Reinforcement(?RF) ^ UnitCost(?RF,?RFUC) swrlb:multiply(?x, ?SV, ?ConUC) ^ swrlb:multiply(?y, ? SRFW, ? RFUC) ^swrlb:add(?SCost, ?x,?y)->SlabCost(?S? SCost)

Figure 3 demonstrates the execution and results in SQWRLQueryTab. It shows the embodied carbon of all the structural frame. From the comparison, it is obvious which structural frame has the minimum embodied carbon, although they belong to different structural frames. For a more in-depth comparison, the outputs from the ontology were switched to Excel and schematically shown in Figures 4.

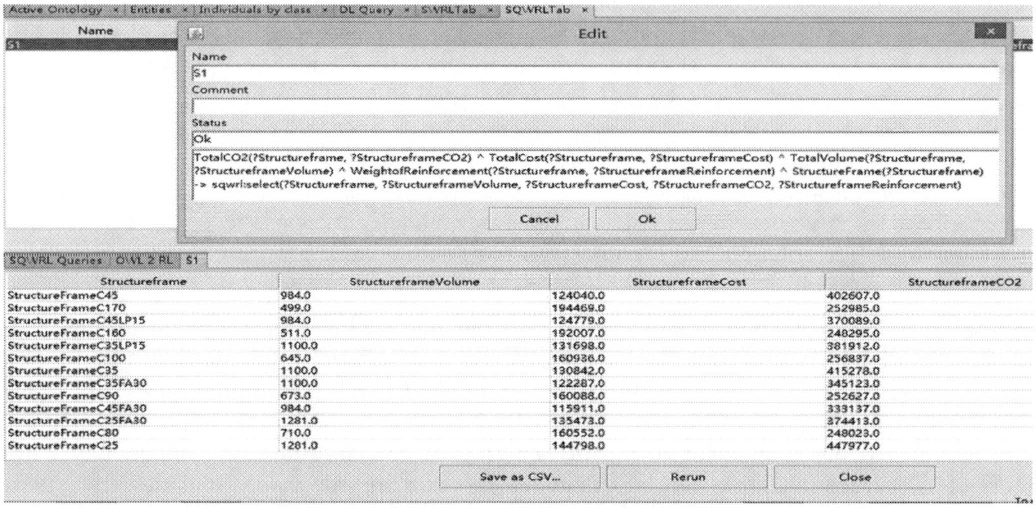

Structureframe	StructureframeVolume	StructureframeCost	StructureframeCO2
StructureFrameC45	984.0	124040.0	402607.0
StructureFrameC170	499.0	194469.0	252985.0
StructureFrameC45LP15	984.0	124779.0	370089.0
StructureFrameC160	511.0	192007.0	248295.0
StructureFrameC35LP15	1100.0	131698.0	381912.0
StructureFrameC100	645.0	160936.0	256837.0
StructureFrameC35	1100.0	130842.0	415278.0
StructureFrameC35FA30	1100.0	122287.0	345123.0
StructureFrameC90	673.0	160088.0	252627.0
StructureFrameC45FA30	984.0	115911.0	333137.0
StructureFrameC25FA30	1281.0	135473.0	374413.0
StructureFrameC80	710.0	160552.0	248023.0
StructureFrameC25	1281.0	144798.0	447977.0

Fig.3 Screenshot of the structural frame selection

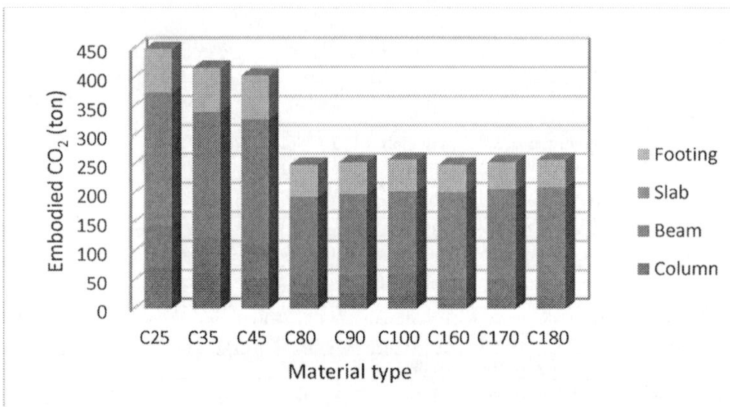

Fig.4 Composition of embodied CO_2 for a structural frame

4. Conclusions

This paper develops a novel and feasible approach for structural engineer to achieve more comprehensive structural designs, where sustainability criteria, e.g. low carbon and CO_2 emission, life cycle costing along with structural safety are holistically considered through reasoning based knowledge processing. A comprehensive knowledge base for multi-perspective structural design across different sectors is developed, which includes relevant taxonomy, ontology, and SWRL rules. The knowledge base has been validated and a full building case study was used to demonstrate its practical use; where NSC, HPC and UHPC different type of materials are used as comparison and alternatives. The approach combines sustainability and cost with safety knowledge; provides multi-perspectives solutions considering safety, low carbon and cost; it demonstrates a new way of working for structural engineer to achieve ultimate sustainable design with the help of intelligent knowledge base.

Within the case study, the NSC, HPC and UHPC, whose concrete classes range from C25 to C180, are selected as fundamental data to calculate the CO_2 and cost of a whole structure. The embodied impact and cost of a structure frame is mainly concentrated in the slab as the volume of the slab is large, regardless of concrete type. Regarding the environmental impact, the structural frame made of UHPC has the least embodied CO_2 compared to that of NSC and HPC. Regarding cost, the structural frame made of NSC shows the minimum cost compared to that of HPC and UHPC. Using the proposed approach, a structural engineer can focus on the important part that most influences CO_2 and cost, and can postpone less urgent decisions to the later design stage.

While the purpose of the approach based on developed ontology is to improve the decision-making process for, in this case, a structure with a concrete frame, the model can be extended to other frame materials including timber and steel. Meanwhile, the method can be further expanded for the use of institutional learning, to conclude from the former design experiences to guide better future designs. It should be mentioned that the developed approach is focused on the environmental impact and cost the of structural frame which is based on the structural components. It is expected that non-structural components in which the mechanical system, electrical system, plumbing system and architectural features can be included from a whole building perspective in the future work. In addition, in terms of cost of a structural frame, the influence of on-site construction (i.e., concrete formwork, labour and equipment for fabrication or erection, construction schedule, etc.) needs to be considered in the future work. Lastly, the case study used in this work is a simple layout of a structural frame with a regular column grid. More complicated case applications will be required to validate the applicability and serviceability of the proposed structural design ontology.

Acknowledgements

The authors gratefully acknowledge use of the services and facilities of Cardiff BIM & Virtual Reality Laboratory and BRE Trust Centre for Sustainable Engineering at the Cardiff University. The authors also would like to acknowledge the support provided by China Scholarship Council (CSC No 201606570007) for partially funding this research.

References

Abanda, F., Tah, J. & Keivani, R., 2013. Trends in built environment semantic Web applications: Where are we today? Expert Systems with Applications, 40(14), pp. 5563-77.

Breitman, K. K., Casanova, M. A. & Truszkowski, W., 2007. Semantic Web: Concepts, Technologies and Applications. London: Springer.

Gluch, P. & Baumann, H., 2004. The life cycle costing (LCC) approach: a conceptual discussion of its usefulness for environmental decision-making. Building and Environment, pp. 571-580.

Grzybek, H., Xu, S., Gulliver, S. & V. F., 2014. Considering the feasibility of semantic model design in the built-environment. Buildings, Volume 4, pp. 849-879.

Hou, S., Li, H. & Rezgui, Y., 2015. Ontology-based approach for structural design considering low embodied energy and carbon. Energy and Buildings, Volume 102, pp. 75-90.

Kohler, N. & Moffatt, S., 2003. Life-cycle analysis of the built environment. Sustainable building and construction, UNEP Industry and Environment April – September, pp. 17-21.

Larrard, F. d. & Sedran, T., 2002. Mixture-proportioning of high-performance concrete. Cement and Concrete Research, 32(11), p. 1699–1704.

Leese , R. & Casey, D., 2015. Embodied CO2e of UK cement, additions and cementitious material, MPA Cement Mineral Products Association. [Online] Available at: http://cement.mineralproducts.org/documents/Factsheet_18.pdf

Lim, C.H., Yoon, Y.S. & Kim, J.H., 2004. Genetic algorithm in mix proportioning of high-performance concrete. Cement and Concrete Research, pp. 409-420.

Miller, D. & Doh, J. H., 2015. Incorporating sustainable development principles into building design: a review from a structural perspective including case study. Struct. Design Tall Spec. Build, Volume 24, pp. 412-439.

Muller, H. S., Haist, M. & Vogel, M., 2014. Assessment of the sustainability potential of concrete and concrete structures considering their environmental impact, performance and lifetime. Construction and Building Materials, 67(C), pp. 321-337.

Noy, N. F. & McGuinness, D. L., 2001. Ontology Development 101: A Guide to Creating Your First Ontology. [Online] Available at: http://protege.stanford.edu/publications/ontology_development/ontology101.pdf

Roussey, C., Pinet, F., Kang, M. . A. & Corcho, O., 2011. An Introduction to Ontologies and Ontology Engineering. In: Ontologies in Urban Development Projects, Advanced Information and Knowledge Processing. London: Springer, pp. 9-38.

Sure, Y., Staab, S. & Studer, R., 2009. Ontology Engineering Methodology. In: Handbook on Ontologies. London: Springer, pp. 135-152.

Wolf, C. D., Pomponi, F. & Moncaster, A., 2017. Measuring embodied carbon dioxide equivanlent of buildings: A review and critique of current industry practice. Energy and Buildings, pp. 68-80.

Wille, K. & Cotulio, C. B., 2015. Material efficiency in the design of ultra-high performance concrete. Construction and Building Materials, Volume 86, pp. 33-43.

Woodward, K., 2014. https://www.worldcement.com. [Online] Available at: https://www.worldcement.com/europe-cis/11082014/the-concrete-centre-reports-on-the-benefits-of-high-strength-concrete-121/

Yang, K. H., Song, J. K. & Song, K. I., 2013. Assessment of CO2 reduction of alkali-activated concrete. Journal of Cleaner Production, pp. 265-272.

Yu, R., Spiesz, P. & Brouwers, H., 2015. Development of an eco-friendly Ultra-High Performance Concrete (UHPC) with efficient cement and mineral admixtures uses. Cement and Concrete Composites, Volume 55, pp. 383-394.

Zhang, J. & Zhao, Y., 2016. The mechanical properties and microstructure of ultra-highperformance concrete containing various supplementary cementitious materials. Journal of Sustainable Cement-Based Materials.

Comparison of machine learning algorithms for forecasting of residential complex energy consumption

Miloš Šipetić, Filip Petrushevski and Florian Judex
Austrian Institute of Technology, Austria
milos.sipetic@ait.ac.at

Abstract. With the advent of building energy production and electrical/heat storage devices, forecasting user consumption patterns on the micro and medium level is becoming more important for optimization of local energy and heat generation and usage. We set up the workflow for automatic data processing in order to train and evaluate a number of prediction models for forecasting of energy consumption. Validation of models has been performed in parallel with the training process using cross-validation and cross-validation with backward feature elimination, in order to reduce the number of features used for training and to optimize the accuracy of the model.

1. Introduction

A major trend in building energy systems is the transition from simply oversizing both production and distribution (Sun, et al., 2014) to flexible and optimized energy systems. The behaviour of the buildings and its tenant then becomes more than just a disturbance variable to be counteracted by a local feedback control. Also, renewable energy production on both building and grid level leads to new business models. The timing of energy consumption becomes important beyond simple off-peak pricing systems. Furthermore, along building integrated energy storages and different approaches to demand response (DR), building energy management systems (BEMS) which balance costs and comfort are deployed increasingly (GlobalData, 2012).

To increase the performance of BEMS, especially when considering the thermal inertia of the building mass, prediction about the behaviour of both energy consumption and production of buildings is a possible option. Therefore, on the one hand, a forecast of renewable energy production is desirable, mostly in the form of solar thermal systems or photovoltaic panels. On the other hand, energy consumption by the heating, cooling and air conditioning (HVAC) as well as by the tenants' usage of electric energy and domestic hot water will help to put this forecast to good use. This is especially important because while the consumption by the tenant does not change much, the ratio increases as building quality increases, making the less predictable part much more important.

On the other hand, although the overall market for DR and BEMS is quite large, the individual benefits for a single user are still quite small (Pinson, et al., 2014). This leads to the need for automating the forecast, reducing the need for manual configuration and optimizations as much as possible, using semantic information alongside recorded data to extract as much knowledge as possible. Thus, this paper explores the various possibilities of clustering building energy consumption data, both thermal and electric, to predict the future of a large residential complex, which in turn could be used to optimize the utilization of various thermal and electric sources and storages.

2. Related work

The residential energy consumption is responsible for 25% of the total energy consumption in Europe (Pérez-Lombard, et al., 2008) which is, with some exceptions, similar to the worldwide average. At the same time there is a big potential for improvement in this sector. This is the reason why the research and development in this area is still very popular.

In their work, Swan and Ugursal reviewed different modeling techniques for end-use energy consumption in the residential sector (Swan & Ugursal, 2009). They group the techniques into two categories, "top-down" and "bottom-up". The former models can estimate of total residential sector energy consumption based on attributes that characterize it. On the other hand, the later models extrapolate the calculated energy consumption of individual households or buildings.

In a recent review Molina-Solana et al. present various data science methods that can be applied to building energy management (Molina-Solana, et al., 2017). They present techniques such as classification, regression, clustering, association rules, sequence discovery, anomaly detection and time series analysis. According to their observation, the combination of various techniques seems to be the most effective approach, especially combining techniques such as clustering within time series analysis.

Clustering techniques are often used to cluster similar patterns of consumption (Rhodes, et al., 2014), (Benitez, et al., 2014), (McLoughlin, et al., 2015). They could be applied purely on time series or be used in combination with additional data sources such as building type, occupants' characteristics or weather data. However, these methods are being used mostly for the descriptive analysis of the data. In order to predict the consumption, additional correlation analysis and models should be used.

3. Methodology

Several methodologies exist that formalize the data science process into distinct steps (Azevedo, 2008). For example, in CRISP-DM (Chapman, et al., 2000) the process starts with understanding the problem at hand, understanding the available data sets and performing various data preparation steps in order to improve the quality of the data. Actual data mining, knowledge discovery and modelling then begin, where new insights are generated from the data using machine learning and statistical methods. The process then allows one to repeat these steps until the goals are reached, at which point the deployment of the system follows. We loosely adopt the steps of this process, as shown in Figure 1.

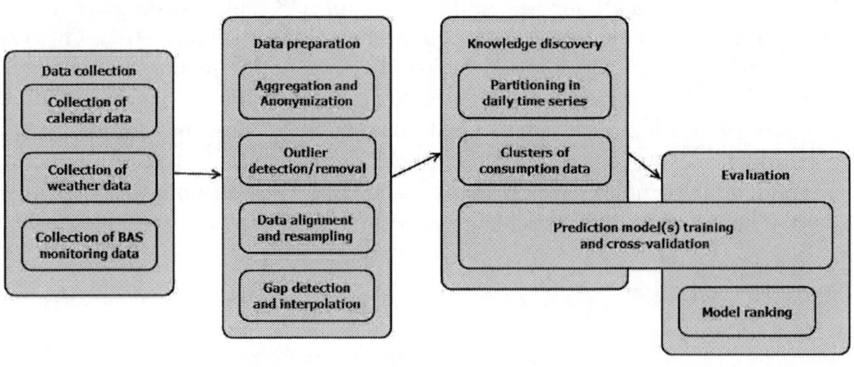

Figure 1 - Data analysis process

In the **data collection** step the data was collected from various sources along with metadata, such as labels, ranges, units etc. Due to privacy requirements, only the aggregated and anonymized data points were used. In the **data preparation** step, the outliers that were attributed to data collection errors were removed. Data gaps were filled when possible, and the datasets were aligned to aid the data mining process. Furthermore, as the goal is to provide day-ahead load forecasting, datasets were split into daily time series. First step in the **knowledge discovery** process was to perform clustering of the available data in order to label the daily time series with a cluster label. Next, the collected features, that are normally available the day before, were used to train the forecasting algorithms to predict the next day's cluster membership, hence predicting next day's consumption pattern. Training of classifier algorithms was directly linked with cross-validation and feature elimination processes, thereby somewhat blurring the line between discovery and **evaluation** phase. This allowed us collect large amount of evaluation data for different combinations of algorithms and to train classifiers with different feature combinations in order to find the optimal feature set for each clusterer/classifier pair.

Knime data analytics framework (Berthold, et al., 2009) was used for most of the aforementioned tasks. Knime is a platform for developing data analytics workflows. It contains a large number of predefined data import, export and transformation blocks, and also provides interfaces to most popular data analytics tools and general programming languages, such as Matlab, R, Python, Java etc. Weka is a library of machine learning algorithms for data mining tasks (Frank, et al., 2010). A number of Weka algorithms had been packaged into Knime blocks, so that they can be used in Knime.

4. Data collection and preparation

Dataset consists of a number of time series from the building automation system of a residential complex in Salzburg, Austria. In this work, following data points are of special interest to us: energy taken from the hot water storage tank (kWh), consumed electric energy (kWh) and consumed domestic hot water (kWh).

Table 1 - Metadata available for collected data points

Description	Unit	Sampling interval	Cumulative	Aggregated	Equidistant samples
Energy extracted from the hot water storage tank	kWh	15'	Yes	Yes	No
Electricity consumption	kWh	15'	No	No (88 data points)	Yes
Domestic hot water consumption	kWh	60'	No	No (88 data points)	Yes

The apartment data was split in three groups: "Main" group, for apartments for which a number of additional data points was provided, such as room temperature, humidity, presence sensors; "control" group, which consists of apartments of the same type and size as the main group, and an "additional" group, consisting of apartments of differing sizes and types. Because of privacy, data was additionally aggregated and anonymized. This was done by calculating the means across groups for each time step, thereby constructing the new time series as in Equation 1.

$$Avg_{group_i} = \sum \frac{c_j}{n} \quad (1)$$

Storage metering data was transformed from cumulative into differential as this form was preferred. Furthermore, as the samples were neither equidistant, nor aligned to the uniform time grid, resampling was performed thereby aligning the samples with other data points.

After the aggregation, the data were manually inspected and some extreme outliers attributed to outages and data collection errors were detected in the datasets. A simple Z-score-based outlier remover was used to filter out the outliers. Z-score was calculated for each value of the time series (as in Equation 2), and all values with z-score less than -4 and more than 4 (range was selected empirically) were removed from the series.

$$Z = \frac{x-\mu}{\sigma} \quad (2)$$

Detailed weather time series for the location of the residential complex and for the monitoring data period were collected from the Weather Underground service (The Weather Company, 2017). Weather dataset consists of the following data points: *temperature*, *relative humidity*, *wind speed*, *sea level pressure* and *conditions* field. *Condition* is represented by a string containing short textual description of current weather conditions such as "*Clear*", "*Fog*", "*Mist*", "*Cloudy*" etc. Other data points are represented by numerical values.

As predictors were intended to be used for day-ahead prediction, it was necessary to split data into a set of daily time series. A number of aggregation functions was applied to each daily time series and each data point, namely, daily means, maximums and minimums were calculated for numerical data points. For the *conditions* field, the string with most occurrences in the daily time series was taken as a value for that day.

Furthermore, holiday data for Austria was collected and included in the dataset from a list of official holidays (OfficeHolidays, 2017). As it is a common practice in Austria take the so called "bridge days" (Fenstertage) off, i.e. Fridays or Mondays in a week where bank holiday occurs on Thursday or Tuesday, respectively, a list of those was compiled and included in the dataset.

Complete list of additional data points is as follows: *temperature(mean)*, *temperature(max)*, *temperature(min)*, each ranged (-90,70°C); *wind speed(mean)*, *wind speed(max)*, *wind speed(min)*, each ranged (0-100km/h); *sea level pressure(mean)*, *sea level pressure(max)*, *sea level pressure(min)*, ranged (0,1085hPa); *humidity(mean)*, *humidity(max)*, *humidity(min)*, ranged (0,100%); *conditions* (textual descriptions), *holiday*, *bridge days*, both given as a Boolean true for official holiday, and bridge day occurrences, respectively; *season*, ranged (1,4), corresponding to astronomical seasons, with 1 being winter; and *day of week*, ranged (1,7) with 1 being Sunday.

5. Clustering methods

A number of Knime blocks integrating algorithms implemented in Weka was used for clustering. The algorithms chosen for comparison were Expectation maximization, self-organizing map (Kohonen map), Hierarchical clustering and XMeans (Friedman, 2008).

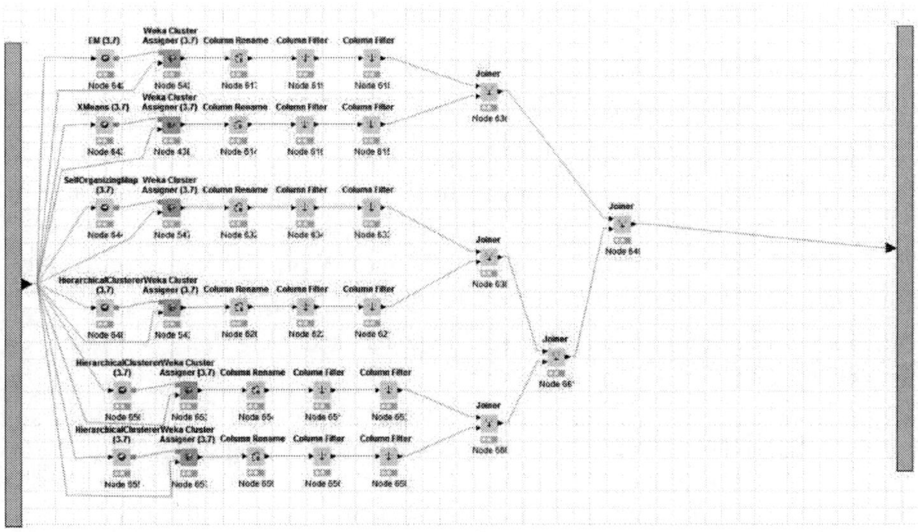

Figure 2 - Subworkflow for clustering input data using the selected clustering algorithms

As a first step in our data mining pipeline, the input data was classified into clusters. Previously described clustering algorithms were used as shown in Figure 2. All the selected algorithms are available in the Knime framework as reusable blocks, and it was possible to configure and set them up using the simple user interface.

SOM, EM and X-means algorithms were able to determine the optimal number of clusters automatically. Hierarchical clustering blocks were preconfigured with 3, 4 and 5 output clusters as it was preliminary determined that other algorithms usually clustered input data in 3, 4 or 5 clusters.

The result of running SOM clustering (Figure 3) on electric energy consumption data illustrates how different consumption patterns were resolved into clusters. All the daily patterns assigned to a particular cluster were drawn on top of each other, and an average consumption pattern was calculated (drawn in thicker line) for each cluster.

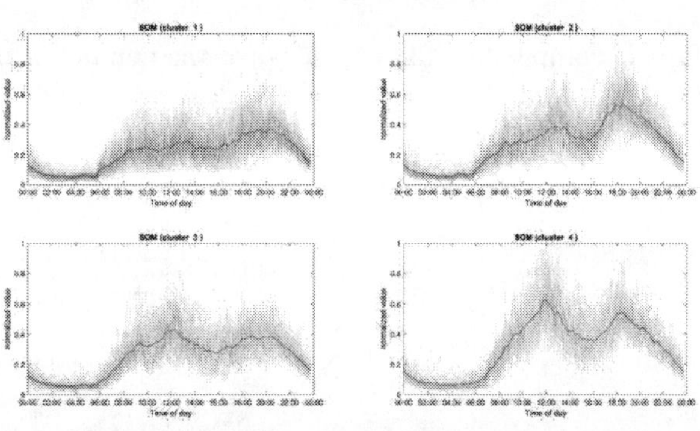

Figure 3 - SOM clustering performed on the electric energy consumption dataset

6. Forecasting and validation

In order to forecast the next day's consumption pattern, additional data points like calendar information and weather forecasts were needed. As cluster membership had been determined for aggregated daily time series, a set of labelled daily data was available for model training and validation. The premise is that based on the available metadata and cluster membership it is possible to forecast a daily consumption pattern, i.e. not only the total consumption for a day, but also the consumption distribution throughout the day.

For cluster membership classification, four different classification algorithms were used: Bayes network, random forest, logistic regression, and support vector machines.

Two different validation techniques were employed, and were run in parallel with the classification process.

Cross-validation is a technique for model validation where an original dataset is split into training and validation sets, the model is then trained on the training set and validated with the validation set. This is performed a number of times for different splits of the original dataset, and the results are then aggregated. Cross-validation is particularly good for avoiding overfitting of the model. There exists a number of different schemes for obtaining the set of splits. In particular for this analysis, the leave-one-out cross-validation was used, where the model is trained on n-1 samples, where n is the size of the dataset. The left-out sample is then forecasted, and the whole process is iteratively performed for each dataset member. The training and validation are performed using all prediction variables.

Sometimes, only some of the used variables contribute to the accuracy of the model, while the others could be left out of the model without consequences. In order to deal with that, a number of feature selection methods have been developed (Guyon & Elisseeff, 2003). **Backward feature elimination** is a feature selection method where a series of training and assessment iterations are made. First, the model is trained with all the available features, and its accuracy is assessed (e.g. using the error rate). Then, the model is trained with one feature left out, this is repeated for all the features, and all the generated models are assessed. Next, the feature whose exclusion contributed the least to the error rate increase is left out. This process repeats until there are no more features left to discard. Combined with leave-one-out cross-validation, as shown in Figure 4, this method enables finding an optimal selection of features for a particular combination of clustering and classifying algorithm.

$$\left(k * \frac{k+1}{2} - 1\right) * n \qquad (3)$$

The resulting workflow is computationally expensive as the number of training iterations is as in Equation 3, with k representing the number of features, and n being the number of rows in the data set.

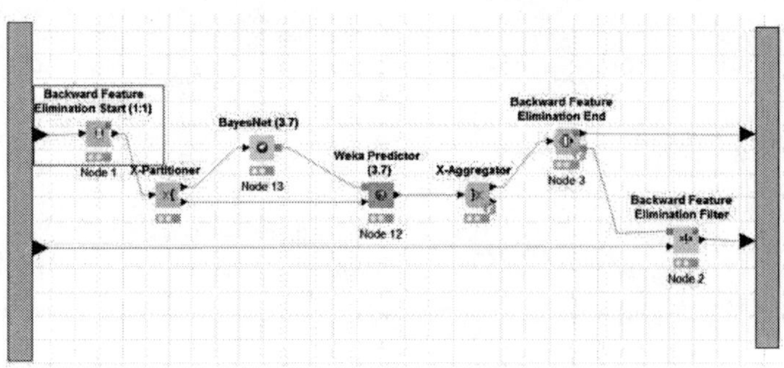

Figure 4 - Cross-validation with backward feature elimination workflow

Furthermore, the whole process had to be performed separately for each combination of clustering (6 times) and classification (4 times) algorithms, and for each data point (3 times).

For our dataset there was an optimal set of features for each combination of clustering and classification algorithms. Namely, starting with a complete set of features, when the feature elimination process starts, the error rate usually decreases for several iterations. Then, as more features get eliminated, it starts to increase again.

Table 3 and Table 2 show the results of running the complete Knime workflow on heat energy consumption, electric energy consumption and domestic hot water consumption datasets. Clusterer and Classifier columns specify the algorithms used for results in the particular row; error shows the error rate, i.e. a percentage of failed cross-validation runs; count specify the optimal number of features to reach this error rate; additionally, Table 3 lists predictors where the optimal set of predictors in reversed order of importance (i.e. the latter predictors are more significant). The results were sorted in the ascending order of error rate.

7. Conclusion and future work

As seen on Table 3**Error! Reference source not found.**, hierarchical clustering configured for 3 or 4 clusters in combination with either random forest or logistic regression produced the most accurate models. The number of features required to reach the optimal accuracy for each combination of clustering and forecasting model varied widely between solutions. Some of the features, such as *mean temperature*, *holidays*, *day-of-week*, and *bridge days* were found to be valuable in most solutions.

Results of forecasting of domestic hot water and electric energy consumption are summarized in the Table 2. Optimal combinations of clustering and classifying model are somewhat different here, as well as optimal number and selection of features. Combination of hierarchical clusterer and random forest classifier again appears near the top of the list for both datasets, as well as xmeans and random forest. Additional factor to consider when selecting best combination is the number of features necessary for optimal forecasting, where using less features is more desirable in order to avoid overfitting the model. Taking this into account some pairs offer considerable advantage. These are xmeans/logistic (5 predictors, 0.195 error rate) and xmeans/random forest (5 predictors, 0.203 error rate) for electric energy consumption, hierarchical(3)/bayes (4 predictors, 0.155 error rate) and hierarchical(3)/random forest (6 predictors, 0.159 error rate) for domestic hot water consumption, and hierarchical(4)/logistic (4 predictors, 0.098 error rate) and hierarchical(3)/svm (3 predictors, 0.108 error rate) for heat energy consumption.

Error rates encountered forecasting the domestic hot water consumption, and especially electric energy consumption need to be addressed further. Possible paths for exploration include data dimensionality reduction (i.e. aggregation of daily time series further, exclusion of low-variance or highly correlated dimensions, e.g. values between 22-05h) or inclusion of additional or constructed features such as previous day temperature, previous day consumption, or the derivatives of some of previously included features.

This combination of methods fared reasonably well for heat energy consumption with available data but it will have to be further validated on another dataset to check whether it is possible to reuse this model construction method for another site. Another interesting question would be whether the model trained on one site would be reusable as-is for similar and similarly used buildings in similar climates and occupied by similar demographics, if consumption data is appropriately normalized beforehand.

Table 2 - Error rates and feature counts for all combinations of clustering and classifying algorithms for electric energy and domestic hot water consumption

Electric energy consumption				Domestic hot water			
Clusterer	**Classifier**	**Error**	**Count**	**Clusterer**	**Classifier**	**Error**	**Count**
XMeans	Logistic	0.195	5	Hierarchical(3)	Bayes	0.155	4
Hierarchical(3)	RandomForest	0.197	12	Hierarchical(3)	RandomForest	0.159	6
XMeans	RandomForest	0.203	5	Hierarchical(4)	RandomForest	0.159	13
XMeans	Bayes	0.224	3	Hierarchical(3)	Logistic	0.167	11
XMeans	SVM	0.227	3	Hierarchical(4)	Bayes	0.179	3
Hierarchical(4)	Bayes	0.237	12	XMeans	RandomForest	0.179	13
Hierarchical(3)	SVM	0.237	3	Hierarchical(4)	Logistic	0.181	7
Hierarchical(3)	Bayes	0.243	4	Hierarchical(3)	SVM	0.184	5
Hierarchical(4)	RandomForest	0.245	9	Hierarchical(5)	Bayes	0.188	13
Hierarchical(3)	Logistic	0.251	4	SOM	Logistic	0.188	8
Hierarchical(5)	RandomForest	0.277	11	Hierarchical(5)	RandomForest	0.188	12
Hierarchical(5)	Bayes	0.288	13	SOM	Bayes	0.191	4
Hierarchical(4)	Logistic	0.296	10	XMeans	Logistic	0.193	6
Hierarchical(5)	Logistic	0.307	6	Hierarchical(5)	Logistic	0.196	7
Hierarchical(4)	SVM	0.309	6	Hierarchical(4)	SVM	0.198	3
Hierarchical(5)	SVM	0.336	9	XMeans	SVM	0.198	4
EM	Bayes	0.355	4	SOM	RandomForest	0.2	4
SOM	RandomForest	0.365	11	XMeans	Bayes	0.205	5
SOM	Bayes	0.373	15	SOM	SVM	0.208	3
EM	SVM	0.4	3	EM	Bayes	0.237	4
EM	RandomForest	0.405	14	EM	RandomForest	0.244	16
EM	Logistic	0.448	11	EM	SVM	0.244	5
SOM	Logistic	0.459	3	EM	Logistic	0.246	6
SOM	SVM	0.523	1	Hierarchical(5)	SVM	0.321	5

The ultimate goal of this research is to develop a consumption forecast model that will help optimize the energy mix and demand response strategy on the building and neighbourhood level. After the consumption forecasting is performed, next step is identifying the gap between available renewable energy and energy needs, taking into account possible demand response signals as well. This analysis will consider if and where potential reductions are possible in order to match needs with availability without compromising comfort. This would have to be done either on a global (e.g. reduction of hot water temperature in the system for the specific period), or local scale (passing the incentive and signals to customers most likely to change their behaviour and consumption pattern).

Acknowledgment

This work was funded by FFG (Austrian Research Promotion Agency) under the BProfEM project (845627).

Table 3 - Error rates and optimal feature sets for all combinations of clustering and classifying algorithms for heat energy consumption

Clusterer	Classifier	Error	Count	Predictors
Hierarchical(3)	Logistic	0.0931	8	Wind (Mean); Fenstertag; Humidity (Mean); Humidity (Min); Pressure (Max); Holiday; DoW; Temperature (Mean)
Hierarchical(4)	Logistic	0.098	4	Fenstertag; Holiday; DoW; Temperature (Mean)
Hierarchical(3)	RandomForest	0.103	9	Conditions; Pressure (Min); Humidity (Min); Wind (Max); Wind (Mean); Holiday; season; Humidity (Mean); Temperature (Mean)
Hierarchical(4)	RandomForest	0.108	8	Humidity (Mean); Fenstertag; Conditions; Humidity (Max); Pressure (Max); DoW; Temperature (Max); Temperature (Mean)
Hierarchical(3)	SVM	0.108	3	Fenstertag; season; Temperature (Mean)
Hierarchical(3)	Bayes	0.123	4	Wind (Max); Pressure (Mean); Temperature (Min); Temperature (Max)
Hierarchical(4)	Bayes	0.137	7	Humidity (Max); Holiday; Fenstertag; Temperature (Min); Humidity (Min); Pressure (Max); Temperature (Max)
XMeans	Logistic	0.137	3	Wind (Max); Humidity (Mean); Temperature (Mean)
Hierarchical(4)	SVM	0.137	4	Holiday; season; Temperature (Mean); Temperature (Max)
SOM	Logistic	0.142	9	Pressure (Mean); season; Wind (Min); Wind (Mean); Temperature (Min); Wind (Max); Pressure (Max); Temperature (Max); Temperature (Mean)
XMeans	RandomForest	0.147	13	Pressure (Max); Conditions; Temperature (Min); Holiday; Wind (Min); Temperature (Max); Pressure (Mean); Wind (Max); Fenstertag; Humidity (Max); season; Wind (Mean); Temperature (Mean)
SOM	RandomForest	0.157	8	Temperature (Min); Humidity (Max); Wind (Mean); DoW; Pressure (Max); season; Conditions; Temperature (Mean)
SOM	Bayes	0.162	5	Pressure (Mean); Pressure (Max); season; Temperature (Min); Temperature (Max)
XMeans	Bayes	0.167	4	Pressure (Max); season; Temperature (Min); Temperature (Max)
Hierarchical(5)	RandomForest	0.167	7	Holiday; Fenstertag; Pressure (Max); DoW; Humidity (Max); Temperature (Max); Temperature (Mean)
Hierarchical(5)	Logistic	0.176	7	season; Wind (Max); Fenstertag; DoW; Holiday; Temperature (Min); Temperature (Max)
SOM	SVM	0.181	6	Holiday; Temperature (Min); Fenstertag; Conditions; season; Temperature (Mean)
EM	Logistic	0.186	6	Wind (Min); DoW; Humidity (Min); Wind (Mean); Wind (Max); Temperature (Mean)
EM	RandomForest	0.196	15	season; Fenstertag; Wind (Min); Conditions; Wind (Mean); Humidity (Min); Holiday; Pressure (Min); Pressure (Mean), Temperature (Max); Humidity (Mean); Wind (Max); Pressure (Max); Humidity (Max); Temperature (Mean)
EM	SVM	0.196	2	Fenstertag; Temperature (Mean)
XMeans	SVM	0.196	2	season; Temperature (Mean)
EM	Bayes	0.206	5	Conditions; Pressure (Min); Temperature (Max); Temperature (Min); Temperature (Mean)
Hierarchical(5)	Bayes	0.206	2	Conditions; Temperature (Mean)
Hierarchical(5)	SVM	0.279	3	season; Temperature (Min); Pressure (Max)

References

Azevedo, A. I. R. L., 2008. KDD, SEMMA and CRISP-DM: a parallel overview. *IADS-DM.*

Ben\'itez, I., Quijano, A., D\'iez, J.-L. & Delgado, I., 2014. Dynamic clustering segmentation applied to load profiles of energy consumption from Spanish customers. *International Journal of Electrical Power \& Energy Systems,* Volume 55, pp. 437-448.

Ben\'itez, I., Quijano, A., D\'iez, J.-L. & Delgado, I., 2014. Dynamic clustering segmentation applied to load profiles of energy consumption from Spanish customers. *International Journal of Electrical Power \& Energy Systems,* Volume 55, pp. 437-448.

Benitez, I., Quijano, A., Diez, J.-L. & Delgado, I., 2014. Dynamic clustering segmentation applied to load profiles of energy consumption from Spanish customers. *International Journal of Electrical Power & Energy Systems,* Volume 55, pp. 437-448.

Berthold, M. R. et al., 2009. KNIME-the Konstanz information miner: version 2.0 and beyond. *AcM SIGKDD explorations Newsletter,* Volume 11, pp. 26-31.

Chapman, P. et al., 2000. CRISP-DM 1.0. *CRISP-DM Consortium,* Volume 76.

Frank, E. et al., 2010. Weka-a machine learning workbench for data mining. *Data mining and knowledge discovery handbook,* pp. 1269-1277.

Friedman, J., 2008. *The elements of statistical learning.* s.l.:Springer-Verlag.

GlobalData, 2012. *Building Energy Management System (BEMS)- Global Market Size, Market Share and Competitive Landscape Analysis to 2020,* s.l.: s.n.

Guyon, I. & Elisseeff, A., 2003. An introduction to variable and feature selection. *Journal of machine learning research,* Volume 3, pp. 1157-1182.

McLoughlin, F., Duffy, A. & Conlon, M., 2015. A clustering approach to domestic electricity load profile characterisation using smart metering data. *Applied energy,* Volume 141, pp. 190-199.

Molina-Solana, M. et al., 2017. Data science for building energy management: A review. *Renewable and Sustainable Energy Reviews,* Volume 70, pp. 598-609.

OfficeHolidays, n.d. *Public Holidays in Austria.* [Online] Available at: http://www.officeholidays.com/countries/austria/ [Accessed 06 2016].

Pérez-Lombard, L., Ortiz, J. & Pout, C., 2008. A review on buildings energy consumption information. *Energy and buildings,* Volume 40, pp. 394-398.

Pinson, P., Madsen, H. & others, 2014. Benefits and challenges of electrical demand response: A critical review. *Renewable and Sustainable Energy Reviews,* Volume 39, pp. 686-699.

Rhodes, J. D. et al., 2014. Clustering analysis of residential electricity demand profiles. *Applied Energy,* Volume 135, pp. 461-471.

Sun, Y., Gu, L., Wu, C. F. J. & Augenbroe, G., 2014. Exploring HVAC system sizing under uncertainty. *Energy and Buildings,* Volume 81, pp. 243-252.

Swan, L. G. & Ugursal, V. I., 2009. Modeling of end-use energy consumption in the residential sector: A review of modeling techniques. *Renewable and sustainable energy reviews,* Volume 13, pp. 1819-1835.

The Weather Company, n.d. *Weather Underground.* [Online] Available at: https://www.wunderground.com [Accessed 7 2016].

Author List

Abanda, Henry	Oxford Brookes University, United Kingdom
Bhatt, Mehul	University of Bremen, Germany
Birch, David	Imperial College London, United Kingdom
Boje, Calin	Cardiff University, United Kingdom
Boonstra, Sjonnie	Eindhoven University of Technology, Netherlands
Borrmann, André	Technical University Munich, Germany
Bres, Aurelien	Austrian Institute of Technology, Austria
Dadi, Gabriel	University of Kentucky, USA
de Wilde, Pieter	Plymouth University, United Kingdom
Dedemen, Gokmen	New York University, USA
Dejaco, Mario Claudio	Politecnico di Milano, Italy
Dragos, Kosmas	Bauhaus University Weimar, Germany
Drewniok, Michał	University College London, United Kingdom
Dunant, Cyrille	University College London, United Kingdom
Eleftheriadis, Stathis	University College London, United Kingdom
Emmerich, Michael	Leiden University, Netherlands
Ergan, Semiha	New York University, USA
Essawy, Yasmeen A. S.	The American University in Cairo, Egypt
Fadoul, Abdelaziz	University of Nottingham, United Kingdom
Farghaly, Karim	Oxford Brookes University, United Kingdom
Farid Alkadri, Miktha	Delft University of Technology, Netherlands
Franz, Steffen	Technische Universitt Darmstadt, Germany
Gao, Shang	Cardiff University, United Kingdom
Geyer, Philipp	Katholieke Universiteit Leuven, Belgium
Grabska, Ewa	Jagiellonian University, Poland
Hakim, Seyedamir	Politecnico di Milano, Italy
Hartmann, Timo	Technical University of Berlin, Germany
Hofmeyer, Hèrm	Eindhoven University of Technology, Netherlands
Hölter, Raoul	Ruhr-Universitt Bochum, Germany
Irmler, Robert	Technische Universitt Darmstadt, Germany
Ismail, Ali	Technische Universitt Dresden, Germany
Jahr, Katrin	Technical University Munich, Germany
Jatmiko	Ministry of Agrarian Affairs and Spatial Planning, Indonesia
Judex, Florian	Austrian Institute of Technology, Austria
Koch, Christian	University of Nottingham, United Kingdom

Kondyli, Vasiliki	University of Bremen, Germany
König, Markus	Ruhr-Universitt Bochum, Germany
Li, Haijiang	Cardiff University, United Kingdom
Long, Stewart	Cardiff University, United Kingdom
Mahmoudi, Elham	Ruhr-Universitt Bochum, Germany
Maltese, Sebastiano	Politecnico di Milano, Italy
Mattern, Hannah	Ruhr-Universitt Bochum, Germany
Michaels, Dominic	University of Kentucky, USA
Nahar, Ahmed	Technische Universitt Dresden, Germany
Nassar, Khaled	The American University in Cairo, Egypt
Ninic, Jelena	University of Nottingham, United Kingdom
Osorio Sandoval, Carlos Arturo	University of Nottingham, United Kingdom
Petrushevski, Filip	Austrian Institute of Technology, Austria
Polter, Michael	Technische Universitt Dresden, Germany
Psimoulis, Panos	University of Nottingham, United Kingdom
Re Cecconi, Fulvio	Politecnico di Milano, Italy
Ren, Guoqian	Cardiff University, United Kingdom
Rogers-Tizard, Will	Price & Myers, United Kingdom
Rüppel, Uwe	Technische Universitt Darmstadt, Germany
Sariyildiz, Sevil	Delft University of Technology, Netherlands
Schanz, Tom	Ruhr-Universitt Bochum, Germany
Scherer, Raimar	Technische Universitt Dresden, Germany
Simondetti, Alvise	Arup, United Kingdom
Singaravel, Sundaravelpandian	Katholieke Universiteit Leuven, Belgium
Smarsly, Kay	Bauhaus University Weimar, Germany
Smith, Ian	École polytechnique fédérale de Lausanne, Switzerland
Soman, Ranjith	Imperial College London, United Kingdom
Strug, Barbara	Jagiellonian University
Suter, Georg	Vienna University of Technology, Austria
Suykens, Johan	Katholieke Universiteit Leuven, Belgium
Taylor, Tim	University of Kentucky, USA
Theiler, Michael	Bauhaus University Weimar, Germany
Tizani, Walid	University of Nottingham, United Kingdom
Turrin, Michela	Delft University of Technology, Netherlands
Ungureanu, Lucian-Constantin	Technical University of Berlin, Germany
van der Blom, Koen	Leiden University, Netherlands
Vidalakis, Christos	Oxford Brookes University, United Kingdom

Wang, Xi	University of Kentucky, USA
Whyte, Jennifer	Imperial College London, United Kingdom
Wood, Brian	Plant Mix Asphalt Institute of Kentucky, USA
Wood, Graham	Oxford Brookes University, United Kingdom
Zhang, Jisong	Cardiff University, United Kingdom
Zhao, Yinghua	Dalian Maritime University, China
Ślusarczyk, Grażyna	Jagiellonian University, Poland
Šipetić, Miloš	Austrian Institute of Technology, Austria

European Group For Intelligent Computing in Engineering (eg-ice)
c/o Andre Borrmann
Arcisstrasee 21
80333 Munich
Germany

ISBN 978-1-5108-4345-5

CURRAN ASSOCIATES INC.
proceedings.com